Adapting and Mitigating Environmental, Social, and Governance Risk in Business

Magdalena Ziolo
University of Szczecin, Poland

IGI Global
PUBLISHER of TIMELY KNOWLEDGE

A volume in the Advances in Business Information Systems and Analytics (ABISA) Book Series

Published in the United States of America by
IGI Global
Business Science Reference (an imprint of IGI Global)
701 E. Chocolate Avenue
Hershey PA, USA 17033
Tel: 717-533-8845
Fax: 717-533-8661
E-mail: cust@igi-global.com
Web site: http://www.igi-global.com

Library of Congress Cataloging-in-Publication Data

Names: Ziolo, Magdalena, 1976- editor.
Title: Adapting and mitigating environmental, social, and governance risk in business / Magdalena Ziolo, editor.
Description: Hershey : Business Science Reference, 2021. | Includes bibliographical references and index. | Summary: "Through theoretical frameworks and empirical research findings, this book explains how enterprises operating in different sectors are adapting their business models towards sustainability and for creating sustainable value"-- Provided by publisher.
Identifiers: LCCN 2020046699 (print) | LCCN 2020046700 (ebook) | ISBN 9781799867883 (hardcover) | ISBN 9781799867890 (paperback) | ISBN 9781799867906 (ebook)
Subjects: LCSH: Industrial management--Environmental aspects. | Business enterprises--Environmental aspects. | Sustainable development.
Classification: LCC HD30.255 .A33 2021 (print) | LCC HD30.255 (ebook) | DDC 658.15/5--dc23
LC record available at https://lccn.loc.gov/2020046699
LC ebook record available at https://lccn.loc.gov/2020046700

This book is published in the IGI Global book series Advances in Business Information Systems and Analytics (ABISA) (ISSN: 2327-3275; eISSN: 2327-3283)

British Cataloguing in Publication Data
A Cataloguing in Publication record for this book is available from the British Library.

Advances in Business Information Systems and Analytics (ABISA) Book Series

Madjid Tavana
La Salle University, USA

ISSN:2327-3275
EISSN:2327-3283

Mission

The successful development and management of information systems and business analytics is crucial to the success of an organization. New technological developments and methods for data analysis have allowed organizations to not only improve their processes and allow for greater productivity, but have also provided businesses with a venue through which to cut costs, plan for the future, and maintain competitive advantage in the information age.

The **Advances in Business Information Systems and Analytics (ABISA) Book Series** aims to present diverse and timely research in the development, deployment, and management of business information systems and business analytics for continued organizational development and improved business value.

Coverage

- Algorithms
- Statistics
- Business Systems Engineering
- Data Management
- Data Strategy
- Business Decision Making
- Big Data
- Business Process Management
- Information Logistics
- Data Governance

IGI Global is currently accepting manuscripts for publication within this series. To submit a proposal for a volume in this series, please contact our Acquisition Editors at Acquisitions@igi-global.com or visit: http://www.igi-global.com/publish/.

The Advances in Business Information Systems and Analytics (ABISA) Book Series (ISSN 2327-3275) is published by IGI Global, 701 E. Chocolate Avenue, Hershey, PA 17033-1240, USA, www.igi-global.com. This series is composed of titles available for purchase individually; each title is edited to be contextually exclusive from any other title within the series. For pricing and ordering information please visit http://www.igi-global.com/book-series/advances-business-information-systems-analytics/37155. Postmaster: Send all address changes to above address.

Titles in this Series

For a list of additional titles in this series, please visit:
http://www.igi-global.com/book-series/advances-business-information-systems-analytics/37155

Innovative and Agile Contracting for Digital Transformation and Inustry 4.0
Mohammad Ali Shalan (Aqarat Real Estate Development Company, Saudi Arabia) and Mohammed Ayedh Algarni (Information and Documents Center, Institute of Public Administration, Saudi Arabia)
Business Science Reference • © 2021 • 415pp • H/C (ISBN: 9781799845010) • US $225.00

Opportunities and Strategic Use of Agribusiness Information Systems
Ferdinand Ndifor Che (W3-Research, USA & APPC Research, Australia) Kenneth David Strang (W3-Research, USA & APPC Research, Australia) and Narasimha Rao Vajjhala (University of New York Tirana, Albania)
Business Science Reference • © 2021 • 333pp • H/C (ISBN: 9781799848493) • US $195.00

Integration Challenges for Analytics, Business Intelligence, and Data Mining
Ana Azevedo (CEOS:PP, ISCAP, Polytechnic of Porto, Portugal) and Manuel Filipe Santos (Algoritmi Centre, University of Minho, Guimarães, Portugal)
Engineering Science Reference • © 2021 • 250pp • H/C (ISBN: 9781799857815) • US $225.00

Managing Business in the Civil Construction Sector Through Information Communication Technologies
Bithal Das Mundhra (Simplex Infrastructures Ltd, India) and Rajesh Bose (Simplex Infrastructures Ltd, India)
Business Science Reference • © 2021 • 254pp • H/C (ISBN: 9781799852919) • US $195.00

Achieving Organizational Agility, Intelligence, and Resilience Through Information Systems
Hakikur Rahman (Institute of Computer Management and Science, Bangladesh)
Business Science Reference • © 2021 • 300pp • H/C (ISBN: 9781799847991) • US $195.00

Handbook of Research on User Experience in Web 2.0 Technologies and Its Impact on Universities and Businesses
Jean-Éric Pelet (ESCE International Business School, INSEEC U Research Center, Paris, France)
Business Science Reference • © 2021 • 426pp • H/C (ISBN: 9781799837565) • US $295.00

Empowering Businesses With Collaborative Enterprise Architecture Frameworks
Tiko Iyamu (Cape Peninsula University of Technology, South Africa)
Business Science Reference • © 2021 • 309pp • H/C (ISBN: 9781522582298) • US $195.00

Natural Language Processing for Global and Local Business
Fatih Pinarbasi (Istanbul Medipol University, Turkey) and M. Nurdan Taskiran (Istanbul Medipol University, Turkey)
Business Science Reference • © 2021 • 452pp • H/C (ISBN: 9781799842408) • US $225.00

IGI Global
PUBLISHER of TIMELY KNOWLEDGE

701 East Chocolate Avenue, Hershey, PA 17033, USA
Tel: 717-533-8845 x100 • Fax: 717-533-8661
E-Mail: cust@igi-global.com • www.igi-global.com

Table of Contents

Detailed Table of Contents

The purpose of the chapter is to present the definition, historical background, and core elements of the concept related to sustainability, corporate social responsibility, and the triple bottom line. Common relationships and the differences between these concepts were indicated on the basis of the gathered information scattered in the scientific literature. The empirical part of the chapter allows the assessment of whether the enterprises really refer to the concepts known in the literature. It also presents an assessment of the stage of business today, referring to the business sustainability typology by using research methods such as case survey and TOPSIS.

This research provides a comprehensive review of corporate sustainability literature in various application areas. The chapter also highlights the gaps in clearly explaining the scope for it extending and incorporating the term of corporate sustainability into other research areas. The main advantage of this study is that it provides an insight into the state of the art of corporate sustainability in various application areas and future development and research directions. In addition to the literature review in this area, the chapter also presents numerous examples of the understanding of corporate sustainability by various business organizations. The chapter analyses nearly 200 different publications in this field available in the Web of Science database. In addition to quantitative analyses, in-depth qualitative research was also carried out.

In a quest for sources of competitive advantage, an insightful tracking and tracing of the changes that take place in their micro and macro environment is a core competence for enterprises to catch up with market trends. Social and economic changes as well as the growing awareness of the negative anthropogenic impact on the climate and the environment increasingly make today's business models evolve towards sustainability. The aim of this chapter is to analyze the concept of a sustainable business model based on the literature review and then to distinguish the driving and limiting factors behind its implementation in enterprises. Based on an empirical study carried out, a diagnosis will be put forward for the awareness of enterprises as regards the business model pursued and the willingness to integrate social, environmental, and governance aspects. The research methods used in this study relied on critical literature review; descriptive, analytic, and synthetic methods; along with in-depth interviews.

The chapter examines the scope of public administration participation in ensuring that entrepreneurs comply with the principles of sustainable development. It was found that the activities of the state administration in this regard may consist in providing entrepreneurs with the status of applying ESG and CSR principles in their activities, then checking compliance with these principles, informing consumers about the consequences of using products and services produced by the entrepreneurs using the ESG and CSR principles. It was determined that the expectation for the application of ESG and CSR principles can also apply to public administration, which in its activity can contribute to environmental protection by reducing energy consumption in various forms, as well as improving social relations by eliminating corruption.

The chapter presents the evolution of potential ESG risks in the healthcare sector related to striving to provide the best care for patients. Based on the literature and selected examples, the analysis of this problem will indicate potential risks of the main factors and tools that can help manage this risk in the healthcare sector. There is a research gap in the literature; there is a lack of detailed discussion and research allowing to establish the relationship between ESG factors and finances. Particular emphasis is placed on social pillar, which in the authors' opinion is critical to the functioning of the healthcare sector, especially from the face of COVID-19. The authors proposed a map to identify potential risk and possible scenarios of action in the long term. The main assumption of the study is that the implementation of ESG potential risk management leads in the long run to sustainable development in the healthcare sector.

Global carbon emissions are contributed by companies significantly. These companies themselves are not insulated from the risks arising from their own irresponsible acts against the climate. Several companies have adopted voluntarily the strategy of acting beyond compliance of existing laws demonstrating proactivity. Climate strategy proactivity (CSP) is the voluntary strategic corporate behavior adopted to satisfy stakeholders' demands which also help respective governments in achieving international commitments. This chapter, amidst the paucity of relevant studies in the context of developing countries, aims to discuss the emerging concept of CSP and underscores an urgent need for more research on CSP setting a research agenda from the perspective of the relevant stakeholders. The chapter concludes that CSP offers huge potentialities for companies more particularly in developing countries such as India attaching greater significance to stakeholders' perspectives.

The COVID-19 pandemic has revealed the failure of the state to withstand emergencies, threatening the lives of millions of citizens. By introducing regimes of social and economic lockdowns in fighting coronavirus, the state faced a societal crisis. Its consequences can't be overestimated, especially due to economic recovery. The growing distrust of households in the state was caused by the disruption of their usual way of living, the growth of unemployment, and the deterioration in their well-being. So people began to distinguish significant differences between their individual values and preferences institutionalized by the state. Hence, the priority for the state should be to restore citizens' confidence by creating a more inclusive societal environment, minimizing the negative consequences of the societal crisis. Infrastructure PPP projects can demonstrate the social preferences' public priority. The "institutional matrix" of PPP organizational forms makes it possible to choose conditions for public projects' implementation with the absolute priority of the healthcare system.

The COVID-19 global pandemic had a shock effect on all spheres of the socio-economic system. It objectively predetermines the urgent necessity to rethink the following phenomena: fundamental foundations of the functioning of modern socio-economic systems and business with capital-centrist principles of their organization, how the shock due to the coronavirus pandemic revealed the marginal possibilities of the existing system of organizing economic activity, patterns of structuring the post-COVID-19 reality and the formation of business principles in the new human-centric socio-economic system. The uncertainty as the fundamental feature of the business environment caused by COVID-19 could become a major challenge for any business in shaping its growth strategy. In this situation, the success of the company depends on managers' understandings of the quality of this uncertainty and the development of an effective strategy for its growth, taking into account the main factors of the formation of the qualitatively new human-centric socio-economic system.

The coronavirus pandemic has predetermined the great priority of protecting public health. The states urgently introduced a regime of economic and social lockdowns to stop the infection. As a result, the activities of firms were suspended or blocked, which caused enormous negative economic and social consequences both for business and for the national societies. The subsequent societal and economic crises predetermined the marginal state of the capital-centric system, which led to the destruction of its structural ties. In the uncertain future, chief executive officers should be prepared to rebuild their businesses. It will be possible if companies take advantage of the opportunities of the 4th technological revolution and rely on the inclusion and diversity strategy to socialize talented people into their organizations. Today, questions remain open, related to both the preparation of future talents and their adequate socialization. The advanced firms will play a leading role in solving these problems to become successful.

Due to the fundamental digitization of social/economic life, it takes on an "on" and "offline" scale image of the world. While analyzing the impact of the ongoing pandemic on the segmentation of world markets, the disruptions in the functioning of some industries, sectors, and entire economies are becoming deeper. The spread of COVID-19 has led to the dysfunction of a known ecosystem, and the destructive force of human isolation and the lockdown of economies have significantly influenced the behavior of societies and governments. Many customer-centric companies have reactively redefined their strategies, and the financial sector, especially banks, was to play an important role in absorbing the shock by providing the necessary credit to businesses and households. Meanwhile, the same institutions have experienced capital and liquidity destabilization due to increased risk reserves created and an operating in conditions of historically low interest rates. Unexpectedly, the pandemic has become another determinant of the new quality of processes, phenomena, and business models.

The CE represents a new model for resilient growth in both developed and developing economies that would help to tackle the causes and devastating effects of climate change and climate change risks, meet the 1.5 degree target of the Paris Agreement, and achieve the Sustainable Development Goals (SDGs). The CE practices can help to reduce greenhouse gases (CO2, methane, and nitro-oxide) to net zero emissions by 2050 through efficient resources use, elongation of product lifetime, recycling, recovery, reuse, materials substitution, efficient waste reduction and management, sharing service, among others.

Preface

Companies undertake adjustment actions for sustainable development. The key issues here are the adjustment of risk management systems in terms of extending risk exposure to environmental and social risk. Due to the fact that sustainable adaptation includes activities aimed at reducing social risk (poverty and, consequently, social exclusion) and environmental risk (climate change), these two categories of risk are particularly taken into account when considering. The criteria for assessing the risk are changing due to changes in the economy. It is especially visible in the conditions of "greening" the economy and social inclusion. These two phenomena referring to the environmental and social pillar of sustainable development strongly weigh on the need to extend the criteria of risk evaluation by financial institutions to ESG risk (environmental, social, corporate governance). Based on research carried it was found that many companies indicated that their mission and vision of action had provisions referring to the concept of sustainable development and that in practice they applied solutions that fit into the sustainable development trend. Companies declared, inter alia, participation in "green" public procurement, recycling, choosing friendly distribution channels, avoiding the implementation of orders that are socially and environmentally harmful, using innovations that have a positive impact on the environment, limiting the share of water in production, or selecting suppliers from the CSR group. Companies are aware of the impact of financial institutions on their business activities. Financial institutions have a significant impact on the effects of actions under sustainable adaptation. Without a developed system of financing environmental protection and social finances, it is not possible to effectively carry out activities in the field of adaptation to climate change or poverty reduction, because each initiative in this area requires dedicated financing. These are extremely capital-intensive activities, and additionally, they are characterized by a specific type of risk - ESG risk, which can be reduced only within the framework of sustainable finance, taking into account this type of risk in the risk assessment. At the same time, sustainable adaptation determines the effectiveness of actions to ensure sustainable development. Green crediting clearly dominates the process of limiting the negative effects of environmental degradation. In turn, in terms of social financing, microfinance and new technologies developing the sharing economy remain the most important. New technologies are characterized by high energy consumption, which in turn has a negative effect on the natural environment. Therefore, it should be assessed individually whether the fight against poverty with the use of new technologies brings effects that in a specific case exceed the environmental costs. The aim of the book is to identify the key divers impacting on adaptation of companies' business models towards sustainability. A summary precedes each chapter in the book and followed by conclusions. Chapter 1 includes introduction. Chapter 2 presents the historical background of the concepts of Sustainability, Corporate Social Responsibility and the Triple Bottom Line. Definitions and descriptions accompanying these concepts are discussed. Also alternative concepts from the literature (such as the CSR pyramid, alternative model M. Schwartz and A. B. Carroll, CSR 2.0, strategic CSR) are considered. Chapter 3 provides an insight into the state of art of corporate sustainability in various application areas and future development and research directions. The chapter also presents numerous examples of the understanding of corporate sustainability by various business organizations. Chapter 4 aims to present the following issues: the theoretical background of sustainable business models, methods of implementation of sustainable business models depending on the size of the company, the barriers to the implementation of sustainable business models and challenges and prospects of the implementation of sustainable business models. Chapter 5 discusses questions and solutions to the problem of necessity or lack of state involvement in stimulating responsible, sustainable development of entrepreneurs conducting consumer education in their creative role in the ESG process. Chapter 6 presents the evolution of potential ESG risks in the healthcare sector related to striving to provide the best care for patients. Based on the literature and selected examples, the analysis of this problem indicates potential risks of the main factors and tools that can help manage this risk in the healthcare sector. Chapter 7 attempts to fill the gap created by the inadequacies of studies in the context of developing countries with respect to the proactivity envisaged by various corporations with respect to the climate strategy adopted by them, and presents the perspective of the relevant stakeholders. Previous studies focused in developed countries have failed to contextualize and conceptualize these issues and concerns of developing countries adequately. The chapter presents a broad view of the concepts of Climate Strategy Proactivity (CSP), competitive advantage, salient stakeholders and their interrelations, also, for an enhanced understanding. Chapter 8 proposes an institutional matrix that allows the government to vary the forms of PPP organization, taking into account the combination of interests of private investors and of the state. Chapter 9 presents with regard to capital-centric and human-centric socio-economic systems, a model description of the shock mechanism' functioning is presented. Chapter 10 assumes that today, in the conditions of an absolutely uncertain post-coronavirus future, only an individual (not a shareholder) with high intellectual autonomy and socially significant values is able to reduce the area of this uncertainty and to rebuild a stronger business taking into account new circumstances. Chapter 11 analyses the impact of the ongoing pandemic on the banking industry. Chapter 12 intends to consider the following: First, climate change, climate change risk and the adaptation and mitigating strategies in dealing with climate change. Second, the role of the CE in dealing with climate change and climate change risk. Third, leverage on the fourth industrial revolution to facilitate CE and mitigate climate change. Chapter 13 the goal of the chapter is to study what effect CSR has on firms' overall performance in a developing country context. The chapter aims to analyze and measure the social and environmental involvement of large Moroccan firms operating in the main sectors of activity and located in different geographical areas.

Acknowledgment

Research results presented in this volume are an element of research project financed by the National Science Center Poland (NCN) OPUS16 2018/31/B/HS4/00570

Chapter 1
The Concept of the Triple Bottom Line as a Link Between Sustainability and CSR

Bartosz Oliwa
University of Szczecin, Poland

ABSTRACT

The purpose of the chapter is to present the definition, historical background, and core elements of the concept related to sustainability, corporate social responsibility, and the triple bottom line. Common relationships and the differences between these concepts were indicated on the basis of the gathered information scattered in the scientific literature. The empirical part of the chapter allows the assessment of whether the enterprises really refer to the concepts known in the literature. It also presents an assessment of the stage of business today, referring to the business sustainability typology by using research methods such as case survey and TOPSIS.

INTRODUCTION

The development of science in Sustainability and Corporate Social Responsibility (CSR) has been going on for at least 50 years. Although the time of origin and development of both concepts are different, they should be considered as complementary. CSR was developed first, but it is narrower than a concept of Sustainability and should be considered as a way of business to achieve the Sustainability. However, fulfilling the Sustainability is not simple and needs a certain path which could be described by a Triple Bottom Line (TBL) model, at least to a certain degree.

Triple Bottom Line (TBL) or People, Planet, Profit (3Ps) model provides a deeper look at both concepts of Sustainability and Corporate Social Responsibility. Figure 1. shows the relationship between Corporate Social Responsibility and Sustainability through the concept of the Triple Bottom Line, which is the fundamental aspect of the considerations in this chapter.

In this chapter the origins, history and ideas of concepts related to Sustainability, CSR and TBL will be presented. The purpose of the chapter is to show how the latter concept can be perceived as a link

DOI: 10.4018/978-1-7998-6788-3.ch001

Figure 1. The relationship between Sustainability and Corporate Social Responsibility through the Triple Bottom Line
Source: own elaboration.

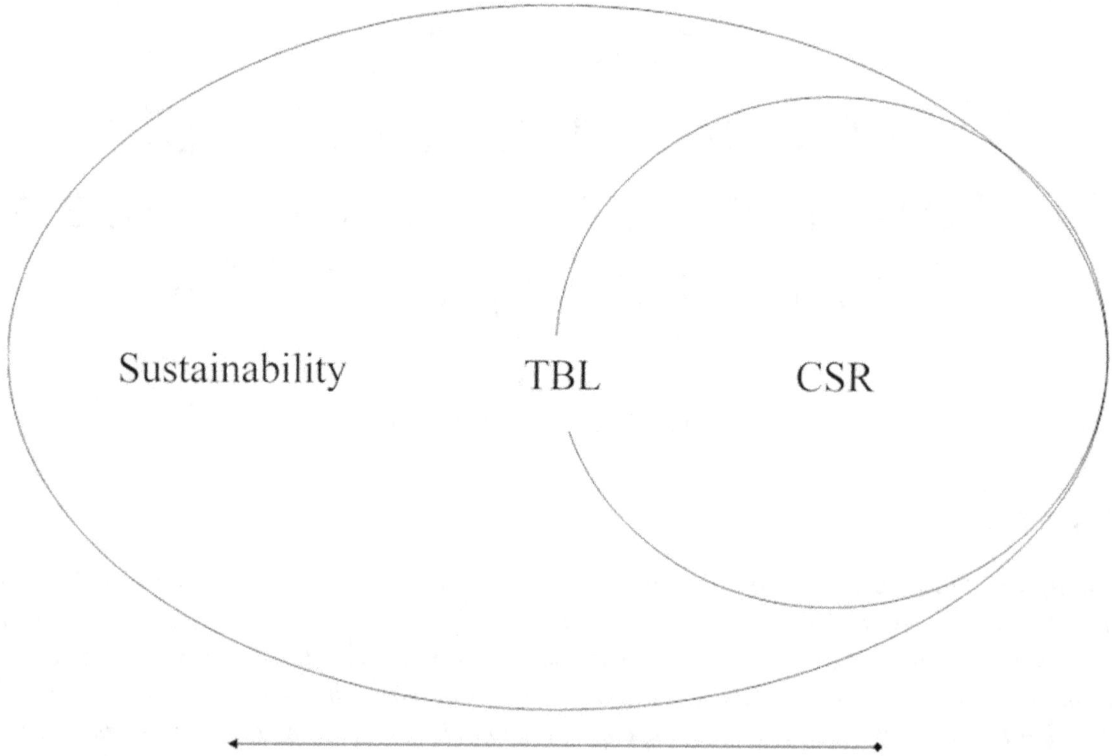

and what are the limitations associated with this kind of thinking. In the empirical part of the chapter, an attempt was made to assess the implementation of the TBL concept by enterprises, as well as the reinvented concept of Corporate Social Responsibility - CSR 2.0, and to examine in which phase of the Business Sustainability Typology enterprises are in.

THE THEORY BEHIND THE CONCEPTS

The Concept of Sustainability

The first records of Sustainability date back to 1713 with the writing of Sylvicultura Oeconomica made by Hans Carl von Carlowitz. This book was the world's first scientific work in forestry (Lusawa, 2009, p. 9). The author presented the 'Sustainability triangle' which consists that the economy is obliged to create the welfare of society and treat nature in gently manner (Lusawa, 2009, p. 10). The 'sustianbility triangle' comprises the following words and their meanings (Lusawa, 2009, p. 10):

- **Immerwährend:** an archaism which corresponds to the English word 'constant';

- **Continuirlich**: the Latin origin archaism used in music which meant lasting in time, and its term is the closest to the English word 'sustained';
- **Perpetuierlich**: the archaism meaning 'perpetual'.

Figure 2. presents a diagram of 'Sustainability triangle' presented by thoughts by H. C. Carlowitz.

Figure 2. Sustainability in terms of the 'Sustainability triangle' by H.C. Carlowitz
Source: own elaboration based on (Lusawa, 2009).

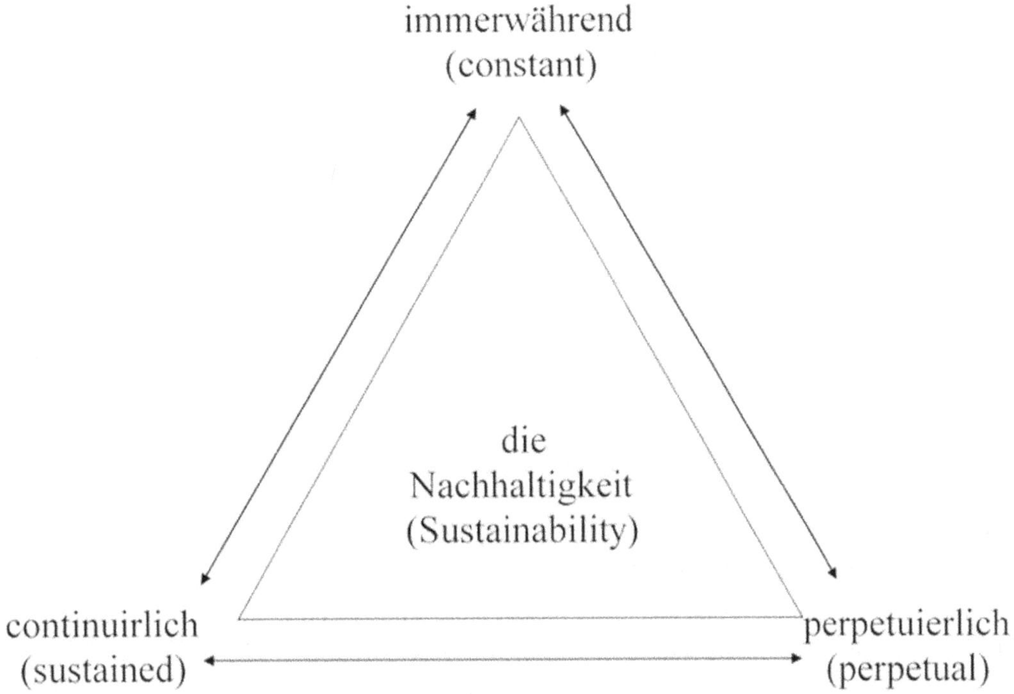

The modern definition of Sustainability was taking its shape in the 1970s when more and more environmental disasters has begun to occur. It has started with huge public responses in North America caused by the environmental disaster associated with the Santa Barbara, California oil spill. This accident led to massive protests in the United States. The protest was backed on the first Earth Day in 1970 by 10% of the US population (20 million people). At the same time thousands of colleges and universities expressed their opposition to the deterioration of the environment. The result of those events was the establishment of the Environmental Protection Agency (EPA) (Earth Day) and the creation of a new regulatory framework that has begun to influence the behavior of enterprises and created additional obligations for corporations (Agudelo, Jóhannsdóttir, & Davídsdóttir, 2019, p. 17) (Carroll, 2015, p. 5).

The most popular definition of Sustainability in contemporary terms is the one proposed by the Brundtland Commission in 1897. According to the presented definition, the idea of Sustainability (or more strict to Sustainable Development) is the one "that meets the needs of the present without compromising the ability of future generations to meet their own needs" (World Commission on Environment and Development, 1987, p. 16). As R. W. Kates, T. M. Parris, A. A. Leiserowitz point out, although the definition of the Brundtland Commission does not directly present environmental issues and economic development, their occurrence is obvious, as indicated in the subsequent paragraphs of the report (Kates, Parris, & Leiserowitz, 2005). Since 1987, the number of definitions presented in the literature has increased enormously: J. Pezzey indicated over 60 definitions (Pezzey, 1992), M. Jacobs - 386 (Jacobs, 1995), B. Carroll - 500 (Carroll B., 2002). Such a large number of definitions according to R. Ciegis, J. Ramansuskiene, B. Martinkus results not so much from different concepts of Sustainability, but rather from emphasizing its various aspects (Ciegis, Ramansuskiene, & Martinkus, pp. 39-40).

It is worth to note that in the literature can be found a distinction between the term Sustainability and Sustainable Development. M. Diesendorf believes that Sustainability is the end point of the process called Sustainable Development (Diesendorf, 2000, pp. 19-37). R. Gray has a similar opinion and defines Sustainability as a state, while Sustainable Development is the process of reaching this state (Gray, 2010, pp. 47-62). A. Benaim, A. Collins and L. Raftis use the term Strategic Sustainable Development, which is the process of reaching the socio-ecological state (Sustainability) in a planned, systematic and scientific manner (Benaim, Collins, & Raftis, 2008, pp. 2-4) based on the FSSD (Framework for Strategic Sustainable Development) by K.H. Robèrt (Robèrt, et al., 2002, p. 197).

The literature relating to the definition of Sustainable Development also emphasizes the importance of technology that should be used to achieve the state of Sustainability (Arena, Ciceri, Terzi, & Bengo, 2009, pp. 229-331). It considers the idea that technology is a supporting factor of achieving Sustainability. However, as considered as a Green Swan, it can also have some black feathers or a Gray one (Elkington, Green Swans: The Coming Boom in Regenerative Capitalism, 2020) because Sustainability is not only about environment but also society. On the one hand, some technologies can help to solve environmental problems, on the other hand other technologies can cause societal problems. It is not said that same technologies cause two impacts at the same time, however they can. For example Social Media can be very good source of spreading the Sustainability idea but also used algorithms in these tools can lead to polarize views of its users (Musco, Musco, & Tsourakakis, 2018, pp. 369-378). Every user has own virtual reality on his screen and the recommendations algorithm can in one user strengthen the beliefs of the dangers of the climate change, other can see that view as a general lie. This polarization effect can lead to ideological tensions between groups which scale could help or prevent to achieve Sustainability. However, this issue is not so simple to solve. The business model of Social Media is developed to fulfill the advisers needs, and if the economic aspect is taking over the societal and environmental ones, achieving Sustainability becomes difficult. So in one time Social Media could help to achieve a Sustainability but on the other hand they can also prevent it. Most issues like that will always come up due to the discrepancies between the short-term view on economic level versus medium to long-term view in environmental and social views. The second thing is that the change must be very wide. Referring to J. Elkington and his book Green Swans: The Coming Boom in Regenerative Capitalism, what is the point in *cleaning up the corporate fish if we then release them back into dirty market waters?* (Elkington, Green Swans: The Coming Boom in Regenerative Capitalism, 2020).

The above example, however very specific, shows that Sustainability is not only about environment but also society and economy, and what is more they are associated together. This relation in the literature is presented as two Sustainability models: the Weak Sustainability and the Strong Sustainability.

Weak Sustainability and Triple Bottom Line Versus Strong Sustainability

The concepts of Sustainability in the literature are most often presented (Giddings, Hopwood, & O'Brien, 2002; Mancebo, 2013; Pelenc & Ballet, Weak Sustainability versus Strong Sustainability, 2015) on the basis of two models: a model consisting of three overlapping circles (Figure 3a), and a model consisting of three nested circles (Figure 3b).

Figure 3. Two concepts of Sustainability
Source: (Giddings, Hopwood, & O'Brien, 2002, pp. 189-192)

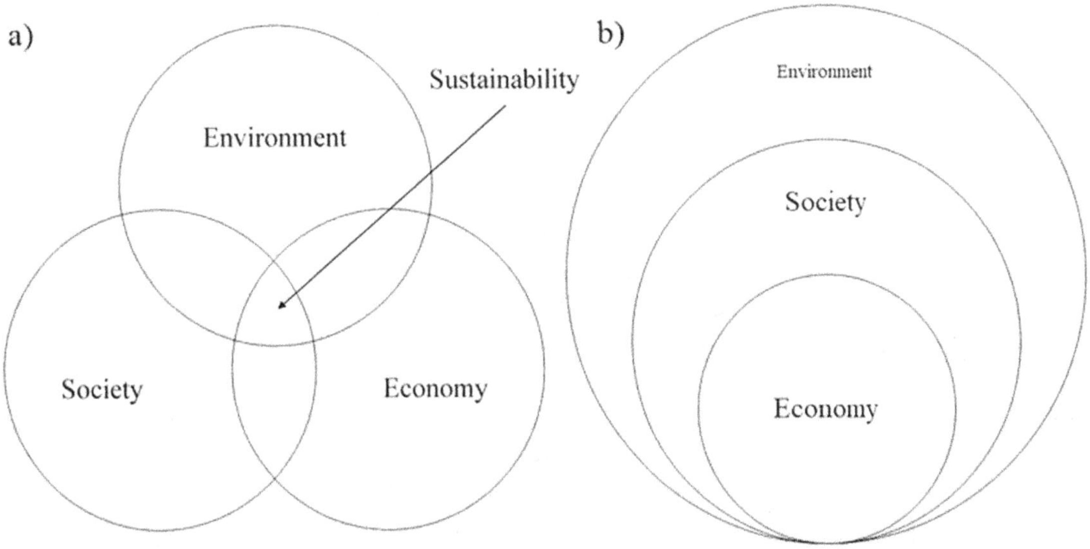

The first of the above-mentioned concepts (Figure 3a.), called the Weak Sustainability is a subject to criticism, mainly due to the trade-offs between environmental, social and economic aspects, while associating the last element as being the most important—which relates to neo-liberal thought (Giddings, Hopwood, & O'Brien, 2002, p. 190). This concept assumes that natural capital and produced capital are substitutable, and there are no fundamental differences between the types of welfare that these capitals generate (Pelenc & Ballet, 2015, p. 1). Representatives of this concept often refer to the development of technology that in the future will slowly use less materials and energy – so the basic assumption of this mechanism is the possibility of decoupling economic growth from resource use (Pearce, 1992, pp. 3-13) (Ekins, Simon, Deutsch, Folke, & Groot, 2003, p. 168).

The model of the Weak Sustainability is similar to the Triple Bottom Line (TBL) model coined in 1994 by J. Elkington (Henriques & Richardson, 2004, pp. xix-xxii) (Elkington, 1997). TBL requires enterprises to include, in addition to financial data, also data related to the impact on the environment and society (Gray & Milne, 2004, pp. 70-80). The term Triple Bottom Line introduces an environmental and social aspect to the traditional bottom line term of total income to expenditure (profit) over a period of time (Lee, 1997, p. 1). "Sustainable development involves the simultaneous pursuit of economic prosperity, environmental quality, and social equity. Companies aiming for Sustainability need to perform not against a single, financial bottom line but against the triple bottom line" (Elkington, 1997, p.

397). This definition implies a shift from the organization's emphasis on short-term financial goals to long-term social, environmental and economic impacts (Arowoshegbe & Emmanuel, 2016, pp. 92-93).

The TBL concept combines three types of capital, that is (note that an order is important (Elkington, 2020)):

1) **social capital (People):** which to some extent is related to human capital, but at the same time covers a broader outline of people's ability to work together for the purposes of the group and the organization, and is associated with values such as: loyalty, honesty, mutual dependence (Elkington, 2020, p. 21);
2) **environmental capital (Planet):** is mainly associated with natural capital in a broad sense, i.e. not only the number of occurrences of a given type of environmental capital (e.g. the number of trees), but also the impact of this type on the ecosystem – air, water, fauna and flora. Natural capital is divided into critical capital (capital that performs important environmental functions that cannot be replaced by productive capital (Ekins, Simon, Deutsch, Folke, & Groot, 2003, p. 169)) and renewable, replaceable, substitutable capital (Elkington, 1998, p. 18);
3) **economic capital (Profit):** which in the simplest sense can be considered the book value constituting the difference between assets and liabilities. In traditional terms, economic capital takes two forms in the form of physical capital (machines, material resources) and financial capital, but it also applies to human capital measured by experience, skills and other knowledge-based assets possessed by the entities that make up a given enterprise (Elkington, 1998, p. 20).

However, the whole argumentation of the Weak Sustainability and thus TBL is based on treating the TBL as just a accounting tool, while the concept was much deeper and was supposed to provoke deeper thinking about capitalism and its future. Hence, considering the Triple Bottom Line as trade-offs between economic (financial), social and environmental elements is fundamentally wrong. "TBL's stated goal from the outset was *system change* — pushing toward the transformation of capitalism. It was never supposed to be just an accounting system. It was originally intended as a genetic code, a triple helix of change for tomorrow's capitalism, with a focus was on breakthrough change, disruption, asymmetric growth (with unsustainable sectors actively sidelined), and the scaling of next-generation market solutions" (Elkington, 2018).

The second model (Figure 3b) is known as the concept of the Strong Sustainability. This concept implies certain limits to which people can use the environment for their own benefit (Biely, Maes, & Passel, 2016, p. 225). Based on this model, it can be concluded that the economy is dependent on society (society creates the economy), while both society and the economy are dependent on the environment (Giddings, Hopwood, & O'Brien, 2002, p. 225) and the capital derived from it (natural capital). It should be mentioned that P. Ekins et al. mentioned four types of natural capital in functional terms. Those are (Ekins, Simon, Deutsch, Folke, & Groot, 2003, p. 192):

- **Type 1:** capital that provides resources for production, which includes, for example, raw materials for the production of food, fuel, metals, etc.;
- **Type 2:** capital derived from absorption of waste from production - this capital can be called investment natural capital and can be divided into positive (for example, animal fertilizer, recycling which is a positive investment contribution) and negative (materials that harm the environment which is a negative investment contribution);

- **Type 3:** capital ensuring the maintenance of basic life functions, which includes, among others: stability of the ecosystem, protection against ultraviolet radiation by the ozone layer;
- **Type 4:** capital that provides 'recreational services', such as the beauty of the landscape - this capital is created directly by ecological capital without human activity, which most often has a negative impact on this type of capital.

The first two types of natural capital can be used for production, as opposed to the other two. This division of capital shows that it is not possible to completely replace natural capital with other capital. P. Ekins et al. argue that without the function of natural capital it is impossible to create welfare because no other functions related to society and the economy can exist. It should be added that the authors also introduce a definition of critical natural capital, which is the key concept of the Strong Sustainability and can be defined as "natural capital, which is responsible for important environmental functions that cannot be replaced by productive capital" (Ekins, Simon, Deutsch, Folke, & Groot, 2003, p. 170).

At the same time, which implies the above, technology in this concept cannot be treated as the only solution to the challenges. As practice shows, technology often leads to a postponement of the problem (Burton, 1968, p. 478) - for example, nuclear energy helps to reduce CO2 emissions, but poses an additional nuclear waste and safety challenge (Biely, Maes, & Passel, 2016, p. 228) - in other words, it delays the problems to the future.

The differences between the two concepts presented are presented in Table 1.

Table 1. Differences between the concepts of sustainable development

	Weak Sustainability	Strong Sustainability
Key idea	Natural capital and other types of capitals (manufactured etc.) are perfectly substitutable	The substitutability of natural capital by other types of capital is severely limited
Consequences	Technological innovation and monetary compensation for environmental degradation	Certain human actions can entail irreversible consequences
Sustainability issue	The total value of the aggregate stock of capital should be at least maintained or ideally increased for future generation	Conserving the irreplaceable « stocks » of critical natural capital for the sake of future generation
Key concept	Optimal allocation of scarce resources	Critical natural capital
Definition of thresholds and environmental norms	Technic/scientific approach for determining thresholds and norms (instrumental rationality)	Scientific knowledge as input for public deliberation (procedural rationality)

Source: (Mancebo, 2013; Pelenc & Ballet, Weak Sustainability versus Strong Sustainability, 2015, p. 1)

The Concept of Corporate Social Responsibility

The another concept is Corporate Social Responsibility (CSR). Ideas about corporate responsibility for community welfare on a voluntary basis stretched back to the nineteenth century but a scientific discussion on the subject began in the 1930s, when E. M. Dodd and C. Bernard started to ask whether large corporation managers had a responsibility to society beyond boundaries of the activities of entities they manage. In the 1950s, H. Bowen (Bowen, 1953), known as the "father of Corporate Social Responsibility", for the first time used the term "Corporate Social Responsibility" extensively developing this area of the subject. Nevertheless, a number of terms have arisen since then and can be confusing. The attention to this problem was drawn in 1975, indicating that everyone has their own definition of CSR, using such terms as: *Corporate Social Responsibility (CSR), Public Affairs, relations with the local community (Community Relations), Urban Affairs, Corporate Responsibility*. The situation did not change in the 1990s, when the World Business Council stated that there was no universally accepted definition of CSR. M. Fifka indicates three reasons for this situation (Fifka, 2009, pp. 312-313):

Reason 1: great interest in the subject of CSR attracts scientists from various research fields in the field of economics, management, law, sociology, philosophy and even theology, which implies many different points of reference, as well as conflicting research methods;

Reason 2: over such a long period, many definitions have been developed, sometimes synonymous and sometimes referring to different concepts, thus creating information noise;

Reason 3: the lack of unity regarding the role of enterprises in society or should be fulfilled – changing the conceptual basis leads to a different definition of CSR.

Currently, there is still a stratification in the area of CSR terminology, as evidenced by a large number of terms used in the literature on the subject and in world business practice, such as: *Corporate Sustainability Management, Business Responsibility Global Business Citizenship, Corporate Social Responsibility, Social Responsibility, Corporate Responsibility, Strategic Corporate Social Responsibility, Total Responsibility Management, Corporate Social Irresponsibility, Corporate Social Responsiveness*.

Although the multitude and variety of definitions always accompany the emerging phase of any new idea, the definition of CSR can be described in terms of its perception dimensions. A. Dahlsrud presented five dimensions of CSR, which include (Dahlsrud, 2006, p. 4):

Dimension 1: the environmental dimension related to the care for the natural environment;

Dimension 2: the social dimension concerning the relationship between business and society;

Dimension 3: economic dimension relating to socio-economic aspects, taking care of the development and profitability of the enterprise;

Dimension 4: the stakeholder group dimension of interaction with and treatment of stakeholders;

Dimension 5: a voluntary dimension relating to activities not required by law.

The dimensions proposed by A. Dahlsrud are presented in Figure 4.

M. Karmasin and M. Litschka made an attempt to unify the issues of the definition of CSR by placing it next to Corporate Governance (CG) and Corporate Citizenship (CC), as part of Corporate Responsibility (CR). The concept of CSR has been assigned to economic, environmental and social responsibility (Karmasin & Litschka, 2017, p. 41), which is common with the Triple Bottom Line concept as Figure 5. presents.

Corporate Governance (CG) arose as a system of rules for managing a company in accordance with legal, economic and ethical conditions, due to the occurrence of scandals published because of some companies. Initially, it was intended to serve shareholders and creditors (Karmasin & Litschka, 2017, p. 47). Currently, it is a system of strategic management, integrated and holistic management in an entrepreneurial way (Hilb, 2006, p. 10). Corporate Citizenship (CC) uses the republican approach (alongside the normative approach) (Tempels, Blok, & Verweij, 2017, p. 93) in which company is treated as an actor that has the private (economic) and public responsibility (ethical) and is obliged to act in such conditions towards society. These conditions should be tightened, especially when national and international regulations are not yet established (Scherer & Palazzo, 2007, pp. 1096-1120). Although Corporate Citizenship is close to the concept of Corporate Social Responsibility (CSR), the field of CC is broader, because company is treated as a citizen. It means that less emphasis is put on the profitability of the enterprise and more on the responsibility towards its stakeholders – especially to community. What distinguishes CSR

Figure 4. The five dimensions of CSR by A. Dahlsrud
Source: own elaboration based on (Dahlsrud, 2006, p. 4)

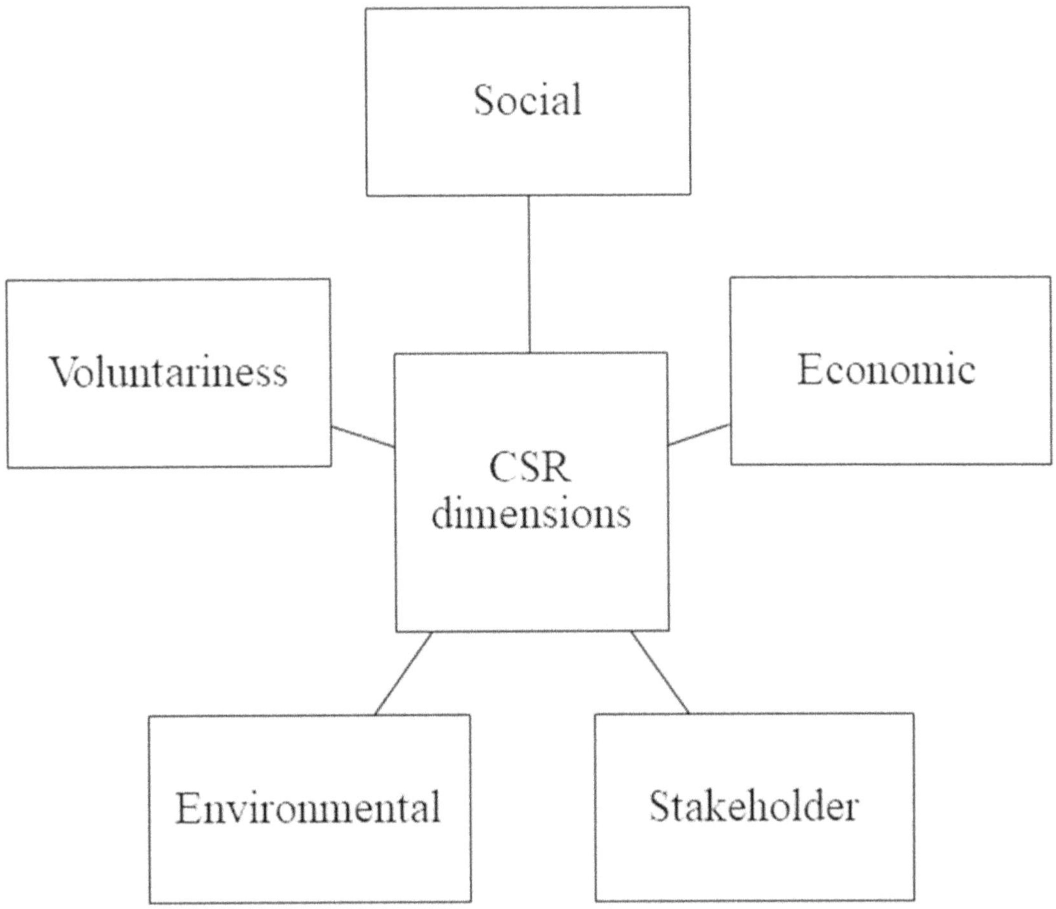

from CG and CC is that CSR values are expressed in three dimensions: economic, environmental and social (Karmasin & Litschka, 2017, pp. 40-41), which is in line with the concept of Triple Bottom Line.

Note that, the whole concept of Corporate Responsibility (which includes CC, CG and CSR) needs an important role, which is assigned to Communication Responsibility. The purpose of Communication Responsibility is to transfer information about Corporate Responsibility in a transparent and reliable manner to the potentially unlimited audience created by the use of various media channels (Karmasin & Litschka, 2017, pp. 45-46).

The attempt to define what CSR is has resulted in the creation of many models. Two of them will be presented as they represent two completely different views (presented on Figure 6.):

- **The CSR Pyramid (1991):** which is an extension of the new understanding of the 1979 definition of CSR and is the following common definition after the one created by H. Bowen in 1953, created by A. B. Carroll;
- **CSR 2.0 DNA:** model presented by W. Visser (Visser, 2010);

Figure 5. The division of Corporate Responsibility
Source: (Karmasin & Litschka, 2017, p. 41)

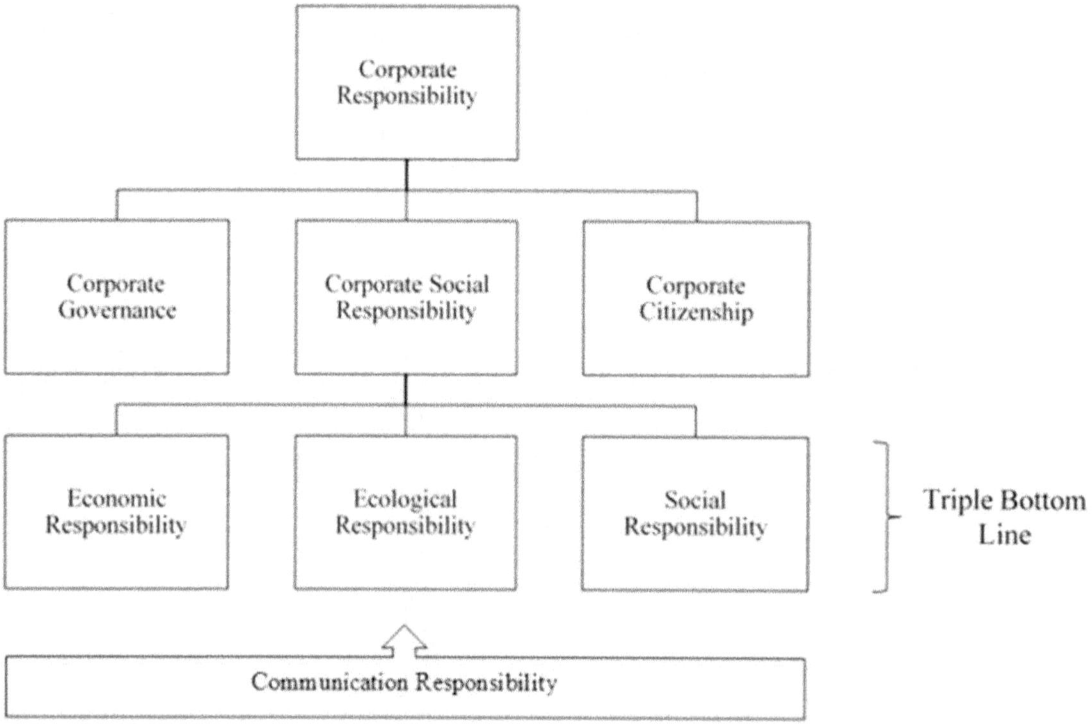

Figure 6. The two different concepts of CSR
Source: (Carroll, 1991; Visser, 2010)

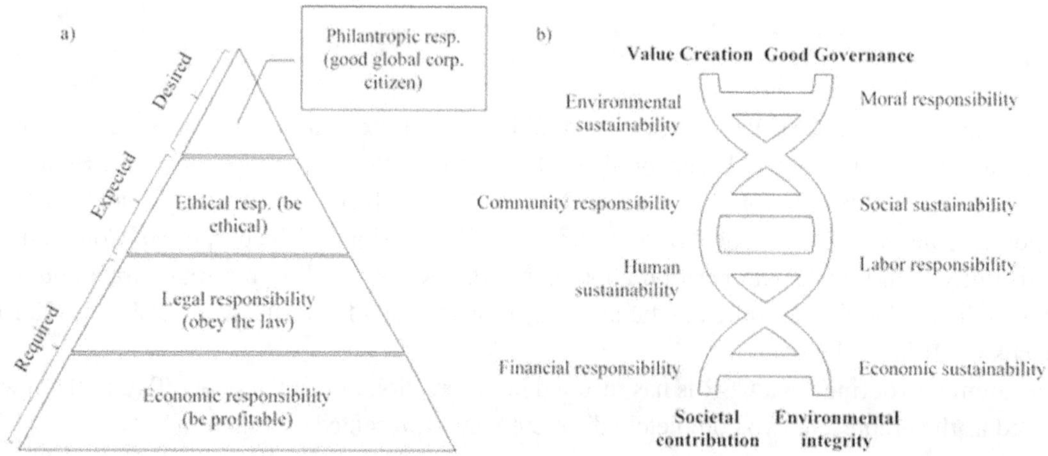

The Figure 6a. presents a model created by A.B. Carroll in 1991 which is based on definition created in 1979. The author described that CSR covers economic, legal, ethical and discretionary (voluntary) expectations that society has towards an organization at a given moment. As the author pointed out, economic obligations are the first and most important social obligations of enterprises, consisting in producing goods and providing services that society needs in return for remuneration in the form of profit. Legal obligations relate to the operation of enterprises on the basis of socially established laws and principles. This means that the society, under the "social contract", expects business to carry out its economic mission in the adopted legal order. Ethical obligations refer to additional obligations expected by the society that go beyond a specific legal framework. Obligations of a volitional (discretionary) nature refer to voluntary obligations not marked with an unambiguous message from the society. They include philanthropic and aid activities towards particular social groups (Carroll A. B., 1979, p. 500).

A characteristic feature of A.B Carroll's CSR Pyramid model is the presence of tensions between individual levels. The author mentions that the greatest tensions exist between the economic level and others above. However, these are not tensions regarding to the choice between profit and activities for the benefit of society (traditional approach). Instead, regarding to stakeholder perspective, the entire pyramid should be considered and then managed in such a way that all the components of the pyramid are met simultaneously (Carroll A. B., 1991, pp. 42-43).

Completely different concept was proposed by M. Visser in 2010, who on the basis of the created CSR 2.0 model in the form of DNA (Figure 6b.) shows that the traditional approaches (CSR 1.0) such as used by A. B. Carroll (CSR Pyramid) are outdated. The one of the reasons is not taking into account the environmental factor (Visser, 2010). Thus, the author proposes to stick to the current acronym of CSR while changing the name to Corporate Sustainability and Responsibility. The purpose of this change with adding the environmental factor into concept was to show the connection between CSR and Sustainability. However, the core change of CSR 2.0 is about changing the whole perception of the enterprises to CSR – in other words the DNA of companies must be change to sustainable one. CSR 2.0. is based on five principles (Visser, 2011, p. 9):

- **the principle of creativity:** this principle requires innovation and creativity, including combining technological solutions in order to solve environmental and social problems;
- **the principle of scalability:** CSR 2.0. requires action on a massive scale, just as the environmental and social needs are immense and urgent. The actions of companies must be large and significant, such as limiting the sale of only organic products, even without the possibility of leaving the choice to the customer;
- **the principle of sensitivity:** CSR 2.0 requires uncomfortable and transformative awareness and an answer to the question whether the industry or the business model used is part of the solution or part of the problem;
- **the principle based on global thinking and local action ('glocality'):** where enterprises will have to be oriented towards local societies by applying global and universal principles of sustainable development;
- **the principle of circularity:** which consists in increasing production while reducing the use of natural and human capital.

The author uses the DNA scheme because it combines CSR (which comes from social aspects) and Sustainability (associated more with the environmental movement) (Visser, 2010). DNA CSR 2.0. it is based on four values: value creation, good governance, social contribution, and environmental integrity (Visser, 2011, p. 9). Value creation is primarily concerned with the company's profitability. The goal is therefore economic development, but not only expressed by contributing to the enrichment of shareholders and management, but the entire economic context in which the company operates by carrying out activities such as investing in infrastructure, creating jobs, providing skills for employees, etc. Good governance refers to the transparency and reporting approach, but in a new version similar to the WEB 2.0 concept and social media, where two-way communication becomes important. Currently, in the field of CSR you can find only one-way communication, where the company only presents a report and data related to Corporate Social Responsibility once in a while (usually once a year). An example of such an approach can be the Patagonia company, which in the online store indicates for each product the environmental impact of its production (however user can decide on this information only to buy the product or not). Social contribution concerns the orientation of activities towards internal (employees, suppliers, consumers, creditors, shareholders) and external (society, government) stakeholders. Environmental integrity is about not only minimizing damage to the environment by businesses, but also maintaining and improving the ecosystem.

The Path of Business to Sustainability

T. Dyllick and K. Muff presented the proposal for the evolution of enterprises towards full sustainable business (Dyllick & Muff, 2016, pp. 156-174) – which can be defined as the path of business to Sustainability. The authors presented three successive phases of transition from the traditional stage of business (*business-as-usual*) to full sustainable business. Traditional business is characterized by taking care of only economic issues. The supporting theory of this model of business is the shareholders' value, using the inside-out organizational perspective, whereby the company's goals are placed at the center of the focus, implying its strategies and actions.

The transition to the next phase (sustainable business 1.0) requires broadening the issues that concern the enterprise to environmental and social issues. A theory supporting sustainable business 1.0. is redefined shareholder value with the same main focus on maximizing value for owners. In this phase, business continues to notice, in addition to economic issues, environmental and social issues. Its organizational orientation, however, does not change.

As the importance of value increases, business moves to the next phase: sustainable business 2.0. The fundamental change compared to the previous phase is the extension of values based on the TBL model and values for stakeholders (Dyllick & Muff, 2016b, p. 400). The company's goal is to create, produce and report results through well-defined areas of Sustainability while maintaining an economic and profitable tone. The enterprise internal perspective is still the focus of attention.

A truly sustainable business (3.0) requires a shift in the organizational perspective, from inside to outside (outside-in). This means that business changes the approach from minimizing negative effects to looking for and implementing solutions supporting society and the environment, focusing primarily on the aspects that require the highest attention (poverty, hunger, environmental degradation, etc.) (Dyllick & Muff, 2016, pp. 164-166). The shift to sustainable business 3.0 needs a change of perspective such as mentioned in CSR 2.0 and truly sustainable companies are looking for answers to questions such as (Dyllick & Muff, 2016, p. 168):

Question 1: Which of the most demanding environmental, social and economic issues can be solved by dedicating resources, competences, talents and experiences by these companies?

Question 2: What are the benefits (and share of these benefits) for society and the environment from the products and services offered by enterprises?

Question 3: How can companies transform their activities to deliver (through the products and services they offer) solutions directly and measurably to pressing environmental and social issues?

Question 4: How can companies open up and develop corporate structures so that they can more effectively respond to the needs of society?

Question 5: What can a single enterprise do? Which sectoral and cross-sectoral strategies should companies be involved in?

Question 6: Which activities must enterprises engage in to change the rules of the game and combine the divergent requirements of the current economic system with the requirements of Sustainability?

Searching by enterprises for answers to the above questions gives them the status of sensitive citizens of society, acting not only individually, but also sectorally and intersectorally. Thanks to such a broad approach, Sustainability will be taken into account throughout the entire supply chain, which will increase the involvement of all its participants. In turn, the increase in the number of participants will affect the "rules of the market game" by combining economic requirements with environmental and social issues, thus bringing the transition to an economy based on Sustainability. This means that "cleaning up the corporate fish if then is released back into dirty market waters?" is over.

Table 2. presents the typology of business towards sustainable business presented by T. Dyllick and K. Muff.

Table 2. The Business Sustainability Typology with key characteristics and shifts

Business Sustainability Typology	Concerns (What?)	Values created? (What for?)	Organizational perspective (How?)	The key shifts involved:
Business-as-usual	Economic concerns	Shareholder value	Inside-out	1st shift: broadening the business concern
Business Sustainability 1.0.	Three dimensional concerns	Refined shareholder value	Inside-out	2nd shift: expanding the value created
Business Sustainability 2.0.	Three dimensional concerns	Triple Bottom Line	Inside-out	3rd shift: changing the perspective
Business Sustainability 3.0.	Starting with Sustainability challenges	Creating value for the good	Outside-in	

Source: (Dyllick & Muff, 2016, p. 169)

The model above shows mainly the way of positive change. Other interesting concept of the future and Sustainability is the Three Horizons model presented by A. Curry and A. Hodgson. The Three Horizons pictured in Figure 7. consist of (Curry & Hodgson, 2008, pp. 2-3):

'1st Horizon': which is the current prevailing system and which loses its strategic fit to external environment with time – the word in this horizon is *in which fossil fuel sources are dominant, in terms of consumption, production, and distribution infrastructure. It is also generally centralized. The prevailing consumption model is that energy is "always on"; continuous power is supplied to whoever wants it and can afford it. This prevailing system is falling away because of concern over carbon emissions and resource shortages (Curry & Hodgson, 2008, p. 3).*

'3rd Horizon': is the horizon where ideas and arguments which have the potential to displace the world of 1st Horizon, because they represent much more effective response to changes in external environment. '3rd Horizon' *advocates propose, generally, the production of energy from renewable energy sources; some also advocate more local or decentralised energy systems; there are some who propose* *reduced consumption. Some link high levels of energy use explicitly to degradation of eco-systems and biodiversity. Emerging technologies (such as combined heat and power) are championed; different energy-based business models are tried (for example service-based energy companies). Other Horizon 3 actors point to hydrogen-based energy futures; some to an energy future based on nuclear fission (Curry & Hodgson, 2008, p. 3).*

'2nd Horizon': is and intermediate space in which first and third horizons collide and where transition is typically unstable, characterized by competing alternative paths to the future proposed by vary actors.

Figure 7. Schematic of the futures-oriented Three Horizons model
Source: (Curry & Hodgson, 2008)

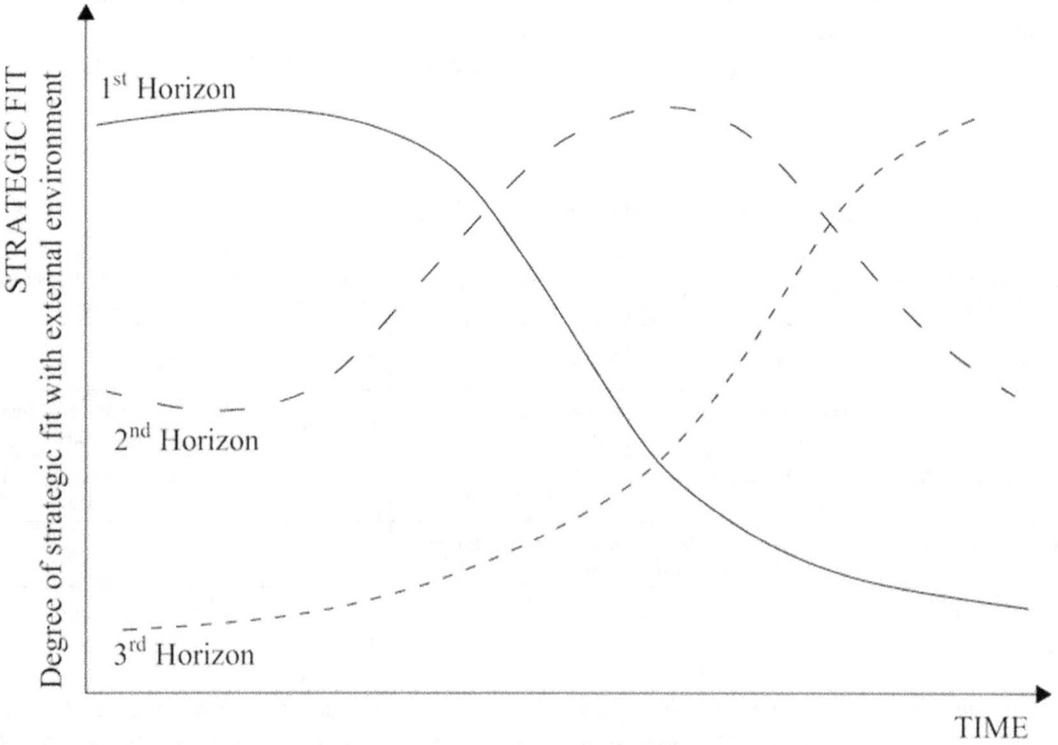

J. Elkington the creator of TBL in the book: *Green Swans: The Coming Boom in Regenerative Capitalism* (Elkington, 2020) divided the Three Horizons into three time frames: 1st Horizon (*business-as-usual; world of the manager)* he dated to 2020, 2nd to 2030 (*world of the entrepreneur*), and the 3rd to 2100 (world of the *visionary*). The last horizon is what J. Elkington hopes: *a time of growing Green Swan solutions and changing the system for the better. But this change needs to have well-tame concepts such as a Triple Bottom Line (Elkington, 2020).*

Corporate Social Responsibility, Triple bottom line and sustainability – where we at?

The purpose of the empirical research

The purpose of this part of the chapter is to make an attempt to assess the level of activities of enterprises in the field of Sustainability on the basis of the collected qualitative research in the form of case studies. To make this assess four questions must be answered:

Question 1: What is the level of enterprises in terms of activities based on the Triple Bottom Line concept in terms of profit, environment and society (separately and together)?

Question 2: What is the level of enterprises in terms of activities based on the CSR 2.0 concept in terms of five principles (creativity, scalability, sensitivity, 'glocality', circularity)

Question 3: Is there a relationship between the level of implementation of activities related to the TBL concept and the CSR 2.0 concept?

Question 4: To which phase, on the basis of the Business Sustainability Typology, enterprises implementing the idea of Sustainability can be assigned?

To answer questions above, the following hypotheses were formulated:

Hypothesis One: Enterprises implementing the idea of the Sustainability do not fully apply the concept of Triple Bottom Line.

Hypothesis Two: Enterprises implementing the idea of Sustainability ascribe the greatest role to profit.

Hypothesis Three: Enterprises implementing the idea of the Sustainability do not fully apply the concept of CSR 2.0.

Hypothesis Four: Enterprises implementing the idea of the Sustainability are in the business-as-usual phase according to the Business Sustainability Typology.

The Methodology Used in the Empirical Part

To answer the questions asked and confirm the hypotheses two research method was used: Case Survey method and Technique for Order of Preference by Similarity to Ideal Solution (TOPSIS).

The Case Survey method provides *bridge the gap between nomothetic surveys and idiographic case studies to combine their respective benefits of generalizable, cross-sectional analysis and in-depth, processual analysis (Larsson, 1993, p. 1515).* According to the methodology, the basic Case Survey procedure consists of (Larsson, 1993, p. 1516):

Step 1: Selecting case studies appropriate to the research questions posed, 2), 3) 4) analysis of coded, quantifiable data
Step 2: Establishing a scheme for coding qualitative information into quantifiable variables
Step 3: Assessing case studies based on specific coding by several raters and measuring interrater reliability
Step 4: Analysis of coded, quantifiable data.

The specific procedure can be broken down to twelve steps, which are (Larsson, 1993, p. 1522):
Step 1: Developing initial research questions
Step 2: Case selection criteria
Step 3: Case sample collection
Step 4: Designing the coding scheme to convert the cases into variables
Step 5: Coding the cases through multiple raters
Step 6: Authors participation.
Step 7: Measuring interrater reliability

Step 8: Resolving coding discrepancies
Step 9: Analyzing the coding validity
Step 10: The analysis of the impact of specific case characteristics;
Step 11: The analysis of case collection;
Step 12: Reporting the study.

The analysis of gathered data using Case Survey method was carried out by the classical TOPSIS method. The TOPSIS belongs to multi-criteria models in making decision (MCDM) (Roszkowska, 2011) and was developed in 1981 by K. Yoon and C. L. Hwang (Yoon i Hwang, 1981). The classical model is similar to method presented by Z. Hellwig in 1968 on the field of economics (taxonomy) (Hellwig, 1968). The main difference is that TOPSIS uses both the positive and negative ideal solutions (patterns), while Hellwig's method uses only positive ideal solution (pattern). TOPSIS also uses the normalization by quotient transform and the Hellwig method uses standardization. Hence the output of TOPSIS is between 0 and 1, and Hellwig method is generally between 0 and 1 but in some cases it can be above 1 (Bąk, 2016) – for this reason the TOPSIS method was used instead of Hellwig method. However empirical studies shows very high positive correlation (0,97-0,98) between both methods (Bąk, 2016).

The procedure of the TOPSIS synthetic measure is as follows (Bąk, 2016, pp. 26-27):

Step 1: Normalization of variables (quotient transformation)
Step 2: Calculating the maximum and minimum value for the stimulants and destimulants of the positive and negative ideal solutions (patterns)
Step 3: Calculation of the Euclidean distances of objects from the positive and negative ideal solutions (patterns);
Step 4: Ranking the results

The TOPSIS method because of being simple, rational, comprehensible concept, its possibility for visualization (Hung & Chen, 2009) and the adaptability to the coding pattern for the variables used in the Case Survey method allows to answer the posed questions.

The Limitations of the Applied Research

The applied research method especially Case Survey method has several limitations. Due to lack of adequate resources the Step 3 in basic procedure had to be modified. Hence in the specific procedure the steps 5 to 9 had to be omitted. The Author was the only person who was assessing the selected case studies. Other limitation was the omitting the stratified random sampling and small worldwide sample size. In the TOPSIS method the step 4 was unnecessary for the research so it has been also omitted.

Data Collection and Sample Description

The Author's resources collected for other research were used for the this study (17 out of 67 scientific articles were used) and supplemented with additional scientific articles collected on the basis of the Microsoft Academic search engine. The following keywords were used to search for additional case studies: sustainability, case studies, case study research. This means that only case studies related to the subject of sustainability were chosen. Initially, abstracts of individual articles from the search engine

(276 articles) were collected and reviewed, and then only those that indicated or could indicate that the article will contain information relevant to the needs of this research (85 articles were identified) were extracted. Finally, information from 13 additional studies was included in the study. In total 30 articles were used related to the subject of sustainability, from which 45 case studies were extracted.

Only those studies that presented sufficient information for their appropriate assessment were selected (e.g. case studies that focused solely on the environment with complete disregard for social issues were not taken into account). Also, the year of 2005 was taken as the minimum date requirement for publication of the article.

In this study, ten variables were used, of which the first three related to the Triple Bottom Line concept and the next five related to the CSR 2.0 concept. The last two variables were a supplement that allowed to determine the phase of Business Sustainability Typology in accordance with the information provided by T. Dyllick, K. Muff (Dyllick & Muff, 2016). All of those variables were coded by using the Lickert scale from 1 to 7, where 1 meant no or weak value of a given feature, and 7 was the opposite. To variables the questions were assigned.

There were also thirteen control variables included such as: year of the publication in the academic journal, three variables about enterprises size (micro sector, SME sector without micro entities, large enterprises), six variables describing the region of headquarters of the enterprise (Europe, North America, Latin America, Asia, Australia, Africa). The last one was categorical variable which described the sector in which enterprise operated. The variable consisted of 4 categories which were Industry sector, Industrial processing sector, Services sector, Trade sector. Affiliation to a given sector depended on the assigned category according to NACE Rev. 2 (Eurostat, 2008). All of the control variables except the year of publication and sector variable were yes-no answers.

Table 3. in Appendix presents the details about the variables, questions, and encoding used.

The sample consists of 45 case studies, which most of them was publicized from 2014 to 2020 (62,2%). Most of the presented enterprises in case studies were from Europe (48,9%), were large (71,1%) and operated in Industrial processing sector (55,6%). Full description of the sample with number of categories and percentage broken down into categories presents Table 4. in Appendix.

Results

The study took into account variables related to the concept of TBL (economic, environmental, social), which were normalized to obtain a value ranging from zero to one. Higher levels of individual variables indicated more sustainable activities of the company. It should be mentioned that the economic variable differs from the other two variables. A value of zero for this variable means that the enterprise is focused primarily on profitability. For the remaining variables zero means no action in a given area (environmental, social). All three variables were also jointly analyzed by establishing a synthetic measure using the TOPSIS procedure. In this method, all the values of the variables were treated as stimulants, because higher results indicated a higher level of Sustainability in terms of the TBL concept.

The synthetic measure obtained by the TOPSIS procedure also reaches values from zero to one, therefore it allows to determine the level for all included variables simultaneously. The value of one is the ideal value, that is, it proves the enterprises' high commitment to Sustainability.

In this study, the TOPSIS method was also used to determine the level of implementation of the CSR 2.0 concept (TOPSIS CSR 2.0 variable) and to assign the studied sample of enterprises to the appropriate Business Sustainability Typology (TOPSIS SUSTAINABILITY variable). In order to define the level of implementation of the CSR 2.0 concept, variables determined on the basis of five CSR 2.0 principles included in the theory were used.

In the case of the TOPSIS SUSTAINABILTY study, all previously captured variables (TBL and CSR 2.0) were used, supplemented with variables related to the orientation of enterprises towards stakeholders and the organizational perspective.

Table 3. Descriptive statistics for Economic, Environmental, Social variables and TOPSIS Performance Scores

Variable	Min	Max	Mean	Q1	Median	Q3	Standard deviation	Skewness	Kurtosis
Economic	0,00	0,67	0,39	0,17	0,33	0,50	0,19	-0,07	-1,12
Environmental	0,17	1,00	0,57	0,50	0,50	0,67	0,20	0,40	-0,57
Social	0,17	0,83	0,46	0,33	0,50	0,50	0,18	0,35	-0,51
TOPSIS TBL	0,00	1,00	0,39	0,21	0,39	0,54	0,22	0,63	-0,15
TOPSIS CSR 2.0	0,06	0,73	0,33	0,20	0,30	0,47	0,19	0,34	-0,72
TOPSIS SUSTAINABILITY	0,54	0,62	0,58	0,58	0,58	0,59	0,03	-0,76	1,00

Source: own elaboration.

Table 3. Provides descriptive statistics for the variables described above.

The data included in Table 3. show that the companies participating in the study were characterized by a moderate implementation of sustainable activities – the mean and median for the TOPSIS TBL variable were 0.39. Broken down into individual variables, it can be seen that enterprises primarily chose environmental activities (average: 0.57), and then social (average: 0.46). Moreover, the economic variable was at a relatively low level, which proves that the profit for the surveyed enterprises was the most important factor. Therefore, the first and second hypotheses should be confirmed.

Data on all three variables calculated with the use of the TOPSIS method show that enterprises are relatively high in the typology of Business Sustainability (average: 0.58). Referring to the theory, it can be stated that the studied companies are in the phase between Business Sustainability 1.0 and Business Sustainability 2.0 (which means the rejection of hypothesis four). The lowest results were observed for the TOPSIS CSR 2.0 variable. That means that it is impossible to reject the third hypothesis. Low level of implementation CSR 2.0 may constitute a serious barrier to entering the phase of sustainable business 3.0. However, it should be emphasized that the correlation between the TOPSIS TBL variable and TOPSIS CSR is strongly positive (the correlation value was 0.752; in order to calculate the correlation, the Shapiro-Wilk tests for the normality of the distribution were first performed; p-values greater than 5% allowed for the Pearson correlation). Such a strong correlation may indicate that the implementation of the TBL concept will support the development of the CSR 2.0 concept, thanks to which enterprises will be able to achieve the business sustainability 3.0 phase. However, it should be borne in mind that this correlation is burdened with a large error due to the omission of methodological steps related to the assessment of case studies by many raters and a limited research sample.

SOLUTIONS AND RECOMMENDATIONS

Research has shown that there is still a need to change the approach of enterprises to Sustainability. Although the development in this area is significant, profit is still the most important criterion among enterprises. It is true that there is also a visible change in attitude and the orientation of activities for the environment, a different, deeper point of reference is still required. Enterprises should adopt the principles of CSR 2.0 in their strategies, i.e. they should realize that they are responsible for the environment and society, in accordance with the Strong Sustainability theory, and then take appropriate actions thinking outside the box, looking for solutions that would support lower resource consumption, and at the same time helping to improve the environment and society. Such an attitude of enterprises will allow for a significant transition from the *world of entrepreneur* (2nd horizon) to the *world of visionary* (3rd horizon).

FUTURE RESEARCH DIRECTIONS

The purpose of the study was to try to determine the implementation of the concept of TBL, CSR 2.0 and to determine in which phase of Business Sustainability the surveyed enterprises were. The study was limited by the lack of other raters assessing the selected sample of enterprises. In addition, the sample of the company was small and there was no stratified sampling made to adapt the sample to the population. Therefore, in future research it is recommended to supplement the above-mentioned limitations and completion of the research sample by using additional sources.

CONCLUSION

The development of science in Sustainability and Corporate Social Responsibility (CSR) has been going on for at least 50 years. Although the time of origin and development of both concepts are different, they should be considered as complementary. CSR was developed first, but it is narrower than a concept of Sustainability and should be considered as a way of business to achieve the Sustainability . However, fulfilling the Sustainability is not simple and needs a certain path which could be described by a Triple Bottom Line (TBL) model.

However, the difficulty of implementing the Triple Bottom Line concept is treating it as purely an accounting tool, while it is much deeper and should provoke deeper thinking about capitalism and its future. A deeper consideration of the TBL concept is also connected with a deeper look at Corporate Social Responsibility, a more thorough view in the CSR 2.0 version.

Currently, a positive trend in the activities of enterprises towards Sustainability is visible. These activities, however, as shown by the conducted research, still rely to a greater extent on neo-liberal thinking, where the most important criterion is profit, and environmental and social issues are placed at a lower place.

The Triple Bottom Line concept cannot be treated as an exchange between its individual areas. All components should be treated at least synonymously or with an appropriate hierarchy according to the Strong Sustainability concept. The concept of TBL, like CSR 2.0, should constitute the main core of the enterprises' activity. As in the case of CSR 2.0, the concept of TBL should be embedded in the DNA of companies. The fulfillment of these conditions will allow to obtain full Sustainability, or as T. Dyllick and K. Muff presented it as a sustainable business 3.0.

REFERENCES

Agudelo, M. L., Jóhannsdóttir, L., & Davídsdóttir, B. (2019). A literature review of the history and evolution of corporate social responsibility. *International Journal of Corporate Social Responsibility.*

Arena, M., Ciceri, S. D., Terzi, S., Bengo, I., Azzone, G., & Garetti, M. (2009). A state-of-the-art of industrial sustainability: Definitions, tools and metrics. *International Journal of Product Lifecycle Management, 4*(1), 207. doi:10.1504/IJPLM.2009.031674

Arowoshegbe, A. O., & Emmanuel, U. (2016). *Sustainability and Triple Bottom Line: an overview of two interrelated concepts* (Vol. 2). Igbinedion University Journal of Accounting.

Bąk, A. (2016). Porządkowanie liniowe obiektów metodą Hellwiga i TOPSIS – analiza porównawcza. *Research Papers of Wroclaw University of Economics.*, (426). Advance online publication. doi:10.15611/pn.2016.426.02

Benaim, A., Collins, A. C., & Raftis, L. (2008). *The Social Dimension of Sustainable Development: Guidance and Application: Thesis submitted for completion of Master of Strategic Leadership towards Sustainability.* Blekinge Institute of Technology.

Biely, K., Maes, D., & Passel, S. V. (2016). *The idea of weak sustainability is illegitimate.* Academic Press.

Bowen, H. R. (1953). *Social responsibilities of the businessman.* Harper & Brothers.

Burton, I. (1968). The quality of the environment: A review. *Geographical Review, 58*(3), 472. doi:10.2307/212567

Carroll, A. B. (1979). A Three-Dimensional Conceptual Model of Corporate Performance. *Academy of Management Review, 4*(4), 497–505. doi:10.5465/amr.1979.4498296

Carroll, A. B. (1991). The pyramid of corporate social responsibility: Toward the moral management of organizational stakeholders. *Business Horizons, 34*(4), 39–48. doi:10.1016/0007-6813(91)90005-G

Carroll, A. B. (2015). Corporate social responsibility: The centerpiece of competing and complementary frameworks. *Organizational Dynamics*, 44.

Carroll, B. (2002). Sustainable development: an eclectic view. *CIWEM International Directory 2003.*

Ciegis, R., Ramansuskiene, J., & Martinkus, B. (n.d.). Ekonomikos plėtra darnaus vystymosi aspektu. *Taikomoji ekonomika: sisteminiai tyrimai, 2*(1).

Curry, A., & Hodgson, A. (2008, August). Seeing in Multiple Horizons: Connecting Futures to Strategy. *Journal of Futures Studies*, (13), 1–20.

Dahlsrud, A. (2006). How Corporate Social Responsibility is Defined an Analysis of 37 Definitions. *Corporate Social Responsibility and Environmental Management, 15*(1), 1–13. doi:10.1002/csr.132

Diesendorf, M. (2000). Sustainability and sustainable development. Sustainability: The corporate challenge of the 21st century.

Dyllick, T., & Muff, K. (2016). Clarifying the meaning of sustainable business introducing a typology from business-as-usual to true business sustainability. *Organization & Environment*, *29*(2), 156–174. doi:10.1177/1086026615575176

Dyllick, T., & Muff, K. (2016b). Transitioning w: Sustainable Business: A One Planet Approach. In *S. Jeanrenaud, J. P. Jeanrenaud, & J. Gosling*. Wiley.

Earth Day. (n.d.). *The history of earth day*. Retrieved November 13, 2020, from https://www.earthday.org/about/thehistory-of-earth-day/

Ekins, P., Simon, S., Deutsch, L., Folke, C., & Groot, R. D. (2003). A framework for the practical application of the concepts of critical natural capital and strong sustainability. *Ecological Economics*, *44*(2-3), 165–185. doi:10.1016/S0921-8009(02)00272-0

Elkington, J. (1997). *Cannibals with forks – Triple bottom line of 21st century business*. Stoney Creek.

Elkington, J. (1998). Accounting for the Triple Bottom Line. *Measuring Business Excellence*, *2*(3), 18–22. doi:10.1108/eb025539

Elkington, J. (2018, June 25). 25 Years Ago I Coined the Phrase 'Triple Bottom Line'. Here's Why It's Time to Rethink It. *Harvard Business Review*. Retrieved September 2020, 2020, from https://hbr.org/2018/06/25-years-ago-i-coined-the-phrase-triple-bottom-line-heres-why-im-giving-up-on-it

Elkington, J. (2020). *Green Swans: The Coming Boom in Regenerative Capitalism*. Fast Company Press.

Eurostat. (2008). NACE Rev. 2: Statistical classification of economic activities in the European Community. *Eurostat Methodologies and Working papers*.

Fifka, M. S. (2009). *Towards a More Business-Oriented Definition of Corporate Social Responsibility: Discussing the Core Controversies of a Well-Established Concept*. J. Service Science & Management.

Giddings, B., Hopwood, B., & O'Brien, G. (2002). Environment, Economy and Society: Fitting them together into Sustainable Development. *Sustainable Development*, *10*(4), 187–196. doi:10.1002d.199

Gray, R. (2010). Is accounting for sustainability actually accounting for sustainability… and how would we know? An exploration of narratives of organisations and the planet. *Accounting, Organizations and Society*, *35*(1), 47–62. doi:10.1016/j.aos.2009.04.006

Gray, R., & Milne, R. M. (2004). Towards reporting on the triple bottom line: Mirages, methods and myths. The Triple Bottom Line does it all add up? Assessing the sustainability of business and CSR.

Hellwig, Z. (1968). Zastosowanie metody taksonomicznej do typologicznego podziału krajów ze względu na poziom ich rozwoju oraz zasoby i strukturę wykwalifikowanych kadr. *Przegląd Statystyczny*, (4).

Henriques, A., & Richardson, J. (2004). Introduction: The Triple Bottom Line does it all add up? *The Triple Bottom Line does it all add up? Assessing the sustainability of business and CSR*.

Hilb, M. (2006). *Integrierte corporate governance. Ein neues Konzept der Unternehmensführung und Erfolgskontrolle*. Springer. doi:10.1007/3-540-32744-4

Hung, C., & Chen, L. (2009). A Fuzzy TOPSIS Decision Making Model with Entropy Weight under Intuitionistic Fuzzy Environment. *Proceedings of the International Multi-Conference of Engineers and Computer Scientists*.

Jacobs, M. (1995). *Sustainable Development-From Broad Rhetoric to Local Reality. Conference Proceedings from Agenda 21 in Cheshire*. Cheshire County Council, Document No. 493.

Karmasin, M., & Litschka, M. (2017). CSR as economic, ethical and communicative concept. In S. Diehl & M. Karmasin (Eds.), *Handbook of Integrated CSR Communication*. Springer International Publishing. doi:10.1007/978-3-319-44700-1_3

Kates, R. W., Parris, T. M., & Leiserowitz, A. A. (2005). What is Sustainable Development? Goals, Indicators, Values, and Practice. *Environment*, *47*(3).

Larsson, R. (1993). Case Survey Methodology: Quantitative Analysis of Patterns Across Case Studies. Academy of Management Journal, 36(6).

Lee, K. M. (1997). So What is the 'Triple Bottom Line'? *The International Journal of Diversity in Organisations, Communities and Nations, 6*.

Lusawa, R. (2009). *Hans Carl Von Carlowitz twórca pojęcia "trwałości"*. Rocznik Naukowy Wydziału Zarządzania w Ciechanowie. Ekonomia i Finanse.

Mancebo, F. (2013). Développement durable (2nd ed.). Paris: Arman Colin.

Musco, C., Musco, C., & Tsourakakis, C. E. (2018). Minimizing Polarization and Disagreement in Social Networks. In *Proceedings of the 2018 World Wide Web Conference (WWW '18)*. International World Wide Web Conferences Steering Committee. 10.1145/3178876.3186103

Pearce, D. (1992). Green economics. *Environmental Values*, *1*(1), 3–13. doi:10.3197/096327192776680179

Pelenc, J., & Ballet, J. (2015). *Weak Sustainability versus Strong Sustainability*. Brief for GSDR.

Pezzey, J. (1992). *Definitions of Sustainability*. UK Center for Economic and Environmental Development, Working Paper No. 9.

Robèrt, K., Schmidt-Bleekh, B., Larderelc, J., Basilede, G., Jansenf, J. L., Kuehrg, R., ... Wackernagelj, M. (2002). Strategic sustainable development - Selection, design and synergies of applied tools. *Journal of Cleaner Production*, *10*(3), 10. doi:10.1016/S0959-6526(01)00061-0

Roszkowska, E. (2011). Multi-Criteria Decision Making Models by applying the TOPSIS method to crisp and interval data. *Multiple Criteria Decision Making, 6*.

Scherer, A. G., & Palazzo, G. (2007). Toward a Political Conception of Corporate Responsibility: Business and Society Seen from a Habermasian Perspective. *Academy of Management Review*, *32*(4).

Tempels, T., Blok, V., & Verweij, M. (2017). Understanding political responsibility in corporate citizenship: Towards a shared responsibility for the common good. *Journal of Global Ethics*, *13*(1), 90–108. doi:10.1080/17449626.2017.1320577

Visser, W. (2010). *CSR 2.0: The Evolution and Revolution of Corporate Social Responsibility. In Responsible Business: How to Manage a CSR Strategy Successfully*. Wiley.

Visser, W. (2011). *The Ages and Stages of CSR. Towards the Future with CSR 2.0*. Social Space.

World Commission on Environment and Development. (1987). *Report of the World Commission on Environment and Development: Our Common Future*. Author.

Yoon, K., & Hwang, C. (1981). *Multiple Attribute Decision Making: Methods and Applications*.

KEY TERMS AND DEFINITIONS

Business Sustainability Typology: The proposal for the evolution of enterprises towards full sustainable business, which can be defined as the path of business to sustainability.

Case Survey: A research method of aggregating qualitative and descriptive information in existing case study literature and making it susceptible to quantitative analysis.

Corporate Social Responsibility (CSR): The concept according to which enterprises take into account social interests and environmental protection in their strategy.

Corporate Social Responsibility 2.0 (CSR 2.0): Reinvented and more radical version of Corporate Social Responsibility concept.

Strong Sustainability: A concept of Sustainability which assumes that social, environmental and economic (financial) capital are complementary, but not interchangeable.

Sustainability: The concept referred as a state of meeting the needs of the present without compromising the ability of future generations to meet their own needs.

Sustainable Development: The concept referred as a process to the state of meeting the needs of the present without compromising the ability of future generations to meet their own needs.

Technique for Order of Preference by Similarity to Ideal Solution (TOPSIS): A research method that creates a synthetic measure on the basis of many features, most often used in the decision-making process.

Triple Bottom Line (TBL, 3BL, 3PP): A sustainability framework that examines the enterprise's social, environment, and economic impact.

Weak Sustainability: A concept of sustainability which assumes that social, environmental and economic (financial) capital are interchangeable.

APPENDIX

Table 4. Variables, related questions and coding used in the study

Name of variable	Question	Scale type	Answers
Economic	How important it is for a company to make a profit?	Lickert	1 - the enterprise's focus is solely on profit; 7 - profit in order to ensure business continuity
Environmental	How important is the environment to the company?	Lickert	1 - the enterprise does not care about environmental matters (internal and external) 7 - the company cares very much about environmental matters (internal and external)
Social	How important are social issues for the company (internal, e.g. employees, clients, and external, e.g. related to the local community)?	Lickert	1 - the enterprise does not care about social matters (internal and external) 7 - the company cares very much about social matters (internal and external)
Stakeholders/ Stakeholders	Towards which group enterprise is oriented the most?	Lickert	1 - The company is exclusively shareholder-oriented 7 - The company is oriented towards a wide range of stakeholders
Inside-out-to-Outside-in	What is the perspective of the organizational orientation of the enterprise?	Lickert	1 - Inside-out perspective 7 - Outside-in perspective
Creativity	What is the level to orientation of innovation and creativity of the enterprise when using various technologies to solve environmental and social problems?	Lickert	1 - No creativity/innovation orientation 7 - Full creativity/innovation orientation
Scalability	What is the company's scalability potential? How much does company use scalability opportunities to achieve sustainability?	Lickert	1 - The enterprise's inability to scale or it does not take the advantage of scalability to achieve sustainability 7 - The enterprise has scalability capabilities and eagerly uses scalability to achieve sustainability
Senitivity	Is the company aware that its business model is a sustainability problem and is making changes to improve?	Lickert	1 - The company does not try to solve the problem in terms of sustainability although it knows that its business model is a problem to achieve sustainability 7 - The company's business model is fully sustainable
Glocality	Is enterprise oriented towards local societies by applying global and universal principles of Sustainability (such as Sustainable Developments Goals)?	Lickert	1 - Enterprise is not oriented to local society and does not apply the global and universal principles of Sustainability 7 - Enterprise is oriented to local society and apply the global and universal principles of Sustainability
Control Variables:	Year of the publication – year; enterprise size sector (micro, SME, large), region of the headquarters of the enterprise (Europe, North America, Latin America, Asia, Australia, Africa, Developing countries, Developed countries – yes/no answers; Sector (1 –Industry, 2 – Industry, 3 – Industrial Processing, 4 – Trade).		

Source: own elaboration.

Table 5. Data collected broken down into categories

Year of publication	Number of enterprises:	Percentage:
2006	2	4,44%
2007	1	2,22%
2008	1	2,22%
2009	1	2,22%
2011	2	4,44%
2012	6	13,33%
2013	4	8,89%
2014	8	17,78%
2015	6	13,33%
2016	1	2,22%
2017	5	11,11%
2018	5	11,11%
2020	3	6,67%
Size of the enterprise		
Micro	2	4,44%
SME	11	24,44%
Large	32	71,11%
Region of the headquarters of the enterprise		
Europe	22	48,89%
North America	6	13,33%
Latin America	6	13,33%
Asia	9	20,00%
Australia	1	2,22%
Africa	1	2,22%
Region of the headquarters of the enterprise broken down into		
Developing countries	13	28,89%
Developed countries	32	71,11%
Sector/branch of the enterprise:		
Industry	4	8,89%
Industrial processing	25	55,56%
Services	12	26,67%
Trade	4	8,89%

Source: own elaboration.

Chapter 2
Corporate Sustainability:
A Review

Iwona Bąk
West Pomeranian University of Technology, Szczecin, Poland

Katarzyna Cheba
https://orcid.org/0000-0001-8753-7764
West Pomeranian University of Technology, Szczecin, Poland

ABSTRACT

This research provides a comprehensive review of corporate sustainability literature in various application areas. The chapter also highlights the gaps in clearly explaining the scope for it extending and incorporating the term of corporate sustainability into other research areas. The main advantage of this study is that it provides an insight into the state of the art of corporate sustainability in various application areas and future development and research directions. In addition to the literature review in this area, the chapter also presents numerous examples of the understanding of corporate sustainability by various business organizations. The chapter analyses nearly 200 different publications in this field available in the Web of Science database. In addition to quantitative analyses, in-depth qualitative research was also carried out.

INTRODUCTION

Economic development, industrialization, and globalization processes have significantly contributed to the degradation of the natural environment. Climate changes, resulting from the emission of carbon dioxide and other greenhouse gases, will negatively influence the functioning of society and the development of countries in the long run (Misztal, 2019, p. 34). Therefore, it is necessary to involve the whole world in activities protecting the natural environment. This applies both to measures taken on a macroeconomic and microeconomic scale, at the level of households and enterprises.

During the past two decades, the concept of corporate sustainability has become increasingly popular. The rapid growth of the research in this area concerning also other directions of world development, such

DOI: 10.4018/978-1-7998-6788-3.ch002

as sustainable development, competitiveness, or sustainable business models is observed. The primary purpose of corporate sustainability is to seek added value to an organization's activities by ensuring they have a positive impact on society, the environment, and the economy. There are usually three areas of corporate sustainability: environmental, social, and economic ones. Some companies also extend this scope to other areas, specifically relating to, e.g., people or organization security. However, the extent of developing this concept and combining it with other business development directions is unknown. In order to explore the issue, this research provides a comprehensive review of corporate sustainability literature in various areas. The paper also highlights the gaps in clearly explaining the scope for it extending and incorporating the term of corporate sustainability into other research areas. The main advantage of this study is providing an insight into the state of the art of corporate sustainability in various application areas, future development, and research directions. In addition to the literature review in this scope, the paper also presents numerous examples of the corporate sustainability understanding by various business organizations. This type of research is particularly important in the current global situation and the threat of a pandemic. A new kind of risk has led to a situation where not only companies but also governments have abandoned their socially responsible actions for the sake of particular benefits.

The paper analyzes publications in this field available in the Web of Science (WoS) database. In addition to quantitative analyzes, in-depth qualitative research was also performed. This research focused mainly on the possibilities of extending the term corporate sustainability and how to combine it with other areas.

Sustainable Development and Corporate Sustainability

The concept of sustainable development was formulated for the first time clearly during the Third UNEP Program in 1975 as "(...) such a course of inevitable and desirable economic development that would not materially and irreversibly affect the human environment and would not lead to the degradation of the biosphere and would not undermine the laws of nature, economics and culture "(UN, 1975). This concept is widespread among researchers from various fields of science. The incorporation of economic issues into this definition has become the basis for formulating a broader concept of sustainable development. In the Brundtland Press Report of the World Commission on Environment and Development of UN in 1987, sustainable development was defined as "... development to meet current needs without the risk that future generations will not be able to meet their needs" (WCED, 1987). In turn, Pearce and Turner (1990) define it as "maximizing the net benefits of economic development while protecting and ensuring the recovery of the usefulness and quality of natural resources in the long term." The main goal of implementing the concept of sustainable development is to reduce the imbalance between economic growth, social development, and the natural environment (Poskrobko, 2009, pp. 25–29).

In the literature, two approaches to this problem can be distinguished (Kozłowski, 2007; Górka, 2007):

- traditional, according to which appropriate relations within economic and social development should be maintained in order to ensure internal compliance,
- a contemporary approach, emphasizing ecological balance and ensuring economic, social, spatial, and environmental order, taking into account the needs of future generations.

The company's efforts to maximize profits or increase market share often violate social and environmental values (Trojanowski, 2015). The accumulation of social and environmental problems contributed to implementing the principles of sustainable development among enterprises. Nowadays, it is believed that sustainable development is a business requirement of the 21st century. When choosing their business partners, companies-customers take into account not only what products and services are offered by a given enterprise, but also whether they act ethically and socially responsible. Nobody will want to work with a company that is known to have, for example, a problem with caring for the environment or do not respect fundamental labor rights. Investors are increasingly aware of the importance of the climate crisis, water scarcity, health and safety in the supply chain, modern slavery, and corruption for their bottom line. Possessing an increasing amount of high-quality data, they increasingly assertively call on companies to address issues related to environmental protection, social responsibility, and corporate governance, striving for a balance between the goals of the organization and the expectations of the entities participating in their operations in increasingly complex ESG (Environmental, Social and Governance). Enterprises all over the world attach increasing importance to ESG factors. Effective management of relationships with various entities (economic, financial, governmental ones) allows companies to manage risk more effectively, take advantage of opportunities, and thus provide themselves with better conditions for achieving long-term success.

The American Business Council declares that the purpose of the corporation is not only to serve its shareholders but to "create value for all our stakeholders," including customers, employees, and local communities. [1] Considering the principles of sustainable development in the functioning of enterprises may contribute to the increase of their value and the strengthening of the competitive position.

Sustainable development is currently one of the most frequently discussed problems, an important area of both scientific considerations and inquiries, as well as decisions regarding the future strategic directions of development of national economies (Bąk, Szczecińska, 2020). This interest is, among others, the effect of the crisis of social trust in commonly used corporate practices, very often focused primarily on maximizing profits for investors. Of course, many of today's corporations are also involved in social activities; however, it is usually classified as cost in the company's budget, a possibly charitable activity that can be deducted from the tax base, an investment in the company's image, or some necessary expenditure, the lack of which can lead to breaking off business contacts (Bąk, Cheba, 2020a).

The literature on the subject (e.g., Sexton et al., 2008; Borys and Czaja, 2009; Płachciak, 2011) indicates that the current stage of the evolution of the idea of sustainable development is primarily its concretization, the aim of which is to develop theoretical foundations of the new development paradigm and its integration with other research areas, including such directions as:

- sustainable transport (e.g., Borys ed. 2008; Bartniczak, 2013),
- sustainable agriculture (e.g., Roling, 2000; Kociszewski, 2013; Altieri, 2018),
- sustainable logistics (e.g., Skowrońska, 2010; Płaczek 2012; Kiba-Janiak, 2015),
- sustainable finance (Fullwiler, 2015; Holmes and Moule, 2016; Aliańska et al. 2018, Zioło et al. 2019),
- sustainable enterprise value (Laszlo, 2003; Bąk, Szczecińska, 2020).

In the subject literature, one can also find references to, for example, "sustainable" urban development (e.g., Girardet, 1999; Mierzejewska, 2009) and the related development of "sustainable" mobility (Kemp and Rotmans, 2004; Banister, 2008; Rudnicki, 2010), "Sustainable" innovations (e.g., Rózicka and Cieślak, 2013) and "sustainable" design (e.g., Bać, 2014; Lechner, 2014), "sustainable" logistics infrastructure (Dembińska, 2018) and relatively new concepts of "sustainable" competitiveness considered in relation to national economies (Aiginger et al., 2013, Cheba, 2019). It is also worth noting that most of these "sustainable" areas are included in sustainable development strategies developed at the international, national, and regional levels.

The assessment of the extent to which the company's activities are sustainable is complex, both due to the complexity of the relationship and the difficulty of their direct measurement. A significant limitation in the multifaceted assessment of sustainable development of enterprises is the moderate availability of statistical data, especially visible, with regard to limited access to qualitative data of a social and environmental nature.

At the present stage of the implementation of the objectives set up in different strategies of sustainable development, including in particular in the latest global strategy for Sustainability 2030 (the 2030 Agenda), we have to deal with significant differentiation of the obtained results in various countries of the world. Sustainable development is particularly important for ensuring proper development and environmental security in both highly developed regions and those that do not develop as dynamically. It is essential both at the level of regions, institutions, and enterprises. It is necessary to establish strategic relations between enterprises and direct and active management thereof, to achieve the goals of the 2030 Agenda (Bąk, Szczecińska, 2020).

The sustainable development of enterprises depends on several factors that can be divided into two main groups (Misztal, 2019a):

- external determinants: political stability, the level of socio-economic development of the country and its growth prospects, legal conditions (including, in particular, national and international regulations and legal norms in the field of environmental protection), social awareness of the impact of human activity on natural resources, financial support for natural environment protection activities, educational programs;
- internal determinants: financial stability of the enterprise, flexibility and the ability to adapt to a changing environment, willingness to take risks, social and environmental awareness, organizational culture and conscious leadership, the size of the enterprise and industries in which it operates externally: macroeconomic conditions, the development directions of the protection environment policy, support from funds for activities aimed at the protection of natural resources, social awareness, the level of competitiveness of enterprises, the level of research development, expenditure on innovative activities;

Economic entities operating on the market often present information on the environmental and social aspects of their activities. It should be noted, however, that both the manner and the scope of disclosures in this field are different. There are no obligatory standards for presenting this type of information, affecting both its quality and credibility. Most often, such a state prompts enterprises to disclose activities that create their positive image, while they ignore behaviors that put them in bad light (Paszkiewicz, Szadziewska, 2011).

Today, more than 90% of CEOs say sustainability is essential to their company's success. That is why they develop sustainability strategies, launch to the market sustainable products and services, create positions such as chief sustainability officers, and publish sustainability reports for consumers, investors, activists, and the general public. This trend is expected to continue in the near future. Research shows that 88% of business school students believe that learning about social and environmental issues in business is a priority, and 67% want to include environmental sustainability in their future work. To meet this demand, the proportion of business schools that require students to attend courses dedicated to business and society increased from 34% in 2001 to 79% in 2011, and specific academic programs on corporate sustainability can now be found at 46% 100 of the Top 100 US Master's Degree Programs in Business Administration (MBA) (Hoffman, 2018).

Bansal and DesJardine (2014) argue that sustainable development takes time into account as it obliges companies to make intertemporal compromises to protect intergenerational equality. In their opinion, sustainable enterprises are those that manage these trade-offs in making strategic decisions in order to take into account both short-term and long-term decisions. Companies must choose between investing less to make lower returns sooner and investing more to make greater returns later (Laverty, 1996).

The growing interest in sustainable development is also visible in the number of publications referring to this term, indexed in the Web of Science (WoS) database between 1987 and 2015. The results of that research were published in 2017 by J. Zhu and Hua [2017]. In that period, as many as 59 926 papers on sustainable development, published by authors from 49 countries, were identified in the WoS database. Also, as many as 149 categories of connections with other research areas were identified. The most significant number of papers in this period was published in the People's Republic of China (11718), then in the United States of America (8839), Great Britain (4905), Australia (2976), and Germany (2298). Throughout the considered period, a systematic increase in the interest in sustainable development was also observed, the most intensive between 2013-2015, when 6189, 6253, and 6087 papers were published in this field, respectively. A further systematic increase in the number of publications is also observed in the following years. Currently, the WoS database includes 33,356 papers referring directly or indirectly to sustainable development and published after 2016. In the first quarter of 2020, the number of publications in this field amounted to over 2,000 (Bąk, Cheba, 2020b). According to the 2011 KPMG survey, 95% of the 250 world largest companies disclose data on their activities in the field of social and environmental responsibility. Most reports were published in Japan, followed by Great Britain and the United States (*KPMG International*, 2011).

Corporate Sustainability in the Web of Science Database

The research was carried out using VOSviewer software version 1.6.14 in order to construct and display bibliometric maps, as well as to identify clusters and their reference networks (van Eck and Waltman 2010; Waltman et al. 2010; Perianes-Rodriguez et al. 2016). We collected 1944 publications indexed in the Web of Science database that were published from 1997 to 2020 containing the term "corporate sustainability" in the title, abstract or keywords. Fig. 1. shows the evolution of the number of publications and citations of these documents in the analysed period. Citations have been increasing significantly, reaching a maximum number in 2019 of 7849 citations. As for the number of publications, the first article appeared in 1997, and, until 2008, only a few articles were published annually in the area under study. The number of publications reached its highest point in 2019 with over three hundred publications. However, it should be noted that in during 8 month of 2020 over 260 publications were already published and the number of citations reached 6840. Table 1 lists the most cited papers.

The main research areas in which the term of "corporate sustainability" were anayalsed are: business economics (1056 papers), environmental sciences ecology (808), science technology other topics (553), engineering (359), social sciences other topics (177). 209 of these articles have appeared in the Journal of Cleaner Production, 192 in Sustainability, 101 in Journal of Business Ethics, and 96 in Busi-

Figure 1. Total publications and citations by year
Source: own elaboration based on WoS

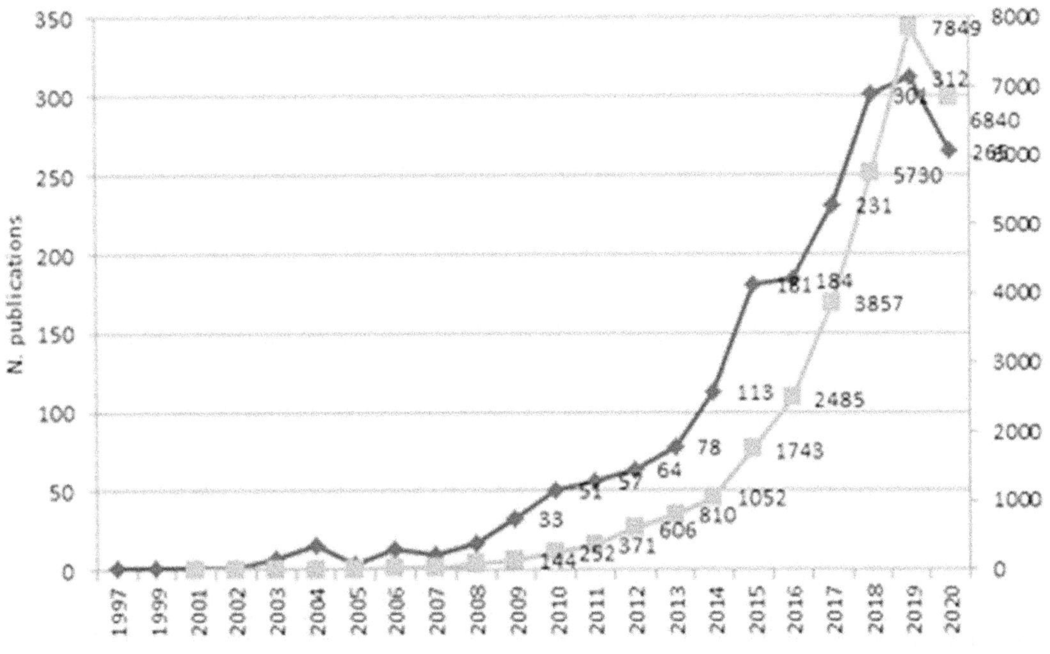

ness Strategy and The Environment. The authors of these studies come mainly from USA (306 papers), England (169), Germay (150), China (141), Australia (133), Brazil (127), Spain (122), and Canada (106).

The author of the first of the presented above papers (Marrewijk, 2003) indicates that the concept of "one solution fits all" in the context of "corporate sustainability" should be abandoned. It is necessary to adopt various and more specific definitions matching the development, awareness and ambition levels of organizations. The authors of this article are of a similar opinion. The authors of subsequent works cited in Table 1 also point out the need to take into account various types of perspectives and points of reference when defining and testing corporate sustainability. Hahn et al. (2010) pointed out that the mainstream of the literature on corporate sustainability is dominated by "the win-win paradigm, according to which economic, environmental and social sustainability aspects can be achieved simultaneously; indeed, corporate sustainability has often been defined by the intersection of these three areas". This means, inter alia, the need to consider trade-offs between the various objectives that make up the overall concept of sustainable development and development of a more inclusive notion of, corporate sustainability. In the next paper of this author (Hahn et al., 2014) it was noted that the corporate sustainability is characterized by conflicting yet interrelated aspects. Linnenluecke and Griffiths (2010) emphasize that there is a link between the cultural orientation of an organization and the pursuit of corporate sustainability principles. The aim of this article is, inter alia, checking the truth of the hypotheses formulated by other authors who suggest that the pathway for the adoption of corporate sustainability principles leads via the adoption of a sustainability-oriented organizational culture.

In order to identify the tendencies of the literature, especially to answer for question how research on this topic is divided into clusters, an analysis of co-citations of references was carried out based on articles with at least 5 co-citations, which resulted in three clusters (see Fig. 2). The clusters are: (1)

Table 1. To ten most cited articles

Paper	Author/year	Journal	Total citations
Concepts and definitions of CSR and corporate sustainability: Between agency and communion	M. van Marrewijk 2003	*Journal of Business Ethics*	889
Conceptualizing a "sustainability business model"	W. Stubbs & Ch. Cocklin 2008	*Organization & Environment*	401
Greening Goliaths versus emerging Davids – Theorizing about the role of incumbents and new entrants in sustainable entrepreneurship	K. Hockerts & R. Wues 2010	*Journal of Business Venturing*	371
The Impact of Corporate Sustainability on Organizational Processes and Performance	R. G. Eccles, I. Ioannou, G. Serafeim 2014	*Management Science*	361
W(h)ither Ecology? The Triple Bottom Line, the Global Reporting Initiative, and Corporate Sustainability Reporting	M. Milne, R. Gray, 2013	Journal of Business Ethics	321
Trade-Offs in Corporate Sustainability: You Can't Have Your Cake and Eat It	T. Hahn, F. Figge, J. Pinkse 2010	Business Strategy and the Environment	277
Corporations, stakeholders and sustainable development I: A theoretical exploration of business-society relations	R. Steure, M. E. Langer, A. Konrad et al. 2005	Journal of Business Ethics	277
Corporate sustainability and organizational culture	M. K. Linnenluecke, A. Griffiths 2010	Journal of World Business	273
Cognitive frames in corporate sustainability: managerial sensemaking with paradoxical and business case frames	T. Hahn, P. Lutz, J. Pinkse et al. 2014	Academy of Management Review	258
Planetary Boundaries: Ecological Foundations for Corporate Sustainability	G. Whiteman, B. Walker, P. Perego 2013	Journal of Management Studies	257

Source: own elaboration based on WoS.

companies, CSR, determinants, environmental, financial, and firm performance, governance, impact, stakeholder theory, strategy; (2) corporate sustainability, framework, green, implementation, innovations, model, organizations, sustainable development, supply chain management; (3) business, management, strategies, perspective.

Analyzes in the first of these areas focus primarily on identifying the factors determining development of corporate sustainability. This problem is presenting in geographical terms: case study from various countries and in firms internal functioning' perspective. The paper of (Crisostomo et al., 2019) aims to analyze corporate sustainability performance (CSP) determinants in Brazil, an important emerging market. Firm CSP is peroxide by the membership to the Corporate Sustainability Index which comprises environmental, social, and economic and governance issues. In this area corporate sustainability is also presenting in relationships with other areas as: investor trust (Suto and Takehara, 2020), government initiatives and internal factors as: environment (e.g. Bansal and Roth, 2000; Banerjee, 2002; Annadale et al., 2004; De Mendonca and Zhou, 2020), corporate sustainability-related awards, global reporting initiatives framework, and organizational strategy (e.g. Zahid et al., 2019), firm financial performance (e.g. Ammer and Othman, 2012). In the second of these cluster focus at the relationships between innovation and corporate sustainability (e.g. Rodrigues et al., 2016; Cherrafi et al., 2018; Xie and Zhu, 2020), while in the third one the relationships with business strategies is the most visible (e.g. Bocken et al., 2014; Schaltegger et al., 2016).

Figure 2. Clusters network
Source: own elaboration in VOSviewer software.

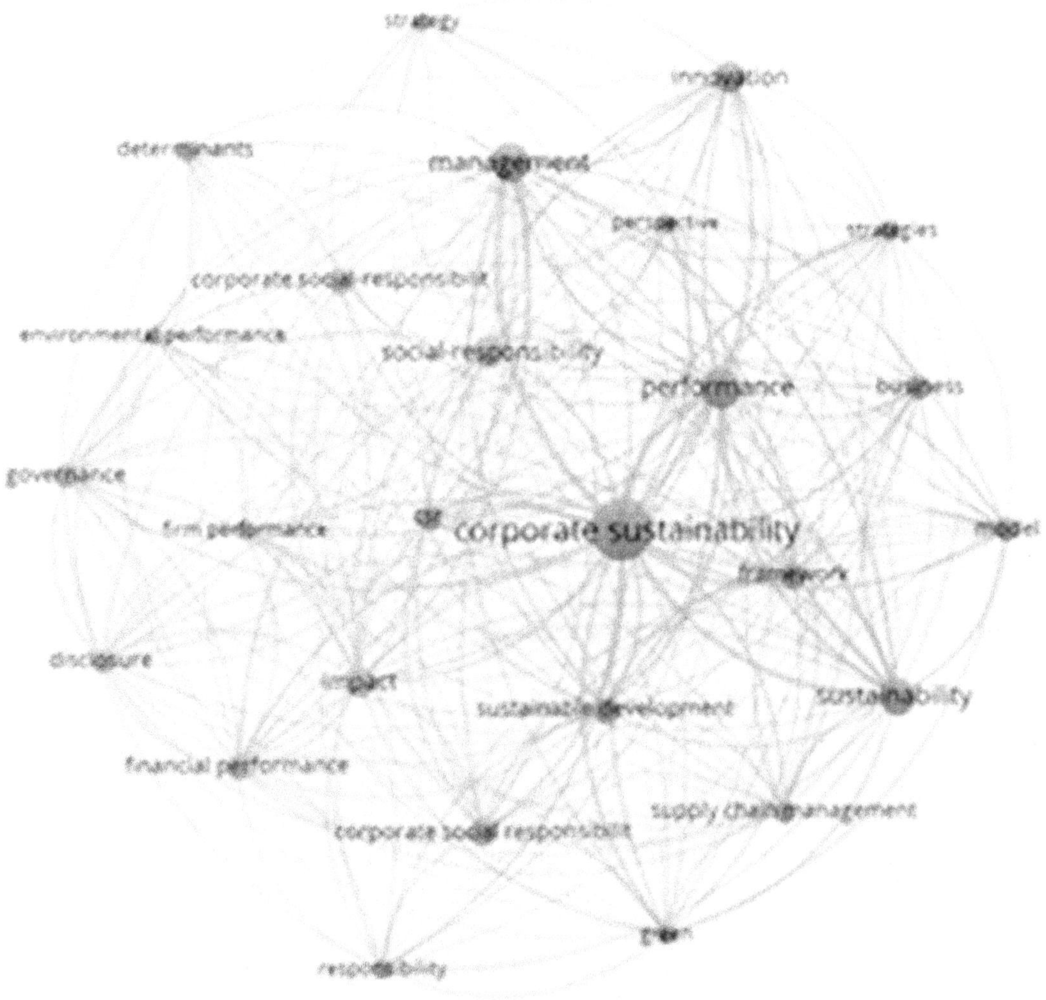

WORLD RANKINGS FOR SUSTAINABLE BUSINESS

Since 2005, the Canadian media and investment advisory firm Corporate Knights has been compiling the annual Global 100 ranking of the world's most sustainable companies. Each year, the last iteration of the index is announced at the World Economic Forum in Davos, Switzerland. All companies with a market capitalization of $ 2 billion or more are included in the ranking. They are compared using 12 key performance indicators (KPIs), which inform how the surveyed companies manage their resources, finances, and employees.

In 2017, the most, 19 companies in the Global 100 ranking, were in the United States. France came second with 12 companies, Great Britain third (11), Canada fourth (6) and Germany, and the Netherlands sixth (5). Of the top ten in the ranking, seven are European companies. Siemens, a German giant whose field of operations ranges from power plants, medical devices to rolling stock, is at the forefront of the ranking as the world's most sustainable company. In its sector, it has proved to be the most energy-efficient company, generating by far the highest income per kilowatt of energy consumed. Siemens also boasts low CO2 emissions and a relatively constant team of employees.[2]

Three years later, the situation in the ranking changed. Almost half (49) of the G100 in 2020 are European companies. The United States and Canada were represented by 29 companies, 18 companies in the ranking come from Asia, only three members from Latin America (all from Brazil), and Standard Bank in South Africa was the only representative of the African continent. The G100 companies represent a wide range of sectors, from the aerospace and clothing industries to wireless telecommunications and energy wholesale companies.

The leader of Global 100 in 2020 was the Danish renewable energy supplier Ørsted, followed by his compatriot - the highest-ranked company in 2019 - Chr. Hansen, Life Sciences, [3] The third in the ranking was another Scandinavian company, Finnish Neste, an oil refinery that is switching from refining crude oil to using kitchen waste and other materials as raw material. The fourth was the US technology conglomerate Cisco, which moved up ten places from 14th thanks to more than $ 25 billion in clean revenues from products with essential environmental characteristics. The American development group Autodesk, which took the fifth place, moved up 43 places from the 2019 ranking. The company uses 99% renewable energy to run its cloud platforms - platforms that help build green buildings, reduce the number of materials in production cycles, and support better designs for the circular economy.

It is worth noting that, in 2020, 28 companies previously did not appear on the Global 100 list. That means that companies increasingly notice the need to pay attention to issues related to sustainable development.

The "Sustainability Leaders Report" is prepared every year by the US-British SustainAbility think tank with the Canadian research company GlobeScan. The basis is the results of a survey conducted among several hundred experts in ecology and social and development problems in dozens of countries worldwide. They answer the question, which company, in their opinion, best implements the principles of sustainable development in its business strategy, and which non-governmental organizations make the most outstanding contribution to the implementation of the 2030 Agenda.

More than 700 experts from 71 countries responded in the latest Leaders Survey (2020). Unilever, Patagonia, and IKEA once again became the most recognizable leaders of the corporation [4]. For the tenth consecutive year, Unilever is ranked first; its position is recognized by 42% of respondents. Patagonia came second (26%), while IKEA came third with a score of 14%. The Interface was ranked fourth (8%), the only company recognized at the forefront of the 23 years in which the survey was conducted.

An exciting event in 2020 is the emergence of four new companies: Microsoft (US-based tech giant), Ørsted, L'Oreal, and Tata. Ørsted is a leading energy company in Denmark, which is particularly recognized for its climate efforts and is at its top in the Global 100 ranking. Meanwhile, the Indian-based Tata conglomerate becomes a South Asian sustainability leader and joins Brazil's Natura & Co. These companies are not based in Europe or North America.

Sustainability specialists point to WWF (World Wide Fund for Nature) as the leading NGO promoting global sustainable development, recognition of which has been growing since last year. However, the perception of Greenpeace, a global organization working to protect the environment, remains unchanged in the high second position. It definitely strengthens its third position compared to 2019 by the World Resources Institute.

Experts assessed how companies deal in various areas of sustainable development. In their opinion, five areas turned out to be the most critical (Leaders Survey, 2020):

1. Having a strategy or plan that defines how the organization will achieve its sustainability ambitions – 87% of experts.
2. Having a corporate culture that fosters innovation and commitment to building and maintaining high performance in terms of sustainable development - 80% of experts.
3. Being goal-driven so that all its activities support sustainable development results that benefit companies and society - 79% of experts.
4. Working with other persons and institutions to improve sustainability performance - 74%.
5. Advocating for new policies and behaviors that enable systemic change, supporting sustainable development - 67% of experts.

The research asked experts how the COVID-19 pandemic crisis will affect the priorities of sustainable development by 2030. Most experts believe the COVID-19 pandemic will have a negative impact on the sustainability agenda, and nearly half expect sustainability to become a less urgent priority. Experts also point out that COVID-19 is likely to exacerbate inequality and poverty even further. Almost a third of experts also believe that the pandemic will re-focus on environmental issues. The essential remarks in this regard concerned the following issues: social, environmental, and financial (Leaders Survey, 2020, p. 26):

- "Companies may postpone some of their sustainability initiatives that do not also reduce cost or increase revenue, as companies activate 'survival mode' to ensure they still exist after the COVID-caused economic recession." (USA);
- "There will be a focus on people first. Now is the time for decent and meaningful jobs, leaving no one behind." (Sweden);
- "There will be a reduction in financial resources available for the SDG agenda and poor institutional capacity at government level to address sustainable development priorities." (Mexico);
- "It will increase the vulnerability of marginalized groups and their exposure to poverty." (Palestine).

In order to increase the resilience of companies to future adverse global events, it is expected that companies will first of all double their ESG commitments (Leaders Survey, 2020, p. 29), including:

- match business goals with social and environmental goals;
- integrate sustainable development into their business strategy;
- include systems thinking in every aspect of business operations;
- set a plan that can be effectively implemented in the event of future systemic shocks;
- increase innovation to adapt to the new reality (e.g., virtual workplaces, education, telemedicine);
- they will focus on employees, their training, and retraining the workforce, which may help the company survive in a crisis.

CASE STUDIES

The following are four companies that, although not included in the Global 100 rankings, appreciate the advantages of sustainable development and its impact on the value of the enterprise, and therefore feel the need to include it in their business models and marketing activities.

Intrum - a leading European company specializing in debt management[5]. It has about 80 thous customers in 25 countries[6]. It conducts three strategic areas of activities for sustainable development: enabling sustainable payments, gaining trust and recognition (both of customers, consumers, and the entire business environment), development (of one's own company and the entire economy and society) by creating new quality.

Every year, Intrum conducts a survey on a group of 10,000 entrepreneurs from all over Europe to learn about their needs related to financial liquidity and receivables. It also regularly analyzes issues related to the indebtedness of European citizens and their approach to spending money and conducts education in the field of personal finance. For example, in Belgium, it supports an organization that operates, inter alia, to raise awareness of personal finance among young citizens. In Sweden, the Spendido mobile application has been created, which is an interactive tool for high school students and their teachers, thanks to which they can gain knowledge about issues related to loans and debt. In the Netherlands, in 2018, Intrum gave seven guest lectures at the Regional Educational Center (ROC) for students aged 16-22 in the field of personal finance and payment habits. In Hungary, Intrum helps foster children and adults to continue their education. In Romania, the company works for an environmental organization: Let's do it Romania and participates in the Free Miorita project, which aims at making renewable energy available to people who do not have access to electricity. In turn, Intrum in Poland takes part in numerous charity initiatives. Importantly, these are not only the activities of the organization but also grass-roots actions organized by the employees.

Henkel - a German chemical concern, specializes in producing auxiliary and hygiene products for domestic and industrial use. It is one of the world's largest producers of detergents and cleaning agents, care and fragrance cosmetics, consumer adhesives and construction chemicals, and industrial technologies and services. Currently, it operates in over 125 countries around the world and employs over 50,000 people.

The company's sustainable development strategy until 2030 assumes a constant reduction in the environmental impact of the company's activities while achieving the set goals. The company also emphasizes that it actively supports the implementation of the 17 Sustainable Development Goals adopted by the United Nations in 2015. In 2019, while meeting its interim targets for 2020, the company achieved the following results (compared to 2010):

- CO2 emissions (per ton of product) lower by 25%;
- The amount of waste (per ton of product) reduced by 29%;
- Water consumption (per ton of product) reduced by 24%;
- Increase in net sales value (per ton of product) by 6%;
- Improved safety (per million hours worked) by 17%.

Thanks to actions undertaken on a global scale, the company increased its efficiency by 43% (compared to 2010).

Henkel wants to contribute to limiting the effect of global warming. It aims to reduce carbon dioxide emissions from production processes by 75% by 2030. The company also wants 100% of the electricity it consumes in the production process to come from renewable sources by 2030. As part of its new packaging strategy, the company has set itself a target - by 2025 - to 100% of its product packaging to be fully recyclable, reusable, or compostable. At the end of 2018, the target was achieved in more than 80% of the packaging. Moreover, by 2025, the plastic packaging of Henkel products on the European market is expected to be made from as much as 35% of plastic waste - by the end of 2018, this figure was almost 10%. In 2018, the effects of the company's pro-environmental activities were once again confirmed by independent experts, rating agencies, and capital markets. For the 18th year in a row, the company has been recognized in the FTSE4Good ethical index. It was also included in the list of many other indices (ECPI, Ethibel Sustainability, Euronext Vigeo Eiris, Global Challenges, MSCI ESG Leaders, and SRI, as well as STOXX Global ESG Leaders). Henkel has also been recognized as a leader in its sector by EcoVadis, Oekom Research, and Sustainalytics.

The BMW Group, representing the brands BMW, MINI, Rolls-Royce, and BMW Motorrad, is one of the world's leading manufacturers of premium cars and motorcycles, as well as a provider of high-quality financial and mobility services. The global employment in the company amounts to approx. 125,000 employees[7].

The company says it takes sustainability into account in all business decisions. It is actively involved in international initiatives, for instance it adheres to the principles of the United Nations Global Compact. It develops innovative solutions that bring tangible benefits to society. The BMW Group has been at the forefront of the most important sustainability rankings for many years: it is the industry leader in both the Dow Jones Sustainability Index and the Carbon Disclosure Project. According to the BMW Group, sustainability makes the business model more competitive and translates into company growth.

The BMW Group has a long tradition of working to minimize environmental impact. Their effect is to reduce the consumption of resources, rationally manage water, reduce the level of CO^2emissions, reduce waste production, and take into account environmental factors when selecting locations for new facilities.

The company's goal is a responsible approach to employees and society and respect for their rights, including the opposition to all forms of discrimination. In order to take full advantage of the opportunities offered by the consistent implementation of the principles of sustainable development, seminars, training, and lectures for buyers and suppliers are organized. The company is also preparing for demographic changes by creating jobs for older workers. It also aims to employ more women in technical and management positions. Another goal of the BMW Group is to promote cultural diversity within the company.

Viessmann[8] is an internationally leading manufacturer of heating, industrial, and cooling systems. It is among 15 companies belonging to the Group for Climate Protection of the German Economy. This organization was established by the Ministry of Environment Protection, Ministry of Economy, and DIHK in 2009. As a third-generation family business, Viessmann clearly declares its social responsibility and the goal of preserving natural living conditions for future generations. Actions to save resources and protect the environment in the sense of a sustainable development approach are also part of the corporate culture, as is the continuous increase in efficiency along the entire process chain from suppliers to customers. The core of the company's sustainability strategy are processes that are directly linked to the product lifecycle. The strategy also covers ecological aspects such as energy and material efficiency, emissions, and biodiversity, as well as social issues such as staff structure, occupational and health protection, employee qualifications, and satisfaction.

All sustainability activities are coordinated by a managing group that reports to the management board. Viessmann has created an online forum - the Alliance for Sustainable Development. This website collects and organizes information on sustainable construction, housing, and modernization, which until now was incomplete or presented in a poorly transparent manner.

Thanks to the use of the technology available on the market, the company not only managed to increase work efficiency and reduce material consumption but, above all, achieved a significant increase in energy efficiency. Fossil energy consumption has fallen by two-thirds; CO2 emissions have fallen by

80%. All essential energy carriers are used in the new energy center - oil and gas, as well as biomass, solar energy, and heat from the air and soil. Highly efficient technologies, such as condensation technology and cogeneration, play an essential role. Woodchips produced on own plantations of fast-growing trees are used in particular for the production of heat and electricity, which is not harmful to the climate. On an area of 180 hectares, poplars and willows are cultivated, which cover nearly half of the annual requirement of 7,000 tons of solid biomass.

CONCLUSION

In order for the company to develop, successfully prosper on the market and gain new customers, the people responsible for it must be aware that there is a relationship between the company's activities and changes, often negative, that it makes in the environment or society. In order to prevent them or eliminate their effects, appropriate solutions must be implemented. Of course, there are no ready-made solutions that will suit every company. However, there are several rules and principles worth following if one wants to ensure sustainability. On a microeconomic scale, the implementation of the company's sustainable development strategy translates into the implementation of this idea on a global basis. Therefore, it is important from a global point of view that this strategy is used by as many organizational units as possible. The research results presented in the paper confirm the increase in the activity of companies in this area.

REFERENCES

Aiginger, K., Bärenthaler-Sieber, S., & Vogel, J. (2013). *Competitiveness under New Perspectives.* Working Paper, 44. www.foreurope.eu

Aliańska, A., Frydrych, S., & Klein, E. (2018). Finanse w koncepcji zrównoważonego rozwoju. *Kwartalnik Kolegium Ekonomiczno-Społecznego, Studia i Prace. Szkoła Główna Handlowa, 1*, 27–44.

Altieri, M. A. (2018). *Agroecology: the science of sustainable agriculture.* CRC Press, Taylor&Francis. doi:10.1201/9780429495465

Ammer, R., & Othman, R. (2012). Sustainability Practices and Corporate Financial Performance: A Study Based on the Top Global Corporations. *Journal of Business Ethics, 108*(1), 61–79. doi:10.100710551-011-1063-y

Annadale, D., Morrison-Saunders, A., & Bouma, G. (2004). The impact of voluntary environmental protection instruments on company environmental performance. *Business Strategy and the Environment, 13*(1), 1–12. doi:10.1002/bse.390

Bać, A. (2014). Idea zrównoważenia i jej wybrane przejawy. *Architectus, 2*(38), 3–13.

Bąk, I., & Cheba, K. (2020a). The Concept of Shared Value in the Theory of Sustainable Finance. An Analysis from the OECD Countries Perspective. In Environmental Impacts Between Sustainable Financial Systems and Financial Markets. IGI Global.

Bąk, I., & Cheba, K. (2020b). Zielona gospodarka jako narzędzie zrównoważonego rozwoju. CeDeWu.

Bąk, I., & Szczecińska, B. (2020). The Value of the Company and Sustainable Development. In Social, Economic Environmental Impacts Between Sustainable Financial Systems and Financial Markets. IGI Global.

Banerjee, S. B. (2002). Corporate environmentalism - The construct and its measurement. *Journal of Business Research*, *55*(3), 177–191. doi:10.1016/S0148-2963(00)00135-1

Banister, D. (2008). The sustainable mobility paradigm. *Transport Policy*, *15*(2), 73–80. doi:10.1016/j.tranpol.2007.10.005

Bansal, P., & DesJardine, M. (2014). Business sustainability: It is about time. *Strategic Organization*, *12*(1), 70–78. doi:10.1177/1476127013520265

Bansal, P., & Roth, K. (2000). Why companies go green: A model of ecological responsiveness. *Academy of Management Journal*, *43*(4), 717–736.

Bartniczak, B. (2013). Zrównoważony transport na poziomie regionalnym jako przedmiot pomiaru wskaźnikowego. Studia Ekonomiczne, *Zeszyty Naukowe Uniwersytetu Ekonomicznego w Katowicach. Uniwersytet Ekonomiczny w Katowicach*, *143*, 11–20.

Bocken, N. M. P., Short, S. W., Rana, P., & Evans, S. (2014). A literature and practice review to develop sustainable business model archetypes. *Journal of Cleaner Production*, *65*, 42–56. doi:10.1016/j.jclepro.2013.11.039

Borys, T. (Ed.). (2008). *Analiza istniejących danych statystycznych pod kątem ich użyteczności dla określenia poziomu zrównoważonego rozwoju transportu wraz z propozycją ich rozszerzenia.* Raport z realizacji ekspertyzy, Jelenia Góra-Warszawa.

Borys, T., Czaja, S. (2009). Badania nad zrównoważonym rozwojem w polskich ośrodkach naukowych. In *Od koncepcji ekorozwoju do ekonomii zrównoważonego rozwoju*. Białystok: Wydawnictwo Wyższej Szkoły Ekonomicznej w Białymstoku.

Cheba, K. (2019). Zrównoważona międzynarodowa konkurencyjność krajów Unii Europejskiej. Studium teoretyczno-empiryczne. CeDeWu.

Cherrafi, A., Garza-Reyes, J. A., Kumar, V., Mishra, N., Ghobadian, A., & Elfezazi, S. (2018). Lean, green practices and process innovation: A model for green supply chain performance. *International Journal of Production Economics*, *206*, 79–92. doi:10.1016/j.ijpe.2018.09.031

Crisostomo, V. L., Freire, F. S., & Freitas, M. R. D. O. (2019). Determinants of corporate sustainability performance – evidence from Brazilian panel data. *Social Responsibility Journal*, *16*(8), 1053–1072. Advance online publication. doi:10.1108/SRJ-04-2018-0102

De Mendonca, T., & Zhou, Y. (2020). When companies improve the sustainability of the natural environment: A study of large US companies. *Business Strategy and the Environment*, *29*(3), 801–811. doi:10.1002/bse.2398

Dembińska, I. (2018). Infrastruktura logistyczna gospodarki w ujęciu środowiskowych uwarunkowań zrównoważonego rozwoju. Uniwersytet Szczeciński, Rozprawy i studia 1010, Szczecin.

Dulewicz, P., Perzyńska, A., & Witkowski, K. (2014). Odpowiedzialność przedsiębiorstwa za zrównoważony rozwój. *Logistyka*, *4*, 3889–3893.

Eccles, R. G., Ioannou, I., & Serafeim, G. (2014). The Impact of Corporate Sustainability on Organizational Processes and Performance. *Management Science*, *60*(11), 2835–2857. doi:10.1287/mnsc.2014.1984

Fullwiler, S. T. (2015). *Sustainable Finance: Building a More General Theory of Finance*. Working Paper No. 106, Binzagr Institute for Sustainable Prosperity.

Girardet, H. (1999). *Creating sustainable cities, Totnes*. Green Books for the Schumacher Society, Dewon.

Górka, K. (2007). Wdrażanie koncepcji rozwoju zrównoważonego i trwałego. *Ekonomia i Środowisko*, *2*(32), 8-20.

Hahn, T., Figge, F., Pinkse, J., & Preuss, L. (2010). Trade-Offs in Corporate Sustainability: You Can't Have Your Cake and Eat It. *Business Strategy and the Environment*, *19*(4), 217–229. doi:10.1002/bse.674

Hahn, T., Lutz, P., Pinkse, J., & Figge, F. (2014). Cognitive frames in corporate sustainability: Managerial sensemaking with paradoxical and business case frames. *Academy of Management Review*, *39*(4), 463–487. doi:10.5465/amr.2012.0341

Hockerts, K., & Wues, R. (2010). Greening Goliaths versus emerging Davids – Theorizing about the role of incumbents and new entrants in sustainable entrepreneurship. *Journal of Business Venturing*, *25*(5), 481–492. doi:10.1016/j.jbusvent.2009.07.005

Hoffman, A. (2018). The Next Phase of Business Sustainability. *Standford Social Innovation Review*. https://ssir.org/articles/entry/the_next_phase_of_business_sustainability

Holmes, I., Moule, S. (2016). *A sustainable finance plan for The European Union*. E3G.

Kemp, R., & Rotmans, J. (2004). Managing the transition to sustainable mobility. In System innovation and the transition to sustainability. Theory, Evidence and Policy. Edward Elgar.

Kiba-Janiak, M. (2015). A Comparative Analysis of Sustainable City Logistics among Capital Cities in the EU. *Applied Mechanics and Materials*, *708*, 113–118. doi:10.4028/www.scientific.net/AMM.708.113

Kociszewski, K. (2013). Ekologizacja polskiego rolnictwa a jego zrównoważony rozwój w warunkach członkostwa w Unii Europejskiej. Wyd. UE we Wrocławiu, Wrocław.

Kozłowski, S. (2007). Przyszłość ekorozwoju. wyd. II, Wydawnictwo KUL, Lublin.

Laszlo, Ch. (2003). *The Sustainable Company: How to Create Lasting Value through Social and Environmental Performance*. Island Press.

Laverty, K. J. (1996). Economic 'Short-Termism': The Debate, the Unresolved Issues, and the Implications for Management Practice and Research. *Academy of Management Review*, *21*(3), 825–860.

Lechner, N. (2014). *Heating, Cooling, Lighting: Sustainable Design Methods for Architects*. John Wiley & Sons Inc.

Linnenluecke, M. K., & Griffiths, A. (2010). Corporate sustainability and organizational culture. *Journal of World Business*, *45*(4), 357–366. doi:10.1016/j.jwb.2009.08.006

Mierzejewska, L. (2009). Rozwój zrównoważony miasta: zagadnienia poznawcze i praktyczne. Wydaw. Naukowe Uniwersytetu im. Adama Mickiewicza, Poznań.

Milne, M., & Gray, R. (2013). W(h)ither Ecology? The Triple Bottom Line, the Global Reporting Initiative, and Corporate Sustainability, *Reporting*. *Journal of Business Ethics*, *118*(1), 13–29. doi:10.100710551-012-1543-8

Misztal, A. (2019a). Zrównoważony rozwój przedsiębiorstw a stopień rozwoju społeczno-gospodarczego. *Studia i Prace Kolegium Zarządzania i Finansów, 174*, 33-45.

Misztal, A. (2019b). *Stabilizacja makroekonomiczna a zrównoważony rozwój przedsiębiorstw – przypadek*. Bułgarii, Czech, Polski i Rumunii. Studia Prawno-Ekonomiczne.

Paszkiewicz, A., Szadziewska, A. (2011). Raportowanie rozwoju zrównoważonego przedsiębiorstw według wytycznych GRI. *Zeszyty Naukowe Uniwersytetu Szczecińskiego, Finanse, Rynki Finansowe, Ubezpieczenia*, *41*(668), 627-643.

Pearce, D., & Turner, R. K. (1990). *Economics of Natural Resources and Environment*. HarvesterWheatsheaf.

Perianes-Rodriguez, A., Waltman, L., & van Eck, N. J. (2016). Constructing Bibliometric Networks: A Comparison of between Full and Fractional Counting. *Journal of Informetrics*, *10*(4), 1–30. doi:10.1016/j.joi.2016.10.006

Płachciak, A. (2011). Geneza idei zrównoważonego rozwoju. *Ekonomia*, *5*(17), 231–248.

Płaczek, E. (2012). Zrównoważony rozwój – nowym wyzwaniem dla współczesnych operatorów logistycznych. *Prace Naukowe Politechniki Warszawskiej Transport*, *84*, 79–92.

Poskrobko, B. (2009). Współczesne trendy cywilizacyjne a idea zrównoważonego rozwoju. *Przegląd Komunalny*, *6*, 7–16.

Rodrigues, V. P., Pigosso, D., & McAloone, T. (2016). Process-related key performance indicators for measuring sustainability performance of ecodesign implementation into product development. *Journal of Cleaner Production*, *139*, 416–428. doi:10.1016/j.jclepro.2016.08.046

Roling, N. G. (2000). *Facilitating sustainable agriculture: participatory learning and adaptive management in times of environmental uncertainty*. Cambridge University Press.

Rózicka, K., & Cieślak, M. (2013). Zrównoważone innowacje – studia przypadków firm polskich i zagranicznych. In Wspólna odpowiedzialność. Rola innowacji, Forum Odpowiedzialnego Biznesu. Warszawa.

Rudnicki, A. (2010). Zrównoważona mobilność a rozwój przestrzenny miasta. *Czasopismo Techniczne. Architektura*, *107*(1-A), 57–74.

Schaltegger, S., Luedeke-Freund, F., & Hansen, E. (2016). Business Models for Sustainability: A Co-Evolutionary Analysis of Sustainable Entrepreneurship, Innovation, and Transformation. *Organization & Environment*, *29*(3), 264–289. doi:10.1177/1086026616633272

Sexton, M. G., Barrett, P. S., & Lu, S. L. (2008). The evolution of sustainable development. University of Salford.

Skowrońska, A. (2010). *Rola polityki logistycznej państwa we wdrażaniu zrównoważonego rozwoju.* Uniwersytet Ekonomiczny we Wrocławiu.

Steure, R., Langer, M. E., Konrad, A., & Martinuzzi, A. (2005). Corporations, stakeholders and sustainable development I: A theoretical exploration of business-society relations,‡ *Journal of Business Ethics, 61*(3), 263–281. doi:10.100710551-005-7054-0

Stubbs, W., & Cocklin, Ch. (2008). Conceptualizing a "sustainability business model". *Organization & Environment, 21*(2), 103–127. doi:10.1177/1086026608318042

Sustainability Leaders. (2019). *The GlobeScan-SustainAbility Survey.* http://odpowiedzialnybiznes.pl/wp-content/uploads/2019/07/the-2019-sustainability-leaders-the-globescan-sustainability-survey.pdf

Sustainability Leaders. (2020). *The GlobeScan-SustainAbility Survey.* https://globescan.com/wp-content/uploads/2020/08/GlobeScan-SustainAbility-Leaders-Survey-2020-Report.pdf

Suto, M., & Takehara, H. (2020). Corporate social responsibility intensity, management earnings forecast accuracy, and investor trust: Evidence from Japan. *Corporate Social Responsibility and Environmental Management, 27*(6), 3047–3059. doi:10.1002/csr.2022

Trojanowski, T. (2015). Przedsiębiorstwa wobec wyzwań zrównoważonego rozwoju. *Zeszyty Naukowe Politechniki Śląskiej. Seria: Organizacja i Zarządzanie, 77*, 239-247.

United Nations (UN). (1975). *United Nations Environment Programme.* Report of the Governing Council on the work pf this third session. United Nations.

van Eck, N. J., & Waltman, L. (2010). Software Survey: VOSviewer, a Computer Program for Bibliometric Mapping. *Scientometrics, 84*(2), 523–538. doi:10.100711192-009-0146-3 PMID:20585380

van Marrewijk, M. (2003). Concepts and definitions of CSR and corporate sustainability: Between agency and communion. *Journal of Business Ethics, 44*(2), 95–105. doi:10.1023/A:1023331212247

Waltman, L., van Eck, N. J., & Noyons, E. C. M. (2010). A Unified Approach to Mapping and Clustering of Bibliometric Networks. *Journal of Informetrics, 4*(4), 629–635. doi:10.1016/j.joi.2010.07.002

WCED (World Commission on Environment and Development). (1987). *Our Common Future. Un Documents: Gathering a Body of Global Agreements has been compiled by the NGO Committee on Education of the Conference of NGOs from United Nations web sites with the invaluable help of information & communications technology.* United Nations.

Whiteman, G., Walker, B., & Perego, P. (2013). Planetary Boundaries: Ecological Foundations for Corporate Sustainability. *Journal of Management Studies, 50*(2), 307–336. doi:10.1111/j.1467-6486.2012.01073.x

Xie, X. M., & Zhu, Q. W. (2020). Exploring an innovative pivot: How green training can spur corporate sustainability performance. *Business Strategy and the Environment, 29*(6), 2432–2449. doi:10.1002/bse.2512

Zahid, M., Rahman, H. U., Muneer, S., Butt, B. Z., Isah-Chikaji, A., & Memon, M. A. (2019). Nexus between government initiatives, integrated strategies, internal factors and corporate sustainability practices in Malaysia. *Journal of Cleaner Production, 241*, 118329. doi:10.1016/j.jclepro.2019.118329

Zhu, J., & Hua, W. (2017). Visualizing the knowledge domain of sustainable development research between 1987 and 2015: A bibliometric analysis. *Scientometrics*, *10*(2), 893–914. doi:10.100711192-016-2187-8

Zioło, M., Filipiak, M.Z., Bąk, K., & Cheba, K. (2019). How to Design More Sustainable Financial Systems: The Roles of Environmental, Social, and Governance Factors in the Decision-Making Process. *Sustainability*, *11*(20), 1-34.

ENDNOTES

1 https://www.corporateknights.com/reports/global-100/global-100-difference-2-15795649/

2 https://www.forbes.pl/rankingi/global-100-najnaj-zrownowazone-firmy-swiata/45stvjs

3 In fact, in 2020, the Danes took three of the first six places, as the biotechnology companies Novozymes qualified in the sixth place.

4 In 2019, the first three places in the ranking were taken by: Unilever, Patagonia and IKEA. The vast majority of them are based in Europe, and Natura is the only emerging market company to be included in the list of the highest rated companies (Leaders Survey, 2019).

5 https://alebank.pl/zrownowazony-rozwoj-nowym-modelem-biznesowym-firm/

6 Annual and Sustainability Report 2019. Leading the way to a sound economy, https://www.intrum.pl/media/7739/intrum_asr_19_eng.pdf

7 https://www.bmw.pl/pl/topics/fascination-bmw/bmw_CSR/zrownowazony-rozwoj.html

8 https://www.viessmann.pl/pl/przedsiebiorstwo/zrownowazony-rozwoj.html

Chapter 3
Sustainable Business Models of Companies:
Challenges and Prospects

Anna Spoz
https://orcid.org/0000-0001-5071-0017
The John Paul II Catholic University of Lublin, Poland

ABSTRACT

In a quest for sources of competitive advantage, an insightful tracking and tracing of the changes that take place in their micro and macro environment is a core competence for enterprises to catch up with market trends. Social and economic changes as well as the growing awareness of the negative anthropogenic impact on the climate and the environment increasingly make today's business models evolve towards sustainability. The aim of this chapter is to analyze the concept of a sustainable business model based on the literature review and then to distinguish the driving and limiting factors behind its implementation in enterprises. Based on an empirical study carried out, a diagnosis will be put forward for the awareness of enterprises as regards the business model pursued and the willingness to integrate social, environmental, and governance aspects. The research methods used in this study relied on critical literature review; descriptive, analytic, and synthetic methods; along with in-depth interviews.

INTRODUCTION

In the era of the intensified domestic and international market competition, progressive globalization of the world economy and advancement of information and digital technologies, the ability of enterprises to compete becomes a prerequisite for their survival and growth. Enterprises pursue competitive advantage, which M.E. Porter says "is at the heart of a firm's performance in competitive markets". However, a reservation must be made that, once gained, competitive advantage is neither permanent nor absolute, which forces enterprises to adapt their business models to the changing operating conditions and customer needs. Research confirms the existence of a positive reinforcing correlation between the

DOI: 10.4018/978-1-7998-6788-3.ch003

level of a company's competitiveness and the performance of a devised business model measured by its profitability (Jabłoński 2010).

Following on social and economic changes and the growing awareness of the negative anthropogenic impact on the environment, companies increasingly often integrate environmental, social and governance aspects in their operating policies, thus modifying their pursued business models towards sustainability.

The aim of this paper is to explain the term of a sustainable business model on the basis of a literature review, and then to discuss the process of its implementation in enterprises. The second part of the paper presents the results of an empirical study conducted in the form of an in-depth interview among entrepreneurs to examine their awareness of the business model implemented, the integration of ESG factors in their operating policies and the willingness to take into account social, environmental and governance factors in newly created business models. At the end of the chapter, the author will consider whether the implementation of a sustainable business model, in addition to the ethical and social aspect, can generate value in terms of financial profitability.

The Nature and Implementation of a Sustainable Business Model

A company's business model reflects the logic of its operation. It structures a certain configuration of interrelated elements, forming an integral whole and reflecting the way the company creates and acquires value (Chesbrough, 2007). The literature has covered the concept of a business model since the 1960s (Bellman et al., 1957), but the interest in this matter has dynamically grown for the last 20 years or so. This issue has become the subject of research in various fields, hence the literature features definitions of this concept as covered from different perspectives, with the emphasis put on different aspects (Table 1). However, the conclusion made by Osterwalder, that "... business models are still relatively poorly understood, particularly as a research area" (Osterwalder et al., 2005), still remains valid.

Table 1. Overview of business model definitions by selected authors

Author	Business model definition
Brandenburger and Stuart (1996)	A business model defines the organization's approach to generating profit at a reasonable cost and integrates the assumptions of value creation and capture
Boulton et al. (1997)	A business model is a unique combination of tangible and intangible assets that provide for an organization's ability to create value,
Linder and Cantrell (2000)	A business model is the core logic of an organization in terms of value creation
Seddon et al. (2004)	A business model describes the fundamental details of a company's value proposition for its various stakeholders and the operational systems that the company uses to create and deliver value to its customers
Malone et al. (2006)	Business models capture what companies do and how they create value
Kujala et al. (2010)	Business models integrate a view on the strategy, the relations of a company and its operations. Business models grow out of value creation for the customer
Osterwalder and Pigneur (2010)	A business model is a reasoned description of how an organization creates, delivers, and captures value
Teece (2010)	A business model articulates the logic of a business's creating and delivering value to customers. It also determines the architecture of the revenues, costs and benefits associated with the enterprise that delivers this value. A business model defines how a company creates and delivers value to customers, and how it converts the payments received into profit

Source: compiled by the author

The integration of social, environmental and governance criteria and practices in business operations has transformed the business models pursued so far into sustainable business models. In their operating policies, companies with a sustainable business model take into account the following aspects:

- environmental aspect, i.e. counteracting climate change by reducing greenhouse gas emissions, protecting biodiversity, treating wastewater and implementing a circular economy by recycling waste (resource efficiency),
- social aspect, i.e. investing in the human capital of the company (employee development) and eliminating inequalities related to gender, ethnic origin, sexual orientation, and taking action to build or strengthen relations with customers or the local community,
- governance aspects, i.e. taking action to improve the organizational structure by increasing its transparency, openness to whistleblowing, detecting corruption, but also improving investor relations and communication with shareholders

Sustainable business models treat sustainability as an integral part of the value proposition. BMfSs (business models for sustainability) provide value both for the customer and for the environment and/or society (Abdelkafi and Tauscher, 2016).

Sustainable business models are based on the triple bottom line approach and cover a wide range of stakeholders, which also include the environment and society (Bocken et al., 2014). Stubbs and Cocklin (2008) see the environment and society as key stakeholders. The implementation of sustainable business models enables companies to pursue competitive advantage by creating the highest value for customers and contributes to the sustainable development of the company and society (Lüdeke-Freund, 2010).

As with the business model, there is no single, universal definition of a sustainable business model. A synthetic list of selected definitions of this concept is given in Table 2.

The question emerges at this point about the very process of creating and implementing sustainable business models and about the driving and limiting factors behind the implementation of an SBM in a company. According to Bocken et al. (2014), in the past, both scholars and business practitioners, instead of transforming existing business models into sustainable business models through relevant corrections, devised them from scratch as new innovative ideas. The process of creating sustainable models is not a simple one and requires an interdisciplinary approach. The most widely known tools designed for this purpose include Business Model Canvas (BMC) (Osterwalder and Pigneur 2010) and its extended version with a triple-layered approach (Joyce and Paquin 2016). Saari et al. (2019) proposed an advanced tool for implementing sustainable business models, named The Impact Canvas Tool (IC). IC is a collaborative platform for ideation based on the involvement of as many stakeholders as possible and the basic principle of equality of perspectives. The IC tool consists of seven different parts representing the key areas in the initial concept development and fine-tuning stages, i.e. vision, customer, solution, competition, resources, actions and team (Saari et al., 2017). Each part is accompanied by three to four guideline questions. Next, Baldassarre et al. (2020) proposed a tool called SBM Pilot Canvas for prototyping and concrete action planning to implement small-scale pilot projects for the deployment of sustainable business models. The tool covers the four core aspects of a project, i.e. business value proposition, sustainability, operational feasibility and financial viability.

Table 2. Overview of sustainable business model definitions by selected authors

Author	Sustainable business model definition
Lüdeke-Freund (2010)	Sustainable business model "creates competitive advantage through superior customer value and contributes to a sustainable development of the company and the society [...]. Since customer value is the strategic nexus of any business model, sustainable business models are crucial for creating extended customer value for individual customers and society, i.e. private and public benefits."
Schaltegger et al. (2012)	Sustainable business model "create customer and social value by integrating social, environmental, and business activities."
Bocken et al. (2014)	"SBM incorporate a triple bottom line approach and consider a wide range of stakeholder interests, including environment and society. They are important in driving and implementing corporate innovation for sustainability, can help embed sustainability into business purpose and processes, and serve as a key driver of competitive advantage."
Breuer and Lüdeke-Freund (2014)	"[A] sustainable business model can be defined as a business model that creates, delivers, and captures value for all its stakeholders without depleting the natural, economic, and social capital it relies on."
Geissdoerfer et al. (2016)	Sustainable business model is "a simplified representation of the elements, the interrelation between these elements, and the interactions with its stakeholders that an organizational unit uses to create, deliver, capture, and exchange sustainable value for, and in collaboration with, a broad range of stakeholders".
Evans et al. (2017)	1. Sustainable value incorporates economic, social and environmental benefits conceptualised as value forms. 2. Sustainable business models require a system of sustainable value flows among multiple stakeholders including the natural environment and society as primary stakeholders. 3. Sustainable business models require a value network with a new purpose, design and governance. 4. Sustainable business models require a systemic consideration of stakeholder interests and responsibilities for mutual value creation. 5.Internalizing externalities through product-service systems enables innovation towards sustainable business models."

Source: compiled by the author

In the process of implementing sustainable business models, enterprises face barriers that result from both the limited resources and the cost of the process itself. The introduction of pro-ecological production methods most often requires immediate capital commitment in investments, the end result of which is uncertain and spread over time (Schaltegger and Synnestvedt, 2002; Wagner, 2007). Schaltegger et al. (2012) emphasize that since companies are primarily oriented on economic results, it is worth considering the introduction by the state of incentives for entrepreneurs to make the effort to modify their business models to sustainable business models. The forms of such assistance may include: reimbursement of part of expenditure related to the purchase of modern machinery and equipment and technologies, reduction of interest rates on bank loans for pro-ecological investments, or through bank guarantees to facilitate their acquisition. Tax exemptions or allowances for entrepreneurs may also be an effective tool in this case.

Schaltegger et al. (2011), on the basis of the conducted research, distinguish three conditions necessary for the effective implementation of environmental and social aspects in the company's operations:

1. Actions for sustainable development must be motivated by a genuine will to solve environmental problems, and not only by compliance with legal requirements.
2. Actions for sustainable development must bring economic benefits in the form of cost savings, improved profitability.
3. The management must be clearly convinced that their business will be successful through voluntary environmental actions.

Companies and a Sustainable Business Model: The Results of Empirical Research

The implementation of sustainable business models is a matter of individual choices. In this part of the paper, the author has verified the following research hypotheses on the basis of the empirical study carried out:

H1: Today's enterprises more and more often integrate ESG (environmental, social and governance) factors in their operating policies.

H2: The awareness of the importance of ESG factors in business operations is rising regardless of the size of the enterprise.

H3 The awareness of the impact of the adopted operating model on business performance is the higher, the larger a company's size. In the case of micro and small-sized enterprises, the business model pursued is intuitive and non-formalized.

In the period from November to December 2019, a study was conducted in a group of 50 companies from the Lubelskie Province, Poland, consisting of small-sized (62%), medium-sized (30%) and large enterprises (8%). The aim of the study was, among others, to find answers to the following questions:

1. What is the share of companies that are aware of the business model pursued?
2. Are environmental, social and governance factors integrated in the existing business models?
3. Which factors would provide the basis for the surveyed companies to build a sustainable business model?

Based on an in-depth interview, an examination was also made whether companies undertake pro-environmental and pro-social activities, even if they do not integrate them in their business models, and if yes, what kind of activities are these.

Along with the increase in the size of the enterprise, the share of companies declaring having a business model increases (Figure 1). This means that as the size of an entity grows, the awareness of what a business model is and its importance in the process of value creation for stakeholders and the ability to generate profit increases. The way micro and small-sized businesses operate is less formalized and more intuitive. In large companies, the business model is most often planned in advance and then implemented, while in the case of small-sized enterprises it is established by business practice.

Figure 1. The share of companies that declare having a business model
Source: own elaboration

As in the case of the declaration of having a business model, the share of enterprises indicating that they have defined and pursue a mission increases with the size of the company (Figure 2). Large companies equally often declared that they integrate environmental, social and sustainable development factors in their mission. In the case of small and medium-sized enterprises, their mission most often covered social aspects, then sustainable development, and lastly environmental issues, although it should be noted that even the latter were indicated by over one out of three of the companies surveyed. This means that regardless of the size of the enterprise, they are aware of the importance of social and environmental aspects as well as sustainable development issues for the operations of the company. Manufacturing processes and service provision in a green approach, however, most often require having modern machinery, plant and equipment, which is why smaller companies do not directly point to these issues in their mission, although their business decision-making takes these factors into account.

Figure 2. Does your company's mission make any reference to the environment, society, sustainable development?
Source: own elaboration

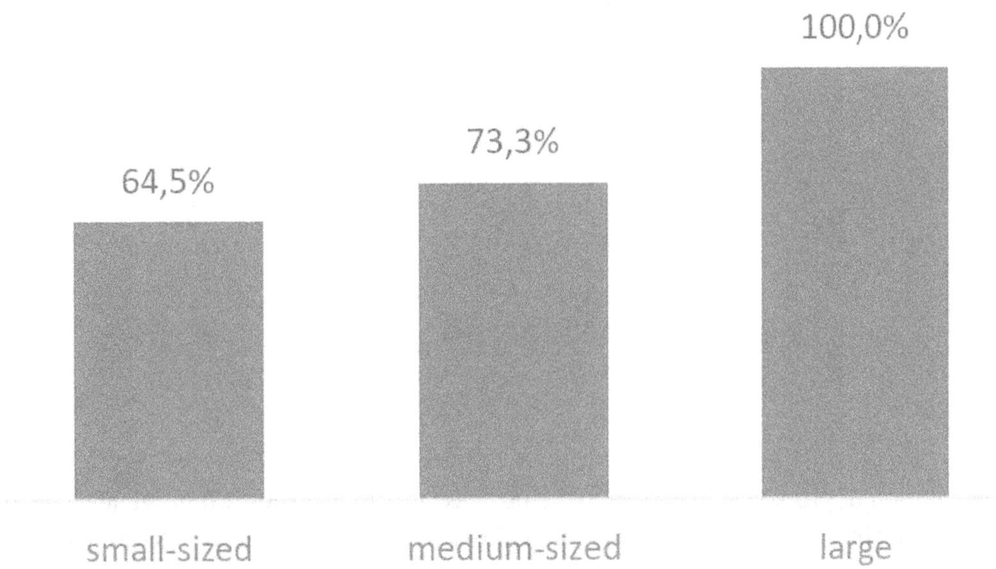

When asked how important the issues in question were in the company's business model, large entities equally often indicated that environmental issues were missing in the business model and that they were a very important part of it (Figure 3). In the case of medium-sized companies, the largest number of surveyed entities (20%) declared that they did not integrate environmental issues. The same share of companies indicated that environmental issues were moderately important. The largest number of small-sized enterprises indicated a minor importance of environmental issues. The above dependencies confirm the previous research results that the larger the size of the company, the higher the share of companies integrating environmental aspects in their business model. This is due to the growing awareness of consumer expectations and resource capabilities to pursue pro-environmental activities.

Figure 3. Integration of environmental aspects in the business model (where: 0 – not integrated, 1 – lowest importance, 5 – highest importance)
Source: own elaboration

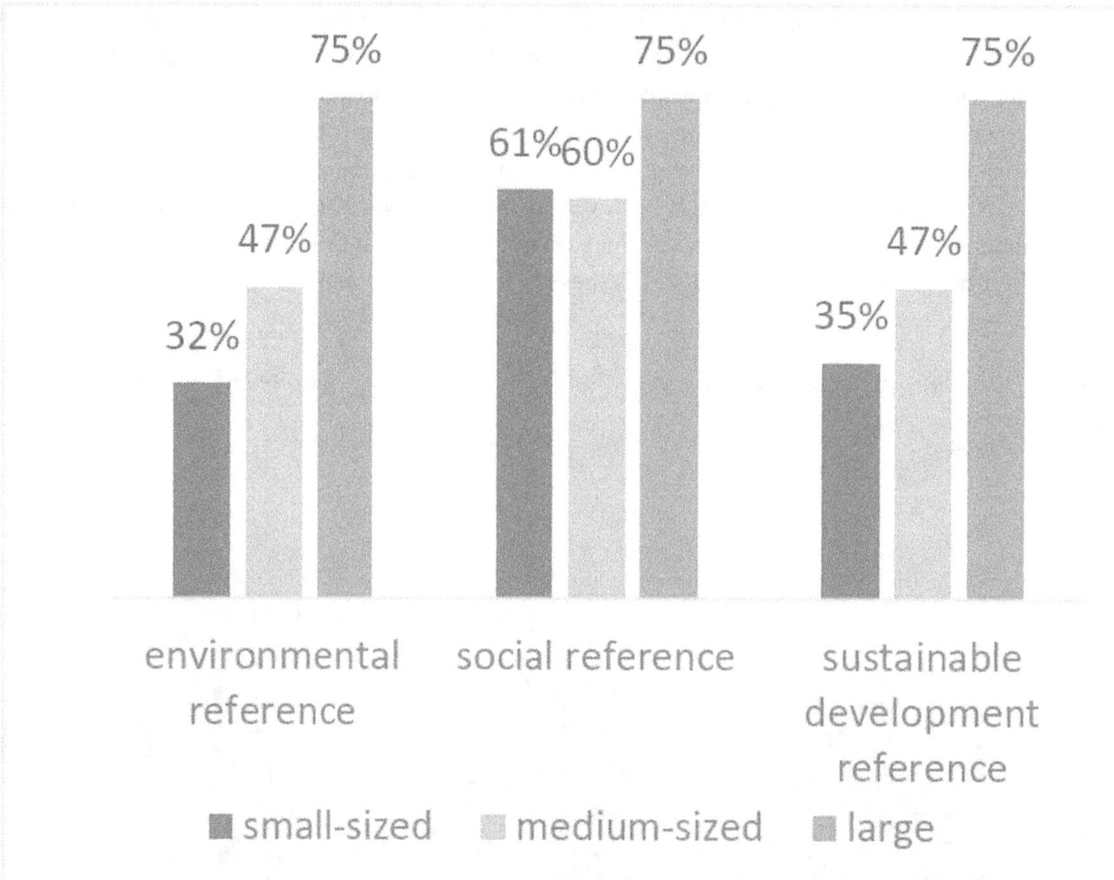

The integration of pro-social activities in the business model was most often acknowledged among large companies (50%) (Figure 4). In the case of medium-sized enterprises, almost one out of three of the surveyed companies equally often indicated a high and a low importance of pro-social activities in the business model. Small-sized companies declared that pro-social activities were of medium importance for them. 13% of small-sized enterprises declared that they did not take into account pro-social issues in the way the company operated and created value.

The importance of sustainable development in the business model was most often recognized by large companies (50%) (Figure 5). This issue was moderately important for medium-sized entities. Small-sized businesses most often assessed sustainable development factors as rather important, with this answer indicated by 19% of the surveyed companies.

50% of large companies indicated governance practices as an important component of the business model. 27% of medium-sized enterprises and only 13% of small-sized ones considered this factor very important. None of the surveyed medium-sized enterprises indicated that governance practices were not integrated in their business model, with such an answer indicated by 6% of small-sized and 25% of large companies.

Figure 4. Integration of pro-social activities in the business model (where: 0 – not integrated, 1 – lowest importance, 5 – highest importance)
Source: own elaboration

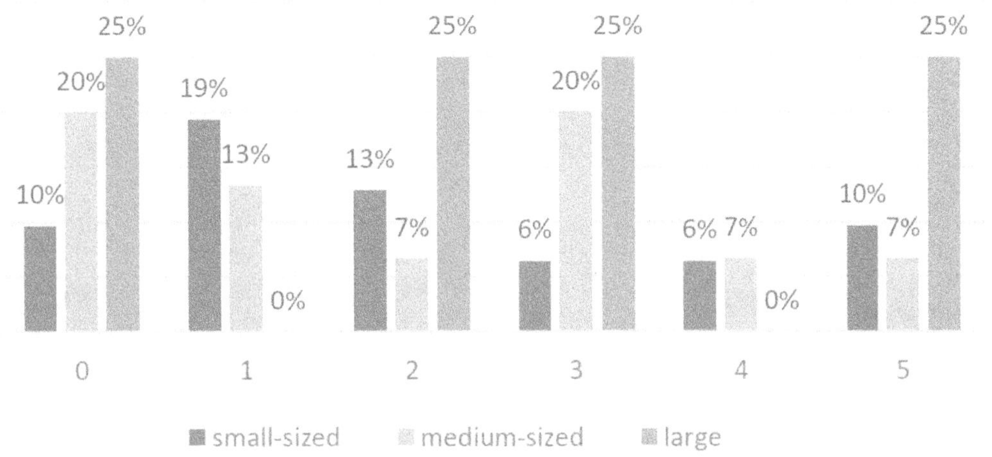

Figure 5. Integration of sustainable development factors in the business model (where: 0 – not integrated, 1 – lowest importance, 5 – highest importance)
Source: own elaboration

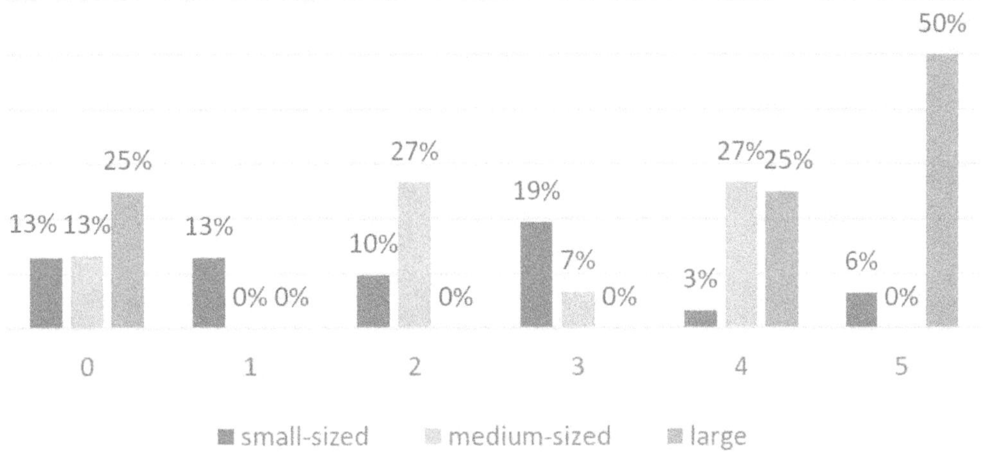

The study also sought answers to the question on which factors would provide the basis for the business models to be built on.

Among the enterprises surveyed, as many as 75% of large companies, 40% of medium-sized and 45% of small-sized enterprises indicated a very high importance of social factors in business model creation (Figure 7). Only small-sized enterprises (16%) declared that they would not take into account social aspects in their new business model.

All the enterprises surveyed, regardless of their size, considered the organizational aspect to be a very important element of the business model being created (Figure 8). As in the previous category, only small-sized enterprises declared that organizational aspects were not taken into account in the entity's operating model. This answer was indicated by 13% of the companies surveyed.

Figure 6. Integration of governance practices in the business model (where: 0 – not integrated, 1 – lowest importance, 5 – highest importance)
Source: own elaboration

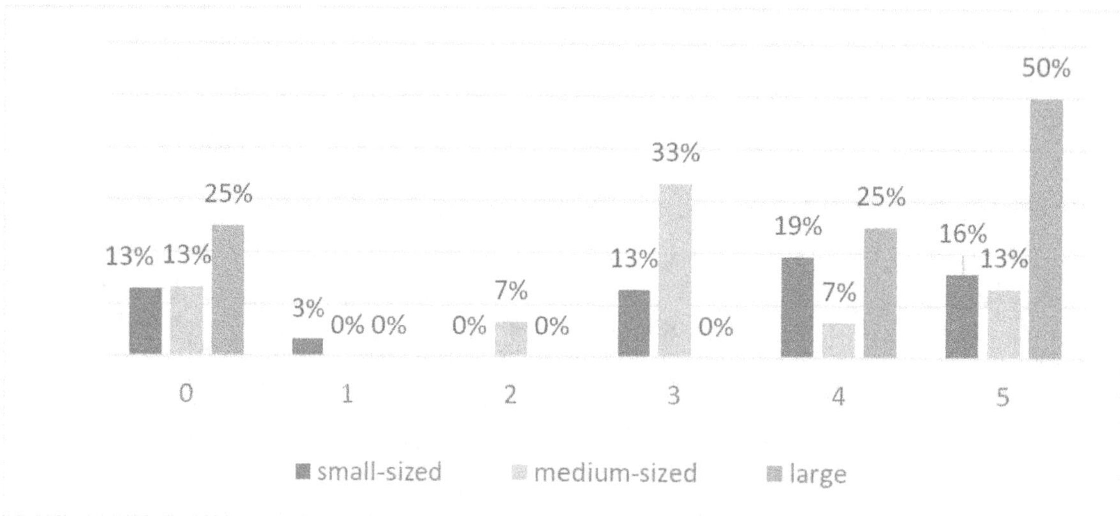

Figure 7. Integration of the social aspect (respecting employee rights, human rights) in the newly created business model (where: 0 – not considered for integration, 1 – lowest importance, 5 – highest importance)
Source: own elaboration

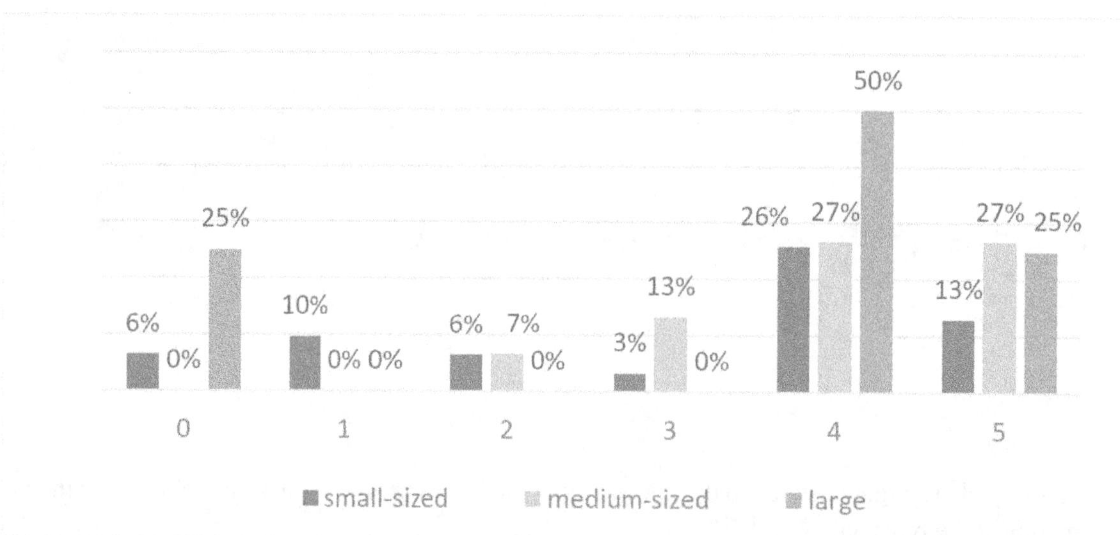

Half of large companies, 40% of medium-sized and 32% of small-sized enterprises considered the technological aspect as very important in the process of building a business model (Figure 9). The other half of large companies and over 30% of medium-sized enterprises considered it important that the enterprise's operations were based on technological innovation that are environmentally and socially friendly. As many as 23% of small-sized enterprises indicated that they would not take this factor into account in the process of building a business model.

Figure 8. Integration of the organizational aspect (digitized approach to the company's organization to eliminate or reduce the consumption of energy, paper, etc.) in the newly created business model (where: 0 – not considered for integration, 1 – lowest importance, 5 – highest importance)
Source: own elaboration

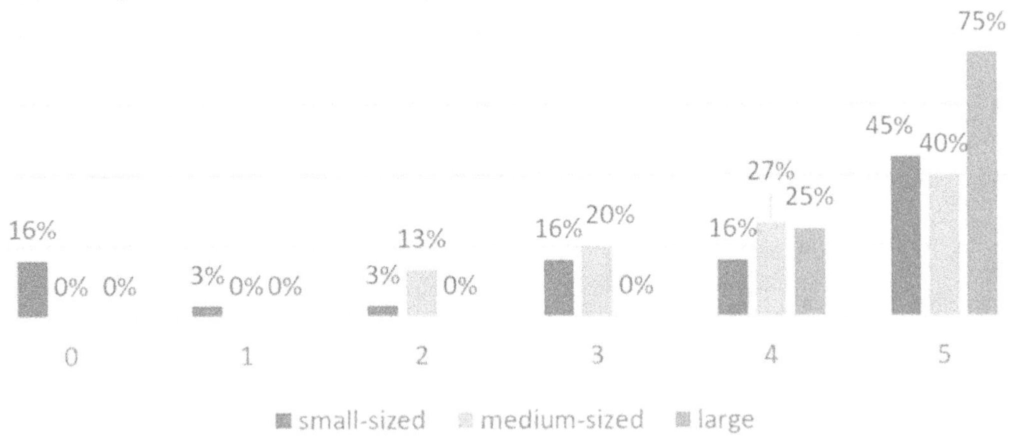

Figure 9. Integration of the technological aspect (putting in place socially and environmentally friendly technological innovations) in the newly created business model (where: 0 – not considered for integration, 1 – lowest importance, 5 – highest importance)
Source: own elaboration

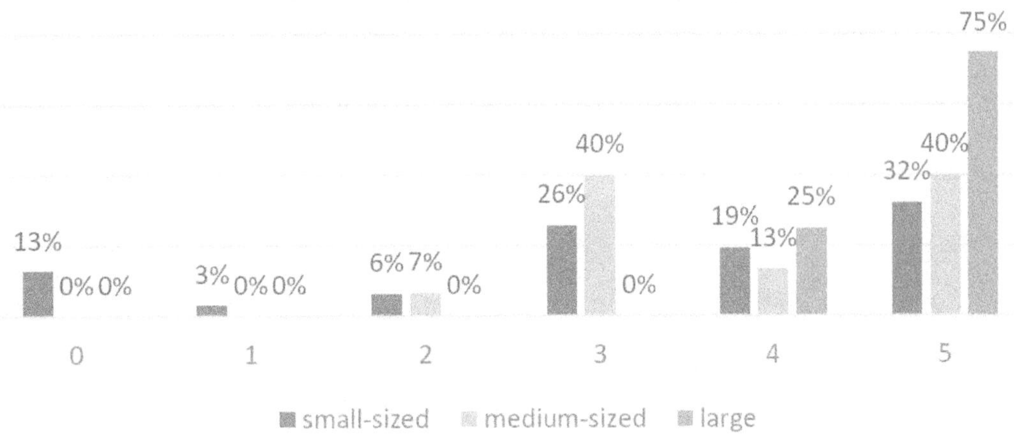

A similar relationship can be seen in the answers to the question whether enterprises would include the provision of services and products that are socially and environmentally friendly (eco-friendly) in the process of building a sustainable business model (Figure 10). Half of large companies each considered this factor to be very and moderately important. Medium-sized entities most often considered this factor as important. Only 16% of small-sized enterprises declared that it was a very important factor for them in the process of building a business model, and as many as 29% of these indicated that they would not take this aspect into account in the process of building a business model.

Figure 10. Integration of environmentally and socially friendly product and service offer in the newly created business model (where: 0 – not considered for integration, 1 – lowest importance, 5 – highest importance)
Source: own elaboration

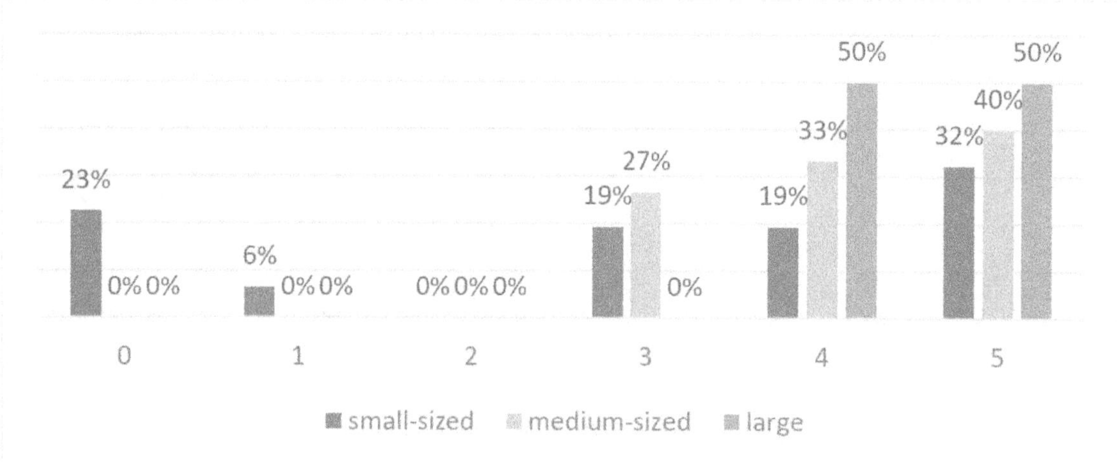

Partnering with environmentally friendly financial institutions is of medium importance for large and small-sized enterprises and of high importance for medium-sized companies (Figure 11). When asked what was important in partnering with financial institutions, the enterprises surveyed indicated the availability and costs of financing.

Figure 11. Integration of partnering with environmentally friendly financial institutions in the newly created business model (where: 0 – not considered for integration, 1 – lowest importance, 5 – highest importance)
Source: own elaboration

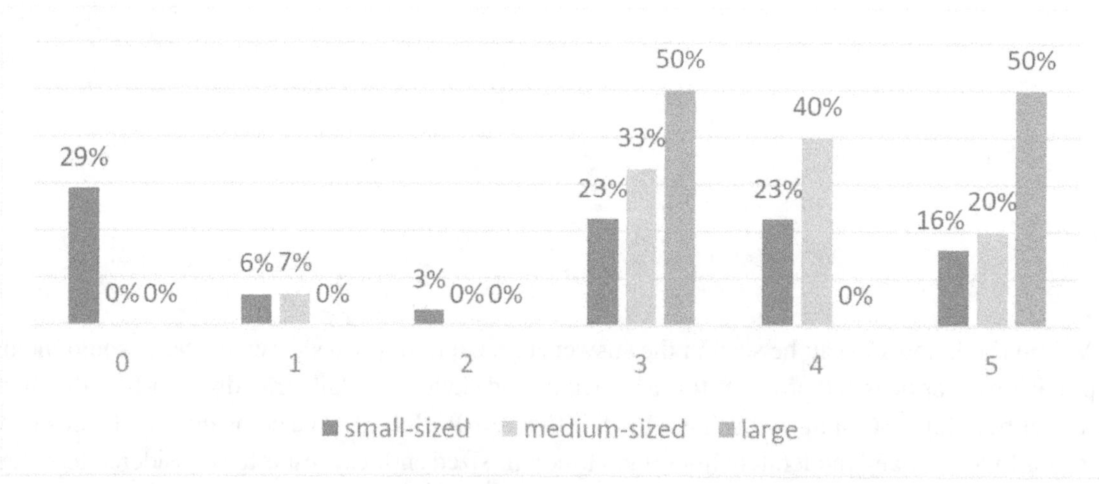

For the entities surveyed, partnering only with entities that pursue a CSR approach was of little importance in the process of building a business model (Figure 12). As many as 32% of small-sized enterprises declared that this factor was of no importance. In the case of medium-sized enterprises, the largest number of companies indicated that business partnerships only with entities that pursue a CSR approach is of little importance. The study shows that when making decisions on partnering with others, companies note whether potential partners pursue a CSR approach, but they do not want and cannot limit their business contacts only to working with such entities.

Figure 12. Integration of partnering with only entities that pursue a CSR approach in the newly created business model (where: 0 – not considered for integration, 1 – lowest importance, 5 – highest importance)
Source: own elaboration

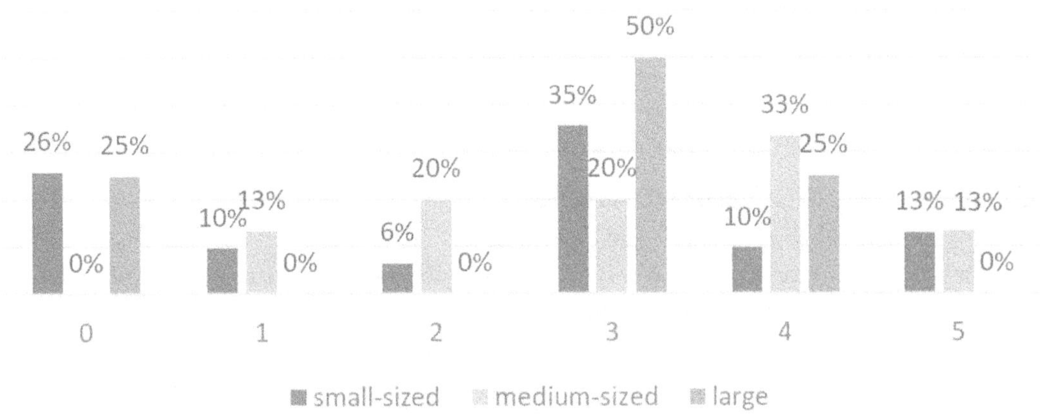

As part of the study, an analysis was made of the share of companies that pursue specific activities in their business practice, even if they do not declare these in their mission (Figure 13).

In the case of some enterprises, especially small-sized enterprises and/or those without a formalized structure, business decision-making processes are intuitive. While they do not have environmental and social aspects or governance practices integrated in the company's mission (as, often, it has not been formalized), such enterprises undertake these activities in their actual operations. As many as 42% of the companies surveyed pursue savings on office supplies by using electronic technologies and use recycling. The smallest number of entities indicated offering environmentally and socially friendly products. This dependence results from the fact that the integration of environmental issues in the operating processes of a company most often entails the need to adapt the resources held to the applicable standards, i.e. the purchase of certified materials, the use of modern eco-friendly machinery, plant and equipment, etc., which require adequate financial expenditure.

Figure 13. The share of enterprises that did not integrate specific activities in the company's mission but pursue them in their business practice
Source: own elaboration

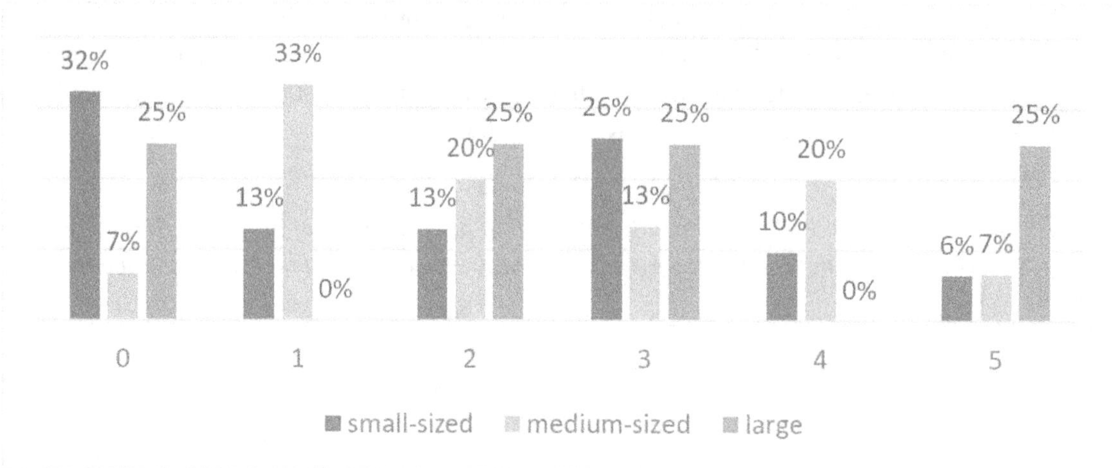

SOLUTIONS AND RECOMMENDATIONS

In view of the fact that enterprises are becoming more and more aware of the importance of including ESG factors in the implemented business model and the benefits of their implementation for enterprises and the economy as a whole, the introduction of countrywide solutions stimulating enterprises to transform their business models towards sustainable ones should be considered. The adoption of a policy in this area in the form of a document will allow entities to structure and systematize the initiatives pursued.

It is recommended to prepare a document containing a list and description of forms of state aid for entities implementing sustainable business models. This solution is particularly desirable from the environmental aspect, when the transition to greener production methods is usually costly, and therefore extremely difficult for SME entities having limited resources.

Never before have there been such favourable conditions for enterprises to invest in pro-climate solutions. In early July 2020, the European Commission announced the launch of the Innovation Fund, i.e. programs to support innovative low-carbon technologies. Over the next 10 years, the Fund is expected to allocate approx. EUR 10 billion to the implementation of technologies for renewable energy, energy-intensive industries, energy storage, and carbon capture, use and storage. The Fund will be financed from the auctions of CO2 emission allowances under the EU emissions trading system.

The Innovation Fund is one of the key elements of the European Green Deal, i.e. a plan that aims to transform the European economy to become climate-neutral by 2050. The importance of the ecological transformation is best demonstrated by the fact that it is one of the three pillars of the Next Generation EU instrument, with a budget of EUR 750 billion.

In addition, in June 2019, the European Union announced guidelines on the (so far voluntary) disclosure of climate-related information by companies. The elements to be communicated to stakeholders include, among others, CO2 emissions reporting along the entire value chain, revenues and investments reporting - broken down into "green" (environmentally sustainable) and "brown" (based on the use of fossil energy sources, highly energy-intensive) and climate policy. Only some companies followed these guidelines, with the scope of the reported data varying widely.

Reporting on ESG-related issues is part of the European sustainable development policy and its task is to direct investment towards "green" enterprises that engage in climate change mitigation efforts. Such efforts now gain an economic dimension. A study by Eliwa et al. (2019) found out that lending institutions value both ESG performance and disclosure and integrate ESG information in their credit decisions - in that firms with stronger ESG performance have a lower cost of debt. The study investigates whether lending institutions reward firms in 15 EU countries for their environmental, social and governance (ESG) performance and disclosure in terms of lowering their cost of debt capital.

Undoubtedly, the greatest incentive for implementing a sustainable business model is the possibility of reducing the cost of financing or increasing the value of the enterprise. Therefore, a recommendation should be put forward to prepare guidelines at the national or EU level, under which the integration of ESG aspects by enterprises would be rewarded by a reduced cost of financing. It is also worth considering the introduction of programs facilitating the change of the business model to a sustainable business model. In this way, these enterprises would gain in attractiveness in the market, ultimately to become of interest for capital market investors.

FUTURE RESEARCH DIRECTIONS

The aim of the study was to present a sustainable business model in companies and to answer the research questions "Do enterprises integrate environmental, social and governance performance in their business models, and if so, are they aware of the implementation of a sustainable business model?" Entrepreneurs were also asked what values they would base the newly created business models on. The study bridges a research gap, as there have been no studies to date on the implementation of a sustainable business model among Polish enterprises.

The empirical study has shown that companies, regardless of their size and industry, are aware of the importance of ESG aspects and increasingly take these into account in their business decision-making. It should be noted that the larger the enterprise, the higher the awareness of the importance of the business model being implemented and its impact on business performance. This dependence most often results from the maturity of a company's organizational structure as well as resource and financial capabilities. It is rather obvious that the transition from a traditional to a sustainable business model most often requires investment in revamping the technical and technological resources, purchase of certified materials, expenditure on employee training, etc.

One of the key challenges in the process of creating sustainable business models is to design such a configuration of interrelated elements forming an integral whole so that a company, in generating value for stakeholders, delivers social and environmental benefits at the same time. This is not an easy task for a company, especially as regards the conversion of social and environmental value proposition into profit.

In the author's opinion, government-funded programs supporting the transformation of traditional into sustainable business models can be extremely useful. Funding for the upgrading of machinery, plant and equipment to be more environmentally friendly, reduced interest rates on loans for the purchase and deployment of green technologies or tax reliefs for enterprises that deliver social and environmental benefits as part of their operations are just examples of possible policy actions. Such initiatives would be especially welcome by micro and small-sized enterprises, which, though aware of the need to transform the traditional model towards a sustainable business model, undertake little effort due to financial constraints.

The direction of future research may be to try to find an answer to the question which state-operated instruments would best encourage economic operators to implement sustainable business models.

CONCLUSION

As a result of social and economic changes, both the concept of sustainability business and the ability to build and implement sustainable business models gained in importance. Implementation of SBM "leads to long-term environmental, social and economic benefits [...]. It makes business to pursue and exploit opportunities that create shared value - value for both the business and the society" (Atiq and Karatas-Ozkan, 2013). The following research hypotheses were verified in the study:

H1: Today's enterprises more and more often integrate ESG (environmental, social and governance) factors in their operating policies.

H2: The awareness of the importance of ESG factors in business operations is rising regardless of the size of the enterprise.

H3 The awareness of the impact of the adopted operating model on business performance is the higher, the larger a company's size. In the case of micro and small-sized enterprises, the business model pursued is intuitive and non-formalized.

Based on the conducted empirical study, all research hypotheses were confirmed.

The ability to quickly and efficiently transition to new business models is an important source of a permanent competitive advantage for enterprises (Geissdoerfer et al., 2018). Unfortunately, in the process of transformation from the traditional to sustainable business model, enterprises encounter barriers, resulting mainly from insufficient resources (material and financial) and legal regulations in this area. The introduction of government programs to reimburse part of firms' expenditure related to the transition to greener production processes or service delivery methods and tax incentives would encourage enterprises to make this effort.

REFERENCES

Abdelkafi, N., & Tauscher, K. (2016). Business models for sustainability from a system dynamics perspective. *Organization & Environment*, *29*(1), 74–96. doi:10.1177/1086026615592930

Atiq, M., & Karatas-Ozkan, M. (2013). Sustainable Corporate Entrepreneurship from a Strategic Corporate Social Responsibility Perspective. *International Journal of Entrepreneurship and Innovation*, *14*(1), 5–14. doi:10.5367/ijei.2013.0102

Baldassarre, B., Konietzko, J., Brown, P., Calabretta, G., Bocken, N., Karpen, I. O., & Hultink, E. J. (2020). Addressing the design-implementation gap of sustainable business models by prototyping: A tool for planning and executing small-scale pilots. *Journal of Cleaner Production*, *255*, 120295. doi:10.1016/j.jclepro.2020.120295

Bellman, R., Clark, Ch., Craft, C., Malcolm, D. G., & Ricciardi, F. (1957). On the Construction of a MultiStage, Multi-Person Business Game. *Operations Research*, *5*(4), 469–503. doi:10.1287/opre.5.4.469

Bocken, N. M. P., Short, S. W., Rana, P., & Evans, S. (2014). A literature and practice review to develop sustainable business model archetypes. *Journal of Cleaner Production*, *65*, 42–56. doi:10.1016/j.jclepro.2013.11.039

Boulton, R. E. S., Libert, B. D., & Samek, S. M. (1997). *Cracking the Value Code: How Successful Businesses are Creating Wealth in the New Economy*. Harper Collins Publishers.

Brandenburger, A. W., & Stuart, S. H. Jr. (1996). Value-based Business Strategy. *Journal of Economics & Management Strategy*, *5*(1), 5–24. doi:10.1111/j.1430-9134.1996.00005.x

Breuer, H., & Lüdeke-Freund, F. (2014). Normative Innovation for Sustainable Business Models in Value Networks. In K. Huizingh, S. Conn, M. Torkkeli, & I. Bitran (Eds.), *The Proceedings of XXV ISPIM Conference – Innovation for Sustainable Economy and Society*. Academic Press.

Chesbrough, H. (2007). Business model innovation: It's not just about technology anymore. *Strategy and Leadership*, *35*(6), 12–17. doi:10.1108/10878570710833714

Eliwa, Y., Aboud, A., & Saleh, A. (2019). ESG practices and the cost of debt: Evidence from EU countries. *Critical Perspectives on Accounting*, *102097*, 102097. Advance online publication. doi:10.1016/j.cpa.2019.102097

Evans, S., Vladimirova, D., Holgado, M., Van Fossen, K., Yang, M., Silva, E., & Barlow, C. (2017). Business model innovation for sustainability: Towards a unified perspective for creation of sustainable business models. *Business Strategy and the Environment*, *26*(5), 597–608. doi:10.1002/bse.1939

Geissdoerfer, M., Bocken, N. M. P., & Hultink, E. J. (2016). Design thinking to enhance the sustainable business modelling process. *Journal of Cleaner Production*, *135*, 1218–1232. doi:10.1016/j.jclepro.2016.07.020

Geissdoerfer, M., Vladimirova, D., & Evans, S. (2018). Sustainable business model innovation: A review. *Journal of Cleaner Production*, *198*, 401–416. doi:10.1016/j.jclepro.2018.06.240

Jabłoński, A. (2013). Modele zrównoważonego biznesu - miejsce i rola w koncepcji zarządzania strategicznego. *Zarządzanie Strategiczne Quo vadis, Prace Naukowe Wałbrzyskiej Wyższej Szkoły Zarządzania i Przedsiębiorczości, red. Krupski, R. T.*, *22*, 283-293.

Joyce, A., & Paquin, R. L. (2016). The Triple Layered Business Model Canvas: A Tool to Design More Sustainable Business Models. *Journal of Cleaner Production*, *135*, 1474–1486. doi:10.1016/j.jclepro.2016.06.067

Kujala, S., Artto, K., Aaltonen, P., & Turkulainen, V. (2010). Business models in project - based firms - Towards a typology of solution - specific business models. *International Journal of Project Management*, *28*(2), 96–106. doi:10.1016/j.ijproman.2009.08.008

Linder, J., & Cantrell, S. (2000). *Changing Business Models: Surveying the Landscape*. Accenture Institute for Strategic Change.

Lüdeke-Freund, F. (2010). Towards a Conceptual Framework of Business Models for Sustainability. In R. Wever, J. Quist, A. Tukker, J. Woudstra, F. Boons, & N. Beute, (Eds.), Knowledge Collaboration and Learning for Sustainable Innovation. Delft: Delft University of Technology.

Malone, T., Weill, P., Lai, R. K., D'Urso, V. T., Herman, G., Apel, T. G., & Woerner, S. (2006). Do Some Business Models Perform Better than Others? MIT Working Paper 4615. doi:10.2139srn.920667

Osterwalder, A., & Pigneur, Y. (2010). *Business Model Generation: A Handbook for Visionaries, Game Changers, and Challengers*. John Wiley and Sons, Inc.

Osterwalder, A., Pigneur, Y., & Tucci, C. (2005). Clarifying Business Models: Origins, Present, and Future of the Concept. *Communications of the Association for Information Systems*, *16*(1). Advance online publication. doi:10.17705/1CAIS.01601

Saari, U. A., Aarikka-Stenroos, L., Boedeker, S., Köppä, L., & Langwaldt, J. (2017). Assessing the usefulness of an early idea development tool among experienced researchers. *CERN ideaSquare Journal of Experimental Innovation*, *1*(2), 3.

Saari, U. A., Aarikka-Stenroos, L., Köppä, L., Langwaldt, J., Boedeker, S., & Mäkinen, S. J. (2019). Sustainable Business Model Ideation and Development of Early Ideas for Sustainable Business Models: Analyzing a New Tool Facilitating the Ideation Process. In A. Aagaard (Ed.), *Sustainable Business Models*. Innovation, Implementation and Success. doi:10.1007/978-3-319-93275-0_5

Schaltegger, S., Hansen, E. G., & Lüdeke-Freund, F. (2012). Business cases for sustainability and the role of business model innovation. *International Journal of Innovation and Sustainable Development*, *6*(2), 95–119. doi:10.1504/IJISD.2012.046944

Schaltegger, S., & Synnestvedt, T. (2002). The link between 'green'and economic success: Environmental management as the crucial trigger between environmental and economic performance. *Journal of Environmental Management*, *65*(4), 339–346. PMID:12369398

Seddon, R. B., Lewis, G. R., Freeman, R., & Shanks, G. (2004). The case for viewing business models as abstractions of strategy. *Communications of the Association for Information Systems*, *13*, 427–442. doi:10.17705/1CAIS.01325

Stubbs, W., & Cocklin, C. (2008). Conceptualizing a "Sustainability Business Model.". *Organization & Environment*, *21*(2), 103–127. doi:10.1177/1086026608318042

Teece, D. I. (2010). Business Model, Business Strategy and Innovation. *Long Range Planning*, *43*(2-3), 172–194. doi:10.1016/j.lrp.2009.07.003

Wagner, M. (2007). Integration of environmental management with other managerial functions of the firm: Empirical effects on drivers of economic performance. *Long Range Planning*, *40*(6), 611–628. doi:10.1016/j.lrp.2007.08.001

Chapter 4
Public Policies and the Role of State vs. Sustainable Business Models and Corporate Sustainability

Wojciech Gonet
https://orcid.org/0000-0003-0066-706X
Siedlce University of Natural Sciences and Humanities, Poland

ABSTRACT

The chapter examines the scope of public administration participation in ensuring that entrepreneurs comply with the principles of sustainable development. It was found that the activities of the state administration in this regard may consist in providing entrepreneurs with the status of applying ESG and CSR principles in their activities, then checking compliance with these principles, informing consumers about the consequences of using products and services produced by the entrepreneurs using the ESG and CSR principles. It was determined that the expectation for the application of ESG and CSR principles can also apply to public administration, which in its activity can contribute to environmental protection by reducing energy consumption in various forms, as well as improving social relations by eliminating corruption.

INTRODUCTION

Limited and declining natural resources, environmental pollution, the greenhouse effect, limited access to drinking water in some regions of the globe mean that concern for the future of the Earth and its inhabitants ceased to be the exclusive domain of international organizations associating states, international private organizations that care for human rights and environmental protection, or national governments. Awareness by entrepreneurs and consumers of the negative impact on the environment is becoming more and more common in the economically developed countries. In the developing countries which want to match economically advanced countries' awareness of the need to conduct business activities taking

DOI: 10.4018/978-1-7998-6788-3.ch004

into account the ESG and CSR principles is lower. In addition, the entrepreneurs from these countries indicate that at the current stage of their development they cannot apply the ESG and CSR principles, because it is too expensive, and the entrepreneurs from highly developed countries, when being in their place several decades ago, were not guided by the ESG and CSR principles. In addition, the entrepreneurs from these countries find that at the current stage of their development it is too expensive for them to apply the ESG and CSR principles. They also indicate that the entrepreneurs from highly developed countries, when being in their place several decades ago, were not guided by the ESG and CSR principles. A few decades ago, their activities were based on the Milton Friedman doctrine, assuming that social responsibility rests solely with individuals, and the entrepreneur's responsibility is limited to ensuring profit for shareholder (Friedman, 1970).

The responsible development of entrepreneurs taking into consideration the care for the environment, society, corporate governance is a bottom-up movement initiated by entrepreneurs. It does not mean giving up profit maximization.

It happens, however, that some entrepreneurs only pretend to apply ESG principles for marketing purposes, while their actual activity contradicts this. It is, therefore, important to verify entrepreneurs whether they apply ESG principles in their activities when they announce it. This implies such questions of who should do this: private rating agencies or government offices? What principles and criteria should be adopted in order to objectively declare that an entrepreneur applies the principles of responsible, sustainable development in his activities, how often an entrepreneur should be checked for compliance with the ESG principles? Who should bear the cost of such audit activities?

In developing countries, it is more difficult for entrepreneurs to apply the ESG principles in their activities, and, in addition, a developing society is more focused on consumerism and the use of the achievements of civilization development.

The role of central and local state administrations in encouraging entrepreneurs to apply the ESG and CSR principles in their activities can be important, in particular, by raising awareness among consumers that it is worth buying the goods and services of these entrepreneurs. The activities of individual countries may be ineffective if the governments of other countries are not interested in encouraging entrepreneurs to apply the ESG and CSR principles. The article also concerns the need to coordinate the actions of the governments of individual countries in the field of compliance by their entrepreneurs with the ESG and CSR principles. Until now, the ESG and CSR principles have been applied to enterprises. Public administration is also an employer for officials, and its functioning affects the environment, e.g. by increasing or reducing the consumption of electricity, heat and paper. In public administration, problems of unequal treatment of officials, corruption and negative impact on the environment can arise. It should be considered whether the ESG and CSR principles can be applied by public, governmental and local administrations. Employee care, equal treatment, and appropriate remuneration in accordance with ESG and CSR principles have so far not been associated with improving the living conditions of socially excluded people such as former prisoners, disabled, homeless, and long-term unemployed people. The existence of the above-mentioned social groups deprived of any sources of income, any job is socially negative. The text also concerns the issue of the possibility of extending the ESG and CSR principles to include the aspirations of entrepreneurs and public administration to eliminate the phenomenon of social exclusion permanently.

COMPANIES USING ESG AND CSR STRATEGIES

The acronym ESG derives from the first letters of the words *environmental, social and governance.* Entrepreneurs voluntarily apply ESG principles, such as the Sullivan Principles (General Motors Board Member) of 1977, which were adopted in South Africa by 125 entrepreneurs. The application of the Sullivan Principles by the entrepreneur meant promoting economic justice, respecting human rights towards employees, applying equal terms of employment, remuneration regardless of race or gender ("The Global Sullivan Principles", n / a). In addition, the application of the Sullivan Principles by the entrepreneur meant ensuring equal participation of employees regardless of race and gender in supervisory positions, training, promotion, improving their quality of life ("The Global Sullivan Principles", n / a). The idea of a socially responsible entrepreneur appeared before World War II. The entrepreneur's goal, in addition to making a profit, should be to act in the public interest, to contribute to the public good (Dodd, 1932, p. 1145). The principle of entrepreneurial mind-set solely for profit began to lose its significance. The activities of entrepreneurs include, in particular, social and environmental effects (Williams, 1999). Entrepreneurs receive privileges from the society; therefore, in their economic activity they must take into account the values important for the society (Wade, 2002, p. 389). The use of privileges by entrepreneurs means that they must accept social values and be responsible, e.g. for their use of slave labor (Backer, 2006, p. 4).

The goal of these entrepreneurs is providing sustainable development for the sake of the environment and employees, taking into account the interests of the owners. Depending on their area of business, there may be many measures to use ESG elements. The environmental element is different for companies from different industries, e.g. pharmaceutical and consulting, whereas the aspect of staff care is the same regardless of the industry of the entrepreneur. For business, sustainable development means an action strategy that, while meeting the current needs of the enterprise and interest groups associated with it, at the same time protects, supports, and strengthens people and sources of resources that will be needed in the future ("Business Strategy", 1992).

Corporate Social Responsibility is defined in GREEN PAPER: Promoting a European framework for Corporate Social Responsibility of July 18, 2001 as "a concept whereby companies decide voluntarily to contribute to a better society and a cleaner environment (…) towards employees and more generally towards all the stakeholders affected by business and which, in turn, can influence its success " (Commission, 2001). The World Business Council for Sustainable Development defines corporate social responsibility as "continuing commitment by business to behave ethically and contribute to economic development while improving the quality of life of the workforce and their families as well as of the local community and society at large" (World, n / a).

In the past, the entrepreneur's possible fulfillment of social obligations was perceived as an interference with the competences reserved for public policy (Friedman, 1962, p. 133-136). An entrepreneur applying the principles of corporate social responsibility in his activities does not replace governmental or local administration in the implementation of public tasks, but supports selected people or social groups, not necessarily his employees or associates. Governmental and local administration supports those people who are dependent, indigent, disabled, etc. An entrepreneur who applies CSR principles can help the above-mentioned people and can also help social groups that cannot get support from public administration, e.g. charities, organizations dealing with disclosing corruption, etc. Visser (2010) went further in terms of the definition of the concept of CSR, pointing out that the starting point for building a company's business model should be the desire to solve a social problem. This view, however, goes too far. An entrepreneur can support governmental or local administration in solving various social problems of groups of people in different parts of the world, but cannot replace the role of the state in this regard. A company's corporate social responsibility performance may be higher in developing countries, where societies are poorer and more people may be at risk of exclusion, for example, due to lack of access to education, communication, the Internet access.

The abovementioned definitions of entrepreneurs applying the ESG and CSR principles in their activities do not indicate who states that a given company can be classified as an entrepreneur guided by the principles of ESG and CSR or not. It is not clear whether a one-off action such as e.g. supporting an organization defending human rights in a country with a totalitarian system is sufficient for granting this status or whether an entrepreneur must be active in the field of responsible development for a longer period. Not every company will be able to demonstrate its achievements in the field of environmental protection. This applies, for example, to consulting companies, service companies, law firms, which from an environmental point of view can only save energy in various forms, such as electricity, heat and fuel. Initially, it can be assumed that for a company to be recognized as adhering to the principles of the ESG and CSR, it is sufficient that its activities comply with one of the following aspects: social, economic or environmental. The analyses and researches conducted so far do not address the issue of who is to state that a company can be granted the status of an entrepreneur applying the ESG and CSR rules, and whether, after receiving this status, still obeys these rules. Currently, it can be noticed that when companies do something that has the features of ESG, CSR, they advertise it on their websites and it is a premise for them to be considered as applying these principles.

Until now, entrepreneurs were expected to comply with the ESG and CSR rules. A question can be asked whether these rules should apply to governmental and local administration offices that employ workers and who may have a negative impact on the environment, e.g. by not segregating waste, not saving electricity and heat. Initially, it can be stated that the social responsibility of conducted activities applies not only to entrepreneurs but also to governmental and local administrations, which, through the activities of offices, may have a negative impact on the environment, society and individual units.

INTERNATIONAL REGULATIONS FOR THE ESG AND CSR PRINCIPLES

In 1999, the United Nations issued *The United Nations Global Compact*, indicating how international enterprises should function (United, 1999). International entrepreneurs should observe the following ten principles in their activities: support and respect the protection of internationally proclaimed human rights, make sure that they are not complicit in human rights abuses, uphold the freedom of association and the effective recognition of the right to collective bargaining, eliminate of all forms of forced and compulsory labor, effectively abolish child labor, eliminate discrimination in respect of employment and occupation, support a precautionary approach to environmental challenges, undertake initiatives to promote greater environmental responsibility, encourage the development and diffusion of environmentally friendly technologies, work against corruption in all its forms, including extortion and bribery (United, nd). The principles of the UN Global Compact are "soft law", they indicate the values that entrepreneurs should take into account in their activities (Bantekas, 2004, p. 312-321). Another document issued by the United Nations on corporate social responsibility is *Norms on the Responsibilities of Transnational Corporations and Other Business Enterprises with Regard to Human Rights* of August 13, 2003 (Norms, 2003). These standards indicate that transnational corporations and other business enterprises should:

- respect economic, social and cultural rights as well as civil and political rights and contribute to their realization, in particular the rights to development, adequate food and drinking water, the highest attainable standard of physical and mental health, adequate housing, privacy, education, freedom of thought, conscience, and religion and freedom of opinion and expression, and refrain from actions which obstruct or impede the realization of those rights (Norms, 2003, p. 6),
- act in accordance with fair business, marketing and advertising practices and take all necessary steps to ensure the safety and quality of the goods and services they provide, including observance of the precautionary principle; nor produce, distribute, market, or advertise harmful or potentially harmful products for use by consumers (Norms, 2003, p. 6),
- carry out their activities in accordance with national laws, regulations, administrative practices and policies relating to the preservation of the environment of the countries in which they operate, as well as in accordance with relevant international agreements, principles, objectives, responsibilities and standards with regard to the environment as well as human rights, public health and safety, bioethics and the precautionary principle, and generally conduct their activities in a manner contributing to the wider goal of sustainable development (Norms, 2003, p. 7),

The Norms enable the governments of developing countries to require from international companies wishing to invest in their territory to comply with the international standards of human rights and environmental protection (Schmidt, 2005, p. 243-246). Tracy Schmidt pointed out that the Norms should be more binding by establishing an effective system of their compliance, monitoring and reporting (Schmidt, 2005, p. 237). The United Nations Special Representative prepared the report *The UN "Protect, Respect and Remedy" Framework for Business and Human Rights* published on April 7, 2008 (Ruggie, 2008). This study highlights the need to exchange experiences on business and human rights. J. Ruggie points out that the activities of multinational enterprises are associated with numerous dangers due to the lack of effective control by international organizations (Ruggie, 2008). The reasons for the difficulties in applying human rights in business are gaps in the management system related to the effects of globalization and the inability of society to exercise effective control over international entrepreneurs (Ruggie, 2008). As a result, multinational companies, which do not respect human rights, are not held responsible for this (Ruggie, 2008). Enterprises should have a human rights risk management system, i.e. enterprises should operate not only in accordance with the laws of the country in which they conduct business activity, but also with human rights in general (Ruggie, 2008). It is not possible to counteract all violations of human rights by entrepreneurs effectively (Ruggie, 2008). It is necessary to have quick access to court and mediation proceedings resolving disputes between employees and entrepreneurs, as well as the adoption of human rights standards by governments and responsible business conduct by entrepreneurs (Ruggie, 2008).

In 2011, the *OECD Guidelines for Multinational Enterprises* were published, defining voluntarily principles and practices related to employment, trade union rights, human rights, environmental protection, disclosure of information, corruption and tax obligations, competition and consumer protection, and the environment (OECD, 2011). They are aimed at the international companies, i.e. those that invest or have their own branches or subsidiaries in other countries (OECD, 2011). The OECD member states are committed to the application by entrepreneurs of the *Guidelines for Multinational Enterprises* on their territory (Deva, 2006, p. 735); conduct promotional and informational activities regarding *the Guidelines ...* by establishing the National Compact Point, which is, inter alia, a place of dissemination of the use of the *Guidelines* ... and an institution responsible for conflict resolution (OECD, 2011). The *OECD*

Guidelines for Multinational Enterprises indicates the legitimacy of taking into account the specificity of the country and community in which the business is conducted by international entrepreneurs, including: human rights, non-discrimination of employees, responsible approach to the environment, health, and safety at work (OECD, 2011). The entrepreneur should take into account the interests of the local community and the natural environment in the plans and effects of his investment (OECD, 2011). Multinational enterprises should promote local capacity building through cooperation with the local society and local entrepreneurs, as well as create and apply internal control methods and management systems that increase the sense of confidence and mutual trust between enterprises and the societies in which the investors operate (OECD, 2011). Investments of multinational enterprises should be based on the local human resources, trainings of local employees, and the investor should comply with the internal law of the country in which the investment is carried out (OECD, 2011).

The International Labor Organization has developed a *Tripartite Declaration of Principles Concerning Multinational Enterprises and Social Policy* encouraging economic and social development and reducing the risks of entrepreneurship (ILO, 2017). In their activities, international entrepreneurs should take into account the local specificity, culture of a given country, and combat discrimination based on: race, sex, religion, political opinions, national and social origin (ILO, 2017). The ILO declaration concerns the rights of workers and trade unions as an area of corporate social responsibility (ILO, 2017).

The European Union has published a document defining the European strategy for promoting corporate social responsibility and its impact on the economy and society (Commission, 2002), which criticized the voluntary approach to the application of corporate social responsibility by entrepreneurs. In 2006, the European Union issued the document *Implementing the Partnership for Growth and Jobs: Making Europe a Pole of Excellence on Corporate Social Responsibility* (Communication, 2006). This document indicates the need to increase awareness of corporate social responsibility, share good practices between small and medium-sized enterprises, cooperate with Member States and acceding states, inform consumers, transparency of actions taken, support for research and education (Communication, 2006).

The documents issued by the above-mentioned institutions constitute "soft law", they indicate how an entrepreneur should act in order to comply with the ESG and CSR principles. These documents define the standards that should be implemented in an enterprise that wants to apply the ESG and CSR principles. They make it possible for the developing countries that are seeking investments by multinational enterprises in their territory to request for this activity to be conducted in accordance with the above-described documents. This applies, in particular, to the cases when the ESG and CSR principles in a developing country are at the initial stage of implementation. Subsequently, international documents indicate what the governments of the developing countries can expect from international entrepreneurs in the field of environmental protection and respect for workers' rights when conducting business activity in their territory. The aforementioned documents do not indicate when a given entrepreneur can be considered as observing the ESG and CSR principles in its operations; who should give such a status and then verify whether the enterprise consistently complies with the ESG and CSR principles in the long term. The documents described above ignore the issue of whether the ESG and CSR principles can be properly applied in public administration offices, where employee rights may also be violated, where corruption and the office's negative impact on the environment may occur. In addition, the above-described documents ignore the issue of the possibility of extending the ESG and CSR rules to combat social exclusion, e.g. of former prisoners, disabled, homeless, and long-term unemployed people.

THE CONFIRAMTION OF THE STATUS OF AN ENTREPRENEUR APPLYING IN HIS ACTIVITY THE ESG AND CSR PRINCIPLES

The determination that entrepreneur can be granted the ESG and CSR status must be made objectively. It can be considered whether it should be done by an organization established by entrepreneurs who follow the ESG and CSR principles, a rating agency or a state office. In the first case, there is a risk of lack of objectivity on the part of entrepreneurs who believe that they meet the ESG and CSR rules and will not want to admit other entrepreneurs to their group. This solution is also opposed by the fact that the fees for the audit confirming the fulfillment of the conditions for obtaining the status of an ESG, CSR company may be set at a too high level, and later, verification of compliance with the ESG and CSR principles in the long term may be too costly and constitute a barrier for smaller entrepreneurs.

Entrusting the task of granting the status of an entrepreneur following the ESG and CSR principles to rating agencies and consulting companies operating on a global scale seems to be a possible solution. In this case, the amount of the fee for conducting an audit before issuing a certificate of an ESG, CSR entrepreneur and subsequent audits confirming compliance with these principles in future activities will be regulated by the government administration of this country in agreement with the branch of an international consulting company or rating agency. This solution would also have the advantage that consulting companies and rating agencies operating globally, when granting the status of an ESG and CSR entrepreneur, would apply the same rules to entrepreneurs from different countries. The disadvantage of this solution is that a private entity, which should be impartial in its activities, obtains rights over the similar private entities, which may lead to a conflict of interest. In this case, it is difficult to indicate who and how should claim compensation, if it turned out that in the analysis of granting the status of an entrepreneur guided by the ESG and CSR principles, a mistake would have been made and the status would have been given to a company that did not deserve it. To whom the consumers from country X, who purchased goods and services of a company with the ESG and CSR status from country Y, granted by a rating agency from country Z, should direct their complaints, if it turned out that the production of the purchased goods was not environmentally friendly.

As a third solution, it can be suggested that the status of an entrepreneur guided in his activities by the principles of ESG and CSR should be granted by a governmental administration office in a given country, whereas the costs of the audit preceding obtaining this status and the subsequent verification of compliance with the ESG and CSR principles would be borne by the entrepreneur. This solution has the advantage that in a given country, when defining the ESG and CSR criteria, one could take into account the level of its economic development and the specificity resulting from its geographical location. Thus, each country could adjust the criteria for granting an entrepreneur the status of a company complying with the ESG and CSR rules slightly differently, depending on the situation in a given country. The responsibility for any mistakes in granting this status would be borne solely by the government of the given country. . This decision has the advantage that the state administration, considering the application for obtaining the status of an entrepreneur, guided by the principles of ESG and CSR in its activities, will be objective in relation to each entrepreneur. Fees for processing the application and its subsequent verification should be at an affordable level so as not to create an obstacle for small and medium enterprises.

Obtaining the status of an entrepreneur driven by ESG and CSR tasks should enable the use of a certificate on the company's products, website, etc., which would be the same in every country, easily recognizable by everyone, especially by consumers.

THE ROLE OF CONSUMERS IN CREATING THE ATTITUDES OF ENTREPRENEURS COMPLIANCE WITH THE ESG AND CSR PRINCIPLES

The consumer, being aware of the risks to which the environment and the society are exposed through the actions of irresponsible entrepreneurs who only care about their profit, will avoid using their services and purchasing products, as long as they can distinguish the entrepreneur who has the status of applying the ESG and CSR principles in his activities from an entrepreneur who does not follow these principles. A simple distinction between these entrepreneurs may occur when the products and goods of the entrepreneur applying the ESG and CSR principles in his activities will have a certificate confirming that they have the status of products that comply with the principles of ESG and CSR. In the case of using the services of companies not involved in production activities, the distinction can be made by posting a certificate on the company's website confirming that the company has a status of an entrepreneur guided by the principles of ESG and CSR in its activities.

Not every consumer is aware of the consequences of their choice and the impact it has on the environment and interpersonal relationships that prevail in the company he purchases goods or services from. Many consumers do not know what the ESG and CSR rules that entrepreneurs apply in their activities are. The government administration should conduct a series of social campaigns explaining what the ESG and CSR rules are, what are the positive effects of applying these rules by entrepreneurs and the role of the consumer in the process of promoting compliance by entrepreneurs with the ESG and CSR rules. These campaigns should be carried out more frequently and on a wider scale in developing countries than in the developed ones, where higher consumer awareness can be expected.

A campaign aimed at consumers may also explain the negative effects of succumbing to advertising campaigns encouraging consumers to thoughtlessly replace goods and products they already have with newer ones. For example, consumers are often unaware of what happens to a mobile phone or a laptop that they change to a newer model after a year of use. Consumers often do not know the details of the process of disposal of electronic equipment which they get rid of, and the disposal of food packaging. As a result of these campaigns, the consumer should stop thinking that nothing can be done to protect the environment, but that he has an important, active role in this regard by choosing the goods and services he purchases.

POSSIBILITIES OF APPLYING THE ESG AND CSR PRINCIPLES BY THE GOVERNMENTAL AND LOCAL ADMINISTRATION

It would be nepotism on the side of international organizations as well as governmental and local administration to expect entrepreneurs to comply with the ESG and CSR principles if these principles were not applied by governmental and local administration. Government administration bodies, while providing services, use the environment and employees; make financial settlements and issue decisions for entrepreneurs. The way they function influences the environment, the quality of relations between employees and managers, and the elimination of corruption. Governmental and local administration offices can strive in their activities to reduce the consumption of electricity and heat, reduce paper consumption by issuing administrative decisions in electronic form, and counteract mobbing among employees. This also includes the creation of support programs for employees in difficult times, such as preschool education; complete elimination of corruption; correct formation of remuneration for employees and managers, that should not be a significant burden for taxpayers; maintaining the employment of workers at the necessary level without creating unnecessary artificial jobs; hiring employees according to the objective criteria after conducting a competition in accordance with their competences and skills. As a criterion for the office functioning in accordance with the ESG and CSR principles, one can add: the speed of processing cases, the quality of service to applicants, issuing appropriate decisions that are not contested by applicants, or in appeal proceedings, the decision issued by the governmental office is not delayed.

By applying similar, analogous and appropriate criteria, government and self-government administration offices may also receive certificates of an entity applying the ESG and CSR principles in its activities. The meaning of this certificate will be different from the one issued for entrepreneurs. An entrepreneur with an ESG and CSR certificate can expect, in the long term, an increase in the popularity of its products and services, as well as an increase in revenues and income. An office that receives a certificate of a unit operating in accordance with the ESG and CSR principles will be a model to follow for other offices. The beneficiary of this certificate will be the state and taxpayers, who will incur lower costs for the functioning of the public administration, since a more efficient office will solve more issues with fewer employees.

POSSIBILITIES FOR EXTENDING THE ESG AND CSR PRINCIPLES TO SOLVING SOCIAL PROBLEMS OF EXCLUDED PERSONS

So far, the ESG and CSR principles concerned reducing the negative impact of an entrepreneur on the environment, proper entrepreneur-employee relations, principles of fair cooperation between entrepreneurs, and eliminating corruption in business. It was assumed that the ESG and CSR principles should only be applied by international entrepreneurs. Public administrations can be guided by the ESG and CSR principles, as these entities may experience negative phenomena such as corruption, mobbing, etc. The problem of the possibility of extending the application of the ESG and CSR principles in the activities of entrepreneurs, public administration for the benefit of socially excluded people, i.e. the disabled, the long-term unemployed, former prisoners, addicted people, the homeless, people without education, illiterate people, elderly people who cannot use digital devices, the Internet, etc., was ignored. Withdrawal from social activity may concern people connected by means of various ties with a socially excluded person, e.g. in a situation where one of the parents or both parents give up professional activity in order to look after a disabled, dependent child. Socially excluded people usually receive support from the public administration in various forms: food, food stamps, accommodation in shelters for the homeless, cash benefits, access to free training, etc. The provision of any assistance by the state administration to socially excluded people ultimately burdens tax payers i.e. entrepreneurs. This assistance is sometimes ineffective, in particular, when it is aimed solely at ensuring a minimum subsistence level, without being aimed at adapting them to functioning in society. Not every socially excluded person can become an active participant in it, because health, age, level of intellectual development may be obstacles that cannot be overcome. In every society of every country there is a group of socially excluded people whose maintenance ultimately burdens the rest of the society paying taxes, and when socially excluded people do not receive any support from the government administration, the costs of their functioning are borne by their individual supporters.

Counteracting social exclusion is a complex problem that can be addressed by entrepreneurs employing socially excluded people, or supporting organizations and public administrations supporting socially excluded people who cannot take up employment. Socially excluded people taking up jobs are often not so effective and flexible workers as the rest. Employing socially excluded people is riskier than with regular employees, as they may require more extensive and more frequent health care. An entrepreneur employing socially excluded people should not bear double costs, i.e. pay taxes, which are in part intended by the public administration to support socially excluded people and help directly, e.g. by employing social excluded people, or help indirectly by supporting organizations that care for socially excluded people. Entrepreneurs cannot replace public administration with its tasks, which include ensuring a minimum subsistence level for every citizen. An entrepreneur who decides to employ socially excluded people or financially supports organizations dealing with the care of socially excluded people who, for various reasons, are not able to exist independently and take up any work, should pay lower taxes to the public administration, which would be a compensation for the risk associated with the employment of socially excluded people. Public administration can also control the number of socially excluded people, e.g. by erasing information about a previous prison sentence. As long as the information about the person's sentencing to imprisonment is included in a public register that is open to the public, this person cannot practice certain professions. Earlier and definitive removal of information about the person's sentencing to prison can help to increase employment opportunities. In this case, it is the public administration that decides how long a person may be socially stigmatized and, thus, socially excluded. There is a difference for public administration whether it is to support socially excluded people who can take up employment and, consequently, become independent from the budget with public money, or whether the state will receive less budget revenue from taxes paid by entrepreneurs employing socially excluded people, but will not have to keep them. The latter solution is more correct socially, as it does not shape the demanding attitudes of socially excluded people. Activities for the benefit of socially excluded people by entrepreneurs should be considered as an application of the ESG and CSR principles.

INTERNATIONAL COOPERATION

The efforts of entrepreneurs and government administration in some countries to pursue activities in accordance with the ESG and CSR principles may be destroyed on a global scale if these principles are not pursued or followed by all the countries. International global corporations should comply with the rules of conducting business activities in accordance with the ESG and CSR principles in each country in which they operate, even if in that country these rules are unknown and not applied. Likewise, the same rules of ESG and CSR should be followed by international organizations, regardless of the country in which their branch is located.

Government and self-government administration of some countries and entrepreneurs from these countries may not be interested in disseminating and implementing the principles of business activity in accordance with the ESG and CSR requirements. It happens that global corporations have a significant influence on the developing countries in which they intend to invest. When negotiating an investment in a given country, a global enterprise may enforce unfavorable wage conditions for employees, as well as lower level of health and safety at work (Bantekas, 2004, p. 314). International industrial groups can transfer toxic production from countries with high environmental standards to countries with lower environmental standards. An attempt of developing countries to impose too high ESG and CSR expectations on potential investors who are global corporations may lead to the loss of investment in favor of another country (Shamir, 2004, p. 637).

Countries where ESG and CSR principles are applied should help, encourage and support those countries that have not yet seen the benefits of ESG and CSR. If this proves to be ineffective, cooperation with entrepreneurs from these countries may be limited or terminated. Such exclusion of entrepreneurs who do not apply ESG and CSR rules is possible if these entrepreneurs are not monopolists or oligopolists in their industries. When an entrepreneur is eliminated from the international or domestic market in terms of the supply of products, services, and the sale and distribution of his goods due to non-compliance with the ESG and CSR rules by consumers and entrepreneurs applying these rules, they will ultimately be forced to apply the ESG and CSR rules. In the long term, the result of such actions should be to promote compliance with the ESG and CSR principles in each country.

CONCLUSION

Operating in accordance with the ESG and CSR principles is more than just operating in accordance with the law. An entrepreneur guided by these principles looks to the future, trying to have a positive impact on the environment and society. His behavior is characterized by responsibility for products, goods and services that he introduces into the environment. Such an entrepreneur is aware that his actions can contribute to the improvement of the environment, the quality of life of a part of the society, improvement of relations with other entrepreneurs as well as governmental and local administration by eliminating corrupt behavior. An objective assessment of the activities of such entrepreneurs and offices is supposed to be honest, which should be the norm. In the history of many countries, the honest behavior of entrepreneurs was perceived as a naive way of functioning and the attitude towards generating the highest profits was glorified. Noticing the negative effects of such activities for the environment, the society and public finances after many years resulted in the desire to change the paradigm of running business. Until now, the ESG and CSR principles were applied only to entrepreneurs. The possibility of their application to the activities of governmental and local administrations, which may also have a negative impact on the environment, society and public finances, was ignored. The ESG and CSR principles can be applied to the activities of public administration offices after their modification. The scope of the ESG and CSR principles should include the assistance of entrepreneurs for socially excluded people, and these activities should be coordinated with tax reliefs. Entrepreneurs engaging in the employment of socially excluded people or helping such people cannot replace public administration in the performance of its tasks, therefore, they should receive a tax relief, which would be their compensation for helping to implement public tasks.

Promoting the activities of entrepreneurs, government and local governments in accordance with ESG and CSR in all countries requires active cooperation from the governments of individual countries, which should strive to develop and implement similar standards in the field of ESG and CSR in their territory. Obtaining the status of an entrepreneur or an office applying the ESG and CSR principles in its activities should be performed by issuing a certificate by an objective state office. Entrepreneurs, government and local administration offices that have obtained the status of an entity operating in accordance with the ESG and CSR principles, should be periodically verified to check whether they still meet the ESG and CSR criteria.

Consumers may play an active role in the process of creating ESG and CSR behaviors by purchasing goods and services more often from entrepreneurs applying ESG and SCR rules. The public administration should conduct educational activities aimed at clarifying the active role of consumers in promoting the application of the ESG and CSR principles by entrepreneurs and the ability of the individual consumer to influence the environment and the consumption of natural resources.

REFERENCES

Backer, L. C. (2006). Multinational corporations, transnational law: The United Nations' norms on the responsibilities of transnational corporations as a harbinger of Corporate Social Responsibility in international law. *Columbia Human Rights Law Review*, *37*(287).

Bantekas, I. (2004). Corporate Social Responsibility in international law. Boston University International Law Review, 22(309).

Business Strategy for Sustainable Development: Leadership and Accountability for the 90s. (1992). IISD, WBCSD Deloitte & Touche.

Commission of the European Communities. (2001). *Green Paper Promoting European framework for Corporate Social Responsibility.* https://ec.europa.eu/employment_social/soc-dial/csr/greenpaper_pl.pdf

Commission of the European Communities. (2002). *Corporate Social Responsibility: A business contribution to Sustainable Development.* https://eur-lex.europa.eu/legal-content/EN/TXT/PDF/?uri=CELEX:52002DC0347&from=EN

Communication from the Commission to the European Parliament, the Council and the European Economic and Social Committee. (2006). *Implementing the partnership for growth and jobs: making Europe a pole of excellence on corporate social responsibility.* https://eur-lex.europa.eu/legal-content/EN/TXT/PDF/?uri=CELEX:52006DC0136&from=PL

Deva, S. (2006). Sustainable good governance and corporations: An analysis of asymmetries. *Georgetown International Environmental Law Review, 18.*

Dodd, E. M. (1932). For Whom are Corporate Managers Trustees? *Harvard Law Review*, *45*(7), 1145. doi:10.2307/1331697

Friedman, M. (1962). *Capitalism and Freedom.* University of Chicago Press.

Friedman, M. (1970). The Social Responsibility of Business Is to Increase its Profits, *New York Times Magazine.* http://umich.edu/~thecore/doc/Friedman.pdf?mod=article_inline

ILO. (2017). *Tripartite Declaration of Principles concerning Multinational Enterprises and Social Policy* (5th ed.). http://www.ilo.org/wcmsp5/groups/public/---ed_emp/---emp_ent/---multi/documents/publication/wcms_094386.pdf

Norms on the Responsibilities of Transnational Corporations and Other Business Enterprises with regard to Human Rights. (2003). https://digitallibrary.un.org/record/501576

OECD. (2011). *OECD Guidelines for Multinational Enterprises.* OECD Publishing. http://www.oecd.org/investment/mne/1922428.pdf doi:10.1787/9789264115415-en

Ruggie, J. (2008). *Protect, Respect and Remedy: a Framework for Business and Human Rights*. https://media.business-humanrights.org/media/documents/files/reports-and-materials/Ruggie-report-7-Apr-2008.pdf

Schmidt, T. M. (2005). Transnational corporate responsibility for international environmental and human rights violations: Will the United Nations' "Norms" provide the required means? *California Western International Law Journal*, *36*(217).

Shamir, S. (2004). Between self-regulation and the Alien Tort Claims Act: On the contested concept of Corporate Social Responsibility. *Law & Society Review*, *38*(635), 635–664. doi:10.1111/j.0023-9216.2004.00062.x

The Global Sullivan Principles. (n.d.). http://hrlibrary.umn.edu/links/sullivanprinciples.html

United Nations Global Compact. (1999). https://www.unglobalcompact.org/what-is-gc/mission/principles

Visser, W. (2010). The Age of Responsibility: CSR 2.0 and the New DNA of Business. *Journal of Business Systems. Governance and Ethics*, *5*(3), 7–22. doi:10.15209/jbsge.v5i3.185

Wade, C. L. (2002). *Racial Discrimination and the Relationship Between the Directorial Duty of Care and Corporate Disclosure* (Vol. 63). University of Pittsburgh Law Review.

Williams, C. A. (1999). The Securities and Exchange Commission and Corporate Social Transparency. *Harvard Law Review*, *112*(6), 1197. doi:10.2307/1342384

World Business Council for Sustainable Development. (n.d.). *Corporate Social Responsibility*. https://growthorientedsustainableentrepreneurship.files.wordpress.com/2016/07/csr-wbcsd-csr-primer

Chapter 5
Potential ESG Risks in Entities of the Healthcare System

Beata Zofia Filipiak
University of Szczecin, Poland

Marcin Kiestrzyn
https://orcid.org/0000-0003-1188-0691
University of Szczecin, Poland

ABSTRACT

The chapter presents the evolution of potential ESG risks in the healthcare sector related to striving to provide the best care for patients. Based on the literature and selected examples, the analysis of this problem will indicate potential risks of the main factors and tools that can help manage this risk in the healthcare sector. There is a research gap in the literature; there is a lack of detailed discussion and research allowing to establish the relationship between ESG factors and finances. Particular emphasis is placed on social pillar, which in the authors' opinion is critical to the functioning of the healthcare sector, especially from the face of COVID-19. The authors proposed a map to identify potential risk and possible scenarios of action in the long term. The main assumption of the study is that the implementation of ESG potential risk management leads in the long run to sustainable development in the healthcare sector.

BACKGROUND

ESG Risk Factors in Sustainable Development and Finance Towards a Sustainable Healthcare System

Sustainability is a broad and debated subject, often difficult to be defined and applied into real projects, especially when dealing with a complex scenario as the one of healthcare. Idea and good practices of sustainability are widespread around several economic sectors and have contributed to the achievement of social welfare, but research shows unlimited economic growth, pursued in business, seems unrealistic (Buys et al., 2014).

DOI: 10.4018/978-1-7998-6788-3.ch005

The interest in researching the relationship between finance and sustainability has increased recently and in particular between sustainable public systems and their impact on the achievement of SDG's objectives (Álvarez-Herranz & Balsalobre-Lorente, 2016; Alińska et al. 2018, Ziolo et al. 2019). Based on the literature review there are many different relationships and possibilities to analyse the involvement between finance and SDG's or sustainable public systems and SDG's objectives. Among them, we can highlight the institutional links in capital markets (Rezende de Carvalho Ferreira et al. 2016; Alińska et al. 2018), the concern with environmental, social and corporate governance (ESG risk) factors (Gray, 2011; Ziolo et al. 2019; Aspinall et al. 2018], the impact of investment (Hebb, 2013), the concern with climate change and human rights (Alm & Sievänen, 2013), sustainable development (Levashova, 2011) socially responsible in investments and effects of decision making (SRI) (Rezende de Carvalho Ferreira et al., 2016; Aspinall et al. 2018). The benefits of sustainable development goals and finance in the health care system are more important than ever before, as it takes into account environmental, social and governance (ESG) factors into decision-making must be ranked as their top concern. (Sepetis, 2020) This problem grew with the change of approaches and goals of sustainable development.

Sustainable finance is defined through the prism of the impact of financial services on environmental, social, and governance (ESG). *(*Gerster, 2011*).* With development of sustainable finance we can observe the increasing role of sustainable healthcare system. With development of sustainable finance we can observe the increasing role of sustainable healthcare system. It can be indicated that along with the development of the concept of sustainable development, health protection is taking an increasingly prominent place.

Socio-economic development, despite the fact that it creates opportunities for universal access to health protection for people, healthcare, pro-health measures paradoxically lead to many threats to human health. Focusing on the environment and the protection of its resources cannot exclude man and the elimination of threats resulting from environmental degradation. There are many health risks that may only become apparent after some time. These threats may result, inter alia, from with increase road traffic, increase in air pollution, water, soil, greenhouse gas emissions, use of toxic chemicals. Risks may also be associated with the release of chemical carcinogens today, consumption of modified products, chemicalisation of agriculture, food or the production of drugs. Human health is also threatened by the existing social and economic inequalities caused by the transfer of production from one country to another. The above dependencies and problems are reflected in the EU strategic documents, which refer both to the problems of sustainable development and constitute the basis for sustainable healthcare.

The EU Strategy on health matters c "Together for Health" (Together for Health, 2007), has adopted as its main goals: promoting health in an aging Europe, protecting citizens from health threats and supporting health systems and new technologies to do so. In this document points out four pillars which are four principles:

- common health values,
- health as the greatest good,
- presence of health issues in all policy areas,
- strengthening the EU position in the world on health matters (Together for Healt, 2007).

The "Together for Health" complements national health protection strategies pursuant to Art. 168 of the Treaty on the Functioning of the European Union (2012).

In turn, the document "Investing in health" (Investing in health, 2013) indicates the need for smart investments in health. This is to include more thoughtful, not necessarily more, investments in sustainable health systems, investing in the health of society, especially through health promotion programs, investing in health insurance as a way to reduce inequalities and fight social exclusion. The goals set in this way are consistent with the pillars of the Europe 2020 strategy.

The main directions of the evolution of the approach to sustainable development in the health care system presented above indicate that sustainability looks at the environmental, social and economic impacts of a healthcare system (table 1). It is an upcoming problem in healthcare leadership and management as the world realizes that climate change is an enormous threat to population health, where we have finite resources to combat these challenges.

Sustainability are changes in socio-technological systems that involve at least three structural levels (fig. 1): 1). micro level - where the technological niches (micro level) of innovation; 2) is included. meso level - where business models are designed; called the regime space; 3). macro level, which captures a wide perspective and the wide landscape (macro level) where hard and soft innovations are adopted, tested, accepted, or rejected by society. (Lopes et al. 2019) Considering the fact that, sustainability presents essentially several separate issues such as protection of ecological systems, inter-generational equity and efficiency of resource use, valuation of environmental assets and recognition of constraints implied by the development and changes of environmental systems (Jones & Dowling 2004; Matthes 2007; Ziolo et al. 2019) then it also implies the need to look at externalities resulting from ESG risks. So that you can determine the types of externalities is to consider axiomata defining sustainability and a number of factors influencing these actions. Earlier research were based on a selected aspects of sustainable finance, which did not show the relation between finance and negative externalities from the perspective of sustainable development. (Ziolo et al., 2019).

The latest research indicates that the existence of externalities has been normal commonly accepted and will confirm the relationship between sustainable finance (the financial system) and ESG (negative externalities) risk factors. Scientific research shows that in addition to mechanisms and classifications, have also discussed external phenomena and appearances of externalities. (Bennett et al. 2017; Jing & Sun 2018). Externalities related to ESG have been analysed in the banking sector (Zang 2016; Smolyansky 2016), financial sector (Ziolo et al. 2019), insurance (Zahou 2014), coal mining (Liu 2014), renewable energy (Sundaraly 2016) and other specific industries. It should also be noted that research on ESG was also carried out on the following topics: ESG reporting, ESG investing and relationships between ESG conduct and corporate financial / economic performance. (Brooks & Oikonomu 2018; Vitolla 2019; Daugaard 2019; Iamandi et al. 2019)

In addition to the above academic research, we can highlight the institutional links in capital markets (Ferreira 2016), the concern with ESG factors (Nikolakis et al. 2012), the impact of investment (Hebb 2013), the focus with climate change and human rights (Alm & Sievänen, 2013), sustainable development (Levashova 2011) and socially responsible investment (SRI) (Rezende de Carvalho Ferreira et al., 2016; Aspinall et al., 2018).

The literature review shows that a significant part of the research is devoted searching to the link between sustainability performance and financial performance. Research by Walley & Whitehead (1994) indicates a negative link between corporate social / environmental performance and financial performance. Dowell, Hart, & Yeung (2000) analysed a positive link between corporate social / environmental performance and financial performance. Some researcher showed no significant, neutral link between corporate performance and financial performance. There are also studies showing the link (positive

Table 1. Evolution of the approach to sustainable development in the healthcare system including sustainable finance

Problems to overcome, which are discuss	Period in which the problem was presented	Author/ Document
Consideration of health in the wider context of sustainable development	the 90s of the 20th century and later	McMichael 2006; Brown et al. 2005, Dooris 1999; Hancock 1996, Labonté 1991; Weisz et al., 2011
Companies, governments and sector organizations are increasingly looking at additional ways of promoting health and safety, by using them as a criteria in procuring products and servlices from other companies. There is a link with social responsibility.	2001	Green Paper: "Promoting a European framework for Corporate Social Responsibility"
Sustainable development is a leading issue with the European Commission, United Nations and World Health Organization (WHO), which are supporting initiatives to integrate sustainable concepts into various sectors of society	2002; 2012	WHO 2002; Brundtland 2012
Many types of tools and beyond-compliance environmental guidelines like environmental management programs, cleaner production, leaner operations, ISO 14001 affects the perception of sustainability health concepts	1987; 2003	Brundtland Report, 1987; Hedberg & Malmborg, 2003
Sustainability in healthcare is understood as a balance of the needs of patients, economic concerns, and environmental costs.	2002; 2012	Jameton & McGuirre 2002; Prada 2012
Sustainability is seen only as one efficiency dimension among others.	2006	Arah et al. 2006
Businesses tend to express sustainability through focusing on environmental aspects of sustainability with social aspects of sustainability rarely mentioned, and that a social vision of sustainability should not emerge "organically from the ranks who have to carry it out," but instead "need more formal, rigorous, and focused research and education that will both push organizational leaders to go further with sustainability practices, and give them a solid grounding from which to work"	2011	Hannon & Callaghan 2011
The wide array of advice, guidelines and information has lead to confusion, not only in the research world, but also for management of health care centers attempting to implement a sustainable health care system	2012	Smith 2012
Increased usage of CSR, and creation of Global Reporting Initiative (GRI), ISO 14001 and ISO 26000, reflect corporate and stakeholders heightened interests and prioritization of sustainability issues that are not only environmental, but are also social	2012	Roca & Searcy 2012
Health improvement as a continuation of the Sustainable Development Goals	2012	Agenda 21(Rio+20)
There have been identified essential factors and key causal relations that affect the patient satisfaction, and ultimately on the level of social sustainability of the healthcare professional	2013	Faezipour & Ferreira 2013
Objective 3 Agenda 2030, which defines the directional activities related to ensuring health and quality of life	2015	Transforming Our World: The 2030 Agenda for Global Action
The EU Commission defines "Sustainable finance" as key area of sustainable development that allow: 1) improving the contribution of finance to sustainable and inclusive growth by funding society's long-term needs, including goods and services; 2) strengthening financial stability by incorporating factors as environmental and social, including by eliminating the risk of ESG and CSR factors into decision-making.	2015; 2018	UN (2015) EU Commission (2018)
It is assumed that a long-term and multidimensional and assume approach to sustainability transitions. Moreover, it is indicated that this process has a key impact on the creation of sociotechnical systems that seek sustainable ways of production and consumption of healtcare services.	2003; 2012; 2019	Kemp, R.& Loorbach 2003; Farla et al. 2012; Lopes et al. 2019
	2019	Lopes et al. 2019
Impact of ESG risk factors on the healthcare system	2020	Sepetis 2020
Proactive and Strategic Healthcare Public-Private Partnerships (PPPs) in the Coronavirus(Covid-19) Epoch, impact of Covid-19 on healthcare sustainable system	2020	Baxter & Casady 2020; UNDP 2020

Source: own study

Figure 1. Sustainability transformation at three structural levels
Source: own elaboration

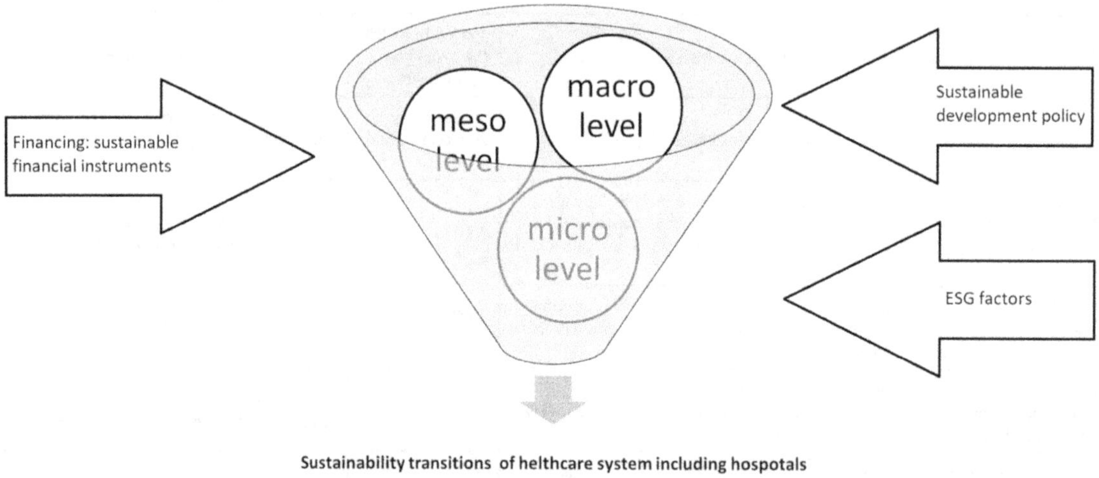

negative, neutral) between ESG criteria and financial performance (Dowell et al. 2000). Important research is the research of Fatemi & Fooladi (2013) in which they show that in a very near future good environmental, social and governance performance will be a new, common standard. Equally important are the studies that refer to the expectations of improvement of social and environmental results over time and their impact on in the valuation of the company on markets.

Highly developed and socially responsible countries, but also those countries that see the benefits of sustainability, are trying to influence the economic situation, and thus implement a policy of sustainable development, using specific macroeconomic policy tools. Among these tools, the most important are: monetary policy and fiscal policy. In its monetary policy, the central bank uses the financial markets in a sense and also affects the situation on these markets. There is an increasing use of instruments related to the sustainable development policy, such as green securities and the policy of preferring projects that take into account environmental elements. Through the market financial impulses of monetary policy are transferred to the real sphere of the economy. An important element is green taxes, which are associated with fiscal policy. The literature review showed that when talking about sustainable development, the impact of ESG factors in healthcare sector entities, one must talk about the use of sustainable finance. A number of financial institutions (market and public financial system) use financial instruments dedicated to sustainable development. The healthcare sector uses sustainable financial instruments to guide its business models or decisions in the area of innovation and investment.

Health Care Sector Business Strategies Towards ESG Factors

Sustainability imperatives, rules and good practices are widespread around many economic sectors, quickly enter also the health care sector entities and have contributed to the achievement of social welfare, but do not always contribute to economic growth. (Buys et al. 2014; Lopes et al. 2019). Health services and products of healthcare entities are considered important and crucial and one have faced considerable changes over recent decades and transformations (WHO 2015). These changes involve the governance of high costs of development for raising quality standards and for the accomplishment of legal aspects for environmental and social activities. (Unger & Landis, 2016; Lopes et al. 2019) This orientation forces actions to change current business strategies and making innovation and implies acquiring financing sources adequate to the adopted strategies.

In the literature on the subject, many definitions of a business model have been proposed. For the healthcare sector, the definition of J. Magretta is important, which defined the business model as a set of assumptions enabling an organization to perform activities that create value for all players on whom it depends, which means that a given organization does not create value only for customers (Magnetta 2010). M. Rappa (2004) believes that a business model be defined as a method of doing business, thanks to which an organization can survive and stay. The business model is also defined by its characteristics. According to Hwang and Christensen (2008), the most important features in the organizations of the healthcare sector include: proposition of value for the customer, profit formula, key resources and processes.

The business model enables easier verification of the strategy of healthcare sector entities. The aim of this model is to achieve, through the strategy, satisfactory results both in the economic area and in the area of improving the quality of services or products provided. The literature on the subject shows practical aspects of how sustainable business models have helped businesses to achieve their sustainability ambitions, which also applies to healthcare sector entities (Boons&Lüdeke-Freund, 2013; Schaltegger et al. 2016; Evans at al. 2017; Geissdoerfer et al. 2018). There is also a perception that sustainable business models are tools for delivering social and environmental sustainability to the industrial systems. (Lüdeke-Freund 2010; Nosratabadi et al., 2019)

In the literature on the subject, Casadesus-Masanell & Ricard (2010) indicate that a very precise distinction should be made between the concepts and components of strategy, business models and tactics. He also shares this view Castano (2014) and team of Nosratabadi). The distinction and definition of sensitive elements in common and connecting strategy, business models and tactics activities can lead to the success of healthcare entities and the implementation of sustainable development goals and the use of public intervention instruments and sources of financing dedicated to innovations dedicated to the implementation of the SDG's. Thus, these activities serve to reduce the ESG risk. Mutual interactions between strategy, business models and tactics are presented in the figure 2.

Figure. 2 indicates the choice of business model should follow from the adopted strategy. The business model implies the tactical decisions that the entities make to compete against, or cooperate with, other enterprises in the marketplace. The same implications apply to entities of the healthcare System. Business models are made of concrete choices of decision making and the consequences of these choices. These choices concern both the degree to which the health goals are met and the goals of the SDG's. Different activities have different specific logics of operation (different for products, different for medical services, and even different with regard to markets on which medical services are offered and on which medical products are sold) and create different value for their stakeholders, including special a value related to sustainability.

The question arises: what ´parts´ are business models made of? The literature indicates that they are composed of two different sets of ´parts´. The first path relates to making the concrete choices made by management about how the organization must operate. The second path involves analyzing and dealing with the consequences of these choices (Casadesus-Masanell & Ricard 2010). It also indicates the methodology of conduct in building a classically understood business model (Hwang and Christensen 2008; Casadesus-Masanell & Ricard 2010; Sharan et al. 2016) and classically understood types of business models (Lopes et al. 2019; Nosratabadi et al., 2019) . It should be emphasized that it is specific values typical for entities from the healthcare sector, the organizational culture, including the elimination of

Figure 2. Mutual interactions between strategy, business models and tactics in healthcare sector entities
Source: own elaboration

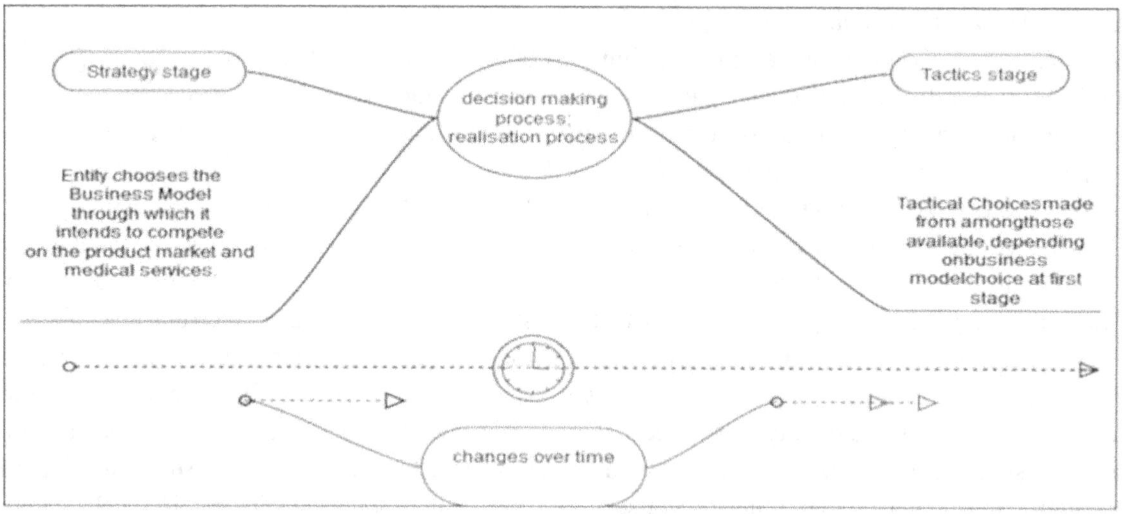

ESG risk, and new trends (indicated as transformation, activities for social responsibility and innovation) that force changes to the classic approach. There are generally four basic questions that need to be reply when creating a business model. (Drucker et al. 2015; Sharan et al. 2016) The first question that any medical entity should ask is, "Who is your base and specific customer?" This is a complex question that needs to be discussed in the financial, legal, and opportunities, opportunities and resources environment. The answer to the first question should be consistent with the second question: "What is the unique value proposition that you are delivering to the customer?" The third question is directly related to the issues of sustainable development. Answer to the question "What resources do we have and what processes / activities will we perform to deliver that unique value?" should at the same time answer the question: "Are resources and processes able to achieve the goals of sustainable development and is there an ESG risk?" The findings should be supplemented by the question "What should be done to improve the achievement of the SDGs and reduce the impact of negative ESG factors?" The final question that needs to be asked when developing a business model is, "What is the cost of purchasing resources as well as performing those activities that are necessary to deliver value to the customer?" Supplementing the last question and extending it, it should be determined: are there any alternative cost options that bring the level of customer satisfaction at a similar or higher level, and better fit into the degree of implementation of the sustainable development goals.

The group of factors that influence the choices both the strategy and the business model are presented in Figure 3. Group of operations consists of three decision keys: (a) key activity: medical processes, medical procedures, production procedures, flexibility, innovation, time, quality, and others; (b) key resources: products, factors of production and logistics, energy, water, supplies, finance and sources of financing, and others; (c) key customers: segment of market, capacity of market, and others.

The group of factors operational and competitive priorities consists: costs, quality of services and products, time to adapt to changes in the market, or changes related to the market. There is also a factor related to the influence of competition and activities related to competition for the patient or recipient of medical products. The policy factor group consists of factors such as national, international and lo-

Figure 3. The group of factors that influence the choices both the strategy and the business
Source: own elaboration based on Cowie & Fisken (2019)

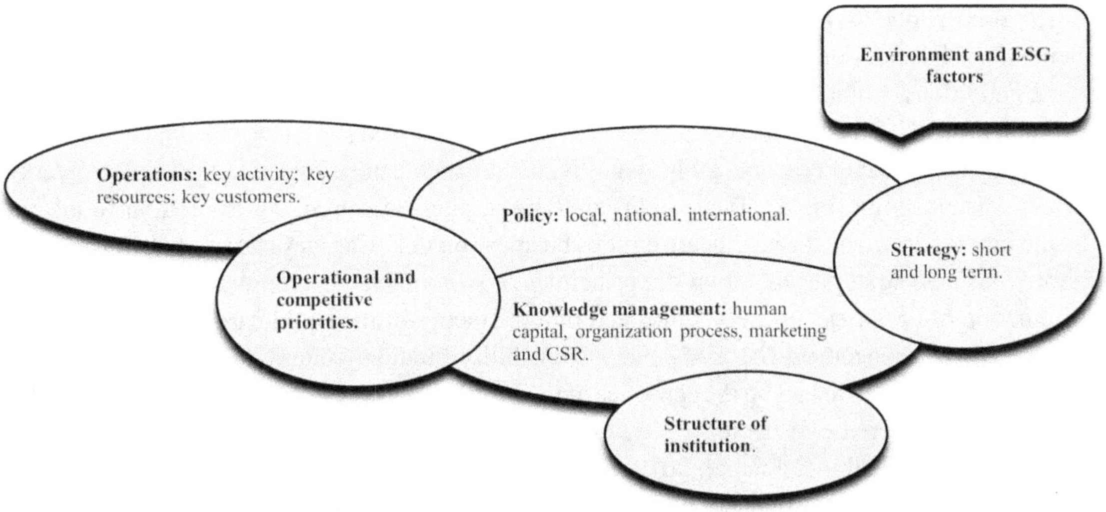

cal law. this group includes a number of factors resulting from the local and national specificity or the policy of governments and international organizations. The knowledge management group includes factors such as human capital management (e.g. selection, training, evaluation of competences, professional development paths); organization process (e.g. databases, document workflow, resource planning programs), marketing activities and CSR activities. The structure of institution group consists of factors influencing the structure of the organization, hierarchy or human resources and their distribution in the organization. Factors related to the construction of industry (short-term) and long-term strategies are in particular: market opportunities, competitive advantage, asset management, market asset (e.g. government contracts, long-term contracts, cooperation, new technologies, accreditations). (Cowie & Fisken 2019)

The indicated groups of factors combine finances and financial resources. They not only provide opportunities to finance activities and processes so that the business model can be successful. But they allow the development of quality, new services and products. The literature on the subject indicates that finance, and especially sustainable finance, contribute to sustainable development and reduce the risk of ESG factors. It should be noted that, in the era of economic crisis caused by the COVID-19 pandemic, the pursuit of the sustainable healthcare system and the SDG's, in order to surpass the coming problems, healthcare entities need to make a total change as far as activity philosophy in the delivery of health services or medical products is concerned, so as to demonstrate their social value awareness, social responsibility and environmental impact friendly policies. An important aspect of the activities undertaken is the development of the Hippocratic Oath of "First Do No Harm" so as to take into account a more global vision of environmental health. Such action allows not only to reduce the risk of conducted activity, but also the risk of financing the sustainable development of healthcare sector entities (innovations) and other ESG risks. (Spetis 2020)

As previously discussed (Fig. 1 and Fig. 3), in the literature review shows strategy and business model as related to each other, but different concepts, especially in terms of time range. Both the strategy, and in particular the business model, must be related to financial issues such as: financing, investment strategies, investment financing strategies, or the cost model. The strategy is part of the ongoing business model to ensure financial stability. Strategy deals with reality and competition. The business model determines how the parts of the business fit together. For healthcare entities available actions for strategy are choices (of target groups, policies, product offering, assets or governance structures) that constitute the constituent elements of business models. Thus, strategy entails designing business models, their adaptation to changing conditions, to changes in policies or preferences of target groups, to allow the healthcare entities to reach its goals. Business models are reflections of the realized strategy of healthcare entities, and factors influencing the choice made, including ESG factors and factors related to the implementation of the idea of sustainability (Fig 3). Tactic plans are current plans of action, which are related take place within the bounds drawn by the healthcare entities business model. (Casadesus-Masanell & Ricart 2010) Therefore, business strategies based on the principles of sustainable development, taking into account the elimination of ESG risks, must be translated into the tactics of the healthcare sector entities.

The effects of management risk ESG and sustainability funding strategy (decision of financial resources in time) from the impact on the activities of the healthcare systems and the healthcare institutions that to factors will increase or decrease environmental, social corporate governance costs or revenue are initially distinguished. (Ziolo et al. 2019; Sepetis, 2020) Direct effects that there are three types of impact. The first is the direct impact on individual health decisions (Kolokotsa et al. 2012; Zamparas 2019) The second is a monetary impact, i.e. an indication of quantitative effects or an indication of qualitative one's effects (Sepetis et al. 2009; Hampton 2012, Azaret al. . 2015, Sepetis, 2020). A third, distinction is microeconomic and macroeconomic impact of environmental, social and governance policies on management risk ESG and sustainability funding strategy. (Sepetis et al. 2009; Sepetis, 2020)

Although most entities of healthcare sector presents their strategic plans, formulate business strategies and make them clear, the SDG's in these plans are not usually detailed and are general in nature. This approach hampers transparency and communication of ways of how sustainability and SDG'S can be pursued. Intervention and actions of external stakeholders are very often required in this respect. It is also necessary to show the ESG factors in the context of sustainable finance, as it shows the relationship of risk elimination through sustainable financing. (Ziolo et al. 2019) Through their activities, various types of entities of healthcare sector limit the usefulness of natural factors to perform their production and consumption functions, resulting in the creation of ecological external costs. The entities which are the perpetrators of this cost are most often aware of their creation and infringement by their activity of the interests of other entities. In the absence of establishment of property rights to the natural environment, there is a tendency to pass these costs on to the whole society, i.e. to make them public. In order to prevent this, state intervention is necessary, which through the use of various instruments may undertake actions that force the entities to behave in a predetermined manner. Without government intervention in this respect, there are no market incentives for polluters to take environmental damage into account. Their impact is spread over many entities and has little or no direct cost to the polluter (European Environment Agency, 1996).

ESG risk factors should be considered in three groups, both classical factors and factors typical for the healthcare sector should be analyzed (table 2). Environmental considerations generally have a limited impact on the performance in healthcare institution. But this is largely because healthcare firms and hospitals tend to have a limited impact on the environment. As a result, environmental factors tend to have a fairly low weighting in our assessment. (Foll, 2018) Environmental criteria, examines how a institution performs as a steward of our natural environment. The impact of its activities on the natural environment is examined and the use of environmental resources is assessed. Social criteria indicate that at the heart of the ESG equation in the healthcare sector is the impact its products have on human health and well-being. Social criteria determine how the institution treats people. This impact covers everything from the unintended side-effects of medicines and product safety as well as quality and value invested money in products and technology to improper marketing practices, affordability concerns and access to healthcare. Governance criteria, which examines how a institution polices itself - how the company is governed. This issue is very important in the healthcare sector.

Table 2. General and specific ESG risk factors for healthcare sector

Types of pillars	Classically understood ESG risk factors	ESG risk factors typical for healthcare institutions
Environmental pillar	• waste and pollution • resource depletion • greenhouse gas emission • deforestation • climate change	• a limited impact of healthcare firms on the environment, • environmental impact of activities related to agrochemical factor and broader chemical activities, • impact of production on: soil depletion, water contamination and biodiversity loss, • the risk of health issues linked to the production and usage of controversial products, • pharmaceutical residues that may be located in food for human consumption as a result of air, soil and water contamination, • river pollution due to the release of antibiotic effluents, • risk related to antimicrobial resistance.
Social pillar	• employee relations & diversity • working conditions, including child labor and slavery • local communities; seeks explicitly to fund projects or institutions that will serve poor and underserved communities globally • health and safety • conflict	• risks related to the illegal or inappropriate marketing of healthcare institution products, which can impact patient safety, • risk related to settling claims and class actions against entities in the healthcare sector, • affordability into account for products of healthcare sector (e.g bills for those who were chronically ill, drug prices, valuation of medical services), • risk of a rapid decline in the value of biotech stocks, • risk of access to healthcare (e.g. access to medicine may and services), • risk of traditional markets of organization of access to medical services and traditional system of healthcare, • risk of facing ever decreasing returns on research and development investment, as well as higher pricing pressures, • innovation to the performance of healthcare companies and human capital (i.e. maintaining knowledge, ensuring innovation capacities, retention strategy), • risk of covid-19 pandemic (i.e impact on health, access to hospitals and drugs).
Economic pillar	• tax strategy • executive remuneration • donations and political lobbying • corruption and bribery • board diversity and structure	• risk of covid-19 pandemic (i.e. changes in investments, priorities, taxation, access to finance, influence on management decisions), • risk of long-term strategy and business models, • risk of R&D intensity, broader market megatrends as well as its M&A strategy, • executives' track records, especially regarding ESG issues, • risk of effectiveness of activity healthcare firms and return on share value, • risk of remuneration of staff.

Source: own elaboration

Table 2 provides a summary of general (classical understanding) ESG factors and specific ESG risk factors for healthcare. The table presents the layout typical for the ESG factor pillars discussed in the literature.

In conclusion, it should be pointed out that the goal of the business model in healthcare sector entities is to achieve, through a strategy (both short-term and long-term), satisfactory results both in the economic area and in the area of improving the quality of medical services or medical products and reducing the impact of ESG risk. Which means not only sustainable development, but it enables access to sustainable finance.

Risks of the ESG Factors and Tools That can Help Manage This Risk[1]

According to Birch et. al. (2014), the financial stability of healthcare systems in many countries consumes an increasing proportion of government spending. Recently, the healthcare system has made several changes, both technological and normative, to increase efficiency. Besides, the biomedical progress in the last decades has contributed to raising the level of organizational complexity in hospitals, which is given by many different factors, such as multiple professional experiences, non-uniform management models, patient specificity, surgery complexity, reduced inpatient days, and a growing number of healthcare service users due to an increase in an average lifetime (Cagliano et. al. 2011). Similar to any other complex system, the complexity of healthcare systems generates adverse events if not controlled (Vincent, 2006). Sustainable healthcare is a burgeoning concept that is gaining momentum as environmental, social, and economic aspects are becoming linked to healthcare activities (Smith 2012). In work Buffoli et. al. (2013) claims that the healthcare structures are supposed to protect and improve public health, but in the meanwhile, they are socially and environmentally impactful structures which can cause negative side effects on the people's health and the context. World Health Organization (2007) in his work shows that there is a problem to get drugs, vaccines, information, and other forms of prevention, care, or treatment – on time, reliably, in sufficient quantity, and at a reasonable cost – to those who need them

Traditional risk management is maturing and expanding its scope. In 2018, the Committee of Sponsoring Organizations of the Treadway Commission (COSO), the main body that guides enterprise risk management (ERM), issued the first revisions to its Framework in over a dozen years. COSO collaborated with the World Business Council for Sustainable Development (WBCSD) to issue draft guidance on the intersection between ERM and ESG (or environmental, social, and governance issues). Figure 4 presents the framework of the ESG management system and the possible path of their implementation as part of the guidance.

For this article, the description of the Framework of the implementation of the ESG risk management system (Figure 4) will be presented in two stages. Stage one from internal oversight for effective risk management to Identify ESG-related risks in this chapter, and the remaining stages in the next chapter.

As shown in Figure 1, in the first place, when implementing ESG risk management, it is necessary for internal oversight, to create the correct manner in which decisions are made and the right pattern of how these decisions are executed. In work, COSO and WBCSD (2018) are written that corporate governance is the set of relationships between the company's management, board, shareholders, and other stakeholders. To do this, it is necessary to build an appropriate awareness of the values of ESG both in the company's management board, team members, and employees. This requires a policy that sets the rules. According to International Finance Corporation IFC (2015), the rules define the limits of what is allowed, in terms of social and environmental issues including working conditions, pollution prevention, safety, community protection, and health. The effective management of risks comes thru an understanding of the business context. According to COSO and WBCSD (2018), a company's strategy and business objectives are established to create value for the organization. This value is based on societal, human, and relationship, natural, intellectual and manufactured capital. Examples of analytical tools used in a business context based on COSO and WBCSD (2018) are presented in Table 3.

Figure 4. The framework of the implementation of the ESG risk management system
Source: own elaboration based on COSO and WBCSD (2018)

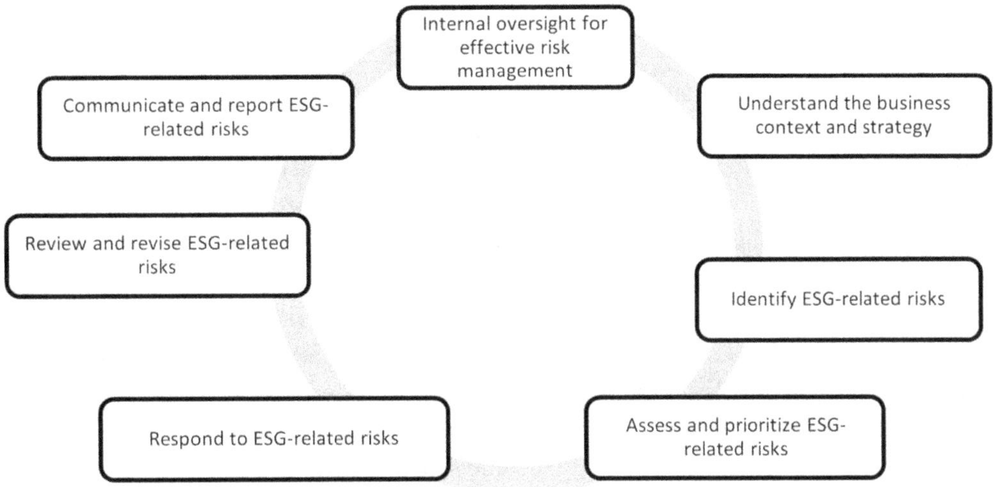

The tools presented in Table 3 are used to assess the internal and external environment and help in making risk inventory.

The next step in implementing ESG risk management is to identify ESG-related risks. Risk is mainly affected by changes in business strategy, goals, or risk appetite. It is necessary to perform the inventory risk in areas related to the conduct of business. Typical risk categories include strategic, operational, financial, and compliance, and some companies have sustainability. To identify risks uses analytical tools described in Table 2.

Table 3. Examples of analytical tools for business context analysis

Tools	Examples
Megatrend analysis	World Economic Forum Global Risk Report; Global Opportunity Report; ESG-focused organizations and conferences, World Health Organization Statistic, local NHS database, political reports
SWOT analysis	Strengths, Weaknesses, Opportunities, Threats
Impact and dependency mapping	The Natural Capital Coalition's Natural Capital Protocol (NCP) and WBCSD's Social Capital Protocol (SCP)24 set out guidance for companies to capture the complexity of impacts and dependencies on natural, human and societal capitals.
Stakeholder engagement	Patients, managers - changes in users preferences for more sustainable products; Suppliers, category managers -shortage of raw materials due to weather, climate change, or environmental impacts
Materiality assessment	Sustainability Accounting Standards Board (SASB); General and industry-specific guidelines for reporting a full range of economic, environmental, social, and governance impacts of operations
ESG-related resource	Natural Capital Protocol Toolkit and Social Capital Protocol Toolkit; Human rights impact assessment; Greenhouse Gas Protocol

Source: own elaboration based on COSO and WBCSD (2018)

The healthcare system is becoming one of the largest industries in the world every year. In work Sepetis (2020) is shown that the public expenditure on health in OECD increase from around 6% of GDP today to almost 9% of GDP in 2030 and as much as 14% by 2060. Service delivery systems are responsible for providing health services for patients, persons, families, communities, and populations in general. The health care system does not function in a political, economic, or institutional vacuum. Its structure and functioning are determined by legal acts of various rank, economic situation, epidemiological status, and internal relations. According to Foll (2018), the healthcare companies operate at the cutting edge of one of the world's biggest long-term challenges – the quest for a longer, better life, which is associated with several risks. In work Cagliano, et. al. (2011) assumes that risk prevention requires the strengthening of procedural, administrative, physical, and individual barriers, .

The transition of environmental, social, and governance (ESG) factors from concept and investor preference to requirements poses a challenge to managers, particularly concerning integrating sustainability risk factors into existing Risk Management Frameworks. The White Paper of Donnelley Financial Solutions (DFIN) (2019) shows a wide range of tools exists to help companies look at ESG risks in a more systematic way. These tools increasingly include scores from credit rating agencies (CRAs), ESG rating firms, and various sustainability and ERM frameworks. As part of ESG risk factors, one of the rating firms (MSCI ESG Research) identifies 37 key issues, the main groups of which are presented in Figure 5.

Figure 5. Main groups of ESG risk factors
Source: own elaboration based on Donnelley Financial Solutions (DFIN) (2019)

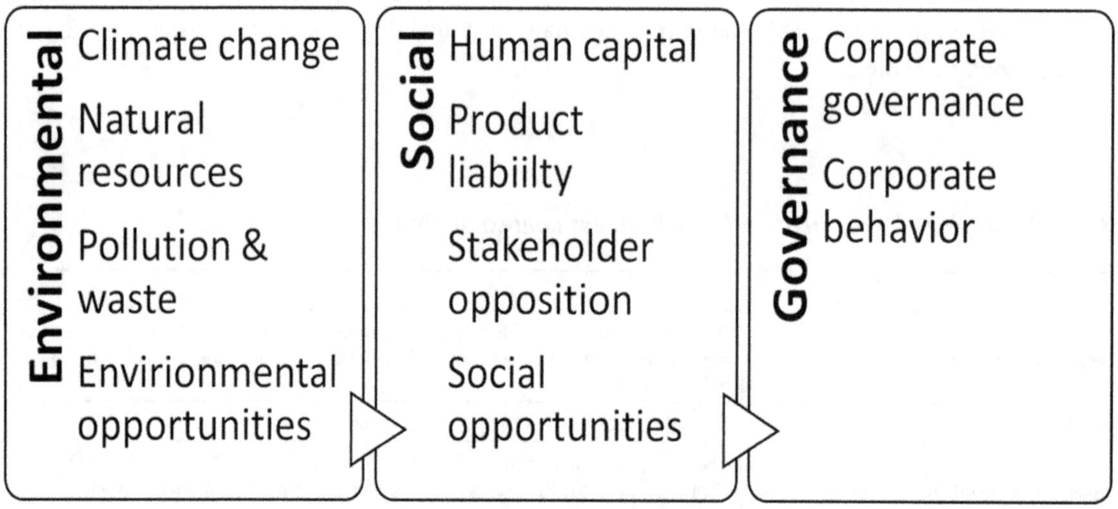

According to the report by Wilkins (2019), the health care industry was ranked 28th out of 34 assessed industries in terms of generating environmental and social risks. Based on the literature Foll (2018) and International Finance Corporation IFC (2015) and report Wilkins (2019), the examples risk factors for the healthcare sector have been identified in Table 4.

According to Wilkins (2019) report among environmental risks, toxicity is a key risk, particularly among pharmaceutical manufacturers, life science companies, and hospitals, because the typical manu-

Table 4. Examples of ESG risk factors in the healthcare sector

Risk areas	Risk factors
Environmental	• toxicity • handle and dispose of bio-hazardous materials • inherent material water-use
Social	• aging population • shortage of health workers such as nurses and doctors • improving access to quality care • pricing policies • reducing costs • side effects of drugs and implanted medical devices • litigation and product recalls • clinical risk (adverse events)
Governance	• noncompliance with regulations • improper billing for services and products • aggressive marketing tactics • pricing manipulation • failure to protect patient privacy • lack of long-term strategy • remuneration

Source: own elaboration based on Donnelley Financial Solutions (DFIN) (2019)and Wilkins (2019)

facturer of pharmaceutical and life sciences products uses products that could harm the environment. Hospitals and health care centers handle and dispose of bio-hazardous materials, which exposes them to the accidental release of potentially toxic agents. Equally notes Foll (2018) that the release of antibiotic effluents into rivers also contributes to a particular topic of interest, namely antimicrobial resistance and that`s a big issue.

In a Case study by Alliance Bernstein (2019) and Lim and Horkova (2019), social factors are prevalent in health care companies because treatments, products, and drugs can benefit society, they can also be costly. Another issue is aging populations, especially in developing counties, that over time, it requires increased care and expenditure. Spitzer and Dawidson (2013) in their work claim that already today, necessary changes in the health care system related to the change in the age structure are indicated. The change in the age structure of society also affects access to qualified medical and nursing staff. The data presented by the World Health Organization WHO (2020) life expectancy and healthy life expectancy have both increased by over 8% globally between 2000 and 2016. The next big social risk is access to medications and care, including a company's pricing policies and keeping underperforming rural or urban hospitals open to serve local communities. In many emerging markets and developing countries, only the wealthy have access to quality care. Pricing politics and reducing costs are some of the topics which apply to both pharmaceutical companies and medical service providers. Lim and Horkova (2019) point out that pharmaceutical companies also face risks related to the illegal or inappropriate marketing of their products, which can impact patient safety and unintended side-effects of medicines and product safety. In work Ross Baker et al., (2004) an adverse event may be defined as an unintended injury or complication resulting in disability, death, or prolonged hospital stay that is caused by healthcare management rather than by the patient's underlying disease process. This includes clinical risks that are common in the health care delivery service. In work Cagliano et. al. (2011), she proposed a methodology to managed clinical risks in four progressive steps, namely:

1. Context analysis - aimed to select and become familiar with the critical healthcare process to be investigated
2. Process mapping - project risk management tools are used to obtain a more in-depth definition of single process activities, also including the identification of actors in charge of them
3. Risk identification and assessment - understanding of the analyzed process to the identification of related risks, again by using project risk management tools.
4. Failure modes and waste analysis (FMEA-Waste analysis) - sources of waste have been adapted to healthcare process analysis from the seven classes of waste defined by the Toyota Production System

These four steps are inspired by Human Reliability Assessment (HRA). A more detailed discussion of clinical risk management and tools can be found in Cagliano et. al. (2011)

Governance risks mainly concern enterprise management. They are related to the pricing policy, unfair practices, remuneration policy, and a long-term approach to management, also in the field of R&D.

After Cagliano et. al. (2011) preventing risk requires understanding how to strengthen those procedural, administrative, physical, and individual barriers intercepting and blocking the deviations.

To manage all risks, also risk factors in ESG, an appropriate management system should be implemented. A properly constructed management system will be monitor emerging issues, so you can prevent potential threats from turning into real problems. In the work of COSO and WBCSD (2018) is described that A management system is a set of appropriate rules and procedures to achieve goals using appropriate tools consistently followed. Also, safety track records among healthcare companies are more and more often implemented to help minimize harm.

A map to Identify Potential Risk and Possible Scenarios of Action in the Long Term

According to IFC (2015), health care facilities are struggling increasingly with environmental and social challenges. To cope with them, they must be effectively assessed so that sustainability is not compromised, especially in the areas of patient care quality, reputation, profitability, and long-term development. Patient care management, quality control, and health and safety is already an essential part of many healthcare institutions.IFC (2015) suggests that the inclusion of an environmental and social management system complements a comprehensive approach to managing healthcare facilities. According to Arrow (1963) professionalism, the not-for-profit status of hospitals, prohibition of advertising and price competition, and lack of an obligation to guarantee good outcomes, are at the heart of medical care values. This comes also with uncertainty and information asymmetries in health care and a supply-sided mindset (Castano, 2014).

According to the guidelines of PN-EN ISO 22301: 2020-04 (ISO) (2020), the PDCA (Plan-Do-Check-Act) model is used for activities related to the implementation and maintenance of the risk management system. The essence of the PDCA model is continuous improvement – an ongoing process of reviewing, correcting, and improving your system. The characteristics of the PDCA model are presented in Figure 6.

Figure 6 shows a simplified PDCA model used in management processes. It covers the basic activities aimed at the continuous improvement of the company.

The ESG risk management system may complement the quality standards applied in a given entity. According to ISO (2020), the use of the PDCA model ensures an appropriate degree of consistency with

Figure 6. PDCA model used in risk management processes
Source: own elaboration based on Donnelley Financial Solutions (DFIN) (2019)and PN-EN ISO 22301: 2020-04 (ISO) (2020)

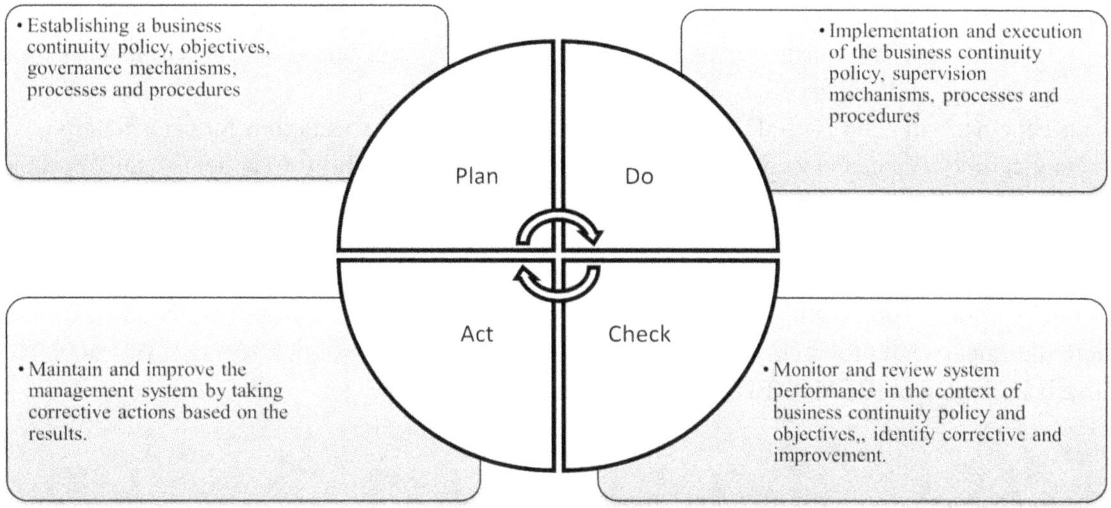

other management system standards such as e.g. ISO 9001, ISO 14001, ISO/IEC 27001, ISO/IEC 20000-1and ISO 28000 and requirements for supply chain security management systems, enabling consistent and integrated implementation and operation with other management systems. The work of Iamandi et. al. (2019) assumes that integrated reporting and the enclosure of ESG goals as part of the sustainable finance desideratum are topical concerns in mainstream academic studies, economic practice, and for European and other international policymakers and organizations.

Another way of managing ESG risk is by entrusting its assessment to specialized rating agencies. After DFIN (2019) there are many ESG rating services out there and their numbers are growing rapidly. Major ones include MSCI ESG Research, RobecoSAM Group, Bloomberg, Thomson Reuters, Sustainalytics, ISS, and Vigeo Eiris.

The work of COSO and WBCSD (2018) shows that enterprises need to assess and prioritize ESG risks due to resource constraints. For this reason, it is impossible to protect against all potential risks. In IFC (2015) the authors maintain that an effective risk assessment examines the extent to which identified risks impact the company's strategy and business objectives. The main points regarding the risk assessment system are outlined below:

1) environmental, OHS, labor and community risks,
2) conduct regular analyzes of risks - specific time intervals,
3) conduct a risk assessment when introducing significant changes to the business,
4) conduct risk analyzes in the event of changes in the environment, e.g. new laws or regulations,
5) include information about risks from both employees and managers,
6) taking into account the comments of external stakeholders, consultants, and experts,
7) prioritize risks in terms of negative effects and probability of occurrence (e.g supply chain, absences of employees, legal regulations),

Although there is no one way to assess risks, companies should adopt a principled approach. Example principles include:

1) relevance - risk assessment is consistent with the risk definition and connected to business context and strategy and risk appetite
2) acceptance - method is used that is similar to the company's expectations for prioritization,
3) replicability - data, and methods used are transparent, traceable, fully documented, and repeatable,
4) consistency - data and methods used for the assessment are compatible with each other.

The principles presented constitute the basis for building a matrix for prioritizing individual risks. One of the prioritization methods is based on the measurement of the impact/likelihood relationship. Where the impact and probability of a given risk are assumed and given a measure. An example of a matrix is presented in [REMOVED REF FIELD]Figure 7.

Figure 7. Example impact and likelihood matrix in Hospital
Source: own elaboration

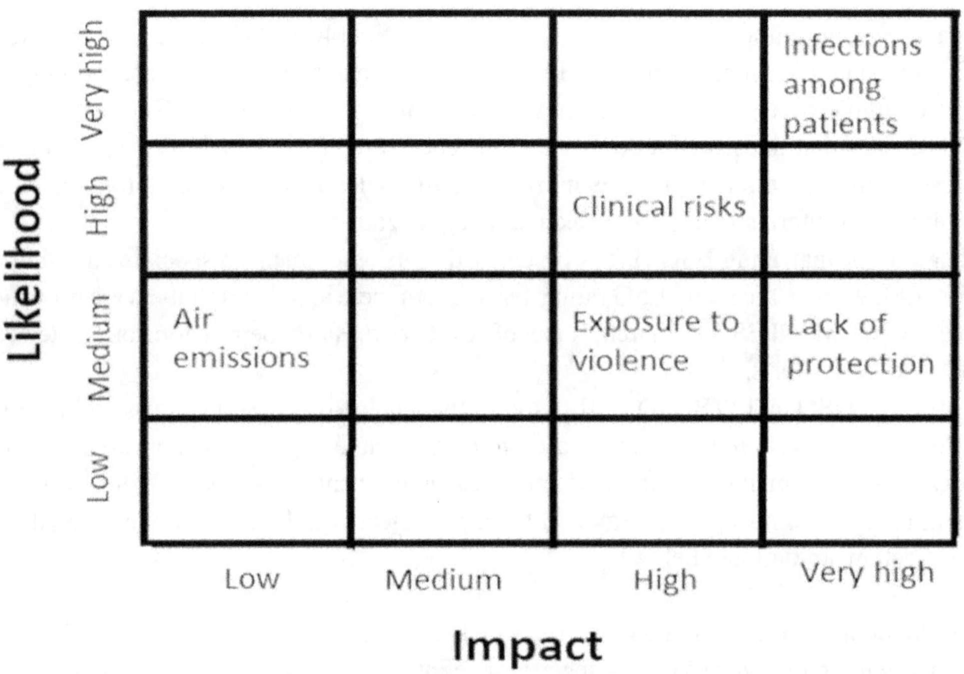

To build a matrix, specific definitions should be assigned to individual measures, from Low to Very High, depending on the specificity of the enterprise. For example, Likelihood maybe once a year or 5 years, the number of cases in a given period or the probability of occurrence, and Impact by affecting the entity's perception (reputation), the number of lawsuits, or a decline in revenue. Individual risk measures can have both monetary and non-monetary dimensions. Measurement approaches depending

Table 5. Examples of measurement approaches

Approach	Description
Expert input	a panel of experts (e.g., Delphi approach) or interviews and discussions with subject matter specialists.
Forecasting and valuation	traditional ERM tools for example statistical regression and Monte Carlo simulation; Natural Capital Protocol and Social Capital Protocol.
Scenario analysis	indicates a possible future event based on probability.
ESG-specific tools	Tools that can be based on the Natural Capital Protocol Toolkit and Social Capital Protocol Toolkit

Source: own elaboration based on COSO and WBCSD (2018)

on a company's prioritization approach and preference are used to measure risk. The work of COSO and WBCSD (2018) shows examples of measurement approaches that have been presented in Table 5.

Presented in Table 5 measurement approaches may be used depending on the data held by the enterprise. They can be both internal and external data sources. Example data sources based on COSO and WBCSD (2018) and IFC (2015) can be grouped into two groups:

1. Internal data sources
    - *patients*
    - *NHS reports*
    - *energy demand*
    - *water usage*
    - *greenhouse gas emissions*
    - *employees*
    - *suppliers*
    - *customer surveys*
    - *quality teams*
    - *management review*
2. External data sources
    - *demographic health surveys*
    - *NHS statistic*
    - *NGOs*
    - *academic research*
    - *experts*
    - *industry or peer company data or reports*
    - *external controls*
    - *existing analysis*
    - *analitics tools*

The choice of the type of database presented above depends on the answers to the question which data is available as input to the measurement tool, what tools and frameworks can be used to support ESG-related risk assessments, how reliable is the data, and does the data apply to the defined scope of the risk.

Respond to ESG-related risks can be deployed within the business context and strategy. COSO and WBCSD (2018) selects and deploys risk responses based on consideration of several options like include accepting, avoiding, pursuing, reducing, and sharing the risk (Table 6).

Table 6. Examples of risk responses in healthcare delivery service

Risk response	Description	Examples
Accept/ Building risk resilience	risks to the strategy and business objectives are within the risk appetite and not likely to become more severe	• aging society • climate change
Avoid	zero tolerance for certain ESG-related risks	• mistakes with diagnoses • ordering the wrong dosage or drug for a patient,
Pursuing	convert risks into opportunities	• cultural context - develop non-discrimination procedures for employees • make electronic health records systems more interoperable
Reducing	risk severity is higher than the risk appetite	• miscommunication among staff • hospital-acquired infections
Sharing	eliminate some risk to individual companies	• building collaborations with NGOs, regulators, suppliers, or other healthcare companies • purchase insurance or reinsurance

Source: own elaboration

The choice of risk response presented in Table 6 depends on the individual characteristics of a given entity. While determining the responses to risk, management may follow the accepted standards, principles, protocols, and management systems to support risk reduction.

The management board may also use its good practices or tools developed in cooperation with academia or stakeholders. Once the risk approach is defined, it is necessary to introduce appropriate models of activities. According to IFC (2015), these are the key questions:

1) Which environmental and social risks you want to address,
2) How to implement the activities and procedures,
3) What are the causes and goals of activities,
4) What are the expected results,
5) What are the time frames and deadlines,

Who is responsible for the areas. The creation of a long-term stable development perspective depends on how the company will react to the identified risk areas. Even if the organization implements appropriate management programs in the defined risk areas, accidents and emergencies can occur. .Therefore it is a necessary review and revises ESG-related risks. Review and revision of ESG-related risks are typically performed by risk owners and sustainability managers. Risk monitoring is done by setting indicators and thresholds to be monitored. An example of a group of indicators was developed by the Sustainability Accounting Standards Board to help companies make sustainable development decisions Table 7).

SASB assumes that the individual thresholds for indicators should correspond to tolerance levels derived from their risk appetite, which is approved by the board. As mentioned earlier in the chapter, the

Table 7. Selected areas and indicators for health protection according to SASB standards

Dimension	General Issue Category	Health Care Delivery Indicators
Environment	Energy Management	1. Total energy consumed 2. Percentage of grid electricity 3. Percentage of renewable
	Waste & Hazardous Materials Management	1. The total amount of medical waste: percentage incinerated; recycled or treated; landfilled 2. The total amount of hazardous and non-hazardous pharmaceutical waste: percentage incinerated; recycled or treated; landfilled
Social Capital	Data Security	1. Percentage of patient records that are EHR that meet requirements 2. Description of policies and practices to secure customers protected health information (PHI) records and other personally identifiable information (PII); percentage involving personally identifiable information (PII) only and protected health information (PHI); 3. Total losses as a result of legal proceedings associated with data security and privacy
	Access & Affordability	1. Discussion of strategy to manage the mix of patient insurance status 2. Amount of Medicare Disproportionate Share Hospital adjustment payments received
	Product Quality & Safety	1. Average Hospital Value-Based Purchasing Total Performance Score and domain score, across all facilities 2. Number of serious Reportable Events 3. Hospital-Acquired Conditions (HAC) Score per hospital 4. Excess readmission ratio per hospital 5. Magnitude of readmission payment adjustment
	Customer Welfare	1. Descriptions of policies and practices to manage the number of prescriptions issued for controlled substances 2. Percentage of controlled substances prescriptions written for which a prescription drug monitoring program (PDMP) database was queried
	Selling Practices & Product Labeling	1. Description of policies or initiatives to ensure that patients are adequately informed about price before undergoing a procedure 2. Discussion of how pricing information for services is made publicly available 3. Number of the entity`s most common services for which pricing information is publicly available, the percentage of total services performed (by volume) that this represents
Human Capital	Employee Health and Safety	1. Total recordable incident rate and days away, restricted, or transferred rate
	Employee Engagement, Diversity & Inclusion	1. Voluntary and involuntary turnover rate for physicians non-physician health care practitioners and all other employees 2. Description of talent recruitment and retention efforts for health care practitioners
	Physical Impacts of Climate Change	1. Description of policies and practices to address: the physical risk due to an increased frequency and intensity of extreme weather events; changes in the morbidity and mortality rates of illness and diseases, associated with climate change 2. Percentage of health care facilities that comply with Emergency Preparedness Rule
Leadership & Governance	Business Ethics	1. Total losses as a result of legal proceedings associated with Medicare and Medicaid fraud under the False Claims Act

Source: own elaboration based on Sustainability Accounting Standards Board (SASB) (2020).

main purpose of the management system is a continual improvement – an ongoing process of reviewing, correcting, and improving your system. That is why regular monitoring of indicators is so important.

The final stage of the process is to communicate and report ESG related risk. This is done through internal and external communication. The differences in the messages depending on the group of stakeholders are can be broken down as follows:

1. Internal stakeholders comunication meaning
   a) educate the board of directors and management to understand how ESG-related risks will impact the business strategy
   b) promote awareness or education of less known but critical risks to thecompany
   c) encourage employee engagement and a culture of risk awareness
2. External stakeholders comunication meaning
   a) mitigating – or reversing – negative ESG impacts
   b) improving reputation and brand loyalty
   c) enabling external stakeholders to understand the organization's true value

The examples given above indicate a different purpose of the information provided depending on the recipients. For the internal group, it is focused on educating the management board and employees and promoting good practices, and external communication - building the image of a responsible company. Stakeholder Engagement builds trust, credibility, and local support. Communication can be two-way in terms of healthcare improvement, facilities amenities, needed prevention actions or critical alerts, both internal and external stakeholders can provide valuable information.

DISCUSION AND CONCLUSION

The management system consists of interdependent elements, each of which plays an important role. According to IFC (2015) implementing an environmental and social management system can have direct financial benefits. Conserving and using energy and water more efficiently helps to reduce operational costs. Reducing waste and discharges can minimize the costs of waste disposal, which have been steadily increasing over time. A management system can help you benchmark your expenditures against industry standards and identify potential operational cost savings.

The growing healthcare and other healthcare sector entities complexity requires management approaches taking into account multiple points of view and by integrating existing tools coming from different fields (Cagliano et. Al. 2011). Tool integration is especially needed by managers of healthcare sector entities. But you have to remember that there will not be a single tool application path here, nor will there be any indication of better or worse tools. These will vary depending on asset type, sector, size, geographic location, and stage in the life cycle.

Although practice shows that it is necessary to implement not only the sustainable development goal, but above all through reported needs, practice shows that it is necessary to implement ideas and recommendations related to the specificity of the health care system. It becomes necessary to modify the goals of sustainable development to the needs of healthcare sector entities and to extend them to the principles and rules typical for ESG risk management and the implementation of sustainable finance. According to Fischer (2015), there is no consensus concerning either the definition of the term or the factors that characterize a "sustainable healthcare system". This shows that practice develops its own paths and solutions. In our considerations, we showed one of the possible tools that integrate the goals of sustainable development, sustainable finance and ESG risk management.

Healthcare managers more and more often show interest and extend the use of already existing procedures or tools in connection with the occurrence and impact of ESG risks.

Specific ESG-related factors or issues may have a direct or indirect, positive, or negative impact on infrastructure assets (Rendlen and Weber, n.d.).

As the authors of the article present, a holistic approach to risk management is necessary. First of all, an appropriate risk management system should be established. It can complement an already existing management system. Also, ESG risks should be identified. These risks are identified based on business tools (Table 3). It may be work at different levels of detail according to the specific case and the information available. Saviano et. al (2018) discus that the management and control tools should be rethought not in terms of the maximization of volumes or reduction of costs per benefit but be oriented towards measurable health indicators. Furthermore, it needs to be determined which risks are relevant to the company's operations and how to respond to them. The manner of reaction depends mainly on the likelihood of a given risk occurring, the impact on the company's operations, and the management's risk appetite (Figure 7). While determining the responses to risk, management may follow the accepted standards, principles, protocols, and management systems to support risk reduction. It should also consider making operators aware of both risks and impact existing in the healthcare process. This includes risk monitoring based on indicators (Table 7). A key feature of the ESG management system is the idea of continual improvement - an ongoing process of reviewing, correcting, and improving your system.

The implementation in the case of healthcare entity delivers revealed difficulty in gathering all the pieces of information necessary to fully apply the system, due to a scarce aptitude for risk management and, as a consequence, for supporting such a comprehensive organizational analysis by both personnel and informational systems. Notwithstanding the implementation of an ESG management system seems inevitable, taking into account even the recommendations Commission Of The European Communities (2001) that companies should endeavour to raise the standards of social development, environmental protection, and respect of fundamental rights and embrace open governance, reconciling interests of various stakeholders in an overall approach of quality and sustainability.

The approach proposed by the authors is aimed at transferring good practice that was used in a medical entity and thanks to which managers have the opportunity not only to manage ESG risk, but also to map the risk and run risk benchmarks with other medical entities. This approach allows for the implementation of sustainable development goals and a broader management and fundraising capacity which enables managers to achieve financial stability.

Furthermore, the authors see the need for further in-depth studies of the analyzed topic, especially in the context of the impact of ESG risks on long term sustainability in the healthcare sector including Covid-19. According to Lopes et. al. (2019) most hospitals organize their strategic plans and make them clear, the sustainability goals in these plans are not usually detailed. It is necessary not only to map strategic goals, but also to relate them to ESG risks, and to impose the effects of the Covid-19 pandemic. For this, a tool in the form of a map, proposed by the authors, may be useful.

REFERENCES

Agenda 21: Implementation of Agenda 21, the Programme for the Further Implementation of Agenda 21 and the outcomes of the World Summit on Sustainable Development. (2012). United Nations. A/C.2/66/L.59. https://www.un.org/ga/search/view_doc.asp?symbol=A/C.2/66/L.59&Lang=E)

Alliance Bernstein. (2019). *Delivering social and environmental impact in the healthcare sector, Principles of Responsible Investments*. https://www.unpri.org/delivering-social-and-environmental-impact-in-the-healthcare-sector/3912.article

Alm, K., & Sievänen, R. (2013). Institutional Investors, Climate Change, and Human Rights. *The Journal of Sustainable Finance & Investment, 3*(3), 177–183. doi:10.1080/20430795.2013.791139

Arah, O. A., Westert, G. P., Hurst, J., & Klazinga, N. S. (2006). A conceptual framework for the OECD health care quality indicators project. *International Journal for Quality in Health Care, 18*(Suppl. 1), 5–13. doi:10.1093/intqhc/mzl024 PMID:16954510

Arrow, K. (1963). Uncertainty and the welfare economics of medical care. *The American Economic Review, 1963*(53), 941–973. http://links.jstor.org/sici?sici=0002-8282%28196312%2953%3A5%3C941%3AUATWEO%3E2.0.CO%3B2-C

Aspinall, N. G., Jones, S. R., McNeill, E. H., Werner, R. A., & Zalk, T. (2018). Sustainability and the financial system. Review of literature 2015. *Br. Actuar, 23*, 1–21. doi:10.1017/S1357321718000028

Baxter, D., & Casady, C. B. (2020). Proactive and Strategic Healthcare Public-Private Partnerships (PPPs) in the Coronavirus (Covid-19) Epoch. *Sustainability, 12*(12), 5097. doi:10.3390u12125097

Bennett, N. J., Roth, R., Klain, S. C., Chan, K., Christie, P., Clark, D. A., Cullman, G., Curran, D., Durbin, T. J., Epstein, G., Greenberg, A., Nelson, M. P., Sandlos, J., Stedman, R., Teel, T. L., Thomas, R., Veríssimo, D., & Wyborn, C. (2017). Conservation social science: Understanding and integrating human dimensions to improve conservation. *Biological Conservation, 205*, 93–108. doi:10.1016/j.biocon.2016.10.006

Birch, S., Murphy, G. T., MacKenzie, A., & Cumming, J. (2014). In place of fear: Aligning health care planning with system objectives to achieve financial sustainability. *Journal of Health Services Research & Policy, 0*(0), 1–6. doi:10.1177/1355819614562053 PMID:25504826

Boons, F., & Lüdeke-Freund, F. (2013). Business models for sustainable innovation: State-of-the-art and steps towards a research agenda. *Journal of Cleaner Production, 45*, 9–19. doi:10.1016/j.jclepro.2012.07.007

Brooks, C., & Oikonomou, I. (2018). The effects of environmental, social and governance disclosures and performance on firm value: A review of the literature in accounting and finance. *The British Accounting Review, 50*(1), 1–15. doi:10.1016/j.bar.2017.11.005

Brown, V., Grootjans, J., Ritchie, J., Townsend, M., & Verrinder, G. (2005). *Sustainability and health: Supporting global ecological integrity in public health*. Earthscan.

Brundtland, G. H. (2012). Health: A pathway to sustainable development. *American Medical Association. Journal of the American Medical Association, 288*(2), 156. PMID:12095374

Buffoli, M., Capolongo, S., Bottero, M., Cavagliato, E., Speranza, S., & Volpatti, L. (2013). Sustainable Healthcare: How to assess and improve healthcare structures' sustainability. *Annali di igiene: medicina preventiva e di comunità, 25*, 411–418. doi:10.7416/ai.2013.1942 PMID:24048179

Burtland Report. (1987). *Report of the World Commission on Environment and Development: Our Common Future*. Available at http://www.un-documents.net/our-common-future.pdf

Buys, L., Mengersen, K., Johnson, S., Buuren, N. V., & Chauvin, A. (2014). Creating a Sustainability Scorecard as a predictive tool for measuring the complex social, economic, and environmental impacts of industries, a case study: Assessing the viability and sustainability of the dairy industry. *Journal of Environmental Management*, *133*, 184–192. doi:10.1016/j.jenvman.2013.12.013 PMID:24374467

Cagliano, A. C., Grimaldi, S., & Rafele, C. (2011). A systemic methodology for risk management in healthcare sector. *Safety Science*, *49*(5), 695–708. doi:10.1016/j.ssci.2011.01.006

Casadesus-Masanell, R., & Ricart, J. E. (2010). From Strategy to Business Models and onto Tactics. *Long Range Planning*, *43*(2-3), 195–215. doi:10.1016/j.lrp.2010.01.004

Castano, R. (2014). *Towards a framework for business model innovation in health care delivery in developing countries*. Medicine for Global Health. https://www.biomedcentral.com/1741-7015/12/233

Commission Of The European Communities. (2001). *Green Paper Promoting a European framework for Corporate Social Responsibility*. https://ec.europa.eu/commission/presscorner/detail/en/DOC_01_9

Commission of the European Communities. (2007). *Together for Health. A Strategic Approach for the EU 2008-2013*. Brussels, 23.10.2007 COM(2007) 630 final.

Committee of Sponsoring Organizations of the Treadway Commission (COSO), World Business Council for Sustainable Development (WBCSD). (2018). *Enterprise risk management: Applying enterprise risk management to environmental, social and governance-related risks*. https://www.coso.org/Documents/COSO-WBCSD-Release-New-Draft-Guidance-Online-viewing.pdf

Consolidated Versions of the Treaty On European Union and the Treaty on the Functioning of the European, Official Journal of the European Union, C 326/122 - C 326/124.

Cowie, J., & Fisken, K. (2019). *Development of the Business Model framework to be used in SURFLOGH*. Transport Research Institute, Edinburgh Napier University.

Daugaard, D. (2019). Emerging new themes in environmental, social, and governance investing: A systematic literature review. *Accounting and Finance*, *60*(2), 1501–1530. doi:10.1111/acfi.12479

Donnelley Financial Solutions (DFIN). (2019). *White Paper. ESG Risks and Opportunities: Understanding the ESG Landscape*. https://www.dfinsolutions.com/sites/default/files/documents/2019-03/dfin_gcm_proxy_whitepaper_ESG_risks_and_oppty_2019223.pdf

Dooris, M. (1999). Healthy cities and local agenda 21: The UK experience – Challenges for the new millennium. *Health Promotion International*, *14*(4), 365–375. doi:10.1093/heapro/14.4.365

Dowel, G., Hart, S., & Yeung, B. (2000). Do Corporate Global Environmental standards create or destroy market value? *Management Science*, *46*(8), 1059–1074. doi:10.1287/mnsc.46.8.1059.12030

Drucker, P. F., Kuhl, J. S., & Hesselbein, F. (2015). *Peter Drucker's Five Most Important Questions: Enduring Wisdom for Today's Leaders*. Jossey-Bass.

EU Commission. (2018). *Action Plan on Sustainable Finance.* Available at https://ec.europa.eu/info/publications/180308-action-plan-sustainable-growth_en

Evans, S., Vladimirova, D., Holgado, M., Van Fossen, K., Yang, M., Silva, E. A., & Barlow, C. Y. (2017). Business model innovation for sustainability: Towards a unified perspective for creation of sustainable business models. *Business Strategy and the Environment*, *26*(5), 597–608. doi:10.1002/bse.1939

Faezipour, M., & Ferreira, S. A. (2013). System dynamics perspective of patient satisfaction in healthcare. *Procedia Computer Science*, *16*, 148–156. doi:10.1016/j.procs.2013.01.016

Farla, J., Markard, J., Raven, R., & Coenen, L. (2012). Sustainability transitions in the making: A closer look at actors, strategies, and resources. *Technological Forecasting and Social Change*, *79*(6), 991–998. doi:10.1016/j.techfore.2012.02.001

Fatemi, A. M., & Fooladi, I. J. (2013). Sustainable finance: A new paradigm. *Global Finance Journal*, *24*(2), 101–113. doi:10.1016/j.gfj.2013.07.006

Fischer, M. (2015). Fit for the Future? A New Approach in the Debate about What Makes Healthcare Systems Really Sustainable. *Sustainability*, *7*(1), 294–312. doi:10.3390u7010294

Foll, J. (2018). *ESG and Healthcare: The challenges ahead.* https://hub.ipe.com/asset-manager/axa-investment-managers/esg-and-healthcare-the-challenges-ahead/10028009.supplierarticle

Geissdoerfer, M., Vladimirova, D., & Evans, S. (2018). Sustainable business model innovation: A review. *Journal of Cleaner Production*, *198*, 104–416. doi:10.1016/j.jclepro.2018.06.240

Gerster, R. (2011). *Sustainable Finance: Achievements, Challenges, Outlook.* Gerster Consulting, Richterswill.

Gray, T. R. (2011). Mapping a Corporate Governance Exchange: A Survey of Canadian Shareholder Resolutions 2000–2009. *The Journal of Sustainable Finance & Investment*, *1*(1), 30–43. doi:10.3763/jsfi.2010.0005

Green Paper. (2001). *Promoting a European framework for Corporate Social Responsibility.* Commission of the European Communities, COM(2001)366/F1. Available at https://ec.europa.eu/transparency/regdoc/rep/1/2001/EN/1-2001-366-EN-F1-1.Pdf

Hancock, T. (1996). Planning and creating healthy and sustainable cities: The challenge for the twenty-first century. In C. Price & A. Tsourus (Eds.), *Our cities, our future: Policies and action for health and sustainable development* (pp. 65–88). World Health Organization, Healthy Cities Project Office.

Hannon, A., & Callaghan, E. (2011). Definitions and organizational practice of sustainability in the for-profit sector of Nova Scotia. *Journal of Cleaner Production*, *19*(8), 877–884. doi:10.1016/j.jclepro.2010.11.003

Hebb, T. (2013). Impact Investing and Responsible Investing: What Does it Mean*? J. Sustain. Financ. Investig*, *3*(2), 71–74. doi:10.1080/20430795.2013.776255

Hedberg, C., & Malmborg, F. (2003). The global reporting initiative and corporate sustainability reporting in Swedish companies. *Corporate Social Responsibility and Environmental Management*, *10*(3), 153–164. doi:10.1002/csr.38

Hwang, J., & Christensen, C. M. (2008). Disruptive Innovation In Health Care Delivery: A Framework For Business-Model Innovation. *Health Affairs*, *27*(5), 1329–1335. doi:10.1377/hlthaff.27.5.1329 PMID:18780919

Iamandi, I.-E., Constantin, L.-G., Munteanu, S. M., & Cernat-Gruici, B. (2019). Mapping the ESG Behavior of European Companies. A Holistic Kohonen Approach. *Sustainability*, *11*(12), 3276. doi:10.3390u11123276

International Finance Corporation (IFC). (2015). *Environmental and Social Management System (ESMS) Implementation Handbook - Health Care Facilities*. https://www.ifc.org/wps/wcm/connect/topics_ext_content/ifc_external_corporate_site/sustainability-at-ifc/publications/publications_handbook_esms-healthcarefacilities

Investing in Health. (2013). *Commission staff working document*. Brussels, 20.02.2013, SWD (2013) 43 final.

Jameton, A., & McGuire, C. (2002). Toward sustainable health-care services: Principles, challenges, and a process. *IJSHE*, *3*(2), 113–127. doi:10.1108/14676370210422348

Janssen, M., & Moors, E. H. (2013). Caring for healthcare entrepreneurs—Toward successful entrepreneurial strategies for sustainable innovations in Dutch healthcare. *Technological Forecasting and Social Change*, *80*(7), 1360–1374. doi:10.1016/j.techfore.2012.12.003

Jing, W., & Sun, B. (2018). Study on the Source of Negative Externality in the Sharing Economy. *Proceedings of the ICCSE'18, 3rd International Conference on Crowd Science and Engineering*. 10.1145/3265689.3265701

Jones, R., & Dowling, P. (2004). *Sustainability, externalities, and economics: the case of temperate perennial grazing systems in NSW. Economic Research Report* (Vol. 24). NSW Department of Primary Industries. Available at http://www.agric.nsw.gov.au/reader/10550

Kemp, R., & Loorbach, D. (2003). *Governance for Sustainability through Transition Management*. Available at https://www.researchgate.net/profile/Derk_Loorbach/publication/2883708_Governance_for_Sustainability_Through_Transition_Management/links/02e7e51a74226aa52c000000/Governance-for-Sustainability-Through-Transition-Management.pdf

Labonté, R. (1991). Econology: Integrating health and sustainable development. Part one: Theory and background. *Health Promotion International*, *6*(1), 49–65. doi:10.1093/heapro/6.1.49

Levashova, Y. (2011). Role of Sustainable Development in Bilateral Investment Treaties: Recent Trends and Developments. *J. Sustain. Financ. Investig*, *1*, 222–229.

Lim, T., & Horkova, M. (2019). *ESG Industry Report Card: Health Care*. S&P Global Ratings. https://www.spglobal.com/en/research-insights/articles/esg-industry-report-card-health-care

Liu, Y. (2014). *Research on the Negative Externalities and Compensation Mechanism of Coal Exploitation*. Institute of Technology.

Lopes, C. M., Scavarda, A. J., Vaccaro, G. L. R., Pohlmann, Ch. R., & Korzenowski, A. L. (2019). Perspective of Business Models and Innovation for Sustainability Transition in Hospitals. *Perspective of Business Models and Innovation for Sustainability Transition in Hospitals Sustainability, 11*(1), 5. doi:10.3390u11010005

Lüdeke-Freund, F. (2010). Towards a conceptual framework of 'business models for sustainability. In R. Wever, J. Quist, A. Tukker, J. Woudstra, F. Boons, & N. Beute (Eds.), *Knowledge Collaboration & Learning for Sustainable Innovation*. SSRN.

Magretta, J. (2002). Why business models matter? *Harvard Business Review*, (5), 86–92. PMID:12024761

Matthes, J. (2007). *Framing-Effekte. Zum Einfluss der Politikberichterstattung auf die Einstellungen der Rezipienten*. Verlag Reinhard Fischer.

McMichael, A. J. (2006). Population health as the "bottom line" of sustainability: A contemporary challenge for public health researchers. *European Journal of Public Health, 16*(6), 579–581. doi:10.1093/eurpub/ckl102 PMID:16857691

Nikolakis, W., Cohen, D. H., & Nelson, H. W. (2012). What Matters for Socially Responsible Investment (SRI) in the Natural Resources Sectors? SRI Mutual Funds and Forestry in North America. *J. Sustain. Financ. Investig, 2*, 136–151.

Nosratabadi, S., Mosavi, A., Shamshirband, S., Kazimieras Zavadskas, E., Rakotonirainy, A., & Chau, K. W. (2019). Sustainable Business Models: A Review. *Sustainability, 11*(6), 1663. doi:10.3390u11061663

PN-EN ISO 22301:2020-04 (ISO) (2020) Bezpieczeństwo powszechne - Systemy zarządzania ciągłością działania – Wymagania.

Prada, G. (2012). Sustainability: What Does This Mean for Canada's Health Care Systems. *Proceedings of the Collaborative Meeting of the Conference Board of Canada's Health-Related Executive Networks.*

Rappa, M. (2004). The utility business model and the future of computing services. *IBM Systems Journal, 43*(1), 32–42. doi:10.1147j.431.0032

Rendlen, B., & Weber, B. (n.d.). *Integrating ESG factors into financial models for infrastructure investments.* WWF Switzerland Guidance Note. http://awsassets.panda.org/downloads/wwf_guidance_note_infra_.pdf

Rezende de Carvalho Ferreira, M. C., Amorim Sobreiro, V., Kimura, H., & Luiz de Moraes Barboza, F. A. (2016). Systematic review of literature about finance and sustainability. *J. Sustain. Financ. Investig, 6*(2), 112–147. doi:10.1080/20430795.2016.1177438

Roca, L., & Searcy, C. (2012). An analysis of indicators disclosed in corporate sustainability reports. *Journal of Cleaner Production, 20*(1), 103–118. doi:10.1016/j.jclepro.2011.08.002

Ross Baker, G., Norton, P. G., Flintoft, V., Blais, R., Brown, A., Cox, J., Etchells, E., Ghali, W. A., Hébert, P., Majumdar, S. R., O'Beirne, M., Palacios-Derflingher, L., Reid, R. J., Sheps, S., & Tamblyn, R. (2004). The Canadian Adverse Events Study: The incidence of adverse events among hospital patients in Canada. *Canadian Medical Association Journal, 170*(11), 1678–1686. doi:10.1503/cmaj.1040498 PMID:15159366

Saviano, M., Bassano, C., Piciocchi, P., Di Nauta, P., & Lettieri, M. (2018). Monitoring Viability and Sustainability in Healthcare Organizations. *Sustainability*, *10*(10), 3548. doi:10.3390u10103548

Scalia, M., Barile, S., Saviano, M., & Farioli, F. (2018). Governance for Sustainability: A triple Helix Model. *Sustainability Science*, *13*(5), 1235–1244. doi:10.100711625-018-0567-0

Schaltegger, S., Hansen, E. G., & Lüdeke-Freund, F. (2016). *Business Models for Sustainability: Origins, Present Research, and Future Avenues*. SAGE Publications Sage CA.

Sepetis, A. (2020). Sustainable Finance in Sustainable Health Care System. *Open Journal of Business and Management*, *8*(01), 262–281. doi:10.4236/ojbm.2020.81016

Sharan, A. D., Schroeder, G. D., West, M. E., & Vaccaro, A. R. (2016). Understanding Business Models in Health Care. *Clinical Spine Surgery*, *29*(4), 158–160. doi:10.1097/BSD.0000000000000380 PMID:27018909

Smith, M. E. F. (2012). *Sustainable Healthcare. A path to sustainability*. The International Institute for Industrial Environmental Economics. https://lup.lub.lu.se/student-papers/search/publication/3126175

Smolyansky, M. (2016). Policy Externalities and Banking Integration; Finance and Economics. Discussion Series 2016-008, Board of Governors of the Federal Reserve System.

Spitzer, W. J., & Dawidson, K. W. (2013). *Future Trends in Health and Health Care*. Implications for Social Work Practice in an Aging Society., doi:10.1080/00981389.2013.834028

Sundaram, A. M. (2016). *Measurement of Externalities for Renewable Energy Investment; Instituto Superior Técnico*. Universidade de Lisboa.

Sustainability Accounting Standards Board (SASB). (2020). *SASB Materiality Map*. https://materiality.sasb.org/

Transforming Our World. (2015). *The 2030 Agenda for Global Action United Nations*. A/RES/70/1. Available at https://www.unfpa.org/sites/default/files/resource-pdf/Resolution_A_RES_70_1_EN.pdf

UN. (2015). *Transforming Our World: The 2030 Agenda for Sustainable Development*. Seventieth United Nations General Assembly. Available at http://www.un.org/ga/search/view_doc.asp?symbol=A/RES/70/1&Lang=E

UNDP. (2020). *Implications of the COVID-19 Pandemic for Global Sustainable Finance*. Working Paper. The International Network of Financial Centres for Sustainability United Nations Environment Programme. Available at https://unepinquiry.org/publication/implications-of-the-covid-19-pandemic-for-global-sustainable-finance/

Unger, S., & Landis, A. (2016). Assessing the environmental, human health, and economic impacts of reprocessed medical devices in a Phoenix hospital's supply chain. *Journal of Cleaner Production*, *112*, 1995–2003. doi:10.1016/j.jclepro.2015.07.144

Vincent, C., Neale, G., & Woloshynowych, M. (2001). Adverse events in British hospitals: Preliminary retrospective record review. *BMJ (Clinical Research Ed.)*, *322*(7285), 517–519. doi:10.1136/bmj.322.7285.517 PMID:11230064

Vitolla, F., Raimo, N., & Rubino, M. (2019). Appreciations, criticisms, determinants, and effects of integrated reporting: A systematic literature review. *Corporate Social Responsibility and Environmental Management, 26*(2), 518–528. doi:10.1002/csr.1734

Walley, N., & Whitehead, B. (1994). It's not easy being green. *Harvard Business Review, 72*, 46–52.

Weisz, U., Haas, W., Pelikan, J. M., & Schmied, H. (2011). Sustainable Hospitals: A Socio-Ecological Approach. *Gaia (Heidelberg), 20*(3), 191–198. doi:10.14512/gaia.20.3.10

Wilkins, M. (2019). *The ESG Risk Atlas: Sector And Regional Rationales And Scores*. S&P Global Ratings. https://www.spglobal.com/_media/documents/ratingsdirect_theesgriskatlassectorandregionalrationalesandscores_41534468_may-15-2019.pdf

World Health Organization. (2002). *Health and Sustainable Development. Report*. WHO. Available at https://www.who.int/mediacentre/events/HSD_Plaq_02.7_def1.pdf

World Health Organization. (2015). *World Health Statistics 2015*. World Health Organization.

World Health Organization (WHO). (2007). *Everybody business: strengthening health systems to improve health outcomes: WHO's framework for action*. https://www.who.int/healthsystems/strategy/everybodys_business.pdf?ua=1

World Health Organization (WHO). (2020). *World health statistics 2020: monitoring health for the SDGs, sustainable development goals*. https://apps.who.int/iris/handle/10665/332070

Xu, Y. (2006). *Public Choice Theory*. Peking University Press.

Zhang, X. (2016). *Research of China Systemically Important Banks Regulation of Negative Externalities*. Shanxi University of Finance & Economics.

Zhou, C. (2014). *Empirical Study on the Economic Externality of Chinese Insurance Industry*. Central South University.

ENDNOTE

[1] This part of the chapter is the result of the management experience of the author who performs managerial functions in the healthcare sector, in particular in healthcare entities. The content presented below is the result of the author's own implementation work and has been generalized in such a way as to constitute good practice for other healthcare sector entities.

Chapter 6
Climate Strategy Proactivity (CSP):
The Perspective of Stakeholders

Nikhil Kant
https://orcid.org/0000-0002-0157-2866
School of Management Studies, Indira Gandhi National Open University (IGNOU), India

Kumari Anjali
School of Sciences, Indira Gandhi National Open University (IGNOU), India

ABSTRACT

Global carbon emissions are contributed by companies significantly. These companies themselves are not insulated from the risks arising from their own irresponsible acts against the climate. Several companies have adopted voluntarily the strategy of acting beyond compliance of existing laws demonstrating proactivity. Climate strategy proactivity (CSP) is the voluntary strategic corporate behavior adopted to satisfy stakeholders' demands which also help respective governments in achieving international commitments. This chapter, amidst the paucity of relevant studies in the context of developing countries, aims to discuss the emerging concept of CSP and underscores an urgent need for more research on CSP setting a research agenda from the perspective of the relevant stakeholders. The chapter concludes that CSP offers huge potentialities for companies more particularly in developing countries such as India attaching greater significance to stakeholders' perspectives.

INTRODUCTION

The risks associated with climate change need adaptation of multilateral mechanisms by the stakeholders. The business community however has shown positive signal, in recent times, through their growing commitment towards the urgent priorities looking beyond their balance sheets, considering the urgent need for a multi-stakeholder approach to negate the impact of these risks (WEF, 2020). This is in contrast of the general tendency amongst corporations to take the least care of the fast depleting natural resources

DOI: 10.4018/978-1-7998-6788-3.ch006

when they pursue their aspirations of attaining competitive advantage. This tendency has irreversibly been damaging the natural climate making our planet highly unlivable so much so that climate change has taken the centre stage amongst the most significant issues across the world in recent times (Kant & Anjali, 2020). The substantiating evidence for the significant contributions in increasing the global carbon emissions by the corporations are visible in the outcome of the Global Risk Report, 2020 (WEF, 2020) which showcases very gloomy picture of the reality. The report identifies all the 05 top risks related to climatic degradations amongst the top 05 global risks on the basis of 'Likelihood' in its 'Global Risks Perception Survey 2019-20' (Figure 1) while there were none a decade ago. The corporations themselves are not insulated from their impact and risks (Kant, 2020a).

Figure 1. Top five global risks in terms of likelihood (WEF, 2020)

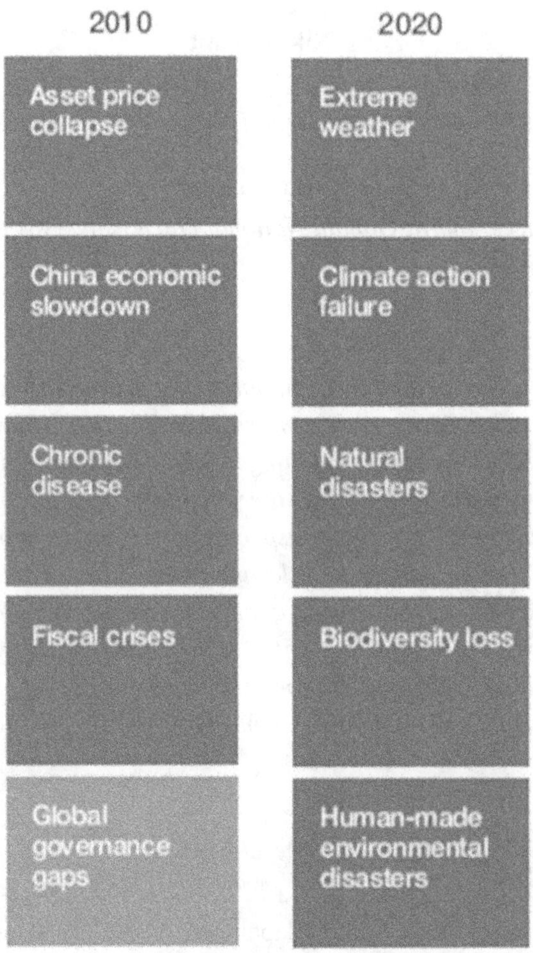

Climate change with its impact on the entire planet is a cruel demonstration of the global inequality showcased by the possessions of the higher incomes by the richest countries/people with much more contributions to climate change than their poor counterparts with lower incomes historically. These poorer counterparts, however, have less resilience and more vulnerability towards the socioeconomic costs of climate change (UN ECLAC, 2020). Here, it is important to remember what the father of the nation of India Mahatma Gandhi had once expressed, “Earth provides enough to satisfy every man’s needs, but not every man’s greed”1, and also what the Brundtland Commission, constituted by the United Nations in 1983, highlighted later in its seminal report ‘Our Common Future’ published in 1987 giving the official and most widely accepted definition of sustainable development as the “...development that meets the needs of the present without compromising the ability of future generations to meet their own needs” (WCED, 1987). Knowing, in brief, about the major events in the last few decades in connection with the efforts towards sustainability would also be helpful in understanding the background of this chapter which is presented in the Figure 2.

Figure 2. Major Events in connection with the efforts towards sustainability

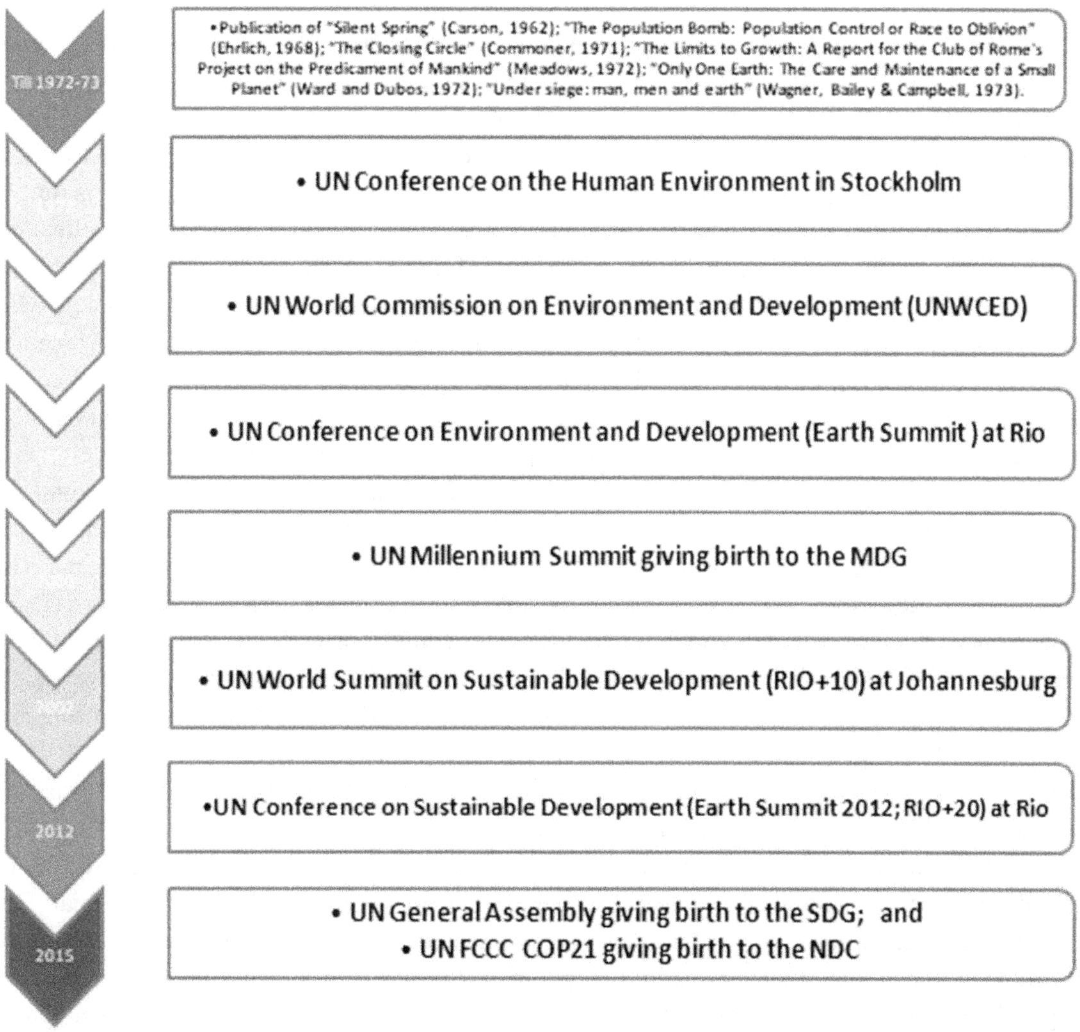

A World Bank arm IFC has estimated that developing countries including India can meet the goals undertaken through their submission of the Nationally Determined Commitments (NDCs) to the United Nations Framework Convention on Climate Change (UNFCCC) under the obligations of Paris Climate Accord with the help of policy reforms, suitable conditions & innovative practices of business thereby underscoring the significance of the corporations by virtue of their possession of innovation, finances and other helpful tools (Kant, 2020c). more than a decade ago, Intergovernmental Panel on Climate Change (IPCC) had underscored the significance of adopting appropriate strategies by different parties urging them to take action for bringing about mitigation and adaptation, technological development and research so that the impact of the climate change risks could be minimized (IPCC, 2007). IPCC has continuously been drawing the attention of the polluting corporations to leverage the carbon markets and products innovations with the supporting initiatives of their respective governments facilitating them with efficient operational strategies, and their investors seeking strong commitments (Kant & Anjali, 2020). It is notable that substantial increase in the number of companies reporting initiatives intended to reduce carbon emission as a sign of their growing inclination towards climate consciousness, reported CDP (formerly known as Carbon Disclosure Project) in its report (CDP, 2017).

Kant and Anjali (2020) remind that the irrecoverable damages meted out to the natural climate on the earth because of the anthropogenic i.e. human induced interferences have been visible through the unusual heat waves, changing weather patterns, rising levels of sea, melting of the glaciers, untimely floods & droughts etc. The transition from the Kyoto protocol towards adoption of the Paris climate deal underscores the efforts being put together by the countries for the emission reduction at the global level. The same type of transition has been witnessed by all the countries in the world with respect to Millennium Development Goals (MDGs) paving way to Sustainable Development Goals (SDGs) in recent past. These transitions also highlight the shift of responsibilities veering towards all categories of countries offloading the developed countries from the compulsory responsibilities by making them non-binding from binding commitments. In other words, the responsibilities have taken the shape of voluntary instead of mandatory in order to ensure climate conservation. Fulfillment of the non binding commitments depends on the organizational voluntariness of sustainable practices displaying latent proactivity which remains beneath the carpet. India is also a responsible party to the international forums where it has made commitments in the form of SDGs of UN and NDCs of UNFCCC under Paris climate accord (Dubash, Khosla, Kelkar, & Lele, 2018). Corporations in India thus cannot shrug the responsibilities of making efforts for the reduction of their carbon footprint in order to help Indian government achieve the goals. It must not be forgotten that climate issues are not only related to the natural climate and resources but have linkage with the society, corporate and governance too (Kant, 2020c).

The incessant growth in the levels of stakeholders' awareness and concerns has not left corporations in India aloof even for a while from analyzing the effect and selecting the suitable strategy (Kant, 2020b). Previous studies focused in developed countries have failed to contextualize and conceptualize these issues and concerns of developing countries adequately (Jayanti & Gowda, 2014; Kant & Anjali, 2020). This chapter, amidst the paucity of relevant studies conducted in the context of developing countries with respect to the proactivity displayed by various corporations highlighting proactive and preventive climate strategy adopted by them, aims to discuss the emerging concept of CSP and underscores the urgent need to undertake research studies setting a research agenda in the field of CSP from the perspective of the relevant stakeholders. The chapter also presents a broad view of the concepts such as CSP, competitive advantage, stakeholders and their interrelations for providing an enhanced understanding.

KNOWING ABOUT CLIMATE STRATEGY PROACTIVITY (CSP)

Kant (2020c) defines CSP as 'the strategic behavior displayed by corporate to meet the stakeholders' expectations by voluntarily adopting such climate conscious preventive practices that are beyond the mandatory regulatory compliance related to pollution and climate conservation.' He further emphasizes that fulfillment of the commitments under the NDCs and the SDGs by the governments requires greater support from the business sector which needs to adopt voluntarily such climate conservation related practices displaying their latent proactivity in view of the political compulsions of the governments in formulating tougher laws (Kant & Agrawal, 2020). Proactivity represents those anticipatory human behaviors which are voluntarily initiated and change oriented as per the demand of the situations (Grant & Ashford, 2008) whereas strategy can be a plan, pattern, position, ploy, perspective or a combination of some or all of them (Mintzberg, Ahlstrand, & Lampel, 1998), or also a human attempt made to meet worthwhile goals of shaping the future amidst real world scarcity of resources (McKeown, 2012). It is noteworthy that In-depth knowledge with respect to the markets, resources, capabilities, competitors, environment and alternatives can help substantially in the development of a strategy. Achievement of organizational goals with limited resources represents an effective corporate strategy which highlights the pattern of adaptation activities towards the natural climate (Freedman, 2013). The components of proactivity and strategy are integral to the concept of CSP which is at the extreme opposite end of the continuum representing the transforming corporate approaches towards natural climate (Moreno & Reyes, 2013) from non compliance passivity to beyond compliance proactivity (Figure 3)

CSP represents the corporate behavior displayed by adopting a set of climate conscious practices with dimensions such as pollution prevention and managerial support to climate (Menguc, Auh, & Ozanne, 2010), and the sum of adopted proactive climate friendly practices (Anton, Deltas, & Khanna, 2004). CSP is the culmination of the organizational efforts under the influence of the consciousness towards

Figure 3. Transforming corporate approaches towards natural climate (Adapted from Berry and Rondinelli, 1998)

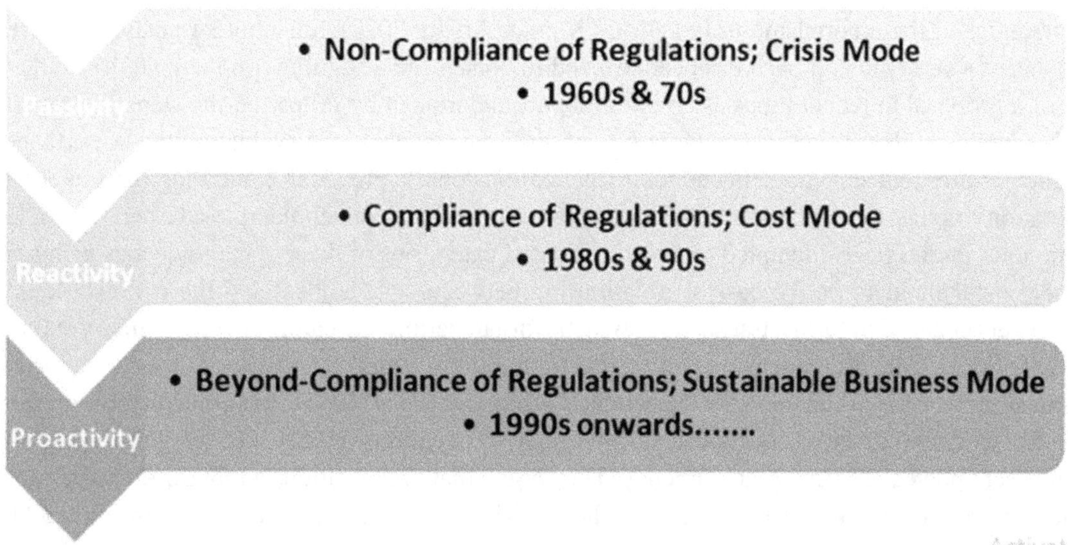

the natural climate (Hunt & Auster, 1990; Kant & Agrawal, 2020) which is underlined by the elementary factors like proactivity towards regulatory compliances, improvement and transformation in the operations, and reporting of the climate actions and practices adopted by them (Delmas, Hoffmann, and Kuss, 2011). CSP denotes the tendency of an organization to anticipate internal as well as external needs and requirements for conservation of natural climate by making voluntarily adopted changes instead of reacting to the mandatory regulatory compliances (Garces-Ayerbe, Rivera-Torres, & Murillo-Luna, 2012; Kant, 2020d).

CSP, assumed to be a motivational factor for adopting those measures which improve the climate positive performances (Valero-Gil, Rivera-Torres, and Garcés-Ayerbe, 2017), is displayed by the corporations to make an advance assessment of the climate conservation related needs voluntarily rather than reacting to them (Garces-Ayerbe et al., 2012) by utilizing conventional corrective and modern preventive climate conscious approaches (Aragon-Correa, 1998). CSP also reflects the systematic pattern of actions voluntarily adopted going beyond minimum compulsory compliance compulsions of the extant laws (Aragon-Correa & Rubio-Lopez, 2007; Kant, 2020a). This implementation voluntariness is displayed clearly by the companies in their different adopted strategies (Hart, 1995). These strategies may be a set of operational, communicational, planning and organizational practices (Kant & Agrawal, 2020; Singh, 2015). Although CSP is an emerging concept in the context of developing countries, Kant & Agrawal (2020) in a recent study has developed a CSPQ Scale to measure CSP displayed by companies in developing countries to attain competitive advantage and sustain it through creation of unique resources and unique capabilities on the basis of the perceptions of their relevant stakeholders.

KNOWING ABOUT STAKEHOLDERS

The seminal book 'Strategic Management: a stakeholder approach' by Freeman in 1984 for exploring and evaluating the stakeholders' perspective with respect to different issues defines stakeholder as 'any group or individual who can affect or is affected by the achievement of the organization's objectives' (Freeman, 1984, p. 46). The continuous growth in the pressure of demand of the stakeholders for fulfilling their respective needs has compelled companies to integrate their concerns in the decision making process and strategies of these companies (Hart, 1995; Kant & Anjali, 2020). Stakeholder analysis undertaken by means of a strategic approach has been utilized to bolster the designing, implementation and evaluation of a proposal in recent times as an integral part undertaken by following the steps of preparing a stakeholders' list, identifying relevant interests of different stakeholders, evaluating the importance and influence of different stakeholders and their implications on the proposal, evaluating the stakeholders' cooperation amongst themselves and determining when/how/which stakeholders to take part (ODA, 1995).

Previous studies have attempted to propose various categories of these stakeholders as primary and secondary stakeholders on the basis of relationship between stakeholders and the organizations. The stakeholders engaged in formal transactions with the organizations are categorized as primary stakeholders whereas they who are not engaged in formal transactions with the organizations are categorized as secondary stakeholders (Clarkson, 1995). Mitchell, Agle, and Wood (1997) have contributed significantly in the classification of stakeholders basing their recommendations on the three attributes. These three attributes are power, legitimacy and urgency. They argue that organizations adopt different strategies to handle different types of stakeholders. 'Stakeholder Theory' (Freeman, 1984) has contributed hugely with wider acceptance for the recognition of the significant elements of social responsibilities of the firms suggesting that a firm may have many stakeholders such as customers, suppliers, mangers, communities, shareholders, workers, unions etc., who can influence the performance of the firm. Corporations must try to ensure satisfaction of all the relevant stakeholders by adopting fitting strategies instead of giving attention to shareholders or managers only (Kant, 2020b).

Corporations try to live up to the expectations of the stakeholders being afraid of the situation that may arise due to their failure in undertaking such activities considered significant by the stakeholders which can compel relevant stakeholders to cancel their support to them (Ravi, 2013). Different level or kind of strategy is desired to be applied for satisfying different stakeholders because of the existence of difference in their interests (Aragon-Correa, Rueda-Manzanares, & Sharma, 2008). In this situation, corporations must be aware of the relevance of different types of stakeholders in order to identify specifically the expectations/demands/requirements/needs of the stakeholders (Freeman, 1984; Kant, 2020b), and hence they use stakeholder analysis to fulfill their strategic objectives (Reed et al., 2009).

Stakeholder theory based studies in the past suggest that corporate efforts are responsible for the adoption of certain strategies which they make in order to meet the needs and expectations of the most salient stakeholders including external and internal stakeholders, community, media, regulators etc. (Buysse & Verbeke, 2003; Henriques & Sadorsky, 1999; Sharma & Henriques, 2005). On the contrary, there are studies which advocate that corporations adopt these strategies under the influence of the pressure of demands of any stakeholders (Aragon-Correa et al., 2008; Darnall, Henriques, and Sadorsky, 2010; Carrascosa-Lopez et al., 2012; Gonzalez-Benito and Gonzalez-Benito, 2006; Murillo-Luna et al., 2008). In recent times, the stakeholder management approaches have laid greater emphasis on the interests and needs of important stakeholders and fulfilling them (Kant, 2020b).

CSP: THE PERSPECTIVE OF STAKEHOLDERS

The companies across the globe have been under compulsion to integrate their climate conservation related strategies in their core corporate strategy in order to negate the consequences of irreversible damages to the natural climate resulting into the disruption of the global and national economy, in recent times (Kant & Anjali, 2020). In the last few decades, the researchers have been paying growing attention to the issues and concerns related to climate change resulting from the irresponsible business practices by the corporations. Their emphasis has been on the task of undertaking studies with respect to the relationship between climate and corporations (Ferguson, Andandarajah, Butnar, Calzadilla, & Dessens, 2020; Kant, 2020c). They got impetus from the work such as "Strategic Management: A Stakeholder Approach" (Freeman, 1984) and "Brundtland Commission Report" (WCED, 1987) which attracted their attention towards the linkage of the corporate strategy with the climate conservation and the approaches of the stakeholders towards the trade-off existing between financial and climate performance of the companies. The transformed approaches have laid greater emphasis on integrating business strategy and climate strategy (Kant, 2020c).

'Stakeholder theory' (Freeman, 1984) contributes immensely which argues that corporations have various stakeholders and these stakeholders can influence their performance making it important that the needs and expectations of all the stakeholders need to be satisfied for protecting the interests of the corporations displaying CSP instead of paying attention to the satisfaction of the investors' needs and expectations only. CSP is believed to be significant strategic behaviour by the stakeholders as they can withdraw their support to the corporations if they witness their failure in satisfying their expectations related to the conservation of natural climate (Ravi, 2013) and sustainable development. Corporations are found to be reluctant, in normal circumstances, towards adopting practices against the degradations of the natural climate. CSP reflects their act of succumbing to the pressure of the stakeholders' needs and expectations (Frooman, 1999) which is a clarion call for them to make every effort to increase awareness regarding relevant stakeholders on the basis of their influence and importance which include customers, managerial and non-managerial employee, prospective employees along with students, different unions, investors, regulators as well as governments, suppliers, Non Government Organizations, various types of communities, financial institutions comprising Banks-Insurance-FIs, academicians etc., in order to identify their climate proactive demands (Freeman, 1984).

Stakeholder analysis is assumed to be a useful tool in the hands of the corporations to meet their strategic objectives (Kant, 2020b; Reed et al., 2009). But, there have been contradictions in the findings of the existing body of knowledge related to CSP. The one group of studies argues that CSP is an outcome of the corporate efforts for meeting the needs and demands of only the most important stakeholders including external and internal stakeholders, regulators, community, media etc. (Buysse & Verbeke, 2003; Henriques & Sadorsky, 1999; Sharma & Henriques, 2005) while the other group argues that the quantum of CSP, which reflects the tendency of the corporations to go beyond regulatory compliance, is an outcome of the impact of the demand of any stakeholder and not the most important stakeholders' pressure (Aragon-Correa et al., 2008; Darnall et al., 2010; Carrascosa-Lopez et al., 2012; Gonzalez-Benito and Gonzalez-Benito, 2006; Murillo-Luna et al., 2008).

The engagement of a growing number of stakeholders for demanding proactive strategies from companies has been increasing with the passage of time which has made identification of relevant stakeholders an important issue for display of CSP by the companies (Kant, 2020b). This can influence the formulation of their climate conservation related policies according to their respective abilities (Kant & Anjali, 2020). The issue has been asking for greater attention from the researchers in recent times. The corporations for the purpose of adoption of different climate friendly strategy take into account a complete range of activities across the continuum starting from as basic as pollution control/ eco-efficiency and as modern as redefinition processes of industrial and business ecosystems with intermediaries like process designing and recycling (Sharma & Henriques, 2005). Inclusion of climate change issues in the business strategy beyond mere regulatory compliances is a token of corporate voluntariness which the corporations show in order to meet the stakeholders' demands related to climate conservation (Gladwin, 1993; Kant & Agrawal, 2020). This makes identification of significant stakeholders very critical for corporate strategy formulation when different stakeholders wield different authority and level of importance and influence for the purpose of display of CSP which are changeable with passage of time and changes in issues (Mitchell et al., 1997).

Henriques & Sadorsky (1999) in their studies undertaken for evaluating the stakeholders' perceived importance concluded that stakeholders like customers, shareholders and communities are the primary stakeholders which are responsible to affect the corporations to adopt climate conservation related strategy in addition to the regulators. Further, Barnett (2007) in his study found that CSP can enhance financial performance of the corporations with the help of suitable positioning of the corporations amongst relevant stakeholders. Competitive advantage with the help of the creation of effective climate proactive reputation by engaging with climate proactivity demanding stakeholders can also be achieved by the corporations as the business sector is believed to be one of the largest polluters which has borne the brunt of this negative image (Kolk & Pinkse, 2005, 2007). This positioning and resultant reputation can further bolster them to gain increased share value gained by means of enhanced competitiveness, increased profits, differentiation and opportunities in newer markets, increased customer loyalty/ attraction, increased employee retention/attraction and enhanced resource price rise resilience as a token of the pressure put by the stakeholders (Kanchan, Kumar, & Gupta, 2015). These positive outcomes can also motivate corporations to gauze that CSP can turn out to be a prominent source of success and competitive advantage in future (Clarkson, Li, Richardson, and Vasvari, 2011).

Managerial perceptions are assumed to be an important determinant for corporate commitment for a specific strategy (Hahn & Scheermesser, 2006; Hou, Al-Tabbaa, Chen, & Mamic, 2014) which have significantly been utilized by majority of studies related to the identification of the salient stakeholder which highlight the biases towards laying more focus on the manager's perceptions instead of perceptions of other stakeholders. It has been found that stakeholders show resistance as their general tendency towards changes because of the prevalence of the uncertainty of the consequential situation but gradually the resistance subsides and they accept changes as their perceptions change witnessing themselves that their problems are being solved. The perceptions further change positively in order to encourage such accommodative behaviors with the increased convincing level towards the benefits arising out of the policies (Steg & Gifford, 2005). The pieces of information that the stakeholders receive are responsible for the stakeholders' perceptions (Hou, 2016) and these perceptions have been found to be highly useful for the purpose of extraction of relevant constructs in order to examine behaviors of the organizations and can reveal the capabilities and willingness of the stakeholders also with respect to the adoption of the strategies (Delmas and Toffel, 2004; Freeman, 1984; Garvare and Johansson, 2010). The distinctiveness of their perceptions survives on account of the difference caused by the organizational objectives, access to information and their own perceptions (Hou, 2016).

The prevailing situations increase the significance of identification of the important, influential and relevant stakeholders because climate conservation related regulations have been found to be significant for display of CSP in developed countries but the situation is not all the same in the context of developing countries (Jones, 2010; Sandhu, Smallman, Ozanne, & Cullen, 2012; Singh, Jain, & Sharma, 2014; Zhang et al., 2008) the reason being the inefficiency of the implementation, monitoring and enforcement mechanisms for the existing regulations (Khanna & Liao, 2014; Qadir & Gorman, 2008). Moreover, studies undertaken in the context of developed countries have not been able to address the issues and concerns of developing countries. The paucity of relevant studies, therefore, calls for more specific studies in the context of developing countries (such as Kant, 2020d, 2020b; Kant & Agrawal, 2020) to provide appropriate insights into the concept of CSP from the stakeholders' perspective.

LIMITATIONS OF THE CHAPTER

This chapter limited itself within the scope of discussing the emerging concept of CSP from the perspective of the relevant stakeholders and proposing a research agenda for future researchers in the context of developing countries.

CONCLUDING COMMENTS

This chapter provides new insights in to the concept of CSP which is not only new but is complex also. Future researchers might receive apt guidance in decision making without getting lost in the comprehensiveness and the complexities of the concept of CSP as this chapter will help them in getting to the right beginning point for further studies to have a more comprehensive and in-depth knowledge bridging the gap between the facts and the stakeholders' perceptions with respect to CSP. Conservation of natural climate has become an important issue in the eyes of the stakeholders of the corporations. Growth in their awareness level has motivated these stakeholders to start paying intense attention to the irreversible consequences of human induced climate change to which corporations have been contributing immensely through their irresponsible practices. In recent times, corporations as well as their stakeholders including governments have started to prepare themselves to fulfill commitments made to the intergovernmental agencies in the form of NDCs and SDGs for ensuring sustainable development by taking suitable mitigation and adaptation measures towards climate change risks and opportunities. This chapter highlights the urgency to speed up the implementations of the suitable actions to mitigate the impact of the huge disconnection between the actions taken and actions desired by corporations in addressing the climate change consequences. The prevailing situation issues a clarion call to undertake adequate studies on the theme underscoring the significance of CSP and its relationship with competitive advantage from stakeholders' perspective because such studies are still in infancy with apparent scarcity of research on such topics which are critical for our own survival.

The identification of indicators of CSP in the context of the companies operating in developing countries like India needs to be given due importance by the researchers in future studies. They need to take into consideration the concerns and awareness of different stakeholders in view of the regulatory mechanism of the developing countries which is different from that of the developed countries. Corporations which have shown their willingness for adoption of climate conscious business practices in developing countries are still very few and far between. Taking a cue from their counterparts in the developed countries, companies in developing countries including India have, however, started to show their inclination towards CSP. Relevant future studies will be helpful in identifying the complete range of measures in order to get rid of the misleading directions coming from the findings of the studies undertaken in the context different from developing countries.

There is a need to widen the perspective of the future researchers without restricting to the mere diagnosis of the prevailing scenario through the perceptual lens of the managers only. They need to bring in to the fold of their research the perceptions of other salient stakeholders also for the evaluation, and need to make effort for proper identification of such stakeholders with respect to CSP. The views and opinions of informed and aware stakeholders in the context of CSP displayed by companies in developing countries must be captured in view of the incessant growth in the stakeholders' awareness. The future researchers ought to pay desired attention to the need of identifying and evaluating the various determinants, antecedents and factors of the corporate CSP in developing countries. This chapter also highlights that the difference, on the basis of the relative importance and influence of various key stakeholders, needs to be examined empirically existing between different categories of stakeholders such as primary stakeholders and secondary stakeholders.

REFERENCES

Agha, S., Alrubaiee, L., & Jamhour, M. (2012). Effect of Core Competence on Competitive Advantage and Organizational Performance. *International Journal of Business and Management*, *7*(1), 192–204.

Anton, W. R. Q., Deltas, G., & Khanna, M. (2004). Incentives for environmental self-regulation and implications for environmental performance. *Journal of Environmental Economics and Management, 48*(1), 632–654. doi:10.1016/j.jeem.2003.06.003

Aragon-Correa, J. (1998). Strategic Proactivity and Firm Approach to the Natural Environment. *Source: The Academy of Management Journal, 41*(5), 556–567. doi:10.5465/256942

Aragon-Correa, J., & Rubio-Lopez, E. A. (2007). Proactive Corporate Environmental Strategies: Myths and Misunderstandings. *Long Range Planning, 40*(3), 357–381. doi:10.1016/j.lrp.2007.02.008

Aragon-Correa, J., Rueda-Manzanares, A., & Sharma, S. (2008). The Influence of Stakeholders on the Environmental Strategy of Service Firms: The Moderating Effects of Complexity, Uncertainty and Munificence. *British Journal of Management, 19*(2), 185–203. doi:10.1111/j.1467-8551.2007.00538.x

Barnett, M. L. (2007). Stakeholder Influence Capacity and the Variability of Financial Returns to Corporate Social Responsibility. *Academy of Management Review, 32*(3), 794–816. doi:10.5465/amr.2007.25275520

Barrett, M., Davidson, E., Prabhu, J., & Vargo, S. L. (2015). Service Innovation in the Digital Age: Key Contributions and Future Directions. *Management Information Systems Quarterly, 39*(1), 135–154. doi:10.25300/MISQ/2015/39:1.03

Berry, M. A., & Rondinelli, D. A. (1998). Proactive corporate environmental management: A new industrial revolution. *The Academy of Management Perspectives, 12*(2), 38–50. doi:10.5465/ame.1998.650515

Brandi, C., Dzebo, A., & Janetschek, H. (2017). *The Case for Connecting the Implementation of the Paris Climate Agreement and the 2030 Agenda for Sustainable Development.* Briefing Paper 21/2017.

Buysse, K., & Verbeke, A. (2003). Proactive Environmental Strategies: A Stakeholder Management Perspective. *Strategic Management Journal, 24*(5), 453–470. doi:10.1002mj.299

Carrascosa-Lopez, C., Segarra-Ona, M.-V., Peiro-Signes, A., & Segura-Garcia-del-Rio, B. (2012). Environmental Proactivity In Manufacturing Industries: Is It Valuable? *International Business & Economics Research Journal, 11*(5), 567–574. doi:10.19030/iber.v11i5.6974

CDP. (2017). CDP India Climate Change Report 2017: India Inc. aligns with NDC and Paris Agreement to seize opportunities. London, UK: CDP.

Clarkson, M. E. (1995). A Stakeholder Framework for Analyzing and Evaluating Corporate Social Performance. *Academy of Management Review, 20*(1), 92–117. doi:10.5465/amr.1995.9503271994

Clarkson, P. M., Li, Y., Richardson, G. D., & Vasvari, F. P. (2011). Does it really pay to be green? Determinants and consequences of proactive environmental strategies. *Journal of Accounting and Public Policy, 30*(2), 122–144. doi:10.1016/j.jaccpubpol.2010.09.013

Crouch, G. I., & Ritchie, J. R. B. (1999). Tourism, competitiveness, and societal prosperity. *Journal of Business Research, 44*(3), 137–152. doi:10.1016/S0148-2963(97)00196-3

Darnall, N., Henriques, I., & Sadorsky, P. (2010). Adopting Proactive Environmental Strategy: The Influence of Stakeholders and Firm Size. *Journal of Management Studies, 47*(6), 1072–1094. doi:10.1111/j.1467-6486.2009.00873.x

Delmas, M., Hoffmann, V. H., & Kuss, M. (2011). Under the Tip of the Iceberg: Absorptive Capacity, Environmental Strategy, and Competitive Advantage. *Business & Society*, *50*(1), 116–154. doi:10.1177/0007650310394400

Delmas, M., & Toffel, M. W. (2004). Stakeholders and environmental management practices: An institutional framework. *Business Strategy and the Environment*, *13*(4), 209–222. doi:10.1002/bse.409

Diab, S. M. (2014). Using the Competitive Dimensions to Achieve Competitive advantage (A Study on Jordanian private hospitals). *International Journal of Academic Research in Business & Social Sciences*, *4*(9), 138–150. doi:10.6007/IJARBSS/v4-i9/1136

Dubash, N. K., Khosla, R., Kelkar, U., & Lele, S. (2018). India and Climate Change: Evolving Ideas and Increasing Policy Engagement. *Annual Review of Environment and Resources*, *43*(1), 395–424. doi:10.1146/annurev-environ-102017-025809

Ferguson, C., Andandarajah, G., Butnar, I., Calzadilla, A., & Dessens, O. (2020). *Costing the earth-climate damage costs and GDP. A summary of the report produced by UCL Energy Institute for CDP.*

Freedman, L. (2013). *Strategy : A history* (1st ed.). Oxford University Press.

Freeman, E. (1984). *Strategic Management: A stakeholder approach*. Pitman.

Frooman, J. (1999). Stakeholder influence strategies. *Academy of Management Review*, *24*(2), 191–205. doi:10.5465/amr.1999.1893928

Gadenne, D. L., Kennedy, J., & McKeiver, C. (2009). An empirical study of environmental awareness and practices in SMEs. *Journal of Business Ethics*, *84*(1), 45–63. doi:10.100710551-008-9672-9

Garces-Ayerbe, C., Rivera-Torres, P., & Murillo-Luna, J. L. (2012). Stakeholder pressure and environmental proactivity. *Management Decision*, *50*(2), 189–206. doi:10.1108/00251741211203524

Garvare, R., & Johansson, P. (2010). Management for sustainability – A stakeholder theory. *Total Quality Management & Business Excellence*, *21*(7), 737–744. doi:10.1080/14783363.2010.483095

Gladwin, T. N. (1993). The Meaning of Greening: A Plea for Organizational Theory. In J. Fischer & K. Schot (Eds.), *Environmental Strategies for Industry: International Perspectives on Research Needs and Policy Implications* (pp. 37–61). Island Press.

Gonzales-Benito, J. C., & Gonzales-Benito, O. C. (2006). A Review of Determinant Factors of Environmental Proactivity. *Business Strategy and the Environment*, *15*(2), 87–102. doi:10.1002/bse.450

Grant, A. M., & Ashford, S. J. (2008). The Dynamics of Proactivity at Work. *Research in Organizational Behavior*, *28*(1), 3–34. doi:10.1016/j.riob.2008.04.002

Hahn, T., & Scheermesser, M. (2006). Approaches to Corporate Sustainability among German companies. *Corporate Social Responsibility and Environmental Management*, *13*(3), 150–165. doi:10.1002/csr.100

Hart, S. L. (1995). A Natural-Resource-Based View of the Firm. *Academy of Management Review*, *20*(4), 986–1014. doi:10.5465/amr.1995.9512280033

Henriques, I., & Sadorsky, P. (1999). The relationship between environmental commitment and managerial perceptions of stakeholder importance. *Academy of Management Journal*, *42*(1), 87–99.

Hou, D. (2016). Divergence in stakeholder perception of sustainable remediation. *Sustainability Science*, *11*(2), 215–230. doi:10.100711625-015-0346-0

Hou, D., Al-Tabbaa, A., Chen, H., & Mamic, I. (2014). Factor Analysis and Structural Equation Modeling of Sustainable Behaviour in Contaminated Land Remediation. *Journal of Cleaner Production*, *84*(1), 439–449. doi:10.1016/j.jclepro.2014.01.054

Hunt, C. B., & Auster, E. R. (1990). Proactive Environmental Management: Avoiding the Toxic Trap. *Sloan Management Review*, *31*, 7–18.

IPCC. (2007). Climate Change 2007: Impacts, Adaptation and Vulnerability. In P. J. van der L. Parry M.L., O.F. Canziani, J.P. Palutikof, & C. E. Hanson (Eds.), Contribution of Working Group II to the Fourth Assessment Report of the Intergovernmental Panel on Climate Change (p. 982). Cambridge, UK: Cambridge University Press.

Jayanti, R. K., & Gowda, M. V. R. (2014). Sustainability dilemmas in emerging economies. *IIMB Management Review*, *26*(2), 130–142. doi:10.1016/j.iimb.2014.03.004

Jones, C. (2010). Exploring new ways of assessing the effect of regulation on environmental management. *Journal of Cleaner Production*, *18*(13), 1229–1250. doi:10.1016/j.jclepro.2010.04.007

Kanchan, U., Kumar, N., & Gupta, A. (2015). Green Business-Way to Achieve Globally Sustainable Competitive Advantage. *Journal of Progressive Research in Social Sciences,* *2*(2), 92–100.

Kant, N. (2020a). Actions beyond Regulatory Compliances: Perceived Climate Strategy Proactivity in Indian Companies. *International Journal of Development Issues*, *ahead-of-print*(ahead-of-print). Advance online publication. doi:10.1108/IJDI-07-2020-0152

Kant, N. (2020b). An analytical Study of Stakeholders' Relevance based on their Perceived Preference in terms of Climate Strategy Proactivity (CSP). *Competitiveness Review*. Advance online publication. doi:10.1108/CR-10-2020-0122

Kant, N. (2020c). Climate Strategy Proactivity (CSP) and its Theoretical Underpinnings. In W. L. Filho, A. M. Azul, L. Brandli, A. L. Salvia, & T. Wall (Eds.), Industry, Innovation and Infrastructure, Encyclopedia of the UN Sustainable Development Goals (Living Reference). Springer Nature. doi:10.1007/978-3-319-71059-4_122-1

Kant, N. (2020d). Primary validation of climate strategy proactivity questionnaire scale measuring relationship of climate strategy proactivity with competitive advantage. *Management of Environmental Quality*. Advance online publication. doi:10.1108/MEQ-07-2020-0161

Kant, N., & Agrawal, N. (2020). Developing a Measure of Climate Strategy Proactivity Displayed to Attain Competitive Advantage. *Competitiveness Review*, *ahead-of-print*(ahead-of-print). Advance online publication. doi:10.1108/CR-06-2020-0079

Kant, N., & Anjali, K. (2020). Climate Strategy Proactivity (CSP): A Stakeholders-Centric Concept. In W. L. Filho, A. M. Azul, L. Brandli, A. L. Salvia, & T. Wall (Eds.), Partnerships for the Goals, Encyclopedia of the UN Sustainable Development Goals (Living Reference). Springer Nature. doi:10.1007/978-3-319-71067-9_121-1

Kasasbeh, E. A., Harada, Y., & Noor, I. M. (2017). Factors Influencing Competitive Advantage in Banking Sector: A Systematic Literature Review. *Research Journal of Business Management, 11*(2), 67–73. doi:10.3923/rjbm.2017.67.73

Khanna, M., & Liao, Y. (2014). Globalization and voluntary environmental management in developing countries. *Frontiers of Economics in China, 9*(1), 138–163.

Kolk, A., & Pinkse, J. (2005). Business Responses to Climate Change: Identifying Emergent Strategies. *California Management Review, 47*(3), 6–20. doi:10.2307/41166304

Kolk, A., & Pinkse, J. (2007). Towards strategic stakeholder management? Integrating perspectives on sustainability challenges such as corporate responses to climate change. *Corporate Governance: The International Journal of Business in Society, 7*(4), 370–378. doi:10.1108/14720700710820452

McKeown, M. (2012). *The Strategy Book* (2nd ed.). Pearson.

Menguc, B., Auh, S., & Ozanne, L. (2010). The interactive effect of internal and external factors on a proactive environmental strategy and its influence on a firm's performance. *Journal of Business Ethics, 94*(2), 279–298. doi:10.100710551-009-0264-0

Mintzberg, H., Ahlstrand, B., & Lampel, J. (1998). *Strategy Safari: A Guided Tour Through the Wilds of Strategic Management*. Free Press.

Mitchell, R. K., Agle, B. R., & Wood, D. J. (1997). Toward a Theory of Stakeholder Identification and Salience:Defining the Principle of Who and What Really Counts. *Academy of Management Journal, 22*(4), 853–886.

Moreno, C. E., & Reyes, J. F. (2013). The Value of Proactive Environmental Strategy: An Empirical Evaluation of the Contingent Approach To Dynamic Capabilities. *Cuadernos Americanos, 26*(47), 87–118.

Murillo-Luna, J. L., Garces-Ayerbe, C., & Rivera-Torres, P. (2008). Why do patterns of environmental response differ? A stakeholders' pressure approach. *Strategic Management Journal, 29*(11), 1225–1240. doi:10.1002mj.711

ODA. (1995). *Guidance Note on How to do Stakeholder Analysis of Aid Projects and Programmes*. Retrieved July 9, 2018, from https://beamexchange.org/uploads/filer_public/5d/4c/5d4c7b02-a25d-43ab-ae33-0e4811b7c5fb/guidance_stakeholderanalysis.pdf

Porter, M. E. (1980). *Competitive Strategy*. Free Press.

Prescott, M. E. (2014). Big data and competitive advantage at Nielsen. *Management Decision, 52*(3), 573–601. doi:10.1108/MD-09-2013-0437

Qadir, S. A., & Gorman, H. S. (2008). The use of ISO 14001 in India: More than a certificate on the wall? *Environmental Practice, 10*(2), 53–65. doi:10.1017/S1466046608080174

Ravi, S. P. (2013). Does Stakeholder Perception of Firm's Corporate Social Responsibility Affect Firm Performance? *International Journal of Asian Business and Information Management*, *4*(1), 67–83. doi:10.4018/jabim.2013010107

Reed, M. S., Graves, A., Dandy, N., Posthumus, H., Hubacek, K., Morris, J., Prell, C., Quinn, C. H., & Stringer, L. C. (2009). Who's in and why? A typology of stakeholder analysis methods for natural resource management. *Journal of Environmental Management*, *90*(5), 1933–1949. doi:10.1016/j.jenvman.2009.01.001 PMID:19231064

Sandhu, S., Smallman, C., Ozanne, L. K., & Cullen, R. (2012). Corporate Environmental Responsiveness in India: Lessons from a Developing Country. *Journal of Cleaner Production*, *35*, 203–213. doi:10.1016/j.jclepro.2012.05.040

Sharma, S., & Henriques, I. (2005). Stakeholder Influences on Sustainability Practices in the Canadian Forest Products Industry. *Strategic Management Journal*, *26*(2), 159–180. doi:10.1002mj.439

Singh, N. (2015). *Environmental Determinants and Their Impact in Various Indian Industries: A Study of Environmental Performance under EMS Framework* (Doctoral Dissertation). Department of Natural Resources Management, TERI University.

Singh, N., Jain, S., & Sharma, P. (2014). Determinants of proactive environmental management practices in Indian firms: An empirical study. *Journal of Cleaner Production*, *66*, 469–478. doi:10.1016/j.jclepro.2013.11.055

Steg, L., & Gifford, R. (2005). Sustainable Transportation and Quality of Life. *Journal of Transport Geography*, *13*(Special Issue), 59–69. doi:10.1016/j.jtrangeo.2004.11.003

UN ECLAC. (2020). *The 2030 Agenda for Sustainable Development in the new global and regional context: Scenarios and projections in the current crisis.* Author.

UNSD. (2019). *The Sustainable Development Goals Report 2019*. Author.

Valero-Gil, J., Rivera-Torres, P., & Garces-Ayerbe, C. (2017). How is Environmental Proactivity Accomplished? Drivers and Barriers in Firms' Pro-environmental Change Process. *Sustainability (Switzerland)*, *9*(8), 1–15. doi:10.3390u9081327

WBCSD. (n.d.). *Moving beyond the "turbulent teens."* Author.

WCED. (1987). *Our Common Future. World Commission on Environment and Development.* World Commission on Environment and Development., doi:10.1080/07488008808408783

WEF. (2020). The Global Risks Report 2020. Insight Report.

Zhang, B., Bi, J., Yuan, Z., Ge, J., Liu, B., & Bu, M. (2008). Why do Firms Engage in Environmental Management? An Empirical Study in China. *Journal of Cleaner Production*, *16*(10), 1036–1045. doi:10.1016/j.jclepro.2007.06.016

ADDITIONAL READING

Anjali, K., Khuman, Y., & Sokhi, J. (2020). A Review of the interrelations of terrestrial carbon sequestration and urban forests. *AIMS Environmental Science*, *7*(6), 464–485. doi:10.3934/environsci.2020030

Barba-Sánchez, V., & Atienza-Sahuquillo, C. (2016). Environmental Proactivity and Environmental and Economic Performance: Evidence from the Winery Sector. *Sustainability*, *8*(10), 1014. doi:10.3390u8101014

Michalisin, M. D., & Stinchfield, B. T. (2010). Climate Change Strategies and The company's performance: An Empirical Investigation of the Natural Resource-Based View of the Firm. *The Journal of Business Strategy*, *27*(2), 123–149.

Sarkis, J. (2003). Corporate environmental benchmarking. *Benchmarking*, *10*(2), 25–33. doi:10.1108/bij.2003.13110baa.001

Yadav, P. L., Han, S. H., & Kim, H. (2017). Sustaining Competitive Advantage Through Corporate Environmental Performance. *Business Strategy and the Environment*, *26*(3), 345–357. doi:10.1002/bse.1921

KEY TERMS AND DEFINITIONS

Climate Strategy Proactivity (CSP): Denotes the strategic behavior demonstrated by corporations for the purpose of meeting the expectations of the stakeholders through adoption of climate conscious preventive practices on voluntary basis moving beyond the compliance of the existing laws for the purpose of conserving natural climate.

Nationally Determined Contributions (NDCs): Denote the national level commitment of different countries under the Paris Climate Agreement of the UNFCCC reflecting the efforts of each country in reducing national level emissions. They are said to be at the heart of the Paris accord urging countries for taking appropriate action for climate change adaptation. As per the paragraph 2 of the Article 4 of the Paris agreement, each country is required to prepare, communicate and maintain post-2020 climate actions which are collectively referred to as its NDCs.

Stakeholder: A stakeholder can be anybody and even a non living entity as it is popularly defined as any individual or group of individuals who has a stake or claim or can affect or is affected by the achievement of the objectives of an organization.

Sustainable Development Goals (SDGs): Denote a universal call to action to end poverty, protect the planet, and ensure peace and prosperity for all by 2030 by all the member countries of the UN in the year 2015 through a set of 17 SDGs which are integrated with one another so that action related to one goal affect outcomes in others. The intention behind SDGs is to achieve sustainable development leaving no one behind keeping it balanced in terms of social, economic, and environmental.

ENDNOTE

1 Mahatma Gandhi, quoted by E. F. Schumacher in Small Is Beautiful: A Study of Economics as if People Mattered (London: Blond and Briggs, 1973), p. 29.

Chapter 7
Public-Private Partnership in the Post-Coronavirus Reality:
The State and Creating a More Inclusive Societal Environment

Irina Vaslavskaya
https://orcid.org/0000-0002-1363-3865
Kazan Federal University, Russia

Yan Vaslavskiy
https://orcid.org/0000-0003-0707-1699
Moscow State Institute of International Relations, MGIMO University, Russia

ABSTRACT

The COVID-19 pandemic has revealed the failure of the state to withstand emergencies, threatening the lives of millions of citizens. By introducing regimes of social and economic lockdowns in fighting coronavirus, the state faced a societal crisis. Its consequences can't be overestimated, especially due to economic recovery. The growing distrust of households in the state was caused by the disruption of their usual way of living, the growth of unemployment, and the deterioration in their well-being. So people began to distinguish significant differences between their individual values and preferences institutionalized by the state. Hence, the priority for the state should be to restore citizens' confidence by creating a more inclusive societal environment, minimizing the negative consequences of the societal crisis. Infrastructure PPP projects can demonstrate the social preferences' public priority. The "institutional matrix" of PPP organizational forms makes it possible to choose conditions for public projects' implementation with the absolute priority of the healthcare system.

DOI: 10.4018/978-1-7998-6788-3.ch007

INTRODUCTION

The rapid spread of COVID-19, deadly dangerous for human life, served as stability test for the existing social foundations of society, as well as for the depth of mutual trust between people and society, citizens and the state. The originality of the crises caused by the COVID-19 pandemic was due to the actions of states that failed to quickly identify the "zero" patient and introduced lockdown regimes that destroyed the structural integrity of national societies and the economics. The severity of such a test, which fell on the shoulders of individuals as their well-being and established way of living was destroyed, turned into an overestimation of the role of state and society in ensuring the stability of households. The most striking demonstration of such individual reassessments was the compliance or non-compliance by citizens with self-isolation regimes, since they became a function of the degree of their trust in the actions of their state and of individual desire to follow the extraordinary norms of behavior imposed in society in connection with the COVID-19 pandemic. Thus, the coronavirus exposed the main "spring" of modern societies, which was unable to dampen the consequences of an unexpected infection, dangerous to human life, and contributed to the development of a societal crisis as a demonstration of national societies' structural disunity. It is in this context the Boston Consulting Group' experts (Boston Consulting Group Perspectives. (2020)) have treated the COVID-19 outbreak as the first and foremost a societal crisis.

Experts' estimates have shown that a social and economic lockdown aimed at halting the exponential growth of coronavirus cases in countries around the world has caused unprecedented losses in both human life and national welfare. At the same time, COVID-19 proved the priority of social problems, which, moreover, were aggravated by the absolute drop in the volume of material production in the world. The pandemic dictated the uncontested subordination of the functions of the state: first, to stabilize the epidemiological situation in the country and only then not to waste time for timely re-opening economics after lockdown. The experts of the Boston Consulting Group (BCG) have designated this newest dualism in government actions as "epinomics" (Gjaja, et al. (2020)). The epinomic policy emphasizes the paramount importance of ensuring the health and life of citizens, the achievement of which is an unconditional factor in the ability to successfully revive the economy. Moreover, the specificity of the first problem is related to the fact that, together with the physical health of citizens in the context of levelling the epidemiological situation in the country, perhaps the most important thing for states becomes to eliminate the negative consequences of the societal crisis. In the latter case, it is about the mechanisms of socialization of individuals in the structure of society (see the chapter in this book titled "Rebuilding a Stronger Business in the Uncertain Post-COVID-19 Future: Factor of Intellectually Autonomous and Adequately Socialized Employees").

As for reducing the scale of uncertainty of the post-coronavirus reality, it is largely associated with creating the more inclusive societal environment, which is predetermined by a change in the functions of the state in the socio-economic system. Moreover, this issue has both a theoretical background and many application problems, since in the past there were no "best practices" of state behavior in situations similar to the COVID-19 pandemic. From the viewpoint of the strategic goals of the social communities' progress in the post-coronavirus future, the most important becomes the restoration of their societal integrity as an objective condition for the rapid economic reopening after the lockdown and for the adequate acceptable scenario of the events in a case of the second wave of the coronavirus pandemic. Actually, the following conclusion of World Health Organisation (WHO) Strategy Update of 14 April 2020 testifies to this: "Governments must also repurpose and engage all available public, community and private sector capacity to rapidly scale up the public health system." It is about restoring the sphere of intersection of the values of society as the integrity of citizens and public choice aggregated by the state.

Almost all experts admit that after the COVID-19 pandemic, the global world will become different, but it will retain both citizens and society and a societal crisis, which must be eliminated by the state as an indispensable condition for further socio-economic progress. In this regard, it should be emphasized that the institutional aspect of the mechanism of public intervention in society and the economy becomes of particular importance. This is due to the fact that it is the formal institutions in the hands of the state that can become an effective tool for restoring the societal integrity of national communities. And in this case, it is not about the mechanism of punishment, which is integrated into the structure of formal institutions, but about the priority of the mechanism of institutionalizing socially significant norms of behavior of citizens in society. And the latter is impossible without restoring the societal integrity of society, and the trust of individuals in their state. It is in this context that public-private partnership (PPP) can become the most acceptable platform for the government to test new mechanisms for resolving the societal crisis. This is due to the fact that PPP forms of organization mediate social interaction of the state with a private investor in the implementation of socially significant projects, mainly in infrastructure. And if successful, all stakeholders of these infrastructure projects will transmit positive results through structural relationships to society: through investors, employees, their relatives, employers, all PPP participants and local communities. And since before COVID-19, nation states could not boast of great success in the development of PPP projects, and formal institutions in the hands of the state largely impeded the expansion of PPP practice, now the state gets the second chance. And now at stake is the most difficult problem of restoring societal integrity, which predetermines the socioeconomic dynamics of local communities in the post-coronavirus future.

Background

So, it should be noted that national governments were forced to resort to emergency measures of fighting the COVID-19 pandemic by introducing a "self-isolation" regime for citizens and blocking the economic and financial systems at the national level. G. Gopinath, Economic Advisor and Director of the IMF Research Department, identified the 2020 global economic crisis as a global "lockdown" due to "great self-isolation" or "great quarantine" (IMF (2020)). In the opinion of Daniel Susskind, the current situation should be associated with "...a self-inflicted economic catastrophe as a necessary policy response to contain its (COVID-19) spread" (Susskind, (2020)). As the first wave of the COVID-19 pandemic has weakened and the real threat of its second wave emerging, the societal problems of national communities force them to turn to the future of creating the more inclusive societal environment with other functions of the state and with another subordination of social and economic priorities.

On the one hand, citizens make their main claims in connection with the coronavirus pandemic, the social and economic lockdown and its devastating consequences for individuals to the state. And it is the state who is accused of all coronavirus problems. (Korchakova-Heeb (2020)). But, on the other hand, their main aspirations to regain the previous well-being position, as well as their social status, are mostly associated with the state. The BCG experts write the following: "At least as important, the willingness for change is there. Citizens want to see a path forward to a bright future. Business leaders will eagerly support the long-term growth it will unleash. And investors will fund it." (Schwaerzler, et al. (2020)).

In other words, the emergency conditions caused by the coronavirus pandemic in 2020 made the national states the last resort, which was forced to bear all the financial costs associated with the lockdown in the national economy, with social support of the population and fiscal and monetary help to private firms which business was blocked. As a result, budgetary expenditures of national governments have reached a marginal level and budget revenues have been reduced to a minimum. As for entrepreneurs whose business has declined or completely closed, they have lost revenue and profits, the ability to pay salaries to employees, repay loans and pay taxes, and also build strategic development prospects. In these conditions, the partnership of national states and private investors in the implementation of socially significant projects becomes not only possible, but even more necessary than before COVID-19. Besides, in crises the importance of socially significant projects, especially in infrastructure, increases greatly due to reducing the period of economic recession.

The urgent need of creating the more inclusive societal environment expansion necessary for the restoration of the societal integrity of society and accelerated economic progress predetermines an increasing demand for a theoretical justification of the new functions of the national state, factors for increasing the effectiveness of formal institutions in its hands. At the same time, it becomes especially important to search for such a structural level of national systems that could serve in practice as a "platform" that allows the state to make systemic decisions and analyze the effect of their implementation in specific projects. In this case, it is about acceptable forms of PPP organization (Déau, (2020)). Their numerous modifications can be conditionally structured in the form of "institutional matrices" (Vaslavskiy, et al. (2019)). Their theoretical justification can serve as a basis for determining the political choice of states in favour of certain forms of PPP taking into account their structural variability, the ability to "design" various partnership options depending on national characteristics, specific requirements of partners, priority sectors and areas of economic activity, and the effectiveness of risk reduction instruments in conditions of increased environmental uncertainty in the post-Covid-19 recovery phase (Vaslavskiy, et al. (2019)).

Back in 2017, the first Sustainable Development Impact Summit of the World Economic Forum was dedicated to the high importance of PPPs for ensuring the sustainable development of national economies all over the world. According to politicians, scientists and practitioners, only expanding the partnership between the state and private business will achieve the United Nations Sustainable Development Goals and implement the provisions of the Paris Climate Agreement by 2030 (World Economic Forum (2017)). Under COVID-19, such importance of PPPs should be interpreted in the context of the need to form and expand the organizational structures of partnerships (cooperation, cooperation) between the state and private business, which potential is huge and can be successfully used to unlock the economic "lockdown" at the national level (World Economic Forum (2019)). Under the current conditions, it would be very important to theoretically rethink the reasons that impeded the widespread practice of PPPs development before COVID-19, as well as the conditions that should be created for the rapid implementation of the diverse forms of such a partnership in the post-Covid-19 recovery phase (Baxter, (2020)).

Taking into account all the above, the structure of the chapter implements the following logic of providing material. The theoretical part examines the problems of inefficiency of the state and of the brightest modern form of the "failures" of the state - a societal crisis caused by the imposition of a state of emergency lockdown as a response to the COVID-19 pandemic. These manifestations of the inefficiency of the state have quite definite estimates in terms of human and economic losses, which indicate the need for a radical change in the functions of the state. As a result, its ineffective operations are very costly to society. So by 2020, the growing public debt due to the coronavirus pandemic will reach its highest level in the recorded history, at 101.5% of Global Gross Domestic Product (GDP) (Gaspar, et al. (2020)). The restoration of missed opportunities is associated with the imperative associated with the state's focus on creating the more inclusive societal environment, first of all, through the implementation of socially significant infrastructure projects. And their organization on the basis of PPP is an acceptable form of reducing the costs of maintaining the state by society and increasing the effectiveness of projects being implemented.

The expansion of the uncertainty field in post-coronavirus reality causes an increase in demand for the applied justification of acceptable forms of PPP organization. Their numerous modifications can be conditionally structured in the form of "institutional matrices" serving the basis for determining the epinomic approach of national states. The choice of certain forms of PPP for the socially significant infrastructure projects should be based on the adaptation of their structural variability, the ability to "design" various partnership options depending on national characteristics, specific requirements of partners, priority sectors and areas of economic activity, and the effectiveness of risk reduction instruments aiming at creating the more inclusive societal environment.

Methodology

State and Development of Societal Crisis Accelerated by the COVID-19 Pandemic

The societal crisis caused by the COVID-19 pandemic has called into question not only the effectiveness of the capital economic system, "that alone rules the world," (Milanovich, (2019)), but also the functions of the state in it as a reflection of the national communities' needs built on this economic foundation. It is the state that is responsible for the public healthcare system that it created, which turned out to be helpless in the face of an unknown deadly virus and could not quickly and effectively resist its exponential spread. As a kind of excuse, it could be noted that national states turned out to be in an absolutely uncertain situation, since there were no precedents like the COVID-19 pandemic in the history. As a result, there were no best national practices of state behaviour in emergency situations of the type that could be resorted to. According to Johns Hopkins Centre for Health Security as of August 26, 2020 the number of people coronavirus infected on the planet reached 24 million people, of which the number of deaths was estimated at 0.8 million. National states independently developed their actions, implementing a certain set of means of combating coronavirus infection.

The BCG experts characterized the process of fighting the COVID-19 pandemic into three phases: flatten, fight, and future. On the first "flatten" phase national governments lock down to flatten the virus's exponential growth curve. On the second "fight" phase, it becomes of the great significance the choice of the moment for "restarts" economic activities while maintaining a low rate of infection and still running the risk of having to implement further lockdowns. A final "future" phase could start only after a vaccine or highly effective treatment has been developed and deployed (Boston Consulting Group. (2020)). According to the BCG experts, the COVID-19 pandemic has reduced the main functions of the state to two main ones: (1) stabilizing the epidemiological situation and (2) economic reopening. The combination of these two goals predetermines the appearance of the term "epinomics" and makes it possible to single out three main epinomic strategies of the state in fighting coronavirus infection: (1) crush and contain, (2) flatten and fight, and (3) sustain and support (Fig. 1).

As a result, almost everywhere in the "flatten" and "fight" stages, national governments made choices in their politics between health outcomes and economic and societal costs. With confirmed cases of coronavirus and fatalities still rising fast, policymakers will have to keep the public health response their first priority. But in any case the coronavirus is still out there, and unemployment and economic activ-

Figure 1. Three specific epinomic strategies of national governments in beating the coronavirus
Source: The World Bank, Oxford COVID-19 Government Tracker, Wordometer, BCG analysis.

	Crush and contain	Flatten and fight (MOST COMMON APPROACH)	Sustain and support
OBJECTIVE	**Full containment** to reduce the number of local coronavirus cases to close to zero through rapid, stringent lockdowns, combined with aggressive testing, tracking, contact tracing, quarantining, and isolating	**Attempted containment** with strong interventions to decrease the number of coronavirus cases and avoid overwhelming the health care system's capacity	**Open containment** with moderate interventions and primary reliance on voluntary restraint to limit the number of coronavirus cases until herd immunity is achieved or a vaccine or cure is developed
IMPLICATIONS FOR RESTART	**Opening the economy in a walled society,** focusing on strict border controls and testing to keep the number of new cases to an absolute minimum and restore economic vitality	**Progressively lifting restrictions and reopening the economy** without surpassing the health care system's limits	**Prolonged quarantining of the vulnerable population,** while the less vulnerable pursue economic activities with few constraints but continued health precautions
PREREQUISITES	• Early, stringent interventions and the acceptance of prolonged lockdowns, when necessary • Strict border control • High volumes of testing and contact tracing relative to the number of cases	• Resources to expand the health care system's capacity • Ability to increase coronavirus monitoring (testing, tracking, and contact tracing) • Adherence to safety protocols during the reopening	• Ability to isolate and support the socioeconomic well-being of the vulnerable • High trust in government translating into high compliance levels • Favorable demographics
EXAMPLES	China, New Zealand, South Korea, and Taiwan	Brazil, Germany, Italy, Nigeria, the UK, and the US	Sweden

ity take huge hits. As a result, the societal crisis deepens and the uncertainties about which strategy to pursue are manifold (Gjaja, et al. (2020)).

It is appropriate to emphasize that the main "failure" of the state in the socio-economic systems that have developed by 2020 is that economic goals are primary in its activity, and that ensuring the life and health of citizens plays a subordinate role. The extreme conditions of the deadly coronavirus pandemic have changed priorities, making the health of citizens an ongoing concern and the first paramount public goal. However, the growing number of infected and deaths from coronavirus, a social lockdown that has led to complete uncertainty about the future welfare of citizens, a radical change in their usual way of life have predetermined the societal crisis. It has manifested itself in the acute discontent of individuals with the state, in all-encompassing opportunism in relation to all of its anti-coronavirus actions. And this, undoubtedly, turns into the main obstacle to an effective strategy of the state aimed at the timely re-opening of the economy. Against this backdrop, rising unemployment and economic lockdown have become extremely expensive public strategy in the fighting COVID-19 pandemic. As a result, all these costs should be attributed to the losses of society due to the fact that the state was unable to build a public healthcare system capable of functioning in anticipation of the huge human and economic losses caused by COVID-19. In fact, they can be interpreted as the price of the fallacy of all the previous practice of national governments that provided rapid growth and optimizing economic output at the expense of underestimating the priority of creating a sustainable public health system. Such misunderstanding of the subordination of the goals of ensuring the health and well-being of citizens and economic growth rates at any cost largely predetermined the transcendental inefficiency of the state in the context of the COVID-19 pandemic, as well as in the implementation of the societal crisis. In practice, this turned into a catastrophic collapse of the global economy and the destruction of the societal integrity of national communities.

State Inefficiency as the Root Cause of the Societal Crisis Brought About by the Coronavirus Pandemic

Long before the COVID-19 pandemic theorists took their best to find out the reasons for the low efficiency of state activity in national socio-economic systems. They linked the main reason with the problem of priority choice of budget expenditures in relation to the three main groups of functions of the state. V. Tanzi (Tanzi, (2011)) called that problem the "triad" of R. Musgrave. Triangle angles were associated with the fundamental state functions: (1) of allocating resources, (2) of redistributing income (equality in income distribution), and (3) of in economic stabilization (economic efficiency) (Musgrave, (1988)). The budgetary constraints of the state did not allow it to finance them equally, which objectively predetermined his choice of any two groups of expenses out of the three available. This essentially fiscal problem was compounded by the fundamental contradiction inherent in the phenomenon of the state itself. On the one hand, the state does not have its own interests, since society created it solely for the purpose of serving the public interest. On the other hand, the society has no adequate means for the operative assessment of the effectiveness of the state's activities. And given the significant financial resources redistributed by society to the state budget for the purpose of financing the production of socially significant goods, its activities become opaque, corrupt and often self-sufficient. This phenomenon is also predetermined by the fact that the state is contradictory in essence, acting both as a subject and as an object of regulation (Pilipenko, et al. (2020)).

In fact, all these theoretical arguments for the ineffectiveness of the state have received practical confirmation in connection with the growth of the already huge expenses of the state aimed at eliminating the consequences of its inappropriate behavior in the emergency conditions of the exponential spread of the deadly coronavirus. This interpretation is based on the fact that the state, on behalf of society implements the functions of strengthening its integrity and stability of functioning. Moreover, the implementation of this public activity is also carried out at the expense of society. In other words, the state disposes of a significant part of the national income that is created in society and is redistributed by all representatives of society in the form of taxes and other contributions to the revenue side of its budget. With this approach, it becomes obvious that society has paid and is paying all the emergency expenses of national state in connection with the COVID-19 pandemic. Only as of June 2020, governments and international organizations have invested close to $9 trillion to try to prevent the most immediate human and economic losses (World Economic Forum, (2020)). But despite these efforts, the global economy is expected to contract by 3% in 2020, affecting the jobs and livelihoods of millions of people. Thus nature-related risks have precipitated a Great Deceleration and a structural economic crisis.

Moreover, in connection with the fiscal support of households and national business, the state itself becomes a huge problem for society. A massive fiscal response has been necessary to increase health capacity, replace lost household income and prevent large-scale bankruptcies. The ongoing COVID-19 pandemic has already prompted an unprecedented fiscal policy response, which could increase close to $11 trillion worldwide (Gaspar,et al., (2020)). And this is happening against the background of the sharp decline in global output, therefore, of the reduction in budget revenues of national governments. As a result growing expenditures of national governments cause an increase of budget deficits and public debts. Moreover, both living generations and future ones will be forced to pay for the huge obligations of their states. In 2020, relative to the January 2020 *World Economic Outlook*, fiscal deficits are expected to be more than five times higher in advanced economies (AEs) and to more than double in emerging market economies (EMEs), leading to an unprecedented jump in public debt of respectively 26 and 7 percentage points of GDP (Fig. 2).

Figure 2. IMF Forecasts for general government gross debt and fiscal balances for 2020
Source: IMF (2020). World Economic Outlook . January. IMF; Gaspar, Vitor, and Gita Gopinath (2020). Fiscal Policies for a Transformed World. July 10. IMF Blog Insights & Analyses on Economics & Finance
Note: Data are as of June 12, 2020.
a. Advanced economies
b. Emerging market economies
c. Low-income developing countries

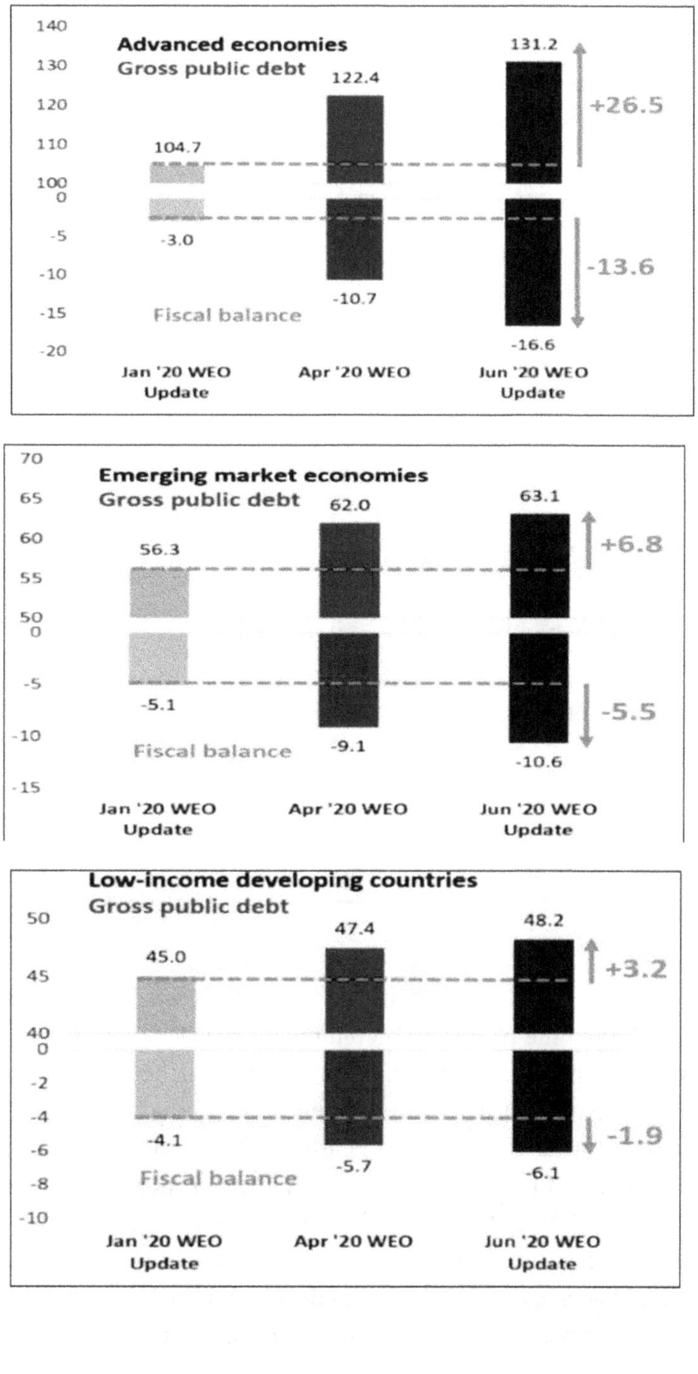

According to preliminary estimates of V. Gaspar and G. Gopinath (Gaspar, (2020)), the global public debt has reached its highest level in recorded history, at 101.5% of Global GDP in 2020 – compared to the post-World War II peaks as well as the highest level ever (Fig. 3).

Figure 3. Soaring public debt for the period 1880-2021 (percent of GDP)
Source: Historical Public Debt Database; IMF World Economic Outlook; Maddison database Project and IMF calculations; IMF (2020). World Economic Outlook . January. IMF; Gaspar, Vitor, and Gita Gopinath (2020). Fiscal Policies for a Transformed World. July 10. IMF Blog Insights & Analyses on Economics & Finance
Note: The aggregate public debt-to-GDP series for advanced and emerging market economies is based on debt-to-GDP data for a constant sample of 25 countries and 27 countries, respectively. The average are calculated using weights derived from GDP in PPP terms.

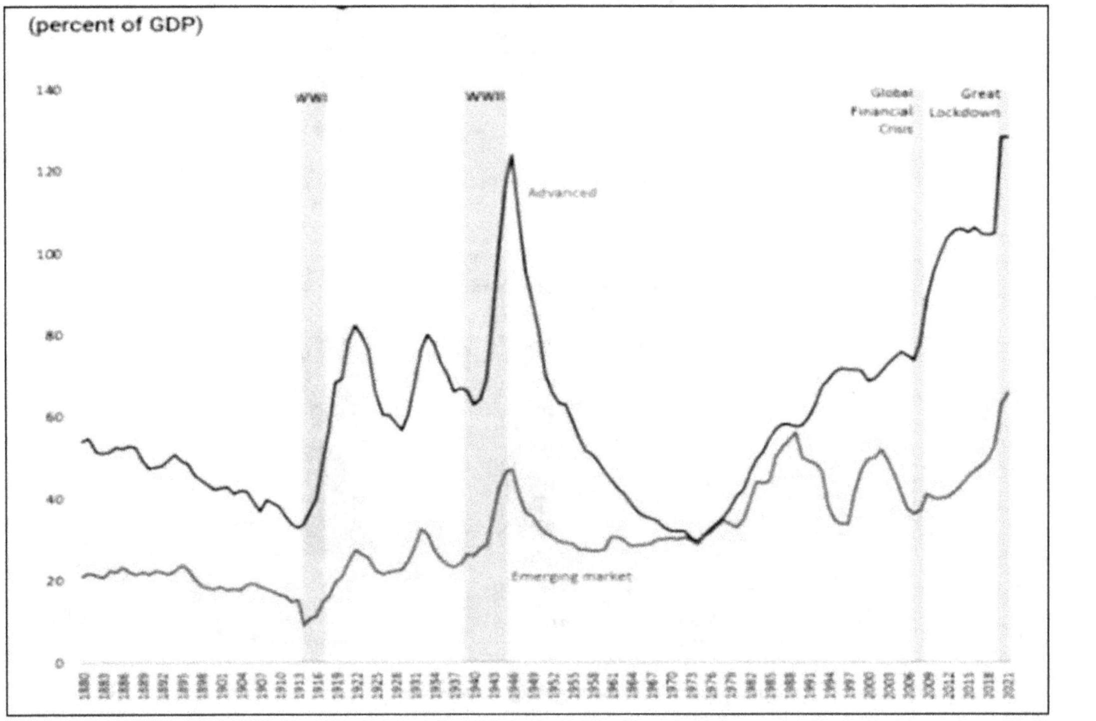

In the absence of a solution to the health crisis, as well as углубляющегося социетального кризиса huge uncertainties remain about the path of the economic recovery. So do the need for increasing fiscal action. The top priority is still public health. Policies that attenuate health risks contribute substantially to the restoration of confidence and trust, thereby helping economic activity and employment and reducing strains on public finances. And going forward, early and targeted containment procedures will have much more limited economic and fiscal costs, as compared to a general lockdown. Once effective vaccine and therapeutics against COVID-19 are widely available, it will be possible to enter a post-COVID world and truly escape the Great Lockdown. That will only be possible if international solidarity allows for access to treatment and vaccines for all people, in developed and developing countries alike. At that stage, governments should redirect fiscal policy toward resilient, sustainable and inclusive growth.

Recovering Missed Opportunities: The State's Focus on Creating the More Inclusive Societal Environment

So the society severely needs deep socio-economic rebuilding on the base clearly expressed the individuals' values. The Covid-19 societal and economic crises bring devastation, but it also brings an opportunity to re-evaluate what kind of a society should be created for future generations. It is about the human-centric system and the state with the health priorities compared to economic benefits. In conditions when the COVID-19 pandemic has not yet ended, it is the state that should evaluate its actions in connection with the stabilization of the epidemiological situation in the country as a serious step towards its rehabilitation in the eyes of society and the return of public confidence and trust. The positive consequences of a successful epinomic policy of states in the categories of lost opportunities can be assessed using the results of the Mckinsey Global Institute experts (Mckinsey Global Institute (2020)). Better health promotes economic growth by expanding the labor force and by boosting productivity as well as by delivering immense social benefits as a basis for eliminating the negative consequences of the societal crisis and restoring societal integrity of the society. Moreover in recent years, a focus on rising healthcare costs, especially in mature economies, has dominated the policy debate. But the health as an investment in national societies has largely been ignored. The COVID-19 pandemic, giving rise to a societal crisis, has put the health system first in the context of its priority for individuals, national societies and economics as well as for the global economic system. This approach makes it possible to assess the missed opportunities for individuals, societies, and economies in the case of effective state policy and prevention of the extreme human and economic losses.

A well-functioning public healthcare system means that over 70% of the gains could be achieved from prevention by creating cleaner and safer environments, encouraging healthier behaviors and addressing the social factors that lie behind these, as well as broadening access to vaccines and preventive medicine. As a result 230 million more people would be alive by 2040 and the welfare value of good health could be as high as $100 trillion. This is a rough estimate of the lost opportunities for society as a result of the failures of the state, which failed to form a highly effective national health system capable of preventing extreme conditions of the COVID-19 pandemic and societal crisis as a manifestation of citizens' distrust of the state. According to the Mckinsey Global Institute evaluations, better health could add $12 trillion to global GDP in 2040, an 8 percent boost that translates into 0.4 percent faster growth every year. About half of these annual economic benefits come from a larger and healthier workforce. The remainder come from expanding the capacity of older people, people with disabilities, and informal caregivers to work as well as from productivity gains as the burden of chronic health conditions is reduced. (Fig. 4)

The economic return could be $2 to $4 for each $1 invested in better health. In higher income countries, implementation costs could be more than offset by productivity gains in healthcare delivery (Fig. 5).

That does not mean capturing the health and economic benefits will be easy. It requires reorienting thinking about and investing in health and healthcare delivery, as well as fostering healthier living conditions and changing behavior. It also requires changes in the workplace and economic policy to allow, among others, increased participation of older people in the workforce. But it's worth. According to early estimates of the Mckinsey Global Institute, the pandemic and its repercussions could lead to a 3 to 8 percent drop in global GDP in 2020 (Mckinsey Global Institute (2020a)). Moreover, each year, poor health reduces global GDP by 15 percent.

Figure 4. Global GDP could rise by about $12 trillion in 2040, an 8 percent increase, mainly from fewer health conditions and expanded participation in the labor force
Source: Mckinsey Global Institute (2020). Prioritizing health: A prescription for prosperity. Executive summary. July.
Note: [1]. Includes impact on older adults (only high- and upper-middle-income countries), informal caregivers (only in OECD), and people with disabilities (global).

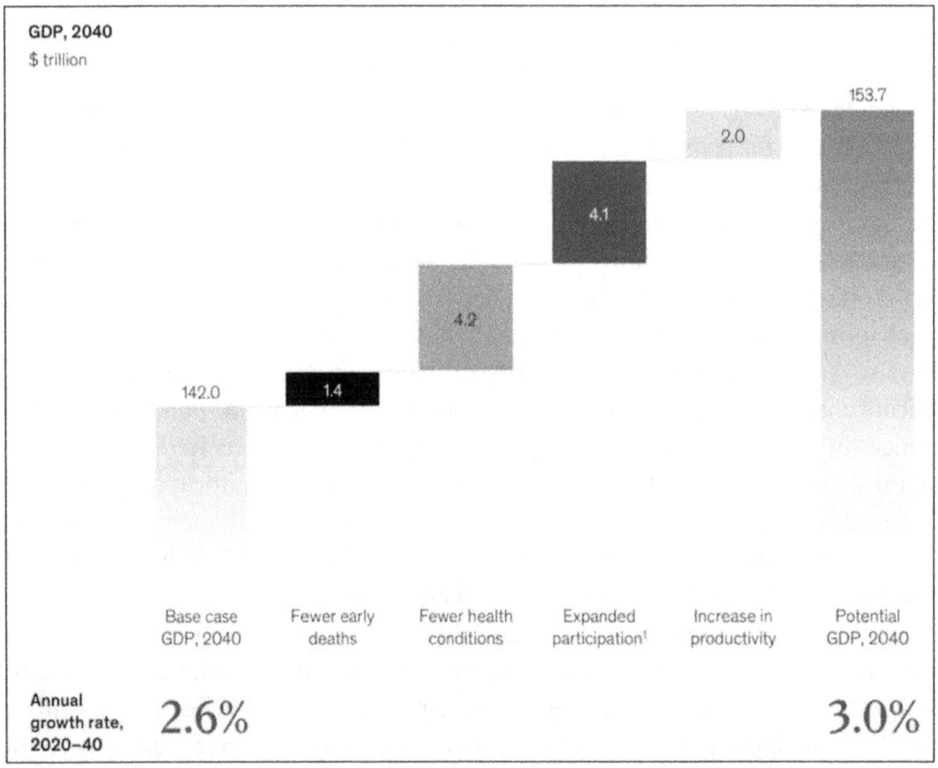

Figure 5. For each $1 invested in improving health, an economic return of $2 to $4 is possible
Source: Source: Mckinsey Global Institute (2020). Prioritizing Health: A Prescription for Prosperity. Executive Summary. July.
Note: Note: Snapshot view of the healthy growth scenario in 2040. Additional healthcare spending, GDP impact, and welfare gains directly attributable to better health only (excluding expanded participation).

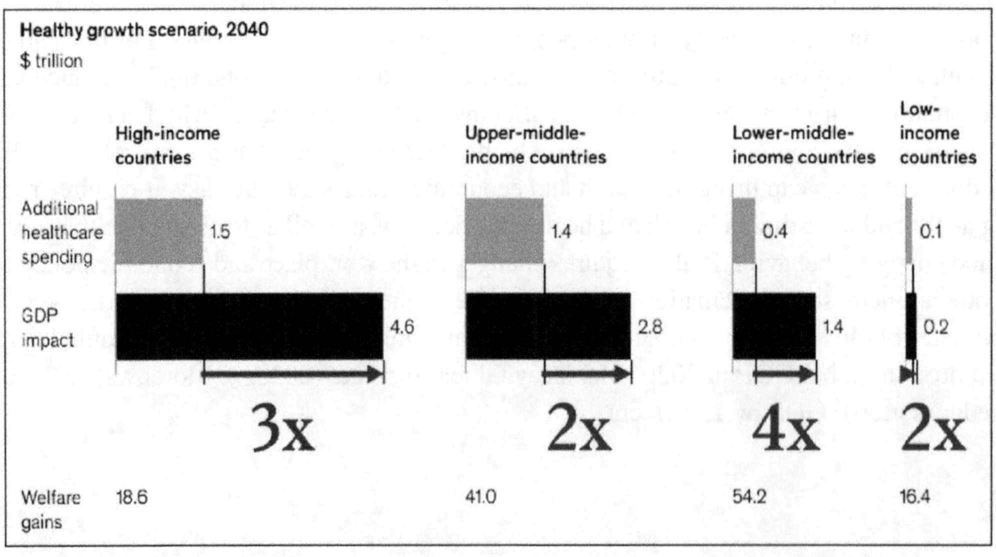

So however tragic and destructive it has been, COVID-19 has placed society at a unique point in time to prioritize health (Fig. 6). Realizing the healthy growth opportunity would require a pivot to prevention both within healthcare systems and beyond. This will not be easy and requires all stakeholders to work together on four imperatives: make health a social and economic priority; keep health on everyone's agenda; transform healthcare systems; and double down on innovation in therapeutics and beyond.

So as countries emerge from the COVID-19 crisis, they meet a once-in-a-generation opportunity to rethink the role of health in a post-pandemic future as well as the quality of the government that could be in a position to fulfil this historic mission. Making health a priority and shifting focus to areas with highest return can improve resilience, reduce health inequity, and promote greater individual, social, and economic well-being. Prevention of diseases is typically less expensive than treatment and reduces the need for more expensive treatment later on, contributing to a high economic return. Capturing the benefits would require dramatic changes that extend beyond what the state typically thinks of as healthcare. It requires substantial changes in where and how healthcare is delivered, as well as changes to communities that would help individuals grow up, work, and age in healthy ways. That means great changes in governments' and regional authorities' way of activities. As to companies, innovators, and communities they need to understand the necessity to shape environments and societies in ways that promote healthy lives and capture the societal and economic benefits. Could there be a better moment to invest in global health to promote well-being and prosperity.

Implementation by the State of Socially Significant Infrastructure Projects as a Prerequisite for the Creation of the More Inclusive Societal Environment

There are a few arguments, which prove that sustainable infrastructure is a key part of rebuilding the post-COVID economy as well as the more inclusive societal environment: the COVID-19 pandemic has shown that access to sustainable infrastructure is far from equitable; investing in sustainable and resilient infrastructure is a critical element of post-pandemic rebuilding economies and health and creating jobs; there are good examples of how to conceive an infrastructure project through the lens of lowering the carbon footprint and integrating ESG principles (The LaGuardia Airport Terminal B reconstruction) (Deau, (2020)).

In other words, if the social and economic lockdown destroyed the structural integrity of socio-economic systems, then only socially significant infrastructure is capable of sharing use of and necessity for the rebuilding a web of collective interdependence, sharing spaces, equity of access and common ground within communities. Developed public infrastructure system refers to the vital physical resources, both public and private, shared by communities in facilitating all aspects our daily lives: transportation (our roads, tunnels, rail lines, airports, bridges); education (schools, universities); health (hospitals, research and testing laboratories, mobile health facilities); civic life (justice centres, government facilities) as well as all of the technology and its related grid that allows us to live, learn, work and circulate every day. And in this sense it is about infrastructure as a core of the post-coronavirus inclusive societal environment (Fig. 7).

This approach includes, among others, moving beyond basic compliance on core labor and human rights standards increase inclusivity, diversity and opportunity for communities and prioritize local recruitment; and using these project platforms to drive local economic development and capacity building, and more broadly improve the quality of life in the surrounding community and region.

Figure 6. The comparison of investment in improving health and economic return (each US$1 invested in improving health / economic return US dollars) in different groups of countries in 2040
Source: Mckinsey Global Institute (2020). Prioritizing health: A prescription for prosperity. Report. July
Note: Snapshot view of the healthy growth scenario in 2040. Additional health spending, GDP impact, and welfare gains directly attributable to better health only (excluding expanded participation).

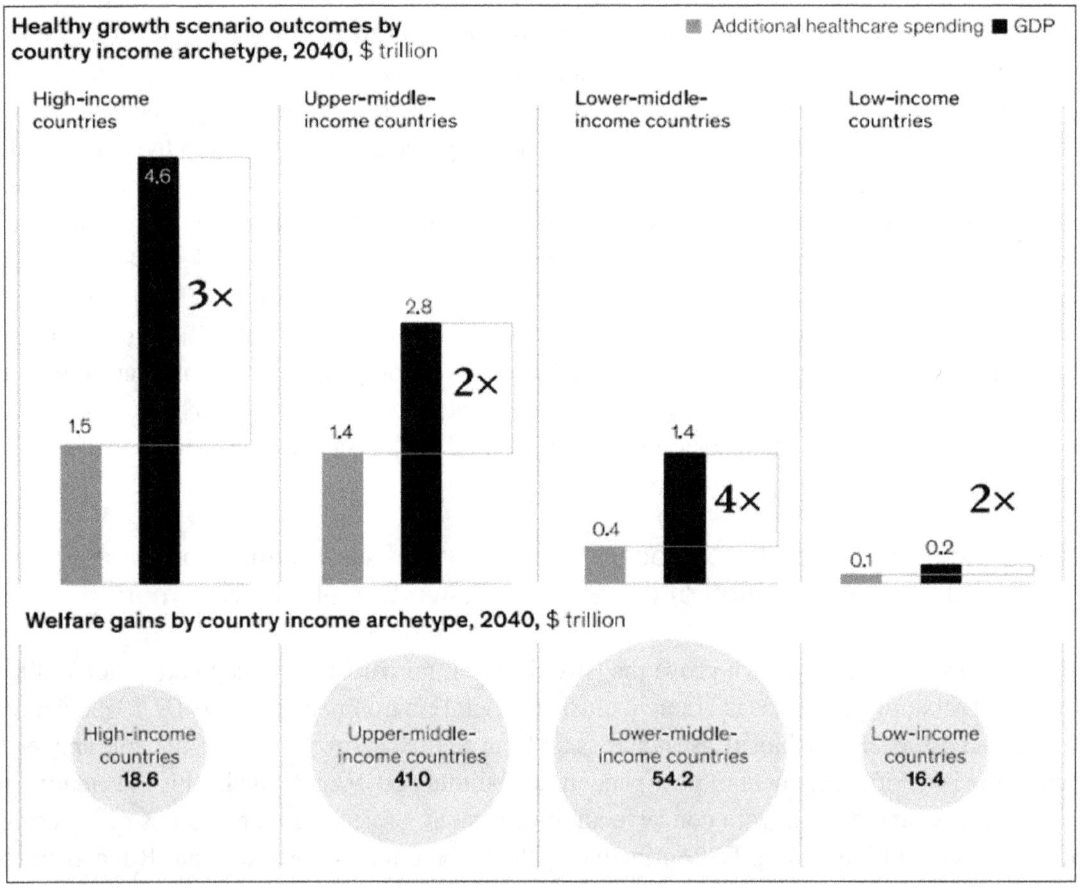

If it is about the uncertainty, then it is the uncertainty surrounding the COVID-19 and its associated health risks has caused many individuals, households, and businesses to opt out of normal activity. Eliminating that uncertainty is essential to restart growth, and to return trust of the households, which is largely predetermined by the development of socially significant infrastructure.

Despite glaring gaps and understood importance of shoring up backbone systems, infrastructure investment actually declined as a share of GDP in 11 of the G20 economies since the global financial crisis of 2008-2009. It was about the European Union, the United States, Russia, and Mexico. By contrast, Canada, Turkey, and South Africa increased investment. If the current trajectory of underinvestment continues, the globe will fall short by roughly 11 percent, or US$350 billion a year. The size of the gap triples if the additional investment required to meet the new UN Sustainable Development Goals is included. So it becomes therefore critical to get finance flowing into urgently needed projects.

Figure 7. The dynamics of the global needs to invest in economic infrastructure for the period of 2016-2030
Source: McKinsey Global Institute (2013). Infrastructure productivity: How to save US$1 trillion a year. McKinsey & Company.
Note: The estimate of total demand is lower than the US$57 trillion projection in previous MGI research. It has been adjusted for the following reasons: the projection covers a 15-year period (2016-2030) rather than an a 18-year period (2013-2030); water numbers have been reduced by 40%, as Global Water Intelligence adjusted its water capital-expenditure definition to exclude equipment spending; base-year prices have been revised from 2010 to 2015; and GDP growth forecasts have been revised downward by IHS.

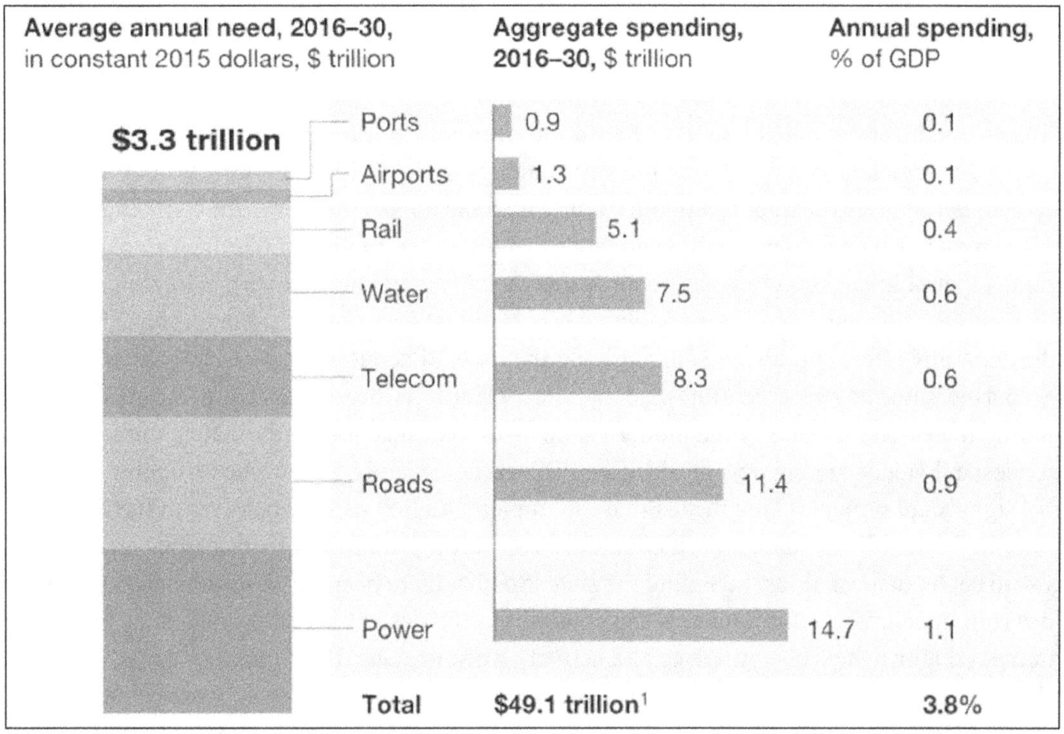

A great deal of attention has focused on connecting institutional investors with projects that need their capital as well as creating an expanded role for public-private partnerships. But the vast majority of infrastructure will likely continue to be financed by the public and corporate sectors.

Even in the face of fiscal concerns, there is substantial scope to increase public infrastructure investment. Governments can increase funding streams by raising user charges, capturing property value, or selling existing assets and recycling the proceeds for new infrastructure. In addition, public accounting standards could be brought in line with corporate accounting so infrastructure assets are depreciated over their life cycle rather than immediately adding to deficits during construction. This change could reduce pro-cyclical public investment behavior.

Corporate finance makes up about three-quarters of private finance. Unleashing investment in privatized sectors requires regulatory certainty and the ability to charge prices that produce an acceptable risk-adjusted return, as well as enablers like spectrum or land access, permits, and approvals. Beyond ramping up finance, there is even bigger potential in making infrastructure spending more efficient and effective. Only improving project selection, delivery, and management of existing assets could translate into 40 percent savings. Virtually every location needs to build expertise and establishing the right organizational structures for developing critical skills and sharing best practices. This effort can pay remarkable dividends, since infrastructure influences the quality of life for citizens everywhere and paves the way to productivity growth and competitiveness.

PPP and the Formalization by the State of Actions on Rebuilding the More Inclusive Societal Environment

The text of this chapter focuses on a deep understanding of the current situation in the world in connection with the COVID-19 pandemic, based on an organic combination of political and economic analysis. This organic connection is emphasized already in the title of the chapter, in which PPP represents a form of business organization and is connected with the economy, but the problem of the formation of the more inclusive societal environment by the state belongs to the field of politics. It is in this aspect that the entire material of the chapter is structured, in which the connection between economic and political analysis is realized. The results obtained are consistent with the findings of Jeffry Frieden (2020), who determines that political economy has become increasingly prominent in both economics and political science in three following ways: (1) in analyzing how political forces affect the economy; (2) in analyzing how the economy affects politics; (3) in applying the tools of economics to study politics.

The partnership between the state and private business is promising from the point of view of eliminating the essential cause of the modern societal crisis, since it is built on the coinciding interests, preferences and values of partners. In addition, PPP refers, as a rule, to long-term, capital-intensive and socially significant projects. This means that the implementation of PPP projects in the field of public goods implies a significant number of stakeholders who, through their actions, transmit consent (disagreement) with each other's actions, including the state. So now there becomes a strong case for PPPs to take a bolder role in addressing the society's major issue. In the case of societal crisis statesmen place the common good above their own interests and actively work to shape the context (Reeves, et al. (2018)).

Public-private partnerships continues to be the dominant procurement option, investment in transport PPPs over the last 25 years has been considerable, adding €203 billion in Europe and US$535 billion in developing countries (Engel, et al. (2020)). According to the available data PPP spending accounts for about 3 percent of global infrastructure spending, and 8 percent of private infrastructure spending (Engel et al. (2014)). Hence, yearly global infrastructure spending is about US$3 trillion, around 5 percentage of world GDP. Around 75 percent of PPP spending is in the transport sector, that is, between US$45 and US$75 billion per year. Another 20 percent of PPP spending finances government services (between US$ 12 and US$ 20 billion per year), while the remainder (between US$3 and US$5 billion per year) is invested in the electricity, telecoms, and water and waste sectors. It follows that PPP spending is only a small fraction of global infrastructure spending: around 3 percent of total world infrastructure spending and around 8 percent of private infrastructure spending.

Private sector participation in building infrastructure and providing infrastructure services could be an important component of a government's infrastructure strategy but goes hand in hand with significantly increased fiscal risks (Schwartz, et al. (2020)). Public-private partnerships can harness private sector innovation and efficiency to improve infrastructure service provision while allowing governments to share project risks with a private partner. But they also usually result in additional debt—both firm and contingent—and are a major source of fiscal risk. E. Bova, and others (2016) estimated that the fiscal cost of contingent liabilities in public private partnerships amounted to 1.2 percent of GDP on average for a sample of 80 advanced economies and emerging markets, with a maximum cost of 2 percent of GDP. In other words, it is difficult to overemphasize the economic aspect of PPP.

On the eve of the COVID-19, the functioning infrastructure of different countries could hardly cope with demand. As for the post-COVID future, while reducing the cost of PPP during a pandemic, the problems will only get worse. Late 2010s the world invested some US$2.5 trillion a year on transportation, power, water, and telecommunications systems. Yet it was not enough—and needs were only growing steeper. The McKinsey Global Institute found that the world needed to invest an average of US$3.3 trillion annually just to support currently expected rates of growth (Fig.7). The partnership between the state and private business is promising from the point of view of eliminating the essential cause of the modern societal crisis, since it is built on the coinciding interests, preferences and values of partners. From viewpoint of the expert of the BCG, there are three priorities that must be priorities for governments around the world (Fig. 8).

Figure 8. The main priorities of the institutional provision of PPP projects by the state, allowing to eliminate the consequences of the societal crisis due to COVID-19 pandemic
Source: Boston Consulting Group analysis

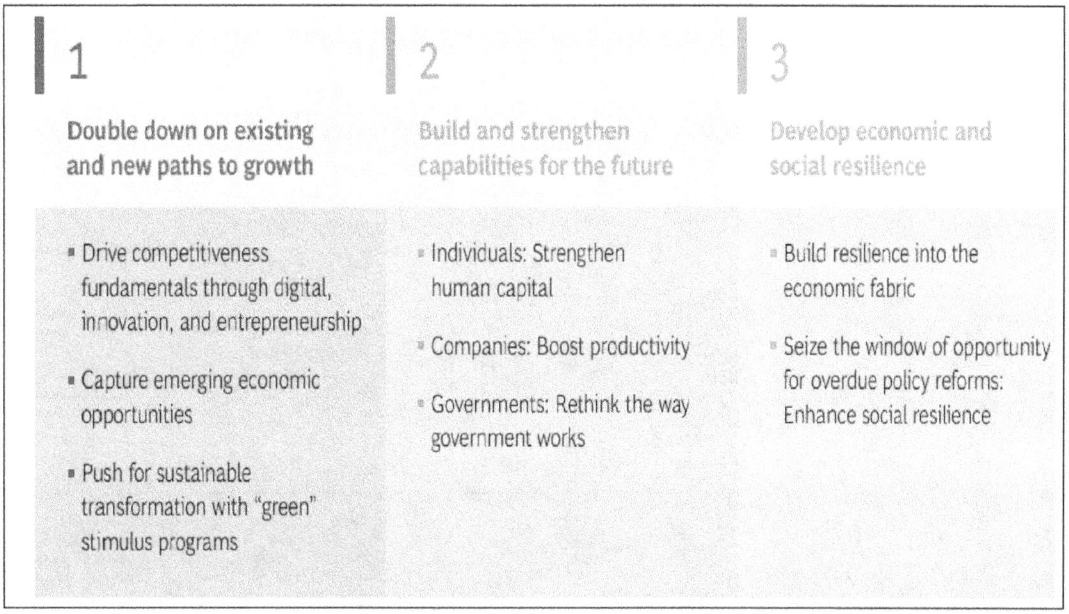

Institutionalization of PPP projects in socially significant areas, in addition to concrete demonstration of a positive effect for citizens, is able to demonstrate to private business that it is increasingly stepping up on sustainability and corporate responsibility. And this is largely due to the growing evidence of a positive link with financial performance. This alignment of finance with corporate responsibility could make a significant contribution to rebuilding the societal integrity in terms of environmental stewardship, workplace conditions, and good governance. In essence corporate responsibility is a long-term maximization of self-interest in which private investors ensure that they don't damage themselves by undermining their own environments.

In other words, the adequate institutionalization by the state of organizational forms for the implementation of PPP projects makes it possible to expand the sphere of coincidence of the priorities of firms (as well as their employees), society and the state. This is where the state policy is being implemented, aimed at minimizing the negative consequences of the societal crisis. Corporate responsibility is fundamentally about individual values and actions, in ways that are compatible with common interest. In other words, it means "doing well by doing good" within an existing policy of fighting the societal crisis caused by COVID-19 shock (Fig. 9).

Figure 9. Fighting the social crisis as institutionalization of the coinciding interests of private business and the state in organizing PPP infrastructure projects
Source: Brimmer, Amanda, Vincent Chin, Patrick Hayden, Troy Thomas, Alexander Türpitz, and Yvonne Zhou (2020). Beyond the Curve. How to Restart in the Wake of COVID-19. The Boston Consulting Group's Henderson Institute. April.

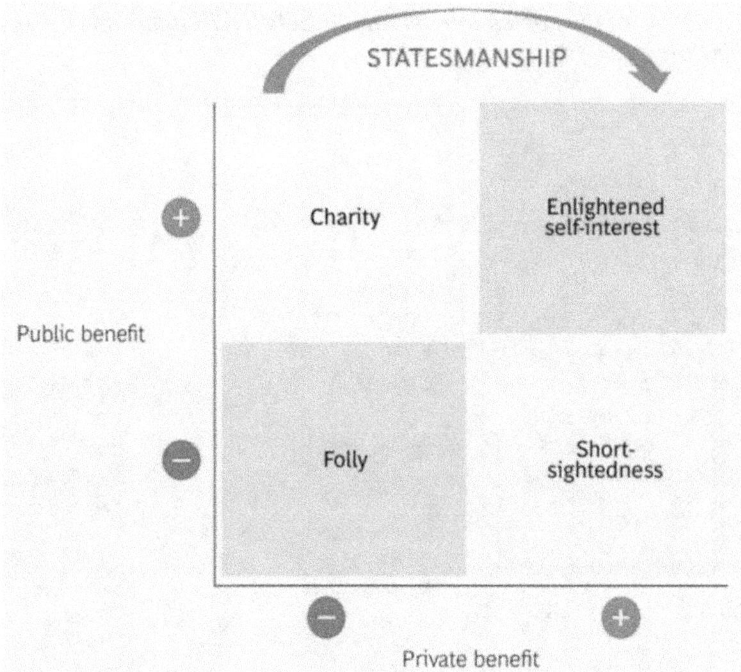

The PPPs specifics due to the dialectic of interaction between the state and private business and the variety of operations with public goods are determined by the functions and fiscal capabilities of the state in society. This is due to the fact that, firstly, the state combines subjective and objective principles; secondly, it institutionalizes the activities of both market agents and business entities acting on behalf of the state; thirdly, in fact, it "uncontrollably" redistributes to its budget a significant part of the national income created by society; fourthly, it follows its own norms of behaviour contrary to the implementation of the function of maximizing public utility, fifthly, it introduces conflict into its relations with society and citizens as a result of inadequate aggregation of individual values in public choice, which, sixthly, it orients all claims of society and citizens to the state for its inability to deal effectively with the crisis caused by COVID-19. Given all these circumstances, it should be emphasized that PPP projects are implemented on conditions dictated by the state.

According to the Boston Consulting Group experts, "those that do will navigate more effectively through the current crisis—will be ready for the next one" (Carrasco, et al. (2020)). For these purposes, it is necessary to prioritize the need to develop policy solutions for the societal crisis at the end of the first wave of the COVID-19 pandemic. First, one should take into account the specifics of formal institutions that mediate the dialectics of interaction between mechanisms for the implementation of socially significant norms of behavior, on the one hand, and punishment for their violation, on the other. Secondly, it is necessary for the state to recognize the phenomenon of social integrity of society as key in any conditions, including the emergency situation with COVID-19 and an understanding that its achievement is possible only with the dominance of the first of the two mechanisms of institutionalizing structural ties in national communities. It is these provisions that should be taken into account by the state when making political decisions in the epinomics. However, these decisions will have an effect with a lag in time, since they should be preceded by the state's awareness of the objective need to revise its role in the institutionalization of structural ties in society. For the effect to be achieved, it is necessary to focus on the constructive (and not destructive) potential of formal institutions. First of all, it is about the adequacy of assessing the individual values of citizens and their families, them as members of society, as employees of firms, as active participants in social interactions, as voters, etc. Having limited itself to the dominant individual priorities, the state must understand the reasons for their differences in understanding by citizens and society, as well as provide an expert assessment of the set of public actions and the specific characteristics of formal institutions that will cause an increase in the sphere of coincidence of individual and socially significant preferences. And it is necessary to understand that the slightest mistake is fraught with significant social and economic losses. Formal institutions modelled by the state should be tested in a systemically important area. And only if successful - the restoration of citizens' loyalty to the policies of national governments - can they be implemented on a large scale, focusing on the successful resolution of the societal crisis caused by the coronavirus pandemic.

So the COVID-19 crisis renews focus on issues that are structural and economic—that transcend the personal and the political ones. Many of those problems could have been addressed a long time ago as well as the tools and techniques. But the COVID-19 pandemic has become the right time to look forward and to begin the hard work of rebuilding national societies and economies for the bright post-COVID days ahead. The resolution of the societal crisis is in many respects consonant with the implementation of the UN people-first model that is meant to be consistent with the Sustainable Development Goals (SDGs). So the public-private partnerships would be made "fit for purpose" and oriented towards meeting the needs of "people-first". In this case the UN people-first model stipulates five desirable outcomes (UN-5) that can be applied to infrastructure PPP projects (Fig. 10).

RESULTS AND DISCUSSION

So the strong economic recovery based on the restored societal unity of the society will benefit everyone if it depends on improved social safety nets and adequate forms of PPPs organization (Pranov, et al. (2019)). In this case, it is necessary to be aware of serious financial problems that can only be solved on the basis of broad-based fiscal partnership. This includes mixed public-private investment in health care, infrastructure, and climate change (IMF (2020a)). This is not an easy task. Policymakers should choose how to invest for the future in a fiscally prudent way, adopt well-planned discretionary policies to stimulate demand, and enhance social safety nets and unemployment benefits (Gaspar, et al. (2020a)).

Figure 10. UN-5 People-first Outcomes
Source: UN, World Economic Forum's Global Future Council

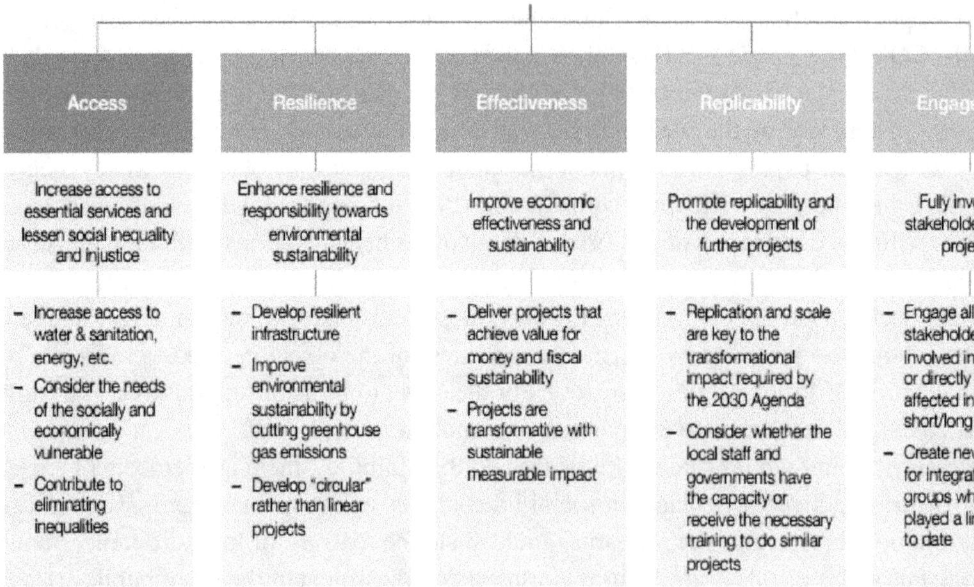

The authors present an experimental model of the institutional matrix (forthcoming Vaslavskiy, et al. (2020). "Institutional matrices: modelling of organizational forms of Public-Private Partnership"), which can be a form of application of the specified parameters of the planned PPP project.

Good infrastructure that fosters and supports economic and human development is a key to growing the economy, creating wealth, and reducing inequalities (Schwartz, et al. (2020)). With the COVID-19 pandemic and its economic fallout, creating good infrastructure through strong infrastructure governance are more important than ever and key to supporting economic recovery. It becomes evident that most countries will find it challenging to meet key public investment needs. A variety of options—raising more revenues, borrowing more, cutting unproductive spending, or getting more private-sector participation—can help to increase infrastructure spending. But all the alternatives have limitations and are insufficient on their own.

Losses and waste in public investment are often systemic. On average, more than one-third of the resources spent on creating and maintaining public infrastructure are lost because of inefficiencies (Fig. 11) (Baum, et al. (2020)). On average, countries waste on average about 1/3 of their infrastructure spending due to inefficiencies (Schwartz, et al. (2020)). These inefficiencies are closely linked to poor infrastructure governance— defined as the institutions and frameworks for planning, allocating, and implementing infrastructure investment spending. Estimates suggest that, on average, better infrastructure governance could make up more than half of the observed efficiency losses (Baum, et al. (2020)). More than two-thirds of the deviations originated from the planning and allocation stages and happened because of government actions or inactions related to, for example, unrealistic costing, expansion of project scope, inadequate coordination across levels of government, or weaknesses in appraisals (Fig. 12). Deviations originating from the implementation stage, which includes procurement, construction, and operation of infrastructure assets, were more diverse, emanating not only from government actions or inactions, but also from factors outside government control, such as project- and market-related risks or force majeure.

Figure 11. Countries waste anywhere from 30 up to 50% of the money spent on infrastructure
Source: Schwartz, Gerd, Manal Fouad, Torben Hansen, and Geneviève Verdier (eds.) (2020). Well Spent: How Strong Infrastructure Governance Can End Waste in Public Investment. Washington, DC: International Monetary Fund

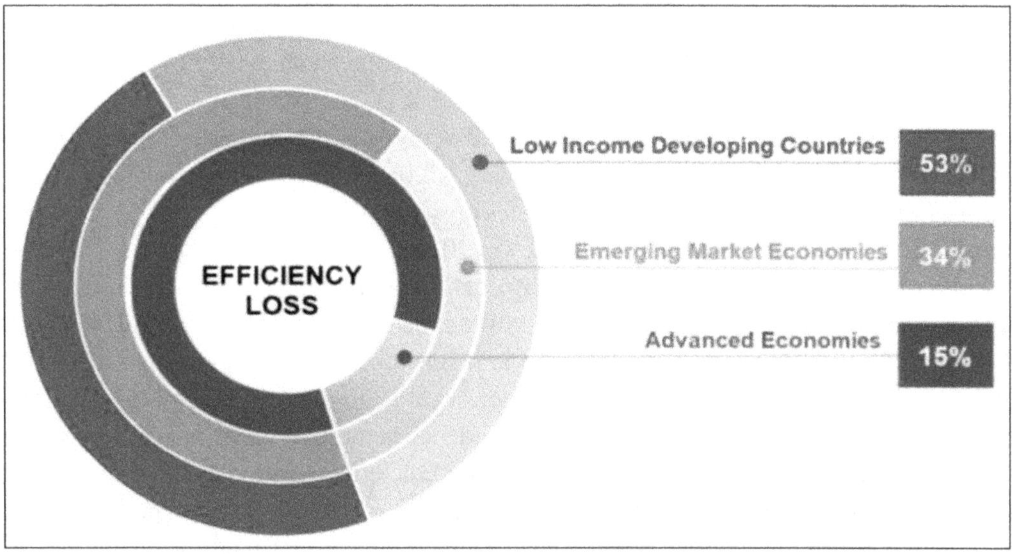

Figure 12. Sources of fiscal risks in realizing infrastructure PPP projects
Source: Monteiro, Rui, Isabel Rial, and Eivind Tandberg (2020). Fiscal risks in infrastructure. In: Schwartz, Gerd, Manal Fouad, Torben Hansen, and Geneviève Verdier, eds. (2020). Well Spent: How Strong Infrastructure Governance Can End Waste in Public Investment. Washington, DC: International Monetary Fund
Note: Percentage is calculated based on the number of projects in the sample (n = 20)

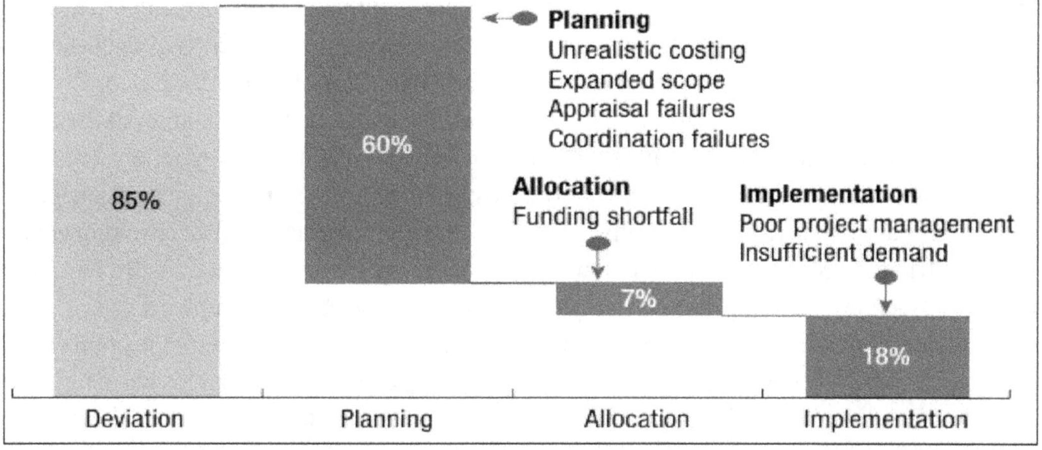

In the wake of *Great Lockdown* and the COVID-19 pandemic, more infrastructure investment and strong infrastructure governance are likely to become even more important, because with economic growth turning negative, public investment will have to be part of stimulating weak aggregate demand (IMF (2020), IMF (2020b)). Public investment can increase demand in the short term and productivity in the long term, sometimes even with limited increases in indebtedness, if spending is done efficiently (IMF (2014), IMF (2015)). Many advanced economies have aging infrastructures and see urgent spending needs for their upkeep and modernization. For example, in the United States, the American Society of Civil Engineers (2017) estimates cumulative spending needs of more than US$10 trillion through 2040 to maintain, repair, or rebuild existing infrastructure. In Europe, in November 2014 the European Commission announced an Infrastructure Investment Plan to unlock more than €315 billion for investment spending. In the same year, the IMF (2014) called for the spending push to help support both short-term demand shortfalls and longer-term development needs (OECD. 2019)).

Under Japan's presidency in 2019, the Group of Twenty (G20) established a set of quality infrastructure investment (QII) principles (Group of Twenty (G20). (2019)), building upon earlier principles established by the Group of Seven (G7) under Japan's presidency in 2016 (Group of Seven (G7) (2016)) and endorsed by the G20 under China's presidency in 2016.

So the numerous experts concluded that PPP projects in any field, especially in infrastructure, should either be very well prepared by the state, or they will not be effective. Moreover, only in the first case the technology of attracting private investment to implement capital-intensive long-term projects will work. But after the COVID-19 the state could be not in a position to provide full budget financing. It turns out that the conditions dictated by the state depend on whether there will be a quality infrastructure after COVID-19 and whether it will have a positive economic effect. National states associate the post-Great Lockdown future with bringing forward rather than the postponement or cancellation of projects to support employment and economic growth. But for this it is necessary to eliminate the consequences of the negative impact that the current economic crisis will most likely affect PPPs. It is about (1) the additional costs for all PPP projects, particularly those that are operational, mostly due to disinfection of equipment and facilities, and workforce shortages; (2) the decreasing revenue of user-funded PPP projects, particularly transportation and energy projects, due to the much-reduced demand; (3) specific challenges to projects that are in the construction phase, such as construction delays and supply chain disruption.

Estimates confirm that there is substantial scope for improving public investment efficiency in most countries (Baum, et al. (2020)). In Figure 13 there are presented the estimations of the investment efficiency for up to 164 countries (using various efficiency score estimation methods) as well as the results. The estimated median efficiency gap is large because over one-third of resources are lost in the public investment process. The gap ranges between 33 percent for the data envelopment analysis estimation and 43 percent for the stochastic frontier analysis (adjusted for skewness), with wide variation across countries around this overall range. Efficiency varies widely across income groups and regions. In general, the size of the gap shrinks as income rises. For example, as shown in Figure 13, panel 1 (data envelopment analysis, non-adjusted efficiency scores), on average, low-income developing countries face an efficiency gap of 53 percent, while emerging markets have a gap of 34 percent, and advanced economies a gap of 15 percent. The range between top and bottom performers declines as income rises. Inefficiencies in public investment spending are therefore substantial. This is a non-negligible source of wasted resources when needs are high and fiscal space is limited, as in the midst of lockdowns. Better infrastructure governance would raise the efficiency of public investment spending and improve infrastructure outcomes. Adopting the public investment practices of best performers could help countries to close about half their efficiency gap.

In this situation, it becomes obvious that, all other things being equal, the adequate use of formal institutions in the hands of the state can give quite tangible economic effect. It is about the professionalism of the state in context of adequate institutionalization of the conditions for the implementation of infrastructure PPP projects, excluding corruption of the top power, reducing the area of shadow business, minimizing socio-economic inequality of citizens and aimed at understanding the value orientations of citizens doomed to poverty due to COVID-19.

Figure 13. Public capital and infrastructure performance: hybrid public investment efficiency score by income level

Source: Anja Baum, Tewodaj Mogues, and Geneviève Verdier (2020) Getting the Most from Public Investment In: Schwartz, Gerd, Manal Fouad, Torben Hansen, and Geneviève Verdier, eds. 2020. Well Spent: How Strong Infrastructure Governance Can End Waste in Public Investment. Washington, DC: International Monetary Fund

Note: Each box shows the median and the 25th and 75th percentiles, and the whiskers show the nonlinear maximum and minimum values. Scores range between 0 and 1. The average efficiency gap is computed as the mean percentage difference between the highest and the average efficiency scores. The four panels reflect different combinations of two aspects in the efficiency score derivation methodology.

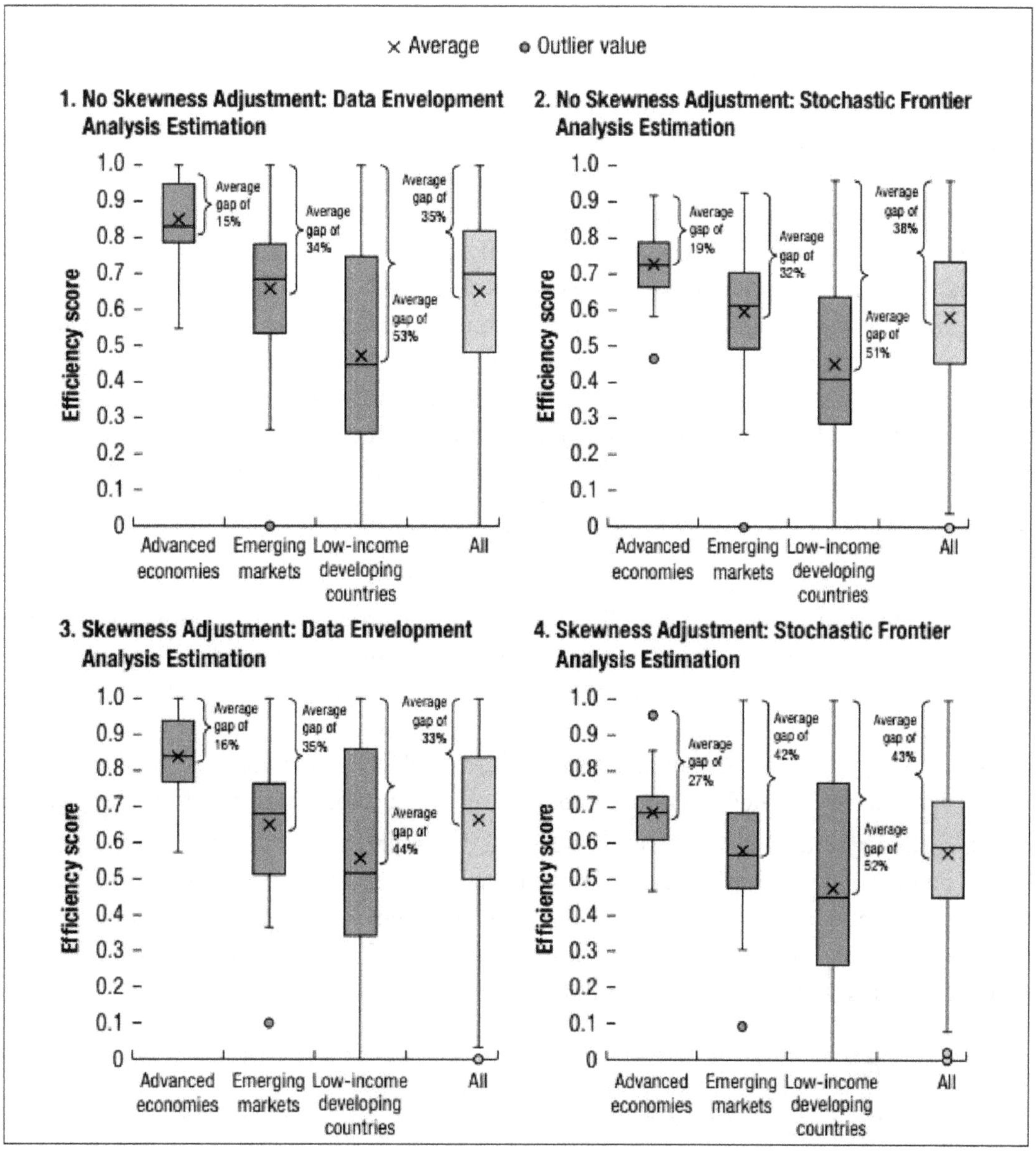

In other words, in the context of the coronavirus pandemic, the state should direct formal institutions, first of all, when implementing capital-intensive socially significant infrastructure PPPs, to create an adequate the more inclusive societal environment. This will reduce the area of distribution of informal institutions that provide irrational antisocial behavior of economic agents. Only this will allow the state to regain the confidence (trust) of citizens, to cooperate joint efforts to reopen the economy in the context of the coronavirus pandemic.

Empirical Evidence

So in the post-COVID-19 future, infrastructure projects can become an effective form of implementation of the UN "human-first" model, since they allow solving the immediate problems of ordinary citizens mostly affected in 2020. It is about the growth of employment, the provision of workforce wages, the development of socially significant infrastructure which contribution to the economic revival of countries can hardly be overestimated. At the same time, the government through PPP gets the opportunity to directly broadcast to society the results of the effectiveness of its epinomic strategy in stabilizing the epidemiological situation and reopening the economy after the lockdown

So the choice of adequate form of PPP organization for implementing socially significant projects as priority actions of the state aimed at restoring the citizens' self-confidence. The authors' approach to the theoretical characterization of PPP forms implies the need to include all the basic types of their organization: quasi-market, hierarchical and hybrid, as well as all of their many modifications. And that is the broad interpretation of public-private partnerships (International Monetary Fund (2020)). Each individual basic type of PPP organization (its institutional matrix) contains many potential sub-options for its reproduction.

In the matrix construction of PPP organization forms, the author limited them to three basic structures (quasi-market, hierarchical, and hybrid). To simplify the construction of the institutional matrix, the author used its square version with three rows and three columns. Let matrix ***A*** represent the preferences of the private partner when choosing PPP organizational forms for the implementation of a transaction with the public good (Vaslavskiy, et al. (2019)). Each element of the row of matrix A indicates the preference of a private business for a particular form of PPP organization. The final preference of a private partner will be indicated with the symbol $\boldsymbol{a}_{ij}$, and their modifications - from the quasi-market to hierarchical and hybrid - will vary from 1 to 2 and 3 depending on transaction costs per line (index ***i***, ***i*** = 1, 2, 3) and depending from delegation of ownership of property in columns (index ***j***, ***j*** = 1, 2, 3). Then the elements of the row with the number ***i*** can be represented as $(\boldsymbol{a}_{i1}, \boldsymbol{a}_{i2}, \boldsymbol{a}_{i3})$, and the elements of column number ***j*** – $(\boldsymbol{a}_{1j}, \boldsymbol{a}_{2j}, \boldsymbol{a}_{3j})$. The following is a matrix ***A*** of preferences of a private partner with respect to PPP organization forms in the form (1)

$$\boldsymbol{A} = \begin{pmatrix} a_{11} & a_{12} & a_{13} \\ a_{21} & a_{22} & a_{23} \\ a_{31} & a_{32} & a_{33} \end{pmatrix} \tag{1}$$

Arguing in a similar way, the author constructs matrix ***B*** (2) taking into account the interests of the state in relation to the forms of organization of PPPs and designates them with a symbol $\boldsymbol{b}_{ij}$, and their modifications - from the quasi-market to hierarchical and hybrid - will vary from 1 to 2 and 3 depending on transaction costs per line (index индекс i, i = 1, 2, 3) and depending from delegation of ownership of property in columns (index j, j = 1, 2, 3). Accordingly, the rows of the matrix B are denoted by (b_{i1}, b_{i2}, b_{i3}), and the columns - by (b_{1j}, b_{2j}, b_{3j}).

$$\boldsymbol{B} = \begin{pmatrix} b_{11} & b_{12} & b_{13} \\ b_{21} & b_{22} & b_{23} \\ b_{31} & b_{32} & b_{33} \end{pmatrix} \tag{2}$$

The final "institutional matrix" C (3) is a form of PPP organization, regarding which the preferences of the state and its private partner coincide. For this purpose the matrices A and B are multiplied, and the rows and columns of the resulting "institutional matrix" C (3) are obtained below:

$$\boldsymbol{C} = \begin{pmatrix} a_{11} & a_{12} & a_{13} \\ a_{21} & a_{22} & a_{23} \\ a_{31} & a_{32} & a_{33} \end{pmatrix} \times \begin{pmatrix} b_{11} & b_{12} & b_{13} \\ b_{21} & b_{22} & b_{23} \\ b_{31} & b_{32} & b_{33} \end{pmatrix}. \tag{3}$$

As a result, below there are the rows and columns of the final "institutional matrix" C (4):

$$\boldsymbol{C} = \begin{pmatrix} c_{11} & c_{12} & c_{13} \\ c_{21} & c_{22} & c_{23} \\ c_{31} & c_{32} & c_{33} \end{pmatrix}, \tag{4}$$

where

$$\boldsymbol{c}_{ij} = \boldsymbol{a}_{i1}\boldsymbol{b}_{1j} + \boldsymbol{a}_{i2}\boldsymbol{b}_{2j} + \boldsymbol{a}_{i3}\boldsymbol{b}_{3j}. \tag{5}$$

Thus, matrix (4) is a set of alternative forms of organizing PPPs ("institutional matrices") of its three basic options (quasi-market, hierarchical, and hybrid), for which the preferences of PPP partners — public and private — coincided. This is the logic of constructing a simple matrix model, which can be applied to any institutional matrix that describes PPPs under the condition of a certain meaningful filling of its cells.

CONCLUSION

The solution to the problems of the societal and economic crises caused by COVID-19 largely depends on the effectiveness of the state based on the restoration of interaction and mutual trust between the state and society. The essential problem of the effectiveness of formal institutions in the hands of the state in the context of eliminating the negative consequences of the societal crisis comes to the fore.

This becomes possible only if the state has a priority focus on creating the more inclusive societal environment. This presupposes the replacement of the redistributive fiscal functions of the state with its mission to professionally assess the value preferences of households that dominate in society and find effective institutional solutions in the mechanism of aggregating public choice. At the same time, private business is becoming a priority structural level that allows the state to work out its practical solutions in the field of restoring the societal integrity of society, since it is the private business that fully represents the interests of numerous stakeholders. In this context, PPP is an adequate platform for testing formal institutions that allow the state to assess the preferences and values of private investors, expand the area of their coincidence with the priorities of state policy, and thus lay the foundations for the more inclusive societal environment.

The latter is most feasible on the example of the sphere of public goods as a priority area of partnership between the state and private business. After COVID-19, the state is forced to consider budgetary constraints and make informed choices among possible forms of "alliances" between the state and private investors. In this case, both the traditional goals of minimizing transaction costs and increasing the efficiency of transactions with public goods, and the time parameters for obtaining socially significant results should be taken into account. The institutional matrix proposed by the authors allows the state to vary the forms of PPP organization, taking into account the combination of preferences of private investors and of the public sector. The variety of forms of PPPs allow the state and private business to optimize the sharing of risks and the burden of expenses as the capabilities of the public segment expand, as well as in the process of creating optimal "rules of the game", conditions and effective incentives to maximize the potential of the national economy.

The success of PPPs on the phase of "fighting" the COVID-19 pandemic largely depends on how much the technology of attracting private investment to the implementation of capital-intensive long-term projects could work. Investments in infrastructure give a quick result in the economy recovering, as jobs are immediately created in construction and industry, and employment growth helps support consumer demand. But most importantly, short-term increase in demand is followed by long-term multiplier effects. In order to achieve these goals everything should be done to create a trust driven recovery environment that is collaborative and partner and stakeholder friendly. National governments should review infrastructure PPP projects in the sectors most affected by the crisis - airports, ports, roads, transport, and energy - to understand demand- and supply-side impacts. At the same time, the paramount importance of creating a national health system capable of promptly taking preventive measures and working to prevent the devastating consequences of infections such as COVID-19 is not discussed. In any case the primary problems that need to be resolved as soon as possible include obtaining an adequate assessment by states of the effectiveness of contractual provisions on PPP projects, expert consideration of restructuring and coordination of sources of contract financing, review of contracts and problem asset management tools. This should be done in discussion of the governments and their private partners and other relevant stakeholders such as financiers and regulators.

As a result of the restoration of social consensus, a significant macroeconomic effect can be obtained. According to the Economic Policy Institute (USA), every US $ 100 billion spent on infrastructure PPP projects leads to the creation of approximately 1 million jobs (full-time), and every dollar invested in transport infrastructure makes an additional contribution to the country's economic growth by the level of US $ 1.5-2 dollars due to the development of trade, activation of business processes in the regions of the country and increasing the mobility of the population. (InfraOne (2020)).

At the same time, the growth of implemented socially significant PPP projects will outwardly demonstrate the professional level of the state and testify to their focus on solving the problems of ordinary citizens. And vice versa: its absence or low rates of involvement of private investors in joint projects with the state will indicate the state's unprofessionalism and inadequate institutionalization of PPP. In fact, it is about the ability of the state to create the more inclusive societal environment. The latter is a fundamental condition for the restoration of societal integrity in the post-coronavirus reality. This can be achieved subject to a change in focus in the organization of PPP projects. Before COVID-19, the state paternalism was typical in everything, since the financial support of socially significant projects was fully or largely provided by budget funds of the state. Consequently, the role of private investors was reduced, rather, to the role of a junior partner in importance. In these conditions, the state tried to neglect the value orientations of partners as insignificant, which largely explains the increase in financial risks and a significant excess of the initial project estimates.

In the context of the coronavirus pandemic, the state is forced to reorganize to adequate institutionalization of the priorities of private partners through the professional use of the formal institutions' potential. The emphasis in the processes of formalizing PPP projects should be shifted from the punishment to the specification of socially acceptable norms of behavior. This actually means creating the more inclusive societal environment for the implementation of private business partnerships with the state. In other words, the resolution of the societal crisis must begin with a change in the functions of the state itself, i.e. their switching from fiscal priorities to value ones related to preferences, for example, of private business as a partner in PPP projects.

REFERENCES

American Society of Civil Engineers. (2017). *Failure to Act: Closing the Infrastructure Investment Gap for America's Economic Future*. American Society of Civil Engineers.

Baum, Mogues, & Verdier. (2020). Getting the most from public investment. In *Well Spent: How Strong Infrastructure Governance Can End Waste in Public Investment*. Washington, DC: International Monetary Fund.

Baxter, D. (2020). *PPP and COVID-19*. 3rd Co-Webinar.

Boston Consulting Group. (2020). *COVID-19: Win the Fight, Win the Future*. Featured Insights. April. BCG.

Boston Consulting Group Perspectives. (2020). *COVID-19: Facts, scenarios, and actions for leaders*. Version 2.2. BCG.

Bova, E., Ruiz-Aranz, M., Toscani, F., & Elif Ture, H. (2016). *The fiscal costs of contingent liabilities: a new dataset*. IMF Working Paper 16/14, International Monetary Fund.

Carrasco, Chandran, Chin, Hayden, Hoteit, Subudhi, & Werfe. (2020). *Start Reimaging Government Now*. Boston Consulting Group.

Déau, T. (2020). *Why Sustainable Infrastructure is a Key Part of Rebuilding the Post-COVID Economy*. World Economic Forum.

Engel, E., Fischer, R., & Galetovic, A. (2014). *Finance and Public-Private Partnerships: A Roadmap.* Background paper for the Global Financial Development Report of the World Bank.

Engel, Fischer, & Galetovic. (2020). *When and how to use public-private partnerships in infrastructure: lessons from the international experience.* NBER Working Paper 26766. Retrieved from: https://www.nber.org/papers/w26766

Frieden, J. (2020). The political economy of economic policy. *Finance & Development, 57*(2), 6-7.

Gaspar & Gopinath. (2020a). *Fiscal Policies for a Transformed World.* Insights & Analyses on Economics & Finance.

Gaspar, Raphael, & Mehdi. (2020). *Fiscal Policies for the Recovery from COVID-19.* Insights & Analyses on Economics & Finance.

Gjaja, Hutchinson, Farber, Brimmer, & Kahn. (2020). *Three Paths to the Future.* Boston Consulting Group Analysis.

Group of Seven (G7). (2016). *G7 Ise-Shima Principles for Promoting Quality Infrastructure Investment.* G7 Ise-Shima Leaders' Declaration.

Group of Twenty (G20). (2019). *G20 Principles for Quality Infrastructure Investment.* G20 Osaka Leaders' Declaration.

IMF. (2014). *Legacies, Clouds, Uncertainties.* World Economic Outlook. October.

IMF. (2015). *Making Public Investment More Efficient.* IMF.

IMF. (2020). The Great Lockdown. World Economic Outlook.

IMF. (2020a). What is the COVID-19 crisis impact on public-private partnerships. Public Financial Management Blog of IMF.

IMF. (2020b). Policies to Support People During the COIVD-19 Pandemic. Fiscal Monitor.

InfraOne. (2020). *Investment in infrastructure: the project market in crisis. Analytical Overview. InfraOne Research.* InfraOne.

International Monetary Fund. (2020). Policies to Support People During the COVID-19 Pandemic. Fiscal Monitor. IMF.

Korchakova-Heeb. (2020). *We Are Building An Airplane While Flying It.* BCG.

McKinsey Global Institute. (2020). *Prioritizing health: A prescription for prosperity.* Executive summary. Author.

Milanovich, B. (2019). *Capitalism, Alone. The Future of the System That Rules the World.* The Belknap Press of Harvard University Press. doi:10.4159/9780674242852

Musgrave, R. (1988). The role of the state in the fiscal theory. In P. B. Sorensen (Ed.), *Public Finance in a Changing World* (p. 105). Macmillan.

OECD. (2019). *Growth Is Taking a Dangerous Downward Turn*. Ecoscope Blog, September 19. Retrieved from: https://oecdecoscope.blog/2019/09/19/growth-is-taking-a-dangerous-downward-turn/.

Pilipenko, O. I., & Pilipenko, A. I. (2020). Mysteries of unsustainable public finance and of low economic growth. In M. Ziolo (Ed.), *Social, Economic, and Environmental Impacts Between Sustainable Financial Systems and Financial Markets*. IGI Global. doi:10.4018/978-1-7998-1033-9.ch009

Pranov B.M., & Rassokhina T.V. (2019). Methodological approaches to the adaptation of the system of global indicators of achieving the goals in the field of sustainable development in the Russian Federation. *Modern Economy Success, 1,* 19-152.

Reeves, M., Kell, G., & Hassan, F. (2018). The Case for Corporate Statesmanship. The Boston Consulting Group. Henderson Institute.

Schwaerzler, Henderon, Patel, Manetti, Chin, Rathore, Mahmoudi, & Osman. (2020). *Beyond the Curve. How Governments Can Galvanize their Nations for the Rebound.* Boston Consulting Group.

Susskind, D. (2020). How will the world be different after COVID-19? *Finance & Development. A Quarterly Publication of the IMF*, *57*(2), 26-27.

Tanzi, V. (2011). *Government versus Markets: The Changing Economic Role of the State.* Cambridge: Syndicate of the Press of the University of Cambridge.

Vaslavskiy, Y., & Vaslavskaya, I. (2019). *Public-private partnership: institutional approach*. Aspect Press.

Vaslavsky, Y., & Vaslavskaya, I. (2019). Infrastructure public-private partnership projects: budget consolidation policy in Russia and government expenditures' efficiency increase. In B. S. Sergi (Ed.), *Modeling Economic Growth in Contemporary Russia* (pp. 199–228). Emerald Publishing. doi:10.1108/978-1-78973-265-820191007

World Economic Forum. (2017). *The Inclusive Growth and Development Report.* Geneva: WEF.

World Economic Forum. (2019). *Transforming Infrastructure: Frameworks for Bringing the Forth Industrial Revolution to Infrastructure*. Community Paper. Geneva: WEF.

World Economic Forum. (2020). *The Future of Nature and Business*. New Nature Economy Report II. Geneva: World Economic Forum.

Chapter 8
COVID-19 Pandemic Shock:
Success of Business in a Human-Centric Socio-Economic System

Zoya Pilipenko
Bank of Russia, Russia

ABSTRACT

The COVID-19 global pandemic had a shock effect on all spheres of the socio-economic system. It objectively predetermines the urgent necessity to rethink the following phenomena: fundamental foundations of the functioning of modern socio-economic systems and business with capital-centrist principles of their organization, how the shock due to the coronavirus pandemic revealed the marginal possibilities of the existing system of organizing economic activity, patterns of structuring the post-COVID-19 reality and the formation of business principles in the new human-centric socio-economic system. The uncertainty as the fundamental feature of the business environment caused by COVID-19 could become a major challenge for any business in shaping its growth strategy. In this situation, the success of the company depends on managers' understandings of the quality of this uncertainty and the development of an effective strategy for its growth, taking into account the main factors of the formation of the qualitatively new human-centric socio-economic system.

INTRODUCTION

The scale of the economic challenge created by the COVID-19 pandemic has not been faced in the global economy in nearly a century since the Great Depression (Wan-Lae Cheng, et al., 2020). The specificity of the COVID-19 shock is due to the fact that it generated a variety of crises, from the societal and economic one, to the food and of public health system. Increasing uncertainty has become a hallmark of post-COVID-19 reality (Okamoto, 2020). This has become the greatest threat to business, which must reopen after the first wave of the COVID-19 pandemic, but cannot build long-term growth strategies in conditions of complete uncertainty and lack of understanding of the shocks' causes and their connection with the socio-economic systems' dynamics. In this regard the first necessary step toward reimagining

DOI: 10.4018/978-1-7998-6788-3.ch008

a more resilient economic future is to understand the COVID-19 shock phenomenon as well as causes of such shocks. Only this will make it possible to highlight the main circumstances that should guide a private business in order to timely reorient from short-term survival plans to long-term growth strategies after its re-opening.

In this situation, there are becoming more and more significant the expert developments of specialists in the field of not only effective anti-shock public policy, but also adequate strategies of firms that re-open after the pandemic. COVID-19 shock has occurred in the modern capital-centric socio-economic system therefore, it is objectively necessary to rethink its basic principles of functioning in the context of the devastating consequences that it caused. This idea is confirmed by the fact that in 2019-2020 several serious books appeared, which describe that the capital-centric model of organizing a socio-economic system has exhausted its potential (passed the optimum point) (Lonergan, and et al., 2020; Milanovic, 2019; Sandbu, 2020). Consequently, in the future, it is not able to provide steadily growing rates of economics and of the welfare of citizens. These thoughts are divided by international expert communities studying the problems of private business development under the COVID-19 pandemic and in the post-pandemic period, as well as specific strategic decisions of companies. Their publications are increasingly discussing categories such as trust, inclusion, openness, belonging, etc. (Smit, et al. 2020; Davies, et al. 2019; Ghose, 2020; Dixon-Fyle, 2020). This is largely due to the fact that the public policy of economic lockdown and the regime of self-isolation of citizens undertaken by the national states as a reaction to the COVID-19 pandemic became a complete shock to all representatives of social system: for citizens, for business, for the state itself as well as for the whole society. Logically, the question arose about the inability of the capital-centric model of the economic system' organization to anticipate future shocks and solve the problems of the uncertain post-COVID-19 future. Indeed, it is difficult to reconstruct the future without a fundamental theoretical understanding of the phenomenon of shock and of the quality of uncertainty of the post-coronavirus reality. In such a situation, businesses are faced with the need for their companies' executive officers (CEOs) to understand the quality of this uncertainty and the new factors of the business success in the emerging human-centric socio-economic system.

To deepen these ideas, the author made an attempt to structure the foundations of the shocks theory and to apply them to understanding the specifics of the COVID-19 shock in the context of the existing capital-centric socio-economic system, which has exhausted its potential. It is about the fact that people-created systems in the sphere of economics, society and technology, both at the national and global levels, acquire the ability to self-organization and self-development in the process of their complication. Self-organization is associated with structural relationships' changes in their quality as they pass definite stages of complication forming dialectically interrelated pairs of phenomena. The marginal efficiency of economic systems is reached at the third stage of their self-organization under the dialectical laws of unity and struggle of opposites and the transition of quantitative changes to a new quality. At the last (fourth) stage of the economic system's self-organization its structural connections are complicated to prepare its leap from one established (existing) "reality" to another - future uncertain future. And in this "discontinuity" the shocks perform the role of the mechanism of structural relationships' breakout and of transmitting this multiplying effect to all interconnected segments of the economy. As a result, shocks change the quality of the system's structure and serve as an impetus for a dynamic change (properly self-development) of the whole system as a result of a "jump" into an uncertain future. Such a shock disruption of structural relationships predetermines the rupture of "continuity" of static economics' changes under the influence of the law of denial of negation, which determines the self-development of systems with self-organizing structure that mediates any human activity.

However, the COVID-19 shock has the specific features comparing to all the previous global economic shocks. It is noteworthy that in 2020, structural relationships in national economic systems were disrupted by the subjective will of national governments, which, on the contrary, should have strengthened them, since societies entrusted that function to them. But in the face of the threat of coronavirus infection fatal to human life, the state was unable to oppose it with anything other than to urgently break all social and economic ties in the system, including financial ones. At the same time, even today, the eternal Russian questions "who is to blame?" and "what to do?" remain open to all representatives of national communities. There are no time-tested answers yet. This chapter is the author's attempt to substantiate the answers to the questions posed and to propose specific conditions for the prosperity of firms in the new post-COVID-19 reality.

Background

Shocks are not easy phenomenon. Over the years of national and global shocks' existence, the theoretical and practical puzzle associated with them has formed. But until now it has remained unsolved. This is due to the fact that the practice of use of the word "shock" (or stress) is rapidly expanding, but the essence of this phenomenon and the forms of its manifestation remain unknown (Hatzius, et al., 2010; Suter, 1992; Yankov, et.al., 2009; Bems, et al., 2019; Easterly, et al., 2000; World Bank, May, 2020; Mutuku, 2012; Lalanne, 2014; IMF, August, 2020). In numerous publications on crisis issues, both in economics and finance, "shocks" have become a common word, the essence of which is supposed to be intuitively clear. That is why shocks began to be widely used with definitions as follows: price shock, currency shock, shock of government debt, shock of liquidity, etc. (Christiano, et al., 1999; Hakro, et al., 2014; Alom Md Fardous, 2012; Bahi, 2015; Rostam, 2017). However, the global financial crisis of 2008-2009 and the inducing it shock in the American market of unsecured mortgage credit, and even more so the COVID-19 shock, exacerbated the importance of theoretical approaches to understanding this phenomenon. It is necessary to obtain a satisfactory explanation of the essential characteristics of shocks, forms of their manifestation, mechanisms of shock's rupture of structural relationships and of the multiplication of this effect on the entire economic structure, as well as of the role of shocks in the progress of economic systems due to the self-organization of their structural relationships and in the self-development of economics in dynamic. Oliver Blanchard (Blanchard, 2009) defined the complexity of the theoretical understanding of the phenomenon of shocks as follows: ".... in each specific case it is difficult to determine what exactly case was the shock" that violated the stability of the economic system, since this violation was preceded by the whole series of events that ultimately caused that shock.

Certain theoretical developments on impulse problems were associated with the name of the famous theorist Ragnar Frisch (Frish, 1933), who became the first to highlight impulse problems in dynamic economics as well as the propagation problems. His interpretation of business cycle transformed under the influence of impulses (shocks) is very important from the viewpoint of the rethinking the COVID-19 shock phenomenon. In 1927 E. Slutsky (Slutsky, 1937) took up to a closer mathematical study of the mechanism by which irregular fluctuations may be transformed into cycles and definitely established that some sort of swings could be produced by the accumulation of erratic influences. In 1959 Irma and Frank Adelman prepared an analytical study of impulse model of business cycle with the help of Klein-Goldberger model (Adelman, et al., 1959).

However, these brilliant scientists did not set themselves the goal of forming the foundations of a full-fledged theory of impulses in a dynamic economy. And the absence of their followers in this area left modern theorists with an unresolved problem of recurring global shocks, including the last one associated with the COVID-19 pandemic and turned out to be the most destructive of all. It is these circumstances that predetermined the author's aspiration to build a methodology for analyzing shocks, as well as the foundations of the full-fledged theory of shocks. Following dialectical logic made it possible to highlight the fundamental quality of the people-created economic system, associated with its ability to self-organization and self-development. As for shocks, the mechanism of shock's disruption of system's structure performs the function of overcoming the marginal limits of its complication in the process of self-organization. This approach makes it possible to give a theoretical interpretation of the shock caused by the COVID-19, correlate it with the marginal state of structural relationships in modern economic systems, and outline the main parameters of the future post-coronavirus reality that private business must take into account in order to be successful.

Taking into account the above, the structure of the chapter highlights the theoretical foundations of the processes of self-organization of structural ties of economic systems and their self-development, as well as the mechanism of shock destruction of vertical structural levels generated by dialectically interacting pairs at the level of real markets. The author formalized the main logical chains associated with the stages of self-organization and self-development of systems, using the dialectical laws of unity and the struggle of opposites, the transition of quantity into quality and double negation.

The applied part of the chapter is devoted to the interpretation of modern economic systems in the categories of their self-organization and self-development, which made it possible to give a theoretical analysis of the COVID-19 pandemic shock, highlight the specifics of the mechanism for its implementation, and determine the main factors, which will allow private business to be successful in the formation of the human-centric economy. With regard to capital-centric and human-centric socio-economic systems, a model description of the shock mechanism' functioning is presented.

Methodology

Laying Foundations for the Theoretical Understanding of the Shocks' Essence and the Forms of Their Manifestation

All the shocks of the late XX and early XXI centuries accompanied by more or less destructive crises were becoming global as a rule. Elimination of the negative consequences of these crises returned economic systems to their original position and after a certain time everything was reproduced with the same result of the shock and subsequent crisis. In textbooks on macroeconomics "shocks" are traditionally interpreted in connection with their causes - non-price determinants, which cause both demand and supply shocks, shifting the curves of aggregate demand and aggregate supply to new points of macroeconomic equilibrium (McConnell, et al., 2008; Sachs, et al., 1993). However, the first in the XXI century global financial shock of 2008-2009 destroyed the idea of automatism of restoring macroeconomic equilibrium in the post-shock period. It served as a "starting button" in the mechanism of multiplying financial and economic imbalances in interconnected national economic systems. Thus, a new aspect has appeared in the problem of shocks, associated with their ability to block the action of the mechanism of "efficient markets".

Modern rethinking of the theoretical developments of R. Frisch (Frisch, 1933) and E. Slutsky (Slutsky, 1927a; Slutsky, 1927b; Slutsky, 1937) makes it possible to doubt the hypothesis according to which it is the random influences - "impulses" on the economic system that cause it to have a cyclical model of response (reaction) to outside influence. Indeed, if from the second half of the twentieth century shocks began to repeat themselves with enviable regularity, and market equilibrium ceased to be effectively restored, then it is logical to raise the question of the immanent internal mechanism of the economic systems' self-movement, which for certain reasons began to fail. At the same time, national economic systems were recovering after shocks and subsequent crises, but it was no longer possible to return the pre-shock growth rates of the global economy as a whole. These and other arguments make it possible to associate the causes of shocks with the economic system itself, and not with the external factors impact on it, as R. Frisch (Frisch, 1933) and E. Slutsky (Slutsky, 1927a) thought. In addition, if global shocks can still be viewed as external to national economies, then for the global economy as a whole they are clearly caused by internal causes. At the same time, it should be noted that shocks also occurred within national borders (in Russia, for example, in 1998) without the fundamental impact of the global economic relationships. If the national economic systems are considered as elements integrated into the system of the global economy, then shocks and crises should be derived from its inherent internal mechanism of self-movement.

Such reasoning contradicts the provisions of R. Frisch and E. Slutsky, but is completely consistent with the dialectical laws of development, infinite in time. To understand the internal causes of shocks, it is necessary to highlight the fundamental feature of any systemic organization created by people, including the economy. From the philosophical point of view, it is about the integrity of the system, when the internal connections of the parts of the system and of the last as a whole prevail comparing with the external influences on them. According to K. Marx (Marx, 1995), the system synthesizes elements in such a way that their absolute (separate, independent) existence becomes impossible as a result of the appearance of their new quality due to the system integrity. In other words, the system as a whole and its elements represent a dialectical unity of contradictions. But, being the integrity, the elements and the system cannot exist as a whole outside of the interaction with each other. Only having such a quality the dialectical couple has the ability to self-organization under the influence of the law of unity and struggle of opposites. As a result, if the elements and the system interact dialectically, then their integrity is ensured by internal relationships, which form a contradictory unity. In other words, dialectical interaction within the framework of system integrity is mediated by its structure. It follows that a shock can be such an impact on the economic system that violates its structure or structural relationships. In the economic system, structural ties mediate the exchange of economic activity, or its results, or tangible and intangible assets (goods, services), etc. Then the shocks that arise in the economy should be associated with the destruction of market exchanges or structural links (structures) that ensure the integrity of the system (Pilipenko, et al. 2016).

In fact, shocks realize the breakout of a dialectically interrelated structural connection that mediates the acts of sale and purchase of a traded asset. And the structural relationship of numerous trade exchanges mediates the transmission of this shock gap along the chain, generating a crisis and more or less deeply violating the integrity of the economic system. As for the form of manifestation of shocks, then for a future understanding of the specifics of the COVID-19 shock, it is advisable to single out its object and subjective components. On the surface of phenomena, shocks are realized in the imbalance between supply and demand for a traded asset, which goes beyond certain limits (point of no return), generates a gap between the base price of the object of exchange and its market price, and destroys the possibility of returning to the original market equilibrium (Pilipenko., et al. 2018). Having overcome the point of no return, market transactions are interrupted and equilibrium price and quantitative proportions in the market cannot be restored. This is how the object component of the shock rupture of structural ties in the economy is realized. In this context, all the forms of shocks' manifestation are realized as price shocks, but differ in the quality of the traded asset and the specific market in which it is traded: for example, a shock on the oil market, stocks market, market of unsecured mortgages credit, of government debts, and etc. At the same time, a shock rupture of market relationships can occur in one market segment, but it can multiply the gap to other markets by structural exchange chains. As a result, conditions arise that violate the integrity of a particular segment of the economy or industry market or regional or national economy.

The subjective component of the mechanism of shock rupture of structural ties is the most important, since the mechanism of self-organization is inherent in dialectically interconnected agents of exchange. They are the ones who realize the market exchange by their behavior in the status of sellers and buyers of assets. The point of no return is reached when a critical mass of market agents en masse either sells a marketable asset or buys it. As a result, structural links of exchange are destroyed by shocks, and this shock's rupture initiates structural breaks along the chain of interconnected market segments from one to another.

Thus, in essence, shocks are a mechanism for breaking structural ties that mediate the exchange of tangible and intangible assets, which destroys the integrity of the economic system and causes economic crises. The external form of manifestation of shocks in the destruction of any market exchange is the price one. But they are often associated with the specific quality of the asset being traded and with the specific market in which the shock occurred. The subjective component of the shock is associated with the opportunistic (spontaneous, asocial) behavior of the subjects of market exchange - sellers and buyers, who are capable of simultaneously and en masse to "dump" an asset on the market or present excessive demand for it. When the critical mass of a particular deal with the tradable goods goes beyond certain limits, structural ties are broken, market deals are destroyed, the point of no return is passed, and the integrity of a particular market or market segment or industry or the economic system as a whole is threatened.

Shocks in the Mechanisms of Self-Organization of Economics in Statics and of Self-Development of Economics in Dynamics

All of the above makes it possible to hypothesize that the mechanism of shock rupture of structural ties performs a specific function in the self-movement of economic systems. Its ambiguity is due to the fact that self-movement of system's integrity integrates self-organization as its evolution in statics as well as the self-development as an interruption of static evolution to implement a dynamic change in the system. All these forms of expression of self-movement of the system as a whole are dialectically interconnected: the dynamics of the system cannot be without statics, and statics is intended to form conditions for its dynamics. At the same time, the mechanism of self-organization is based on the complication of the structural links of the system, aimed at strengthening its integrity, and the mechanism of self-development of system integrity is implemented through the shock destruction of the existing structural links. This occurs at the moment when they have reached their limit of self-organization in a static economy and their further self-organization can occur only after dynamic transformations of the system and the formation of a structure of a new quality. In other words, a new quality of a static economy cannot exist without its dynamic changes, and dynamics as self-development of the economy cannot but end with the formation of a new quality of structure in a new static economy.

The complexity of the above construction is due to the fact that it deals with such dialectically interrelated categories as static economics and dynamic one, self-organization of static economics and self-development of dynamic economics. This list should be continued by including two dialectical laws, which are related to each other as dialectical pairs of phenomena. As a result, the economy appears as the integrity in its two forms of manifestation - in statics and in dynamics. Moreover, in both cases, the economic system is in the process of its constant change (complication). The integrity of such a system is ensured by its structure, represented by the structural relationships of dialectical pairs, which are first formed at the horizontal level in connection with ensuring the stability of the exchange of material goods and services. According to Fig. 1, this occurs in the time interval $t_0 - t_1$, in which the structure at the horizontal level ensures the self-organization of the integral system under the influence of the law of unity and struggle of opposites.

Figure 1. General model of interaction of self-organization and self-development mechanisms of economic systems: shocks in the mechanisms of implementation of dialectical laws
Source: the author's development

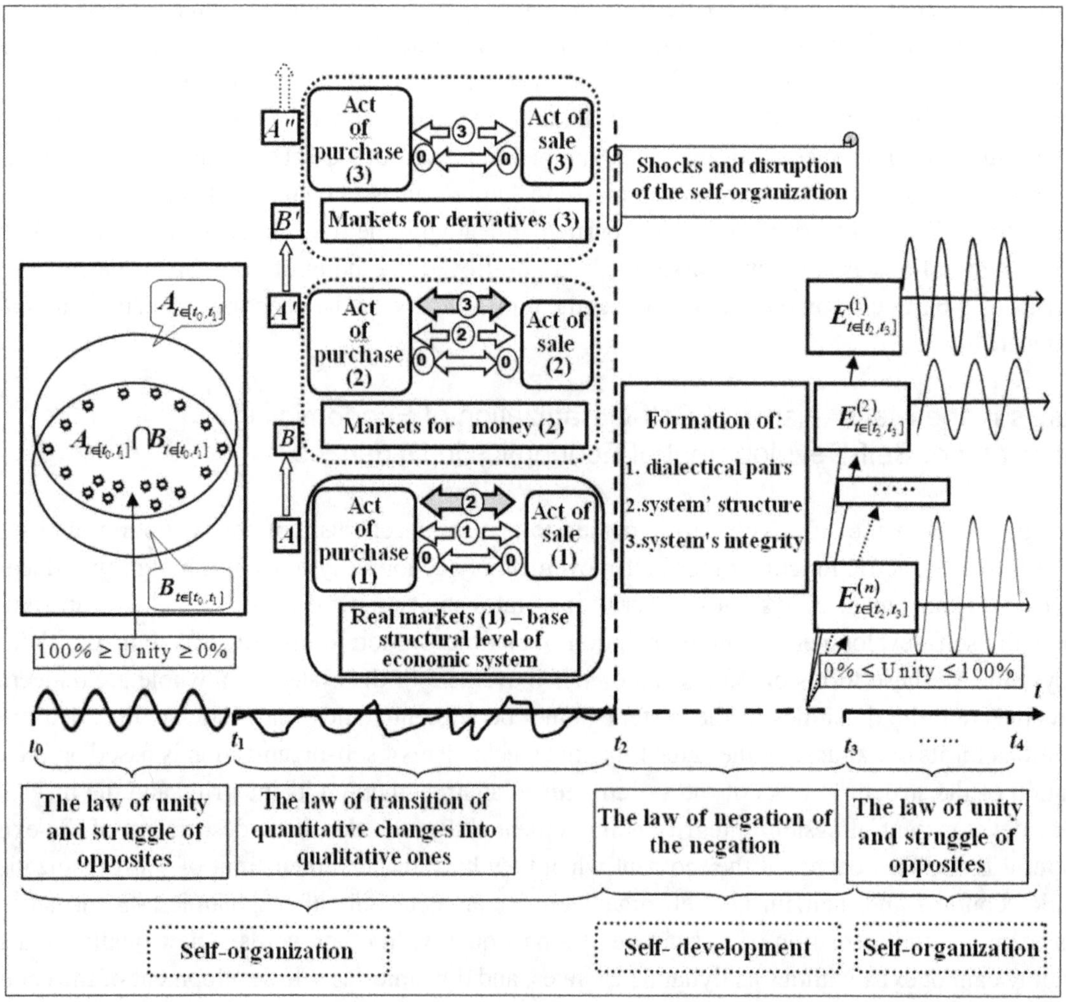

The specificity of this time interval of the system' self-organization is predetermined by the priority importance of maintaining the consensus of interests of the subjects of dialectical pairs participating in the exchange. These changes in consensus are predetermined by the combination between the unity and contradictions of participants in structural relations, which is represented by overlapping segments of dynamic sets (Fig. 1). Theoretically, they range from 100% coincidence of interests of dialectically related participants to zero, since in the process of economic system' complication, the above unity is replaced by opposites. This is the subjective essence of structural changes aimed at ensuring systemic integrity. The shock breakdown of all the structural ties that hinder the strengthening of systemic integrity is the key to stabilizing the system. If at the stage $t_0 - t_1$ of the self-organization mechanism' implementation the law of unity and struggle of opposites has exhausted its possibilities, it will be substituted by the law of transition of quantitative changes into qualitative ones. The mechanism of self-organization realized by the last law is illustrated at the stage $t_1 - t_2$.

So, as the complexity of the self-organizing economic system, structural ties, in which the opposites of the participants' interests prevail, and their quantitative diversity increases, cannot ensure its integrity. Under the influence of the law of transition of quantitative changes into qualitative ones, the horizontal structure of the system generates additional vertically located structural levels that allow maintaining the integrity of the entire system under new conditions. Fig. 1 shows that the basic structural level represented by the real markets is forced to form vertical structural levels, first in the form of money markets, and then of the derivatives' markets. The separation of causes and consequences between these levels under the influence of the law of the transition of quantitative changes into qualitative ones, on the one hand, strengthens the integrity of the whole system, but on the other hand, makes this process multi-step and the entire system increasingly fragile. Shocks realize their function of destroying ineffective structural connections both at the margin of complexity established by the law itself during the transition from quantity to a new quality, and during the transition of the structure from the mechanism of self-organization under the influence of one dialectic law to another. The process of self-organization itself ends with the structural hierarchy generation. Indeed, as soon as the higher structural level-consequence ceases to solve the problems of the lower level-cause, conditions are created for the inclusion of a shock mechanism for the destruction of non-working structural links and the subsequent generation of a working structure during a crisis.

However, shocks are built into the mechanism for the implementation of all dialectical laws. So in the time interval $t_2 - t_3$ the process of self-organization (Fig. 1) of the system, its structure, designed to strengthen its integrity and the operation of the laws of unity and struggle of opposites and the law of transition of quantitative changes into qualitative ones cease to operate due to tectological intersystem opposites, which cannot be resolved by self-organizing systems already established. And we are not talking about the economic system and its national and global forms of organization (although this too). The main thing is the lack of opportunities to reconcile the established principles of structural changes and self-organization of the economics, society and technological system. This phenomenon is shown in Fig. 1 by a shock break in the continuity of the previous evolution of the system at the stages of its self-organization and by a dashed line of time of the uncertainty of the future structure. At the time interval $t_2 - t_3$, the law of double negation is realized by shock destruction (negation) of both the structural levels-consequences and the structural levels-causes, and the dialectical pairs and principles associated with them under the laws of unity and struggle of opposites, and of quantity transition into new quality. And it is this period that is the dynamics of the economic system - its true self-development. At the same time, the principles on which the new systemic integrity and the structures serving them will be built will be different in essence, but the forms of their implementation in terms of self-organization and self-development, the dialectics of existing laws and shock mechanisms for eliminating non-working structural ties will remain the same.

All this must be understood with a small amendment, which is fundamental: the efficiency of the economy, social consensus and the degree of implementation of technological progress at new stages of self-organization will depend on the adequacy of mankind's choice of the principles of coordinating intersystem interactions (between the economy, society and the technological foundation). In any case, this will be a step forward in the progressive self-movement of mankind, but its value depends on many circumstances, which are conditionally summarized in three scenarios for the implementation of self-organization of system integrity ($\boldsymbol{E}^{(1)}$, $\boldsymbol{E}^{(2)}$,..., $\boldsymbol{E}^{(n)}$) on its first stage - actions in the time frame $t_3 - t_4$.

Fig. 2 deepens the model understanding of the generation of a vertical hierarchy of structural levels of the economic system in the process of its self-organization (at stage $t_1 - t_2$ in Fig. 1).

The logic of the formation of a vertical hierarchy of structural levels is predetermined by the needs of their basic horizontal level. It mediates the functioning of real markets, represented by the market for consumer (material) goods and services, the market for investment goods, and the labor market. Arrows with index 0 show equilibrium in these markets, as well as the unity of interests of the participants, which prevails over their opposite. However, as transactions with delayed payment increase, there is a need for intermediary transactions related to lending the borrowers against their obligations to repay the debt. The problem of transactions with real goods with delayed payment is depicted by a dashed arrow with index 1. The increase of such transactions to a critical level is the reason for the formation of a vertical structural level represented by money markets. This dependence is depicted by dashed lines with an arrow with index 1 to square A - the reason for the formation of a new level-consequence - square B. The dashed line with an index of 2, which returns to the level of real markets, solves the problem of non-monetary loans when purchasing material goods and services and restores the broken equivalence in transactions with deferred payment. It is in this connection that all vertical structural levels arise, realizing the causal subordination of higher levels to the solution of problems of lower structural levels. Fig. 2 reproduces the same logic of interaction in the relationship between money markets and markets for financial derivatives.

In this situation, shocks form the conditions for the self-development, i.e. the dynamic stage of self-movement of economic systems, which is realized in the form of a gap in the continuity of its static evolution. But this process is slow. On the one hand, it presupposes the "necessity" of a shock rupture of system-forming structural ties, which would throw to the point of "no return" both the entire hierarchy of structural levels and the fundamental horizontal structure, dialectically connecting all real markets. This is important, since the latter act as a fundamental basis that ensures the self-organization of structural ties and the integrity of the economics in statics. On the other hand, by the time the system "leaps" from a static state to a dynamic one, "sufficient" conditions must be formed, which are associated with the technological, object and subjective components of structural relationships. They are the only ones who can provide their new quality and dynamic transformation of economic integrity. If these necessary and sufficient conditions do not coincide, then shocks and subsequent crises will realize the typical scenario of the "step forward - two back" type. It will presuppose a "reset" of structural links, i.e. their restoration in their previous pre-shock form and the continuation of the process of self-organization of structural connections to the next limit of complexity, which will be reached by one or another structural level.

Figure 2. A model of the formation of vertical structural levels of the system in the process of its self-organization according to the causes-consequences principle of their dependence
Source: the author's development

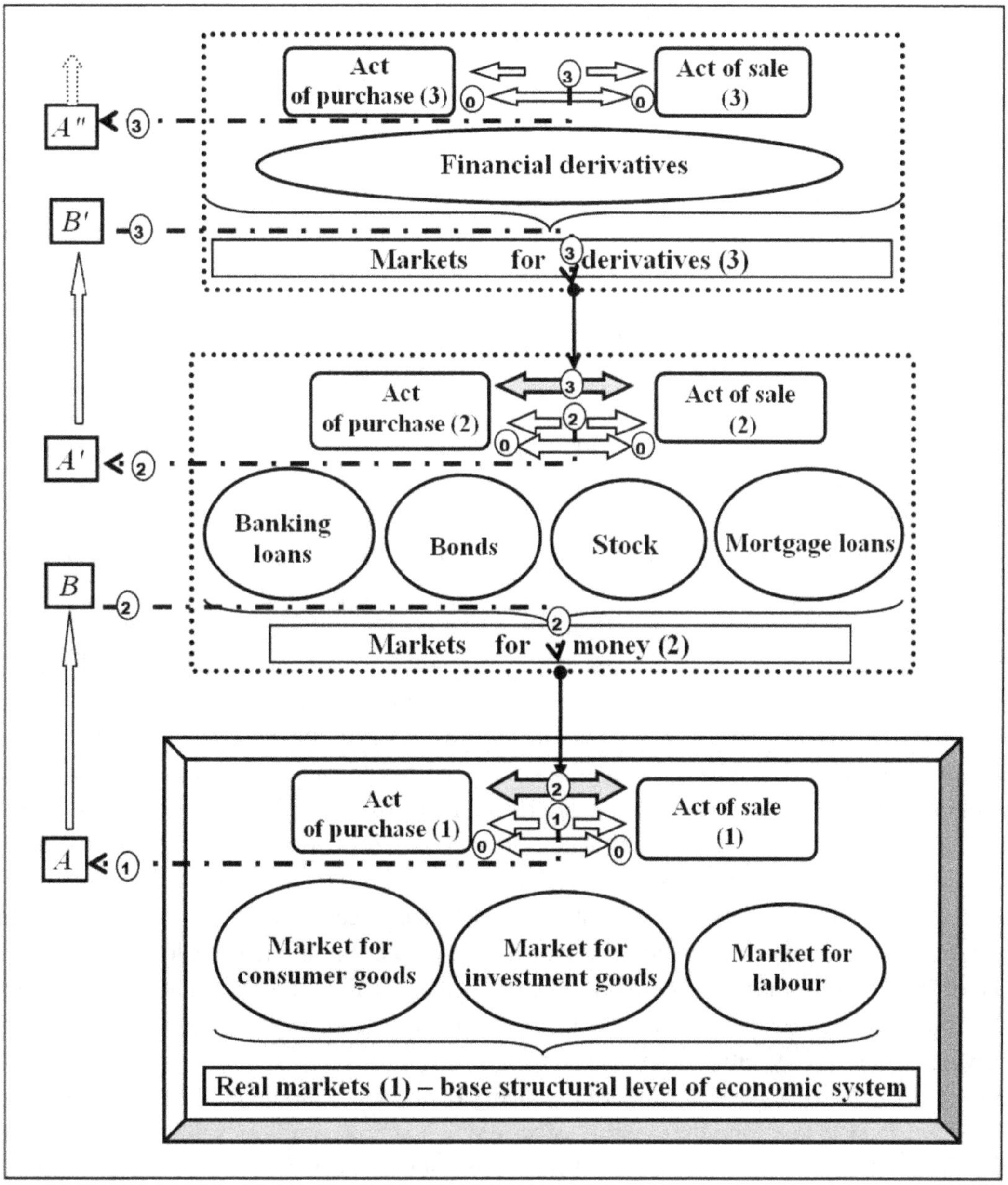

Then, as a result of the opportunism of market players or the reckless actions of national governments, structural ties will be severed in a shock manner and the crisis will begin to realize its typical phases. This scenario is associated with Groundhog Day and is described in Fig. 3. Lower structural levels, represented by dialectical pairs exchanging a traded asset, face a problem (for example, a lack of money or, conversely, the need to invest in a profitable asset). If such problems become widespread, then additional structures are formed vertically to solve them. As a result, a vertical hierarchy of structural levels is built, in which any higher structure is designed to solve the problems of a lower level. In other words, the entire hierarchy of structural levels is built according to the principle of cause-and-consequence relationships over the real markets. As long as this subordination remains, such self-organization of the structural ties of the economic system strengthens its integrity (the left panel of Fig. 3). However, the rush demand or supply of an asset as a subject component of the shock triggers it (the right panel of Fig. 3) and, under certain circumstances, structural relationships begin to break (Pilipenko, 2020). The structures-causes and structures-consequences change places and instead of strengthening the integrity of the economic system, they multiply the breakdown of ties and weaken the integrity of the entire system.

Only private business, which represents the most important structural level of national economic systems, can break the vicious circle of repeated shocks and subsequent crises. In addition, businesses become the main beneficiary of the dynamic changes in the economic system.

Understanding the COVID-19 Shock in Terms of the Shocks' Theory

COVID-19 was first detected at Hubei province in China in December 2019, and within three months, it acquired all the signs of a pandemic, quickly spreading throughout the planet. On March 11, 2020, the World Health Organization described the spread of coronavirus in the world as a pandemic. According to Johns Hopkins Centre for Health Security as of June 24, 2020, the number of people infected on the planet reached 9.26 million people, of which the number of deaths from coronavirus was estimated at 0.48 million.

The specificity of the shock associated with the COVID-19 pandemic is due to the fact that national communities and their governments did not expect such a rapid exponential increase in the number of patients with coronavirus and the death rate (Fig. 4). According to Johns Hopkins Centre for Health Security and to the World Bank, as of April, 2020, deaths from coronavirus ranged from 14% of all infected in Belgium, 12,44% - in Italy, about 12% - in France, 9,5% - in Sweden, to 3,5% - in the USA and 1,7% - in Germany. The phenomenon of such a rapid spread of the COVID-19 virus around the world has called into question the ability of national health systems to withstand the COVID-19 pandemic.

They failed to quickly adapt to the extreme conditions of fighting an unknown infection that threatens human life. The high mortality rate from coronavirus has raised a lot of questions to the institution of the state, the most important function of which is to protect the life and health of its citizens. The practice of ineffective fighting the coronavirus pandemic has called into question the effectiveness of formal institutions created by the state to ensure sustainable interaction between society and the state, the individuals and society, citizens and the state.

In this regard, based on the categories of the theory of shocks, it should be stated that the mission of the state is inadequate to ensure the stability of society in extreme conditions that threaten human life. In other words, the entire previous period of time, the state, as a central element of the mechanism of structural self-organization of economic systems, was honed to maintain a balance between the object components of exchange both at the horizontal structural level of real markets and on the structural hierarchies that rise above them, represented by markets for money, financial instruments, etc. And in this, the national states have succeeded enough, operating with quantitative and qualitative parameters for regulating aggregate supply and demand, GDP, as well as interest rates, exchange rates, etc.

Figure 3. Model of shock's realization in the process of self-organization of structural links, built as a vertical hierarchy of structural levels-causes and structural levels-consequences in case of strengthening the integrity of the economic system (the left panel) and in case of their shock's destruction (the right panel)
Source: the author's development
Note: **A (A', A")** *stands for* **CAUSES**; **B (B', B")** *stands for* **CONSEQUENCE**

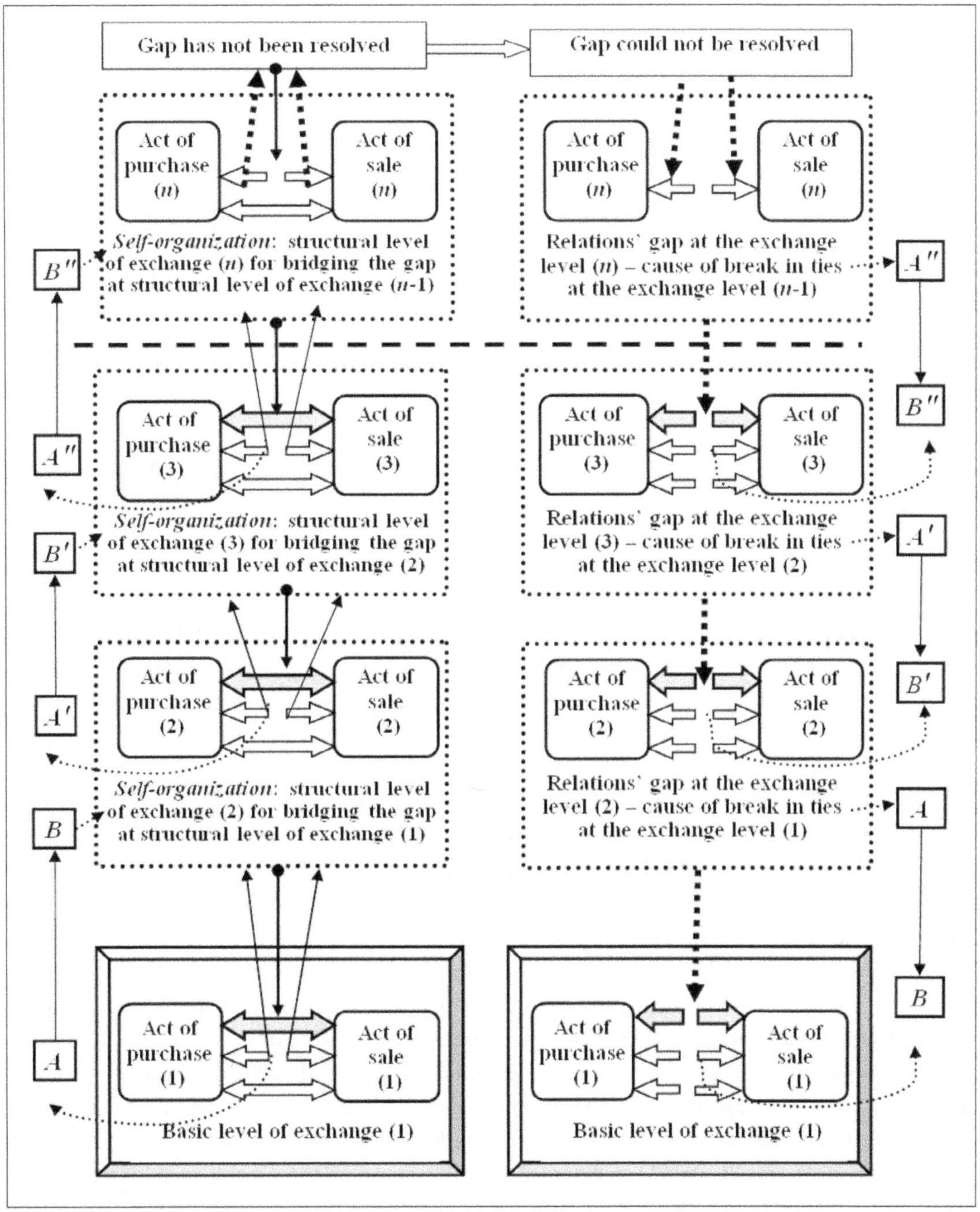

Figure 4. Doubling days as an early indicator of распространения коронавирусной инфекции в ряде стран мира на апрель 2020 г

Source: Disease Progression, Health Care System Capacity, and Response (2020). COVID-19: BCG Perspectives. Version: 20 April

Notes: [1] Includes Middle East. [2] Countries selected from the left chart. [3] # of days after exceeding 100 confirmed cases. [4] Excludes Brazil

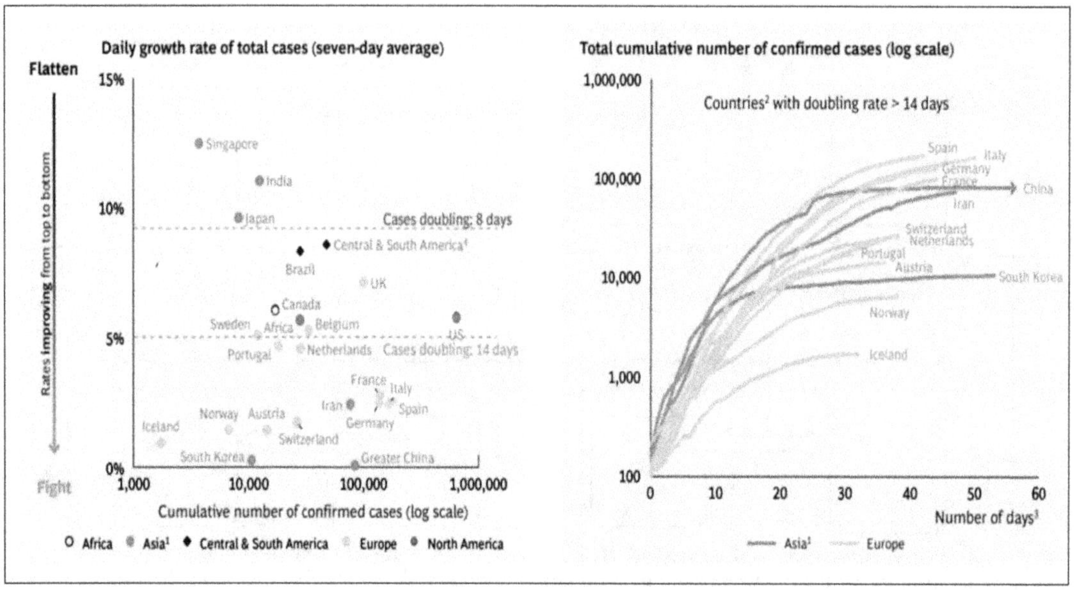

And now the threat of imbalance in national systems arose in connection with the subject component represented by people who carried out all exchange operations both in horizontal and vertical structural levels. Such a reformatting of the importance of the object and subjective components in the structural links mediating the exchange, which determines the quantitative and qualitative parameters of the stability of economic systems, has become fatal for national states in the context of the COVID-19 pandemic. Public sectors simply did not have the experience of effective management of the subject component of the structure of the economic system, and, therefore, formal institutions were not oriented towards it. In addition, in the past, there were absent "the best practices" of public administration in such situations, and the state and policy-makers were forced to independently make decisions at their own risk and peril in an extreme situation

Based on the data obtained since the beginning of the spread of COVID-19, experts from the Boston Consulting Group (BCG) conditionally divided the entire period of the spread of the infection into three phases, depending on the response of national governments to this disaster (Boston Consulting Group, 2020). The first phase after the outbreak of the pandemic was called "Flatten" and was characterized by public measures aimed at reducing the number of new cases of diseases and, mainly, of deaths. It was at this stage that the regimes of social distancing (lockdown) and partial business closures were introduced in most countries of the world as extraordinary measures. In the second stage of the COVID-19 pandemic, called by BCG experts "Fight", national governments were looking for ways to collectively fight the virus, restart the economy, and support society in balancing lives and livelihood. In other words, it was about the timeliness of taking measures to increase economic activity with recovering GDP, some business re-openings, and social distancing on sustainable level. As to the last phase - the "Future" one, then it will come only under conditions when disease could be controlled through vaccine/cure/herd immunity, and treatment within sustainable medical capacities possible.

On this basis, it should be concluded that national governments deliberately severed structural ties both horizontal and vertical, destroying dialectical interactions between their objective and their subject components. Then, in terms of the theory of shocks, it turns out that the actions of national governments destroyed the structure that realizes the self-organization of the entire system, its stability and stability. Moreover, it should be emphasized that the structural ties in modern developed economies are distinguished by a variety of horizontally intersecting dialectical pairs. And, in addition, since the "Great Depression" dialectical pairs have arisen in them vertically interacting with each other according to the cause-and-consequence principle. It is about a hierarchy of financial markets, dialectically related to real markets. And in connection with the COVID-19 pandemic, the actions of states, and not the agiotage behavior of speculators of financial instruments, generated a shock gap in both vertical and horizontal structural ties through the introduction of a social and economic lockdowns. The ensuing recession was unprecedented. The "Great Lockdown" all over the world triggered the worst economic downturn since the Great Depression and much more serious than the 2008-2009 global financial crisis (World Economic Outlook Update, 2020) (Fig. 5, 6).

Figure 5. Economic impact of the Great Lockdown compared to the 2008-2009 global financial crisis
Source: IMF (2020). World Economic Outlook

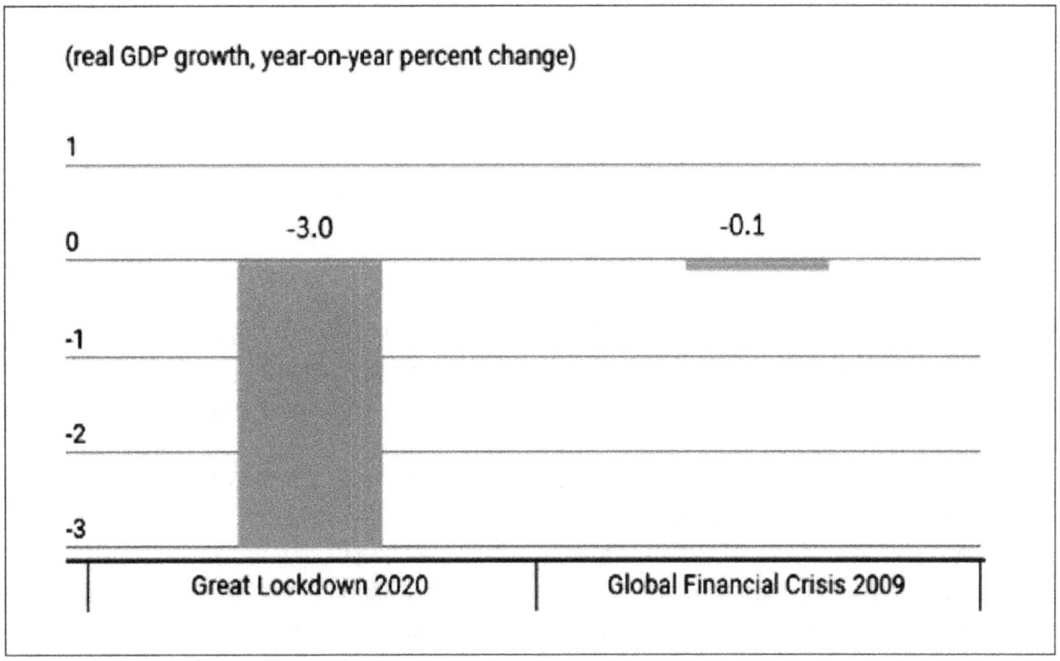

The cumulative output loss over 2020 and 2021 from the pandemic crisis could be around US9 trillion dollars, which is larger than the economies of Japan and Germany combined. And for the first time both advanced economies and emerging market and developing economies are in recession. As to the major economies they have been significantly downgraded. And this is not surprising, because in the blink of an eye, all obligations, cause and consequence relationships, i.e. everything that formal institutions specified for a stable state of economic systems, ceased to exist. The fundamental structural link that powers the movement of real markets disappeared by shock, the economy stopped.

Figure 6. The cumulative output loss over 2020 and 2021 from the COVID-19 shock and pandemic crisis
Source: IMF (2020). World Economic Outlook

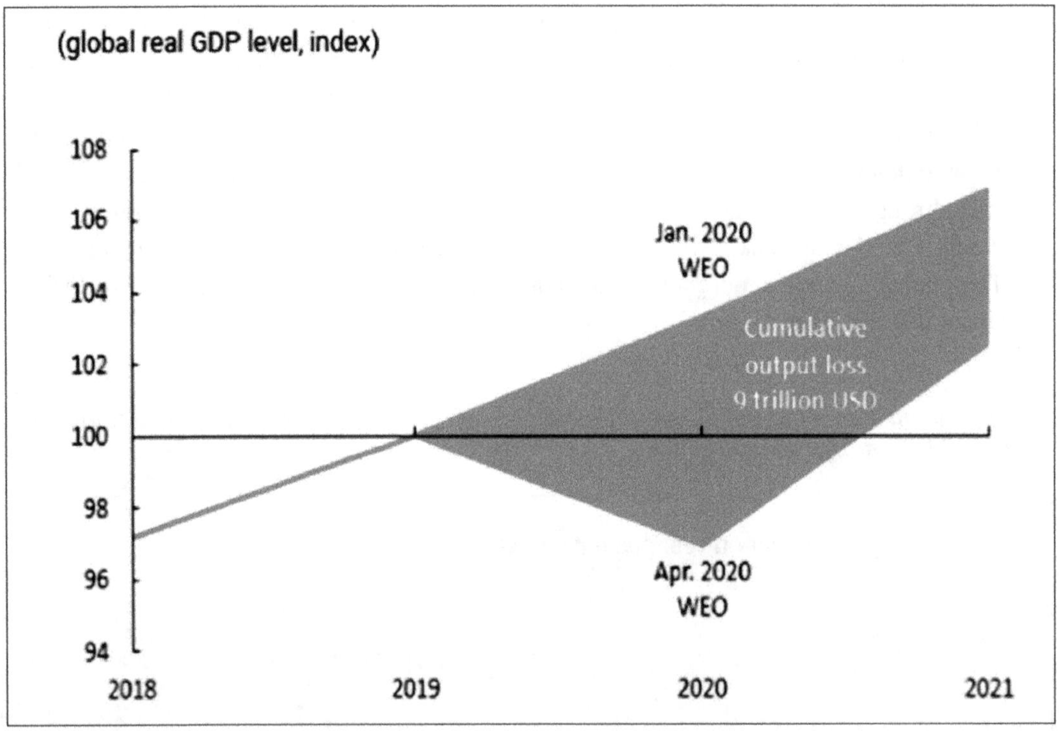

All other structural connections that were initially due to its functioning and its problems got up too. In a structural form, these problems are presented by BCG experts in Fig. 7. They are sure that the COVID-19 shock uniquely raises liquidity and capital risks in both the financial system and the real economy simultaneously.

However, this is only the "visible part of the iceberg". The point is that the stress caused by the shock actions of national governments, which broke the object component of all structural interactions (market exchanges), was shock-multiplied by their subjective component. In this regard, the shock effect of social distancing can be considered the main feature of the COVID-19 shock. This is its main difference from all previous shocks, since the form of its manifestation has ceased to be price one and associated with a certain market of the traded asset. Perhaps this subjective aspect indicates the onset of the moment of the marginal level of the system in statics. It can go beyond it only through the realization of its dialectical leap into an uncertain post-coronavirus future. And the main thing that will predetermine the successful implementation of such a "dynamic" scenario is the willingness of the business to implement it.

Figure 7. BCG experts' views on the interconnectedness of structural problems in financial and real markets
Source: BCG Center for Macroeconomics analysis

Let's make a reservation right away that the state will be ready only for «the Great Reset» (Patterson, 2020), since it will strive with all its might to restore what ensures the stability of the system in its before-COVID-19 structural form. Like the structure of the system, the state is intended to strengthen the stability of the socio-economic system in its previous state. Being empowered by this society, the state cannot go beyond this fundamental mission: to preserve the integrity of the system in statics. Following this logic, it could be assumed that "if the top (the state) cannot", then the mission of transferring the system in statics to its dynamics - as the realization of the moment of self-development - must be fulfilled by another structural level, which is represented by private business.

Human-Centric System: Business Success Factors in the Post-COVID-19 Reality

Whether companies can take advantage of the COVID-19 opportunity to become successful depends on many circumstances. It is necessary to highlight just some of them. First, the quality (complexity) of the horizontal and vertical structural ties of the economic system on the eve of COVID-19 shock in the country is of paramount importance. It is about the extent to which they characterize the position of the national economics in statics relative to its marginal structural level. Secondly, it becomes of the great importance to correctly evaluate the degree of readiness of structural ties to massively implement the transition to a digital base in the context of realizing the possibilities of the 4th technological revolution.

And, third, it becomes apparently most important the extent to which businesses are aware of the limits of the national capital-centric economic system. This is due to the fact that this system, being dominant in almost all countries of the world, demonstrated its great failure when the state, on its behalf, destroyed all structural ties in an attempt to stop or slow down the threat to human life that COVID-19 brought. Branco Milanivich (Milanovic, 2019) described that system as follows: "…the entire globe now operates according to the same economic principles – production organized for profit using legally free wage labour and mostly privately owned capital, with decentralized coordination." So, for the first time in the long years of triumphant march across the world capital-centric socio-economic system it demonstrated its inability to protect all social strata of society (ordinary people, asset owners, officials from the state, etc.) from the lethal effects of COVID-19. This situation is theoretically explained by the fact that the system, which is based on capital-centrist principles of organization, has passed the marginal point (optimum) in its development. Under the new conditions, such a system is not capable of solving the problems of the post-COVID-19 uncertain future. In this situation, the success of the company depends on managers' understanding of the quality of this uncertainty and the development of an effective strategy for its growth, taking into account the main factors of the of the human-centric socio-economic system.

Understanding the fundamental changes that COVID-19 has brought to the future of socio-economic systems is important for chief executive officers (CEOs) not so much from the standpoint of macroeconomics, but in the context of the need for a radical restructuring of intra-firm relations with personnel. Distant forms of work predetermined the need to increase the importance of horizontal structural ties in companies with an emphasis on the priority of the subject factor in all restored relationships (Chapter in this book titled «Rebuilding a Stronger Business in the Uncertain Post-COVID-19 Future: Factor of Intellectually Autonomous and Adequately Socialized Employees»). In other words to succeed, organizations must blend digital and human capabilities (Grasshoff, et al., 2020). In many ways, it is these new realities of the future practice of successful firms that predetermine uncertainty as the fundamental feature of the post-coronavirus future. Moreover, in any case, national economic systems structurally prepared or not prepared for a dynamic leap will sooner or later begin to form the foundations of human-centric fundamentals (Carlsson-Szlezak, et al., 2020). Therefore, for firms, digitalization and the priority of the subjective component of horizontal and vertical structural ties in teams becomes an uncontested scenario of their successful future in an uncertain post-coronavirus reality. But many companies have not appeared to recognize the imperative of making long-term such moves being on the stage of fighting the pandemic.

So, in the future human-centric system, the main factor for the success of firms is the priority of the human factor. To a large extent, this is predetermined by the factors indicated above, which generated uncertainty as the main property of future reality. And in this regard, the role of a person capable of making decisions and choosing directions for the further development of firms becomes the main feature not only for CEOs, but also for leading employees of companies. It is no coincidence that such a priority predetermines success of businesses that build their status as an 'employer of choice' to attract, retain and grow their talent. BCG provides proof of the correctness of this conclusion: highly engaged workplaces have 67% less employee turnover (Gallup), and highly engaged teams bring in 21% greater profitability (Forbes) (Mattey, et al., 2020).

In this regard, it could be possible to interpret the main feature of the human-centric socio-economic system from the point of view of the theory of shocks. All the people-created systems - economic, technological, social ones - are characterized by the fact that at a certain stage of their complication they acquire the ability to self-organization and to self-development. This happens as the fundamental structural level is formed horizontally. It is represented by dialectically interacting pairs of participants of exchange operations. Moreover, all self-organization processes are based on the interaction of two dialectically related processes - of disintegration and of integration. The meaning of their interaction is very simple: the more specialized types of activity can be combined into a cooperative system, the more the latter benefits. The famous Russian scientist A.A. Bogdanov (Bogdanov, 1934) paid great attention to those general organizational processes back in the 1930s. A modern interpretation of these phenomena, adapted to the practice of firms, appeared in the interpretation of the experts from Mckinsey & Company. So in 2015 there appeared the publication titled «Why diversity matters», in 2018 – «Delivering through diversity», and in 2020 – «Diversity wins: How inclusion matters». In other words, the phenomenon that A.A. Bogdanov defined as "specialization.", "division", "disintegration" applied to the macro-level of the economics in the modern sense is adapted as "diversity" to the level of firms. In fact, this is the most important component of those fundamental transformations that the people-created capital-centric system came close to. And achieving this stage it cannot progress any more, being dependent on capital and its investment preferences, which predetermine the division of society (disintegration, diversity) rather than its integration (inclusion). The dominance of this particular principle of organization predetermines the polarization of wealth and income, and the shrinking of the middle class and the growth of antagonism between different segments of the population, as well as between citizens and the state. The fundamental foundations of the new macro-system should be based on the dialectical combination of the principals of diversity (specialization/disintegration) and of inclusion (cooperation /integration) (Fig. 8) of people of various specializations (and not capital-financed spheres of the economy) within the framework of a human-centric system with the priority of inclusion.

Judging by Fig. 8, the differentiation of economic activity realizes a positive choice of its specialized types, increasing their diversity and endlessly delving into economic activity, creating the labor processes' coexistence. Integration, using various types of specialized labor, realizes the negative selection of its types of organization, forms connections between them and coordinates the forms of their manifestation. That is why the results of integration are significantly inferior in scale to the variety of differentiated types of activities. A.A. Bogdanov (1934) compared the processes of differentiation and integration with a universal regulatory mechanism in all spheres of human activity. At the same time, the differentiation of human activity (positive selection), "by complicating the forms, increases the heterogeneity of being, delivers material for it that is ever increasing" (Bogdanov, 1934) (Fig. 8). As for integration (negative selection), it simplifies this material, removes from it everything that is fragile, inconsistent, contradictory, brings homogeneity and consistency in its connections. Complementing each other, both processes spontaneously organize the world (Bogdanov, 1934).

Surprisingly, in the context of the COVID-19 pandemic, these theoretical positions were quickly and efficiently realized by analytical agencies serving CEOs requests. In fact the experts of Mckinsey & Company (Dixon-Fyle, 2020) were among the first to adapt this idea to private businesses' practice in connection with post-COVID-19 future. This allowed firms to be the first to take these fundamental processes into account and adequately translate them into their strategies to adapt to the conditions of the coronavirus. Indeed, a successful firm should focus on building a team (the factor of including everyone in the success of the firm) of people who have a highly professional specialization and who are united by a common goal. According to Mckinsey & Company, as to the trajectories of hundreds of companies (more than 1,000 large companies from 15 countries) since 2014 the overall slow growth in diversity in fact masks a growing polarization among these organizations.

Figure 8. The model of interaction of the process of specialization (disintegration) and cooperation (integration) of economic activity
Source: the author's development

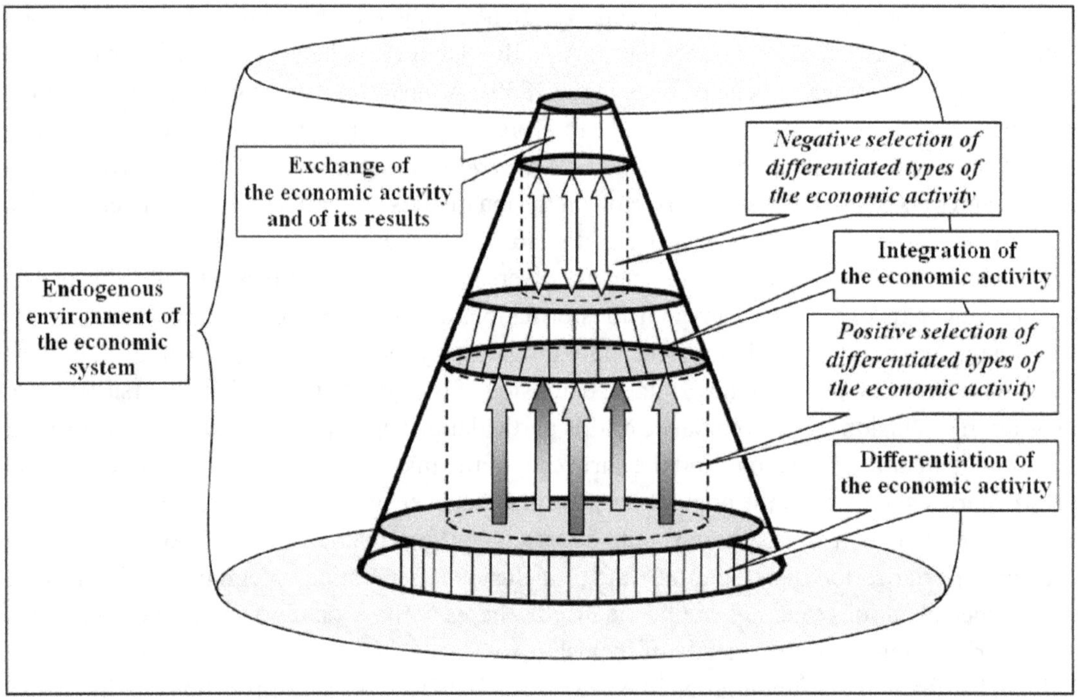

These diversity winners are adopting systematic, business-led approaches to inclusion and diversity (I&D) as well as to create a long-lasting inclusive culture and to promote inclusive behavior. This conclusion is proved by specific data (Fig. 9). Before COVID-19 pandemic this growing polarization between high and low performers was reflected in an increased likelihood of a performance penalty. In 2019, fourth-quartile companies for gender diversity on executive teams were 19 percent more likely than companies in the other three quartiles to underperform on profitability—up from 15 percent in 2017 and 9 percent in 2015. At companies in the fourth quartile for both gender and ethnic diversity, the penalty was even steeper in 2019: they were 27 percent more likely to underperform on profitability than all other companies in our data set. As a result, the experts of Mckinsey & Company (Dixon-Fyle, et al., 2020) suggest 2 fundamental factors of successful survival when fighting the coronavirus pandemic: a permanent business-led approach to inclusion and diversity organizational principals, and bold action on inclusion.

So, the actions of companies and their CEOs in the direction of optimizing the I&D approach as the basis for the successful use of digital and human capabilities is a decisive factor in building up a critical mass of companies in national economies as an indispensable condition for the formation of the foundations of a human-centric socio-economic system. This is where the dialectic of self-development of man-made systems is realized. In this context, there is also a mechanism of shocks that destroy structural ties that have reached their ultimate state and require their replacement with qualitatively new ones, which will accelerate progress in the future.

Figure 9. Financial outperformance of the business diversity in executive teams
Source: Dixon-Fyle, Sundiatu, Vivian Hunt, and Sara Prince (2020). Diversity wins: How inclusion matters. Mckinsey & Company. May 19 Data Set
Notes: [1] Likelihood of financial outperformance vs the national industry median; p-value <0.05, except 2004 data where p-value <0.1, [2] n=383; Latin America, UK, and USA; earning before interest and taxes (EBIT) margin 2010-13. [3] n=991; Australia, Brazil, France, Germany, India, Japan, Mexico, Nigeria, Singapore, South Africa, UK, and US; EBIT margin 2011-15. [4] n=1,039; 2017 companies for which gender data available in 2019, plus Denmark, Norway, and Sweden; EBIT margin 20141-18. [5] n=364; Latin America, UK, and US; EBIT margin 2010-13. [6] n=589; Brazil, Mexico, Singapore, South Africa, UK, and US; EBIT margin 2011-15. [7] n=533; Brazil, Mexico, Nigeria, Singapore, South Africa, UK, and US, where ethical data available in 2019; EBIT margin 2014-18.

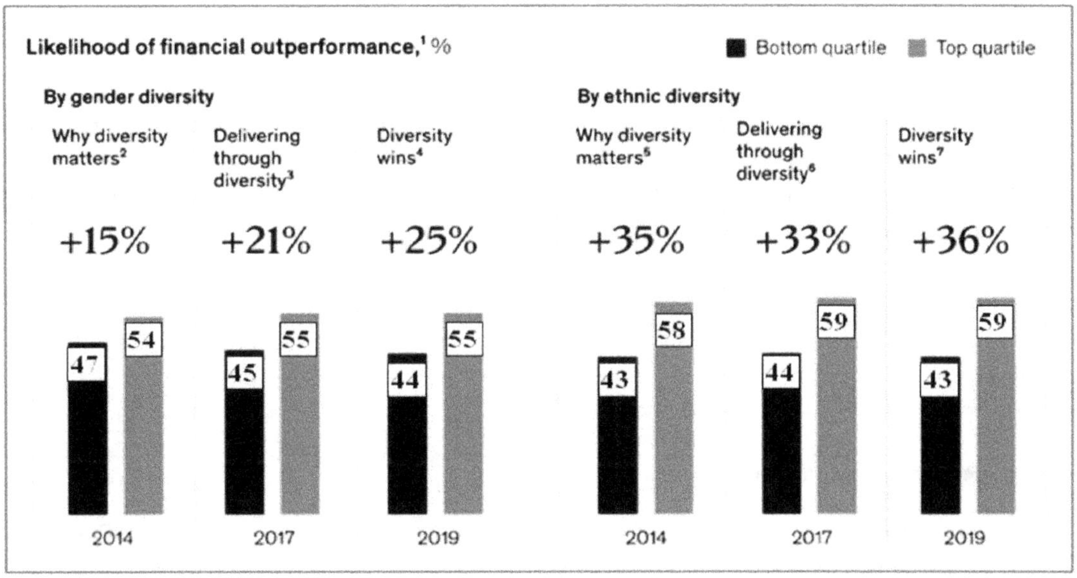

RESULTS AND DISCUSSION

Taking into account all of the above, it is necessary to highlight the fundamental processes that occur at the structural level of the business. It is about dialectically interconnected phenomena of "diversity" and "inclusion" (D&I), which are directly related to the transformation of the capital-centric system into a human-centric one. In the categories of shocks' theory, it is about the essence and forms of manifestation of an objectively operating mechanism of self-organization of systemic integrity.

The founder of the organizational theory A.A. Bogdanov (Bogdanov, 1934) argued that a different degree of organization of any systemic integrity is predetermined by a combination of the principles of specialization (division, disintegration) and cooperation (integration) of economic activities (subjects and objects). Then any organization is the result of unification (cooperation, integration) of specialized types of activities (subjects and objects). However, the line between these dialectically interrelated processes is very fluid. Moreover, at each stage of the organization's development, either specialization (division, disintegration) or unification (cooperation, integration) dominates. From the standpoint of macroeconomics, the capital-centric system is a systemic integrity dominated by disintegration over integration. And while capital is the driver of this system, it exacerbates these differences in the form of quantitative indicators of GDP, GDP per capita in the regional context, in country's comparisons, as well as in the form of social imbalances, such as inequality of opportunities for citizens, population polarization in income, increasing poverty with acceleration of wealth' concentration in the hands of a few, etc. At the same time, the capital-centric system has been fulfilling its main mission of increasing the total productivity of labor for a long time. However, with the general slowdown of the economic growth rates the fact of the disintegration of society, social stratification, and social confrontation becomes more and more noticeable. It is these imbalances that uncover the shock caused by the COVID-19 pandemic, which theoretically indicates the extreme stage of the structural complication of the capital-centric system.

Almost a mirror image of the dialectic of specialization (separation) and cooperation (unification) processes occurring in the system at the macro level is the structural level represented by business. Only in modern publications on the organizational problems of firms in the before-coronavirus and post-coronavirus reality these processes are concretized as diversity (the result of specialization, division) and inclusion (for the purposes of unification, cooperation). In the capital-centric system before COVID-19, with a dialectical combination of diversity and inclusion as organizational principles for structuring the organizational unity of firms, diversity dominated. The validity of these conclusions is proved by the results of CEOs' surveys conducted by the Mckinsey & Company experts for the period from 2012 to 2019. (Fig. 10). They encompassed 15 countries and more than 1,000 large companies.

Figure 10. Overall sentiment on diversity was more positive than negative, but sentiment on inclusion was markedly worse
Source: Mckinsey & Company data set. May 19, 2020

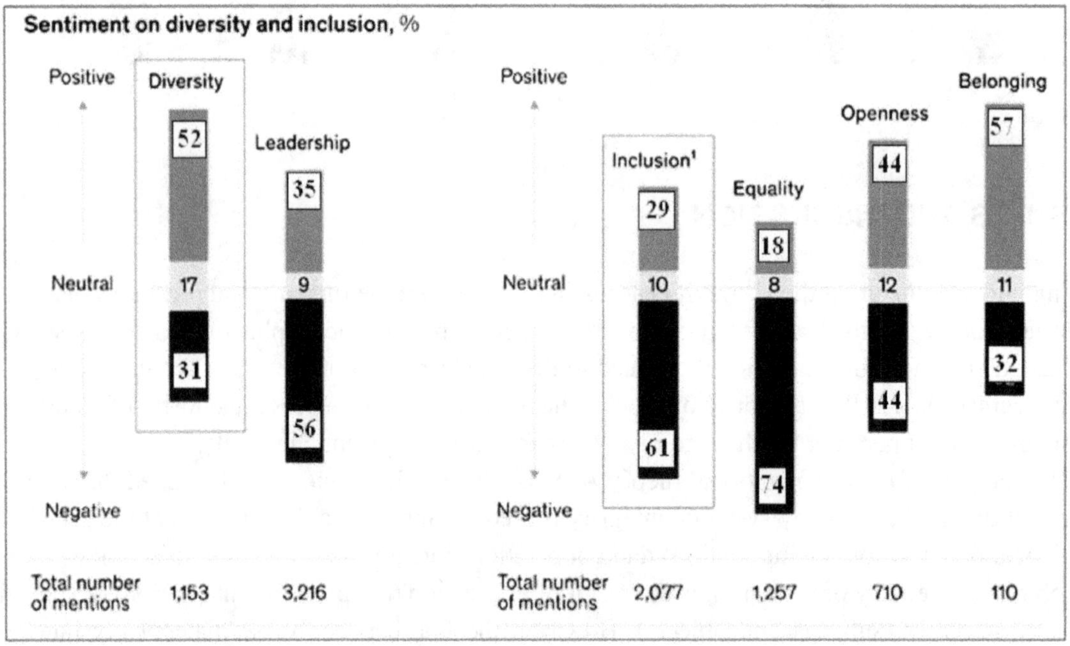

According to two indicators characterizing diversity - diverse representation and leadership accountability, a positive attitude towards this organizational principle steadily prevails (52% - positive and 31% - negative). This is a reflection of the dominance of the principle of diversity versus inclusion as the essence of the organizational principle of the capital-centrist system, which had already passed its optimum by the beginning of the COVID-19 pandemic. Actually, this is the main obstacle on the way of constructing post-coronavirus reality, which presupposes not so much equalizing the significance of the diversity (disintegration)-inclusion (integration) principles of constructing a new system, as raising the significance of unifying (inclusive) tendencies in its organization. Not coincidentally, CEOs' polls on inclusion are counterproductive: 61% of the answers are negative, and 29% - positive. Moreover, of the three main indicators of inclusion - equality, openness, and belonging – the answers are differentiated as follows: as to equality 74% of answers – negative (only 18% - positive), openness has 44% positive and negative answers, but belonging are positively assessed by 57% of respondents (32% - negatively).

On this basis, it could be concluded that the main problem of the capital-centric system is the dominance of the disintegration principle of organization at the macro level and of the diversity at the level of firms. And it is possible to remove this obstacle and radically transform organizational principles towards the dominance of unifying tendencies in comparison with dividing ones at the macro-level (and at the level of firms - increased inclusion versus diversity) only if the sentiment of CEOs changes to such a criterion of inclusion as equality. By the way, it is possible to achieve such fundamental transformation as the basis for the human-centric system only by changing the ratio between the principles of diversity and inclusion (D&I) towards inclusion and diversity (I&D) at the business level. Only a critical mass of firms with I&D priority will serve as a necessary condition for adjusting the disintegration-integration principles towards integration–disintegration ones in macroeconomics and society. And only these fundamental changes at the business level will predetermine the change of the state's activities. They should be aimed at fulfilling the priority mission of ensuring and supporting the all-encompassing unity of a society that integrates diversity of citizens, enterprises, municipalities, regions, etc.

From these positions, the relationship between the acceleration of digitalization at the firm level with the increase in the number of specialized activities and the deepening of specialization (as the basis for differentiation) of employees of firms in the context of diversity of their skills becomes obvious. In fact, CEOs can only professionally use the organizational mechanism of including a growing number of professionally specialized employees in the team's activities. The more optimally the employees will be included, taking into account their differentiated abilities, the more successful the company will be. It is no coincidence that the Mckinsey & Company experts emphasize, that the most diverse companies recognize I&D as more than a social-justice imperative; they also see it as a core enabler of growth and value creation. These diversity winners are pulling ahead of the rest. It is their critical mass that is capable of creating the foundation of a human-centric society in which the state will perform at the macro level the same function as firms: to expand the inclusiveness of the growing diversity of specialized representatives of society.

Empirical Evidence

The authors consider it appropriate to present a formalized model of the organizational principals of economic activity (and of its results) as differentiation (specialization, diversity) and integration (cooperation, inclusion). There are introduced a number of notations, generally speaking, depending on time, in the form of a dynamic volume set ranked by quality. In particular, the author outlined a very wide diversity of qualitative characteristics of the differentiation (specialization) of economic activity $\{\boldsymbol{D}\}$, generally speaking, depending on time, ranked by quality ($\boldsymbol{i}$) of a dynamic set (Yaryomenko, 1997) of volume $\boldsymbol{n}$

$$D = \{D_1, ..., D_i, ..., D_n\}, \tag{1}$$

where the index $i \in [1, 2, ..., n]$.

Moreover, each object of the set (1) is a combination of various types of specialized activities $k \in [1, 2, ..., K]$ i-th quality rank:

$$D_i = \bigcup_{k=1}^{K} D_i^{(k)}. \tag{2}$$

Let us represent the entire volume of specializations of the k-th type of activity as the union of all these specializations extracted from all ranked by $i \in [1, 2, ..., n]$ of qualitative characteristics of differentiation the dynamic set (1):

$$D^{(k)} = \bigcup_{i=1}^{n} D_i^k. \tag{3}$$

Here, the index k means, for example, the following: $k = 1$ - the level of preparedness of human capital (education and qualifications), $k = 2$ - the level of advanced technology, $k = 3$ - the level of energy availability, and etc.

In the notation (3), the dynamic set (1) appears as a hierarchy of levels of economic activity by type of specialization

$$D = \{D^{(1)}, ..., D^{(k)}, ..., D^{(K)}\}. \tag{4}$$

Similarly, we introduce the integration (cooperation) of economic activity (and of its results). Thus, the range of qualitative characteristics of integration (cooperation, inclusion) as forms of organization of economic activity $\{In\}$, generally speaking, depending on time, is denoted as ranked by quality (j) in the form of a dynamic set, which volume $m < n$

$$In = \{In_1, ..., In_j, ..., In_m\}, \tag{5}$$

where the index $j \in [1, 2, ..., m]$.

Moreover, each object of the set (5) is a combination of various types of cooperative activities $l \in [1, 2, ..., L]$ with this characteristic of a qualitative level j:

$$In_j = \bigcup_{l=1}^{L} In_j^{(l)}. \tag{6}$$

We represent the entire volume of cooperation (integration, inclusion) of type l activity as the union of all these forms of cooperation, extracted from all qualitative integration characteristics ranked by $j \in [1, 2, ..., m]$ from the set (5):

$$In^{(l)} = \bigcup_{j=1}^{m} In_j^l . \tag{7}$$

Here, the index l means, for example, the following: $l = 1$ - the level of preparedness of human capital (education and qualifications), $l = 2$ - the level of advanced technology, $l = 3$ - the level of energy availability, and etc.

In the notation (7), the dynamic set (5) appears as a hierarchy of levels of economic activity by type of inclusive organization

$$In = \left\{ In^{(1)}, ..., In^{(l)}, ..., In^{(L)} \right\} . \tag{8}$$

Using the Venn-Euler diagram, it becomes possible to clearly illustrate the logic of selection by cooperation as a form of economic activity of the currently required specializations from all possible ones offered by such a form of economic activity as differentiation (Fig. 11). This design uses a series of notations that were introduced earlier (Fig. 8). In particular, dynamic sets (4) and (8) are considered on the set of all types of economic activity of the economic system E_t. And the intersection of these sets acts as one in many.

Figure 11. Logical scheme: at the moment, the state of the economic system Et determines the inclusion in economic activity by cooperation of only those types of specialization – $D_{t\in[t_0,t_1]} \cap In_{t\in[t_0,t_1]}$*, which are claimed by the system Et*

Source: the author's development

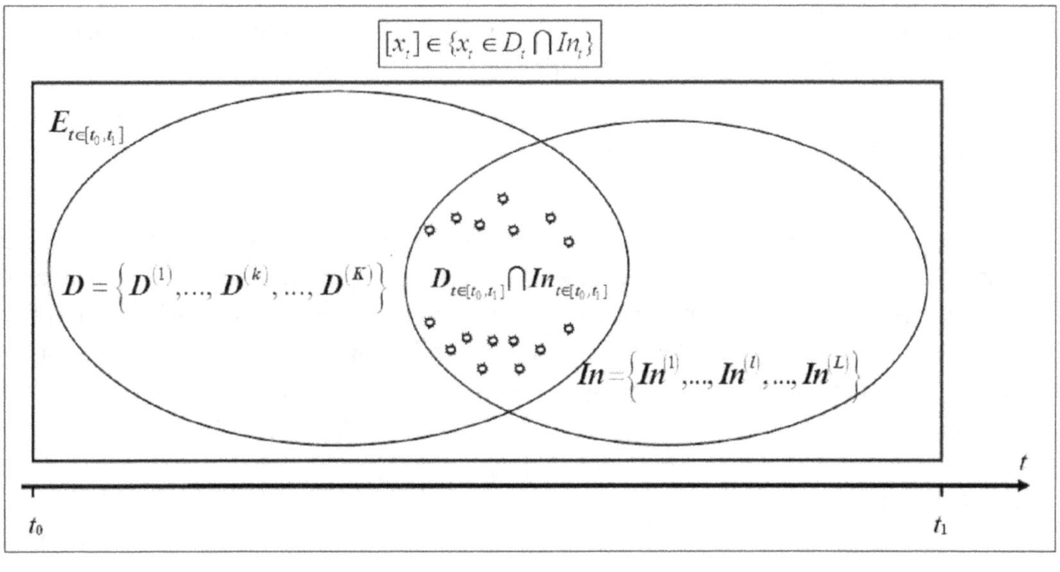

Based on the developed model concepts, it can be argued that there are certain dependencies in the distributions of differentiation and integration as forms of economic activity. In particular, it is, for example, about the distribution function of cooperation of the type of ***l***-activity according to a qualitative criterion ***j*** (Fig. 12).

Figure 12. The function Fl(In) of the distribution of cooperation of the type of l-activity according to the qualitative criterion j is given. Of course, this distribution function may change over time.
Source: the author's development

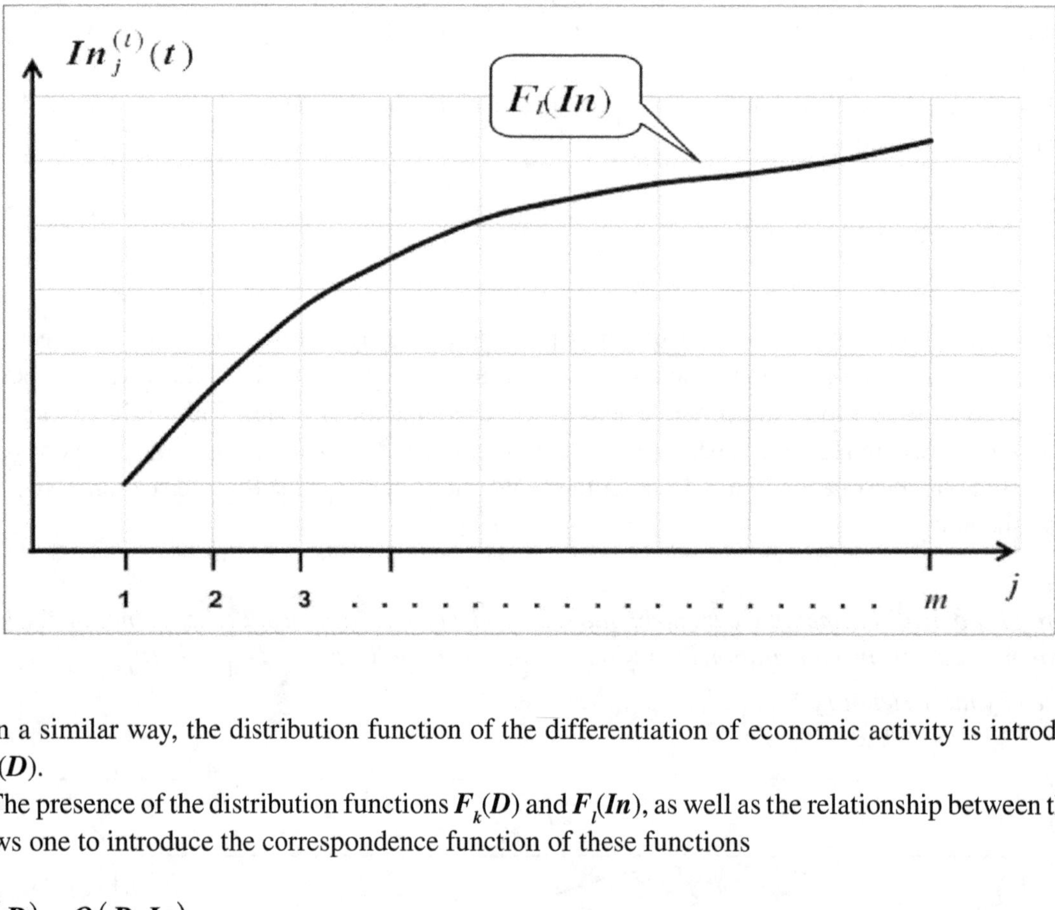

In a similar way, the distribution function of the differentiation of economic activity is introduced – $F_k(D)$.

The presence of the distribution functions $F_k(D)$ and $F_l(In)$, as well as the relationship between them, allows one to introduce the correspondence function of these functions

$$Q_j(D) = Q(D, In). \tag{9}$$

This correspondence function displays a negative selection of specialized activities carried out by cooperation (as a form of economic activity) at each qualitative level ***j*** at the current time ***t***. In other words, relation (9) reflects the dynamics of the formation of an endogenous environment, which determines the change in the mechanism of self-development of the economic system: for example, substitution of the capital-centric system by the human-centric system in the post-COVID-19 reality.

CONCLUSION

The COVID-19 pandemic caused a fundamental shock for all socio-economic systems, which has multidimensional forms of manifestation both in relation to the entire capital-centric organization of economic activity and business. The latter found itself in a difficult situation caused by the economic lockdown negatively affecting the companies' operational activities and financial consequences, as well as the organizational principles of the business. Social lockdown and distant work of company's employees have changed the attitude of people to the system of social communication, including vertical and horizontal ties and their professional activities in the team. Fundamental changes took place both in the demand of households and other exchange participants, and in the supply of goods and services. As a result, COVID-19 made the business vision of the future completely uncertain. And it becomes a major obstacle to the implementation of business long-term growth strategy. This means that the business will not expand its activities in the economy, the parameters of which are not known to CEOs.

In this regard, a theoretical understanding of the phenomenon of shock caused by the COVID-19, the uncertainty of the post-COVID-19 future generated by it, becomes objectively necessary. All these phenomena take place within the framework of the modern capital-centric socio-economic system, and, therefore, are somehow connected with the basic principles of its functioning. It was the shock of COVID-19 that showed, as Branko Milanovic (Milanovic, 2019) wrote, that for the first time in many years of its triumphant march across the countries of the world, the capital-centric socio-economic system was unable to reflect the lethal impact of coronavirus infection on all social strata of society, starting with ordinary people, and ending with asset owners, government officials, etc. It turns out to become surprising that the state, traditionally responsible for the stability of the economic system, resorted to a regime of social and economic lockdown, which destroyed all structural ties that ensure its stability and integrity. It is no coincidence that this came as a shock to all representatives of society: citizens, business, the state itself and the entire society.

From a theoretical point of view, the destruction by the state of a systemic structure with a capital-centrist principle of organization, created by people for many decades, means that it has passed its marginal level. And in the new conditions of the post-coronavirus reality, even a capital-centric system restored by the state in its previous form (many think tanks around the world write about the Great Resert) will not be able to solve the problems of reducing the uncertainty of the post-COVID-19 future. The same conclusion unambiguously applies to the state, which was focused on ensuring the integrity of the economic system with the capital-centric principle of organization. It is simply not capable of generating new conditions for the functioning of the socio-economic system and radically different functions. In these conditions, private business has a "historical" mission to form a new socio-economic system with human-centric principles of organization at its core. Only this structural level, having become a massive one, can serve as a factor in adjusting the functions of the state, subordinate to the task of maintaining the integrity of the qualitatively new system.

These findings are consistent with the categories established by the author in the shocks theory. If any systemic organization - in technology, production, economy, society - is in statics, then its complication occurs in the process of self-organization of its structural relationships. During this period, it is the self-organizing structure that ensures systemic integrity by strengthening the structural interaction of dialectical pairs of phenomena. However, the countries of the world faced the COVID-19 pandemic at a time when in the most developed economic systems, structural ties have reached their marginal level. And the shock caused by COVID-19 has fulfilled its function of disrupting the causal relationships of vertically aligned structures generated by real markets. If the countries have not yet realized their potential for self-organization in the event of the complication of vertical structural ties in the economy, then the national states will restore them in their former form. And then their self-organization will bring the system closer to the marginal level of its structural relationships, and the next shock will lead the system to the need to make a dynamic leap into a new reality with human-centric principles of systemic organization. As for the developed countries of the world, their structural ties have reached their marginal stage therefore, the "Great Reset" will not help them to accelerate economically in conditions when social imbalances are aggravated because of the societal crisis due to the COVID-19 pandemic. This means that under the influence of the dialectical law of double negation, even the restored structural ties in their previous guise will not give the desired progress and will be objectively replaced by others that will be oriented towards human-centrism.

Under such conditions, in any economic system that is prepared to break the continuity of its static complication or is not prepared for immediate dynamic changes, private business creates conditions that will structure the uncertain post-coronavirus reality aiming to get a success. However, this business success will depend on how correctly it evaluates the factors of future progress within the framework of the new human-centric system. The main thing here is the understanding of the universal law of any organizational processes as well as the optimum of combination of dialectically interacting principles of "separation" and "unification" in organizational processes. Disintegrating tendencies in systemic integrity are predetermined by the deepening specialization of economic activity, participants, objects, etc. In the modern world, this process is deepening and accelerating many times, or rather, it becomes multidimensional as a result of digitalization and grandiose perspectives due to the 4th technological revolution. However, startling results are possible if multidimensional specialized activities and their professionals are included in the teams united within the firms. This aspect, adapted to organizational processes at the level of firms, was combined by experts of the Mckinsey & Company, of the World Economic Forum, into the "I&D" approach. It turned out that being dialectically interconnected these processes still differ in priority. Thus, in the capital-centric system, the "I&D" approach is implemented with the dominance of diversity. In the new conditions of the formation of post-coronavirus reality, priority importance is shifting to inclusion in the policy of CEOs to success. And on this path, purely human sentiment of CEOs on inclusion appears in the context of their positive or negative attitude to such parameters of inclusion as equality, openness, and belonging.

The future post-COVID-19 reality environment will undoubtedly provide firms with a huge set of alternatives to I&D approaches from much more complex specialized building blocks. At the same time, the choice will depend on the firms represented by stakeholders, employees, managers, CEOs and, of course, shareholders (but not primarily). In other words, in the new reality, value preferences of shareholders, owners of financial assets are becoming secondary. The main "creators" of this self-organizing reality are no longer financial assets (capitals) and their owners. Their functions are transferred to individuals with the quality of intellectual autonomy, a critical mass of which solves the problem of optimizing I&D processes in relation to the activities of firms that will succeed in the new conditions of post-COVID-19 reality. And this reality differs significantly from the capital-centric socio-economic system because the new principles of integrity functioning are guided by the realization of human abilities in the human-centric socio-economic system.

REFERENCES

Adelman & Adelman. (1959, Oct.). The dynamic properties of the Klein-Goldberger model. *Econometrica*.

Alom, M. F. (2012). *Volatility and Spillover Effects of Oil and Food Price Shocks*. Lambert Academic Publishing.

Bahi, D. R. (2015). *Energy Price Shocks and Macroeconomics Performance*. RFF Press.

Bems, Caselli, Grigoli, & Gruss. (2019). *Gains from anchoring inflation expectations: evidence from the taper tantrum shock*. IMF Working Paper, WP/19/75.

Blanchard, O. (2009). *Macroeconomics* (5th ed.). MIT.

Bogdanov, A. A. (1934). *Tectology or General Organizational Science*. Conjuncture Institute publishing house.

Boston Consulting Group. (2020). *COVID-19: Win the Fight, Win the Future*. Featured Insights. Boston Consulting Group.

Carlsson-Szlezak, Reeves, & Swartz. (2020). Understanding the economic shock of coronavirus. *HBR Newstand Special Edition*.

Cheng, D., Jacobs, K., Law, S., & Schubert, W. Xu, & Zegeye. (2020). Reimagining the postpandemic economic future. McKinsey & Company.

Christiano, L. J., Eichenbaum, M., & Evans, C. L. (1999). Monetary policy shocks: what have we learned and to what end? In J.B. Taylor & M. Woodford (Eds.), Handbook of Macroeconomics (Vol. 1A). Amsterdam: Elsevier. doi:10.1016/S1574-0048(99)01005-8

Davies, B., Diemand-Yauman, C., & van Dam, N. (2019). *Competitive advantage with a human dimension: From lifelong learning to lifelong employability. McKinsey Quarterly*.

Dixon-Fyle, Hunt, & Prince. (2020). *Diversity wins: How inclusion matters*. McKinsey & Company.

Easterly, Islam, & Stiglitz. (2000). *Shaken and Stirred: Explaining Growth Volatility. Macroeconomic Paradigms for Less Developed Countries*. World Bank.

Frish, R. (1933). Propagation problems and impulse problems in dynamic economics. In *Economic Essays in Honour of Gustav Cassel*. Allen and Unwin.

Ghose, B. (2020). *Why 2020 will see the birth of the 'trust economy'*. World Economic Forum.

Grasshoff, G., Coppola, M., Pfuhler, T., Bochtler, S., Gittfried, N., Vogt, P., & Wiegand, C. (2020). Global Risk 2020: It's Time for Banks to Self-Disrupt. Boston Consulting Group.

Hakro, A. N., & Omezine, A. M. (2014). *Oil Price Shocks and Macroeconomic Fundamentals of Oman Economy*. Lambert Academic Publishing.

Hatzius, J., Hooper, P., Mishkin, F., Schoenholtz, K. L., & Watson, M. W. (2010). *Financial conditions indexes: a fresh look after the financial crisis*. NBER Working Paper Series. 16150. Retrieved from: https://www.nber.org/papers/w16150

IMF. (2020). External stress and the international investment position. In External Sector Report: Global Imbalances and the COVID-19 Crisis. Washington, DC: IMF.

Lalanne, C. (2014). *Mechanical Vibration and Shock Analysis (3rd ed., vol. 5).* Wiley.

Lonergan, E., & Blyth, M. (2020). *Angrynomics*. Columbia University Press. doi:10.2307/j.ctv13840ch

Marx, K. (1995). *Capital: A New Abridgement*. Oxford University Press.

Mattey, C., Hilberath, C., Sibilio, N., Aurora, J., & Ruiz, H. (2020). *Personalisation for your people: How COVID-19 is reshaping the race for talent*. June. Mckinsey & Company.

McConnell, C., & Brue, S. (2008). *Economics* (17th ed.). McGraw-Hill.

Milanovic, B. (2019). Capitalism, Alone: The Future of the System that Rules the World. Harvard University Press. doi:10.4159/9780674242852

Mutuku, C. (2012). *Monetary and Fiscal Policy Shocks: VAR Econometrics*. Lambert Academic Publishing.

Okamoto, G. (2020). Knightmare Uncertainty. *IMF Finance & Development, 57*(3).

Patterson, G. (2020). *How to get your company strategy ready for the Great Reset*. World Economic Forum.

Pilipenko, Z. A. (2016). Impulse transmission model of macroeconomic cycle within the framework of the theory of shocks: aspect of economic security. In *Dependability Engineering and Complex Systems: Advances in Intelligent Systems and Computing* (Vol. 470). Springer International Publishing Switzerland. doi:10.1007/978-3-319-39639-2_32

Pilipenko, Z. A. (2020). Shocks' theory: financial mechanism of economic systems' destabilization. In Social, Economic, and Environmental Impacts Between Sustainable Financial Systems and Financial Markets. IGI Global.

Pilipenko, Z. A., & Pilipenko, A. I. (2018). Shocks in global economy: impulse model of macroeconomic cycle. In B. S. Sergi, F. Fidanoski, M. Ziolo, & V. Naumovski (Eds.), *Regaining Global Stability After the Financial Crisis*. Advances in Finance, Accounting, and Economics. IGI Global. doi:10.4018/978-1-5225-4026-7.ch012

Rostam, B. (2017). *Stock Markets and Oil Price Shocks*. Lambert Academic Publishing.

Sachs, J. D., & Larrain, F. B. (1993). *Macroeconomics in the Global Economy*. Prentice Hall.

Sandbu, M. (2020). *The Economics of Belonging*. Princeton University Press.

Slutsky, E. (1927b). The summation of random causes as the source of cyclic processes. The Questions of Conjuncture. Conjuncture Institute of Moscow.

Slutsky, E. (1937). The summation of random causes as the source of cyclic processes. Econometrica, 5(2), 105–146.

Slutsky, E. E. (1927a). The accumulation of accidental causes as the source of cyclic processes. In *Problems of Economic Conditions*. Conjuncture Institute publishing house.

Smit, S., Hirt, M., Dash, P., Lucas, A., Latkovic, T., Wilson, M., Greenberg, E., Buehler, K., & Hjartar, K. (2020). *Crushing coronavirus uncertainty: The big 'unlock' for our economies. To safeguard lives and livelihoods, we must restore confidence. In Strategy & Corporate Finance Practice*. McKinsey & Company.

Suter, C. (1992). *Debt Cycles in the World-Economy. Foreign Loans, Financial Crises, and Debt Settlements, 1820-1990*. Westview Press, Inc.

World Bank. (2020). *The COVID-19 Pandemic: Shocks to Education and Policy Responses*. World Bank.

World Economic Outlook Update. (2020). A Crisis Like No Other: an Uncertain Recovery. Washington, DC: IMF.

Yankov & Zakrajsek. (2009). Credit market shocks and economic fluctuations: evidence from corporate bond and stock markets. *Journal of Monetary Economics*.

Yaryomenko, Yu. V. (1997). *Theory and Methodology of Research of a Multilevel Economy*. Moscow: Publishing House.

Chapter 9
Rebuilding a Stronger Business in the Uncertain Post-COVID-19 Future:
Factor of Intellectually Autonomous and Adequately Socialized Employees

Andrey I. Pilipenko
The Russian Presidential Academy of National Economy and Public Administration, Russia

Zoya A. Pilipenko
Bank of Russia, Russia

Olga I. Pilipenko
https://orcid.org/0000-0001-5734-5673
The Russian Presidential Academy of National Economy and Public Administration, Russia

ABSTRACT

The coronavirus pandemic has predetermined the great priority of protecting public health. The states urgently introduced a regime of economic and social lockdowns to stop the infection. As a result, the activities of firms were suspended or blocked, which caused enormous negative economic and social consequences both for business and for the national societies. The subsequent societal and economic crises predetermined the marginal state of the capital-centric system, which led to the destruction of its structural ties. In the uncertain future, chief executive officers should be prepared to rebuild their businesses. It will be possible if companies take advantage of the opportunities of the 4th technological revolution and rely on the inclusion and diversity strategy to socialize talented people into their organizations. Today, questions remain open, related to both the preparation of future talents and their adequate socialization. The advanced firms will play a leading role in solving these problems to become successful.

DOI: 10.4018/978-1-7998-6788-3.ch009

INTRODUCTION

The COVID-19 pandemic has caused crises in almost all areas of human activity. Paradoxical theoretical assessments suggest themselves in connection with the desire of national states to slow down the exponential growth of the COVID-19 pandemic by actions that contradict their stabilization mission: the emergency introduction of lockdown regimes destroyed the structural ties of societies, and, consequently, their integrity. As a result, the "order" of the capital-centric model of economic organization, which won all over the world, instantly transformed into a "chaos" of intersecting shocks and crises increasing the uncertainty of the post-COVID-19 future. But the dialectic of self-organization and self-development of complex systems created by man, the interaction of the dialectical laws of unity and struggle of opposites, the transition of quantity into quality and the negation of negation makes it possible to see a natural order in any chaos. The COVID-19 marked the end of human childhood: the period of static is over, the capital-centric system created by people has reached the margin of its complexity, and it must be prepared for the leap into the post-coronavirus future (the chapter in this book "COVID-19 Pandemic Shock: Success of Business in Human-centric Socio-economic System").

Capital as a driver will definitely be replaced by an adequately socialized person with intellectual autonomy qualities. This would be possible to avoid the effect of Grigory Perelman, who became the first to brilliantly prove the Poincaré hypothesis of a hundred years ago and after that refused all social contacts. In order to form a humane system in the future, it is necessary not only to understand the patterns of self-organization and self-development of systems, their reaching the limits of complexity and mechanisms for implementing crises, but also to find a solution of the fundamental problem of the indefinite post-COVID-19 future. If the latter takes the form of a human-centric system, then its specificity will be predetermined by the dialectic of the Scylla of education and the Charybdis of socialization. It is about the education of intellectually autonomous individuals capable of adapting the achievements of the 4th technological revolution to the tasks of socio-economic progress. This opens up an opportunity to accelerate the development of human society in the "two steps forward - one back" regime, instead of the modern version of "one step forward - two back". It should be emphasized that such a scenario is possible only under the condition of adequate socialization of intellectually autonomous individuals. The latter is predetermined by the structure of the national society, the level of expert qualities of the state, which, with the help of formal institutions, is able to motivate citizens to unlimited creativity in the name of the prosperity of the society of the future.

The necessary and sufficient conditions for the success of the above scenario are undoubtedly associated with private business, capable and interested in implementing the latest trends in transforming the organizational structure of society. Companies lost a lot as a result of lockdowns, may lose even more in the event of the second wave of the COVID-19 pandemic. Thus, business rebuilding becomes a chance - the moment of truth, which must be realized on the fundamental basis of a theoretical understanding of chief executive officers (CEOs) of the current situation and optimal practical solutions with a focus on people with the qualities of intellectual autonomy, provided that they could be adequately socialized at the firm level. In this regard, many problems arise, the most important of which is the level of education of people capable to overcome psychological and cognitive barriers (PCB) and share the standards of socially significant principles of behavior within the company. This is on the one hand. On the other hand, CEOs have to understand the conditions that must be created for such employees so that they could realize all their enormous intellectual potential in the company. In this regard, great opportunities are associated with the implementation of the inclusion and diversity (I&D) strategy in the activities of firms by advanced CEOs.

Background

The COVID-19 pandemic has negatively affected almost all structure-forming spheres of human life, from the economic system and circulation of goods and other assets to society, relations with the state, organizational structures in companies and family ties. On this occasion, the experts of the World Economic Forum spoke as follows: “We are at a critical juncture for the future of human societies: we face an unprecedented global humanitarian and health crisis with the COVID-19 pandemic while the hour is late to stave off the worst of the climate and nature crises” (WEF, 2020). In other words, nature has demonstrated to the human community the result that its socio-economic progress has brought without taking into account harmony with the ecological environment. From a philosophical viewpoint, it is about the need to return the human principle to the person-created self-organizing systems. This is a unique chance to rethink the universal laws of development and take the path of forming a person who is able to understand them and use them wisely, both in organizing his systemic integrity and in interconnection with nature.

COVID-19 illustrated the marginal state of the economic system, since it is only in this capacity that its structural ties can instantly collapse, despite the fact that they have ensured its integrity and progress for a long time. It is from these positions it becomes possible to assess the economic and social lockdown regimes introduced by the state in an effort to stop the spread of coronavirus infection. And this phenomenon is additional evidence of the exhaustion of the positive potential of a human-created system with an emphasis on capital-centrist principles of organization. This is also true for the national state created to ensure the system’s structural integrity. In this regard, all the rationales for a strategy focused on the Great Reset (Sutcliffe, 2020; Billimoria, et al., 2020; Doumba, 2020; Schwab, et al., 2020) are meaningless, since the restoration of structural ties that are broken by the state in a system that has passed its optimum point means opposition to the fundamental laws of self-organization and self-development or regression (see the chapter in this book “COVID-19 Pandemic Shock: Success of Business in Human-centric Socio-economic System”).

It is no coincidence that many experts identify uncertainty as the main quality of the post-COVID-19 future. To eliminate it, it is necessary to theoretically determine its causes and identify the factors that will determine the structuring of the post-coronavirus economic and social reality. So, people-created systems are packed into a capital-centrist model of organization, the peculiarity of which is that, being created by man, it subordinated him to its rules of behaviour (Milanovic, 2019; Lonergan, et al., 2020; Sandbu, 2020). Influenced by the self-organization mechanisms, the dominant all over the world capital-centric system was constantly becoming more complex, moving from one marginal level of self-organization to another. The passage of the optimum point was accompanied by the deepening of the problem associated with the fact that capital as a priority factor of its self-development and the owner of capital (assets) as the main driver of self-organization of the capital-centric system stopped being the driver of its progress and became its main brake. The most complex system of structural connections and the variety of possible alternatives for constructing an indefinite post-COVID-19 reality are predetermined not so much by the owners of capital as by individuals able to use this capital to construct the new system, to build alternatives of inclusion of the rapidly increasing diversified types of activity. Intellectually autonomous and adequately socialized individuals are capable to become such drivers in the new uncertain reality of the post-coronavirus future (Pilipenko, et al., 2019; Pilipenko, 2020). Moreover, this reveals the dynamic aspect of a self-developing system with human-centric principles of organization at the base, which can be implemented only if a critical mass of intellectually autonomous and adequately socialized individuals is formed. The solution to this problem brings both theorists, and practitioners, and policy-makers back to the understanding of the priority importance of the person himself, i.e. every individual who must first be educated so as to understand this, and then adequately socialized in order to serve the society that enlightened him about this.

Only with such qualities a person is able to construct a post-coronavirus reality in the form of a human-centric system. The path to this is long and thorny, since there are subjective factors that impede its successful completion due to the high inertia of the behavior of the main drivers of the previous system. In addition, no universal best practices have been identified for achieving high quality education for all students at all times (Boston Consulting Group, 2017; De Smedt, 2014). According to experts, the level of education of people in recent years has generally been falling (Kautz, et al., 2014), which does not allow the former socio-economic system to dynamically jump into the "bright future" of post-coronavirus reality. As a result, the prospects that the 4th industrial revolution provides to new generations can turn into missed opportunities. Meanwhile, according to the authors, the "crisis" of education is due to the unresolved essential problem, the significance of which in modern conditions of growing uncertainty and the emergence of unexplored possibilities of human organizations on a new technological basis is associated with the answer to the question "how to teach an individual to learn." And answering this question, it is necessary to realize the main obstacle to mutual understanding between students and teachers, associated with the presence of psychological and cognitive barriers (PCB) in their consciousness and the lack of generally accepted technologies to overcome them (Pilipenko, 1997; Kuhl, 2010; Neisser, et al., 1996). However, the most difficult problem of forming the main demiurge of the new human-centric system does not finish with an excellent education. The quality of intellectual autonomy is realized in the individual's ability to identify problems in professional activity, determine the reasons for their occurrence, outline a set of solutions, conditions for their successful implementation and justify the choice of the one that will definitely give the optimal result.

However, the educational level of a person capable of constructing the indefinite reality of the post-coronavirus future is only a necessary condition for him to realize his unlimited creative potential. A sufficient condition is his desire to realize his intellectual potential for the benefit of society in general and the company as a place of professional activity, in particular. In the capital-centric system, this aspect of human inclusion into the society was largely polemical. This was due to the fact that formal institutions and the punishment mechanism integrated into them were sufficient to suppress the opportunistic actions of individuals and their violations of formal rules of behavior. In other words, the priority of society and the indisputability of the state's rightfulness were not questioned. However, in the context of COVID-19, the economic and social lockdowns made all citizens think about the advisability of government actions in a pandemic, which instantly brought down the welfare of most households, complicated their social interactions, and disrupted the usual way of life of their entire environment. In these conditions the problem of discrepancy between individual values and priorities of society as a whole, which the state implements, became obvious.

As for people with a high intellectual level, they, as a rule, are self-sufficient. Therefore, they are able to share social preferences and follow the norms of behavior accepted in society only if they share them completely or at least partially. Therefore, the problem of socialization of highly intellectual individuals into the national community as the basis of its societal integrity is no less, and perhaps a more complex puzzle, which did not have much significance within the framework of the capital-centric system. In conditions of uncertain reality everything changes. In its structuring, the main participants become companies that can revive and be successful only if they take into account the latest trends and if their CEOs are able to optimize diversity and inclusion in organizational processes within firms.

In accordance with the above stated logic, the material of the chapter is structured as follows. The theoretical section of the chapter is subordinated to the presentation of methodological approaches to understanding the effect of the rapid destruction of the national systems based on capital-centric principles of organization, as a result of the introduction by states of emergency regimes of economic and social lockdown. The dialectical approach made it possible to see the signs of the marginal state of the previous system, which, as a result of the COVID-19 pandemic, will objectively be transformed by constructing structural ties based on human-centric principles of organization. The replacement of capital by a person as a driver of a new post-coronavirus reality highlights two of its qualities necessary for this. It is about education that forms individuals with the qualities of intellectual autonomy, capable of overcoming psychological and cognitive barriers. But for an active participation in the structuring the new human-centric reality, a person must be capable of transcending, integration into society, which will allow him to socialize and restore its societal integrity.

Practical conclusions are based on the fact that it is the companies represented by their CEOs who are called upon to carry out adequate socialization of educated individuals with the qualities of intellectual autonomy. In this context, the main problem areas are highlighted related to the optimization at the firm level of such organizational principles as inclusion and diversity (I&D). The lack of significant progress in the context of raising the level of education of talented employees and their accelerated socialization into the firms' teams lies in the minds of the CEOs themselves, who bear all the negative manifestations of the capital-centric system: rejection of leadership as a manifestation of diversity and a negative attitude towards such signs of inclusion as equality and openness. Meanwhile, the effective implementation of the I&D strategy of firms could significantly accelerate the formation of structural links of the future human-centric reality, minimizing its current high uncertainty. This will undoubtedly serve as the basis for rebuilding a stronger business in the post-COVID-19 future. Empirical estimates are presented to prove the validity of this conclusion. Based on the results of the discussion of the above problems, conclusions are substantiated.

Methodology

Puzzle, Caused by COVID-19: Structural Relationships Have Been Destroyed, What Next?

The COVID-19 pandemic caused economic and societal crises, changing the concept of the subordination of the economy and society from the standpoint of the importance of restored integrity for designing the future. The effect of a rather rapid destruction of structural ties in both the economy and the social sphere should be considered phenomenal, which suggests that their structures have reached the point of no return. From the point of view of philosophy, this means that the structural relationships in their previous form go beyond the scope of the law of transition of quantitative changes into qualitative ones into the sphere of influence of the law of double negation (Pilipenko, Z.A., et al., 2016; Pilipenko, Z.A. 2020; Pilipenko, et al., forthcoming book). In other words, the structure that has passed the optimum point, which is responsible for the integrity of the system, is no longer able to provide it and it will gradually be replaced by new structural links. The specificity here is manifested in the fact that if in previous crises the restoration of structural ties in the economy unambiguously predetermined the stable state of society, then after the coronavirus pandemic everything changed. It became obvious that without restoring the societal integrity of the system, it is hardly possible to restore the functioning of the balanced economy. In addition, the situation is aggravated by the fact that the results of the 4th technological revolution cannot be widely replicated in areas of activity, industries, regions, etc. without participation of professionally trained and adequately integrated (socialized, included) in the social activities of individuals. In other words, capital and its owners cease to be the basis for the formation of new structural relationships. Only individuals with the qualities of intellectual autonomy and adequate socialization can re-construct structural ties on a new technological basis. Moreover, the construction of a new reality is beyond the power of individuals, intellectuals of a new type must constitute the critical mass of all professionals.

However, the specificity of their inclusion is predetermined not so much by unifying tendencies as by disintegrative ones. The point is that the generation of new structural ties is preceded by the differentiation of the professional activity of economic entities and participants in social relations. And only by being adequately separated, at least in terms of professional training, the subjects are able to construct new dialectically interacting structural relationships in society and in the economy. Many publications are devoted to diversity (disintegration, division) (Hunt, et al., 2018), there are also those ones that emphasize the need for inclusion (unification, integration) (Bailinson, et al., 2020). So the essence of the puzzle of "including the diversified" as applied to the structuring of post-coronavirus reality is that both are right. And the puzzle can easy be settled interpreting this phenomena on a theoretical basis using the principles of dialectical logic. Back in the 1930s, the Russian theoretician A.A. Bogdanov (Bogdanov, 1934) was the first to dialectically connect disintegrating and integrating processes (tendencies) in systems created by man, calling them universal mechanisms that spontaneously organize (structure) the reality. In other words, the puzzle that emerged due to the coronavirus pandemic associated with the uncertainty of the future social and economic reality is nothing more than the beginning of the formation of a new order (the law of self-organization) or of the new optimum in the interaction of disintegrating and integrating processes. And the unification (integration, inclusion) of the disconnected (specialized, diversified) types of activity (processes, trends and phenomena) will certainly be achieved in the new post-coronavirus reality, but on the basis of the human-centric principle. It is the letter that will gradually replace capital-centric principle that led to the collapse of structural relationships as a result of the COVID-19 pandemic. As a result, theoretically, the puzzle is easy enough: the main creator of new structure is a person, who must possess such qualities that will form the societal integrity of society, uniting a huge variety of diverse individuals. It is about intellectually autonomous individuals with multifunctional professional capabilities (potential), who, at the same time, have basically the same social values (with a huge variety of them). As a result, societal integrity is formed, which will predetermine the growing diversity of economic activities.

If all the previous reasoning is correct, then in terms of the formation of economic integrity on the basis of new structural ties, it is necessary to determine that aspect of human activity that will maximize the possibilities of his specialization. On this basis, the division of economic activity is multiplied, its types and forms are deepened using the achievements of the 4th industrial revolution, new goods and services are generated, i.e. other technologies to meet human needs. Education plays a decisive role in these processes with human participation. However, the differentiation (separation, diversity) of activities (processes, trends and phenomena) is important for the structure formation in human-created systems only if they are integrated. And in this context, the socialization of a person comes to the fore, which can only be based on the coincidence in the main value priorities of intellectually autonomous individuals. Thus, in the formation of the structure of a new human-centric system, the dialectic of two phenomena that determine the primary importance of a person in it - education and socialization - becomes paramount. Only their optimal combination will allow the formation of a critical mass of individuals with the qualities of intellectual autonomy and adequate (socially significant) socialization. Thus, the structuring of the new post-coronavirus reality and the strengthening of its integrity will take place by coordinating the processes of separation and unification, diversity and inclusion, the participants of which are persons who differ in the level of education and who share in general socially significant norms that ensure societal integrity.

Education as a Necessary Condition for the Emergence of Intellectually Autonomous Individuals: Overcoming Psychological and Cognitive Barriers

The problem of education is eternal. They describe it, highlighting the main reasons for the decline in the quality of knowledge and justifying the latest new technologies (Romer, 1986; UNESCO, 2016; UNESCO, 2016a). However, in 2018, in its World Development Report, the World Bank (World Bank, 2018) formulated a disappointing conclusion that the education system was in a state of crisis (The Economist, 2020). Following dialectical logic, the authors tried to highlight the essence of the problem of the ineffectiveness of the educational process, taking into account more and more advanced methods of presenting material, more and more skillful teaching technologies, etc.

The starting point of the research was the basic methodological principles of teaching, which were systematized by the famous Soviet researcher A.A. Pinskiy (Pinsky, 1978) in the form of the following three: "what to teach", "how to teach" and "how to learn". As for the first two - "what to teach", "how to teach", they are quite skillfully implemented in the educational process. But the 3rd component of the Pinsky triad - «how to learn» turned out to be the weakest element of the modern education system. This is largely due to the fact that the problem of implementing this principle became the most difficult. Meanwhile, the current state of the education system has made the principle of "how to learn" the most popular, especially in connection with the massive transition to distance learning during the COVID-19 pandemic. Indeed, not having taught the student to learn, the teacher makes the first two components - "what to teach" and "how to teach" - meaningless. The main reason for the unresolved problem of "how to learn" (or rather, "to teach how to learn") lies in the fact that the modern education system simply ignores it. From the philosophical viewpoint, this problem can be presented structurally as follows. If the teacher and the learner are the dialectical pair, then their connection can be represented by the methodological principles of teaching: then the teacher is associated with "how to teach", and the learner is associated with "how to learn". Their dialectical unity is determined by the quality of mastering the subject - "what to teach" (and at the same time "what to learn"). If the degree of the student's mastery of the academic discipline is high, then the gap between "what to teach" (in teaching by the teacher) and "what to learn" (on the part of the learner) is minimized. Otherwise, this gap increases. It follows that the degree of mismatch between "what to teach" and "what to learn" predetermines the quality of education in all disciplines in general. What predetermines the gap between "what to teach" and "what to learn", provided that both the student and the teacher strive to increase the level of mastery of the subject. According to the authors, this phenomenon is predetermined by the psychological and cognitive barriers (PCB), functioning both in the educational consciousness of students and in the professional consciousness of teachers.

It follows that the main reason for the low level of education is explained by the presence of PCB, or rather, by the fact that they are not overcome both in the educational consciousness of students and in the professional consciousness of teachers due to the different levels of their philosophical level (Pilipenko, 1997; Pilipenko, et al., 1999; Pilipenko A.I., at al. 2015). The methodology of the teacher's thinking operates with a theoretical understanding of the taught discipline, and the methodology of the student's thinking is based on everyday consciousness. The resolution of this dialectical contradiction is associated with overcoming the PCB in the learning process by both learners and teachers. So ***"how to learn"*** is concretized on the PCB theory platform as a new didactic principle: "***I know...... how I know***". And the latter means a fundamental transfer of emphasis in the system of education to the student, who himself must and is able to assess the degree of his learning. In this sense, he becomes capable of self-reflection, acquires a new quality of a self-learning (self-developing) subject. In this sense, it becomes possible to resolve the crisis in education, turning learning and schooling into the same thing (Schönfeld, 2017; Pritchett, 2013).

The PCB theory structures the problem of the difficulties of mastering scientific knowledge, typical mistakes and misconceptions in the most general form, serving explanatory, diagnostic and predictive tools. It is aimed at identifying the sources of many students' difficulties in the process of mastering an education subject, at developing general approaches to prevent and overcome the PCB. Comprehensive, multidisciplinary analysis of the phenomenon of PCB, presupposing historical and philosophical, psycholinguistic, psychological, categorical and subject aspects, allow lining up the model of real cognitive consciousness of students (Fig.1).

Figure 1. The model of real cognitive consciousness of students
Source: authors' development

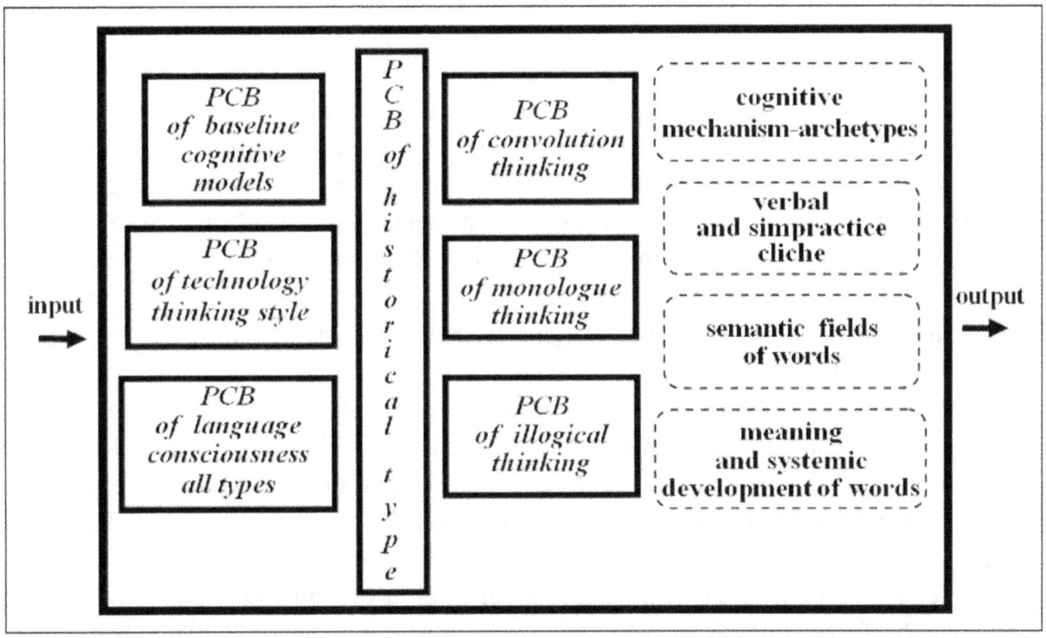

It is this typology that can become in the teachers' hands an effective means of diagnosing various difficulties (PCB) of students, as well as a real mechanism for optimizing the educational process as a whole. The theory of PCB in education focuses on any teacher' and student' problems and reviews determinants of the educational activity success connected with systematic prevention and overcoming the psychological and cognitive barriers of various types, objectively inherent in the student's educational consciousness. It means that definitely authentic failures of mental activity learning (in the Fig.1) should be defined at the "entrance" of educational information before it passes through the "potential psychological boxes".

If the student does not know how to overcome these psychological-cognitive barriers then he ***doesn't know how he knows***. The students' learning could be of a high level as a result of their successful overcoming of the PCB system, objectively inherent in the minds of students. The methodological basis of the PCB theory in teaching, which represents a fundamentally new basis for the creation of innovative educational technologies, combined with the model of real cognitive consciousness of students, represents a fundamentally new basis for the creation of innovative educational technologies focused on the development of the intellectually autonomous personalities for the post-COVID-19 reality (Maor, et al., 2017). At the same time, the model of real cognitive consciousness of students could become a new pedagogical tool designed to identify cognitive difficulties, their diagnostics, and to organize their reflection (self-reflection) by students (in the minds of students).

The methodological basis of the Pilipenko theory of PCB to learning and the generalized model of the real cognitive consciousness of students act as a new multifunctional pedagogical tool that allows:1) to carry out a causal diagnosis of students' cognitive difficulties; 2) to organize reflection and self-reflection of the students for the identifying unproductive cognitive strategies; 3) to design innovative educational technologies focused on the development of human capital as an important factor of the formation and development of the knowledge economy; 4) to solve effectively the third problem of the Pinsky triad - ***how to learn*** or, somewhat broader, ***how to teach to learn***. The psycho-pedagogical activity organized in this way could significantly increase the effectiveness of studying.

The problems of modern education are largely predetermined by the fact that the traditional learning paradigm dominates in the educational process (Fig.2). In its framework the learner is considered as an object of influence of a teacher (subject – object influence). Mass errors, cognitive difficulties and other negative results of such educational process lead to the conclusion of its methodological, methodical and didactic inconsistency because the real cognitive representations of students are ignored. The PCB theory allowed revealing the phenomenon of risk behaviour of students, predetermined with the presence of many irresistible PCB in their educational consciousness. It is this phenomenon that is manifested in the students' stress, in the formation of their image of complete uncertainty and, naturally, in their weak current educational results, which today is defined as school (educational) failure. And, meanwhile, the ability of a student to overcome their own PCBs in the learning process is the most important quality of an intellectually autonomous personality. A high level of education allows an individual to adapt to any uncertain environment, identify problems in professional activity, understand the reasons for their occurrence and make a non-trivial decision from a multitude for their successful solution (The Economist, 2020a; Dam van, 2019).

However, for all the importance of the educational level of the individual and his quality of self-sufficiency, suitable for behavior in any uncertain situation, education, in which the student is freed from PCBs, is destined to predetermine the tendencies of specialization (division, diversity) in the economy and in society. At the same time, the main participant of these processes is an individual with the quality of intellectual autonomy and the ability to overcome his own PCBs. However, it should be emphasized that only adequate socialization will allow the formation of a critical mass of people with such qualities that will be able to interact and correct socially significant rules of social behavior in accordance with their own ideas about public welfare.

To summarize the above, then the learning crisis due to the COVID-19 pandemic, according to the World Bank (World Bank, 2020) manifests itself in the following: (1) 258 million children and youth of primary- and secondary-school age are out of school; (2) ... the Learning Poverty rate in low- and middle-income countries was 53 percent; (3) … the crisis was not equally distributed: the most disadvantaged children and youth had the worst access to schooling, highest dropout rates, and the largest learning deficits; (4) the world was already far off track for meeting Sustainable Development Goal 4.… However, the above forms of manifestation of the learning crisis rather reflect the crisis of socialization of young people both in education and in the employment system.

Figure 2. Comparison of classical and modern learning paradigms

Source: authors' development on the base of "main differences of empirical and theoretical abstractions, generalizations and concepts" in Davidova, V.V., and Davidov, V.V. (1996). The Theory of Developmental Education, INTOR, Moscow, pp. 72-73.

Classical learning paradigm	Modern learning paradigms
1. The main mission of education: *preparing* the younger generation for life and work	1. The main mission of education: ensuring the conditions of self-determination and *self-realization* of the individual
2. The student is a *simple* system	2. The student is a *complex* system
3. Knowledge is based on the *past* ("school of memory")	3. Knowledge is based on the *future* (*"school of thinking"*)
4. Education as the *transfer to the student of well-known samples* of knowledge and skills ("sampling")	4. Education as the *creation* by the student of an image of the world in himself through active self-reliance of the student into the world of objective, social and spiritual culture
5. The student - as an *object* of pedagogical influence, he *undergoes* studying	5. The student - as a *subject* of pedagogical influence, he is *self-learning*
6. The *subject – object*, monologue relations of the teacher and of the *student*	6. The *subject – subject*, dialogue relations of the teacher and of the *learner*
7. "Response", *reproductive*, student' activity	7. Active, *creative* activity of the learner

Socialization as a Sufficient Condition for the Integration of Intellectually Autonomous Individuals Into the Structural Relationships of the Human-Centric System

Since the mid-2010s, the problems of socialization of individuals (comparable in meaning with the category of "inclusion") have begun to be actively discussed as at the macro-level (WEF, 2015, 2016, 2017, 2018; Breen, 2016) and at the level of companies (The business case for inclusive growth, 2018;

Dixon-Fyle, et al., 2020). At the same time, the mechanism of socialization or inclusion of individuals in the economic and social systems as a whole differs significantly from inclusion of employees into companies' teams. Running a little ahead, it should be emphasized that in the current conditions of the coronavirus, the processes of socialization at the firm level ultimately predetermine the features of socialization at the macro level.

At the same time, socialization as inclusion of employees is predetermined by the quality of their education. The features of such socialization at the firm level are predetermined by the quality of diversity of employees, which, in turn, is the result of their education. It is about the ability or inability of individuals at the end of their learning to reflect, self-reflect and, most importantly, to transcend. Without going deep into the characteristics of the specific mechanism of inclusion, it should be noted that it is largely due to the experience acquired by the individual at the end of the educational process from the following list: (1) experience of cognitive activity, recorded in the form of knowledge (cognitive component); (2) experience in the implementation of known methods of activity in the form of the ability to act according to a model (operational component); (3) experience of creative activity - in the form of the ability to make effective decisions in problem situations (creative component); (4) experience in the implementation of emotional-value relationships - in the form of personal orientations (motivational-orientation component). The acquisition by a student of a certain set of experiences as a result of education serves as the basis for diversity in society and predetermines the possibilities of his inclusion (socialization) into the company's team. The latter is of decisive importance for understanding the situation that has developed due to COVID-19, in which companies and their CEOs are destined to form structural relationships of a new reality based on human-centrism, which should replace capital-centrism.

Based on the developments of Russian scientists in the field of human psychology (Slobodchikov, et al., 1995; Slobodchikov, et al., 2000), human development psychology (Slobodchikov, et al., 2000) and educational psychology (Slobodchikov, et al., 2013), the authors identified fundamental changes associated with education in the context of the conditions for constructing a human-centric system on the technological basis of the 4th industrial revolution. For the purposes of constructing post-coronavirus reality, education should be aimed at the formation of an intellectually autonomous personality capable of self-development on the basis of the qualities of reflection (self-reflection) and transcending acquired in the educational process (Ananiev, 1977; Ushinsky, 2005; Elkonin, 1989; Piaget, 2008; Vygotsky, 1960; Slobodchikov, et al., 2013). This is preceded by the minimization of the gap between "what to teach" (from the side of the teacher) and "what to learn" (from the side of the student) in the learning process, which indicates the formation of the participants' ability to overcome their PCBs in the educational process. Then, upon graduation, individuals capable of self-development objectively need socialization (integration, inclusion into the various structures of society), since it mediates their self-development. In other words, in the human-centric system, education has a special mission - to create conditions for the formation of a critical mass of individuals with the qualities of intellectual autonomy, capable of adequately socializing and self-developing for the purpose of ensuring societal integrity and social progress. Thus, it is only as a result of education that a person develops dialectically interconnected abilities for reflection and for transcending, which predetermine his socialization. In this interpretation, education becomes a necessary condition for constructing the future post-COVID-19 reality in the form of a human-centric system, and socialization becomes its sufficient condition. In this process, a self-developing personality structures his inner subjectivity in the process of his self-organization, and objectifies it outwardly through transcending.

From a theoretical point of view, a self-developing intellectually autonomous individual is distinguished by the ability to reflect or to realize the boundaries of his own subjectivity and the ability to transcend these boundaries, opening up new opportunities for the realization of the individual self outside him (in society). The latter is the content of the process of socialization (inclusion) of the individual into various structures in society. It is in this sense that the content of the human-centric system is accompanied by the deepening of knowledge about properly human nature in man. The dialectics of the interaction of reflection as a result of training an individual and transcending as the basis of his socialization predetermines the essence of the mechanism of human self-development. If a person in the process of education was unable to form the ability to transcend, then this means that in the process of self-reflection he did not learn to overcome his PCBs. As a result, his level of education and ability for self-reflection are insufficient to become an intellectually autonomous person in an uncertain reality, and fully realize himself through transcending. If the individual's abilities for self-development are limited, then he has not learned to overcome the PCBs in the educational process. This makes him helpless in overcoming the manifold PCBs that he may face in an external uncertain reality.

It is logical to assume in this regard that the crisis of modern education is caused by the growing gap between a person's ability to self-reflection and his ability to transcend, i.e. between the self-organization of his inner subjectivity and self-development as a manifestation of his individuality (selfhood) outside in the form of intellectual autonomy. In addition, from a philosophical point of view, the crisis of modern education can be defined from the point of its impact on the integrity of society and the individual as dialectic of unity in diversity. If an individual has not acquired the ability to transcend in education then his socialization into the structure of society does not strengthen it (at best, does not change). In such a state, society is ready for a quick break of its structural relationships due to extreme conditions, since only a self-developing personality with a high ability to transcend is capable of quickly solving extraordinary problems. Here is another explanation why societies, represented by their states, took unprecedented measures to combat COVID-19 by breaking structural ties that will be restored already in the process of constructing a new reality. In other words, the societal crisis, as well as the economic crisis itself, were objectively predetermined by the state of structural ties, which gradually lost their integrity as a person lost (or decrease) the ability for self-reflection and transcending as a result of the learning process. Thus, education has a priority role in the construction of the future reality.

Recent innovations in education, which have already begun to respond to the above-mentioned problems, are associated with the competence-based approach as a reaction to the widening gap between theoretical thinking (associated with education) and social practice (the mechanism of socialization) (Schleicher, et al., 2016). It is no coincidence that it was originally initiated by the Western business representing this social practice. On the one hand, CEOs needed graduates who would be ready to immediately get involved in work, and, on the other hand, firms were interested in young people being able to flexibly retrain and master new knowledge and technologies throughout their professional life. The competence-based approach to education assumes that educational competence should include both cognitive and operational-technological components, as well as motivational, ethical and social ones. In this case, educational competence must implement a predetermined social requirement (normal) for educational training. It is about a specific set of interrelated orientations, knowledge, abilities, skills, real experience of the student's activity in relation to a certain range of objects of reality, necessary for the implementation of personally and socially significant productive activity.

The positive in the competence-based approach is that it does not deny the importance of knowledge, but focuses on the ability to acquire, process and use the knowledge gained, including independently in practical life. As a negative aspect in the competence-based approach, it should be singled out its goals (i.e. content) of education, dictated by the requirements of society (or of its social order), implemented by the state on behalf of society and due to its needs. In other words, the competence-based approach lacks the fundamental mission of education - to create conditions for the self-development of the individual. It is focused on identifying and transforming only individual, fragmentary human potentials into purely useful resources for their utilization in a particular social production. This is the main difference between the mission of education in the human-centric systems and capital-centric one, the structure of which was destroyed by the first wave of the COVID-19 pandemic (Fig. 3).

Figure 3. OECD: Model of educational achievements - 2030
Source: OECD, (2016). Schleicher A., Ramos G. Global competency for an inclusive world (online) Retrieved from: https://www.oecd.org/pisa/aboutpisa/Global-competency-for-an-inclusive-world.pdf

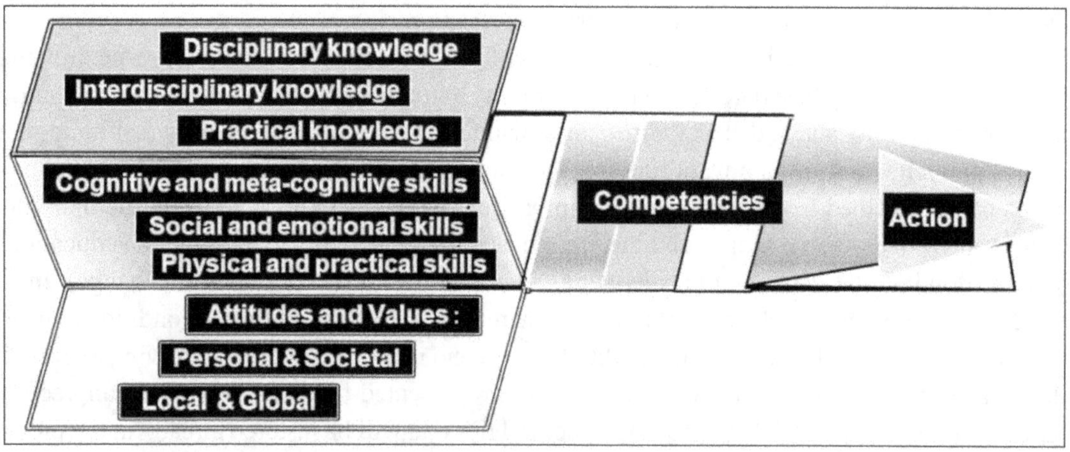

This specificity of the competence-based approach to the content of education is well traced in the components of the OECD model of educational achievements (OECD, 2016) (Fig. 3). This quality "human resource" is quite useful for society at a specific stage of its development, but not for the formation of "properly human in a person". Man as a natural social being appears in the aggregate of his essential forces, generic abilities, and the world as a unity of nature and society appears as a universe of objective forms of culture. These two poles - the objectivity of culture (in the broad sense) and the inner world, the essential forces of a person - are connected in education, conjugated in the content of education.

It is logical that education, in the context of preparing an intellectually autonomous personality capable of self-development, performs the function of ensuring the dominance of human-centric principles in the organization of a new post-COVID-19 social reality. And its main creator is a self-developing person who can fully realize his subjectivity only in society. And the quality of an intellectually autonomous personality allows him to socialize (self-develop in society) consciously, since his success is predetermined by his individual ability to overcome PCBs both in education and in social reality. For such an individual, the digitalization of society does not threaten with the loss of a job, since he is able to create cyber-human systems that involve people and machines and combine the wisdom of humans with the capabilities of technology for the greater good. According to Thomas W. Malone (Malone, 2018), «people should move from thinking about *putting humans in the loop* to *putting computers in the group*».

With the increasing importance of the intellectually autonomous personality, it is the individual who begins to predetermine the dialectical unity of the individual and society through his socialization, since the prosperity of society depends on his diverse abilities. From a philosophical point of view, this can be explained by the fact that the basis of the mechanism of self-development of society and the self-organization of its structural ties is the unity of goals (needs, motivations) set by a person, and the means of achieving them (satisfying human needs as the realization of his goals). It is this dialectic that predetermines the complication of all systems with the participation of a person in all spheres of his activity and his socialization as a dialectic of the relationship between the individual and society as a whole. If society evaluates the abilities of intellectually autonomous individuals highly, then it will provide him with all the external attributes of success in the profession and in society. If society does not do this, then the intellectually autonomous person will socialize on the conditions that suit him, or will prefer not to socialize at all, as the Russian mathematician Grigory Perelman did after his epoch-making contribution to the development of mathematics. In other words, society should be ready to socialize intellectually autonomous individuals on their terms, since only in this case they will basically share the value priorities of society. The priority of people capable of intellectual autonomy predetermines the functional dependence of society on them, the integrity of which depends on their desire to self-develop within its boundaries. These fundamental changes in the context of the COVID-19 pandemic were first felt by CEOs while rebuilding a stronger business after lockdown

J. Schumpeter is Right: Chief Executive Officers are the Main Demiurges of the New Post-COVID-19 Reality

The specificity of the situation that has developed as a result of the coronavirus, associated with the complete uncertainty of the future reality, is manifested in the fact that the structural level of firms is called upon to design it. It is they who, for objective reasons, cannot finish their activities as a result of an economic lockdown. Such a situation is predetermined by many essential features of entrepreneurs in the person of CEOs of modern companies, as well as their innovative function deeply described by J. Schumpeter (Schumpeter, 1949). As a result of the economic and social lockdown, the business was forced to abandon its long-term development strategies due to the complete uncertainty of the future. But in the short run, CEOs are forced to take swift steps to minimize the negative impact of this uncertainty. In the figurative expression of the KPMG specialists, advanced firms represented by their CEOs focus on finding opportunity in adversity (KPMG, 2020).

It's amazing that firms have begun to rethink their mission in a new social reality due to the coronavirus pandemic. According to KPMG experts, the most CEOs have shifted their organizations' purpose from purely profit to its social valuation. As a result 54 percent of the respondents have taken a broader, purpose-driven approach aimed at multiple stakeholders' needs. And around 22 percent have connected their primary objective with improving society. Only less than a quarter (23 percent) of CEOs continued to view the overall purpose of the organization in the narrow sense of "governance for shareholder value". Thus more then 79 percent of CEOs had to re-evaluate their purpose as a result of COVID-19 (Fig. 4).

CEOs recognize that recovery from the pandemic does not mean a return to 'normal'. Instead, there is an opportunity to define a new future. According to Fig. 3, COVID-19 has forced CEOs to radically adjust the goals of their organizations by increasing the importance of social aspects of activities. B 2020 CEOs became increasingly prepared to personally take part in tackling society's major challenges. Ac-

Figure 4. The impact of the pandemic: more powerful and relevant than ever purposes of CEOs
Source: KPMG (2020). CEO Outlook: COVID-19. Special Edition. Executive summary. KPMG International

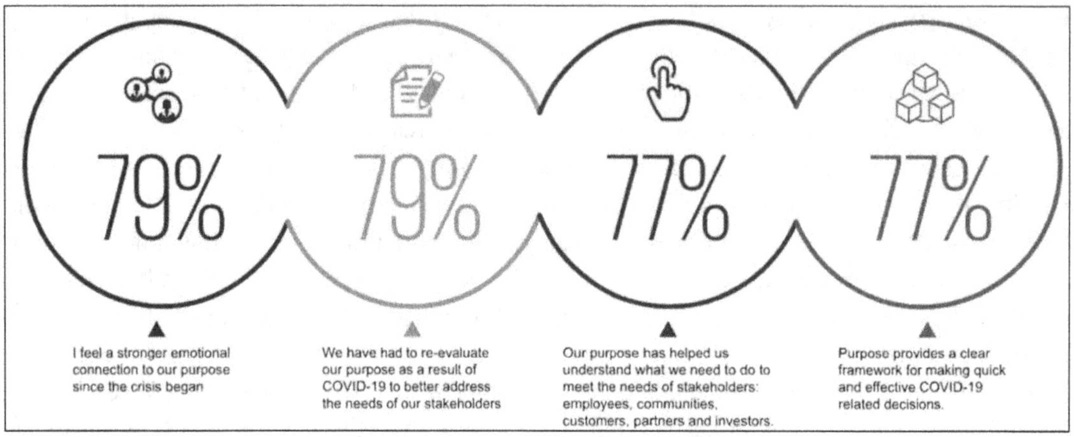

cording to 65 percent of the respondent CEOs, the importance of business in solving the societal crisis will increase as the trust of society and citizens in the state falls. Under these conditions, it becomes clear why 76 percent of the respondent CEOs mention their personal responsibility to be a ‘leader for change on societal issues’. These results generally indicate the peculiarities of business socialization in the new conditions of the COVID-19 pandemic, which manifests itself both in the process of adapting it to new realities and of structuring it to fit your requirements. In fact, this is how the dialectic of interaction of factors of self-organization and self-development of firms is realized in conditions when they are forced to turn into active participants in the processes of structuring a new reality. Moreover, a tendency is gradually established to replace adaptive methods of doing business in society with creative actions creating reality as desired by practical organizations.

It is symptomatic that the adjustment of the internal self-organization of companies is carried out, first of all, in connection with the conditions for attracting and inclusion (socialization) of talents. It is with them that companies associate their accelerated digitalization and their future success in the new reality. This proves, in general, the validity of the above theoretical conclusions of the authors regarding the dialectics of the interaction of education and socialization of individuals and their place in the modern societal and economic crisis. As for CEOs, in a crisis state of society, they come to the need to rebuild the mechanism of their socialization in society, as well as internal structures, focusing on personnel with extraordinary abilities, which distinguishes intellectually autonomous individuals (Fig. 5). And if the future reality in the context of society or the environment of the firm’s functioning is uncertain, therefore, the employee is needed in the totality of all his potential abilities, which predetermines his own socialization and success, as well as the successful socialization of the organizations in which he will work. In fact, CEOs evaluate and test a variety of mechanisms for socializing their firms into an uncertain future reality. As a result, theoretical conclusions and practical results are reduced to the same. The problem of talented employees (with the qualities of intellectual autonomy) comes to the fore, since it is they who, adequately socializing through inclusion in companies’ teams, mediate technologies for minimizing the uncertainty of future reality and are able to simulate a variety of mechanisms for strengthening the position of business in the future post-coronavirus reality.

Figure 5. The companies' need of building employees' skills in critical thinking, leadership and management, and advanced data analysis
Source: Agrawal, Sapana, Aaron De Smet, Pawel Poplawski, and Angelika Reich (2020). Beyond hiring: How companies are reskilling to address talent gaps. Organization Practice and McKinsey Accelerate. January. McKinsey & Company
Note: [1]Out of 35 skills included in the Survey. Question was asked only of respondents who say their organizations have a re-skilling program currently under way or have already re-skilled >1 group, or class of employees; n= 394

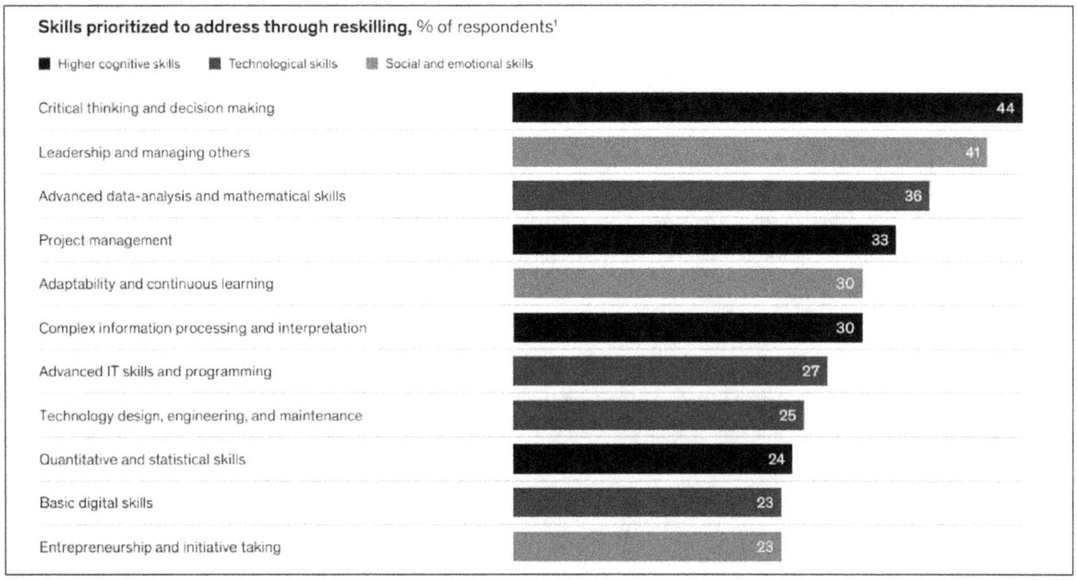

CEOs came to this conclusion quickly enough. Thus, if at the beginning of 2020 CEOs ranked 'talent risk' behind 11 other ones, то уже спустя полгода it becomes the number one threat to long-term growth. According to the new McKinsey Global Survey on future workforce needs (Agrawal, et al., 2020), nearly nine in ten executives and managers say their organizations either face skill gaps already or expect gaps to develop within the next five years. There is a need for their organizations to address potential skill gaps in a wide range of business areas (Fig. 5). Nearly all respondents classify closing potential skill gaps as a priority for their organizations, and about one-third put it among the top three priorities. Furthermore, organizations are acutely aware of the importance of learning in today's business environment. They also understand that the ability of the workforce to learn new skills, model new behavior, and adapt continuously is key to sustained success (Nielsen, et al., 2020). And these requirements for the employee's abilities are obviously associated with the qualities of an intellectually autonomous personality capable of self-development. The experts express this idea as follows: "....only if the individual intentionally treat every moment as a learning opportunity, then everyday experiences and interactions could be accepted (treated) as tremendous learning opportunities" (Christensen, et al., 2020; Mattey, et al., 2020).

By prioritizing their requirements for the conditions of socialization in the current uncertain environment due to COVID-19, CEOs understand the need to adapt to the priority preferences of talented employees. As self-organizing, intellectually autonomous individuals, they will choose their future jobs and companies in accordance with their individual values. It is no coincidence that recently more and more organizations write about their aspiration to become an Employer of Choice in the new reality. It is about more holistic Employee Value Proposition (EVP) that matches their employees' needs and aspirations. A talented, happy and consistent workforce adds to an organisation's overall competitive advantage. Given COVID-19 is a public health crisis, and the most common positive impact felt by people during this period was 'feeling safe', trust is increasingly important in times of uncertainty (Boston Consulting Group, 2020) (Fig. 6). This is backed by 83% of employees stating that trust in their employer is important. While trust during COVID-19 restrictions is often linked to physical safety (e.g., hygiene protocols), it is also related to psychological factors such as job stability and security, as well as autonomy to get work done. Considering the preferences of their future employees, CEOs highlight the conditions that must be created in the organization in order to attract talented employees, i.e. possessing the qualities of intellectual autonomy, in the author's interpretation

Figure 6. Top 10 ways employers can gain their employees' trust
Source: BCG (2020). Workforce Sentiment Survey. Boston Consulting Group.
Note: n=1002, Australia only

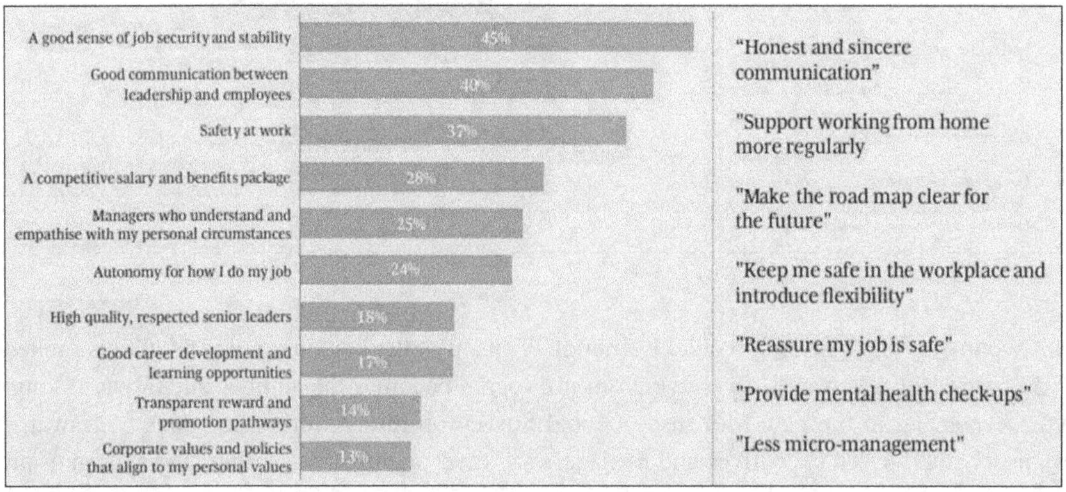

In other words, CEOs recognize that the success of their company depends on the internal environment that will initiate employees to continuous learning and improving their professional skills. Numerous studies of companies' practices in this area have shown a strong correspondence between employees' stated needs and the underlying drivers of their engagement, well-being, and work effectiveness. Table 2 shows the top employee needs and outcome drivers, grouped by core themes of employee experience.

Jointly, ten employee experience elements accounted for approximately 60 percent of differences in outcomes. Thus as organizations continue to adapt to the crisis, they can meaningfully improve employee experience. Even if organizations may not be able to take compensate right now, they can achieve a 55 percent improvement in engagement by addressing employees' need for work recognition through non-financial means (Emmett, et al., 2020). To resume it should be noted that to address employees' needs and help them thrive during the return, organizations should focus on four areas: safety and security, relationships, culture, and purpose. It is because, according to the CEO of one organization, they are putting teams of their best people on the hardest problems – if they can't solve it no one can. CEOs of the most advanced organizations interpret this strategy as the art of the possible (COVID-19: Briefing materials, 2020) (Fig. 7).

In other words, in connection with employees with the qualities of intellectual autonomy, it is the companies, represented by their CEOs, that must create the necessary conditions for their socialization (inclusion) taking into account those aspirations that will strengthen the integrity of the company and contribute to its rebuilding as a strong business in the conditions of uncertainty due to pandemic coronavirus. This approach differs significantly from the parameters of the capital-centric system, in which the parameters of success were set by capital owners and CEOs at the firm level, and by the state - at the social level. They also dictated the basic conditions of socialization (inclusion), which were to be accepted by individuals unconditionally, as a given. The progress of the emerging reality with a self-developing person as a driver of the principles of its organization dictates new conditions for his socialization: the priority of individual requirements is gradually becoming unconditional both for the company and for society.

Figure 7. Employees' engagement, well-being, and effectiveness, driven by a set of employee experience factors

Source: Jonathan Emmett, Gunnar Schrah, Matt Schrimper, and Alexandra Wood (2020). COVID-19 and the employee experience: How leaders can seize the moment. Organization Practice. June. Mckinsey&Company

Top employee needs and experience factors by core themes of employee experience

Theme	Need (rank)	Employee experience factors	Improvement		
			Work effectiveness	Engagement	Well-being
Stable, secure work experience	Job security (1) Financial stability (2)	Organizational stability	+16.9%	+52.9%	+53.3%
	Physical and mental health (6) Being rewarded (8)	Compensation and benefits	+21.2%	+45.6%	+44.5%
Trusting relationships	Working with people I can trust (5)	Trust in leadership	+23.7%	+47.6%	+45.4%
		Relationship with company	+20.9%	+49.9%	+51.3%
	Being recognized for my work (10)	Nonfinancial recognition	+20.4%	+55.1%	+49.3%
Social cohesion and inclusion	Being treated fairly (4)	Fairness	+22.3%	+48.0%	+52.3%
		Involvement	+14.8%	+32.4%	+51.1%
	Having supportive coworkers (9)	Respect	+15.7%	+51.8%	+49.8%
		Equality	+16.2%	+50.8%	+50.9%
Individual purpose and contribution	Achieving work goals (7) Balance of work and private life (3) Fulfilling my personal purpose at work (12)	Alignment with organizational purpose and values	+20.3%	+49.0%	+49.3%

Unsurpassed PCBs of CEOs: What Hinders Optimization of Tectological Principles of Diversity (Disintegration) and Inclusion (Integration) in the Firms

Socialization, as the realization of a person's ability to self-development, not only depends on the level of education of the individual, but itself can be realized only under the condition of optimizing the tectological processes (Bogdanov, 1934)) of separation (specialization, disintegration, diversity) and unification (cooperation, integration, inclusion) in the structures of society. Moreover, these processes are differently implemented at the macro level of society and at the micro level of firms. The COVID-19 pandemic and the destruction of structural ties as a result of lockdown dictated new conditions for the subordination of these processes: companies, represented by their CEOs, become drivers of the processes of socialization (as a result of diversity and inclusion) of individuals. Consequently, it is they who are forced to be the first to structure organizational processes at the level of firms, rebuilding them on the human-centric principles (Küpper, et al., 2020). Gradually, they will predetermine the structuring of the future post-COVID-19 reality at the macro level of society.

Socialization at the firm level is based on the coordination of processes of diversity and inclusion. In publications on this issue, inclusion is put in the first place, and diversity – in the second, therefore the firms' strategy is called inclusion and diversity (I&D) one. However, theoretically, although these phenomena are dialectically interdependent, the priority still belongs to diversity. This is due to the fact that inclusion is advisable in the case of diversity of phenomena, subjects, objects, processes, etc. The less diverse (specialized, disconnected) the phenomena, the less expedient the inclusion, since the resulting effect will be small. And vice versa: the more diverse subjects are in terms of their abilities, specialization, professionalism, the more effective their inclusion becomes. In our case, it is the training of educated individuals capable of self-reflection and self-development that serves as the basis for the inclusion of the organizational structure of the company. And the greater the diversity of intellectually autonomous individuals included into the organizations' team, the more opportunities the firm has to succeed in an uncertain environment. The diversity of extraordinary talented personalities allows, under adequate conditions of their socialization (inclusion), to give a diversity of extraordinary solutions that allow structuring an indefinite environment. But at the same time, adequate inclusion (socialization) of talented individuals in the team of the organization becomes a serious problem.

It should be noted that the explanation of the reasons for the not-so-obvious progress of firms implementing an I&D strategy lies in the attitude of the CEOs themselves to the conditions that optimize I&D processes in organizations in relation to talented employees. Moreover, it is possible to concretize this situation as a consequence of the unresolved PCBs of the CEOs themselves. This is manifested in their individual attitude to those components that predetermine diversity and inclusion separately. The fact is that the negative attitude of CEOs towards them erects a few critical barriers in the way of the sustained change in company's culture, and the individual mindsets and behavior, that are needed to build a truly inclusive and diverse culture. The first barrier is a lack of purposeful follow through on diversity and inclusion pledges. It means that public commitments to build a diverse and inclusive company culture should be followed by systematic, business-led approach to I&D on the behalf of CEOs. The latter is necessary to translate these pledges into actual changes. HR director of one of the companies expressed this idea as follows: "A disconnect between what the company says and the progress it is making on the ground can seriously erode credibility both inside and outside of the organization, and further contribute to a lack of experienced inclusion". In other words, it is about the intentions of CEOs to implement the I&D strategy in their organizations and the absence of real steps to implement it in the activities of all departments and employees.

The second obstacle is more fundamental, and it largely explains the presence of the first one. The fact is that both inclusion and diversity imply the presence of certain parameters that determine them. Generally unaddressed misconceptions about fairness and meritocracy are one critical issue. The Mckinsey&Company' experts (Hunt, et al., 2015; Hunt, et al., 2018; Dixon-Fyle, et al., 2020) quite rightly noted that, that the logic behind prioritizing inclusion alongside diversity is coming more clearly into focus—but the full dynamics of the different aspects of inclusion, and their relative importance, are not yet fully understood. Inclusion is closely linked to employee engagement, itself in turn a critical component of employee retention, productivity and financial performance (Fig. 8).

So it becomes possible to выделить two indicators of a systematic approach to I&D, including diverse representation itself, and leadership accountability for I&D. As to core indicators of

inclusion, its three core indicators are researched as follows (Dixon-Fyle, 2020): "equality" is defined as fairness and transparency in promotion, pay and recruitment, and equal access to sponsorship opportunities as well as other resources and retention support; "openness" is defined as an organizational culture where people treat each other with mutual respect, and where bias, bullying, discrimination and micro-aggressions are actively tackled; "belonging" is defined as an outcome resulting from the organization's demonstrating commitment to support the well-being and contributions of diverse and other employees. Leaders and managers foster connection with their diverse talent and between all employees, building a sense of community and encouraging them to contribute their diverse talents fully.

According to Mckinsey&Company' research (Hunt, 2018; Dixon-Fyle, 2020), overall sentiment of CEOs on diversity is 52 percent positive and 31 percent negative. As to sentiment of CEOs on inclusion the results have become markedly worse at only 29 percent positive and 61 percent negative. Moreover, as far as "equality" is concerned, in the structure of assessments of CEOs who are inclined to implement the I&D strategy more broadly, 74% assess this position as negative. With regard to the 'openness' indicator, sentiments of 44% of respondent CEOs are negative, and together with the neutral assessments of the respondents, the negative attitude of CEOs to this indicator exceeds 50% of all respondents. These data indicate that CEOs themselves are not ready to create normal conditions for the socialization of gifted talented individuals capable of intellectual autonomy and realizing their potential for the benefit of rebuilding a stronger business in the face of uncertainty due to COVID-19.

RESULTS AND DISCUSSION

The above conclusions lead to the question: if CEOs are forced to rebuild a stronger business in the face of uncertainty due to COVID-19 and realize that only people are the key factor in their success, then why do they have such a contradictory attitude towards the conditions of their socialization into the firm? The problem is that a firm is a structure that, on the one hand, socializes itself, i.e. is forced to integrate (be included) into the structural relationships of society, and on the other hand, it itself must socialize (include in the organization's team) individuals with different levels of education. So, when socializing into the structure of society, the company adapts to the environment in order to continue its activities in society. When it comes to socializing individuals into its structure, the firm must take into account the requirements of those individuals whose qualities meet the firm's top needs for employees. There are no questions about the growing demand for talented firms capable of adapting to the uncertain external environment of firms. They must be able to tackle the non-trivial challenges faced by employers due to the COVID-19 pandemic.

Figure 8. Sentiments on inclusion are on average more negative than those on diversity (% of negative sentiments[1])

Source: Dixon-Fyle, Sundiatu, Vivian Hunt, Kevin Dolan, and Sara Prince (2020). Diversity wins. How inclusion matters. Mckinsey&Company. May

Note: [1] total number of mentions by theme: Diversity 1,153; Leadership 3,216; Inclusion 2, 077; Equality 1,257; Openness 710; Belonging 110.

[2] Weighted average of Equality, Openness and Belonging

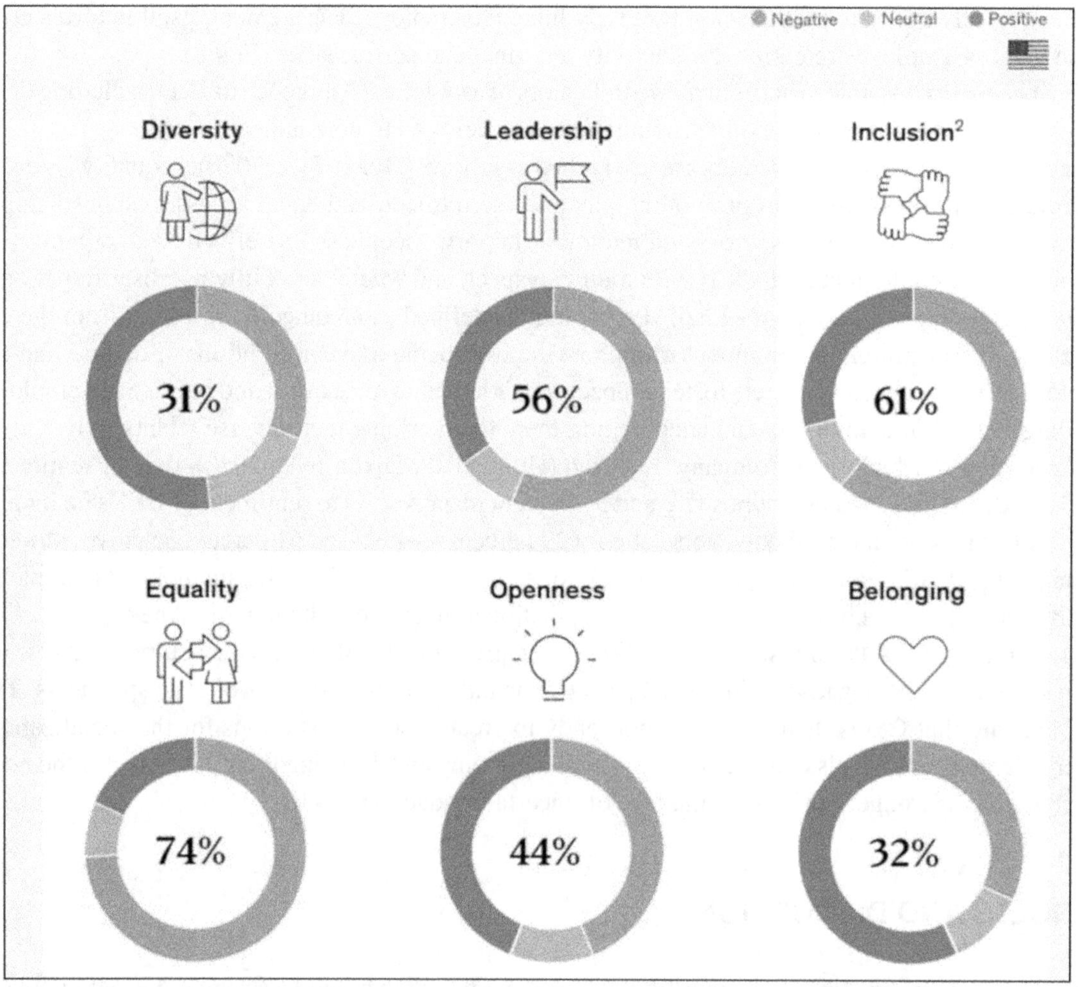

If over the past five years the process of socialization of talented employees at the firm level has not been proceeding at a rapid pace, then, all other things being equal, the question of the mechanisms for implementing CEOs I&D strategy becomes paramount. What's wrong here?

From a theoretical and practical point of view, it turns out that the mechanism for optimizing such tectological principles as diversity and inclusion within a firm is a serious problem. As noted above, diversity is determined by the different level of education of employees, and inclusion is the ability of firms to include them into a single effective organization's team. Moreover, all the prerequisites for the formation of such teams are obvious. So, back in 2019 according to the Mckinsey&Company' experts (McConnell, et al., 2019), the resulting job displacement could be massive—think Industrial Revolution massive—affecting as many as 800 million people globally by 2030 and requiring up to 375 million of them to switch occupational categories and learn new skills. As a whole the companies lack the talent they will need in the future: 44 percent of respondents say their organizations will face skill gaps within the next five years, and another 43 percent report existing skill gaps (Fig. 9) (Agrawal, et al., 2020). In other words, 87 percent of respondents either are experiencing gaps now or expect them within a few years.

Figure 9. Respondents' expectations for skill shortages due to market and technology trends that are changing the talent needs of organizations
Source: Küpper, Daniel, Tom Reichert, Tom Reichert, Vaishali Rastogi, *and* Ryoji Kimura *(2020). How CEOs (chief executive officer) Can Win the Fight and Transform to Win the Future. Boston Consulting Group. June 8*
Note: [1] Figures may not sum to 100%, because of rounding; n=1,216

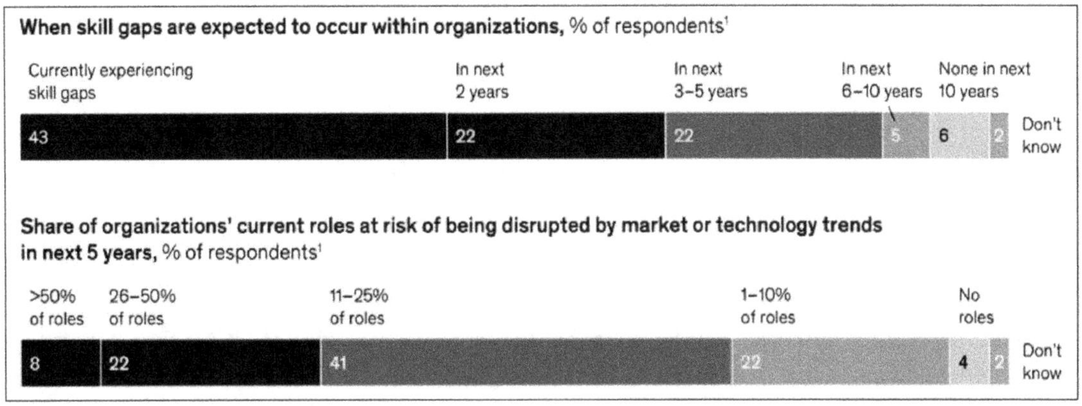

For CEOs today it becomes obvious that achieving strong performance in the new reality will require more than a rapid crisis response. Winning the fight will be a marathon and during this period, business continuity and competitive position will constantly be at risk and require active management. And, winning the future will demand making long-term, proactive moves even as the fight phase persists (Küpper, et al., 2020). To respond proactively, CEOs must focus on five priorities (Fig. 10).

The framework provides the key activities that companies must pursue in five functional areas. And practically all of them are somehow connected with the socialization of talented individuals into the team of their organizations. And today the directions of the CEOs' policy aimed at solving the problems of the personnel gap are also known. It is about optimizing diversity and inclusion processes in the organizations through the development and implementation of the I&D strategy. The main problem is in the details. The point is that each of the components of the mechanisms of diversity and inclusion of talented employees in the firms' team, imply the introduction of certain behavioral norms that must be followed by all representatives of firms from lower to upper levels of management. For example, "gender" and "ethical" parameters, as well as "leadership" refer to the parameters of diversity, while "equality", "openness", "belonging" are characteristics of inclusion. As a result, among all firms that stepped up their efforts to implement the I&D strategy, financial performance improved among those that were able to more or less fully implement the conditions for the implementation of the processes of diversity and of inclusion in the teams of their organizations. And those firms that inconsistently implemented all these parameters either did not receive any return, or even worsened their financial performance.

Figure 10. CEOs: framework for addressing five critical priorities
Source: Küpper, Daniel, Tom Reichert, Tom Reichert, Vaishali Rastogi, *and* Ryoji Kimura *(2020). How CEOs (chief executive officer) Can Win the Fight and Transform to Win the Future. Boston Consulting Group. June 8*

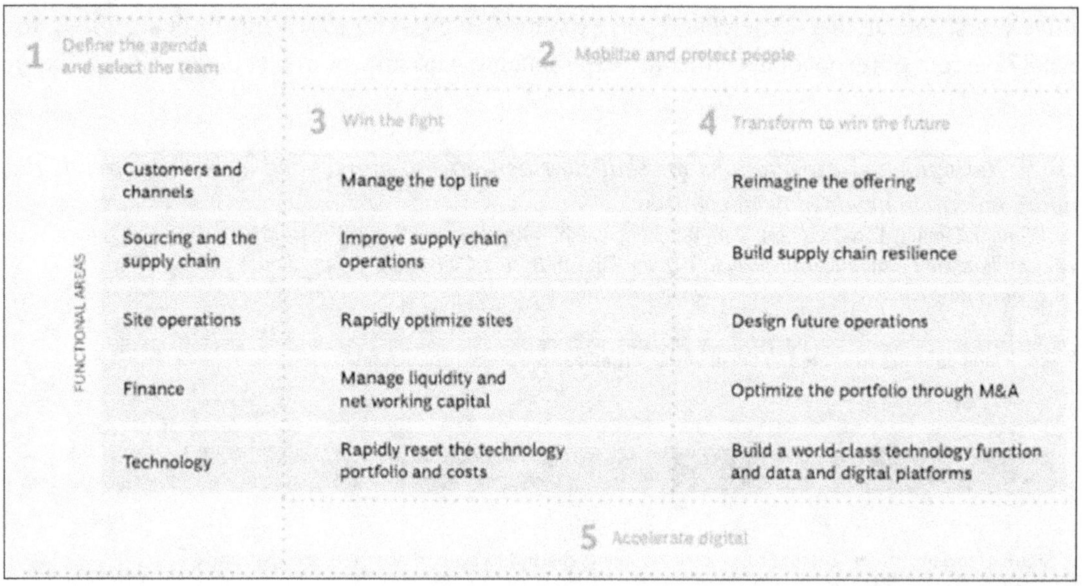

The main problem of unsuccessful firms is that the negative attitudes of CEOs themselves towards certain I&D parameters, especially in terms of "leadership", "equality" and "openness". In fact, in this way, there appear the insurmountable PCBs of CEOs themselves, who formed as persons with qualities of intellectual autonomous in the capital-centric system. To rebuild a stronger business in the uncertain environment and achieve longer-term objectives, CEOs must learn to overcome their PCBs as to positive attitude to such parameters as "leadership" and "equality", as well as to "openness" and "belonging" to socialize talented employees for their organizations' success. By applying the lessons learned from implementations of the I&D strategy across businesses, CEOs can optimize these practices and enhance the efficiency, satisfaction, and engagement of the workforce over the long term. Satisfaction and engagement will also be crucial for retaining employees, especially as the market for talent heats up again during the recovery.

Empirical Evidence

So, the authors' assessments based on the data of Mckinsey & Company (Dixon-Fyle, 2020) showed the validity of the above conclusions that the I&D strategy is a promising mechanism for the socialization of talented individuals at the firm level under conditions of uncertainty. However, for all the seeming simplicity of its implementation in the practice of firms, it turned out that the subjective aspect associated with the seriousness of the CEOs' intentions plays a predominant role in obtaining results in the context of financial indicators.

Thus, the Mckinsey&Company' experts (Dixon-Fyle, 2020) identified five groups of companies, that participated in the poll: (1) Diversity Leaders (5 percent of the data set); (2) Fast Movers (28 percent of the data set); (3) Resting on Laurels (29 percent of the data set); (4) Moderate Movers (10 percent of the data set); (5) Laggards (28 percent of the data set).

Diversity Leaders distinguishes a systematic, business-led approach to I&D for at least five years. For such companies the following is typical: a strong culture of accountability, deployment of innovative and ambitious interventions, and strong leadership commitment.

Fast Movers have strongly focused on I&D, including developing a bespoke business case with ambitious I&D targets, promotion of full transparency including talent processes, pay, and effective retention initiatives.

Resting on Laurels features a less systematic approach to I&D, including initiatives such as employee resource groups but with less emphatic efforts to tackle the barriers connected with other parameters of diversity.

For **Moderate Movers** it is typical to have failing commitments to I&D to translate them into tangible progress on representation, including workplace culture. This is largely due to the lack of a robust articulation of a "reason why" for diversity at all levels, and insufficient attention to inclusive mindsets and behaviour.

Laggards have typically not embarked on a purposeful I&D strategy. This is accompanied by lack of data and of insight into the I&D performance and by the fragmentation of the sparse efforts of fledgling employee resource groups. These companies typically have limited accountability for I&D at all levels, and significant challenges with inclusion.

The estimates below are based on data only for two parameters characterizing diversity: gender and ethnicity. The results are tabulated in Fig. 11.

Figure 11. Data describing the shares of companies implementing certain elements of the diversity strategy and their different results for the period of 2014 and 2019
Source: authors' development on the base of the Mckinsey&Company' research (Dixon-Fyle, 2020)

	i	share of companies (p_i)	2014 Gender	2019 Gender	share of companies (p_i)	2014 Ethnicity	2019 Ethnicity
Diversity leaders	1	0.05	26	40	0.15	17	32
Fast movers	2	0.28	7	27	0.24	1	18
Resting on laurels	3	0.29	28	22	0.22	18	12
Moderate movers	4	0.10	12	19	0.11	3	10
Laggards	5	0.28	9	8	0.28	1	0
Weighted mathematical expectation (μ)			15.100	20.080		7.360	12.860
Weighted standard deviation (σ)			9.162	10.005		7.872	10.424
Coefficient of variation (CV)			0.607	0.498		1.070	0.811

Obviously, the distribution of such values as "Diversity leaders", "Fast movers", "Resting on laurels", "Moderate movers" and "Laggards" in a sample of 1000 firms is random. Analyzing this information, the authors introduced into the consideration generalized characteristics both according to gender and ethnic indicators:

weighted mathematical expectation $$\mu = \sum_{i=1}^{5} p_i a_i , \quad (1)$$

weighted standard deviation $\sigma = \sqrt{\sum_{i=1}^{5} p_i \left(a_i - \mu\right)^2}$, (2)

coefficient of variation ! $V = \frac{\sigma}{\mu}$, (3)

where a_i – gender or ethnic data for the corresponding years.

In addition, it is interesting to estimate the value (***H***) entropy as an uncertainty measure of information:

$$H = \sum_{i=1}^{5} p_i \log_2 p_i . \quad (4)$$

For practical applications, it is convenient to express entropy in terms of binary logarithms In this case the unit of entropy has a special name of *bit*. Estimates obtained using formulas (1) – (4) make it possible to explore the statistical content of tabular data. In particular, based on, for example, an estimate of expectation $\boldsymbol{\mu}$ = 20.080 it becomes possible to build a confidence interval (10.075; 30.085), into which the real value of this quantity will fall with the probability 0.68. On the other hand, coefficients of variation clearly demonstrate how much of the data spread $\boldsymbol{\sigma}$ falls on each unit $\boldsymbol{\mu}$.

It should be noted that in comparison with gender data the value of weighted standard deviation rises sharply for ethnic data. Thus for 2014 the weighted standard deviation $\boldsymbol{\mu}$ = 7.872 is more than weighted mathematical expectation $\boldsymbol{\mu}$ = 7.360. For 2019 these values are also very close: $\boldsymbol{\mu}$ = 12.860 and $\boldsymbol{\sigma}$ = 7.872. Moreover entropy as a measure of information uncertainty for ethnic data ***H*** = 2.25 bit is more than ***H*** = 2.09 bit - for gender data.

The above estimates confirm that the actions of companies in relation to the orientation towards diversity should be systematic. This means that the sustained change in company culture, and the individual mindsets and behaviour are needed to build a truly diverse and inclusive culture. Inclusion is closely linked to employee engagement, itself in turn a critical component of employee retention, productivity and financial performance. According to the State of the Global Workplace report, (Gallup, 2017), business units successful in the I&D strategy are 17% more productive and 21% more profitable than those unsuccessful. They also have 20% higher sales, 10% higher customer metrics. Besides the above results show that even where companies are more diverse, many appear unable to cultivate inclusive work environments in an effective and consistent way. Such environments promote inclusive leadership and accountability among managers, equality and fairness of opportunity, and openness and freedom from bias and discrimination. More than that, fostering a diverse and inclusive culture is a critical success factor: it enables individuals both to shine in their own right and to pull together as a team.

CONCLUSION

In a situation full of uncertainty about the post-coronavirus future, to rebuild business and make it more stronger CEOs should single out those factors that will determine the mechanisms for structuring the future socio-economic system. Now there is reopening the monumental task of rethinking how to govern and manage. The reality of systemic hazards—with their complexity, uncertainty, and ambiguity—calls for decision criteria based on a new set of principles: robust decision-making, multilayered governance, empowered self-organization and more. And in this context, the strategy of socializing talented individuals into company teams based on the optimization of diversity and inclusion has promising prospects. At the same time, the individual, as the main participant in the construction of the future reality on behalf of firms, must be endowed with the qualities of intellectual autonomy and adequately socialized. The fundamental essence of this problem is predetermined by its complexity and dialectical interrelation of two mechanisms of human inclusivity: education and socialization. Without each other, they will not provide the phenomenon of inclusiveness as a quality of the social environment, and their combination is a fundamental problem that has not been solved in any country in the world. The national community that will be the first in this race for a creative person capable of autonomously solving complex problems and serving the fatherland with all its talent will be a leader in moving forward.

Thus, the rapidly becoming complex system has demanded not just owners of capital, but those who, with the help of this capital, will solve increasingly complex problems of the system's self-movement, build alternatives to inclusiveness from the rapidly increasing diversification of specialized types of activity and its main carriers, i.e. individuals with abilities for self-reflection and transcending. The dialectic of these abilities of a person as a constructor of the future social reality is predetermined by the dialectics of Scylla of education and Charybdis of socialization. We are talking about the formation of intellectually autonomous individuals capable of adapting the 4th technological revolution to the tasks of socio-economic progress, which will accelerate it in the "two steps forward - one back" mode, instead of its modern version as "one step forward - two back". However, this is possible only under the condition of adequate socialization of intellectually autonomous individuals, which is predetermined by the structure of the national society, the maturity of leading national firms, the level of expert qualities of the state, which, with the help of formal institutions, is able to motivate citizens to unlimited creativity in the name of the prosperity of the society of the future.

REFERENCES

Agrawal, S., De Smet, A., Poplawski, P., & Reich, A. (2020). *Beyond hiring: How companies are reskilling to address talent gaps. In Organization Practice and McKinsey Accelerate*. McKinsey & Company.

Ananiev, B. G. (1977). The problems of modern human science. Academic Press.

Bailinson, P., Decherd, W., Ellsworth, D., & Guttman, M. (2020). *Understanding organizational barriers to a more inclusive workplace*. Mackinsey and Company. June.

Billimoria, J., & Bishop, M. (2020). How COVID-19 can be the Great Reset toward global sustainability. In *Sustainable Development Impact Summit.* World Economic Forum.

Bogdanov, A. A. (1934). *Tectology or General Organizational Science*. Conjuncture Institute publishing house.

Boston Consulting Group. (2017). Russia 2025: From Average Students to Talents. Boston Consulting Group.

Boston Consulting Group. (2020). *Workforce Sentiment Survey*. Boston Consulting Group.

Breen, K. (2016). *Why does inclusive growth matter?* The World Economic Forum.

Christensen, L., Gittleson, J., & Smith, M. (2020). The most fundamental skill: Intentional learning and the career advantage. In *McKinsey Accelerate*. McKinsey & Company.

COVID-19. Briefing Materials. (2020). Global health and crisis response. McKinsey & Company.

Dam. (Ed.). (2019). Elevating Learning & Development: Insights and Practical Guidance from the Field. McKinsey & Company.

De Smedt, B. (2014). Advances in the use of neuroscience methods in research on learning and instruction. *Frontline Learning Research*, *2*(4).

Dixon-Fyle, Hunt, Dolan, & Prince. (2020). *Diversity wins: How inclusion matters*. McKinsey & Company.

Doumba, M. (2020). The Great reset must place social justice at its centre. In *Sustainable Development Impact Summit*. World Economic Forum.

Elkonin, D. B. (1989). *Selected Psychological Works*. Pedagogy Publisher.

Emmett, J., Schrah, G., Schrimper, M., & Wood, A. (2020). *COVID-19 and the employee experience: How leaders can seize the moment. In Organization Practice*. June. Mckinsey&Company.

Hunt, Layton, & Prince. (2015). *Diversity Matters*. McKinsey & Company.

Hunt, Prince, Dixon-Fyle, & Yee. (2018). Delivering through Diversity. Executive summary. *McKinsey Quarterly*.

Kautz, T., Heckman, J. J., Diris, R., Ter Weel, B., & Borghans, L. (2014). *Fostering and measuring skills: improving cognitive and non-cognitive skills to promote lifetime success*. NBER Working Paper, 20749. National Bureau of Economic Research.

KPMG. (2020). CEO Outlook: COVID-19. Special Edition. Executive summary. KPMG International.

Kuhl, P. K. (2010). Brain mechanisms in early language acquisition. *Neuron*, *67*(5), 713–727. doi:10.1016/j.neuron.2010.08.038 PMID:20826304

Küpper, Reichert, Reichert, Rastogi, & Kimura. (2020). *How CEOs Can Win the Fight and Transform to Win the Future*. Boston Consulting Group.

Lonergan, E., & Blyth, M. (2020). *Angrynomics*. Columbia University Press. doi:10.2307/j.ctv13840ch

Malone, T. W. (2018). *Superminds. The Surprising Power of People and Computers Thinking Together*. Little, Brown Spark.

Maor, D., Reich, A., & Yocarini, L. (2017). *The people power of transformations*. Mckinsey&Company.

Mattey, Hilberath, Sibilio, Aurora, & Ruiz. (2020). *Personalisation for Your People. How COVID-19 is reshaping the race for talent*. Boston Consulting Group.

McConnell, M., & Schaninger, B. (2019). *Are we long—or short—on talent? McKinsey Quarterly*.

Milanovic, B. (2019). Capitalism, Alone: The Future of the System that Rules the World. Harvard University Press. doi:10.4159/9780674242852

Neisser, U., Boodoo, G., Bouchard, T. J. Jr, Boykin, A. W., Brody, N., Ceci, S. J., Halpern, D. F., Loehlin, J. C., Perloff, R., Sternberg, R. J., & Urbina, S. (1996). Intelligence: Knowns and unknowns. *The American Psychologist*, *51*(2), 77–101. doi:10.1037/0003-066X.51.2.77

Nielsen, N. C., Dotiwala, F., & Murray, M. (2020). *A transformation of thelearning function: Why it should learn new ways. In McKinsey Accelerate*. McKinsey & Company.

OECD. (2016). *Global Competency for an Inclusive World.* Retrieved from: https://www.oecd.org/pisa/aboutpisa/Global-competency-for-an-inclusive-world.pdf

Piaget, J. V. F. (2008). *The Psychology of Intelligence*. Direct-Media.

Pilipenko, A., Pilipenko, O., & Pilipenko, Z. (2019). Education and inclusive development: puzzle of low-learning equilibrium. In Modeling Economic Growth in Contemporary Russia. Bradford, UK: Emerald Publishing Limited. doi:10.1108/978-1-78973-265-820191006

Pilipenko, A. I. (1997). *Cognitive barriers in teaching physics and methodological principles for overcoming them.* The Dissertation Abstract for a Scientific Degree of Doctor of Pedagogics. Moscow: Russian Academy of Education Publisher.

Pilipenko, A. I. (2015). *Innovative Models of Education: The Aspect of Psychological and Cognitive Barriers.* http://ssrn.com/abstract=2597968

Pilipenko, A. I. (2020). Education and theory of psychological and cognitive barriers: human capital as driver of stable economic growth. In Social, Economic, and Environmental Impacts Between Sustainable Financial Systems and Financial Markets. IGI Global. doi:10.4018/978-1-7998-1033-9.ch011

Pilipenko, A. I., & Solomenik, V. D. (1999). *To the Future Teacher About the Psychological and Cognitive Barriers: Tutorial.* Publishing House of Bryansk Pedagogical University.

Pilipenko, O.I., Pilipenko, Z.A., & Pilipenko, A.I. (n.d.). *Theory of Shocks, COVID-19, and Normative Fundamentals for Policy Responses: Emerging Research and Opportunities*. IGI Global Publishers.

Pilipenko, Z. A. (2016). Impulse transmission model of macroeconomic cycle within the framework of the theory of shocks: aspect of economic security. In *Dependability Engineering and Complex Systems: Advances in Intelligent Systems and Computing* (Vol. 470). Springer International Publishing Switzerland. doi:10.1007/978-3-319-39639-2_32

Pilipenko, Z. A. (2020). Shocks' theory: financial mechanism of economic systems' destabilization In: Edited by Magdalena Ziolo. In Social, Economic, and Environmental Impacts Between Sustainable Financial Systems and Financial Markets. IGI Global.

Pinsky, A.A. (1978). Methodology as a science. *Soviet Pedagogy, 12.*

Pritchett, L. (2013). *The Rebirth of Education: Schooling Ain't Learning*. Centre for Global Development, Brookings Institution Press.

Romer, P. M. (1986, October). Increasing returns and long-run growth. *Journal of Political Economy, 94*(5), 1002–1037. doi:10.1086/261420

Sandbu, M. (2020). *The Economics of Belonging*. Princeton University Press.

Schleicher, A., & Ramos, G. (2016). *Global Competency for an Inclusive World.* OECD. Retrieved from: https://www.oecd.org/pisa/aboutpisa/Global-competency-for-an-inclusive-world.pdf

Schönfeld, M. (2017). *Work Readiness Assessment Tools in Comparison: From Administration to Z-scores*. World Bank.

Schumpeter, J. A. (1949). The Theory of Economic Development: An Inquiry into Profits, Capital, Credit, Interest, and the Business Cycle. Cambridge, MA: Harvard University Press.

Schwab, K., & Malleret, T. (2020). *COVID-19's legacy: This is how to get the Great Reset right. In Sustainable Development Impact Summit.* WEF.

Slobodchicov, V. I., & Isaev, E. I. (1995). Human Psychology. Academic Press.

Slobodchicov, V. I., & Isaev, E. I. (2000). Psychology of Human Development. Academic Press.

Slobodchicov, V. I., & Isaev, E. I. (2013). Psychology of Human Education. Formation of Subjectivity in Educational Processes. Moscow: Academic Press.

Sutcliffe, H. (2020). COVID-19: The 4 building blocks of the Great Reset. In *Sustainable Development Impact Summit*. World Economic Forum.

The business case for inclusive growth. (2018). Deloitte Global Inclusive Growth Survey.

The Economist. (2020). *Covid-19 and the crisis for higher education*. Report. London: The Economist.

The Economist. (2020a). *Leading From Afar. The new world of work calls for a more creative and adaptable approach to leadership*. London: The Economist Intelligence Unit Limited.

UNESCO. (2016). *Education for People and Planet: Creating Sustainable Futures for All.* Global Education Monitoring Report 2016. Paris: UNESCO Publishing. Retrieved from: https://unesdoc.unesco.org/images/0024/002457/245752e.pdf

UNESCO. (2016a). *Contemporary learning crisis: education' failure in "creating sustainable future for all". In The Global Education Monitoring Report* (2nd ed.). UNESCO Publishing.

Ushinsky, K. D. (2005). *Selected Works (vol. 4). Academic Press.*

Vygotsky, L. S. (1960). *Development of Higher Mental Functions*. Nauka Publisher.

WEF. (2018). *The Inclusive Growth and Development Report*. The World Economic Forum.

WEF. (2020). *The Future of Nature and Business*. New Nature Economy Report II. World Economic Forum.

World Bank. (2018). *World Development Report 2018: Learning to Realize Education's Promise*. World Bank.

World Bank. (2020). *The COVID-19 pandemic: shocks to education and policy responses*. World Bank Report.

Chapter 10
The Impact of the Pandemic (COVID-19) on the Change of Business Models on the Example of the Banking Industry

Przemyslaw Jacek Sawicki
University of Szczecin, Poland

ABSTRACT

Due to the fundamental digitization of social/economic life, it takes on an "on" and "offline" scale image of the world. While analyzing the impact of the ongoing pandemic on the segmentation of world markets, the disruptions in the functioning of some industries, sectors, and entire economies are becoming deeper. The spread of COVID-19 has led to the dysfunction of a known ecosystem, and the destructive force of human isolation and the lockdown of economies have significantly influenced the behavior of societies and governments. Many customer-centric companies have reactively redefined their strategies, and the financial sector, especially banks, was to play an important role in absorbing the shock by providing the necessary credit to businesses and households. Meanwhile, the same institutions have experienced capital and liquidity destabilization due to increased risk reserves created and an operating in conditions of historically low interest rates. Unexpectedly, the pandemic has become another determinant of the new quality of processes, phenomena, and business models.

INTRODUCTION

The rise of the Internet and the digital transformation of highly developed countries that has been going on for several decades led to the fourth industrial (Schwab, 2016) revolution. Observing this year's changes caused by the risk of COVID-19, it can be argued that the pandemic has a chance to become

DOI: 10.4018/978-1-7998-6788-3.ch010

a catalyst for technological and model improvements accelerating the emergence of another in a much shorter time.

For several decades, the finance sector has been the most efficient in implementing technological innovations, redefining product distribution channels and ways of effectively interacting with customers. In the 1960s, banks introduced ATMs, in the early 1970s they enabled electronic card payments, in the first decade of the 21st century, online banking was made available to financial services recipients on a large scale, and from 2010 on-line forms of contact in the "e" and "m" banking (Accenture, 2020) formats were becoming more and more common.

In the era of digitization of economies, new driving forces appeared to support the development of the banking industry. One of them is Big Data (Marz, Warren, 2015). which facilitates the processing of collected data in terms of, inter alia, customer segmentation and personalization of offers. In one of the largest Polish banks, its clients perform 6 million transactions and 4 million logins to electronic banking (Jagiełło, Kubisiak, 2020) every day. Every year, the bank processes the data provided by the execution of 2.5 billion payment transactions. Processing such resources requires state-of-the-art computing units and the use of resources from another breakthrough in the computing system - cloud computing (IDG Research, 2020). In Europe, the Scandinavian countries are the leaders in cloud computing applications. The percentage of companies using data processing in the cloud reaches 70%.

At the MIT Sloan School of Management, management professor Eryk Brynjolfsson, together with his colleagues, compared the performance of companies where decisions were made on the basis of data analysis with the performance of other companies (Brynjolfsson, Hitt, Kim, 2011). The team found that they were 6% more productive than companies that did not make much use of the available data when making decisions. Currently, the skillful processing of Big Data is a source of profitability optimization and a sustainable competitive advantage (Mayer-Schönberger, Cukier, 2013) for many companies.

Parallel to the development of cloud computing, the impact of another field of science was discovered - artificial intelligence (Redefine banking with Artificial Intelligence, 2020) on the reduction of data storage and processing costs and the relationship between Internet access, user connectivity in the network and the emergence of innovative forms of contact between the customer and the bank (biometrics, voice assistant, chatbots, video consultant).

In the financial industry, it is estimated that artificial intelligence has the potential to unlock $ 1 trillion a year in additional value for banks (McKinsey&Company, 2020). Both disciplines complement each other creating a new conceptualization of business assumptions.

The advent of advanced technologies is an example of the dynamics of discoveries in the early 2000s. In the management sphere, their key consequence is a new format for business scaling - platformization of services breaking with the hierarchical structure of work in favor of collaborative (Srinival, Schoeps, 2019) network models. The new model gives a scale effect and increases the contact with mass customers to the level of a prosumer. According to experts, in the digital age, service platforms will become the future of e.g. banks forced to compete on the payments market with the largest technology companies.

In the face of economic disruptions manifested by the current epidemic situation, the ability to adapt high technologies is described as one of the main factors determining the post-pandemic positioning of a company. The example of Bigtechs (Business Insider Inteligence, 2019) or Fintechs (EBA, 2019) shows that operating globally even in the period of economic downturn due to Covid-19, there is the potential to achieve financial inclusion (Spence, 2019).

A comparison of data from 2019/2020 confirms that the reactions of bigtechs to market stimuli during the economic slowdown due to the pandemic in most cases showed an increase in brand value.

Figure 1. The top most valuable tech brands of 2020 (brand value in $US billions and rounded to the nearest billion)
Source: BrandZ, Global Top 100 Most Valueble Brands/Kantar (including data from Bloomberg) 2020.

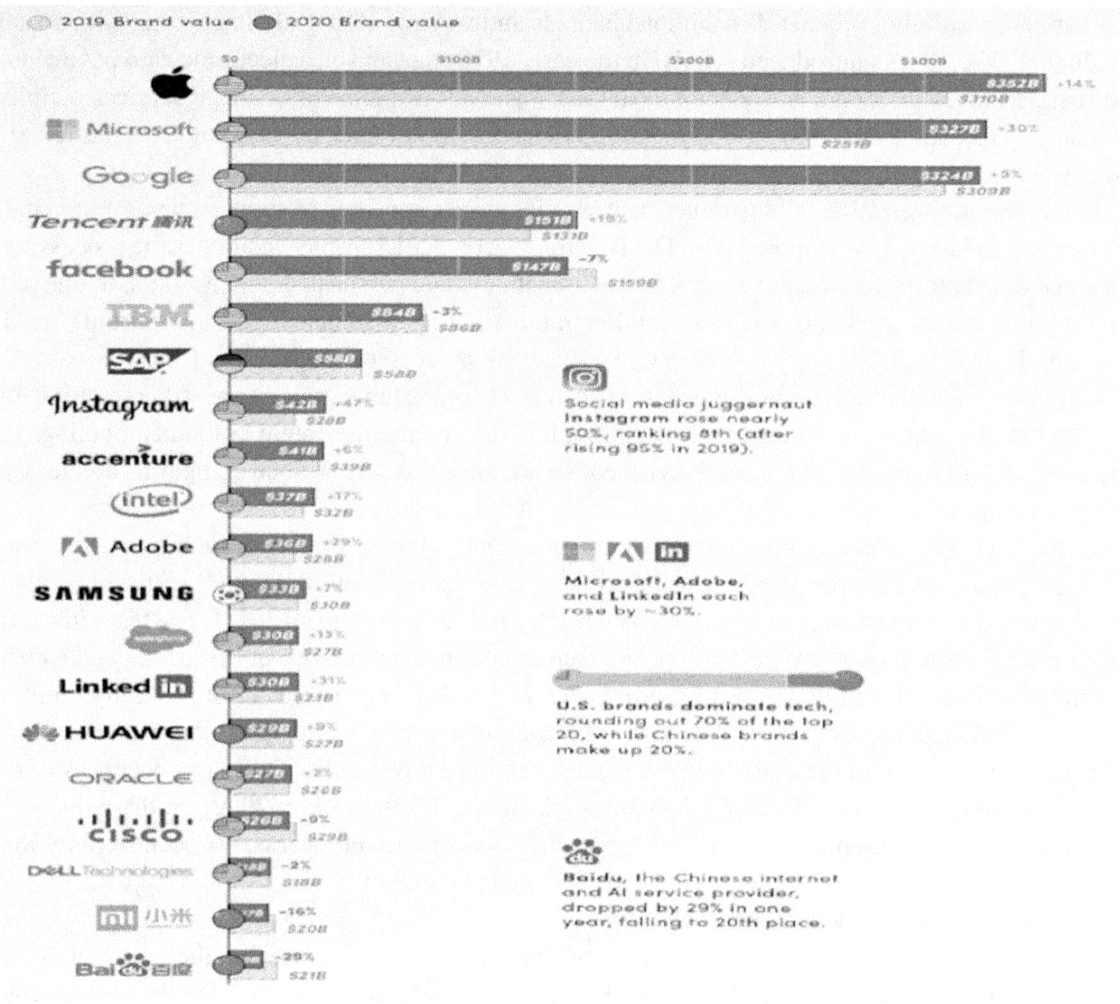

The functioning of Bigtechs based on platform strategies is based on the use of advanced IT algorithms in positioning, exploration and comprehensive analysis of the client's image. This approach shifts the main burden in the business model from selling products to delivering services (this solution is successfully used by, among others, Uber, Airbnb, Amazon). The inversion of vectors indirectly allocates the costs of product service to the customer, making the final recipient a kind of "free and invisible" employee of a given institution. Research by the MIT Sloan School of Management showed that in 2013, out of the top 30 brands in terms of market capitalization, 14 were platform-oriented.

Many banks will be forced to compete with the same tool, i.e. platform technology (KPMG International Cooperative, 2020) in order to survive and face large international platform businesses. As a result, the transformation of traditional financial intermediaries into technology companies will become a reality (Kelly, 2016).

The Banking Industry is one of the Most Innovative in the World

The devaluation of thinking about social and economic progress drew the attention of economists to entrepreneurship and innovation. There has been a decline in the value of the traditional approach to the enterprise, understood through the prism of the profit brought to the owners. The new approach indicated the important role of innovative enterprises in generating economic growth (Schumpeter, 1960). In the mid-90s of the last century, a breakthrough innovation with a global impact was created. The consequences of the emergence of the Internet in the context of social phenomena and economic processes were not foreseen at that time, nor the pace of implementation by the banking industry most prone to this innovation.

The technological advancement inscribed in the banks' DNA and the openness to digitization of services resonated with the interest in new possibilities of operation, and the simultaneous formation of the information society (Wang, 2014) stimulated a new quality of the service. The classic model of the bank's operation (execution of customer operations in a branch at the so-called window) has largely been replaced by a new service quality, which is a derivative of complex efficiency mechanisms, including:

the strategy of multi-channel touchpoints on the purchasing (Kotler, Kartayaja, Setiawan, 2017) path,
real-time event monitoring architecture,
prediction of revenues on the client,
a model for suggesting purchases.

Technologically oriented banks noticed new growth potential by developing silos for on and off line services. The operational models supporting this division (Business Intelligence (Wikipedia, 2020) Customer Relastionship Management (Deloitte Digital, 2020) from the point of view of growth have become strategic and even fundamental for the entire industry, they are accelerated by the context of increasing mobility of societies (Report Mobirank, 2018) the phenomenon of global Smartphoneization (Clearbridge Mobile, 2020) and the ongoing pandemic.

The illustration shows data on the penetration of the population of the modern world with a smartphone. Few of the remaining countries have a population greater than the number of subscribed phones. Consumers are rapidly becoming digital, creating new economic value (Surma, 2017) for businesses. In the financial services market, the term "digital customer" (Gartner, 2020) is known by implication as a mobile one, who contacts the bank via mobile devices, mainly via a smartphone. This segment includes the majority of age groups with the largest share of people aged 20-35. Banks are the most striving for this client group (Dimock, 2019).

The growing mobility of banking customers, the convergence of mobile telephone devices and the exponentially growing number of banking application users have clearly dominated the processes of technological change in terms of online services (The First News, 2020). Adjusting current strategies to market trends has become a direct goal of banks. A number of innovations were supposed to improve the profitability of operating activities. The axis of changes has become the relocation of contact with the client. Actions taken in this direction optimized the branch network, leading to a reduction in the number of branches and front office employees, on the other hand, they contributed to the strengthening of the positive experience as a result of a much better identification of unique customer needs and, not least, an increase in employment in IT departments and back office departments.

Figure 2. World smartphone penetration
Source: Harvard Business Review magazine (2019, September).

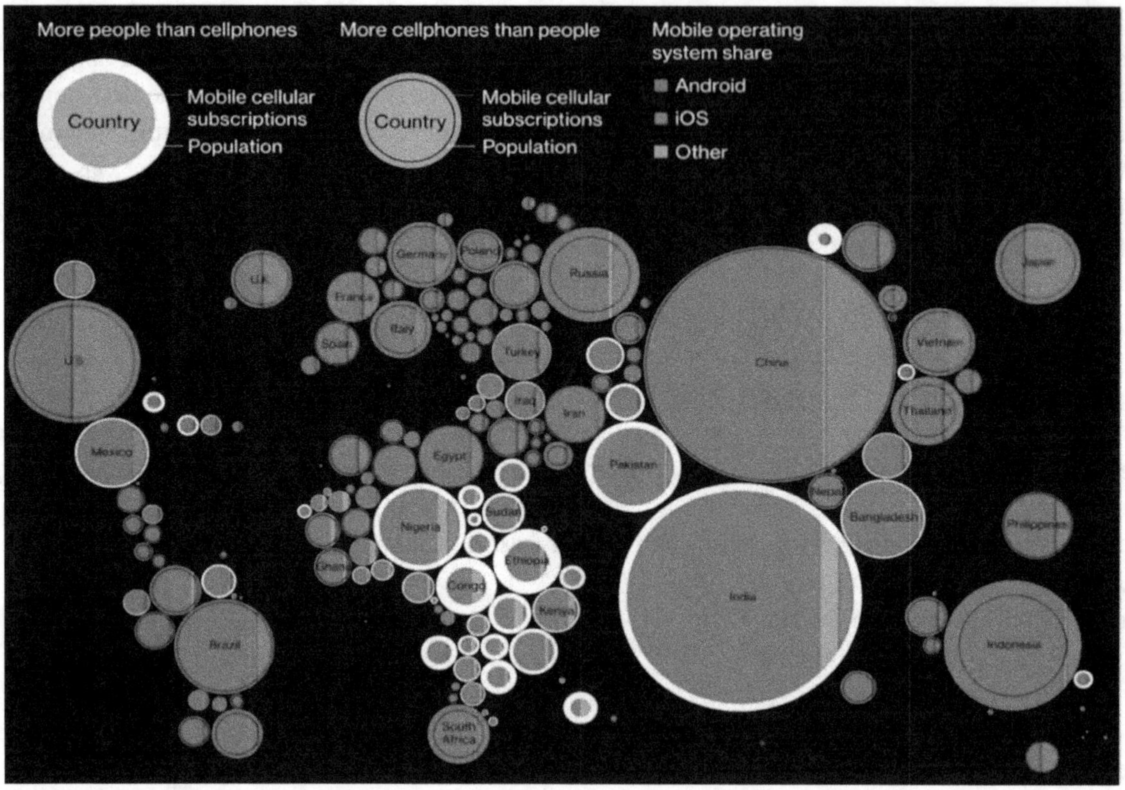

Using the consortium, the banking industry proposed to the newly formed customer group its own mobile payment system on the Internet and in brick-and-mortar stores (Wikipedia, 2020) as well as convenient interaction through robotization and a virtual banking assistant that performs transfers based on voice commands. A functional solution is also the form of contact with the client via a video consultant. The actions taken significantly affect the customer's autonomy and loyalty, and most importantly attract new customers.

The new approach is reflected in banks' greater share of socially responsible environmental impact – CRS (Unido, 2020). As a result of the growing dematerialisation of financial services and the increase in non-cash circulation of money (contactless payments), the demand for paper and cash transport is falling. The impact of digitization not only optimizes costs and increases operating profit, but also indirectly supports the implementation of sustainable economy demands by banks.

For the past three decades, the financial sector (Drucker, 1999) has been the most dynamic and profitable industry in the world. At this point it should be said that the most innovative is also. Both in the past and now, financial intermediaries were one of the first to face development challenges. In the last decade, while monitoring the customer and employee market, banks noticed the need to manage customer relationships more effectively. The result of the work was the implementation of a CRM system with a modern front end supported by an in-depth Big Data analysis. Banks were one of the first to start processing customer data in the cloud. Achievements in the field of implementation of elements of artificial intelligence and biometrics, e.g. increasing the security of logins, have found many different useful applications.

However, there is a conviction among financial services specialists that the current models of banking operations are not adequate to the pace of changes in market trends. Currently, due to the progressive deregulation and de-monopolization of the payments market, the financial industry is facing fundamental challenges. Recently, the most technologically advanced companies known as Bigtechs eg Google, Apple, Facebook, Amazon, Alibaba (Miklaszewska, Folwarski, 2020) have become the greatest threat to banks. Defending against their expansion in acquiring payment markets is another determinant of innovation in the banking industry. The EU PSD2 (Europa, 2020b) directive, which opens the way for open banking API (Deloitte, 2020) and third parties TPP (Europa, 2020c) contributes to the dismantling of the provision of financial services by banks. The situation of banks is not facilitated by the over-regulation of the banking system, which has a significant impact on the maintenance of financial liquidity of these institutions.

The Economic Shock of the Pandemic

The McKinsey&Company (Chong, Handscomb, Wiliams, 2020) publishing house published the results of the analysis of daily prices, stock prices and selected balance sheet items from the first wave of the pandemic. The sample included, among others banks from 53 countries and selected companies. The study was carried out in two stages. In the first, the impact of the pandemic on the banking sector was assessed. The study was intended to show how varied the impact of the shock caused by the pandemic on banks and businesses was. In the second, the role of various policy initiatives in alleviating the tensions of the banking system rated on an ongoing basis by the markets was analyzed using a global database and survey methodology.

The results suggest that the negative impact of the COVID-19 shock on banks was more severe and had a significantly longer impact on the financial sector than on enterprises and non-bank financial institutions, revealing the expectation that banks will absorb at least part of the corporate sector shock. Another result of this analysis was that banks with lower liquidity buffers before the crisis and higher exposure to certain sectors (tourism, aviation, catering, transport, culture and arts, event business) experienced greater drops in share prices.

The second part of the study analyzed over 400 initiatives to support the financial sector by the monetary authorities of individual economies. Announcements of liquidity support correlated with large increases in banks' share prices. Access to refinancing by central banks and initiatives to address bank funding shortfalls had a calming effect on markets, as evidenced by the stabilization of bank stock valuations in global markets in the first half of 2020 (WSJ, 2020).

During this period, the unexpected effect of the actions of central banks in the form of investors' greater appetite for risk was noteworthy. In many countries, interest rates have been lowered to historically low levels, projected to remain very low for several years. The state budgets of advanced economies have increased significantly as a result of asset purchases, support for the liquidity of the banking system, the opening of US dollar swap lines and other instruments designed to sustain the flow of credit to the economy (Visual Capitalist, 2020). The aggregate assets of the group of ten central banks G10 (Cukiermann, 2020) grew by around $ 6 trillion from mid-January to the end of June 2020, more than double the amount in the two years of the global financial crisis from December 2007 to December 2009, representing nearly 15 percent G10 GDP. The data is presented in the table.

Figure 3. G10 central bank assets
Source: Global Financial Stability Update, June 2020. Note: G10 = Group of Ten; other G10 central banks = central banks of Canada, Sweden, Switzerland, and the United Kingdom.

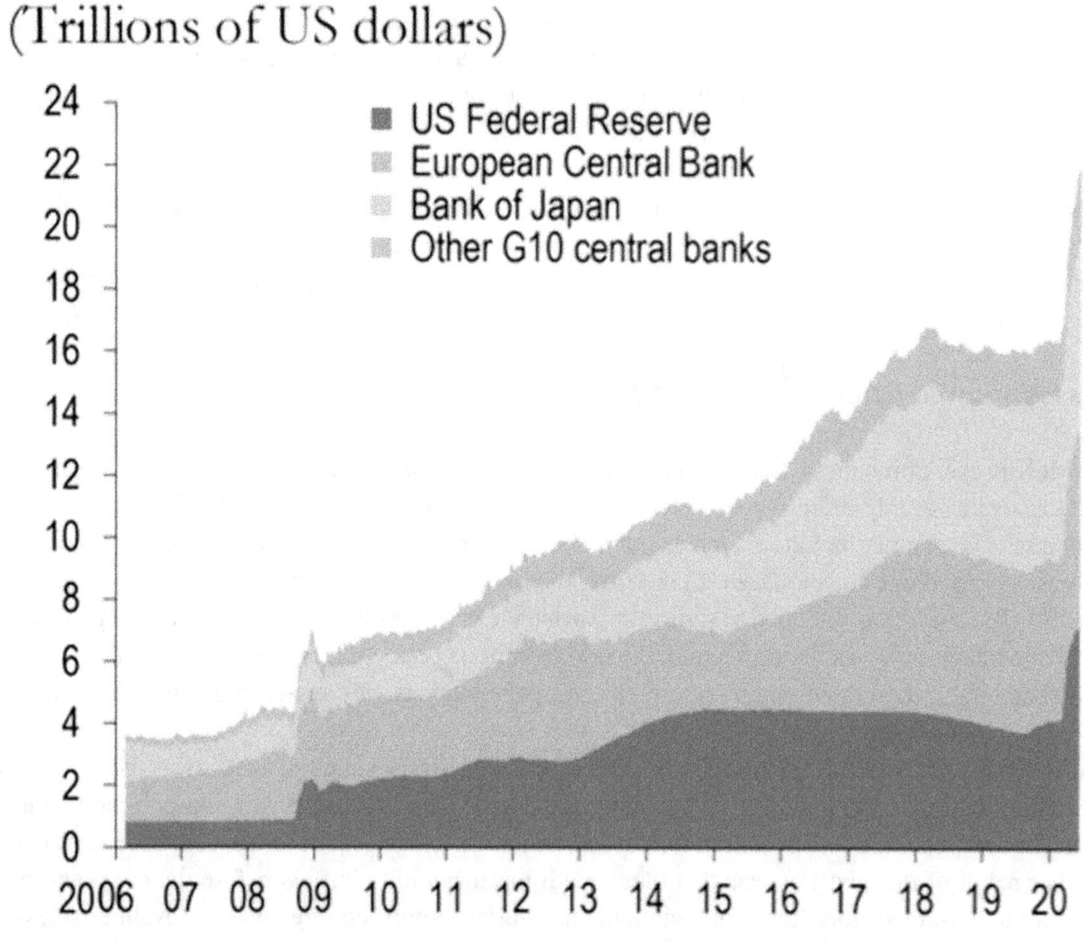

Fiscal and financial policy measures helped to improve investor sentiment. Governments around the world have provided companies with nearly $ 11 trillions (International Monetary Fund, 2020) in anti-crisis financial shields through the banking system. As a result of these actions, confidence in the markets increased.

The impulse for the improvement of market sentiment after the first wave of the disease was the opening of some economies and the easing of restrictions related to COVID-19. In addition, investors apparently expected to continue monetary policy supporting the global economy for an extended period of time and further bolster sentiment by announcing the use of a range of policies, including government loan guarantees, supporting loan restructuring and encouraging banks to use available capital and liquidity buffers to lend (International Monetary Fund, 2020a)

At the same time, there was a discrepancy between the optimism in the financial markets and the evolution of the world economy. The prosperity among investors was based on strong support from state policy in the face of uncertainty about the scope and speed of economic recovery. Markets expected a quick V-shaped rebound, while the World Economic Outlook of June 2020 (International Monetary Fund,

2020b) pointed to the apparent discrepancy between risk pricing in financial markets and the economic outlook as expressed by consumer sentiment. This situation may raise concerns about the persistence of increases in share prices, strongly correlated with the support from central banks.

IMF experts estimate that the difference between market prices and fundamental values in most major equity and bond markets in developed economies is close to historic highs, although the opposite is true for equities in some emerging economies (International Monetary Fund, 2020c). Hence the thesis that the recession may be deeper and longer than currently predicted by investors. If the vaccine does not appear on the market after the second, a third wave of the virus is expected, which will result in the return of restrictions. In this situation, market expectations regarding the retention of financial markets by central banks may turn out to be wrong, prompting investors to reassess their risk appetite. The resurgence of trade tensions and deepening social unrest around the world, as a consequence, may reveal many financial weaknesses that have been accumulating for decades in the economies of highly developed and developing countries.

The Global Stability of the Financial System (Cavallino, De Fiore, 2020) report mentions that aggregate corporate debt has been increasing for several years and has remained historically high relative to GDP. At the same time, household indebtedness rose to record levels, especially in countries that managed to avoid the impact of the global financial crisis of 2007-2008. This means that there are currently many economies with high levels of indebtedness, which could be conducive to a sudden economic slowdown. This deterioration in economic fundamentals led to the highest rate of corporate bond defaults since the 2008 global financial crisis and a decline in bond yields, oil prices and equity prices. In the United States, 10-year bond yields fell below 0.5%, and stock prices of major stock indices around the world fell. The data is presented in the table below.

The above-mentioned phenomena pose a risk of a wider impact on the solvency of enterprises and households. Potential bankruptcies will test the resilience of the banking sector.

Figure 4. The 10-year US Treasury yield has been falling to record-low levels
Source: Federal Reserve Bank of St. Louis.

Changing consumer behavior as a new paradigm for banking business models. The Covid-19 pandemic has increased the urgency to digitize banking financial services, but it is not its only determinant. In the course of the spread of the Covid-19 virus, short-term humanitarian challenges are of particular importance, as they accelerate banks' medium-term strategies in the financial sector. The axis of change is the digital transformation that has been influencing the demand and supply sides for a decade. Taking into account the pace of technology development in recent years, including the development of the bigtech sector, digitization, next to the pandemic, today creates the most important factors accelerating the transformation of the industry. At the same time, it is estimated that the risks caused by the risk of disease accelerated the implementation of new technologies by a minimum of two years, regardless of whether they relate to videoconferencing, peer-to-peer (Investopedia, 2020) transactions or internet banking (The Financial Brand, 2020).

The increasing comfort of service in the field of remote forms of contact thanks to digitization and reduced dependence on physical branches in the future will further accelerate the transformation of the industry by privileging entities with an appropriate capital buffer and greater digital opportunities. In China and Italy, four weeks after the coronavirus began to spread, the estimated increase in customer engagement with digital technologies was 10 to 20 percent (Adarkar, Hyde, Sridharan, 2020). In contrast, the Royal Bank of Canada (RBC) saw impressive online growth during the COVID-19 pandemic, bringing 400,000 new digital customers to market, leading to an overall increase in digital re-engagement of 29% (Borndigital, 2020). The potential of the digital market seems endless.

Figure 5.
Source: Digital Banking Report, The Financial Brand, (2020, August).

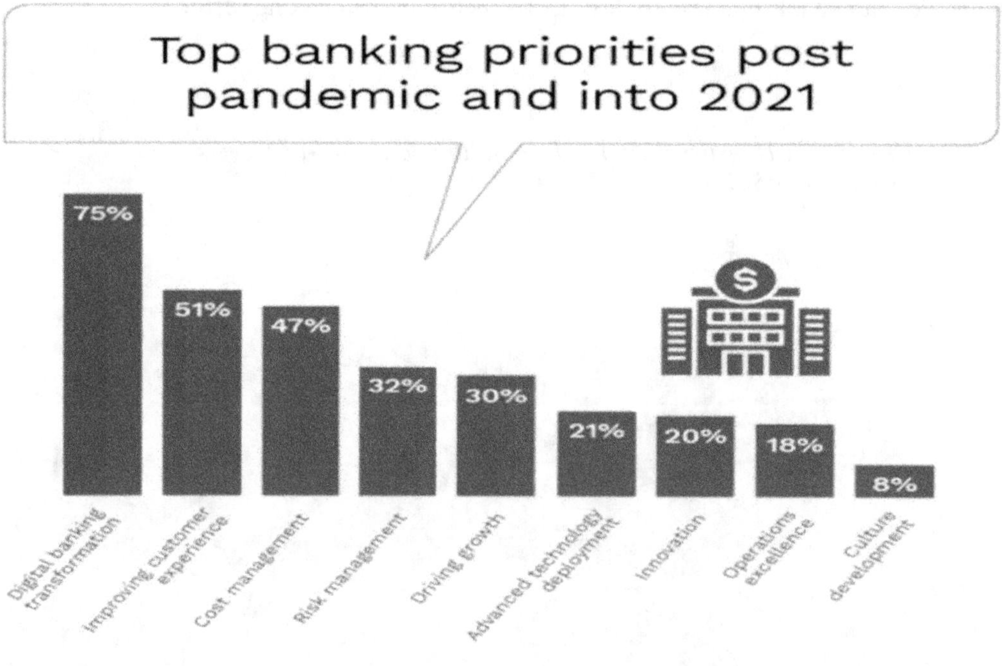

According to the Digital Banking Report, digital transformation took the first place among the post-pandemic priorities of the banking industry. If customers perceive the new experience as positive, the changes can be groundbreaking and long-term.

Purely digital banks have an average cost-to-income ratio of 47% well below the average (73%) of the less prominent and universal banks (Deloitte IIF, 2020). In this context, financial leaders are wondering what business model versus changing consumer habits would be the most appropriate and perspective.

Ad hoc support is provided by the tactic of agile management of short-term projects and mergers with selected Fintech market representatives specializing in artificial intelligence applications. The value of the Fintech market has decreased due to the pandemic, making some deals attractive (Handscomb, Mahadevan, Naidoo, Schor, Sieberer, Srinivasan, 2020). Financial entities around the world have quickly adapted their formations to the dynamically changing environment, but only the largest ones include them in their medium-term strategies. Deloitte in the Insight edition published conclusions (Baret, Celner, O'Reilly, Shilling, 2020) after interviews with dozens of banking leaders in order to probe the transformative potential of the industry. Contrary to the declaration for Digital Banking (Tab. 6), Deloitte summed up that the most common initiatives they undertook during the pandemic were proactive measures to protect health and raise employee morale, modify the operating model for branches and develop contingency plans.

Meanwhile, the earlier, and during the pandemic, even clearer changes in customer preferences, for example in the area of communication, create space for building new models based on the possessed or available business analytics (BI) and Big Data analysis. Adaptation of CRM, remote forms of contact or analysis of the customer's digital footprint can determine the sphere of completely new experiences both on the part of the bank's customer and its employee.

After the first wave of coronavirus, some intermediaries have attempted to reach a different level of interaction with the client. She proposed a new standard of banking service, effective and safe in terms of communication in the age of health threats. The implemented service format not only meets the modern expectations of customers, but is intended to shape new habits in the relationship with the bank, regardless of the customer's age. The sales process is based on the end-to-end formula. The purchase of the product is initiated by the customer in an out-of-office channel on a portable device, and electronic documents are approved in a trusted profile with an e-signature. The client, and in fact the user of the banking application using this form of cooperation, obtains a number of incentives and a bonus in the form of access to practical non-financial functionalities embedded in the application (including e-exchange, parking and motorway fees, for transport tickets, gift cards, transfers to phone number, ATM withdrawals without a payment card, the number of functions is constantly growing). Traditional banking enthusiasts do not receive these advantages. Improving the effectiveness of the new service standard is supported by telephone assistance of an advisor, consultation with a video advisor and the use of artificial intelligence in the form of a voice assistant built into the application. Call center voice bots are to facilitate quick contact by offering educational facilities "at a distance".

The expansion of online infrastructure brings banks closer to another dimension of business identity. Platformization of services with a remodeled range of functionalities is to be the pillar of the new ecosystem in the structure of the largest banks in the world. The originality of the new format is significant considering the fact that so far the banking industry has been associated with a classic, branch-centric business model. However, taking into account the deregulation of the transaction market (KPMG, 2020) the further expansion of bigtechs and the dynamically growing mobility of consumers, the choice of

Figure 6.
Source: Digital Banking Report, The Financial Brand, (2020, August).

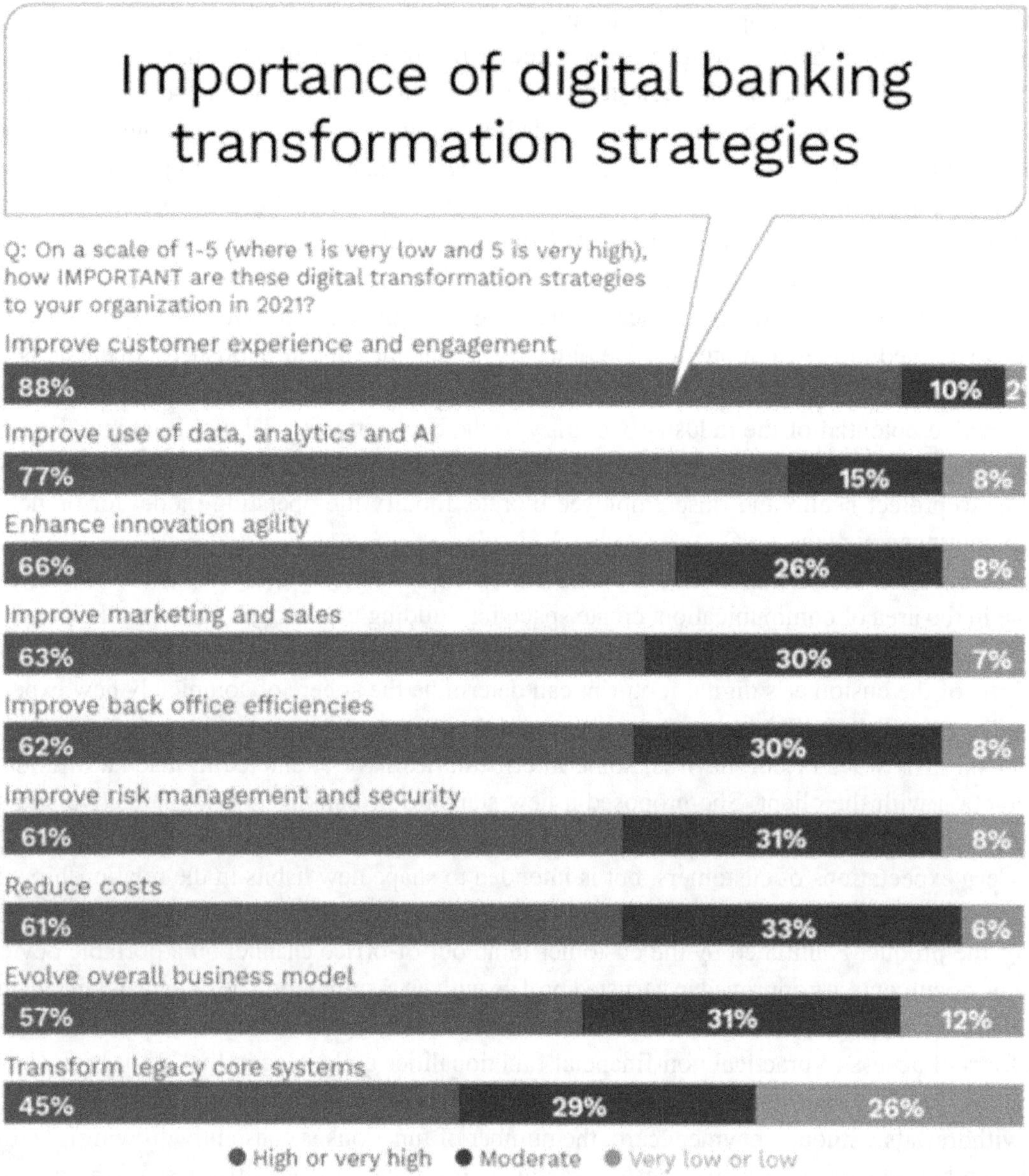

the platform as the target model for the largest banks seems natural and logical. Megatrends confirm this direction.

According to PwC, the largest increase in the number of banking customers occurs in the digital channel. The number of customers in the hybrid and offline channels is decreasing every year.

Regardless of the digitization of the services offered, work continues on the aspect of relationality, which is extremely important in the new model of banking transformation. Practice shows that clients, regardless of gender and belonging to target groups, accept virtual service, appreciate its advantages and meet expectations. On the other hand, they demand the availability of consultations and banking support

Figure 7.
Source: PwC, The Financial Brands, (2017, June).

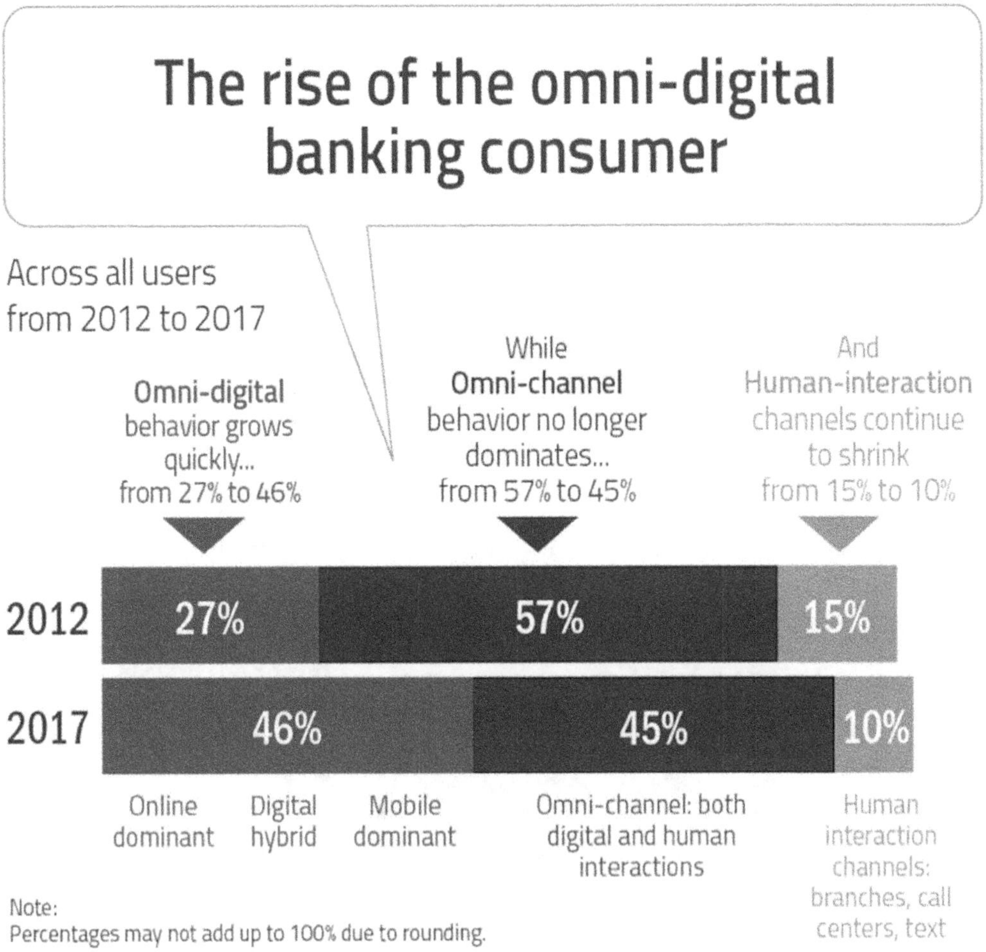

from an advisor / expert (Migliorelli, 2018). Research shows that direct contact with another person carries a strong emotional charge resulting from mutual knowledge and trust. In this field, the author of Duena Blomstrom in her book Emotional Banking (Blomstrom, 2018) formulates the concept of *human touch*, seeing in it the potential to achieve lasting and much greater value in the mutual relationship with the bank. This relationship would be based on meeting the emotional needs of the property owner. Other inspiring theories about the need to experience feelings in a relationship with a bank include the thread of the so-called caring banking compared to parental care. This aspect could successfully complete a new chapter in banking related, for example, to wealth management as part of individual or entrepreneurial succession. Despite the dynamic development of digital forms of contact and the decline in the importance of traditional forms, digitization will not always replace traditional interaction.

Financial institutions are aware of the transformation inside and outside their organizations, however, many projects require shierarching and timming. Besides, not every company has the appropriate transformational capital and the ability to use high technologies. These factors are nowadays significant barriers to development and competitiveness.

Figure 8.
Source: Efma/Synechrome, (2020, September).

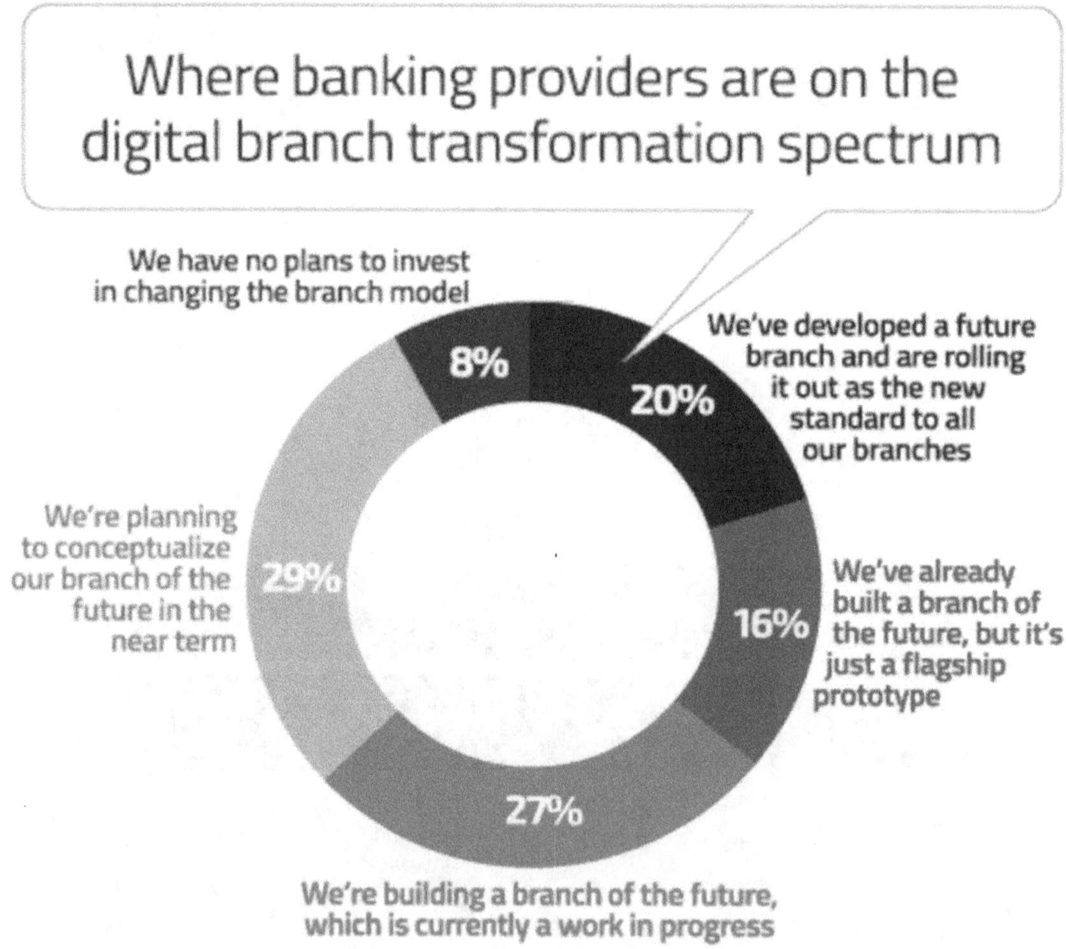

Efma's study confirms that not all bankers are aware of the path they want to follow. One in five financial institutions say they have already embarked on a journey to digitally transform the industry and are in the process of implementing their future branch model, while one in four believe the answer is both to increase the size of the network and to invest in a model change. Bank leaders agree on the approach, however, show different opinions as to the choice of the best model.

SUMMARY

The challenges facing the banking industry are growing not only for pandemic reasons. The changes are nothing new in this sector. The industry operates in one of the most turbulent environments that are sensitive to consumer behavior and depend increasingly on the development of advanced technologies. But never before has customer behavior changed so quickly. The progressive digitization of society and pandemic circumstances accelerate it even more. There are many possible scenarios and none of them seems final. The next 10 years will verify the correctness of the elections.

Chris Skinner (Skinner, 2018) the founder of the European network of financial professionals, claims that banks are facing the choice of one of several leading business models correlating with operational ones in order to meet growing customer demands and market competition. Industry leaders are considering the classic universal bank model, the ecosystem technology provider model, the financial services aggregator model, and the open, vertically integrated service platform model. Each of these models is distinguished by a different cost structure, product offer, required capital buffer and forecast profitability level.

Regardless of the choice of the model, ultimately the market will primarily maintain these banks, perhaps technology companies with a banking license (Jagiełło, Kubisiak, 2020) which, apart from transaction centers supported by artificial intelligence, will agilely form an ecosystem of targeted, not necessarily financial advisory services.

The main goal of such organizations will be to offer a completely new experience of deep fragmentation and customization of the customer base. Time saving and emotional component - mutual trust, positive experience will be a common value and a "currency" in mutual settlements. Banks supported by the power of Big Data analysis will shorten the purchasing distance to the maximum by using the digital footprint and user behavioral profile (a new type of mass customer). The assembly of AI with cloud computing will define a new approach to the assessment of creditworthiness and risk exposure. In this field, the competition for customer retention will be the greatest. Only a small group of clients with graded income and specific professions will receive the care of a certified advisor. Experiencing emotional coherence in mutual relations between the counselor and the consumer will be of particular importance in this segment.

In the near future, banking activities will be further de-segmented and legally deregulated (PSD3). With time, banks will take over the role of multiagents responsible for creating needs that go far beyond the financial area of customer interests. The financial services market as a result of Smartphoneization, demonopolization and further digitization - blockchain (Szpringer, 2019) will be embedded in the constantly expanding platform offer that affects many spheres of life. The mass customer will become the beneficiary of a narrower range of services performed remotely and in real time, but in a fully automated form.

Until recently, this picture was a vision for most representatives of the banking industry. The current visions of industry leaders are now becoming an element of medium-term management strategies.

REFERENCES

Accenture. (2020, September). *Banking Technology Vision 2020, Raport.* Author.

Adarkar, A., Hyde, P., & Sridharan, A. (2020). *Leading a consumer bank through the coronavirus pandemic.* McKinsey&Company.

Arnon, A.D., Ricco, J.A., Smetters, K.A. (2020, September). Epidemiological and economic effects of lockdown. *Brookings.*

Baret, S., Celner, A., O'Reilly, M., & Shilling, M. (2020). *COVID-19 potential implications for the banking and capital markets sector*. Deloitte Insight.

Blomstrom, D. (2018). *Emotional Banking: Fixing Culture*. In *Leveraging FinTech and Transforming Retail Banks into Brands*. Palgrave McMillan. doi:10.1007/978-3-319-75653-0

Brynjolfsson, E., Hitt, L., & Kim, H. (2011, April). *Strength in Number: How does data driven decision making affect firm performance*. SSoM MIT.

Business Insider Intelligence. (2019, January). *40 Bigtech predictions. Moody's, Big Tech – a real threat to financial firms in retail services*. Author.

Capgemini Research Institute. (2020). *The Great Digital Divide Report, Offline Population Survey*. Author.

Cavallino, P., & De Fiore, F. (2020, June). Central banks' response to Covid-19 in advanced economies. *BIS Bulletin*.

Chong, E., Handscomb, CH., & Wiliams, O. (2020, October). *Agile resilience in the UK: Lessons from COVID-19 for the 'next normal'*. McKinsey and Company.

Clearbridge Mobile. (2020). The 2020 Enterprise Mobility Trends Report. Retrieved from: https://clearbridgemobile.com/enterprise-mobility-trends/

Corporate Social Responsibility. (2020). Retrieved from: https://www.unido.org/our-focus/advancing-economic-competitiveness/competitive-trade-capacities-and-corporate-responsibility/corporate-social-responsibility-market-integration/what-csr

Cukiermann, A. (2020, July). *Quantitative easing and helicopter money: Not so distant cousins*. Retrieved from: https://voxeu.org/article/quantitative-easing-and-helicopter-money-not-so-distant-cousins

Deloitte IIF. (2020). *Realizing of digital promise: COVID19 catalyzes and accelerates transformation in financial services*. Author.

Deloitte Digital. (2020). *Digital CRM 2.0 Building customer relationships in the digital landscape*. Author.

Dimock, M. (2019). *Defining generations: Where Millennials end and Generation Z begins*. Retrieved from: https://www.pewresearch.org/fact-tank/2019/01/17/where-millennials-end-and-generation-z-begins/

Drucker, P. (1999). *Management Challenges For The 21st Century*. Academic Press.

EBA. (2019). *Report on the impact of FinTech on payment institutions' and e-money institutions' business models*. EBA.

European Commission. (2020). *Banks and third party providers agree on joint efforts regarding the transition to new payment rules*. Retrieved from: https://ec.europa.eu/info/publications/190726-joint-statement-psd2_en

Handscomb, CH., Mahadevan, D., Naidoo, E., Schor, L., Sieberer, M., & Srinivasan, S. (2020, June). *An operating model for the next normal: Lessons from agile organizations in the crisis*. McKinsey.

IDG Research, . (2020). The state of the cloud: How enterprise adoption is taking shape. *InfoWorld*.

IMF Fiscal Monitor Country Fiscal Measures in response on COVID-19. (2020, October). Retrieved from: https://www.imf.org/en/Topics/imf-and-covid19/Fiscal-Policies-Database-in-Response-to-COVID-19

IMF Policy Tracker. (2020, October). *COVID-19 Financial Assistance and Debt Service Relief.* Retrieved from: https://www.imf.org/en/Topics/imf-and-covid19/COVID-Lending-Tracker

International Monetary Fund. (2020, June). *Global Financial Stability Report*. Author.

Jagiełło, Z., & Kubisiak, P. (2020). *From the moneybox to the cloud computing*. ICAN Institute.

Jagiełło, Z., & Kubisiak, P. (2020). *From the moneybox to the cloud computing*. ICAN Institute.

Kelly, K. (2016). *The inevitable. Understanding the 12 technological Forces That Will Shape Our Future*. Academic Press.

Kotler, P., Kartayaja, H., & Setiawan, I. (2017). *Marketing 4.0, Moving from Traditional to Digital*. J. Wiley & Sons.

KPMG. (2020, April). *Report: PSD2 and Open Banking. Revolution or evolution?* Retrieved from: https://ec.europa.eu/info/law/payment-services-psd-2-directive-eu-2015-2366_eu

KPMG International Cooperative. (2020). *Banking on consumer platforms, Reshaping the banking experience*. Author.

Marz, N., & Warren, J. (2015). *Big Data Best Practices of Scaling Data System in real time*. Manning Publication Co.

Mayer-Schönberger, V., & Cukier, K. (2013). *Big Data Effective Data Analysis, A revolution that will change our thinking, work and life*. MT Business Ltd.

McKinsey & Company. (2020, September). *AI-bank of the future: Can banks meet the AI challenge*. Author.

Migliorelli, M. (2018). *New Cooperative Banking in Europe Strategies for Adapting the Business Model Post Crisis*. Palgrave Macmillan. doi:10.1007/978-3-319-93578-2

Miklaszewska, E., & Folwarski, M. (2020). *Emotional banking. Digital transformation of banks and customer expectations*. Poltex.

MobirankR. (2018). Retrieved from:https://mobirank.pl/2018/02/02/mobile-i-digital-w-2018-roku-w-polsce-i-na-swiecie/

Redefine banking with Artificial Intelligence. (2020). Retrieved from: https://www.accenture.com/_acnmedia/pdf-68/accenture-redefine-banking.pdf

Schumpeter, J. (1960). *The Theory of Economic Development*. PWN.

Schwab, K. (2016). *The fourth Industrial revolution*. Deloitte, World Economic Forum.

Skinner, C. (2018). *Digital Human: The Fourth Revolution of Humanity Includes Everyone*. Academic Press.

Spence, M. (2019, July). *Impact of the form of revolution on welfare*. Retrieved from: https://www.obserwatorfinansowy.pl/bez-kategorii/rotator/wplyw-cyfrowej-rewolucji-na-dobrobyt/

Srinival, V., & Schoeps, J.T. (2019, December). *Platform banking as a new business model.* Deloitte Center for FS.

Surma, J. (2017). *Digitization of life in the era of Big Data.* Academic Press.

Szpringer, W. (2019). *Blockchain as a system innovation, Challenges for financial sector.* Poltext.

Szpringer, W. (2019). *Blockchain as a system innovation, Challenges for financial sector.* Poltext.

The best banking app. (2020). Retrieved from: https://www.thefirstnews.com/article/youre-simply-the-best-pko-bank-polski-app-takes-top-spot-in-global-ranking-4783

Wang, V. X. (2014). *Handbook of Research on Education and Technology in a Changing Society.* Scopus. doi:10.4018/978-1-4666-6046-5

World Economic Outlook Update. (2020, June). *A Crisis Like No Other, An Uncertain Recovery.* IMF.

Chapter 11
Circular Economy and Climate Change in Developing Economies

James Osabuohien Odia
University of Benin, Benin City, Nigeria

ABSTRACT

The CE represents a new model for resilient growth in both developed and developing economies that would help to tackle the causes and devastating effects of climate change and climate change risks, meet the 1.5 degree target of the Paris Agreement, and achieve the Sustainable Development Goals (SDGs). The CE practices can help to reduce greenhouse gases (CO2, methane, and nitro-oxide) to net zero emissions by 2050 through efficient resources use, elongation of product lifetime, recycling, recovery, reuse, materials substitution, efficient waste reduction and management, sharing service, among others. Given the numerous economic opportunities, innovation, and policy progresses, developing countries should transit to the CE pathway by aligning the CE strategies with the mitigation of climate change and the achievement of SDGs, synergize the CE practices with the existing national policies, and mainstream across sectoral strategy and policy development.

INTRODUCTION

The circular economy (CE) is a system where the products of today are the raw materials of tomorrow, reducing the need for resources, and waste and emissions. This is in contrast to the linear or traditional economy where products are manufactured, used and discarded. The CE concept is a new sustainability paradigm (Geissdoerfer, Savaget, Bocken & Hultink, 2017) and business transformation model (Frishammar & Parida,2019).It depicts a radical shift from the liner economy of "take-make-dispose" step-by-step plan, whereby raw materials are collected and transformed into products which are used until they are finally discarded as wastes.The CE is built on the three principles of input, sustainable cycles and output (Ellen MacArthur, 2012).The CE principles design out waste, strictly differentiate between consumable and durable product components, rely on renewable energy, decrease resource dependence

DOI: 10.4018/978-1-7998-6788-3.ch011

and increase system resilience. Forgarassy and David (2020) identified three principles for the optimal design of CE systems will include keeping resources under control, and balancing the material flow of renewable energy sources (principles of inputs) as well as preserving and increasing natural resource systems (principle of sustainable cycles) and principles of outputs. There is currently a growing discussions on CE in relation to developing countries. Apart from China, in Sub-Saharan, East and Southern Africa, South and Southeast Asia and Latin America are also adopting national policies and launching initiatives to promote CE (Wright et al,2019). This is because circular strategies tend to reduce the GHGs emission. Circularity also makes the society more climate-resilient.

According to the United Nations Framework Convention on Climate Change (2015), transformation in the usage of natural resources is a requirement to achieve a prospered, secured and resilient nations. Specifically, the developing countries require transformation in models of resources usage in order to address climate change and maintain ecosystem stability. Basically, the CE has the potentials to unleash sustainable development and to attain the social, environmental and economic benefits. It has been argued that circularity will help build resilience and climate adaptation and mitigation through efficient water and energy use, improved management of land resources, increase the quality of life, and attain the 1.5° C target (Ellen MacArthur Foundation, 2019).The CE can support a successful climate policy by reducing the high climate impact of materials consumption. The CE offers a concrete perspective on how sustainable production and consumption can be organized to emit less carbon dioxide (Co_2). Therefore, the promotion of circular production and consumption model, and synergizing with climate mitigation and adaptation is key to meeting the global commitments to the Paris Agreement, particularly by developing countries.

Therefore, this chapter examines how the circular economy can assist to mitigate and tackle the climate change impacts of material consumption and production in developing economies. The rest of the chapter is sub-divided as follows: the immediate section considers background on circular economy as new business paradigm, climate change and climate change risk. The third section on the issues, controversies and problems It addresses the issues of linear vs circular economy; and the climate math of obtaining the 1.5 target. The fourth section is the solution and recommendation on circular economy and its roles in addressing climate change and climate change risks. In this section, we explore the adaptation and mitigation strategies, and CE practices to deal with climate change. The last section is the concluding remarks

BACKGROUND

The Circular Economy and the New Business Paradigm

Gan, Zhang, Liang, Zhao and Li (2013) have argued that although there is no commonly accepted definition of CE so far, the focal point of CE is the closed flow of materials and the use of raw materials and energy through multiple phases. According to the Ellen MacArthur Foundation (2015), the CE "replaces the 'end-of-life' concept with restoration, shifts towards the use of renewable energy, it removes the use of toxic chemicals, which impair re-use, and aims for the elimination of waste through a superior design of materials, products, systems, and, within this, business models".The CE is similar but distinct from "cradle to cradle", "performance economy" and "industrial ecology". Other related CE terms often used are resource efficiency, green economy, waste management or recycling While most attention goes to recycling and/or waste management, there are some signs of increasing attention also for other parts of the life-cycle of goods and services.

According to Fogarassy and David (2020), circularity involves a shift from a simple mitigation model to an absolute value creation model.It involves the decoupling of economic growth from increased use of resources in order to reduce the negative environmental impacts. The CE refers to the "production and consumption of goods through closed loop material flows that internalize environmental externalities linked to virgin resource extraction and the generation of waste including pollution" (Sauvé, Bernard & Sloan,2016).Mitchell (2015) emphasized the CE importance in extending the resources usage in order to extract the maximum value of material and product, and subsequently recover and reuse. Murray et al. (2017) opined that CE integrates economic activities with environmental issues in a sustainable way, revealing the relationship between CE and the delivery on the sustainable development goals (SDGs) (Preston & Lehne, 2017; Schroeder, Anggraeni & Weber, 2018).

Horvath, Mallinguh and Fogarassy (2018) noted that in circular economic models, there is integration between the economic actors and members of the supply chain. Hence the business ecosystems can constantly redesign or self- regulate. Basically, CE helps to transform business processes into sustainable, closed-loop resource system (Fogarassy & David, 2020).The CE improves the air quality, reduce water contamination, and protect biodiversity. It offers innovation opportunities to businesses to reduce materials costs, increase asset utilization and respond to dynamic customer demands. The CE implies change to the business model, consumer preference and individual ownership. It emphasizes shared use and renting, value of second-life (recycled) products and asset sharing over single, independent use. It is one in which products and materials are recycled, repaired and reused rather than thrown away or discarded, and waste from one industrial process becomes a valued input for another. The creating and optimizing resource 'loops' along value chains help to meet the material needs of growing populations through drastically lower rates of per capita primary resource use.

The vision of a CE rests on a systemic approach to resource efficiency in which 'end-of-life' products and materials at the end of their original service lifespan are not discarded but recycled, repaired or reused (3Rs) through the circular value chains. Willemsz (2020) argued that the CE follows the 3Rs where resources use are minimized (reduce); products and parts are reused; and raw materials are recycled to a high standard. The goals of 3Rs have become an acceptable way of disposing wastes (Ahmadi,2017; Huang, Wang, Kua, Geng, Bleischwitz & Ren, 2018) and a potential strategy to solve existing environmental problems (Preston & Carr, 2018).Neverthless, CE goes beyond recycling; it entails a critical review of products and the systems. It comprises "longer lifecycle, reduced materials impact, reusability, ease of disassembly for repair and replacement, introduction of new revenue models, such as product-service systems, and supporting other consumption models based on shared use. In the CE system, value is created by focusing on value preservation. The CE helps to promote eco-effectiveness through the development of new products with a long life cycle (Braungart & McDonough, 2009). Circular Economy is based on the establishment of closed production systems where resources are reused and kept in a loop of production and usage, allowing generating more value and for a longer period (Urbanatu,Chiawni & Chiesa, 2017)

A CE can be helpful in reducing conservatory gases because it uses renewable energy in the long run which is less polluting than remnant fuels.There is combination of efficiency usage and savings or potential gain of resources in a CE model (Ghisellini, Cialani & Ulgiati,2016).It reduces emissions from materials and also improves the availability of raw materials, ideally supported by an effective policy framework (Faure-Schuyer et al.,2018). Circular economy is restorative and regenerative by design; it optimizes value circulation, not prevention of waste generation. It is a continuous positive development cycle that preserves and enhances natural capital, optimizes resource yields and minimizes system risks by managing finite stocks and renewable flows. Murray, Skene and Haynes (2017) believed that emerging technologies can support the CE transition through radical increase in virtualization, de-materialization, transparency and feedback-driven intelligence.

Table 1. Ladders/Levels of Circularity-9 Rs

Level	R's	Description
HIGHEST	Refuse	Prevent the use of resources
	Rethink and Reduce	Decrease the use of resources
	Re-use	Find new product use (second hand)
	Repair	Maintain and repair
	Refurbish	Improve the product
	Remanufacture	Create new product from second hand
	Re-purpose	Re-use product for different purpose
	Re-cycle	Re-use raw materials of product
LOWEST	Recover	Recover energy from waste
	Disposal	

Climate Change

Climate change is currently one of the environmental phenomena threatening economic development and sustainability globally. It represents a change in climate due to human activity which has affected the composition of the global atmosphere as well as the natural climate variability over an observed period of time. The natural climate cycle and human activities have contributed to an increase in the accumulated heat-trapping of greenhouse gases (GHGs) in the atmosphere thereby causing global warming (Nwalem, 2015). Global warming results in the rise in the sea levels, oceans warm and glaciers melt, changes in rainfall patterns and increase in soil erosion, storms, floods and drought problems, coastal inundation and ecological destabilization thereby threatening agricultural productivity, human settlements, natural capital and ultimately a creating food crisis, worsening weather, energy decrease and general environmental breakdowns. The Mckinsey Global Intitute [MGI] (2020a) argued that changing climate would create a lot of economic, business and social risks over the next three decades because the increasing physical risks such as rising temperatures, heat waves, floods, droughts and sea levels will translate to increased socioeconomic risks. According to the UNEP, the projected impacts of unmitigated climate change in Africa are likely to have significant impacts on human livelihoods, health, water resources, agricultural production and food security, as well as nature-based tourism.

Climate change constitutes serious risk to poverty reduction and other sustainable development goals because it can undermine the efforts and progresses made so far. Again, MGI (2020a) posits the impact of climate change could affect human beings, human-made physical assets, and the natural world. A global temperature average of an increase of 2.3°C by 2050 could trigger physical feedback loops (such as the thawing of permafrost leading to the release of significant amounts of methane) that might cause the planet to warm for hundreds or thousands of years. The rising temperature and heat waves in India pose increasing risk that will drive reduce the GDP growth, labour workforce employment rate and productivity. The rise in sea level in Florida will lead to more storms and flooding in Florida's vulnerable coastline, cause $75 billion worth of damage to Florida real estate, drop in home price, mortgage rates could rise leading to increasing defaults and reduction in property revenue tax.

Climate change entails the release of GHGs such as CO_2, carbon monoxide, methane nitrous oxide and chloro-fluorocarbons leading to the progressive depletion of the ozone layer in the stratosphere. A United Nations report of 2018 found the 1.5° C target may not be met by 2030 because of the continuous increase in the emission of CO_2 by countries. The resultant effect could be an increase of 3°C or 4° C by 2100. According to Ellen MacArthur Foundation (2019), agriculture, forestry, and other land use (AFOLU) contribute around a quarter of global GHG emissions. Industry account for 21% of total global CO_2 emissions; the manufacture of cement, steel, plastics and aluminium make up about 60% of these emissions. The cement industry is a top source of CO_2 emission (Czigler et al,2020). The extraction and processing of resources account for over 90% of land-and water-related environmental impacts (water stress and biodiversity loss). The production of plastic using fossil fuels is a major source of GHG emission. Plastics can stay in the environment for a long time, thereby causing lots of damage and harm to biodiversity, and depletion of the ecosystem services that is needed to support life.

Table 2. Anthropogenic greenhouse-gas (GHG) emissions per sector and type of gas

	Sectors	CO_2 (%)	Mechane (%)	Other GHGs (%)	Total GHG per gigaton (%)	Share of Total gigaton (%)
1	Industry	46	46	8	25	33
	Agriculture/Livestock	6	80	14	15	20
	Power	100			12	17
	Transport	100			8	10
	Waste	-	98	2	6	8
	Net Deforestation	100			6	7
	Building	100			3	4

Source: Adapted from Henderson et al (2020)

Climate Change Risks

Engel, Enkvist and Henderson (2015) classified climate change risks into value- chain risks (physical, price, product risks) and external-stakeholders risks (rating, regulation, reputation risks).Physical risks relate to damage to infrastructure and other assets like factories and supply chain by extreme weather like wildfires, floods or hurricanes. According to MGI (2020a), there are seven characteristics of physical climate risks viz: rising heat and humidity, flooding, storms, rising sea levels, increasing across the globe, spatial or local, ever-changing and non-stationery, non-linear and breaching thresholds, systemic, regressive with greater impacts on emerging economies and unprepared and slow adaptability by companies and communities. Price risks refer to increased price volatility of raw materials due to drought unstable climate or climate-related regulation. Product risks refer to core products turning unpopular or usellable as a result of new or greener products in the market, regulatory or production costs. Rating risks refer to possible high cost of capital due to climate related exposure like carbon pricing, disruption in supply chain or product obsolescence. Regulation risks refer to government action such as carbon-trading programme,renewable portfolio standard, circular economy prompted by climate change. Reputation risks is the probability of profitability loss following a business' activities or position tht the public considers harmful.

ISSUES, CONTROVERSIES AND PROBLEMS

Linear vs Circular Economy

The linear approach to industrialization has come under strain because of its environmental and economic implications (Nguyen, Stuchtey & Zils, 2014). The linear has fuelled the depletion of natural resources, waste, environmental degradation, climate change and negative human health effects (Barra & Leonard,2018).The production of goods and services exerts excessive pressures on the ecosystems thereby affecting the provision of essential services such as water, air and soil cleaning (Michelini, et al.,2017). Again, the raw materials collection and product formation are associated with high energy and water consumption, toxic emissions and the disruption of natural capital such as forests and lakes. The toxic substances emitted when these products are discarded, cause climate change. The economic model in the linear economy affects the supply of materials creating uncertainty due to increasing demands, scarcity and fluctuating in prices of raw materials and geopolitical dependence on different materials. Michelini, et al (2017) have argued that there has to be transition to a resource-efficient and regenerative circular economy if the world wants to tackle the effects of climate change by 2050 (Ellen MacArthur Foundation, 2019). Also, it has become increasingly apparent that the 'business as usual'(BAU) is not an option for a sustainable future owing to the rising global population, increasing resources consumption and negative environmental impacts (Wautelet, 2018). The threats posed by BAU to companies include volatile price of resources, decline supply chain efficiency, increase bans on waste trading, decreasing costs of renewable energy sources among others (Horvath, Mallinguh & Fogarassy,2018) and exposure to "linear risks", higher resource prices and supply disruptions (Ramkumar,et al, 2018).There are also significant losses of value and negative effects all along the material chains (Ellen MacArthur Foundation, 2013).

According to Bocken, Ritala and Huotari (2017), a CE model aims to close the gap between production and the natural ecosystem's cycles in which humans ultimately depend upon. The transition to a CE not only reduce the negative impacts of the linear economy, it also represents a systemic shift that builds long-term resilience, generates business and economic opportunities, and provides environmental and societal benefits. The CE promotes resilience, alternative strategy for industrial development, job creation and sustainable growth for developed and developing in comparison to the traditional manufacturing-led growth pathway in most developing economies (Roges, Koacic & Tulkers,2020). Stahel (2016) found that a shift to a circular economy would guarantee low-carbon economy, reduce each of the seven European nation's GHG emissions by 70% and increase the workforce by about 4%. Also, CE can dampen the effects of price volatility and losses resulting from the (unexpected) unavailability of raw materials. Also, circular practices can reduce negative externalities such as CO_2 emissions, heavy ecological footprint and significant land use through efficient resource use, and promotion of innovation and increased security of resources supply (Sijbren de Jong et al, 2016). The use of clean, renewable energy sources for household lighting is found to reduce resources consumption in sub-Saharan Africa (Schroeder et al, 2018).

Challenges to the Circular Economy Implementation

Although there are high hopes that CE will help to tackle climate through the reduction of greenhouse gases, some researchers have argued that there needs to some requirements for a CE implementation to be successful. These include: new methods of regulation such as the extended producer responsibility (EPR) policies, technology push and market pull policies, creation of lead market and low carbon products, robust and transparent carbon accounting system, integration of informal workers skill base and resource efficiency towards CE, trade policy favouring reduced import duties and removal of restrictions on trade related to CE activities (Schroeder, Anantharaman, Anggraeni & Foxon, 2019; Preston,Lehne, Wellesley & Sugathan,2019; Rizos et al, 2019). Preston et al (2019) have contended that robust regulation is required to create the right incentive structures for a transition to the CE and ensure that businesses comply with the highest labour, health and environmental standards when implementing CE practices. It should support and enable the existing CE expertise, practitioners and innovators in the informal sector must also be captured, preserved and utilized, mitigate displacement of informal workers and attract foreign investment and trade.

The survey by Chatham House-UNIDO found the major limitations to CE to be limited institutional capacity and weak regulation, lack of access to finance and technology, less cooperation between sectors, persistent infrastructural deficits, low skills, high resistant from incumbent industries, a glowing urban population, a lack of consumer awareness, the absence of a stronger legal definition of waste, and a scarcity of adequate CE-related policies. There is also the undeveloped and fragmented private sector as well as an active informal economy beyond the reach of market interventions (Preston et al, 2019).

Circular Economy and Sustainable Development Goals in Developing Countries

A CE is seen route into a genuinely sustainable economy in which material, information and value circulate together. Although CE has gained traction in developed countries, this is little understanding by most developing countries of how the application of CE practices can contribute positively towards economic growth, jobs, sustainable development and climate change. Nevertheless, the CE is gaining popularity as a complete or partial solution or model to address the challenges of sustainable development (Geissdoerfer et al.,2017a) and meet the SDGs. The CE is relevant to various SDGs such as Goal 12, "ensure sustainable consumption and production patterns'' and Goal 13 on "climate action (Rizos, Elkerbout & Egenhofer,2019). The CE can also support developing economies to achieve sustainable production and consumption (SDG 12) and other SDGs like Sustainable Cities and Communities (SDG 11), Good Health and Well-Being (SDG 3), clean water and sanitation (SDG 6), affordable and clean energy (SDG7), life on earth (SDG 15), decent work and economic growth (SDG 8), end hunger (SDG 2) and poverty (SDG1) (Wright et al, 2019). It will also enable meeting the 1.5 degree target, drive sustainable and resilient economic growth and development.

According to Ashraf, Knaepen, van Seters and Mackie (2020), there should an integration of the CE and climate change in foreign policies in the areas of development cooperation, trade and investments, international diplomacy, migration and security, as well as international dimensions of environmental policy. The need to integrate climate change in foreign policies is in line with the 2030 Agenda which emphasizes the importance of balancing the economic, social and environmental dimensions of sustainable development in order to achieve the SDGs (Mackie et al., 2017).The CE is a societal transition in which the circulation of materials eventually contributes to economic, environmental and societal benefits of current and future generations (Homrich, Galvao, Abadia & Carvalho 2018; Reichel, De Schoenmakere & Gillabel 2016).

Climate Change, Climate math of 1.5 Degree Target and the Circular Economy

The world faces great challenges to mitigate the effects of climate change in order to achieve the global 1.5 degree target. It is argued this would take rapid action as well as a global, comprehensive, near-term action. Companies must invest in massive decarbonization efforts and individual must make change to their consumption and modes of transportation. Henderson et al (2020) outlined five major five major business, economic and societal shifts that would make the 1.5-degree target possible. These shifts include (1) reforming food and industry by change our modes of consumption, farming and waste. This involves reducing CO_2 emission from the production of ruminants (especially beef and lamb) meat, changing the agricultural system of cultivation to deal with CO_2 and methane emission (2) electrifying our lives, road transport and buildings (3) adapting industrial operations by electrifying industries, ensuring greater efficiency and reducing the methane emission (4) decarbonize power and fuel through expanding the use of renewable energy, bioenergy, bio-kerosene, biogas and biodiesel, blue hydrogen produced from natural gas and (5) ramp up carbon capture and carbon sequestration activity through developing the "carbon capture, use, and storage (CCUS) industry" and increasing the rate of reforestation The CCUS prevent CO2 emissions from entering the atmosphere as it compress, transport and store prevent CO2 underground.

Ellen MacArthur Foundation (2019) has found increased circularity of resources use and decarbonization of energy production will result in the reduction of CO_2 emission.Circularity is critical to meet the net-zero emission reduction objective by 2050 (OECD, 2018,Material Economics, 2018; Ellen MacArthur Foundation, 2019). Basically, the CE tilts towards processes such as material substitution, higher utilization of products through sharing models, reduced raw material needs in the production processes, product design aimed at achieving higher resource efficiency, waste heat recovery and biomass cascading, and approaches that hold potentials to transform industrial value chains (Rizos et al, 2019). According to UNCTAD (2018), circularity can be promoted through the emergence or collaboration of sectors or economy, movement from the ownership of goods towards accessibility to services, encouraging consumer education, awareness and behavioural shifts.The alignment of enablers in various markets and shifting consumer preferences can make the CE an important contributor to achieve the SDGs and the 1.5 degree target of the Paris Agreement.

The Chatham House (2017) classified the instruments for promoting circularity into command and control, economic and public-private dimensions. The command and control instruments include waste disposal, recycling, warranties refund system and streamlined regulations. The economic instruments include the use of taxes and other incentives (See Table 2).

Table 3. Instruments for promoting circularity

Command and Control	Economic	Public-Private
Waste disposal and trade standards	Landfill and/or incineration taxes	Improved legislature and infrastructures
Minimum recycling requirements	Different taxation for reused or recycled products	Circularity certificate and labelling schemes
Deposit refund system-plastic bottles	Reduced value added taxes for repairs and re-used services	Extended producer responsibility scheme
Circular public procurement	Increased taxes for non-reparable products	Discounts for efficiency
Extended legal warranties	Tax shifts from labour to consumption	Products designed for recycling
Streamlined regulations for leasing and shared businesses	Incentives for access over ownership	Virtual platform for asset sharing

Source: Chatham House (2017)

SOLUTIONS AND RECOMMENDATIONS

Adaptation and Mitigation Strategies, and Climate Change

Climate policy responses consist of adaptation measures (for managing near-term physical climate risks) and mitigation measures (for lessening greenhouse-gas emissions eventually reducing them to net zero to reduce future physical climate risk).Both adaptation and mitigation strategies are necessary to address the impacts of climate change. The MGI report of 2020 has shown that adaptation to climate change is very critical because of the increasing rise in the risks of physical hazards and non-linear socioeconomic jolts.There is also the major challenge of mitigating climate change through de-carbonization, renewable energy efficiency and circularity. While adaptation is urgent, further warming and risk increase can only tackled by achieving net-zero greenhouse-gas emission which is possible though the mitigation strategies The adaptation strategies include protecting people and assets, building resilience, reducing exposure, and ensuring that appropriate insurance and financing are in place

Circular Economy Strategies and Climate Change Risks

The CE can help to address climate change and achieve low carbon economy by 2050. The CE through reducing, reusing and recycling avoid GHGs emission from traditional waste management systems like energy, recovery and landfills; it also helps to reduce the GHG emission by cutting down the energy required for industrial production in converting raw materials to usable products (Deloitte, 2016). The CE strategies or measures to mitigate the impacts of climate change include the use of more efficient design and production, shorter transport distances, shared use and recycling. Other strategies are reuse, refurbishment, remanufacture, recovery, repairs, lifetime extension, material efficiency, packaging, waste reduction and management. The combination of various circular strategies has greater effect than the sum of separate strategies. The CE practices of recycling and reuse can save between 13% and 66% of GHGs embedded in products in sectors like food, material intensive industries and construction. The CE offers significant and cost-effective solutions to reduce GHG emissions related to food waste between 33% and 38%.Circular economy in the automotive industry is more from refurbishment, remanufacturing and recycling. In the construction industry, the CE practices include recycling, recovery and reuse.

Table 4. Adaptation and Mitigation strategies for addressing Climate Change

Adaptation Strategies	Mitigation Strategies	
Protect people and assets -Increased emergency preparedness; -Harden infrastructure -Build protective structures like sea walls	**Decarbonization** **Reduce demand through efficiency and optimization** - energy efficiency improvement, -process optimization - shifts in consumer patterns	**Circular Economy Practices** -Reuse -Repair -Refurbish -Remanufacture -Recovery -Recycling -Extend product lifetime -Resources use efficiency -Material substitution -Industrial symbiosis -Sharing and service models -Design for disassembly
Building resilience -Raise inventory levels in production -Build back up power capacity	**Change power and fuel mix** -Deploy renewable resources - Electrify transport, buildings and industry -Use of biomass, biofuel and bioenergy -Grow the blue / green hydrogen market	
Reducing exposure -Relocate assets and communities that are too difficult to protect -Redesign physical assets footprints based on full life cycle.	**Lower methane and nitro-oxide (GHGs) emission** -Reform agricultural and food system -Eliminate fugitive methane emissions	
Insurance and Finance -Subsidize premiums for vulnerable stakeholders; -Encourage parametized insurance and catastrophic bonds -Mobilize finance to fund adaptation measures	**Scale up a carbon-management industry** - Expand CCUS -Stop deforestation and support afforestation	

Adapted from MGI (2020c)

The report by Material Economics (2018) found that a shift towards CE could reduce EU emissions from heavy industry to as much as 56% by 2050 relative to a baseline scenario. According to the International Resource Panel (IRP), more resource-efficient practices would be critical to achieving the commitments to the Paris Agreement of 1.5 degree target. The IRP projects that resource efficiency approaches could reduce GHG emissions by 60 per cent by 2050. Savings on individual resources could be higher: producing aluminum from scrap results in a 90–95% reduction in energy inputs and GHGs emissions (Ekins & Hughes, 2017; Gardner, 2017). An economy with net zero emissions requires renewable and energy efficiency measures and reduction in material use and tackling the global waste crisis. Barra and Leonard (2018) summarized the CE solutions to address emissions from plastics to entail: producing plastics from alternative non-fossil fuel feed stocks; using plastic wastes as a resource; redesigning plastic manufacturing processes and products to enhance longevity, reusability and waste prevention; collaboration between businesses and consumers to encourage recycling and increase the value of plastic products; encouraging sustainable business models which promote plastic products as services, and encourage sharing and leasing; developing robust information platforms to aid circular solutions; and adopting fiscal and regulatory measures to support the circular economy".

CONCLUSION AND SUGGESTIONS FOR FURTHER RESEARCHES

The CE presents numerous opportunities for developing and developed countries to mitigate the devastating influence of climate change and climate change risks with better results compared to the adaptation strategies. It will also enable the world to achieve the sustainable development goals especially SDGs 12, 11, 13, 6, by 2030, and meet the 1.5 degree target of the Paris Agreement by 2050. The CE offers an alternative strategy to developing countries to developed industrially, create numerous jobs and employments, resilient growth and sustainable development. The CE transition of circularity of materials and optimizing closed resources loop along value chains contribute immensely to economic, environmental and societal developments. CE strategies offer counter measures to tackle the devastating effects of climate change globally. In addition to the great impact of the decarbonization measures, the CE practices will help to reduce negative externalities and greenhouse gases ($CO_{2,}$ methane and nitro-oxide) to net zero emissions through the deployment of strategies of efficient resources use, elongation of product lifetime, recycling, recovery, reuse, materials substitution, efficient waste reduction and management, sharing service among others.

Only a few developing countries have started to transit and implement the CE principles even though there are reported advantages and benefits of opening up economic opportunities, innovation and policy progresses for developing countries that decide to follow the CE pathway. The CE strategies should be aligned with the mitigation of climate change and the achievement of the sustainable development goals. Also, the governments of developing countries should synergize the CE practices with the existing national policies and mainstream across sectoral strategy and policy development, and invest in the key fundamentals- good governance and regulatory frameworks, inclusive policies and integration of the informal and existing CE sector, investment in critical infrastructure, pooled financing partnerships at bilateral and plurilateral leves and trades at regional and international levels

REFERENCES

Ahmadi, M. (2017). Evaluating the performance of 3Rs waste practices: Case study-region one municipality of Tehran. *Advance Recycling Waste Management, 2*(130), 2. doi:10.4172/2475-7675.1000130

Ashraf, N., van Seters, J., & Mackie, J. (2020). *The integration of climate change and circular economy in foreign policies*. ECDPM Discussion No.274.

Baporikar, N. (Ed.). (2020). *Handbook of research on entrepreneurship development and opportunities in circular economy*. doi:10.4018/978-1-7998-5116-5

Barra, R., & Leonard, S. A. (2018). *Plastics and the circular economy*. Scientific and Technical Advisory Panel to the Global Environment Facility.

Bocken, N. M. P., Ritala, P., & Huotari, P. (2017). The circular economy: Exploring the introduction of the concept among S&P 500 firms. *Journal of Industrial Ecology, 21*(3), 487–490. doi:10.1111/jiec.12605

Braungart, M., & McDonough, W. (2009). Cradle to cradle. Re-making the way we make things. London: Vintage Books Chatham House.

Czigler, T., Reiter, S., Schulze, P., & Somar, K. (2020). *Laying the foundation for zero-carbon cement.* McKinsey and Company May.

de Jong, S., van der Gaast, M., Kraak, J., Bergema, R., & Usanov, A. (2016). *The circular economy and developing countries: A data analysis of the impact of a circular economy on resource-dependent developing nations.* Centre of Expertise on Resources, The Hague Centre for Strategic Studies.

Deloitte. (2016). *Circular economy potentials for climate change.* Deloitte Sustainability Team.

Material Economics. (2018). *The circular economy – A powerful force for climate mitigation. Transformative innovation for prosperous and low-carbon industry.* Academic Press.

Ekins, P., & Hughes, N. (2017). *Resource efficiency: potential and economic implications.* UN Environment Programme (UNEP). Https://europa.eu/ capacity4dev/unep/documents/resource-efficiency-potential-and-economic-implications

Ellen MacArthur Foundation. (2012). *Towards the circular economy: An economic and business rationale for an accelerated transition.* The Ellen MacArthur Foundation.

Ellen MacArthur Foundation. (2015). *Towards a circular economy: Business rationale for an accelerated transition.* The Ellen MacArthur Foundation.

Ellen MacArthur Foundation. (2017). *What is a circular economy?* The Ellen MacArthur Foundation.

Ellen MacArthur Foundation. (2019). *Completing the picture: How the circular economy tackles climate change.* www.ellenmacarthurfoundation.org/publications

Faure-Schuyer, A., Egenhofer,C & Elkerbout, M. (2018). *Value chains based on mineral raw materials – challenges for European policy and industry.* CEPS Policy Insights No 2018/07.

Forgarassy, C., & David, F. (2020). Theoretical and practical approaches of circular economy for business models and technological solutions. *Resources, 9*(76), 1–9. doi:10.3390/resources9060076

Gan, Y., Zhang, T., Liang, S., Zhao, Z., & Li, N. (2013). How to deal with resource productivity. *Journal of Industrial Ecology, 17*(3), 440–451. doi:10.1111/j.1530-9290.2012.00547.x

Gardner, J. (2017). *Circular economy and decarbonisation: lessons from industry.* Hoffmann Centre for Sustainable Resource Economy.

Geissdoerfer, M., Savaget, P., Bocken, N. M. P., & Hultink, E. J. (2017). The circular economy – a new sustainability paradigm? *Journal of Cleaner Production, 143*(6), 757–768. doi:10.1016/j.jclepro.2016.12.048

Ghisellini, P., Cialani, C., & Ulgiati, S. (2016). A review on circular economy: The expected transition to a balanced interplay of environmental and economic systems. *Journal of Cleaner Production, 114*(7), 11–32. doi:10.1016/j.jclepro.2015.09.007

Henderson, K., Pinner, D., Rogers, M., Smeets, B., Tryggested, C., & Vargas, D. (2020). Climate math: What a 1.5 degree pathway would take. *The McKinsey Quarterly.*

Homrich, A. S., Galvao, G., Abadia, L. G., & Carvalho, M. M. (2018). The circular economy umbrella: Trends and gaps on integrating pathways. *Journal of Cleaner Production, 175*, 525–543. doi:10.1016/j.jclepro.2017.11.064

Horvath, B., Mallinguh, E., & Fogarassy, C. (2018). Designing business solutions for plastic waste management to enhance circular transitions in Kenya. *Sustainability, 10*(5), 1664. doi:10.3390u10051664

Huang, B., Wang, X., Kua, H., Geng, Y., Bleischwitz, R., & Ren, J. (2018). Construction and demolition of waste management in China through the 3Rs principle. *Resources, Conservation and Recycling, 129*, 36–44. doi:10.1016/j.resconrec.2017.09.029

Mackie, J., Ronceray, M., & Spierings, E. (2017). *Policy coherence and the 2030 Agenda: Building on the PCD experience*. Discussion Paper 210. Maastricht: ECDPM.

McKinsey Global Institute (MGI). (2020a). Climate risks and response: Physical hazards and socioeconomic impacts. *McKinsey Quarterly*.

MGI. (2020b). Confronting climate risk. *McKinsey Quarterly*.

MGI. (2020c). *Leading the battle against climate change: Action for China*. McKinsey and Company.

Michelini, G., Moraes, R. N., Cunha, R. N., Costa, J. M. H., & Ometto, A. R. (2017). From linear to circular economy: PSS conducting the transition. *Procedia CIRP, 64*, 2–6. doi:10.1016/j.procir.2017.03.012

Murray, A., Skene, K., & Haynes, K. (2017). The circular economy: An interdisciplinary exploration of the concept and application in a global context. *Journal of Business Ethics, 140*(3), 369–380. doi:10.100710551-015-2693-2

Nguyen, H., Stuchtey, M., & Zils, M. (2014). *Remaking the industrial economy*. Available at https://www.McKinsey.com

OECD. (2018). *Global material resources outlook to 2060 - Economic drivers and environmental consequences*. OECD.

Preston, F., & Lehne, J. (2017). *A wider circle? The circular economy in developing countries*. https://www.chathamhouse.org/sites/default/files/publications/research/2017-12-05-circular-economy-preston-lehne-final.pdf

Preston, F., Lehne, J., Wellesley, L., & Sugathan, M. (2019). An inclusive circular economy: Priorities for developing countries. The Royal Institute of International Affairs, Chatham House.

Ramkumar, S., Kraanen, F., Plomp, R., Edgerton, B., Walrecht, A., Baer, I., & Hirsch, P. (2018) Linear risks. *Amst. Circular Economy*, 9. https://www.ebrd.com/news/publications/essays-and-glossaries/ linear-risk-business-impacts-of-linear-consumption-practices.htm

Reichel, A., De Schoenmakere, M., & Gillabel, J. (2016). *Circular economy in Europe, developing the knowledge base*. European Environmental Agency.

Rizos, V., Elkerbout, M., & Egenhofer, C. (2019). *Circular economy for climate neutrality: Setting the priorities for the EU*. CEPS Policy Brief No 2019/04.

Schroeder, P., Anantharaman, M., Anggraeni, K., & Foxon, T. J. (2019). The circular economy and the global South: Sustainable lifestyles and green industrial development. Abingdon: Routledge.

Schroeder, P., Anggraeni, K., & Weber, U. (2018). The relevance of circular economy practices to the sustainable development goals. *Journal of Industrial Ecology*, *23*(1), 77–95. doi:10.1111/jiec.12732

Schwerdtle, P. N. (2019). Circular economy and environmental health in low- and middle-income countries. *Globalization and Health*, *15*(1), 65. doi:10.118612992-019-0501-y PMID:31847867

Stahel, W. R. (2016). The circular economy. *Nature: International weekly. Journal of Science*, *531*(7595).

The Stanley Foundation. (2017). *The circular economy pathway to pursuing 1.5°C*. Available at https://www.stanleyfoundation.org/resources.cfm?id=1630

UNCTAD. (2018). *Circular economy: The new normal?* Policy Brief, No.61 UNCTAD.

Wautelet, T. (2018). *The concept of circular economy: its origins and it evolution.* Retrieved from: https://www.researchgate.net/publication/322555840

Webster, K. (2017). *The circular economy. A wealth of flows*. Ellen MacArthur Foundation.

Wright, C. Y., Godfrey, L., Armiento, G., Haywood, L. K., Inglesi-Lotz, R., Lyne, K., & Schwerdtle, P. N. (2019). Circular economy and environmental health in low-and middle-income countries. *Globalization and Health*, *15*(65), 1–5. doi:10.118612992-019-0501-y PMID:31847867

Chapter 12
The Impact of Adopting CSR on the Firm's Overall Performance:
Empirical Evidence From Large Moroccan Firms

Abdelmajid Ibenrissoul
ENCG, ISO, Hassan II University of Casablanca, Morocco

Khawla Bouraqqadi
FSJES, FBGR, Hassan II university of Casablanca, Morocco

Souhaila Kammoun
IHEC, CODECI, University of Sfax, Tunisia

ABSTRACT

The purpose of the chapter is to study what effect CSR has on firms' overall performance in a developing country context. While most of the previous empirical researches focused on the relationship between CSR and financial performance, the present study suggests exploring the impact of CSR on overall performance which encompasses economic, environmental, and social dimensions as well as stakeholders. The empirical study aims to analyze and measure the social and environmental involvement of large Moroccan firms operating in the main sectors of activity and located in different geographical areas. Using multiple linear regression analysis, the authors empirically test the impact of CSR on overall performance on a sample of 44 companies. The main findings reveal that CSR is a driver for improving image and reputation, enabling the firm to achieve overall corporate performance. On the basis of the main results, they set out some managerial implications and further directions for CSR research in developing countries.

DOI: 10.4018/978-1-7998-6788-3.ch012

INTRODUCTION

Over the last decades, the interest in Corporate Social Responsibility (CSR) has steadily growing in developed and developing countries. CSR has gained in prominence on the part of both practitioners and researchers, becoming an integral part of the business and an indispensable concern in the contemporary corporate world in a broad spectrum. Moreover, CSR is seen as a real strategic necessity (Falkenberg and Brunsael, 2011; Kammoun et al., 2020a; 2020b). To engage in CSR means that a firm is taking into account environmental issues, integrating them into the scope of the firm's strategic decisions and operating in ways that improve society and the environment. As outlined by Pesqueux (2002), CSR is concretized through economic prosperity, respect for the environment and respect and improvement of social cohesion, which are the main dimensions of sustainable development at the firm level. To put it briefly, companies are called to adopt a strategic approach to CSR, with the aim of reconciling the need for competitiveness and social responsibility (European Commission, 2011). In this framework, the work of Porter and Kramer (2006, 2011) on strategic social responsibility is of key importance for the analysis of CSR practices. Their work brings out a new paradigm showing that when CSR is strategic, it becomes a tool for gaining sustainable competitive advantage (Kammoun et al., 2020a).

The adoption of social responsibility strategies leads us to assess their impacts in terms of firms' performance. When CSR becomes an important component of a firm's overall strategy, it can increase firm performance as well as generating positive social impact. In this line of thinking, companies that approach CSR strategically can leverage CSR to benefit both the firm and society (Vallaster et al., 2012). Predominantly, the commitment to a CSR strategy has an influence on firm performance that has long been reduced to its financial and economic dimensions. Within the current economic context, it makes more sense to move from a financial representation of performance to more global approaches by including the social and environmental dimensions. Therefore, performance is not long reduced to its financial dimension, but performance encompasses the economic, social and environmental dimensions. The aggregation of economic, social and environmental performance represents firm's overall performance (Renauld, 2003). In other words, overall performance encompasses the following dimensions: economic, environmental, social and stakeholders. Herein, overall performance would be the apparent face of the implementation of sustainable development strategies by companies (Capron & Quairel, 2005). Within this context, firm's responsibility is no longer limited only to direct shareholders, but incorporates other stakeholders (associations, NGOs, trade unions, customers, suppliers, etc.). Henceforth, to be socially responsible, companies need to be accountable to themselves and their shareholders.

The underlying purpose of the present paper is to study what effect CSR has on the firm's overall performance in large companies in a developing country context. The choice of large companies is justified by two reasons. Firstly, the majority of large firms are engaged in CSR and today, many of them voluntarily provide reports on their CSR practices, risks, and activities. Secondly, the implementation of CSR approach and its integration into all aspects of the businesses become mainly effective for large companies subject to intense competitive pressures and image risks. While most of the previous empirical researches focused on the relationship between CSR and financial performance, the present study suggests exploring the impact of CSR on overall performance.

This research adds to the empirical literature on the impact of corporate social behaviour on firm-level performance and provides practical insights into how firms might improve their overall performance by integrating CSR into all aspects of business and performing financial, environmental, social responsibilities and dialogue with stakeholders. Focusing on four dimensions of CSR, we contribute to understanding how the overall performance encompasses the following dimensions: economic, environmental, social and the consideration of stakeholders. To our knowledge, the present study is among the first attempts to investigate the impact of CSR commitment on firm's overall performance in a developing country such as Morocco.

The chapter is set out as follows. The second section provides an overview on the relationship between CSR and corporate performance in order to formulate the hypotheses underlying our research question. The third section outlines the dataset and the research methodology to examine the impact of CSR on firm's overall performance. The final section depicts the main results and sets out some managerial implications, conclusion and further directions for CSR research respectively.

Theoretical Background

What is CSR?

CSR is a broad and multidimensional concept (Karyawati et al., 2018; Kooskora et al., 2019; Kammoun et al., 2020b) that includes economic, environmental and social dimensions and has become increasingly important in recent years, giving rise to different theories that attempt to serve as a framework for analyzing CSR. Nevertheless, there is neither a global and standardized definition (Dahlsrud, 2008; van Marrewijk, 2013; Kammoun et al., 2020b; Hiswåls et al., 2020) nor a common way of quantifying CSR at the firm level (Crifo, and Forget, 2015; Newman et al., 2019). Dahlsrud (2008) identified at least 37 definitions of CSR. Contrary to the general accepted beliefs that the doctrine of CSR is a new paradigm or just a managerial fad, the concept of CSR is a fairly old concept that has found its roots in practices, known through philanthropy, of companies more than a century old, first in America and then in the rest of the world. Nevertheless, the development of the concept of CSR is not new and has its beginnings in the work of Bowen (1953), who is considered the "founding father" of the academic conception of CSR. Indeed, his book explains the religious roots of CSR and brings a great evolution of the concept both theoretically and conceptually.

Born in an industrialized world, CSR is the response to pressure from NGOs and associations to take social and ecological aspects into consideration in their activities. In other words, the importance of CSR lies in the respect of obligations towards individuals and the environment. Any firm that wants to be socially responsible, must act beyond the legal and regulatory aspects, i.e., invest in human capital, the environment, and consolidate relations with all stakeholders. As a response to the challenge of globalization, CSR helps the firm to balance economic, environmental and social requirements through the satisfaction of the needs of all stakeholders. Stakeholders' CSR awareness can gain more benefits from a firm's CSR initiatives and thereby improving firm performance (Rhou et al., 2016; Kammoun et al., 2020b). According to The World Business Council for Sustainable Development, CSR is the ongoing commitment of companies to act ethically and contribute to economic development while improving the quality of life of its employees and their families, the local community and society as a whole. Being a universal concept, CSR represents the voluntary decision of companies to contribute to a better society and a healthier environment. From this point of view, CSR seems to be crucial to sustainable economic development and the well-being of societies (Garde-Sanchez et al., 2018; Zelazna et al., 2020).

Through these definitions, it appears that CSR goes beyond legal obligations and is based on criteria of sustainable development, ethics and good governance, taking into account the social and environmental aspects, without forgetting the economic aspect, which is characterized by profitability and the production of wealth. At the organizational level, CSR can be a source of efficiency and sustainable financial performance. In other words, CSR presents a real growth factor for the firm since it is part of a long-term strategic vision. The integration of CSR in the firm's strategy does not aim to modify the firm's main role, which is to create wealth, but to take into account performance factors while respecting the social and environmental aspect. CSR strategy contributes to the improvement of the firm's reputation and brand image as well as the exclusion of managerial instability. Therefore, responsible management will help the firm gain competitive advantage and acquire a profitable position.

CSR in Moroccan Context

Even though CSR in Morocco is relatively recent compared to some developed countries, it's steadily taking its roots in the corporate environment. CSR enables Moroccan companies to take advantage of several opportunities and to rise to the occasion by integrating new management practices that increase their performance and the value created for them and their stakeholders. In this context, Moroccan companies have been implementing a major project for the past two decades in which social and economic innovation is in full development, as well as the introduction of new practices to create a new mode of management. With the adoption of the CGEM's social responsibility charter, business leaders have taken up the challenge of committing to this program and showing that CSR could be a practice that brings opportunities to improve the firm's relationship with its environment. As a result, in order to maintain their reputation, companies are required to demonstrate the legitimacy of their actions.

Within the framework of CSR, a program has been introduced and financed by several large, certified companies. This program aims to combat dropping out of school, to consolidate students' skills by providing them with continuing education, and to promote the development of students from disadvantaged backgrounds through the introduction of extracurricular activities. As part of their societal practices, these companies attach great importance to the partners with which they operate, emphasizing customer satisfaction, the health safety of their products, pollution control and environmental protection, as well as the establishment of social dialogue to ensure overall cohesion.

Similarly, the majority of the companies surveyed pay attention to the ethical dimension in terms of codes of conduct that encourage partners, especially employees, to comply with an ethics charter that aims to specify commitments in terms of equality, discrimination and common law. This approach enhances the value of any firm's human resources, builds shareholder loyalty, helps satisfy customer needs and, lastly, fulfills commitments to society as a whole. Several companies conduct their societal practices in collaboration with several NGOs, including the association, Injaz Al Maghrib, Al JISR, Insaf, l'Heure Joyeuse, SOS Village, Les Rangs d'Honneur, etc. This policy allows companies to benefit from various advantages including the CSR Label by the CGEM, the "Top-performer" Trophy by Vigeo, and the "Pioneers of CSR and the Green Economy in Africa" Prize at the 2nd Africa CSR Forum in Tunis in 2013.

Relationship Between CSR and Performance

Contrary to the short-term vision, which considers the firm as "*a thing, a property, a package of shares whose value must be maximized*" (Albert; 2003), we are now opting for a long-term vision that considers the firm as an institution that, in order to achieve its goals, must have not only a financial responsibility, but also social and environmental responsibilities. The firm aims to reconcile the expectations of all stakeholders, thus achieving collective success.

Nevertheless, the study of corporate performance has long been reduced to its financial dimension and a significant number of empirical studies have tried to investigate the relationship between CSR and financial performance (Orlitzky et al., 2003, Portney, 2008; Margolis et al. 2009; Galant and Cadez, 2017: Maqbool and Zameer, 2017; Kooskora et al., 2019; Cho et al., 2019; Kammoun et al., 2020b; Kammoun et al., 2020c). The relationship between CSR and performance is still subject to debate as both CSR and performance are multidimensional and there are several ways to measure the relationship between these two variables (Galant and Cadez, 2017; Kooskora et al., 2019; Kammoun et al., 2020a). That being said, it's noteworthy that financial performance consisted in measuring the profitability desired by shareholders only with quantified results. However, this approach often did not allow managers to make better decisions because they adopted a narrow vision of the situation. In a similar vein, Porter and Kramer (2006) stated that the solution for CSR lies in the principle of 'shared value'. Porter and Kramer (2011) propose an approach to value creation that alerts on the need to adopt a new management model that breaks with the model of maximising value for shareholders alone. Therefore, in order to better assess performance, it would be necessary to analyze performance in its entirety in order to understand it. This approach requires that the factors that contribute to measuring performance be identified beforehand.

This notion of overall performance designates a more accurate vision that goes beyond the economic competitiveness of companies, but this concept integrates the societal and environmental costs generated in terms of unemployment, de-skilling, stress-related pathologies, pollution, etc. The overall performance of companies is thus defined by Baret (2006) as "the aggregation of economic, social and environmental performance". Its measurement represents a renewal of evaluation systems. There has, in recent times, been an increasing interest in determining the impact of CSR commitment on firm's overall performance. Following on from the work of Caroll (1979) and Wartick and Cochran (1985), the broad conception of corporate performance emerged in the 1990s and formalizes the idea that the firm assumes a multidimensional responsibility encompassing social, ecological, political and economic aspects, and focuses in particular on the evaluation of human resources as a source of value creation and competitive advantage.

Within this context, the business world has seen a shift from a restrictive financial approach to a more global approach integrating the material and immaterial (social and environmental) aspects. Henceforth, corporate performance is no longer based solely on profit, but also on the achievement of social and environmental objectives and on taking into account the interests of all stakeholders. Thus, the global vision of performance was born thanks to the emergence of the notions of Sustainable Development and Corporate Social Responsibility.

In this study, the notion of overall performance is considered as a multidimensional notion that aims at creating homogeneity between the three financial, social and environmental performances, i.e., it allows the combination of economic growth, respect for the environment as well as the improvement of social cohesion. In addition, there is a relationship between CSR and the overall performance insofar as the latter's primary objective is to steer the firm towards performance that is more respectful of stakeholders and less focused on short-term profit-making. Similarly, overall business performance is considered to be a concept of crucial importance because it provides a basis for arbitrating the development of CSR policies implemented by the firm. In what follows, the empirical study attempts to investigate the relationship between overall performance and social responsibility variables. CSR can therefore have a direct or indirect, immediate or medium to long-term impact on a firm's overall performance. This analysis brings us to the following central research hypothesis: CSR has a positive effect on firm's overall performance.

EMPIRICAL ANALYSIS

Research Methodology

In order to verify the impact of CSR on overall performance, the survey was based on a sample of 44 companies that we selected using the non-probability sampling technique. This gives us a response rate of approximately 22% when compared to the entire target population (N=200). This result is a success given the conditions and constraints under which this survey was conducted. The variable coding and data entry phase was based on a methodical approach that respected the nature of the variables and the types of analysis we wished to apply for each variable. The dependent variable of this research, i.e. the firm's overall performance, is operationalized by three performance measures: the financial aspect, the environmental aspect, the social aspect and the consideration of stakeholders. The choice of the main explanatory variable is based on the research hypothesis stated earlier.

Table 1. Measurement structure of the variables

	Variable name	Number of items
Dependent variable	PERFORMANCE	6 items
Independent variables	Environmental aspect	3 items
	Social aspect	16 items
	Financial aspect	4 items
	Stakeholders	3 items

Source: Authors' calculations

3.2. Exploratory Factor Analysis

Exploratory factor analysis (EFA) aims to identify latent dimensions from observable individual variables (items), it also allows to explain a large part of the variance with a minimum of factors. To determine whether existing correlations are sufficient for factor analysis, the Bartlett sphericity test, the KMO (Kaiser Meyer Olkin) test, and Cronbach's alpha index will be used in this research. Once the analysis of the correlation matrix has been verified, the number of factors to be retained through PCA and MCA should be determined.

The results of the Factor Analysis are summarised in the table below:

Table 2. Thresholds and choices made in the exploratory factor analysis

Factor extraction mode	Axes of analysis	Thresholds and choices selected
Principal Component Analysis	KMO: Kaiser-Meyer-Olkin	³ 0,7
	Bartlett Sphericity Test	Close to 0 (less than 5%)
Multiple Correspondence Analysis	Reliability	Alpha of Cronbach > 0,7

Source: Authors' calculations

Table 3. Results of PCA analysis of items

Variables	Number of items	Factor analysis methods	Factors identified*	Quality of representativeness of items*
Overall Performance	6 items	ACP	Only one factor	KMO = 74,6% Bartlett Sign: 0,00
Environmental aspect	3 items	ACM	Only one factor	Alpha of cronbach 73,3%
Social aspect	16 items	ACP	Only one factor	KMO = 60,00% Bartlett Sign: 0,00
Financial aspect	4 items	ACM	Only one factor	Alpha of cronbach 81,1%
Stakeholders	4 items	ACM	Only one factor	Alpha of cronbach 85,8%

Source: Authors' calculations

Each factor gives a significant percentage of information that is considered to be satisfactory enough to draw reliable conclusions. The KMO index has a significance that exceeds 70% for the majority of the variables, so we can say that the index can be qualified as good or meritorious and tells us that the items are of good quality.

The Cronbach Alpha index is satisfactory since the significance exceeds 70%. We can say that we have a very good representativeness of the items by the factor that we found. For the qualitative variables, the Barlett's Sphericity Test aims to measure the sample adequacy. The index is significant since $P < 0.005$.

3.3. Multiple Regression Analysis

The regression analysis helps us to give an idea of the quality of representation of our model and to identify the variables that have a real influence on the overall performance of the firm. It also allows us to identify the degree of influence of each independent variable by assigning a coefficient for each variable.

The multiple linear regression model is one of the most commonly used statistical methods for studying multidimensional data. This model has long dominated research in economics and management. It consists in interpreting a dependent variable or more precisely in explaining the variance of a phenomenon (endogenous variable or explaining Y_i) according to a linear relationship as a function of two or more independent variables (exogenous or explanatory variables $X_{i1}, \ldots, X_{ip}$) and an error term (ε_i). It should be noted that the variable to be explained is always a continuous variable while the explanatory variables can be continuous or categorical (ordinal or dichotomous). This method makes it possible to estimate the extent to which exogenous variables allow the variable to be explained through their regression coefficients.

The relationship between the variable to be explained Y and the p explanatory variables (X_p) is expressed by the following equation:

$$Y_i = a_0 + a_1 X_{i1} + a_2 X_{i2} + a_3 X_{i3} + \ldots + ap X_{ip} + \varepsilon_i, i = 1, 2, 3, \ldots, n$$

The objective of a linear regression is to predict the regression coefficients (ai), which minimize the sum of the squares of the minimum errors or deviations, using the ordinary least squares (OLS) method, such as:

$$Min\ (\Sigma \hat{\varepsilon}\ i2ni{=}0) = min\ (\Sigma\ (Yi - (\hat{a}0 + \hat{a}1\ Xi1 + \hat{a}_2\ Xi_2 + \hat{a}3\ Xi3_{+\dots} + \hat{a}p\ Xip_{)2})$$

The coefficient a0 is called the regression constant. It represents the base value that the variable to be explained Yi would take if all the explanatory variables in the regression had a zero value. Generally, this coefficient is of little interest because of the rarity of such a situation. The ap coefficients can be interpreted as the variation in Yi if each explanatory variable was increased by one unit. Thus, we observe that each explanatory variable (Xp) is multiplied by its own coefficient beta (ß) which in its standardized form represents its relative contribution in the model. In addition, the error terms εi are random variables that cover phenomena (or variables) not clearly considered by the regression model. They can be related to measurement errors or to the unanticipated nature of human behaviour. The mean of each error term is equal to zero: E (εi) = 0.

The conceptual research model can be tested using the following regression equation:

$$Y\ \text{overall}\ Performance = a0 + \beta 1 environmental\ aspect + \beta 2 social\ aspect + \beta 3 financial aspect + \beta 4 Actors + \varepsilon i$$

After applying the multiple linear regression model on our data, the results were as follows:

Table 4. Multiple Regression Model Estimate

		Dependent variable
		Overall Performance
R		0,76
R^2		0,59
Standard error of the estimate		0,63
Constant		1,577
Environnemental aspect	*ß*	0,27*
	Sig	(0,000)
Social aspect	*ß*	0,16*
	Sig	(0,000)
Financial aspect	*ß*	0,59*
	Sig	(0,000)
Actors	*ß*	0,20*
	Sig	(0,000)

Source: Authors' calculations

The multiple correlation (R) is a standardized index that presents the degree of strength of the relationship between the dependent variable and the set of independent variables. It is an index that varies between -1 and 1; in this case, R = 0.76. Thus, the relationship between the dependent variable and the independent variables is very significant.

- The multiple correlation squared (R2) is an index that estimates the explanatory power of the explanatory variables in the model. This coefficient varies between 0 and 1, i.e. between a low and a high predictive power.

The closer R2 is to 1 means, the better the dependent variable (Y) is explained by the independent variables X1…. X_k. Consequently, the results show that the explanatory power of the variables is very strong.

- The regression model shows that we can identify four statistically significant influence relationships at one level (0.000) for the variables: (environmental aspect, social aspect, financial aspect and stakeholders).
- Standardized coefficients ß allow us to know the direction of the relationship between each predictor and the dependent variable (positive or negative relationship).
- The values of the ß coefficient are respectively (0.27; 0.16; 0.59 and 0.20), the result shows that these variables have a positive influence on overall performance.

Based on these results, we can write the estimated equation as follows:

Y Overall Performance = 1,57 + 0,59 financial performance +0,27 environmental performance + 0,16 social performance + 0,2 stakeholders+ 0,63

As mentioned earlier, the empirical study has been conducted in order to determine financial and non-financial factors that can boost or have negative effect on the firm's overall performance. Broadly, the results of the regression analysis reveal that financial performance, environmental performance, social performance and stakeholders have positive and significant impact on the firm's overall performance. This brings us to validate our research hypotheses and to confirm that the CSR approach could be an important determinant of overall Performance. We discuss, in what follows, how each CSR dimension can be an important determinant of overall performance.

Importantly, we find that items measuring financial performance have significant and positive impact on overall performance. The results reveal that financial performance contributes in a large part to the overall performance of large Moroccan companies. For Moroccan companies, the improvement of overall performance is mainly due to the increasing of financial performance (turnover, profitability, market share). This result brings us to conclude that the primary vocation of a firm remains the generation of long-term economic profitability.

Besides this, large Moroccan companies have to contribute to the achievement of other major objectives, such as employability and environmental protection. Especially since several factors converge to favour the emergence of CSR practices in Morocco, including: the evolution of the labour code, commitments in favour of environmental protection, respect for human rights associated with a societal commitment to fight against poverty, the development of socially responsible investment, etc. From a CSR perspective, the survival of companies no longer depends on the only financial dimension of the performance, but also how they behave.

With regards to the environmental aspect, the companies interviewed confirm that they use innovative technologies that are less polluting and save water, energy and non-renewable resources, and ensure that greenhouse gas emissions are constantly kept below the limit values imposed by law. Other companies interviewed have set up wind farms with the same objectives. The regression analysis reveals that environmental performance, which means preserving the environment by recycling polluting waste or waste water and making an effort in terms of employment, has a positive and significant impact on the firm's overall performance. To put it another way, overall performance depends on the importance given by Moroccan companies to improving environmental management and the evolution of environmental performance by adopting approaches such as ISO 14001 or equivalent. Indeed, environmental performance enhances the value of companies with production methods that respect the environment and make it possible to achieve long-term savings in terms of water, energy and raw material consumption. This result is consistent with the findings of previous empirical studies. Environmental performance can yield many benefits for companies, including costs and resources savings, sales growth (Amato and Amato, 2012), increased satisfaction and loyalty of customers and morale of employees (Tran et al., 2020; Zelazna et al., 2020). The attitude of CSR firms towards environmental risks can affect their social reputation and improve their image (Stanwick and Stanwick, 1998; Banerjee and Shogren, 2010; Fukuda and Ouchida, 2020). CSR proves to be a driver for improving image and reputation, creating a persistent and stable competitive advantage and thus achieving firm's overall performance.

The third outcome of the regression analysis is the positive and significant impact of social performance on the overall performance of Moroccan companies. This implies that improving social performance is an important means of achieving overall performance. In other words, improving the overall performance of the firm is closely linked to improvements in the conditions of employment of human resources. Henceforth, the firm must meet the expectations of workers, by paying satisfactory wages and creating a safer work environment in order to improve its performance. This result is in line with previous studies (Greening and Turban, 2000; Hopkins, 2003; Bode et al., 2015; Mory et al., 2016; De Roeck et al., 2016 ; El Akremi et al., 2018; Vishwanathan et al., 2019). These studies acknowledge that CSR can affect a firm's ability to retain, develop and motivate employees (Hopkins, 2003; Bode et al., 2015; Mory et al., 2016; De Roeck et al., 2016) and could be particularly helpful in recruiting high quality employees who have a high degree of employment choice (Greening and Turban, 2000). If many business organizations see employees' wellbeing as their first priority (Chaudhary, 2017), it's because employees as internal stakeholders have a direct impact on business performance and profitability (Chaudhary, 2017; Omer, 2018; et al., 2020). In sum, employees of CSR companies benefit from social practices such as fair pay, favourable working climate, and professional opportunities (El Akremi et al., 2018) and, in turn, CSR companies profit from such motivated employees (Vishwanathan et al., 2019).

A further aspect to be underlined concerns the identification of stakeholders and their relationship with the firm. Companies must be aware of their impact on society and the environment and have to work with stakeholders to understand their views and concerns on various environmental, social and economic issues. Interestingly, we find that items measuring the variable stakeholders (employees, investors, owners and banks; public authorities, local and regional authorities; the media, competitors; NGOs, local communities; suppliers and customers) have significant and positive impact on overall performance. Another key factor in achieving the overall performance seems to be the stakeholders' satisfaction. These new actors require to be heard and dialogue becomes a vital goal for the firm's overall performance and sustainability. To improve overall performance, Moroccan companies must implement stakeholder based-CSR. The Commitment to CSR strengthens the linkages that companies have with their stakeholders and this improvement, in turn, impacts positively on overall performance. This result is consistent with the findings of Greening and Turban (2000) and Vishwanathan et al. (2019). According to them, CSR companies have access to a larger pool of stakeholders with whom they can develop productive relationships and this may enhance firm performance.

On the basis of the foregoing developments, it appears that performance cannot be reduced to its financial dimension but it extends to a more global approach including social and environmental dimensions as well as stakeholders. Hence, Moroccan companies should introduce new dimensions that are essential for their viability and performance such as environmental and social aspects and also the role of stakeholders. Certainly, financial performance is of vital importance for investors and stakeholders. In fact, a well performing business can bring high and long-term returns for their investors, and enhance the income of employees, generate more investments and employment opportunities, bring better quality products for customers, and have better environment friendly production (Sultan, 2014). In addition to the financial aspect, the empirical results confirm that the implementation of socially responsible practices contributes positively and significantly to increase the overall performance of Moroccan companies. Evidently, the performance of each dimension such as economic, environmental, and social and stakeholders plays a great role in this process.

4. CONCLUSION

The purpose of this study was to study the impact that the choice to comply with the principles of Social Responsibility can have on firm's overall performance. This paper provides some contributions to the literature on the relationship between CSR and firm performance. Although extant research has examined the effect of CSR commitment on financial performance, in an attempt to justify its impact on obtaining profits, albeit with divergent and inconclusive results, the effect of CSR on overall performance remains largely unexplored. Also, we add to the literature by proposing and empirically testing the impact of each dimension on the overall performance on a sample of 44 companies by opting for multiple linear regression analysis.

Within this framework, we aimed to achieve three main objectives. The first objective is to analyze and measure the social and environmental involvement of large Moroccan firms operating in the main sectors of activity and located in different geographical areas, while taking into account that the financial aspect probably has a direct link with the overall performance. This involvement is studied by taking into account the specific characteristics of the companies (size, region, sector, nature of activity). The second objective is to make overall performance a constant variable, i.e., the variable that explains the research model. The third objective is to verify the existence of a relationship between CSR and firm's overall performance, i.e., the positive or negative effects of CSR dimensions on the overall performance of Moroccan companies.

On the basis of the foregoing results, it is deduced that firms' overall performance can be directly influenced by their CSR practices. That is, the majority of firms surveyed perceive CSR as an asset, while a small number of firms see it as a constraint. In other words, the hypotheses of financial (already theoretically proven), social and environmental impact are strongly supported for all the companies in the sample.

The empirical findings have important practical implications. The ðndings suggest that ðrms pursuing an improved overall performance could do so by undertaking socially responsible actions and by incorporating them in the overall strategy of the firm. Because the ðndings suggest that the positive iñuence of CSR on firm performance is due principally to the financial performance, we suggest that practitioners in large Moroccan companies need to continuously improve environmental performance, social performance and the dialogue with internal and external stakeholders. In other words, practitioners have to make well-targeted investments in CSR activities to achieve better performance. The adoption of a CSR approach could be a method for developing the overall performance of the large Moroccan companies. Moreover, CSR would be an excellent instrument to contribute to the reduction of social and environmental problems and the generation of sustainable development. In brief, large Moroccan companies can only ensure their sustainability and evolution if they operate in a favourable environment.

Despite our important ðndings, the study is not without limitations. In fact, the study put focus on large Moroccan companies and we must be cautious when applying these results to SMEs and to other contexts. Further investigations on small and medium Moroccan companies are needed to provide insights on how the relationship between the firm and its internal and external stakeholders will serve to develop a global vision of the firm's CSR strategy and open up a relevant line of research, especially since CSR is still evolving in developing countries. Moreover, CSR is considered as a cause of growth and, from a managerial standpoint, it should be studied in the future as an instrument of progress that affects the entire value chain of the firm (R&D, production, marketing, commercialisation, etc.). This enhances greatly the need for well-designed CSR strategies to ensure sustainable integration of Moroccan companies into global supply chains.

REFERENCES

Agbodan, M. M., & Amoussouga, F. G. (1995). *Les facteurs de performance de l'entreprise*. John Libbey Eurotext.

Albert, M. (2003). Une nouvelle économie sociale de marche? Quels modèles d'entreprise pour un développement durable? *Futuribles (Paris, France)*, (287), 5–21.

Amato, L. H., & Amato, C. H. (2012). Environmental policy, rankings and stock values. *Business Strategy and the Environment*, *21*(5), 317–325. doi:10.1002/bse.742

Banerjee, P., & Shogren, J. F. (2010). Regulation, reputation, and environmental risk. *Economics Letters*, *106*(1), 45–47. doi:10.1016/j.econlet.2009.09.021

Baret, P. (2006). L'évaluation contingente de la Performance Globale des Entreprises: une méthode pour fonder un management socialement responsable? In Responsabilité sociale de l'entreprise, (pp. 135-152). De Boeck Supérieur.

Ben Yedder, M. & Zaddem, F. (2009). La Responsabilité Sociale de l'Entreprise (RSE), voie de conciliation ou terrain d'affrontements? *Revue multidisciplinaire sur l'emploi, le syndicalisme et le travail*, *4*(1), 84-103.

Bode, C., Singh, J., & Rogan, M. (2015). Corporate social initiatives and employee retention. *Organization Science*, *26*(6), 1702–1720. doi:10.1287/orsc.2015.1006

Bourguignon, A. (1995). La performance, essais de definition. *Revue Française de Comptabilité*, 269.

Bowen, H. R. (1953). *Social responsibility of the businessman*. Harpers and Brothers.

Capron, M., & Quairel-Lanoizelée, F. (2004). *Mythes et réalités de l'entreprise responsable*. La Découverte.

Carroll, A. B. (1979). A three-dimensional conceptual model of corporate performance. *Academy of Management Review, 4*(4), 497–505. doi:10.5465/amr.1979.4498296

Chaudhary, R. (2017). Corporate social responsibility and employee engagement: Can CSR help in redressing the engagement gap? *Social Responsibility Journal, 13*(2), 323–338. doi:10.1108/SRJ-07-2016-0115

Cho, S. J., Chung, C. Y., & Young, J. (2019). Study on the relationship between CSR and financial performance. *Sustainability, 11*(2), 343. doi:10.3390u11020343

Crifo, P., & Forget, V. D. (2015). The economics of corporate social responsibility: A firm-level perspective survey. *Journal of Economic Surveys, 29*(1), 112–130. doi:10.1111/joes.12055

Dahlsrud, A. (2008). How Corporate Social Responsibility Is Defined: An Analysis of 37 Definitions. *Corporate Social Responsibility and Environmental Management, 15*(1), 1–13. doi:10.1002/csr.132

De Roeck, K., El Akremi, A., & Swaen, V. (2016). Consistency matters! How and when does corporate social responsibility affect employees' organizational identification? *Journal of Management Studies, 53*(7), 1141–1168. doi:10.1111/joms.12216

Dohou, A., & Berland, N. (2007). *Mesure de la performance globale des entreprises. 28 ème*. Congrès de l'Association Francophone de Comptabilité.

El Akremi, A., Gond, J. P., Swaen, V., De Roeck, K., & Igalens, J. (2018). How do employees perceive corporate responsibility? Development and validation of a multidimensional corporate stakeholder responsibility scale. *Journal of Management, 44*(2), 619–657. doi:10.1177/0149206315569311

European Commission. (2011). *Communication from the Commission to the European Parliament, the Council, the European Economic and Social Committee and the Committee of the Regions: a renewed EU strategy 2011–14 for corporate social responsibility.* Available from: https://publications.europa.eu/en/publication-detail/-/publication/ae5ada03-0dc3-48f8-9a32-0460e65ba7ed/language-en

Falkenberg, J., & Brunsæl, P. (2011). Corporate Social Responsibility: A Strategic Advantage or a Strategic Necessity? *Journal of Business Ethics, Springer, 99*(1), 9–16. doi:10.100710551-011-1161-x

Freeman, R. E. (1984). *Strategic Management: A stakeholder approach*. Pitman.

Friedman, M. (1993). *The Social Responsibility of Business is to Increase it Profits*. Chapman & Hall.

Fukuda, K., & Ouchida, Y. (2020). Corporate social responsibility (CSR) and the environment: Does CSR increase emissions? *Energy Economics, 104933*. Advance online publication. doi:10.1016/j.eneco.2020.104933

Galant, A., & Cadez, S. (2017). Corporate social responsibility and financial performance relationship: A review of measurement approaches. *Economic Research-Ekonomska Istraživanja, 30*(1), 676–693. doi:10.1080/1331677X.2017.1313122

Garde-Sanchez, R., López-Pérez, M. V., & López-Hernández, A. (2018). Current Trends in Research on Social Responsibility in State-Owned Enterprises: A Review of the Literature from 2000 to 2017. *Sustainability, 10*(7), 2403. doi:10.3390u10072403

Germain, C., & Trebucq, S. (2004). La performance globale de l'entreprise et son pilotage: quelques réflexions. *Semaine sociale Lamy, 1186*, 35-41.

Greening, D. W., & Turban, D. B. (2000, September). Corporate Social Performance as a Competitive Advantage in Attracting a Quality Workforce. *Business & Society*, *39*(3), 254–280. doi:10.1177/000765030003900302

Henri, J., & Giasson, A. (2006). Measuring environmental performance: A basic ingredient of environmental management. *CMA Management*, *80*(5), 28.

Hiswåls, A.S., Hamrin, C.W., Vidman, A., & Macassa, V. (2020). Corporate social responsibility and external stakeholders' health and wellbeing: A viewpoint. *Journal of Public Health Research*, *9*(1), 1742. doi:10.4081/jphr.2020.1742

Hopkins, M. (2003). The business case for CSR: Where are we? *International Journal of Business Performance Management*, *5*(2-3), 125–140. doi:10.1504/IJBPM.2003.003261

Kammoun, S., Lebas, C., & Mercuri-Chapuis, S. (2020a). Types de RSE, types d'innovation: un bilan de travaux empiriques. In La responsabilité sociale des entreprises. Des relations sociales à la dimension stratégique, (pp. 113-128). Editions EMS. Management et Société. Collection Questions de société.

Kammoun, S., Loukil, S., & Ben Romdhane Loukil, Y. (2020b). The impact of Firm Performance and Corporate Governance on Corporate Social Responsibility: Evidence from France. In I. S. Paiva & L. C. Carvalho (Eds.), *Conceptual and Theoretical Approaches to Corporate Social Responsibility, Entrepreneurial Orientation, and Financial Performance* (pp. 266–288). IGI Global., doi:10.4018/978-1-7998-2128-1.ch014

Kammoun, S., Loukil, S., Ben Romdhane, Y., & Ibenrissoul, A. (2020c). The relationship between CSR, Corporate Governance and Firm Performance: Evidence from Moroccan listed firms. In I. S. Paiva & L. C. Carvalho (Eds.), *Conceptual and Theoretical Approaches to Corporate Social Responsibility, Entrepreneurial Orientation, and Financial Performance* (pp. 289–304). IGI Global., doi:10.4018/978-1-7998-2128-1.ch015

Karyawati, P. G., Subroto, B., Sutrisno, T., & Saraswati, E. (2018). The Complexity of Relationship between Corporate Social Responsibility (CSR) and Financial Performance. *Emerging Markets Journal*, *8*(2), 2018. doi:10.5195/emaj.2018.155

Kooskora, M., Juottonen, M. & Cundiff, K. (2019). The Relationship Between Corporate Social Responsibility and Financial Performance (A Case Study from Finland). *Social Responsibility and Sustainability*, 471–491. doi:10.1007/978-3-030-03562-4_25

Lebas, M. (1995). Oui, il faut définir la performance. *Revue française de comptabilité, 269*, 66-71.

Lepetit, M. (1997). *Performance globale: vers une prise en compte des effets non marchands. Commissariat Général du Plan, ouvrage collectif. In Entreprise et performance globale-outils, évaluation, pilotage*. Economica.

Maqbool, S., & Zameer, M. N. (2017). An Empirical Examination of the Relationship between Corporate Social Responsibility and Profitability: Evidence from Indian Commercial Banks. *Pacific Business Review International*, *9*(12), 39–47.

Margolis, J. D., Elfenbein, H. A., & Walsh, J. P. (2009). *Does It Pay to Be Good and Does It Matter? A Meta-Analysis of the Relationship between Corporate Social and Financial Performance.* Working paper.

Marion, A., Asquin, A., & Everaere, C. (2012). *Diagnostic de la performance de l'entreprise: Concepts et méthodes*. Dunod. doi:10.3917/dunod.mario.2012.01

Mercier, S. (2001). *L'apport de la théorie des parties prenantes au management stratégique: une synthèse de la littérature*. Xième Conférence de l'Association Internationale de Management Stratégique.

Mory, L., Wirtz, B. W., & Göttel, V. (2016). Factors of internal corporate social responsibility and the effect on organizational commitment. *International Journal of Human Resource Management*, *27*(13), 1393–1425. doi:10.1080/09585192.2015.1072103

Newman, C., Rand, J., Tarp, F. & Trifkovic, N. (2019). Corporate Social Responsibility in a Competitive Business Environment. *The Journal of Development Studies*, *56*(8), 1455-1472. doi:10.1080/00220388.2019.1694144

Omer, S.K. (2018). The impact of corporate social responsibility on employee's job satisfaction. Journal of Process Management. *New Technologies*, *6*(3), 56-64.

Orlitzky, M., Frank, L., Schmidt, F. L., Sara, L., & Rynes, S. L. (2003). Corporate social and financial performance: A meta-analysis. *Organization Studies*, *24*(3), 403–441.

Pasquero, J. (1997). Business ethics and national identity in Quebec: Distinctiveness and directions. *Journal of Business Ethics*, *16*(6), 621–633.

Pasquero, J. (2004). Responsabilités sociales de l'entreprise: Les approches nord-américaines. In *Jacques Igalens (dir.), Tous responsables*. Éditions d'Organisation.

Pasquero, J. (2005). La responsabilité sociale de l'entreprise comme objet des sciences de gestion: un regard historique. In Responsabilité sociale et environnementale de l'entreprise, (pp. 80-111). Presses de l'Université du Québec.

Porter, M. E. (1985). *Competitive Advantage*. Free Press.

Porter, M.E. & Kramer, M.R. (2006). Strategy and Society: The Link Between Competitive Advantage and Corporate Social Responsibility. *Harvard Business Review*, *84*(12), 78-92.

Porter, M. E., & Kramer, M. R. (2011). Creating shared value: How to reinvent capitalism – and unleash a wave of innovation and growth. *Harvard Business Review*, *89*(1-2), 62–77.

Portney, P. R. (2008). The (Not So) New Corporate Social Responsibility: An Empirical Perspective. *Review of Environmental Economics and Policy*, *2*(2), 261–275.

Reed, D. (1999). Stakeholder management theory: A critical theory perspective. *Business Ethics Quarterly*, *9*(03), 453–483.

Reynaud, E. (2003). Développement durable et entreprise: Vers une relation symbiotique. *Journée AIMS, Atelier développement durable. ESSCA Angers*, *15*, 1–15.

Rhou, Y., Singal, M., & Koh, Y. (2016). CSR and Financial Performance: The Role of CSR Awareness in the Restaurant Industry. *International Journal of Hospitality Management*, *57*(1), 30–39.

Stanwick, P. A., & Stanwick, S. D. (1998). The relationship between corporate social performance, and organizational size, financial performance, and environmental performance: An empirical examination. *Journal of Business Ethics*, *17*(2), 195–204.

Sultan, A. S. (2014). Financial Statements Analysis - Measurement of Performance and Profitability: Applied Study of Baghdad Soft-Drink Industry. *Research Journal of Finance and Accounting*, *5*(4), 49–56.

Torugsa, N. A., O'Donohue, W., & Hecker, R. (2013). Proactive CSR: An empirical analysis of the role of its economic, social and environmental dimensions on the association between capabilities and performance. *Journal of Business Ethics*, *115*(2), 383–402. doi:10.100710551-012-1405-4

Tran, K. T., & Nguyen, P. V. (2020). Corporate Social Responsibility: Findings from the Vietnamese Paint Industry. *Sustainability*, *12*(3), 1044. https://doi.org/10.3390/su12031044

Van Marrewijk, M. (2013). Concepts and definitions of CSR and corporate sustainability: between agency and communion. *Journal of Business Ethics*, 641–655.

Vishwanathan, P., van Oosterhout, H. J., Heugens, P. P. M. A. R., Duran, P., & Van Essen, M. (2019). Strategic CSR: A concept building meta-analysis. *Journal of Management Studies*. Advance online publication. doi:10.1111/joms.12514

Wartick, S. L., & Cochran, P. L. (1985). The evolution of the corporate social performance model. *Academy of Management Review*, *10*(4), 758–769.

Zelazna, A., Bojar, M., & Bojar, E. (2020). Corporate Social Responsibility towards the Environment in Lublin Region, Poland: A Comparative Study of 2009 and 2019. *Sustainability*, *12*, 4463. doi:10.3390u12114463

KEY TERMS AND DEFINITIONS

Corporate Social Responsibility (CSR): CSR covers all the practices implemented by companies in order to respect the principles of sustainable development (social, environmental, and economic) and to establish dialogue with all stakeholders.

Environmental Performance: It means preserving the environment by recycling polluting waste or wastewater and making an effort in terms of employment.

Financial Performance: A firm's ability to make profits, to be profitable by creating added value and achieving the objectives set. It can be measured through different indicators such as ROA (Return on Assets) and ROE (Return on Equity).

Social Performance: A practice used to assess the well-being of employees in the firm and to find factors for improvement compatible with the performance to be achieved by the firm. The assessment of the performance of employees is part of a sustainable development approach.

Sustainable Development: A mode of development that meets the needs of present generations without compromising the ability of future generations to meet their own needs. This implies taking into account imperatives such as the preservation of the environment and natural resources or social and economic equity.

Chapter 13
The Integration of CSR Practices in the Investment Decision:
Evidence From Moroccan Companies in the Mining Industry

Abdelmajid Ibenrissoul
ENCG, ISO, Hassan II University of Casablanca, Morocco

Souhaila Kammoun
IHEC, CODECI, University of Sfax, Tunisia

Abdelaziz Tazi
ENCG, ISO, Hassan II University of Casablanca, Morocco

ABSTRACT

The purpose of the chapter is to understand the practices of decision makers in relation to financial, societal, and environmental concerns and apprehend the appropriateness of integrating CSR practices in the investment decision. The chapter purports to highlight the link between a business strategy based on development investments and the normative or moral obligations of its stakeholders as well as progress in terms of the impact of the proactive integration of societal concerns alongside concerns about value creation for stakeholders. The exploratory study examines the operationalization of CSR practices in the Moroccan mining industry with a focus on the integration of the criteria of four dimensions related to local development, reputation and environmental improvement, water conservation, as well as governance and ethics and their impact on value creation. The chapter sets out some practical implications and further research directions.

DOI: 10.4018/978-1-7998-6788-3.ch013

INTRODUCTION

In a rapidly-changing business world, industries as well as companies are facing new environmental, social and economic challenges that in large part determine their ability to operate and manage rapid change in a time of uncertainty, to protect their market share, maintain their level of performance, and to deliver sustainable, profitable growth without degrading environment. With these new challenges facing today's companies come economic, social and environmental responsibilities. Moreover, tensions between financial objectives on the one hand, and those relating to the principles of Corporate Social Responsibility (CSR) on the other, have become real issues to be addressed at the highest level of organizations.

Within this context, companies are called to assess their operating methods, rethink their role and design innovative strategies by integrating, in addition to traditional financial considerations, other social, environmental and ethical considerations. Several companies, from all sectors, sizes and countries have understood that they can no longer simply aim for purely financial performance; rather they seek multidimensional performance, integrating social, societal and environmental aspects such as working conditions, human rights, ecological footprint, governance methods, etc. Profit is no longer the main objective, but a means to serve other purposes related to the common good and related to other spheres of responsible management, namely social, environmental, governance and ethics.

The chapter put focus on the link between a company strategy based on development investments and the normative or moral obligations of its stakeholders and attempts to identify practices related to the proactive integration of CSR principles in investment decisions. From a methodological standpoint, we choose the interpretivist approach. As an epistemological position, interpretativism considers that social reality is primarily the result of actions, meanings, symbolic products and social practices (Geertz, 1973). More precisely, we have opted for a triangulation method by combining two methods that allow us to draw valid conclusions, following five steps: the census of decision-makers' impressions of the expansion of their investment procedures, the formulation of research proposals, the main exploratory study, triangulation based on a longitudinal analysis and then the design of an interpretative model.

The underlying objectives of the chapter are to understand the practices of decision-makers in relation to financial, societal and environmental concerns and apprehend the appropriateness of integrating CSR practices in the investment decision. Indeed, the interest for the scientific community is to present a meaning to the practices related to the integration of the CSR principles in the investment decision and for practitioners to contribute to the formalization of the criteria related to the integration of CSR principles in the investment decision, in line with the evolution of national and international standards and regulations. Several studies have pointed out that the mining industry is paying increasing attention to the environmental and social impacts of its activities, particularly with the adoption of the concept of sustainable development (Whitmore, 2006). However, mining companies' efforts to ensure that their activities are environmentally and socially responsible are often below the aspirations of the population (Prno, 2013). The operationalization of the theoretical framework aims to understand the practices related to the integration of CSR principles in investment decision-making. Four dimensions are considered in this study: "People" by contributing to local development, "Profit" by improving reputation and "Planet" by improving the environment and preserving water and the dimension related to "Governance & Ethics".

The chapter is organized as follows. Following the introductory section, we provide an overview of the debate on the achievement of sustainable development goals and commitment to CSR in the Moroccan mining industry and bring to the fore the importance of the integration of CSR principles in the investment decisions. After that, we present the data and methodology of the research. The chapter sets out the main empirical findings with the ideas advanced in the theoretical literature review. And lastly, the chapter summarizes the main conclusions drawn from the exploratory study and puts into perspective further research directions.

THEORETICAL FRAMEWORK

In this overview, we provide a brief summary of the background literature relevant to our research in order to underline the urgency for achieving sustainable development goals and to advance CSR from the Moroccan institutional framework and the imperatives of the new mining industry strategy. We begin by first setting out the relevance of the integration of CSR practices in the Moroccan mining industry. We then present the link between a business strategy based on development investments and the normative or moral obligations of its stakeholders as well as progress in terms of the impact of the proactive integration of societal concerns alongside concerns about value creation for stakeholders.

Sustainable Development in the Corporate Moroccan Mining Context

As in the global economy, the Moroccan mining industry plays a great economic role. In fact, Morocco's mining industry contributes about 10 per cent of the country's GDP (with 90% coming from phosphates), represents 30 per cent of its exports, accounts for majority of sea and rail freight and employs over 40,000 people (Ministry of mining). Nevertheless, mining activities, in general, have an impact on the environment in the broadest sense of the term. In fact, most extractive industry sites in Morocco are located in very poor villages where inhabitants are directly exposed to environmental and health risks related to the mining activity. As in other countries, the Moroccan mining industry is also characterized by the cascade effect on other sectors. In brief, mining companies are contributing to the deterioration of the environment by emitting many dangerous pollutants in large quantities and by over-using available natural resources. There is an urgent need to establish effective regulatory framework reducing potential environmentally adverse impact of mining (mining laws, environmental regulations, CSR, etc.). This all hinges on the achievement of all sustainable development goals.

Accordingly, a key challenge for the sector is to demonstrate that it contributes to the welfare and wellbeing of the current generation without compromising the quality of life of future generations (WCED, 1987; Azapagic, 2004). Henceforth, the main challenge is to manage mining in a way that contributes to sustainable development (Whitmore, 2006; Zelazna et al., 2020). The concept of sustainable development is commonly divided into three "pillars" or "dimensions": economic, environmental and social and all three pillars have to be considered in order to achieve sustainable development (Hojem, 2014). These issues are increasingly mentioned in sustainability reports published by mining companies (Hilson, 2000; Horowitz, 2006; Worrall et al., 2009).

In recent years, many countries have adopted laws and regulations that require mining companies to consult with local communities that will be affected by mining operations. Aware of the costs generated in the long term (health, mine rehabilitation, etc.), the mining industry has begun to take an interest in assessing the environmental and social impacts of its activities, in particular by adopting the principles of sustainable development (Whitmore, 2006). Notwithstanding, the several efforts made by mining industries to implement environmentally and socially responsible activities (Bhattacharya, 2000; Hilson, 2001) often fall short of public expectations (Himley, 2010; Holden, 2011; Prno, 2013). In the Moroccan's case, new laws for the mining sector recognize the importance of site restoration and include strict regulations on water, air and soil quality. Furthermore, in order to reduce the harmful impact of the mining industry on the environment and face the growing social challenges across the mining sites, the mining industry is called to undertake diverse actions and to integrate ethical values and sustainable development principles in the organization to support good governance and to make more commitment to the economic, social and environmental issues. Like many other industries, the mining industry is increasingly becoming aware of these environmental and social impacts. It's worth stating that respect for the environment and society are the fundamental cornerstones of CSR. In what follows, we will explain what CSR is, and why organisations have to adopt a CSR strategy and integrate Socially Responsible Investment (SRI) into their decision-making.

Advancing CSR and SRI in the Moroccan Mining Industry

CSR is a broad and complex concept that has come to the forefront in recent years, in both developed and developing countries and even though the concept has come a long way, it still continues to gain the attention of researchers and practitioners alike (George et al., 2020; Kammoun et al., 2020b; Venkatesh et al., 2020). Even though CSR is a recurring theme in both economic and research contexts, there is no agreed or universal definition of CSR (Dahlsrud, 2008; Newman et al., 2019; Kammoun et al., 2020c; Rodriguez-Gomez et al., 2020) nor a common agreement on the hierarchy of its component aspects and the way of measuring or quantifying CSR at the firm level (Crifo and Forget, 2015; Newman et al., 2019; Rodriguez-Gomez et al., 2020). This may be due to the fact that CSR is multidimensional and has evolved considerably over time, and there is no consensus on the aspects that make it up (Kooskora et al., 2019; Kammoun et al., 2020a; Rodriguez-Gomez et al., 2020). All this raises the question as to what can be considered to be CSR.

A thorough review of the extant literature reveals that there are about 37 definitions of CSR (Dahlsrud, 2008). Through these definitions, the main areas recurring in most definitions of CSR are economic, social, and environmental (Marí-Farinós 2017; Chowdhury et al., 2019). To engage in CSR, the company must implement actions that promote sustainable development, environmental protection and social progress. The ISO 26000 standard defines CSR as "*an organization's responsibility for the impacts of its decisions and activities on society and the environment, through transparent and ethical behaviour that contributes to Sustainable Development, including health and the welfare of society; takes into account the expectations of stakeholders; is in compliance with applicable law and consistent with international norms of behavior; and is integrated throughout the organization and implemented in its relations*" (NF ISO 26 000, 2010). The ISO 26000 definition of CSR, which is based on stakeholder theory, is aligned with the CSR as defined in 2001 by the European Union and that's why in many organizations it is considered a fundamental part of their CSR strategy. A CSR strategy can be defined as "*a set of measures that complement the company's core business activities and contribute to the overall mission of the company*" (Burke & Logsdon, 1996). Furthermore, the United Nations Principles for Responsible Investment (PRI, 2006) propose integrating ESG issues in the decision making and investment analysis processes. The Socially Responsible Investment (SRI) can be defined as a form of investment integrating respect for ethical values, the protection of the environment, and the improvement of social conditions or "good" governance (Revelli and Viviani, 2015).

Henceforth, the integration of SRI in the decision-making and the adoption of a CSR strategy will impact the way many companies, including the largest groups, are now managed and operate, and how they communicate with their stakeholders. The formulation of a CSR strategy requires that social, societal and environmental aspects be placed at the heart of the company's concerns. A CSR strategy that complements the company's strategy should enable the company to appropriate some of the positive externalities created while contributing to the common good; select CSR actions that are important to the company's main stakeholders; and clearly communicate the measures taken to stakeholders through "*storytelling*" actions. Herein, the CSR strategy associated with care of the environment, social issue, and ethical conduct of enterprises, appears as a mean of operationalization of sustainable development at the lowest level (Zelazna et al., 2020). To engage in CSR, the company must implement actions that promote sustainable development, environmental protection and social progress. In this line of thinking, Wheeler et al. (2003) have tried to reconcile the concepts of corporate social responsibility and sustainable development (or sustainability) with a stakeholder approach. Their model of sustainable development encompasses the concepts of CSR, corporate citizenship and stakeholder theory.

Throughout the last years, a growing number of Moroccan mining companies are committed to a process of CSR. Admittedly, CSR refers to the responsibility of the company towards its stakeholders, including employees, customers, the natural environment and the community. However, the commitment to CSR in the mining industry goes beyond making profit and obeying the law to increasing the social and environmental sustainability of the community in which they operate. Also, CSR commitment implies permanent collaboration and dialogue with the various stakeholders concerned with the problematic of local development. Through CSR, mining companies can frame their attitudes and strategies towards stakeholders, be they investors, employees or communities (Jenkins, 2004). In addition to the evolution of the mining sector, there is also pressure from external stakeholders, including customers and suppliers, NGOs and any other parties interacting with mining companies (local residents, local authorities). In recent years, the mining industry has demonstrated a willingness to commit itself to a policy of social responsibility through numerous actions that converge towards Socially Responsible Investments. This commitment stems mainly from the normative or moral obligations of the stakeholders. Nevertheless, this situation poses a problem for these companies, which are accustomed to making their investment decisions on the basis of procedures based on financial criteria.

Impact of CSR on Value Creation

Porter and Kramer (2006) have argued that the solution to CSR lies in the principle of "shared value". According to Porter and Kramer (2011), there are three levers that contribute to the creation of shared value and are mutually reinforcing: (1) a new design of products and markets can foster innovation and the development of products with "social and environmental benefits"; (2) by rethinking their value chain, companies can reduce their energy use and improve the allocation of their resources; (3) the integration into a local cluster can foster synergies between companies, but also bring together public and private players, universities and research centres, administrations and local populations with companies established in the area. For Porter and Kramer (2011), the opportunity to create "shared value" must guide the company's CSR commitment.

The empirical literature review on the topic reveals that CSR initiatives contribute to creating value for firms such as differentiation assets (Flammer, 2015; Fosfuri et al., 2015), customer loyalty (Du et al., 2001), attracting and retaining key employees (Flammer and Luo, 2016; Bode et al., 2016) or gaining better access to capital (Cheng et al., 2014). Investments aim to increase profitability, as stakeholders - such as customers and employees - often value commitment to social causes such as environmental conservation or the defence of human rights (Fosfuri et al., 2015; Bode et al., 2016; Flammer and Kacpercyzk, 2016).

Furthermore, it's worthy of note that the ethical and responsible attitude advocated by CSR, which is increasingly favoured by investors and managers, is likely to win companies points by improving their image and reputation (Abbott and Morsen, 1979; Fombrun and Shanley, 1990) or by improving managerial skills and knowledge of the business environment and its stakeholders (Barney 1991; Russo and Fouts 1997; Wernerfelt 1984). In the same vein, Fosfuri and Asmussen (2016) developed a model that considers the impact of investment decisions on social brand value. In brief, companies that "*build a moral reputation through CSR will reap rewards in the form of favourable environmental conditions and relationships with key stakeholders, which will lead to long-term competitive advantage*" (Kaul and Luo, 2016). In the similar vein, many other empirical studies have been carried out on the link between CSR and financial performance and found divergent results (Karyawati et al., 2018; Kammoun et al., 2020a). While some empirical studies suggest both a potentially negative or positive relationship between CSR and financial performance, other studies have found no significant relationship (Orlitzky et al., 2003, Margolis et al. 2009; Mouatassim and Ibenrissoul, 2016; Galant and Cadez, 2017: Maqbool and Zameer, 2017; Kooskora et al., 2019; Broadstock et al., 2019; Kammoun et al., 2020b; Kammoun et al., 2020c). This relationship is still generating debate among researchers in both developed and developing countries. In the same vein, some other researchers have investigated the relationships between the company's social, environmental, and ðnancial and economic performance (Brogi and Lagasio, 2019; Chowdhury et al., 2019), and found that three dimensions (economic, social and environmental) are interconnected, and joint action ensures long-term commitment and sustainability (Rodriguez-Gomez et al., 2020).

Similarly, according to the concept known as the "Tripple_Bottom Line" and its synonym People, Planet, Profit (3P), Elkington (1997) emphasizes three types of responsibility: social responsibility (people), environmental responsibility (planet) and economic responsibility (profit). This type of reporting addresses the three main areas affecting society, i.e. the social, environmental and economic dimensions of CSR, and is also in line with the consideration and information of stakeholders required by CSR (Mintz, 2011). Put briefly, what is good for society and good for the environment is obviously good for financial performance.

In what follows, we use a qualitative approach to test if the integration of the criteria of the Social Responsibility of Organisations presents an advantage for Moroccan mining companies and if there is a difficulty in integrating CSR practices into investment decisions. The empirical analysis aims to provide insights on how the implementation of CSR dimensions as well as the dimension related to "Governance and Ethics" may create "Shared Value".

DATA DESCRIPTION AND RESEARCH METHODOLOGY

The empirical study was conducted at three Moroccan mining companies, coded A, B and C for confidentiality reasons. The points of convergence of the three selected companies are the membership of the Moroccan mining sector, the significant economic stakes and the important environmental, social and ethical issues. The points of divergence are the nature of the Public vs. Private shareholder, the size of the companies (turnover, workforce and number of subsidiaries) and the geographical location. The study

Table 1. Size of the target population for the field survey

	Preliminary study	Main study	Total
Human Capital	6	7	13
Investment Project Manager	5	4	9
Financiers	3	3	6
Top Management	3	4	5
Purchasing	0	1	1
Risk Management	1	1	2
Total	18	20	38

Source: Authors' development

used a qualitative approach, consisting of 2 steps: a preliminary exploratory study and a main exploratory study. The following table illustrates the size of the population solicited as part of our field survey:

The interviewees were selected among the managers (Middle and Top Management) of the 3 mining groups at the head office level and various operating sites. The targeted respondents were from different business lines concerned by the investment decision, i.e. senior executives, Directors of major investment projects or heads of major projects, Human Resources Directors and Financial Managers. Interviewees were selected according to the criteria of suitability, accessibility and geographical proximity (Yin, 1994).

The central question is to identify the practices that fall within the scope of the Corporate Social Responsibility of Organizations with regard to the investment decision making of Moroccan companies in the mining sector and to understand how CSR-related practices are integrated in investment decisions in the Moroccan mining sector by Economic, Environmental and Social categories and Ethics (People, Planet and Profit) and whether practices change according to decision-making power.

The two research proposals are as follows:

Proposal 1: the integration of the criteria of the Social Responsibility of Organisations presents an advantage for Moroccan companies in the mining sector;

The aim of this proposal is to understand the managers' perception of the integration of criteria relating to the social responsibility of organisations in the investment decision. The response of senior and middle managers to the various questions will make it possible to understand the advantages and shortcomings in relation to the integration of CSR practices and therefore identify the possible creation of 'Shared Value'.

Proposal 2: there is a difficulty in integrating CSR practices into investment decisions.

The answers to the questions addressed to the senior executives and middle managers will make it possible to understand the presence or absence of this difficulty as well as the proposal of ways to overcome the difficulties.

The scoping study began with data collection, development of the interview guide, testing of the guide, and then the conduct of the interviews. The analysis of the collected data was carried out using Thematic Content Analysis (TCA), using NVivo qualitative data analysis software. It should be noted that the interviews were transcribed using coding to facilitate processing by the NVivo software. The coding made it possible to exploit the maximum amount of information collected during the interviews by assigning each statement to the corresponding research proposal. Each interview lasted approximately one hour, for a total of 20 hours, and took approximately three hours to transcribe and classify the responses according to the coding carried out in the Nvivo software, for a total of approximately 60 hours.

RESULTS AND DISCUSSION

Officials interviewed expressed the view that mining companies integrate CSR principles to respond to stakeholder pressure, meet regulatory and normative obligations, and strengthen the image and reputation of their companies. All the more so as some customers demand to ensure, before purchasing mining products, that the entire value chain is socially responsible. Respondents stated that mining areas are found in remote regions that need the means necessary for local development.

Admittedly, the contribution of mining companies to local development will help to build trusting and lasting relationships with stakeholders, while changing negative perceptions due mainly to the nature of territories marked by a fragile economic and social situation. For instance, trust is built by improving communication skills, showing commitment, establishing common goals, etc. The environmental dimension presents considerable challenges to be taken into consideration, such as mine tailings, energy efficiency, biodiversity and water-related risks. Working conditions are a central element to be taken into consideration in the mining industry through a Quality, Safety and Environment (QSE) approach.

The issue of obtaining better access to capital was raised by the financiers interviewed and project managers. The protection of human rights is a major issue that mining companies must manage. The benefit of improving organisational governance and good business practice was mentioned by top managers and investment project managers. Energy efficiency was seen as a factor, among others, that has improved the financial profitability of several investment projects.

The above-mentioned benefits provide their companies with a Sustainable Competitive Advantage. With regard to shortcomings, respondents cited confusion between the services to be provided by the state and those that could be provided by the company. This confusion stems from the fact that all the mining areas are located in remote regions that need infrastructure, health services, access to drinking water, electricity, education, etc. The respondents also mentioned the fact that the State is not responsible for the provision of these services. When investments are made, mining companies naturally begin by setting up technical equipment, road networks and other infrastructure to launch mining activity. However, the population/residents express needs related to employment, health, education and this as early as the phase of geotechnical studies - exploration techniques of mining deposits.

This situation causes in some projects a relative overspending of the human, material and technical means allocated for the investment project. Taking into account the needs of stakeholders in several fields, the identification of expectations remains difficult. This difficulty is the result of several socio-economic factors that vary from one mining site to another.

Analysis by number of occurrences using the Nvivo software revealed that the priority criteria for the four dimensions are:

- Financial criteria: Net Present Value (NPV), Internal Rate of Return (IRR) and Return on Investment (ROI),
- Social criteria: Local job creation (local recruitment rate), contribution to local development, education, health and societal acceptability,

- Environmental criteria: Resource preservation / Water recycling, use of renewable energy, pollution prevention.
- Governance and Ethics criteria: Integration of environmental, social and ethical clauses in purchasing, ecosystem development, Good Governance Charter.

Table 2. Criteria related to the 4 dimensions of CSR

Financial criteria	Environmental criteria	Societal criteria	Governance and ethics criteria
Net Present Value (NPV)	CO2 emission	Local job creation (local recruitment rate)	Number of companies referenced for purchase/ ecosystem development
Internal rate of return (IRR)	Use of renewable energy	Gender/women/nationality/ age diversity	Integration of environmental, social and ethical clauses (in purchasing, choice of partners, etc.)
Return on investment (ROI) period	Resource preservation /recycling of water	Contribution to local development Education	Amicable land purchases
Cash flows generated	Vegetation degradation/land rehabilitation	Contribution to local development Health	Dedicated budget for Social Responsibility for Organizations
Profitability index (PI)	Pollution prevention	Contribution to Local development Infrastructure	Consumer/Customer Issues
Dividends	Sound	Access for people with disabilities	Awareness of project managers on standards and certifications (ISO 26000, GRI)
Tax benefits	Vibration	Integration of Occupational Health and Safety actions	Management Involvement
The budget allocated	Environmental acceptability	Employee participation in community activities	Mediation Stakeholders
	Depletion of reserves and natural resources	Psychosocial risk assessment	Independent Reporting (Environmental Impacts)
	Climate and hydrology	Skills development (employability)	SAR reporting and communication
	Waste treatment	Social Acceptability	Fighting Corruption / Fraud
	waste recycling/Circular economy	Ratio of Acting to Incumbents	Charter of good governance / deployment of internal procedures
	Regulatory compliance rate soil	Skills transfer in the broadest sense	Human rights
	Contamination/ groundwater table	Contribution to industrial ecosystem development	Integrity
	Air/dust contamination		Transparency in project management
	Biodiversity		Clear and defined processes: Purchasing
	Stability of the area		Digitization
	Tailings dams/discharges from waste rock		Project management by mixed teams
	Explosives management		**Continuous transformation/ Agility**

Source: Authors' development

The following table presents the criteria for the four dimensions of CSR:

The integration of the criteria of the four dimensions in the investment decision allows to reach a "Global Return" expected by the stakeholders. The longitudinal study elaborated over a period of 10 years allowed to apprehend the opportunity of integrating Socially Responsible Investment (SRI) and to appreciate the real orientations in terms of SRI.

This triangulation has shown that the social responsibility practices of organisations depend on the macroeconomic environment and in particular on the pressure and needs of stakeholders. Prior to 2011, CSR practices were mainly oriented towards actions related to environmental protection. From 2011 until the end of 2014, special attention was paid to local employment, education, infrastructure development and health. This distribution of practices was well observed during the qualitative study which showed that the pressure exerted by stakeholders was materialized by the needs of mining regions and this by an intensification, in the period from 2015 to 2018, of practices related to the creation of local jobs, the setting up of basic infrastructures, then education and health.

The analysis of the verbatins has enabled us to understand that all the players in Moroccan companies in the mining sector are aware of the opportunity presented by the integration of practices relating to the social responsibility of organisations in investment decisions throughout the value chain, as well as the need to develop a formalism for the multi-criteria evaluation of investment projects. In terms of Governance and Ethics, the study reveals very important issues and fundamental balances to be taken into consideration, such as the development of the Ecosystem. Taking into account the three dimensions "Profit", "Planet", and "People" in the different phases of an investment project requires a commitment throughout the different phases of the project but also a synergy between the different actors, from the critical phase of expropriation of land for mining needs to the rehabilitation of the mine after depletion of the deposit.

To take into account the CSR principles in the three dimensions mentioned above, with the addition of the Governance and Ethics dimensions, may create "Shared Value". Decision-makers and managers have expressed that consideration of practices related to Corporate Social Responsibility does not allow the rejection of the investment, since it has a positive impact on the investment decision. The creation of Shared Value was manifested by the number of citations of benefits related to Shared Value creation. An illustration of this is good governance (cited 74 times), manifested by anti-corruption actions, management involvement and independent reporting. Ethics (cited 68 times) is part of moral and also regulatory obligations, particularly in terms of environmental protection legislation and personal data protection.

On the basis of the empirical investigation, it can be deduced that decision-makers in the mining industry should consider four dimensions in the creation of shared value as a result of an investment decision. The three main dimensions are the following: firstly, practices related to "Profit" through traditional financial criteria such as Internal Rate of Return, Net Present Value and Return on Investment (ROI); secondly, practices related to "Planet" through environmental criteria such as water conservation, limiting the waste of natural resources and loss of biodiversity; thirdly, practices related to "People", in particular by taking into consideration societal acceptability by improving the conditions of local residents through actions related to the employability of young people (Education), the improvement of basic infrastructure and health services. In addition to these three dimensions, we mention the dimension relating to governance and ethics which include responsible purchasing, the charter of good governance and respect for human rights.

CONCLUSION AND FUTURE DIRECTIONS RESEARCH

The main purpose of this chapter was to delve deeper into understanding the practices of Moroccan mining companies with regard to the integration of "Profit", "Planet" and "People" practices in investment decisions, which justifies our choice of content analysis. Using a mixed methodology of triangulation (qualitative and quantitative), the empirical investigation attempted to operationalize the practices related to the integration of the CSR principles in the Moroccan mining industry. To this end, the empirical study tried to identify three main dimensions: "People" through contribution to local development, "Profit" through reputation improvement and "Planet" through environmental improvement and water conservation. A fourth dimension related to "Governance and Ethics" was added in order to address the main shortcomings such as the difficulties in assessing the impact of actions undertaken and their prioritization.

The research adds to the understanding of the practical level of CSR and SRI in mining industry and its impact on value creation. In fact, the modelling of the integration of practices relating to the Social Responsibility of Organizations for the four above-mentioned dimensions constitutes an attempt to formalize the interaction between the creation of national wealth (in the broad sense, not only budgetary) and its effective application in economic and social structural policies.

Despite these contributions, the study has some limitations. Indeed, the population interviewed is essentially composed of managers working in the mining sector. Because of their interest, interviewing other stakeholders such as local residents, political representatives and clients would enrich the research proposals and the understanding of the practices applied during the decision-making process of investments. Therefore, further empirical investigations have to increase the size of the respondents for the different stakeholders (local residents, clients, suppliers, etc.) in order to provide practical insights into how stakeholders' perceptions change with the evolution of socially responsible investment in the Moroccan mining industry.

REFERNCES

Abbott, W. F., & Monsen, R. J. (1979). On the measurement of corporate social responsibility: Self-reported disclosures as a method of measuring corporate social involvement. *Academy of Management Journal*, *22*(3), 501–515.

Azapagic, A. (2004). Developing a Framework for Sustainable Development Indicators for the Mining and Minerals Industry. *Journal of Cleaner Production*, *12*, 639–662.

Barney, J. (1991). Firm resources and sustained competitive advantage. *Journal of Management*, *17*, 99–120.

Bhattacharya, J. (2000). Sustainable development of natural resources: Implications for mining of minerals. *Mineral Resources Engineering*, *9*, 451–464.

Bode, C., & Singh, J. (2016). *Employee Engagement through Corporate Social Initiatives: an intrapreneurship perspective*. INSEAD.

Brogi, M., & Lagasio, V. (2019). Environmental, social, and governance and company proðtability: Are ðnancial intermediaries different? *Corporate Social Responsibility and Environmental Management, 26*, 576–587.

Burke, L., & Logsdon, J. M. (1996). How Corporate Social Responsibility Pays Off. *Long Range Planning, 29*, 495–502.

Cheng, B., Ioannou, I., & Serafeim, G. (2014). Corporate social responsibility and access to finance. *Strategic Management Journal, 35*(1), 1–23.

Chowdhury, R.H., Choi, S., Ennis, S. & Chung. D. (2019). Which Dimension of Corporate Social Responsibility is a Value Driver in the Oil and Gas Industry? *Canadian Journal of Administrative Sciences/ Revue Canadienne des Sciences de l'Administration, 36*, 260–72.

Crifo, P., & Forget, V. D. (2015). The economics of corporate social responsibility: A firm-level perspective survey. *Journal of Economic Surveys, 29*(1), 112–130.

Dahlsrud, A. (2008). How Corporate Social Responsibility Is Defined: An Analysis of 37 Definitions. *Corporate Social Responsibility and Environmental Management, 15*(1), 1–13. https://doi.org/10.1002/csr.132

Du, S., Bhattacharya, C. B., & Sen, S. (2007). Reaping relational rewards from corporate social responsibility: The role of competitive positioning. *International Journal of Research in Marketing, 24*(3), 224–241.

Elkington, J. (1997). *Cannibals with forks: The triple bottom line of 21st century*. Capstone Publishing Ltd.

Flammer, C. (2015). Does corporate social responsibility lead to superior financial performance? A regression discontinuity approach. *Management Science, 61*(11), 2549–2568.

Flammer, C., & Kacpercyzk, A. (2016). The Impact of Stakeholder Orientation on Innovation: Evidence from a Natural Experiment. *Management Science, 62*(7), 1982–2001.

Flammer, C., & Luo, J. (2016). Corporate Social Responsibility as an Employee Governance Tool: Evidence From a Quasi-Experiment. *Strategic Management Journal.*

Fombrun, C., & Shanley, M. (1990). What's in a Name? Reputation Building and Corporate Strategy. *Academy of Management Journal, 33*, 233–258. doi:10.2307/256324

Fosfuri, A., & Asmussen, G. (2016). *Strategic Corporate Social Responsibility in Multinational Enterprises*. Bocconni University & Copenhagen Business School, Working paper.

Fosfuri, A., Giarratana, M. S., & Roca, E. (2015). Walking a slippery line: Investments in social values and product longevity. *Strategic Management Journal, 36*(11), 1750–1760.

Galant, A., & Cadez, S. (2017). Corporate social responsibility and financial performance relationship: A review of measurement approaches. *Economic Research-Ekonomska Istraživanja, 30*(1), 676–693. doi:10.1080/1331677x.2017.1313122

Geertz, C. (1973). *The Interpretation of Cultures*. Basic Books.

George, N. A., Aboobaker, N., & Edward, M. (2020). Corporate social responsibility, organizational trust and commitment: a moderated mediation model. *Personnel Review*. doi:10.1108/pr-03-2020-0144

Hilson, G. (2000). Sustainable development of policies in Canada's mining sector: An overview of government and industry efforts. *Environmental Science & Policy*, *3*(4), 201–211.

Hilson, G. (2001). Putting theory into practice: How the gold mining industry interpreted the concept of sustainable development? *Mineral Resources Engineering*, *10*(04), 397–413. doi:10.11420950609801000725

Hojem, P. (2014). *Making Mining Sustainable: Overview of Private and Public Responses*. Published by Luleå University of Technology.

Horowitz, L. (2006). Section 2: Mining and sustainable development. *Journal of Cleaner Production*, *14*(3-4), 307–308. doi:10.1016/j.jclepro.2005.03.005

Jenkins, H. (2004). Corporate social responsibility and the mining industry: Conflicts and constructs. *Corporate Social Responsibility and Environmental Management*, *11*(1), 23–34. doi:10.1002/csr.50

Kammoun, S., Lebas, C., & Mercuri-Chapuis, S. (2020a). Types de RSE, types d'innovation: un bilan de travaux empiriques. In La responsabilité sociale des entreprises. Des relations sociales à la dimension stratégique, (pp. 113-128). Editions EMS. Management et Société. Collection Questions de société.

Kammoun, S., Loukil, S., & Ben Romdhane Loukil, Y. (2020b). The impact of Firm Performance and Corporate Governance on Corporate Social Responsibility: Evidence from France. In I. S. Paiva & L. C. Carvalho (Eds.), *Conceptual and Theoretical Approaches to Corporate Social Responsibility, Entrepreneurial Orientation, and Financial Performance (pp. 266-288)*. IGI Global. doi:10.4018/978-1-7998-2128-1.ch014

Kammoun, S., Loukil, S., Ben Romdhane Loukil, Y., & Ibenrissoul, A. (2020c). The relationship between CSR, Corporate Governance and Firm Performance: Evidence from Moroccan listed firms. In I. S. Paiva & L. C. Carvalho (Eds.), *Conceptual and Theoretical Approaches to Corporate Social Responsibility, Entrepreneurial Orientation, and Financial Performance (pp. 289-304)*. IGI Global. doi:10.4018/978-1-7998-2128-1.ch015

Karyawati, P. G., Subroto, B., Sutrisno, T., & Saraswati, E. (2018). The Complexity of Relationship between Corporate Social Responsibility (CSR) and Financial Performance. *Emerging Markets Journal*, *8*(2), 2018. doi:10.5195/emaj.2018.155

Kaul, A., & Luo, J. (2016). An Economic Case for CSR: The Comparative Efficiency of For-Profit Firms in Meeting Consumer Demand for Social Goods. *Strategic Management Journal*.

Kooskora, M., Juottonen, M. & Cundiff, K. (2019). The Relationship Between Corporate Social Responsibility and Financial Performance (A Case Study from Finland). *Social Responsibility and Sustainability*, 471–491. doi:10.1007/978-3-030-03562-4_25

Maqbool, S., & Zameer, M. N. (2017). An Empirical Examination of the Relationship between Corporate Social Responsibility and Profitability: Evidence from Indian Commercial Banks. *Pacific Business Review International*, *9*(12), 39–47.

Margolis, J. D., Elfenbein, H. A., & Walsh, J. P. (2009). *Does It Pay to Be Good and Does It Matter? A Meta-Analysis of the Relationship between Corporate Social and Financial Performance.* Working paper.

Marí-Farinós, J. (2017). Sustainability as an object of corporate social responsibility. *VITRUVIO-International. Journal of Architectural Technology and Sustainability*, *2*, 13–22.

Mintz, S. M. (2011). Triple Bottom Line Reporting for CPAs. *The CPA Journal*, *81*(12), 26–33.

Mouatassim, L. & Ibenrissoul, A. (2016). *Y a-t-il un impact de la RSE sur la performance financière de l'entreprise: Etude empirique sur les Sociétés marocaines cotées à la bourse de Casablanca.* hal-01351951/document.

Newman, C., Rand, J., Tarp, F., & Trifkovic, N. (2019). Corporate Social Responsibility in a Competitive Business Environment. *The Journal of Development Studies*, *56*(8), 1455-1472. doi:10.1080/00220388.2019.1694144

Norme, I. S. O. 26000. (2010). *Responsabilité sociétale.* https://www.iso.org/fr/iso-26000-social-responsibility.html

Orlitzky, M., Frank, L., Schmidt, F. L., Sara, L., & Rynes, S. L. (2003). Corporate social and financial performance: A meta-analysis. *Organization Studies*, *24*(3), 403–441.

Porter, M. E., & Kramer, M. R. (2006, December). Strategy and Society: The Link Between Competitive Advantage and Corporate Social Responsibility. *Harvard Business Review*, 78–92.

Porter, M. E., & Kramer, M. R. (2011). Creating shared value: How to reinvent capitalism – and unleash a wave of innovation and growth. *Harvard Business Review*, (January/February), 62–77.

Postel, N., & Sobel, R. (2019). Corporate social responsibility (CSR): An institutionalist Polanyian analysis. *Society and Business Review*, *14*(4), 381–400.

Prno, J. (2013). An analysis of factors leading to the establishment of a social license to operate in the mining industry. *Resources Policy, Elsevier*, *38*(4), 577–590. doi:10.1016/j.resourpol.2013.09.010

Revelli, C. & Viviani, J.L. (2015). Financial performance of socially responsible investing (SRI): what have we learned? *A meta-analysis Business Ethics: A European Review*, *24*(2), 158-185.

Rodriguez-Gomez, S., Arco-Castro, M. L., Lopez-Perez, M. V., & Rodríguez-Ariza, L. (2020). Where Does CSR Come from and Where Does It Go? A Review of the State of the Art. *Administrative Sciences*, *10*(3), 60. https://dx.doi.org/10.3390/admsci10030060

Russo, M. V., & Fouts, P. A. (1997). A resource-based perspective on corporate environmental performance and profitability. *Academy of Management Journal*, *40*, 534–559.

Thietard, R. (2014). *Méthodes de recherche en Management.* Dunod.

Venkatesh, U., Mathew, J., & Chaudhuri, A. (2020). *Corporate social responsibility as an antecedent of brand valuation, Mandated Corporate Social Responsibility.* Springer.

Wernerfelt, B. (1984). A resource-based view of the firm. *Strategic Management Journal*, *5*, 171–180.

Wheeler, D., Colbert, B., & Freeman, R. E. (2003). Focusing on value: Reconciling corporate social responsibility, sustainability and a stakeholder approach in a network world. *Journal of General Management*, *28*(3), 1–28.

Whitmore, A. (2006). The emperor's new clothes: Sustainable mining? *Journal of Cleaner Production*, *14*(3-4), 309–314. doi:10.1016/j.jclepro.2004.10.005

Worrall, R., Neil, D., Brereton, D., & Mulligan, D. (2009). Towards a sustainability criteria and indicators framework for legacy mine land. *Journal of Cleaner Production*, *17*(16), 1426–1434. doi:10.1016/j.jclepro.2009.04.013

Yin, R. K. (1994). *Case study research: Design and method*. Sage Publications.

Zelazna, A., Bojar, M., & Bojar, E. (2020). Corporate Social Responsibility towards the Environment in Lublin Region, Poland: A Comparative Study of 2009 and 2019. *Sustainability*, *12*, 4463. doi:10.3390u12114463

KEY TERMS AND DEFINITIONS

CSR Strategy: Is a set of measures related to the integration of CSR practices that complement the firm's core business activities and contribute to the overall mission of the firm.

Developing Country: Is a country with a less developed industrial base and a low Human Development Index (HDI) relative to other countries.

Qualitative Research: Is a method of inquiry in social science and related disciplines. This method relies on data obtained by the researcher from first-hand observation, interviews, questionnaires, focus groups, participant-observation.

Socially Responsible Investment: Is an investment that is considered socially responsible due to the nature of the activities the firm conducts.

Shared Value: It can be defined as policies and operating practices that enhance the competitiveness of a company and advance the economic and social conditions in the communities in which it operates.

Triangulation: Is a qualitative research strategy to test validity through the convergence of information from different sources. It refers to the use of multiple methods or data sources in qualitative research to develop a comprehensive understanding of phenomena.

Compilation of References

Abbott, W. F., & Monsen, R. J. (1979). On the measurement of corporate social responsibility: Self-reported disclosures as a method of measuring corporate social involvement. *Academy of Management Journal*, *22*(3), 501–515.

Abdelkafi, N., & Tauscher, K. (2016). Business models for sustainability from a system dynamics perspective. *Organization & Environment*, *29*(1), 74–96. doi:10.1177/1086026615592930

Accenture. (2020, September). *Banking Technology Vision 2020, Raport*. Author.

Adarkar, A., Hyde, P., & Sridharan, A. (2020). *Leading a consumer bank through the coronavirus pandemic*. McKinsey&Company.

Adelman & Adelman. (1959, Oct.). The dynamic properties of the Klein-Goldberger model. *Econometrica*.

Agbodan, M. M., & Amoussouga, F. G. (1995). *Les facteurs de performance de l'entreprise*. John Libbey Eurotext.

Agenda 21: Implementation of Agenda 21, the Programme for the Further Implementation of Agenda 21 and the outcomes of the World Summit on Sustainable Development. (2012). United Nations. A/C.2/66/L.59. https://www.un.org/ga/search/view_doc.asp?symbol=A/C.2/66/L.59&Lang=E)

Agha, S., Alrubaiee, L., & Jamhour, M. (2012). Effect of Core Competence on Competitive Advantage and Organizational Performance. *International Journal of Business and Management*, *7*(1), 192–204.

Agrawal, S., De Smet, A., Poplawski, P., & Reich, A. (2020). *Beyond hiring: How companies are reskilling to address talent gaps. In Organization Practice and McKinsey Accelerate*. McKinsey & Company.

Agudelo, M. L., Jóhannsdóttir, L., & Davídsdóttir, B. (2019). A literature review of the history and evolution of corporate social responsibility. *International Journal of Corporate Social Responsibility*.

Ahmadi, M. (2017). Evaluating the performance of 3Rs waste practices: Case study-region one municipality of Tehran. *Advance Recycling Waste Management*, *2*(130), 2. doi:10.4172/2475-7675.1000130

Aiginger, K., Bärenthaler-Sieber, S., & Vogel, J. (2013). *Competitiveness under New Perspectives*. Working Paper, 44. www.foreurope.eu

Albert, M. (2003). Une nouvelle économie sociale de marche? Quels modèles d'entreprise pour un développement durable? *Futuribles (Paris, France)*, (287), 5–21.

Aliańska, A., Frydrych, S., & Klein, E. (2018). Finanse w koncepcji zrównoważonego rozwoju. *Kwartalnik Kolegium Ekonomiczno-Społecznego, Studia i Prace. Szkoła Główna Handlowa*, *1*, 27–44.

Alliance Bernstein. (2019). *Delivering social and environmental impact in the healthcare sector, Principles of Responsible Investments*. https://www.unpri.org/delivering-social-and-environmental-impact-in-the-healthcare-sector/3912.article

Alm, K., & Sievänen, R. (2013). Institutional Investors, Climate Change, and Human Rights. *The Journal of Sustainable Finance & Investment, 3*(3), 177–183. doi:10.1080/20430795.2013.791139

Alom, M. F. (2012). *Volatility and Spillover Effects of Oil and Food Price Shocks*. Lambert Academic Publishing.

Altieri, M. A. (2018). *Agroecology: the science of sustainable agriculture*. CRC Press, Taylor&Francis. doi:10.1201/9780429495465

Amato, L. H., & Amato, C. H. (2012). Environmental policy, rankings and stock values. *Business Strategy and the Environment, 21*(5), 317–325. doi:10.1002/bse.742

American Society of Civil Engineers. (2017). *Failure to Act: Closing the Infrastructure Investment Gap for America's Economic Future*. American Society of Civil Engineers.

Ammer, R., & Othman, R. (2012). Sustainability Practices and Corporate Financial Performance: A Study Based on the Top Global Corporations. *Journal of Business Ethics, 108*(1), 61–79. doi:10.100710551-011-1063-y

Ananiev, B. G. (1977). The problems of modern human science. Academic Press.

Annadale, D., Morrison-Saunders, A., & Bouma, G. (2004). The impact of voluntary environmental protection instruments on company environmental performance. *Business Strategy and the Environment, 13*(1), 1–12. doi:10.1002/bse.390

Anton, W. R. Q., Deltas, G., & Khanna, M. (2004). Incentives for environmental self-regulation and implications for environmental performance. *Journal of Environmental Economics and Management, 48*(1), 632–654. doi:10.1016/j.jeem.2003.06.003

Aragon-Correa, J. (1998). Strategic Proactivity and Firm Approach to the Natural Environment. *Source: The Academy of Management Journal, 41*(5), 556–567. doi:10.5465/256942

Aragon-Correa, J., & Rubio-Lopez, E. A. (2007). Proactive Corporate Environmental Strategies: Myths and Misunderstandings. *Long Range Planning, 40*(3), 357–381. doi:10.1016/j.lrp.2007.02.008

Aragon-Correa, J., Rueda-Manzanares, A., & Sharma, S. (2008). The Influence of Stakeholders on the Environmental Strategy of Service Firms: The Moderating Effects of Complexity, Uncertainty and Munificence. *British Journal of Management, 19*(2), 185–203. doi:10.1111/j.1467-8551.2007.00538.x

Arah, O. A., Westert, G. P., Hurst, J., & Klazinga, N. S. (2006). A conceptual framework for the OECD health care quality indicators project. *International Journal for Quality in Health Care, 18*(Suppl. 1), 5–13. doi:10.1093/intqhc/mzl024 PMID:16954510

Arena, M., Ciceri, S. D., Terzi, S., Bengo, I., Azzone, G., & Garetti, M. (2009). A state-of-the-art of industrial sustainability: Definitions, tools and metrics. *International Journal of Product Lifecycle Management, 4*(1), 207. doi:10.1504/IJPLM.2009.031674

Arnon, A.D., Ricco, J.A., Smetters, K.A. (2020, September). Epidemiological and economic effects of lockdown. *Brookings*.

Arowoshegbe, A. O., & Emmanuel, U. (2016). *Sustainability and Triple Bottom Line: an overview of two interrelated concepts* (Vol. 2). Igbinedion University Journal of Accounting.

Arrow, K. (1963). Uncertainty and the welfare economics of medical care. *The American Economic Review, 1963*(53), 941–973. http://links.jstor.org/sici?sici=0002-8282%28196312%2953%3A5%3C941%3AUATWEO%3E2.0.CO%3B2-C

Ashraf, N., van Seters, J., & Mackie, J. (2020). *The integration of climate change and circular economy in foreign policies*. ECDPM Discussion No.274.

Aspinall, N. G., Jones, S. R., McNeill, E. H., Werner, R. A., & Zalk, T. (2018). Sustainability and the financial system. Review of literature 2015. *Br. Actuar, 23*, 1–21. doi:10.1017/S1357321718000028

Atiq, M., & Karatas-Ozkan, M. (2013). Sustainable Corporate Entrepreneurship from a Strategic Corporate Social Responsibility Perspective. *International Journal of Entrepreneurship and Innovation, 14*(1), 5–14. doi:10.5367/ijei.2013.0102

Azapagic, A. (2004). Developing a Framework for Sustainable Development Indicators for the Mining and Minerals Industry. *Journal of Cleaner Production, 12*, 639–662.

Bać, A. (2014). Idea zrównoważenia i jej wybrane przejawy. *Architectus, 2*(38), 3–13.

Backer, L. C. (2006). Multinational corporations, transnational law: The United Nations' norms on the responsibilities of transnational corporations as a harbinger of Corporate Social Responsibility in international law. *Columbia Human Rights Law Review, 37*(287).

Bahi, D. R. (2015). *Energy Price Shocks and Macroeconomics Performance*. RFF Press.

Bailinson, P., Decherd, W., Ellsworth, D., & Guttman, M. (2020). *Understanding organizational barriers to a more inclusive workplace*. Mackinsey and Company. June.

Bąk, I., & Cheba, K. (2020a). The Concept of Shared Value in the Theory of Sustainable Finance. An Analysis from the OECD Countries Perspective. In Environmental Impacts Between Sustainable Financial Systems and Financial Markets. IGI Global.

Bąk, I., & Cheba, K. (2020b). Zielona gospodarka jako narzędzie zrównoważonego rozwoju. CeDeWu.

Bąk, I., & Szczecińska, B. (2020). The Value of the Company and Sustainable Development. In Social, Economic Environmental Impacts Between Sustainable Financial Systems and Financial Markets. IGI Global.

Bąk, A. (2016). Porządkowanie liniowe obiektów metodą Hellwiga i TOPSIS – analiza porównawcza. *Research Papers of Wroclaw University of Economics.*, (426). Advance online publication. doi:10.15611/pn.2016.426.02

Baldassarre, B., Konietzko, J., Brown, P., Calabretta, G., Bocken, N., Karpen, I. O., & Hultink, E. J. (2020). Addressing the design-implementation gap of sustainable business models by prototyping: A tool for planning and executing small-scale pilots. *Journal of Cleaner Production, 255*, 120295. doi:10.1016/j.jclepro.2020.120295

Banerjee, P., & Shogren, J. F. (2010). Regulation, reputation, and environmental risk. *Economics Letters, 106*(1), 45–47. doi:10.1016/j.econlet.2009.09.021

Banerjee, S. B. (2002). Corporate environmentalism - The construct and its measurement. *Journal of Business Research, 55*(3), 177–191. doi:10.1016/S0148-2963(00)00135-1

Banister, D. (2008). The sustainable mobility paradigm. *Transport Policy, 15*(2), 73–80. doi:10.1016/j.tranpol.2007.10.005

Bansal, P., & DesJardine, M. (2014). Business sustainability: It is about time. *Strategic Organization, 12*(1), 70–78. doi:10.1177/1476127013520265

Bansal, P., & Roth, K. (2000). Why companies go green: A model of ecological responsiveness. *Academy of Management Journal, 43*(4), 717–736.

Bantekas, I. (2004). Corporate Social Responsibility in international law. Boston University International Law Review, 22(309).

Baporikar, N. (Ed.). (2020). *Handbook of research on entrepreneurship development and opportunities in circular economy*. doi:10.4018/978-1-7998-5116-5

Baret, P. (2006). L'évaluation contingente de la Performance Globale des Entreprises: une méthode pour fonder un management socialement responsable? In Responsabilité sociale de l'entreprise, (pp. 135-152). De Boeck Supérieur.

Baret, S., Celner, A., O'Reilly, M., & Shilling, M. (2020). *COVID-19 potential implications for the banking and capital markets sector*. Deloitte Insight.

Barnett, M. L. (2007). Stakeholder Influence Capacity and the Variability of Financial Returns to Corporate Social Responsibility. *Academy of Management Review*, *32*(3), 794–816. doi:10.5465/amr.2007.25275520

Barney, J. (1991). Firm resources and sustained competitive advantage. *Journal of Management*, *17*, 99–120.

Barra, R., & Leonard, S. A. (2018). *Plastics and the circular economy*. Scientific and Technical Advisory Panel to the Global Environment Facility.

Barrett, M., Davidson, E., Prabhu, J., & Vargo, S. L. (2015). Service Innovation in the Digital Age: Key Contributions and Future Directions. *Management Information Systems Quarterly*, *39*(1), 135–154. doi:10.25300/MISQ/2015/39:1.03

Bartniczak, B. (2013). Zrównoważony transport na poziomie regionalnym jako przedmiot pomiaru wskaźnikowego. Studia Ekonomiczne, *Zeszyty Naukowe Uniwersytetu Ekonomicznego w Katowicach. Uniwersytet Ekonomiczny w Katowicach*, *143*, 11–20.

Baum, Mogues, & Verdier. (2020). Getting the most from public investment. In *Well Spent: How Strong Infrastructure Governance Can End Waste in Public Investment*. Washington, DC: International Monetary Fund.

Baxter, D. (2020). *PPP and COVID-19*. 3rd Co-Webinar.

Baxter, D., & Casady, C. B. (2020). Proactive and Strategic Healthcare Public-Private Partnerships (PPPs) in the Coronavirus (Covid-19) Epoch. *Sustainability*, *12*(12), 5097. doi:10.3390u12125097

Bellman, R., Clark, Ch., Craft, C., Malcolm, D. G., & Ricciardi, F. (1957). On the Construction of a MultiStage, Multi-Person Business Game. *Operations Research*, *5*(4), 469–503. doi:10.1287/opre.5.4.469

Bems, Caselli, Grigoli, & Gruss. (2019). *Gains from anchoring inflation expectations: evidence from the taper tantrum shock*. IMF Working Paper, WP/19/75.

Ben Yedder, M. & Zaddem, F. (2009). La Responsabilité Sociale de l'Entreprise (RSE), voie de conciliation ou terrain d'affrontements? *Revue multidisciplinaire sur l'emploi, le syndicalisme et le travail*, *4*(1), 84-103.

Benaim, A., Collins, A. C., & Raftis, L. (2008). *The Social Dimension of Sustainable Development: Guidance and Application: Thesis submitted for completion of Master of Strategic Leadership towards Sustainability*. Blekinge Institute of Technology.

Bennett, N. J., Roth, R., Klain, S. C., Chan, K., Christie, P., Clark, D. A., Cullman, G., Curran, D., Durbin, T. J., Epstein, G., Greenberg, A., Nelson, M. P., Sandlos, J., Stedman, R., Teel, T. L., Thomas, R., Veríssimo, D., & Wyborn, C. (2017). Conservation social science: Understanding and integrating human dimensions to improve conservation. *Biological Conservation*, *205*, 93–108. doi:10.1016/j.biocon.2016.10.006

Berry, M. A., & Rondinelli, D. A. (1998). Proactive corporate environmental management: A new industrial revolution. *The Academy of Management Perspectives*, *12*(2), 38–50. doi:10.5465/ame.1998.650515

Bhattacharya, J. (2000). Sustainable development of natural resources: Implications for mining of minerals. *Mineral Resources Engineering*, *9*, 451–464.

Biely, K., Maes, D., & Passel, S. V. (2016). *The idea of weak sustainability is illegitimate*. Academic Press.

Billimoria, J., & Bishop, M. (2020). How COVID-19 can be the Great Reset toward global sustainability. In *Sustainable Development Impact Summit.* World Economic Forum.

Birch, S., Murphy, G. T., MacKenzie, A., & Cumming, J. (2014). In place of fear: Aligning health care planning with system objectives to achieve financial sustainability. *Journal of Health Services Research & Policy*, *0*(0), 1–6. doi:10.1177/1355819614562053 PMID:25504826

Blanchard, O. (2009). *Macroeconomics* (5th ed.). MIT.

Blomstrom, D. (2018). *Emotional Banking: Fixing Culture.* In *Leveraging FinTech and Transforming Retail Banks into Brands.* Palgrave McMillan. doi:10.1007/978-3-319-75653-0

Bocken, N. M. P., Ritala, P., & Huotari, P. (2017). The circular economy: Exploring the introduction of the concept among S&P 500 firms. *Journal of Industrial Ecology*, *21*(3), 487–490. doi:10.1111/jiec.12605

Bocken, N. M. P., Short, S. W., Rana, P., & Evans, S. (2014). A literature and practice review to develop sustainable business model archetypes. *Journal of Cleaner Production*, *65*, 42–56. doi:10.1016/j.jclepro.2013.11.039

Bode, C., & Singh, J. (2016). *Employee Engagement through Corporate Social Initiatives: an intrapreneurship perspective.* INSEAD.

Bode, C., Singh, J., & Rogan, M. (2015). Corporate social initiatives and employee retention. *Organization Science*, *26*(6), 1702–1720. doi:10.1287/orsc.2015.1006

Bogdanov, A. A. (1934). *Tectology or General Organizational Science.* Conjuncture Institute publishing house.

Boons, F., & Lüdeke-Freund, F. (2013). Business models for sustainable innovation: State-of-the-art and steps towards a research agenda. *Journal of Cleaner Production*, *45*, 9–19. doi:10.1016/j.jclepro.2012.07.007

Borys, T. (Ed.). (2008). *Analiza istniejących danych statystycznych pod kątem ich użyteczności dla określenia poziomu zrównoważonego rozwoju transportu wraz z propozycją ich rozszerzenia.* Raport z realizacji ekspertyzy, Jelenia Góra-Warszawa.

Borys, T., Czaja, S. (2009). Badania nad zrównoważonym rozwojem w polskich ośrodkach naukowych. In *Od koncepcji ekorozwoju do ekonomii zrównoważonego rozwoju.* Białystok: Wydawnictwo Wyższej Szkoły Ekonomicznej w Białymstoku.

Boston Consulting Group Perspectives. (2020). *COVID-19: Facts, scenarios, and actions for leaders.* Version 2.2. BCG.

Boston Consulting Group. (2017). Russia 2025: From Average Students to Talents. Boston Consulting Group.

Boston Consulting Group. (2020). *COVID-19: Win the Fight, Win the Future.* Featured Insights. April. BCG.

Boston Consulting Group. (2020). *COVID-19: Win the Fight, Win the Future.* Featured Insights. Boston Consulting Group.

Boston Consulting Group. (2020). *Workforce Sentiment Survey.* Boston Consulting Group.

Boulton, R. E. S., Libert, B. D., & Samek, S. M. (1997). *Cracking the Value Code: How Successful Businesses are Creating Wealth in the New Economy.* Harper Collins Publishers.

Bourguignon, A. (1995). La performance, essais de definition. *Revue Française de Comptabilité*, 269.

Bova, E., Ruiz-Aranz, M., Toscani, F., & Elif Ture, H. (2016). *The fiscal costs of contingent liabilities: a new dataset.* IMF Working Paper 16/14, International Monetary Fund.

Bowen, H. R. (1953). *Social responsibilities of the businessman.* Harper & Brothers.

Bowen, H. R. (1953). *Social responsibility of the businessman.* Harpers and Brothers.

Brandenburger, A. W., & Stuart, S. H. Jr. (1996). Value-based Business Strategy. *Journal of Economics & Management Strategy, 5*(1), 5–24. doi:10.1111/j.1430-9134.1996.00005.x

Brandi, C., Dzebo, A., & Janetschek, H. (2017). *The Case for Connecting the Implementation of the Paris Climate Agreement and the 2030 Agenda for Sustainable Development.* Briefing Paper 21/2017.

Braungart, M., & McDonough, W. (2009). Cradle to cradle. Re-making the way we make things. London: Vintage Books Chatham House.

Breen, K. (2016). *Why does inclusive growth matter?* The World Economic Forum.

Breuer, H., & Lüdeke-Freund, F. (2014). Normative Innovation for Sustainable Business Models in Value Networks. In K. Huizingh, S. Conn, M. Torkkeli, & I. Bitran (Eds.), *The Proceedings of XXV ISPIM Conference – Innovation for Sustainable Economy and Society.* Academic Press.

Brogi, M., & Lagasio, V. (2019). Environmental, social, and governance and company proðtability: Are ðnancial intermediaries different? *Corporate Social Responsibility and Environmental Management, 26,* 576–587.

Brooks, C., & Oikonomou, I. (2018). The effects of environmental, social and governance disclosures and performance on firm value: A review of the literature in accounting and finance. *The British Accounting Review, 50*(1), 1–15. doi:10.1016/j.bar.2017.11.005

Brown, V., Grootjans, J., Ritchie, J., Townsend, M., & Verrinder, G. (2005). *Sustainability and health: Supporting global ecological integrity in public health.* Earthscan.

Brundtland, G. H. (2012). Health: A pathway to sustainable development. *American Medical Association. Journal of the American Medical Association, 288*(2), 156. PMID:12095374

Brynjolfsson, E., Hitt, L., & Kim, H. (2011, April). *Strength in Number: How does data driven decision making affect firm performance.* SSoM MIT.

Buffoli, M., Capolongo, S., Bottero, M., Cavagliato, E., Speranza, S., & Volpatti, L. (2013). Sustainable Healthcare: How to assess and improve healthcare structures' sustainability. *Annali di igiene: medicina preventiva e di comunità, 25,* 411–418. doi:10.7416/ai.2013.1942 PMID:24048179

Burke, L., & Logsdon, J. M. (1996). How Corporate Social Responsibility Pays Off. *Long Range Planning, 29,* 495–502.

Burtland Report. (1987). *Report of the World Commission on Environment and Development: Our Common Future.* Available at http://www.un-documents.net/our-common-future.pdf

Burton, I. (1968). The quality of the environment: A review. *Geographical Review, 58*(3), 472. doi:10.2307/212567

Business Insider Intelligence. (2019, January). *40 Bigtech predictions. Moody's, Big Tech – a real threat to financial firms in retail services.* Author.

Business Strategy for Sustainable Development: Leadership and Accountability for the 90s. (1992). IISD, WBCSD Deloitte & Touche.

Buys, L., Mengersen, K., Johnson, S., Buuren, N. V., & Chauvin, A. (2014). Creating a Sustainability Scorecard as a predictive tool for measuring the complex social, economic, and environmental impacts of industries, a case study: Assessing the viability and sustainability of the dairy industry. *Journal of Environmental Management, 133,* 184–192. doi:10.1016/j.jenvman.2013.12.013 PMID:24374467

Buysse, K., & Verbeke, A. (2003). Proactive Environmental Strategies: A Stakeholder Management Perspective. *Strategic Management Journal*, *24*(5), 453–470. doi:10.1002mj.299

Cagliano, A. C., Grimaldi, S., & Rafele, C. (2011). A systemic methodology for risk management in healthcare sector. *Safety Science*, *49*(5), 695–708. doi:10.1016/j.ssci.2011.01.006

Capgemini Research Institute. (2020). *The Great Digital Divide Report, Offline Population Survey*. Author.

Capron, M., & Quairel-Lanoizelée, F. (2004). *Mythes et réalités de l'entreprise responsable*. La Découverte.

Carlsson-Szlezak, Reeves, & Swartz. (2020). Understanding the economic shock of coronavirus. *HBR Newstand Special Edition.*

Carrasco, Chandran, Chin, Hayden, Hoteit, Subudhi, & Werfe. (2020). *Start Reimaging Government Now*. Boston Consulting Group.

Carrascosa-Lopez, C., Segarra-Ona, M.-V., Peiro-Signes, A., & Segura-Garcia-del-Rio, B. (2012). Environmental Proactivity In Manufacturing Industries: Is It Valuable? *International Business & Economics Research Journal*, *11*(5), 567–574. doi:10.19030/iber.v11i5.6974

Carroll, B. (2002). Sustainable development: an eclectic view. *CIWEM International Directory 2003.*

Carroll, A. B. (1979). A Three-Dimensional Conceptual Model of Corporate Performance. *Academy of Management Review*, *4*(4), 497–505. doi:10.5465/amr.1979.4498296

Carroll, A. B. (1991). The pyramid of corporate social responsibility: Toward the moral management of organizational stakeholders. *Business Horizons*, *34*(4), 39–48. doi:10.1016/0007-6813(91)90005-G

Carroll, A. B. (2015). Corporate social responsibility: The centerpiece of competing and complementary frameworks. *Organizational Dynamics*, 44.

Casadesus-Masanell, R., & Ricart, J. E. (2010). From Strategy to Business Models and onto Tactics. *Long Range Planning*, *43*(2-3), 195–215. doi:10.1016/j.lrp.2010.01.004

Castano, R. (2014). *Towards a framework for business model innovation in health care delivery in developing countries.* Medicine for Global Health. https://www.biomedcentral.com/1741-7015/12/233

Cavallino, P., & De Fiore, F. (2020, June). Central banks' response to Covid-19 in advanced economies. *BIS Bulletin.*

CDP. (2017). CDP India Climate Change Report 2017: India Inc. aligns with NDC and Paris Agreement to seize opportunities. London, UK: CDP.

Chaudhary, R. (2017). Corporate social responsibility and employee engagement: Can CSR help in redressing the engagement gap? *Social Responsibility Journal*, *13*(2), 323–338. doi:10.1108/SRJ-07-2016-0115

Cheba, K. (2019). Zrównoważona międzynarodowa konkurencyjność krajów Unii Europejskiej. Studium teoretyczno-empiryczne. CeDeWu.

Cheng, D., Jacobs, K., Law, S., & Schubert, W. Xu, & Zegeye. (2020). Reimagining the postpandemic economic future. McKinsey & Company.

Cheng, B., Ioannou, I., & Serafeim, G. (2014). Corporate social responsibility and access to finance. *Strategic Management Journal*, *35*(1), 1–23.

Cherrafi, A., Garza-Reyes, J. A., Kumar, V., Mishra, N., Ghobadian, A., & Elfezazi, S. (2018). Lean, green practices and process innovation: A model for green supply chain performance. *International Journal of Production Economics, 206*, 79–92. doi:10.1016/j.ijpe.2018.09.031

Chesbrough, H. (2007). Business model innovation: It's not just about technology anymore. *Strategy and Leadership, 35*(6), 12–17. doi:10.1108/10878570710833714

Chong, E., Handscomb, CH., & Wiliams, O. (2020, October). *Agile resilience in the UK: Lessons from COVID-19 for the 'next normal'*. McKinsey and Company.

Cho, S. J., Chung, C. Y., & Young, J. (2019). Study on the relationship between CSR and financial performance. *Sustainability, 11*(2), 343. doi:10.3390u11020343

Chowdhury, R.H., Choi, S., Ennis, S. & Chung. D. (2019). Which Dimension of Corporate Social Responsibility is a Value Driver in the Oil and Gas Industry? *Canadian Journal of Administrative Sciences/Revue Canadienne des Sciences de l'Administration, 36*, 260–72.

Christensen, L., Gittleson, J., & Smith, M. (2020). The most fundamental skill: Intentional learning and the career advantage. In *McKinsey Accelerate*. McKinsey & Company.

Christiano, L. J., Eichenbaum, M., & Evans, C. L. (1999). Monetary policy shocks: what have we learned and to what end? In J.B. Taylor & M. Woodford (Eds.), Handbook of Macroeconomics (Vol. 1A). Amsterdam: Elsevier. doi:10.1016/S1574-0048(99)01005-8

Ciegis, R., Ramansuskiene, J., & Martinkus, B. (n.d.). Ekonomikos plėtra darnaus vystymosi aspektu. *Taikomoji ekonomika: sisteminiai tyrimai, 2*(1).

Clarkson, M. E. (1995). A Stakeholder Framework for Analyzing and Evaluating Corporate Social Performance. *Academy of Management Review, 20*(1), 92–117. doi:10.5465/amr.1995.9503271994

Clarkson, P. M., Li, Y., Richardson, G. D., & Vasvari, F. P. (2011). Does it really pay to be green? Determinants and consequences of proactive environmental strategies. *Journal of Accounting and Public Policy, 30*(2), 122–144. doi:10.1016/j.jaccpubpol.2010.09.013

Clearbridge Mobile. (2020). The 2020 Enterprise Mobility Trends Report. Retrieved from: https://clearbridgemobile.com/enterprise-mobility-trends/

Commission Of The European Communities. (2001). *Green Paper Promoting a European framework for Corporate Social Responsibility*. https://ec.europa.eu/commission/presscorner/detail/en/DOC_01_9

Commission of the European Communities. (2001). *Green Paper Promoting European framework for Corporate Social Responsibility*. https://ec.europa.eu/employment_social/soc-dial/csr/greenpaper_pl.pdf

Commission of the European Communities. (2002). *Corporate Social Responsibility: A business contribution to Sustainable Development*. https://eur-lex.europa.eu/legal-content/EN/TXT/PDF/?uri=CELEX:52002DC0347&from=EN

Commission of the European Communities. (2007). *Together for Health. A Strategic Approach for the EU 2008-2013*. Brussels, 23.10.2007 COM(2007) 630 final.

Committee of Sponsoring Organizations of the Treadway Commission (COSO), World Business Council for Sustainable Development (WBCSD). (2018). *Enterprise risk management: Applying enterprise risk management to environmental, social and governance-related risks*. https://www.coso.org/Documents/COSO-WBCSD-Release-New-Draft-Guidance-Online-viewing.pdf

Communication from the Commission to the European Parliament, the Council and the European Economic and Social Committee. (2006). *Implementing the partnership for growth and jobs: making Europe a pole of excellence on corporate social responsibility*. https://eur-lex.europa.eu/legal-content/EN/TXT/PDF/?uri=CELEX:52006DC0136&from=PL

Consolidated Versions of the Treaty On European Union and the Treaty on the Functioning of the European, Official Journal of the European Union, C 326/122 - C 326/124.

Corporate Social Responsibility. (2020). Retrieved from: https://www.unido.org/our-focus/advancing-economic-competitiveness/competitive-trade-capacities-and-corporate-responsibility/corporate-social-responsibility-market-integration/what-csr

COVID-19. Briefing Materials. (2020). Global health and crisis response. McKinsey & Company.

Cowie, J., & Fisken, K. (2019). *Development of the Business Model framework to be used in SURFLOGH*. Transport Research Institute, Edinburgh Napier University.

Crifo, P., & Forget, V. D. (2015). The economics of corporate social responsibility: A firm-level perspective survey. *Journal of Economic Surveys*, *29*(1), 112–130. doi:10.1111/joes.12055

Crisostomo, V. L., Freire, F. S., & Freitas, M. R. D. O. (2019). Determinants of corporate sustainability performance – evidence from Brazilian panel data. *Social Responsibility Journal*, *16*(8), 1053–1072. Advance online publication. doi:10.1108/SRJ-04-2018-0102

Crouch, G. I., & Ritchie, J. R. B. (1999). Tourism, competitiveness, and societal prosperity. *Journal of Business Research*, *44*(3), 137–152. doi:10.1016/S0148-2963(97)00196-3

Cukiermann, A. (2020, July). *Quantitative easing and helicopter money: Not so distant cousins*. Retrieved from: https://voxeu.org/article/quantitative-easing-and-helicopter-money-not-so-distant-cousins

Curry, A., & Hodgson, A. (2008, August). Seeing in Multiple Horizons: Connecting Futures to Strategy. *Journal of Futures Studies*, (13), 1–20.

Czigler, T., Reiter, S., Schulze, P., & Somar, K. (2020). *Laying the foundation for zero-carbon cement*. McKinsey and Company May.

Dahlsrud, A. (2006). How Corporate Social Responsibility is Defined an Analysis of 37 Definitions. *Corporate Social Responsibility and Environmental Management*, *15*(1), 1–13. doi:10.1002/csr.132

Dahlsrud, A. (2008). How Corporate Social Responsibility Is Defined: An Analysis of 37 Definitions. *Corporate Social Responsibility and Environmental Management*, *15*(1), 1–13. https://doi.org/10.1002/csr.132

Dam. (Ed.). (2019). Elevating Learning & Development: Insights and Practical Guidance from the Field. McKinsey & Company.

Darnall, N., Henriques, I., & Sadorsky, P. (2010). Adopting Proactive Environmental Strategy: The Influence of Stakeholders and Firm Size. *Journal of Management Studies*, *47*(6), 1072–1094. doi:10.1111/j.1467-6486.2009.00873.x

Daugaard, D. (2019). Emerging new themes in environmental, social, and governance investing: A systematic literature review. *Accounting and Finance*, *60*(2), 1501–1530. doi:10.1111/acfi.12479

Davies, B., Diemand-Yauman, C., & van Dam, N. (2019). *Competitive advantage with a human dimension: From lifelong learning to lifelong employability. McKinsey Quarterly.*

de Jong, S., van der Gaast, M., Kraak, J., Bergema, R., & Usanov, A. (2016). *The circular economy and developing countries: A data analysis of the impact of a circular economy on resource-dependent developing nations*. Centre of Expertise on Resources, The Hague Centre for Strategic Studies.

De Mendonca, T., & Zhou, Y. (2020). When companies improve the sustainability of the natural environment: A study of large US companies. *Business Strategy and the Environment*, *29*(3), 801–811. doi:10.1002/bse.2398

De Roeck, K., El Akremi, A., & Swaen, V. (2016). Consistency matters! How and when does corporate social responsibility affect employees' organizational identification? *Journal of Management Studies*, *53*(7), 1141–1168. doi:10.1111/joms.12216

De Smedt, B. (2014). Advances in the use of neuroscience methods in research on learning and instruction. *Frontline Learning Research*, *2*(4).

Déau, T. (2020). *Why Sustainable Infrastructure is a Key Part of Rebuilding the Post-COVID Economy*. World Economic Forum.

Delmas, M., Hoffmann, V. H., & Kuss, M. (2011). Under the Tip of the Iceberg: Absorptive Capacity, Environmental Strategy, and Competitive Advantage. *Business & Society*, *50*(1), 116–154. doi:10.1177/0007650310394400

Delmas, M., & Toffel, M. W. (2004). Stakeholders and environmental management practices: An institutional framework. *Business Strategy and the Environment*, *13*(4), 209–222. doi:10.1002/bse.409

Deloitte Digital. (2020). *Digital CRM 2.0 Building customer relationships in the digital landscape*. Author.

Deloitte IIF. (2020). *Realizing of digital promise: COVID19 catalyzes and accelerates transformation in financial services*. Author.

Deloitte. (2016). *Circular economy potentials for climate change*. Deloitte Sustainability Team.

Dembińska, I. (2018). Infrastruktura logistyczna gospodarki w ujęciu środowiskowych uwarunkowań zrównoważonego rozwoju. Uniwersytet Szczeciński, Rozprawy i studia 1010, Szczecin.

Deva, S. (2006). Sustainable good governance and corporations: An analysis of asymmetries. *Georgetown International Environmental Law Review*, *18*.

Diab, S. M. (2014). Using the Competitive Dimensions to Achieve Competitive advantage (A Study on Jordanian private hospitals). *International Journal of Academic Research in Business & Social Sciences*, *4*(9), 138–150. doi:10.6007/IJARBSS/v4-i9/1136

Diesendorf, M. (2000). Sustainability and sustainable development. Sustainability: The corporate challenge of the 21st century.

Dimock, M. (2019). *Defining generations: Where Millennials end and Generation Z begins*. Retrieved from: https://www.pewresearch.org/fact-tank/2019/01/17/where-millennials-end-and-generation-z-begins/

Dixon-Fyle, Hunt, & Prince. (2020). *Diversity wins: How inclusion matters*. McKinsey & Company.

Dixon-Fyle, Hunt, Dolan, & Prince. (2020). *Diversity wins: How inclusion matters*. McKinsey & Company.

Dodd, E. M. (1932). For Whom are Corporate Managers Trustees? *Harvard Law Review*, *45*(7), 1145. doi:10.2307/1331697

Dohou, A., & Berland, N. (2007). *Mesure de la performance globale des entreprises. 28 ème*. Congrès de l'Association Francophone de Comptabilité.

Donnelley Financial Solutions (DFIN). (2019). *White Paper. ESG Risks and Opportunities: Understanding the ESG Landscape*. https://www.dfinsolutions.com/sites/default/files/documents/2019-03/dfin_gcm_proxy_whitepaper_ESG_risks_and_oppty_2019223.pdf

Dooris, M. (1999). Healthy cities and local agenda 21: The UK experience – Challenges for the new millennium. *Health Promotion International*, *14*(4), 365–375. doi:10.1093/heapro/14.4.365

Doumba, M. (2020). The Great reset must place social justice at its centre. In *Sustainable Development Impact Summit*. World Economic Forum.

Dowel, G., Hart, S., & Yeung, B. (2000). Do Corporate Global Environmental standards create or destroy market value? *Management Science*, *46*(8), 1059–1074. doi:10.1287/mnsc.46.8.1059.12030

Drucker, P. (1999). *Management Challenges For The 21st Century*. Academic Press.

Drucker, P. F., Kuhl, J. S., & Hesselbein, F. (2015). *Peter Drucker's Five Most Important Questions: Enduring Wisdom for Today's Leaders*. Jossey-Bass.

Dubash, N. K., Khosla, R., Kelkar, U., & Lele, S. (2018). India and Climate Change: Evolving Ideas and Increasing Policy Engagement. *Annual Review of Environment and Resources*, *43*(1), 395–424. doi:10.1146/annurev-environ-102017-025809

Dulewicz, P., Perzyńska, A., & Witkowski, K. (2014). Odpowiedzialność przedsiębiorstwa za zrównoważony rozwój. *Logistyka*, *4*, 3889–3893.

Du, S., Bhattacharya, C. B., & Sen, S. (2007). Reaping relational rewards from corporate social responsibility: The role of competitive positioning. *International Journal of Research in Marketing*, *24*(3), 224–241.

Dyllick, T., & Muff, K. (2016). Clarifying the meaning of sustainable business introducing a typology from business-as-usual to true business sustainability. *Organization & Environment*, *29*(2), 156–174. doi:10.1177/1086026615575176

Dyllick, T., & Muff, K. (2016b). Transitioning w: Sustainable Business: A One Planet Approach. In *S. Jeanrenaud, J. P. Jeanrenaud, & J. Gosling*. Wiley.

Earth Day. (n.d.). *The history of earth day*. Retrieved November 13, 2020, from https://www.earthday.org/about/thehistory-of-earth-day/

Easterly, Islam, & Stiglitz. (2000). *Shaken and Stirred: Explaining Growth Volatility. Macroeconomic Paradigms for Less Developed Countries*. World Bank.

EBA. (2019). *Report on the impact of FinTech on payment institutions' and e-money institutions' business models*. EBA.

Eccles, R. G., Ioannou, I., & Serafeim, G. (2014). The Impact of Corporate Sustainability on Organizational Processes and Performance. *Management Science*, *60*(11), 2835–2857. doi:10.1287/mnsc.2014.1984

Ekins, P., & Hughes, N. (2017). *Resource efficiency: potential and economic implications*. UN Environment Programme (UNEP). Https://europa.eu/ capacity4dev/unep/documents/resource-efficiency-potential-and-economic-implications

Ekins, P., Simon, S., Deutsch, L., Folke, C., & Groot, R. D. (2003). A framework for the practical application of the concepts of critical natural capital and strong sustainability. *Ecological Economics*, *44*(2-3), 165–185. doi:10.1016/S0921-8009(02)00272-0

El Akremi, A., Gond, J. P., Swaen, V., De Roeck, K., & Igalens, J. (2018). How do employees perceive corporate responsibility? Development and validation of a multidimensional corporate stakeholder responsibility scale. *Journal of Management*, *44*(2), 619–657. doi:10.1177/0149206315569311

Eliwa, Y., Aboud, A., & Saleh, A. (2019). ESG practices and the cost of debt: Evidence from EU countries. *Critical Perspectives on Accounting, 102097*, 102097. Advance online publication. doi:10.1016/j.cpa.2019.102097

Elkington, J. (2018, June 25). 25 Years Ago I Coined the Phrase 'Triple Bottom Line'. Here's Why It's Time to Rethink It. *Harvard Business Review*. Retrieved September 2020, 2020, from https://hbr.org/2018/06/25-years-ago-i-coined-the-phrase-triple-bottom-line-heres-why-im-giving-up-on-it

Elkington, J. (1997). *Cannibals with forks – Triple bottom line of 21st century business*. Stoney Creek.

Elkington, J. (1997). *Cannibals with forks: The triple bottom line of 21st century*. Capstone Publishing Ltd.

Elkington, J. (1998). Accounting for the Triple Bottom Line. *Measuring Business Excellence*, *2*(3), 18–22. doi:10.1108/eb025539

Elkington, J. (2020). *Green Swans: The Coming Boom in Regenerative Capitalism*. Fast Company Press.

Elkonin, D. B. (1989). *Selected Psychological Works*. Pedagogy Publisher.

Ellen MacArthur Foundation. (2012). *Towards the circular economy: An economic and business rationale for an accelerated transition*. The Ellen MacArthur Foundation.

Ellen MacArthur Foundation. (2015). *Towards a circular economy: Business rationale for an accelerated transition*. The Ellen MacArthur Foundation.

Ellen MacArthur Foundation. (2017). *What is a circular economy?* The Ellen MacArthur Foundation.

Ellen MacArthur Foundation. (2019). *Completing the picture: How the circular economy tackles climate change*. www.ellenmacarthurfoundation.org/publications

Emmett, J., Schrah, G., Schrimper, M., & Wood, A. (2020). *COVID-19 and the employee experience: How leaders can seize the moment. In Organization Practice*. June. Mckinsey&Company.

Engel, E., Fischer, R., & Galetovic, A. (2014). *Finance and Public-Private Partnerships: A Roadmap*. Background paper for the Global Financial Development Report of the World Bank.

Engel, Fischer, & Galetovic. (2020). *When and how to use public-private partnerships in infrastructure: lessons from the international experience*. NBER Working Paper 26766. Retrieved from: https://www.nber.org/papers/w26766

EU Commission. (2018). *Action Plan on Sustainable Finance*. Available at https://ec.europa.eu/info/publications/180308-action-plan-sustainable-growth_en

European Commission. (2011). *Communication from the Commission to the European Parliament, the Council, the European Economic and Social Committee and the Committee of the Regions: a renewed EU strategy 2011–14 for corporate social responsibility*. Available from: https://publications.europa.eu/en/publication-detail/-/publication/ae5ada03-0dc3-48f8-9a32-0460e65ba7ed/language-en

European Commission. (2020). *Banks and third party providers agree on joint efforts regarding the transition to new payment rules*. Retrieved from: https://ec.europa.eu/info/publications/190726-joint-statement-psd2_en

Eurostat. (2008). NACE Rev. 2: Statistical classification of economic activities in the European Community. *Eurostat Methodologies and Working papers*.

Evans, S., Vladimirova, D., Holgado, M., Van Fossen, K., Yang, M., Silva, E., & Barlow, C. (2017). Business model innovation for sustainability: Towards a unified perspective for creation of sustainable business models. *Business Strategy and the Environment*, *26*(5), 597–608. doi:10.1002/bse.1939

Faezipour, M., & Ferreira, S. A. (2013). System dynamics perspective of patient satisfaction in healthcare. *Procedia Computer Science*, *16*, 148–156. doi:10.1016/j.procs.2013.01.016

Falkenberg, J., & Brunsæl, P. (2011). Corporate Social Responsibility: A Strategic Advantage or a Strategic Necessity? *Journal of Business Ethics, Springer*, *99*(1), 9–16. doi:10.100710551-011-1161-x

Farla, J., Markard, J., Raven, R., & Coenen, L. (2012). Sustainability transitions in the making: A closer look at actors, strategies, and resources. *Technological Forecasting and Social Change*, *79*(6), 991–998. doi:10.1016/j.techfore.2012.02.001

Fatemi, A. M., & Fooladi, I. J. (2013). Sustainable finance: A new paradigm. *Global Finance Journal*, *24*(2), 101–113. doi:10.1016/j.gfj.2013.07.006

Faure-Schuyer, A., Egenhofer,C & Elkerbout, M. (2018). *Value chains based on mineral raw materials – challenges for European policy and industry*. CEPS Policy Insights No 2018/07.

Ferguson, C., Andandarajah, G., Butnar, I., Calzadilla, A., & Dessens, O. (2020). *Costing the earth-climate damage costs and GDP. A summary of the report produced by UCL Energy Institute for CDP.*

Fifka, M. S. (2009). *Towards a More Business-Oriented Definition of Corporate Social Responsibility: Discussing the Core Controversies of a Well-Established Concept*. J. Service Science & Management.

Fischer, M. (2015). Fit for the Future? A New Approach in the Debate about What Makes Healthcare Systems Really Sustainable. *Sustainability*, *7*(1), 294–312. doi:10.3390u7010294

Flammer, C. (2015). Does corporate social responsibility lead to superior financial performance? A regression discontinuity approach. *Management Science*, *61*(11), 2549–2568.

Flammer, C., & Kacpercyzk, A. (2016). The Impact of Stakeholder Orientation on Innovation: Evidence from a Natural Experiment. *Management Science*, *62*(7), 1982–2001.

Flammer, C., & Luo, J. (2016). Corporate Social Responsibility as an Employee Governance Tool: Evidence From a Quasi-Experiment. *Strategic Management Journal*.

Foll, J. (2018). *ESG and Healthcare: The challenges ahead*. https://hub.ipe.com/asset-manager/axa-investment-managers/esg-and-healthcare-the-challenges-ahead/10028009.supplierarticle

Fombrun, C., & Shanley, M. (1990). What's in a Name? Reputation Building and Corporate Strategy. *Academy of Management Journal*, *33*, 233–258. doi:10.2307/256324

Forgarassy, C., & David, F. (2020). Theoretical and practical approaches of circular economy for business models and technological solutions. *Resources*, *9*(76), 1–9. doi:10.3390/resources9060076

Fosfuri, A., & Asmussen, G. (2016). *Strategic Corporate Social Responsibility in Multinational Enterprises*. Bocconni University & Copenhagen Business School, Working paper.

Fosfuri, A., Giarratana, M. S., & Roca, E. (2015). Walking a slippery line: Investments in social values and product longevity. *Strategic Management Journal*, *36*(11), 1750–1760.

Freedman, L. (2013). *Strategy : A history* (1st ed.). Oxford University Press.

Freeman, E. (1984). *Strategic Management: A stakeholder approach*. Pitman.

Frieden, J. (2020). The political economy of economic policy. *Finance & Development*, *57*(2), 6-7.

Friedman, M. (1970). The Social Responsibility of Business Is to Increase its Profits, *New York Times Magazine*. http://umich.edu/~thecore/doc/Friedman.pdf?mod=article_inline

Friedman, M. (1962). *Capitalism and Freedom*. University of Chicago Press.

Friedman, M. (1993). *The Social Responsibility of Business is to Increase it Profits*. Chapman & Hall.

Frish, R. (1933). Propagation problems and impulse problems in dynamic economics. In *Economic Essays in Honour of Gustav Cassel*. Allen and Unwin.

Frooman, J. (1999). Stakeholder influence strategies. *Academy of Management Review*, *24*(2), 191–205. doi:10.5465/amr.1999.1893928

Fukuda, K., & Ouchida, Y. (2020). Corporate social responsibility (CSR) and the environment: Does CSR increase emissions? *Energy Economics*, *104933*. Advance online publication. doi:10.1016/j.eneco.2020.104933

Fullwiler, S. T. (2015). *Sustainable Finance: Building a More General Theory of Finance*. Working Paper No. 106, Binzagr Institute for Sustainable Prosperity.

Gadenne, D. L., Kennedy, J., & McKeiver, C. (2009). An empirical study of environmental awareness and practices in SMEs. *Journal of Business Ethics*, *84*(1), 45–63. doi:10.100710551-008-9672-9

Galant, A., & Cadez, S. (2017). Corporate social responsibility and financial performance relationship: A review of measurement approaches. *Economic Research-Ekonomska Istraživanja*, *30*(1), 676–693. doi:10.1080/1331677X.2017.1313122

Gan, Y., Zhang, T., Liang, S., Zhao, Z., & Li, N. (2013). How to deal with resource productivity. *Journal of Industrial Ecology*, *17*(3), 440–451. doi:10.1111/j.1530-9290.2012.00547.x

Garces-Ayerbe, C., Rivera-Torres, P., & Murillo-Luna, J. L. (2012). Stakeholder pressure and environmental proactivity. *Management Decision*, *50*(2), 189–206. doi:10.1108/00251741211203524

Garde-Sanchez, R., López-Pérez, M. V., & López-Hernández, A. (2018). Current Trends in Research on Social Responsibility in State-Owned Enterprises: A Review of the Literature from 2000 to 2017. *Sustainability*, *10*(7), 2403. doi:10.3390u10072403

Gardner, J. (2017). *Circular economy and decarbonisation: lessons from industry*. Hoffmann Centre for Sustainable Resource Economy.

Garvare, R., & Johansson, P. (2010). Management for sustainability – A stakeholder theory. *Total Quality Management & Business Excellence*, *21*(7), 737–744. doi:10.1080/14783363.2010.483095

Gaspar & Gopinath. (2020a). *Fiscal Policies for a Transformed World*. Insights & Analyses on Economics & Finance.

Gaspar, Raphael, & Mehdi. (2020). *Fiscal Policies for the Recovery from COVID-19*. Insights & Analyses on Economics & Finance.

Geertz, C. (1973). *The Interpretation of Cultures*. Basic Books.

Geissdoerfer, M., Bocken, N. M. P., & Hultink, E. J. (2016). Design thinking to enhance the sustainable business modelling process. *Journal of Cleaner Production*, *135*, 1218–1232. doi:10.1016/j.jclepro.2016.07.020

Geissdoerfer, M., Savaget, P., Bocken, N. M. P., & Hultink, E. J. (2017). The circular economy – a new sustainability paradigm? *Journal of Cleaner Production*, *143*(6), 757–768. doi:10.1016/j.jclepro.2016.12.048

Geissdoerfer, M., Vladimirova, D., & Evans, S. (2018). Sustainable business model innovation: A review. *Journal of Cleaner Production*, *198*, 401–416. doi:10.1016/j.jclepro.2018.06.240

George, N. A., Aboobaker, N., & Edward, M. (2020). Corporate social responsibility, organizational trust and commitment: a moderated mediation model. *Personnel Review*. doi:10.1108/pr-03-2020-0144

Germain, C., & Trebucq, S. (2004). La performance globale de l'entreprise et son pilotage: quelques réflexions. *Semaine sociale Lamy, 1186*, 35-41.

Gerster, R. (2011). *Sustainable Finance: Achievements, Challenges, Outlook.* Gerster Consulting, Richterswill.

Ghisellini, P., Cialani, C., & Ulgiati, S. (2016). A review on circular economy: The expected transition to a balanced interplay of environmental and economic systems. *Journal of Cleaner Production, 114*(7), 11–32. doi:10.1016/j.jclepro.2015.09.007

Ghose, B. (2020). *Why 2020 will see the birth of the 'trust economy'.* World Economic Forum.

Giddings, B., Hopwood, B., & O'Brien, G. (2002). Environment, Economy and Society: Fitting them together into Sustainable Development. *Sustainable Development, 10*(4), 187–196. doi:10.1002d.199

Girardet, H. (1999). *Creating sustainable cities, Totnes.* Green Books for the Schumacher Society, Dewon.

Gjaja, Hutchinson, Farber, Brimmer, & Kahn. (2020). *Three Paths to the Future.* Boston Consulting Group Analysis.

Gladwin, T. N. (1993). The Meaning of Greening: A Plea for Organizational Theory. In J. Fischer & K. Schot (Eds.), *Environmental Strategies for Industry: International Perspectives on Research Needs and Policy Implications* (pp. 37–61). Island Press.

Gonzales-Benito, J. C., & Gonzales-Benito, O. C. (2006). A Review of Determinant Factors of Environmental Proactivity. *Business Strategy and the Environment, 15*(2), 87–102. doi:10.1002/bse.450

Górka, K. (2007). Wdrażanie koncepcji rozwoju zrównoważonego i trwałego. *Ekonomia i Środowisko, 2*(32), 8-20.

Grant, A. M., & Ashford, S. J. (2008). The Dynamics of Proactivity at Work. *Research in Organizational Behavior, 28*(1), 3–34. doi:10.1016/j.riob.2008.04.002

Grasshoff, G., Coppola, M., Pfuhler, T., Bochtler, S., Gittfried, N., Vogt, P., & Wiegand, C. (2020). Global Risk 2020: It's Time for Banks to Self-Disrupt. Boston Consulting Group.

Gray, R., & Milne, R. M. (2004). Towards reporting on the triple bottom line: Mirages, methods and myths. The Triple Bottom Line does it all add up? Assessing the sustainability of business and CSR.

Gray, R. (2010). Is accounting for sustainability actually accounting for sustainability… and how would we know? An exploration of narratives of organisations and the planet. *Accounting, Organizations and Society, 35*(1), 47–62. doi:10.1016/j.aos.2009.04.006

Gray, T. R. (2011). Mapping a Corporate Governance Exchange: A Survey of Canadian Shareholder Resolutions 2000–2009. *The Journal of Sustainable Finance & Investment, 1*(1), 30–43. doi:10.3763/jsfi.2010.0005

Green Paper. (2001). *Promoting a European framework for Corporate Social Responsibility.* Commission of the European Communities, COM(2001)366/F1. Available at https://ec.europa.eu/transparency/regdoc/rep/1/2001/EN/1-2001-366-EN-F1-1.Pdf

Greening, D. W., & Turban, D. B. (2000, September). Corporate Social Performance as a Competitive Advantage in Attracting a Quality Workforce. *Business & Society, 39*(3), 254–280. doi:10.1177/000765030003900302

Group of Seven (G7). (2016). *G7 Ise-Shima Principles for Promoting Quality Infrastructure Investment.* G7 Ise-Shima Leaders' Declaration.

Group of Twenty (G20). (2019). *G20 Principles for Quality Infrastructure Investment.* G20 Osaka Leaders' Declaration.

Hahn, T., Figge, F., Pinkse, J., & Preuss, L. (2010). Trade-Offs in Corporate Sustainability: You Can't Have Your Cake and Eat It! *Business Strategy and the Environment, 19*(4), 217–229. doi:10.1002/bse.674

Hahn, T., Lutz, P., Pinkse, J., & Figge, F. (2014). Cognitive frames in corporate sustainability: Managerial sensemaking with paradoxical and business case frames. *Academy of Management Review, 39*(4), 463–487. doi:10.5465/amr.2012.0341

Hahn, T., & Scheermesser, M. (2006). Approaches to Corporate Sustainability among German companies. *Corporate Social Responsibility and Environmental Management, 13*(3), 150–165. doi:10.1002/csr.100

Hakro, A. N., & Omezine, A. M. (2014). *Oil Price Shocks and Macroeconomic Fundamentals of Oman Economy.* Lambert Academic Publishing.

Hancock, T. (1996). Planning and creating healthy and sustainable cities: The challenge for the twenty-first century. In C. Price & A. Tsourus (Eds.), *Our cities, our future: Policies and action for health and sustainable development* (pp. 65–88). World Health Organization, Healthy Cities Project Office.

Handscomb, CH., Mahadevan, D., Naidoo, E., Schor, L., Sieberer, M., & Srinivasan, S. (2020, June). *An operating model for the next normal: Lessons from agile organizations in the crisis.* McKinsey.

Hannon, A., & Callaghan, E. (2011). Definitions and organizational practice of sustainability in the for-profit sector of Nova Scotia. *Journal of Cleaner Production, 19*(8), 877–884. doi:10.1016/j.jclepro.2010.11.003

Hart, S. L. (1995). A Natural-Resource-Based View of the Firm. *Academy of Management Review, 20*(4), 986–1014. doi:10.5465/amr.1995.9512280033

Hatzius, J., Hooper, P., Mishkin, F., Schoenholtz, K. L., & Watson, M. W. (2010). *Financial conditions indexes: a fresh look after the financial crisis.* NBER Working Paper Series. 16150. Retrieved from: https://www.nber.org/papers/w16150

Hebb, T. (2013). Impact Investing and Responsible Investing: What Does it Mean*? J. Sustain. Financ. Investig, 3*(2), 71–74. doi:10.1080/20430795.2013.776255

Hedberg, C., & Malmborg, F. (2003). The global reporting initiative and corporate sustainability reporting in Swedish companies. *Corporate Social Responsibility and Environmental Management, 10*(3), 153–164. doi:10.1002/csr.38

Hellwig, Z. (1968). Zastosowanie metody taksonomicznej do typologicznego podziału krajów ze względu na poziom ich rozwoju oraz zasoby i strukturę wykwalifikowanych kadr. *Przegląd Statystyczny,* (4).

Henderson, K., Pinner, D., Rogers, M., Smeets, B., Tryggested, C., & Vargas, D. (2020). Climate math: What a 1.5 degree pathway would take. *The McKinsey Quarterly.*

Henri, J., & Giasson, A. (2006). Measuring environmental performance: A basic ingredient of environmental management. *CMA Management, 80*(5), 28.

Henriques, A., & Richardson, J. (2004). Introduction: The Triple Bottom Line does it all add up? *The Triple Bottom Line does it all add up? Assessing the sustainability of business and CSR.*

Henriques, I., & Sadorsky, P. (1999). The relationship between environmental commitment and managerial perceptions of stakeholder importance. *Academy of Management Journal, 42*(1), 87–99.

Hilb, M. (2006). *Integrierte corporate governance. Ein neues Konzept der Unternehmensführung und Erfolgskontrolle.* Springer. doi:10.1007/3-540-32744-4

Hilson, G. (2000). Sustainable development of policies in Canada's mining sector: An overview of government and industry efforts. *Environmental Science & Policy, 3*(4), 201–211.

Hilson, G. (2001). Putting theory into practice: How the gold mining industry interpreted the concept of sustainable development? *Mineral Resources Engineering*, *10*(04), 397–413. doi:10.1142095060980100 0725

Hiswåls, A.S., Hamrin, C.W., Vidman, A., & Macassa, V. (2020). Corporate social responsibility and external stakeholders' health and wellbeing: A viewpoint. *Journal of Public Health Research*, *9*(1), 1742. doi:10.4081/jphr.2020.1742

Hockerts, K., & Wues, R. (2010). Greening Goliaths versus emerging Davids – Theorizing about the role of incumbents and new entrants in sustainable entrepreneurship. *Journal of Business Venturing*, *25*(5), 481–492. doi:10.1016/j.jbusvent.2009.07.005

Hoffman, A. (2018). The Next Phase of Business Sustainability. *Standford Social Innovation Review*. https://ssir.org/articles/entry/the_next_phase_of_business_sustainability

Hojem, P. (2014). *Making Mining Sustainable: Overview of Private and Public Responses*. Published by Luleå University of Technology.

Holmes, I., Moule, S. (2016). *A sustainable finance plan for The European Union*. E3G.

Homrich, A. S., Galvao, G., Abadia, L. G., & Carvalho, M. M. (2018). The circular economy umbrella: Trends and gaps on integrating pathways. *Journal of Cleaner Production*, *175*, 525–543. doi:10.1016/j.jclepro.2017.11.064

Hopkins, M. (2003). The business case for CSR: Where are we? *International Journal of Business Performance Management*, *5*(2-3), 125–140. doi:10.1504/IJBPM.2003.003261

Horowitz, L. (2006). Section 2: Mining and sustainable development. *Journal of Cleaner Production*, *14*(3-4), 307–308. doi:10.1016/j.jclepro.2005.03.005

Horvath, B., Mallinguh, E., & Fogarassy, C. (2018). Designing business solutions for plastic waste management to enhance circular transitions in Kenya. *Sustainability*, *10*(5), 1664. doi:10.3390u10051664

Hou, D. (2016). Divergence in stakeholder perception of sustainable remediation. *Sustainability Science*, *11*(2), 215–230. doi:10.100711625-015-0346-0

Hou, D., Al-Tabbaa, A., Chen, H., & Mamic, I. (2014). Factor Analysis and Structural Equation Modeling of Sustainable Behaviour in Contaminated Land Remediation. *Journal of Cleaner Production*, *84*(1), 439–449. doi:10.1016/j.jclepro.2014.01.054

Huang, B., Wang, X., Kua, H., Geng, Y., Bleischwitz, R., & Ren, J. (2018). Construction and demolition of waste management in China through the 3Rs principle. *Resources, Conservation and Recycling*, *129*, 36–44. doi:10.1016/j.resconrec.2017.09.029

Hung, C., & Chen, L. (2009). A Fuzzy TOPSIS Decision Making Model with Entropy Weight under Intuitionistic Fuzzy Environment. *Proceedings of the International Multi-Conference of Engineers and Computer Scientists*.

Hunt, Layton, & Prince. (2015). *Diversity Matters*. McKinsey & Company.

Hunt, Prince, Dixon-Fyle, & Yee. (2018). Delivering through Diversity. Executive summary. *McKinsey Quarterly*.

Hunt, C. B., & Auster, E. R. (1990). Proactive Environmental Management: Avoiding the Toxic Trap. *Sloan Management Review*, *31*, 7–18.

Hwang, J., & Christensen, C. M. (2008). Disruptive Innovation In Health Care Delivery: A Framework For Business-Model Innovation. *Health Affairs*, *27*(5), 1329–1335. doi:10.1377/hlthaff.27.5.1329 PMID:18780919

Iamandi, I.-E., Constantin, L.-G., Munteanu, S. M., & Cernat-Gruici, B. (2019). Mapping the ESG Behavior of European Companies. A Holistic Kohonen Approach. *Sustainability*, *11*(12), 3276. doi:10.3390u11123276

IDG Research, . (2020). The state of the cloud: How enterprise adoption is taking shape. *InfoWorld.*

ILO. (2017). *Tripartite Declaration of Principles concerning Multinational Enterprises and Social Policy* (5th ed.). http://www.ilo.org/wcmsp5/groups/public/---ed_emp/---emp_ent/---multi/documents/publication/wcms_094386.pdf

IMF Fiscal Monitor Country Fiscal Measures in response on COVID-19. (2020, October). Retrieved from: https://www.imf.org/en/Topics/imf-and-covid19/Fiscal-Policies-Database-in-Response-to-COVID-19

IMF Policy Tracker. (2020, October). *COVID-19 Financial Assistance and Debt Service Relief.* Retrieved from: https://www.imf.org/en/Topics/imf-and-covid19/COVID-Lending-Tracker

IMF. (2014). *Legacies, Clouds, Uncertainties.* World Economic Outlook. October.

IMF. (2015). *Making Public Investment More Efficient.* IMF.

IMF. (2020). External stress and the international investment position. In External Sector Report: Global Imbalances and the COVID-19 Crisis. Washington, DC: IMF.

IMF. (2020). The Great Lockdown. World Economic Outlook.

IMF. (2020a). What is the COVID-19 crisis impact on public-private partnerships. Public Financial Management Blog of IMF.

IMF. (2020b). Policies to Support People During the COIVD-19 Pandemic. Fiscal Monitor.

InfraOne. (2020). *Investment in infrastructure: the project market in crisis. Analytical Overview. InfraOne Research.* InfraOne.

International Finance Corporation (IFC). (2015). *Environmental and Social Management System (ESMS) Implementation Handbook - Health Care Facilities.* https://www.ifc.org/wps/wcm/connect/topics_ext_content/ifc_external_corporate_site/sustainability-at-ifc/publications/publications_handbook_esms-healthcarefacilities

International Monetary Fund. (2020). Policies to Support People During the COVID-19 Pandemic. Fiscal Monitor. IMF.

International Monetary Fund. (2020, June). *Global Financial Stability Report.* Author.

Investing in Health. (2013). *Commission staff working document.* Brussels, 20.02.2013, SWD (2013) 43 final.

IPCC. (2007). Climate Change 2007: Impacts, Adaptation and Vulnerability. In P. J. van der L. Parry M.L., O.F. Canziani, J.P. Palutikof, & C. E. Hanson (Eds.), Contribution of Working Group II to the Fourth Assessment Report of the Intergovernmental Panel on Climate Change (p. 982). Cambridge, UK: Cambridge University Press.

Jabłoński, A. (2013). Modele zrównoważonego biznesu - miejsce i rola w koncepcji zarządzania strategicznego. *Zarządzanie Strategiczne Quo vadis, Prace Naukowe Wałbrzyskiej Wyższej Szkoły Zarządzania i Przedsiębiorczości, red. Krupski, R. T., 22*, 283-293.

Jacobs, M. (1995). *Sustainable Development-From Broad Rhetoric to Local Reality. Conference Proceedings from Agenda 21 in Cheshire.* Cheshire County Council, Document No. 493.

Jagiełło, Z., & Kubisiak, P. (2020). *From the moneybox to the cloud computing.* ICAN Institute.

Jameton, A., & McGuire, C. (2002). Toward sustainable health-care services: Principles, challenges, and a process. *IJSHE*, *3*(2), 113–127. doi:10.1108/14676370210422348

Janssen, M., & Moors, E. H. (2013). Caring for healthcare entrepreneurs—Toward successful entrepreneurial strategies for sustainable innovations in Dutch healthcare. *Technological Forecasting and Social Change*, *80*(7), 1360–1374. doi:10.1016/j.techfore.2012.12.003

Jayanti, R. K., & Gowda, M. V. R. (2014). Sustainability dilemmas in emerging economies. *IIMB Management Review*, *26*(2), 130–142. doi:10.1016/j.iimb.2014.03.004

Jenkins, H. (2004). Corporate social responsibility and the mining industry: Conflicts and constructs. *Corporate Social Responsibility and Environmental Management*, *11*(1), 23–34. doi:10.1002/csr.50

Jing, W., & Sun, B. (2018). Study on the Source of Negative Externality in the Sharing Economy. *Proceedings of the ICCSE'18, 3rd International Conference on Crowd Science and Engineering*. 10.1145/3265689.3265701

Jones, C. (2010). Exploring new ways of assessing the effect of regulation on environmental management. *Journal of Cleaner Production*, *18*(13), 1229–1250. doi:10.1016/j.jclepro.2010.04.007

Jones, R., & Dowling, P. (2004). *Sustainability, externalities, and economics: the case of temperate perennial grazing systems in NSW. Economic Research Report* (Vol. 24). NSW Department of Primary Industries. Available at http://www.agric.nsw.gov.au/reader/10550

Joyce, A., & Paquin, R. L. (2016). The Triple Layered Business Model Canvas: A Tool to Design More Sustainable Business Models. *Journal of Cleaner Production*, *135*, 1474–1486. doi:10.1016/j.jclepro.2016.06.067

Kammoun, S., Lebas, C., & Mercuri-Chapuis, S. (2020a). Types de RSE, types d'innovation: un bilan de travaux empiriques. In La responsabilité sociale des entreprises. Des relations sociales à la dimension stratégique, (pp. 113-128). Editions EMS. Management et Société. Collection Questions de société.

Kammoun, S., Loukil, S., & Ben Romdhane Loukil, Y. (2020b). The impact of Firm Performance and Corporate Governance on Corporate Social Responsibility: Evidence from France. In I. S. Paiva & L. C. Carvalho (Eds.), *Conceptual and Theoretical Approaches to Corporate Social Responsibility, Entrepreneurial Orientation, and Financial Performance* (pp. 266–288). IGI Global., doi:10.4018/978-1-7998-2128-1.ch014

Kammoun, S., Loukil, S., Ben Romdhane, Y., & Ibenrissoul, A. (2020c). The relationship between CSR, Corporate Governance and Firm Performance: Evidence from Moroccan listed firms. In I. S. Paiva & L. C. Carvalho (Eds.), *Conceptual and Theoretical Approaches to Corporate Social Responsibility, Entrepreneurial Orientation, and Financial Performance* (pp. 289–304). IGI Global., doi:10.4018/978-1-7998-2128-1.ch015

Kanchan, U., Kumar, N., & Gupta, A. (2015). Green Business-Way to Achieve Globally Sustainable Competitive Advantage. *Journal of Progressive Research in Social Sciences*, *2*(2), 92–100.

Kant, N. (2020c). Climate Strategy Proactivity (CSP) and its Theoretical Underpinnings. In W. L. Filho, A. M. Azul, L. Brandli, A. L. Salvia, & T. Wall (Eds.), Industry, Innovation and Infrastructure, Encyclopedia of the UN Sustainable Development Goals (Living Reference). Springer Nature. doi:10.1007/978-3-319-71059-4_122-1

Kant, N., & Anjali, K. (2020). Climate Strategy Proactivity (CSP): A Stakeholders-Centric Concept. In W. L. Filho, A. M. Azul, L. Brandli, A. L. Salvia, & T. Wall (Eds.), Partnerships for the Goals, Encyclopedia of the UN Sustainable Development Goals (Living Reference). Springer Nature. doi:10.1007/978-3-319-71067-9_121-1

Kant, N. (2020a). Actions beyond Regulatory Compliances: Perceived Climate Strategy Proactivity in Indian Companies. *International Journal of Development Issues*, *ahead-of-print*(ahead-of-print). Advance online publication. doi:10.1108/IJDI-07-2020-0152

Kant, N. (2020b). An analytical Study of Stakeholders' Relevance based on their Perceived Preference in terms of Climate Strategy Proactivity (CSP). *Competitiveness Review*. Advance online publication. doi:10.1108/CR-10-2020-0122

Kant, N. (2020d). Primary validation of climate strategy proactivity questionnaire scale measuring relationship of climate strategy proactivity with competitive advantage. *Management of Environmental Quality*. Advance online publication. doi:10.1108/MEQ-07-2020-0161

Kant, N., & Agrawal, N. (2020). Developing a Measure of Climate Strategy Proactivity Displayed to Attain Competitive Advantage. *Competitiveness Review, ahead-of-print*(ahead-of-print). Advance online publication. doi:10.1108/CR-06-2020-0079

Karmasin, M., & Litschka, M. (2017). CSR as economic, ethical and communicative concept. In S. Diehl & M. Karmasin (Eds.), *Handbook of Integrated CSR Communication*. Springer International Publishing. doi:10.1007/978-3-319-44700-1_3

Karyawati, P. G., Subroto, B., Sutrisno, T., & Saraswati, E. (2018). The Complexity of Relationship between Corporate Social Responsibility (CSR) and Financial Performance. *Emerging Markets Journal, 8*(2), 2018. doi:10.5195/emaj.2018.155

Kasasbeh, E. A., Harada, Y., & Noor, I. M. (2017). Factors Influencing Competitive Advantage in Banking Sector: A Systematic Literature Review. *Research Journal of Business Management, 11*(2), 67–73. doi:10.3923/rjbm.2017.67.73

Kates, R. W., Parris, T. M., & Leiserowitz, A. A. (2005). What is Sustainable Development? Goals, Indicators, Values, and Practice. *Environment, 47*(3).

Kaul, A., & Luo, J. (2016). An Economic Case for CSR: The Comparative Efficiency of For-Profit Firms in Meeting Consumer Demand for Social Goods. *Strategic Management Journal.*

Kautz, T., Heckman, J. J., Diris, R., Ter Weel, B., & Borghans, L. (2014). *Fostering and measuring skills: improving cognitive and non-cognitive skills to promote lifetime success.* NBER Working Paper, 20749. National Bureau of Economic Research.

Kelly, K. (2016). *The inevitable. Understanding the 12 technological Forces That Will Shape Our Future*. Academic Press.

Kemp, R., & Loorbach, D. (2003). *Governance for Sustainability through Transition Management.* Available at https://www.researchgate.net/profile/Derk_Loorbach/publication/2883708_Governance_for_Sustainability_Through_Transition_Management/links/02e7e51a74226aa52c000000/Governance-for-Sustainability-Through-Transition-Management.pdf

Kemp, R., & Rotmans, J. (2004). Managing the transition to sustainable mobility. In System innovation and the transition to sustainability. Theory, Evidence and Policy. Edward Elgar.

Khanna, M., & Liao, Y. (2014). Globalization and voluntary environmental management in developing countries. *Frontiers of Economics in China, 9*(1), 138–163.

Kiba-Janiak, M. (2015). A Comparative Analysis of Sustainable City Logistics among Capital Cities in the EU. *Applied Mechanics and Materials, 708*, 113–118. doi:10.4028/www.scientific.net/AMM.708.113

Kociszewski, K. (2013). Ekologizacja polskiego rolnictwa a jego zrównoważony rozwój w warunkach członkostwa w Unii Europejskiej. Wyd. UE we Wrocławiu, Wrocław.

Kolk, A., & Pinkse, J. (2005). Business Responses to Climate Change: Identifying Emergent Strategies. *California Management Review, 47*(3), 6–20. doi:10.2307/41166304

Kolk, A., & Pinkse, J. (2007). Towards strategic stakeholder management? Integrating perspectives on sustainability challenges such as corporate responses to climate change. *Corporate Governance: The International Journal of Business in Society*, *7*(4), 370–378. doi:10.1108/14720700710820452

Kooskora, M., Juottonen, M. & Cundiff, K. (2019). The Relationship Between Corporate Social Respon- sibility and Financial Performance (A Case Study from Finland). *Social Responsibility and Sustainability*, 471–491. doi:10.1007/978-3-030-03562-4_25

Korchakova-Heeb. (2020). *We Are Building An Airplane While Flying It*. BCG.

Kotler, P., Kartayaja, H., & Setiawan, I. (2017). *Marketing 4.0, Moving from Traditional to Digital*. J. Wiley & Sons.

Kozłowski, S. (2007). Przyszłość ekorozwoju. wyd. II, Wydawnictwo KUL, Lublin.

KPMG International Cooperative. (2020). *Banking on consumer platforms, Reshaping the banking experience*. Author.

KPMG. (2020). CEO Outlook: COVID-19. Special Edition. Executive summary. KPMG International.

KPMG. (2020, April). *Report: PSD2 and Open Banking. Revolution or evolution?* Retrieved from: https://ec.europa.eu/info/law/payment-services-psd-2-directive-eu-2015-2366_eu

Kuhl, P. K. (2010). Brain mechanisms in early language acquisition. *Neuron*, *67*(5), 713–727. doi:10.1016/j.neuron.2010.08.038 PMID:20826304

Kujala, S., Artto, K., Aaltonen, P., & Turkulainen, V. (2010). Business models in project - based firms - Towards a typology of solution - specific business models. *International Journal of Project Management*, *28*(2), 96–106. doi:10.1016/j.ijproman.2009.08.008

Küpper, Reichert, Reichert, Rastogi, & Kimura. (2020). *How CEOs Can Win the Fight and Transform to Win the Future*. Boston Consulting Group.

Labonté, R. (1991). Econology: Integrating health and sustainable development. Part one: Theory and background. *Health Promotion International*, *6*(1), 49–65. doi:10.1093/heapro/6.1.49

Lalanne, C. (2014). *Mechanical Vibration and Shock Analysis (3rd ed., vol. 5)*. Wiley.

Larsson, R. (1993). Case Survey Methodology: Quantitative Analysis of Patterns Across Case Studies. Academy of Management Journal, 36(6).

Laszlo, Ch. (2003). *The Sustainable Company: How to Create Lasting Value through Social and Environmental Performance*. Island Press.

Laverty, K. J. (1996). Economic 'Short-Termism': The Debate, the Unresolved Issues, and the Implications for Management Practice and Research. *Academy of Management Review*, *21*(3), 825–860.

Lebas, M. (1995). Oui, il faut définir la performance. *Revue française de comptabilité*, *269*, 66-71.

Lechner, N. (2014). *Heating, Cooling, Lighting: Sustainable Design Methods for Architects*. John Wiley & Sons Inc.

Lee, K. M. (1997). So What is the 'Triple Bottom Line'? *The International Journal of Diversity in Organisations, Communities and Nations, 6.*

Lepetit, M. (1997). *Performance globale: vers une prise en compte des effets non marchands. Commissariat Général du Plan, ouvrage collectif. In Entreprise et performance globale-outils, évaluation, pilotage*. Economica.

Levashova, Y. (2011). Role of Sustainable Development in Bilateral Investment Treaties: Recent Trends and Developments. *J. Sustain. Financ. Investig, 1*, 222–229.

Lim, T., & Horkova, M. (2019). *ESG Industry Report Card: Health Care.* S&P Global Ratings. https://www.spglobal.com/en/research-insights/articles/esg-industry-report-card-health-care

Linder, J., & Cantrell, S. (2000). *Changing Business Models: Surveying the Landscape*. Accenture Institute for Strategic Change.

Linnenluecke, M. K., & Griffiths, A. (2010). Corporate sustainability and organizational culture. *Journal of World Business, 45*(4), 357–366. doi:10.1016/j.jwb.2009.08.006

Liu, Y. (2014). *Research on the Negative Externalities and Compensation Mechanism of Coal Exploitation*. Institute of Technology.

Lonergan, E., & Blyth, M. (2020). *Angrynomics*. Columbia University Press. doi:10.2307/j.ctv13840ch

Lopes, C. M., Scavarda, A. J., Vaccaro, G. L. R., Pohlmann, Ch. R., & Korzenowski, A. L. (2019). Perspective of Business Models and Innovation for Sustainability Transition in Hospitals. *Perspective of Business Models and Innovation for Sustainability Transition in Hospitals Sustainability, 11*(1), 5. doi:10.3390u11010005

Lüdeke-Freund, F. (2010). Towards a Conceptual Framework of Business Models for Sustainability. In R. Wever, J. Quist, A. Tukker, J. Woudstra, F. Boons, & N. Beute, (Eds.), Knowledge Collaboration and Learning for Sustainable Innovation. Delft: Delft University of Technology.

Lüdeke-Freund, F. (2010). Towards a conceptual framework of 'business models for sustainability. In R. Wever, J. Quist, A. Tukker, J. Woudstra, F. Boons, & N. Beute (Eds.), *Knowledge Collaboration & Learning for Sustainable Innovation.* SSRN.

Lusawa, R. (2009). *Hans Carl Von Carlowitz twórca pojęcia "trwałości"*. Rocznik Naukowy Wydziału Zarządzania w Ciechanowie. Ekonomia i Finanse.

Mackie, J., Ronceray, M., & Spierings, E. (2017). *Policy coherence and the 2030 Agenda: Building on the PCD experience*. Discussion Paper 210. Maastricht: ECDPM.

Magretta, J. (2002). Why business models matter? *Harvard Business Review*, (5), 86–92. PMID:12024761

Malone, T. W. (2018). *Superminds. The Surprising Power of People and Computers Thinking Together.* Little, Brown Spark.

Malone, T., Weill, P., Lai, R. K., D'Urso, V. T., Herman, G., Apel, T. G., & Woerner, S. (2006). Do Some Business Models Perform Better than Others? MIT Working Paper 4615. doi:10.2139srn.920667

Mancebo, F. (2013). Développement durable (2nd ed.). Paris: Arman Colin.

Maor, D., Reich, A., & Yocarini, L. (2017). *The people power of transformations*. Mckinsey&Company.

Maqbool, S., & Zameer, M. N. (2017). An Empirical Examination of the Relationship between Corporate Social Responsibility and Profitability: Evidence from Indian Commercial Banks. *Pacific Business Review International, 9*(12), 39–47.

Margolis, J. D., Elfenbein, H. A., & Walsh, J. P. (2009). *Does It Pay to Be Good and Does It Matter? A Meta-Analysis of the Relationship between Corporate Social and Financial Performance.* Working paper.

Marí-Farinós, J. (2017). Sustainability as an object of corporate social responsibility. *VITRUVIO-International. Journal of Architectural Technology and Sustainability, 2*, 13–22.

Marion, A., Asquin, A., & Everaere, C. (2012). *Diagnostic de la performance de l'entreprise: Concepts et méthodes*. Dunod. doi:10.3917/dunod.mario.2012.01

Marx, K. (1995). *Capital: A New Abridgement*. Oxford University Press.

Marz, N., & Warren, J. (2015). *Big Data Best Practices of Scaling Data System in real time*. Manning Publication Co.

Material Economics. (2018). *The circular economy – A powerful force for climate mitigation. Transformative innovation for prosperous and low-carbon industry*. Academic Press.

Mattey, Hilberath, Sibilio, Aurora, & Ruiz. (2020). *Personalisation for Your People. How COVID-19 is reshaping the race for talent*. Boston Consulting Group.

Mattey, C., Hilberath, C., Sibilio, N., Aurora, J., & Ruiz, H. (2020). *Personalisation for your people: How COVID-19 is reshaping the race for talent*. June. Mckinsey & Company.

Matthes, J. (2007). *Framing-Effekte. Zum Einfluss der Politikberichterstattung auf die Einstellungen der Rezipienten*. Verlag Reinhard Fischer.

Mayer-Schönberger, V., & Cukier, K. (2013). *Big Data Effective Data Analysis, A revolution that will change our thinking, work and life*. MT Business Ltd.

McConnell, C., & Brue, S. (2008). *Economics* (17th ed.). McGraw-Hill.

McConnell, M., & Schaninger, B. (2019). *Are we long—or short—on talent? McKinsey Quarterly*.

McKeown, M. (2012). *The Strategy Book* (2nd ed.). Pearson.

McKinsey & Company. (2020, September). *AI-bank of the future: Can banks meet the AI challenge*. Author.

McKinsey Global Institute (MGI). (2020a). Climate risks and response: Physical hazards and socioeconomic impacts. *McKinsey Quarterly*.

McKinsey Global Institute. (2020). *Prioritizing health: A prescription for prosperity*. Executive summary. Author.

McMichael, A. J. (2006). Population health as the "bottom line" of sustainability: A contemporary challenge for public health researchers. *European Journal of Public Health*, *16*(6), 579–581. doi:10.1093/eurpub/ckl102 PMID:16857691

Menguc, B., Auh, S., & Ozanne, L. (2010). The interactive effect of internal and external factors on a proactive environmental strategy and its influence on a firm's performance. *Journal of Business Ethics*, *94*(2), 279–298. doi:10.100710551-009-0264-0

Mercier, S. (2001). *L'apport de la théorie des parties prenantes au management stratégique: une synthèse de la littérature*. Xième Conférence de l'Association Internationale de Management Stratégique.

MGI. (2020b). Confronting climate risk. *McKinsey Quarterly*.

MGI. (2020c). *Leading the battle against climate change: Action for China*. McKinsey and Company.

Michelini, G., Moraes, R. N., Cunha, R. N., Costa, J. M. H., & Ometto, A. R. (2017). From linear to circular economy: PSS conducting the transition. *Procedia CIRP*, *64*, 2–6. doi:10.1016/j.procir.2017.03.012

Mierzejewska, L. (2009). Rozwój zrównoważony miasta: zagadnienia poznawcze i praktyczne. Wydaw. Naukowe Uniwersytetu im. Adama Mickiewicza, Poznań.

Migliorelli, M. (2018). *New Cooperative Banking in Europe Strategies for Adapting the Business Model Post Crisis*. Palgrave Macmillan. doi:10.1007/978-3-319-93578-2

Miklaszewska, E., & Folwarski, M. (2020). *Emotional banking. Digital transformation of banks and customer expectations*. Poltex.

Milanovich, B. (2019). *Capitalism, Alone. The Future of the System That Rules the World*. The Belknap Press of Harvard University Press. doi:10.4159/9780674242852

Milne, M., & Gray, R. (2013). W(h)ither Ecology? The Triple Bottom Line, the Global Reporting Initiative, and Corporate Sustainability, *Reporting*: *Journal of Business Ethics*, *118*(1), 13–29. doi:10.100710551-012-1543-8

Mintzberg, H., Ahlstrand, B., & Lampel, J. (1998). *Strategy Safari: A Guided Tour Through the Wilds of Strategic Management*. Free Press.

Mintz, S. M. (2011). Triple Bottom Line Reporting for CPAs. *The CPA Journal*, *81*(12), 26–33.

Misztal, A. (2019a). Zrównoważony rozwój przedsiębiorstw a stopień rozwoju społeczno-gospodarczego. *Studia i Prace Kolegium Zarządzania i Finansów*, *174*, 33-45.

Misztal, A. (2019b). *Stabilizacja makroekonomiczna a zrównoważony rozwój przedsiębiorstw – przypadek*. Bułgarii, Czech, Polski i Rumunii. Studia Prawno-Ekonomiczne.

Mitchell, R. K., Agle, B. R., & Wood, D. J. (1997). Toward a Theory of Stakeholder Identification and Salience:Defining the Principle of Who and What Really Counts. *Academy of Management Journal*, *22*(4), 853–886.

MobirankR. (2018). Retrieved from:https://mobirank.pl/2018/02/02/mobile-i-digital-w-2018-roku-w-polsce-i-na-swiecie/

Moreno, C. E., & Reyes, J. F. (2013). The Value of Proactive Environmental Strategy: An Empirical Evaluation of the Contingent Approach To Dynamic Capabilities. *Cuadernos Americanos*, *26*(47), 87–118.

Mory, L., Wirtz, B. W., & Göttel, V. (2016). Factors of internal corporate social responsibility and the effect on organizational commitment. *International Journal of Human Resource Management*, *27*(13), 1393–1425. doi:10.1080/09585192.2015.1072103

Mouatassim, L. & Ibenrissoul, A. (2016). *Y a-t-il un impact de la RSE sur la performance financière de l'entreprise: Etude empirique sur les Sociétés marocaines cotées à la bourse de Casablanca*. hal-01351951/document.

Murillo-Luna, J. L., Garces-Ayerbe, C., & Rivera-Torres, P. (2008). Why do patterns of environmental response differ? A stakeholders' pressure approach. *Strategic Management Journal*, *29*(11), 1225–1240. doi:10.1002mj.711

Murray, A., Skene, K., & Haynes, K. (2017). The circular economy: An interdisciplinary exploration of the concept and application in a global context. *Journal of Business Ethics*, *140*(3), 369–380. doi:10.100710551-015-2693-2

Musco, C., Musco, C., & Tsourakakis, C. E. (2018). Minimizing Polarization and Disagreement in Social Networks. In *Proceedings of the 2018 World Wide Web Conference (WWW '18)*. International World Wide Web Conferences Steering Committee. 10.1145/3178876.3186103

Musgrave, R. (1988). The role of the state in the fiscal theory. In P. B. Sorensen (Ed.), *Public Finance in a Changing World* (p. 105). Macmillan.

Mutuku, C. (2012). *Monetary and Fiscal Policy Shocks: VAR Econometrics*. Lambert Academic Publishing.

Neisser, U., Boodoo, G., Bouchard, T. J. Jr, Boykin, A. W., Brody, N., Ceci, S. J., Halpern, D. F., Loehlin, J. C., Perloff, R., Sternberg, R. J., & Urbina, S. (1996). Intelligence: Knowns and unknowns. *The American Psychologist*, *51*(2), 77–101. doi:10.1037/0003-066X.51.2.77

Newman, C., Rand, J., Tarp, F. & Trifkovic, N. (2019). Corporate Social Responsibility in a Competitive Business Environment. *The Journal of Development Studies*, *56*(8), 1455-1472. doi:10.1080/00220388.2019.1694144

Nguyen, H., Stuchtey, M., & Zils, M. (2014). *Remaking the industrial economy*. Available at https://www.McKinsey.com

Nielsen, N. C., Dotiwala, F., & Murray, M. (2020). *A transformation of thelearning function: Why it should learn new ways. In McKinsey Accelerate*. McKinsey & Company.

Nikolakis, W., Cohen, D. H., & Nelson, H. W. (2012). What Matters for Socially Responsible Investment (SRI) in the Natural Resources Sectors? SRI Mutual Funds and Forestry in North America. *J. Sustain. Financ. Investig*, *2*, 136–151.

Norme, I. S. O. 26000. (2010). *Responsabilité sociétale*. https://www.iso.org/fr/iso-26000-social-responsibility.html

Norms on the Responsibilities of Transnational Corporations and Other Business Enterprises with regard to Human Rights. (2003). https://digitallibrary.un.org/record/501576

Nosratabadi, S., Mosavi, A., Shamshirband, S., Kazimieras Zavadskas, E., Rakotonirainy, A., & Chau, K. W. (2019). Sustainable Business Models: A Review. *Sustainability*, *11*(6), 1663. doi:10.3390u11061663

ODA. (1995). *Guidance Note on How to do Stakeholder Analysis of Aid Projects and Programmes*. Retrieved July 9, 2018, from https://beamexchange.org/uploads/filer_public/5d/4c/5d4c7b02-a25d-43ab-ae33-0e4811b7c5fb/guidance_stakeholderanalysis.pdf

OECD. (2011). *OECD Guidelines for Multinational Enterprises*. OECD Publishing. http://www.oecd.org/investment/mne/1922428.pdf doi:10.1787/9789264115415-en

OECD. (2016). *Global Competency for an Inclusive World*. Retrieved from: https://www.oecd.org/pisa/aboutpisa/Global-competency-for-an-inclusive-world.pdf

OECD. (2018). *Global material resources outlook to 2060 - Economic drivers and environmental consequences*. OECD.

OECD. (2019). *Growth Is Taking a Dangerous Downward Turn*. Ecoscope Blog, September 19. Retrieved from: https://oecdecoscope.blog/2019/09/19/growth-is-taking-a-dangerous-downward-turn/.

Okamoto, G. (2020). Knightmare Uncertainty. *IMF Finance & Development, 57*(3).

Omer, S.K. (2018). The impact of corporate social responsibility on employee's job satisfaction. Journal of Process Management. *New Technologies*, *6*(3), 56-64.

Orlitzky, M., Frank, L., Schmidt, F. L., Sara, L., & Rynes, S. L. (2003). Corporate social and financial performance: A meta-analysis. *Organization Studies*, *24*(3), 403–441.

Osterwalder, A., & Pigneur, Y. (2010). *Business Model Generation: A Handbook for Visionaries, Game Changers, and Challengers*. John Wiley and Sons, Inc.

Osterwalder, A., Pigneur, Y., & Tucci, C. (2005). Clarifying Business Models: Origins, Present, and Future of the Concept. *Communications of the Association for Information Systems*, *16*(1). Advance online publication. doi:10.17705/1CAIS.01601

Pasquero, J. (2005). La responsabilité sociale de l'entreprise comme objet des sciences de gestion: un regard historique. In Responsabilité sociale et environnementale de l'entreprise, (pp. 80-111). Presses de l'Université du Québec.

Pasquero, J. (1997). Business ethics and national identity in Quebec: Distinctiveness and directions. *Journal of Business Ethics*, *16*(6), 621–633.

Pasquero, J. (2004). Responsabilités sociales de l'entreprise: Les approches nord-américaines. In *Jacques Igalens (dir.), Tous responsables*. Éditions d'Organisation.

Paszkiewicz, A., Szadziewska, A. (2011). Raportowanie rozwoju zrównoważonego przedsiębiorstw według wytycznych GRI. *Zeszyty Naukowe Uniwersytetu Szczecińskiego, Finanse, Rynki Finansowe, Ubezpieczenia*, *41*(668), 627-643.

Patterson, G. (2020). *How to get your company strategy ready for the Great Reset.* World Economic Forum.

Pearce, D. (1992). Green economics. *Environmental Values*, *1*(1), 3–13. doi:10.3197/096327192776680179

Pearce, D., & Turner, R. K. (1990). *Economics of Natural Resources and Environment*. HarvesterWheatsheaf.

Pelenc, J., & Ballet, J. (2015). *Weak Sustainability versus Strong Sustainability*. Brief for GSDR.

Perianes-Rodriguez, A., Waltman, L., & van Eck, N. J. (2016). Constructing Bibliometric Networks: A Comparison of between Full and Fractional Counting. *Journal of Informetrics*, *10*(4), 1–30. doi:10.1016/j.joi.2016.10.006

Pezzey, J. (1992). *Definitions of Sustainability.* UK Center for Economic and Environmental Development, Working Paper No. 9.

Piaget, J. V. F. (2008). *The Psychology of Intelligence*. Direct-Media.

Pilipenko, A. I. (1997). *Cognitive barriers in teaching physics and methodological principles for overcoming them.* The Dissertation Abstract for a Scientific Degree of Doctor of Pedagogics. Moscow: Russian Academy of Education Publisher.

Pilipenko, A. I. (2015). *Innovative Models of Education: The Aspect of Psychological and Cognitive Barriers.* http://ssrn.com/abstract=2597968

Pilipenko, A. I. (2020). Education and theory of psychological and cognitive barriers: human capital as driver of stable economic growth. In Social, Economic, and Environmental Impacts Between Sustainable Financial Systems and Financial Markets. IGI Global. doi:10.4018/978-1-7998-1033-9.ch011

Pilipenko, A., Pilipenko, O., & Pilipenko, Z. (2019). Education and inclusive development: puzzle of low-learning equilibrium. In Modeling Economic Growth in Contemporary Russia. Bradford, UK: Emerald Publishing Limited. doi:10.1108/978-1-78973-265-820191006

Pilipenko, O.I., Pilipenko, Z.A., & Pilipenko, A.I. (n.d.). *Theory of Shocks, COVID-19, and Normative Fundamentals for Policy Responses: Emerging Research and Opportunities*. IGI Global Publishers.

Pilipenko, Z. A. (2020). Shocks' theory: financial mechanism of economic systems' destabilization In: Edited by Magdalena Ziolo. In Social, Economic, and Environmental Impacts Between Sustainable Financial Systems and Financial Markets. IGI Global.

Pilipenko, Z. A. (2020). Shocks' theory: financial mechanism of economic systems' destabilization. In Social, Economic, and Environmental Impacts Between Sustainable Financial Systems and Financial Markets. IGI Global.

Pilipenko, A. I., & Solomenik, V. D. (1999). *To the Future Teacher About the Psychological and Cognitive Barriers: Tutorial*. Publishing House of Bryansk Pedagogical University.

Pilipenko, O. I., & Pilipenko, A. I. (2020). Mysteries of unsustainable public finance and of low economic growth. In M. Ziolo (Ed.), *Social, Economic, and Environmental Impacts Between Sustainable Financial Systems and Financial Markets*. IGI Global. doi:10.4018/978-1-7998-1033-9.ch009

Pilipenko, Z. A. (2016). Impulse transmission model of macroeconomic cycle within the framework of the theory of shocks: aspect of economic security. In *Dependability Engineering and Complex Systems: Advances in Intelligent Systems and Computing* (Vol. 470). Springer International Publishing Switzerland. doi:10.1007/978-3-319-39639-2_32

Pilipenko, Z. A., & Pilipenko, A. I. (2018). Shocks in global economy: impulse model of macroeconomic cycle. In B. S. Sergi, F. Fidanoski, M. Zioło, & V. Naumovski (Eds.), *Regaining Global Stability After the Financial Crisis*. Advances in Finance, Accounting, and Economics. IGI Global. doi:10.4018/978-1-5225-4026-7.ch012

Pinsky, A.A. (1978). Methodology as a science. *Soviet Pedagogy, 12.*

Płachciak, A. (2011). Geneza idei zrównoważonego rozwoju. *Ekonomia*, *5*(17), 231–248.

Płaczek, E. (2012). Zrównoważony rozwój – nowym wyzwaniem dla współczesnych operatorów logistycznych. *Prace Naukowe Politechniki Warszawskiej Transport*, *84*, 79–92.

PN-EN ISO 22301:2020-04 (ISO) (2020) Bezpieczeństwo powszechne - Systemy zarządzania ciągłością działania – Wymagania.

Porter, M.E. & Kramer, M.R. (2006). Strategy and Society: The Link Between Competitive Advantage and Corporate Social Responsibility. *Harvard Business Review*, *84*(12), 78-92.

Porter, M. E. (1980). *Competitive Strategy*. Free Press.

Porter, M. E. (1985). *Competitive Advantage*. Free Press.

Porter, M. E., & Kramer, M. R. (2006, December). Strategy and Society: The Link Between Competitive Advantage and Corporate Social Responsibility. *Harvard Business Review*, 78–92.

Porter, M. E., & Kramer, M. R. (2011). Creating shared value: How to reinvent capitalism – and unleash a wave of innovation and growth. *Harvard Business Review*, *89*(1-2), 62–77.

Portney, P. R. (2008). The (Not So) New Corporate Social Responsibility: An Empirical Perspective. *Review of Environmental Economics and Policy*, *2*(2), 261–275.

Poskrobko, B. (2009). Współczesne trendy cywilizacyjne a idea zrównoważonego rozwoju. *Przegląd Komunalny*, *6*, 7–16.

Postel, N., & Sobel, R. (2019). Corporate social responsibility (CSR): An institutionalist Polanyian analysis. *Society and Business Review*, *14*(4), 381–400.

Prada, G. (2012). Sustainability: What Does This Mean for Canada's Health Care Systems. *Proceedings of the Collaborative Meeting of the Conference Board of Canada's Health-Related Executive Networks.*

Pranov B.M., & Rassokhina T.V. (2019). Methodological approaches to the adaptation of the system of global indicators of achieving the goals in the field of sustainable development in the Russian Federation. *Modern Economy Success, 1,* 19-152.

Prescott, M. E. (2014). Big data and competitive advantage at Nielsen. *Management Decision*, *52*(3), 573–601. doi:10.1108/MD-09-2013-0437

Preston, F., & Lehne, J. (2017). *A wider circle? The circular economy in developing countries.* https://www.chathamhouse.org/sites/default/files/publications/research/2017-12-05-circular-economy-preston-lehne-final.pdf

Preston, F., Lehne, J., Wellesley, L., & Sugathan, M. (2019). An inclusive circular economy: Priorities for developing countries. The Royal Institute of International Affairs, Chatham House.

Pritchett, L. (2013). *The Rebirth of Education: Schooling Ain't Learning*. Centre for Global Development, Brookings Institution Press.

Prno, J. (2013). An analysis of factors leading to the establishment of a social license to operate in the mining industry. *Resources Policy, Elsevier*, *38*(4), 577–590. doi:10.1016/j.resourpol.2013.09.010

Qadir, S. A., & Gorman, H. S. (2008). The use of ISO 14001 in India: More than a certificate on the wall? *Environmental Practice*, *10*(2), 53–65. doi:10.1017/S1466046608080174

Ramkumar, S., Kraanen, F., Plomp, R., Edgerton, B., Walrecht, A., Baer, I., & Hirsch, P. (2018) Linear risks. *Amst. Circular Economy*, 9. https://www.ebrd.com/news/publications/essays-and-glossaries/ linear-risk-business-impacts-of-linear-consumption-practices.htm

Rappa, M. (2004). The utility business model and the future of computing services. *IBM Systems Journal*, *43*(1), 32–42. doi:10.1147j.431.0032

Ravi, S. P. (2013). Does Stakeholder Perception of Firm's Corporate Social Responsibility Affect Firm Performance? *International Journal of Asian Business and Information Management*, *4*(1), 67–83. doi:10.4018/jabim.2013010107

Redefine banking with Artificial Intelligence. (2020). Retrieved from: https://www.accenture.com/_acnmedia/pdf-68/accenture-redefine-banking.pdf

Reed, D. (1999). Stakeholder management theory: A critical theory perspective. *Business Ethics Quarterly*, *9*(03), 453–483.

Reed, M. S., Graves, A., Dandy, N., Posthumus, H., Hubacek, K., Morris, J., Prell, C., Quinn, C. H., & Stringer, L. C. (2009). Who's in and why? A typology of stakeholder analysis methods for natural resource management. *Journal of Environmental Management*, *90*(5), 1933–1949. doi:10.1016/j.jenvman.2009.01.001 PMID:19231064

Reeves, M., Kell, G., & Hassan, F. (2018). The Case for Corporate Statesmanship. The Boston Consulting Group. Henderson Institute.

Reichel, A., De Schoenmakere, M., & Gillabel, J. (2016). *Circular economy in Europe, developing the knowledge base*. European Environmental Agency.

Rendlen, B., & Weber, B. (n.d.). *Integrating ESG factors into financial models for infrastructure investments*. WWF Switzerland Guidance Note. http://awsassets.panda.org/downloads/wwf_guidance_note_infra_.pdf

Revelli, C. & Viviani, J.L. (2015). Financial performance of socially responsible investing (SRI): what have we learned? *A meta-analysis Business Ethics: A European Review*, *24*(2), 158-185.

Reynaud, E. (2003). Développement durable et entreprise: Vers une relation symbiotique. *Journée AIMS, Atelier développement durable. ESSCA Angers*, *15*, 1–15.

Rezende de Carvalho Ferreira, M. C., Amorim Sobreiro, V., Kimura, H., & Luiz de Moraes Barboza, F. A. (2016). Systematic review of literature about finance and sustainability. *J. Sustain. Financ. Investig*, *6*(2), 112–147. doi:10.1080/20430795.2016.1177438

Rhou, Y., Singal, M., & Koh, Y. (2016). CSR and Financial Performance: The Role of CSR Awareness in the Restaurant Industry. *International Journal of Hospitality Management*, *57*(1), 30–39.

Rizos, V., Elkerbout, M., & Egenhofer, C. (2019). *Circular economy for climate neutrality: Setting the priorities for the EU*. CEPS Policy Brief No 2019/04.

Robèrt, K., Schmidt-Bleekh, B., Larderelc, J., Basilede, G., Jansenf, J. L., Kuehrg, R., ... Wackernagelj, M. (2002). Strategic sustainable development - Selection, design and synergies of applied tools. *Journal of Cleaner Production, 10*(3), 10. doi:10.1016/S0959-6526(01)00061-0

Roca, L., & Searcy, C. (2012). An analysis of indicators disclosed in corporate sustainability reports. *Journal of Cleaner Production, 20*(1), 103–118. doi:10.1016/j.jclepro.2011.08.002

Rodrigues, V. P., Pigosso, D., & McAloone, T. (2016). Process-related key performance indicators for measuring sustainability performance of ecodesign implementation into product development. *Journal of Cleaner Production, 139*, 416–428. doi:10.1016/j.jclepro.2016.08.046

Rodriguez-Gomez, S., Arco-Castro, M. L., Lopez-Perez, M. V., & Rodríguez-Ariza, L. (2020). Where Does CSR Come from and Where Does It Go? A Review of the State of the Art. *Administrative Sciences, 10*(3), 60. https://dx.doi.org/10.3390/admsci10030060

Roling, N. G. (2000). *Facilitating sustainable agriculture: participatory learning and adaptive management in times of environmental uncertainty*. Cambridge University Press.

Romer, P. M. (1986, October). Increasing returns and long-run growth. *Journal of Political Economy, 94*(5), 1002–1037. doi:10.1086/261420

Ross Baker, G., Norton, P. G., Flintoft, V., Blais, R., Brown, A., Cox, J., Etchells, E., Ghali, W. A., Hébert, P., Majumdar, S. R., O'Beirne, M., Palacios-Derflingher, L., Reid, R. J., Sheps, S., & Tamblyn, R. (2004). The Canadian Adverse Events Study: The incidence of adverse events among hospital patients in Canada. *Canadian Medical Association Journal, 170*(11), 1678–1686. doi:10.1503/cmaj.1040498 PMID:15159366

Rostam, B. (2017). *Stock Markets and Oil Price Shocks*. Lambert Academic Publishing.

Roszkowska, E. (2011). Multi-Criteria Decision Making Models by applying the TOPSIS method to crisp and interval data. *Multiple Criteria Decision Making, 6.*

Rózicka, K., & Cieślak, M. (2013). Zrównoważone innowacje – studia przypadków firm polskich i zagranicznych. In Wspólna odpowiedzialność. Rola innowacji, Forum Odpowiedzialnego Biznesu. Warszawa.

Rudnicki, A. (2010). Zrównoważona mobilność a rozwój przestrzenny miasta. *Czasopismo Techniczne. Architektura, 107*(1-A), 57–74.

Ruggie, J. (2008). *Protect, Respect and Remedy: a Framework for Business and Human Rights*. https://media.business-humanrights.org/media/documents/files/reports-and-materials/Ruggie-report-7-Apr-2008.pdf

Russo, M. V., & Fouts, P. A. (1997). A resource-based perspective on corporate environmental performance and profitability. *Academy of Management Journal, 40*, 534–559.

Saari, U. A., Aarikka-Stenroos, L., Boedeker, S., Köppä, L., & Langwaldt, J. (2017). Assessing the usefulness of an early idea development tool among experienced researchers. *CERN ideaSquare Journal of Experimental Innovation, 1*(2), 3.

Saari, U. A., Aarikka-Stenroos, L., Köppä, L., Langwaldt, J., Boedeker, S., & Mäkinen, S. J. (2019). Sustainable Business Model Ideation and Development of Early Ideas for Sustainable Business Models: Analyzing a New Tool Facilitating the Ideation Process. In A. Aagaard (Ed.), *Sustainable Business Models*. Innovation, Implementation and Success. doi:10.1007/978-3-319-93275-0_5

Sachs, J. D., & Larrain, F. B. (1993). *Macroeconomics in the Global Economy*. Prentice Hall.

Sandbu, M. (2020). *The Economics of Belonging*. Princeton University Press.

Sandhu, S., Smallman, C., Ozanne, L. K., & Cullen, R. (2012). Corporate Environmental Responsiveness in India: Lessons from a Developing Country. *Journal of Cleaner Production, 35*, 203–213. doi:10.1016/j.jclepro.2012.05.040

Saviano, M., Bassano, C., Piciocchi, P., Di Nauta, P., & Lettieri, M. (2018). Monitoring Viability and Sustainability in Healthcare Organizations. *Sustainability, 10*(10), 3548. doi:10.3390u10103548

Scalia, M., Barile, S., Saviano, M., & Farioli, F. (2018). Governance for Sustainability: A triple Helix Model. *Sustainability Science, 13*(5), 1235–1244. doi:10.100711625-018-0567-0

Schaltegger, S., Hansen, E. G., & Lüdeke-Freund, F. (2012). Business cases for sustainability and the role of business model innovation. *International Journal of Innovation and Sustainable Development, 6*(2), 95–119. doi:10.1504/IJISD.2012.046944

Schaltegger, S., Hansen, E. G., & Lüdeke-Freund, F. (2016). *Business Models for Sustainability: Origins, Present Research, and Future Avenues.* SAGE Publications Sage CA.

Schaltegger, S., Luedeke-Freund, F., & Hansen, E. (2016). Business Models for Sustainability: A Co-Evolutionary Analysis of Sustainable Entrepreneurship, Innovation, and Transformation. *Organization & Environment, 29*(3), 264–289. doi:10.1177/1086026616633272

Schaltegger, S., & Synnestvedt, T. (2002). The link between 'green' and economic success: Environmental management as the crucial trigger between environmental and economic performance. *Journal of Environmental Management, 65*(4), 339–346. PMID:12369398

Scherer, A. G., & Palazzo, G. (2007). Toward a Political Conception of Corporate Responsibility: Business and Society Seen from a Habermasian Perspective. *Academy of Management Review, 32*(4).

Schleicher, A., & Ramos, G. (2016). *Global Competency for an Inclusive World.* OECD. Retrieved from: https://www.oecd.org/pisa/aboutpisa/Global-competency-for-an-inclusive-world.pdf

Schmidt, T. M. (2005). Transnational corporate responsibility for international environmental and human rights violations: Will the United Nations' "Norms" provide the required means? *California Western International Law Journal, 36*(217).

Schönfeld, M. (2017). *Work Readiness Assessment Tools in Comparison: From Administration to Z-scores.* World Bank.

Schroeder, P., Anantharaman, M., Anggraeni, K., & Foxon, T. J. (2019). The circular economy and the global South: Sustainable lifestyles and green industrial development. Abingdon: Routledge.

Schroeder, P., Anggraeni, K., & Weber, U. (2018). The relevance of circular economy practices to the sustainable development goals. *Journal of Industrial Ecology, 23*(1), 77–95. doi:10.1111/jiec.12732

Schumpeter, J. A. (1949). The Theory of Economic Development: An Inquiry into Profits, Capital, Credit, Interest, and the Business Cycle. Cambridge, MA: Harvard University Press.

Schumpeter, J. (1960). *The Theory of Economic Development.* PWN.

Schwab, K. (2016). *The fourth Industrial revolution.* Deloitte, World Economic Forum.

Schwab, K., & Malleret, T. (2020). *COVID-19's legacy: This is how to get the Great Reset right. In Sustainable Development Impact Summit.* WEF.

Schwaerzler, Henderon, Patel, Manetti, Chin, Rathore, Mahmoudi, & Osman. (2020). *Beyond the Curve. How Governments Can Galvanize their Nations for the Rebound.* Boston Consulting Group.

Schwerdtle, P. N. (2019). Circular economy and environmental health in low- and middle-income countries. *Globalization and Health, 15*(1), 65. doi:10.118612992-019-0501-y PMID:31847867

Seddon, R. B., Lewis, G. R., Freeman, R., & Shanks, G. (2004). The case for viewing business models as abstractions of strategy. *Communications of the Association for Information Systems, 13*, 427–442. doi:10.17705/1CAIS.01325

Sepetis, A. (2020). Sustainable Finance in Sustainable Health Care System. *Open Journal of Business and Management, 8*(01), 262–281. doi:10.4236/ojbm.2020.81016

Sexton, M. G., Barrett, P. S., & Lu, S. L. (2008). The evolution of sustainable development. University of Salford.

Shamir, S. (2004). Between self-regulation and the Alien Tort Claims Act: On the contested concept of Corporate Social Responsibility. *Law & Society Review, 38*(635), 635–664. doi:10.1111/j.0023-9216.2004.00062.x

Sharan, A. D., Schroeder, G. D., West, M. E., & Vaccaro, A. R. (2016). Understanding Business Models in Health Care. *Clinical Spine Surgery, 29*(4), 158–160. doi:10.1097/BSD.0000000000000380 PMID:27018909

Sharma, S., & Henriques, I. (2005). Stakeholder Influences on Sustainability Practices in the Canadian Forest Products Industry. *Strategic Management Journal, 26*(2), 159–180. doi:10.1002mj.439

Singh, N. (2015). *Environmental Determinants and Their Impact in Various Indian Industries: A Study of Environmental Performance under EMS Framework* (Doctoral Dissertation). Department of Natural Resources Management, TERI University.

Singh, N., Jain, S., & Sharma, P. (2014). Determinants of proactive environmental management practices in Indian firms: An empirical study. *Journal of Cleaner Production, 66*, 469–478. doi:10.1016/j.jclepro.2013.11.055

Skinner, C. (2018). *Digital Human: The Fourth Revolution of Humanity Includes Everyone*. Academic Press.

Skowrońska, A. (2010). *Rola polityki logistycznej państwa we wdrażaniu zrównoważonego rozwoju.* Uniwersytet Ekonomiczny we Wrocławiu.

Slobodchicov, V. I., & Isaev, E. I. (1995). Human Psychology. Academic Press.

Slobodchicov, V. I., & Isaev, E. I. (2000). Psychology of Human Development. Academic Press.

Slobodchicov, V. I., & Isaev, E. I. (2013). Psychology of Human Education. Formation of Subjectivity in Educational Processes. Moscow: Academic Press.

Slutsky, E. (1937). The summation of random causes as the source of cyclic processes. Econometrica, 5(2), 105–146.

Slutsky, E. (1927b). The summation of random causes as the source of cyclic processes. The Questions of Conjuncture. Conjuncture Institute of Moscow.

Slutsky, E. E. (1927a). The accumulation of accidental causes as the source of cyclic processes. In *Problems of Economic Conditions*. Conjuncture Institute publishing house.

Smith, M. E. F. (2012). *Sustainable Healthcare. A path to sustainability.* The International Institute for Industrial Environmental Economics. https://lup.lub.lu.se/student-papers/search/publication/3126175

Smit, S., Hirt, M., Dash, P., Lucas, A., Latkovic, T., Wilson, M., Greenberg, E., Buehler, K., & Hjartar, K. (2020). *Crushing coronavirus uncertainty: The big 'unlock' for our economies. To safeguard lives and livelihoods, we must restore confidence. In Strategy & Corporate Finance Practice*. McKinsey & Company.

Smolyansky, M. (2016). Policy Externalities and Banking Integration; Finance and Economics. Discussion Series 2016-008, Board of Governors of the Federal Reserve System.

Spence, M. (2019, July). *Impact of the form of revolution on welfare.* Retrieved from: https://www.obserwatorfinansowy.pl/bez-kategorii/rotator/wplyw-cyfrowej-rewolucji-na-dobrobyt/

Spitzer, W. J., & Dawidson, K. W. (2013). *Future Trends in Health and Health Care.* Implications for Social Work Practice in an Aging Society., doi:10.1080/00981389.2013.834028

Srinival, V., & Schoeps, J.T. (2019, December). *Platform banking as a new business model.* Deloitte Center for FS.

Stahel, W. R. (2016). The circular economy. *Nature: International weekly. Journal of Science, 531*(7595).

Stanwick, P. A., & Stanwick, S. D. (1998). The relationship between corporate social performance, and organizational size, financial performance, and environmental performance: An empirical examination. *Journal of Business Ethics, 17*(2), 195–204.

Steg, L., & Gifford, R. (2005). Sustainable Transportation and Quality of Life. *Journal of Transport Geography, 13*(Special Issue), 59–69. doi:10.1016/j.jtrangeo.2004.11.003

Steure, R., Langer, M. E., Konrad, A., & Martinuzzi, A. (2005). Corporations, stakeholders and sustainable development I: A theoretical exploration of business-society relations,ʃ *Journal of Business Ethics, 61*(3), 263–281. doi:10.100710551-005-7054-0

Stubbs, W., & Cocklin, Ch. (2008). Conceptualizing a “sustainability business model”. *Organization & Environment, 21*(2), 103–127. doi:10.1177/1086026608318042

Sultan, A. S. (2014). Financial Statements Analysis - Measurement of Performance and Profitability: Applied Study of Baghdad Soft-Drink Industry. *Research Journal of Finance and Accounting, 5*(4), 49–56.

Sundaram, A. M. (2016). *Measurement of Externalities for Renewable Energy Investment; Instituto Superior Técnico.* Universidade de Lisboa.

Surma, J. (2017). *Digitization of life in the era of Big Data.* Academic Press.

Susskind, D. (2020). How will the world be different after COVID-19? *Finance & Development. A Quarterly Publication of the IMF, 57*(2), 26-27.

Sustainability Accounting Standards Board (SASB). (2020). *SASB Materiality Map.* https://materiality.sasb.org/

Sustainability Leaders. (2019). *The GlobeScan-SustainAbility Survey.* http://odpowiedzialnybiznes.pl/wp-content/uploads/2019/07/the-2019-sustainability-leaders-the-globescan-sustainability-survey.pdf

Sustainability Leaders. (2020). *The GlobeScan-SustainAbility Survey.* https://globescan.com/wp-content/uploads/2020/08/GlobeScan-SustainAbility-Leaders-Survey-2020-Report.pdf

Sutcliffe, H. (2020). COVID-19: The 4 building blocks of the Great Reset. In *Sustainable Development Impact Summit.* World Economic Forum.

Suter, C. (1992). *Debt Cycles in the World-Economy. Foreign Loans, Financial Crises, and Debt Settlements, 1820-1990.* Westview Press, Inc.

Suto, M., & Takehara, H. (2020). Corporate social responsibility intensity, management earnings forecast accuracy, and investor trust: Evidence from Japan. *Corporate Social Responsibility and Environmental Management, 27*(6), 3047–3059. doi:10.1002/csr.2022

Szpringer, W. (2019). *Blockchain as a system innovation, Challenges for financial sector.* Poltext.

Tanzi, V. (2011). *Government versus Markets: The Changing Economic Role of the State.* Cambridge: Syndicate of the Press of the University of Cambridge.

Teece, D. I. (2010). Business Model, Business Strategy and Innovation. *Long Range Planning, 43*(2-3), 172–194. doi:10.1016/j.lrp.2009.07.003

Tempels, T., Blok, V., & Verweij, M. (2017). Understanding political responsibility in corporate citizenship: Towards a shared responsibility for the common good. *Journal of Global Ethics, 13*(1), 90–108. doi:10.1080/17449626.2017.1320577

The best banking app. (2020). Retrieved from: https://www.thefirstnews.com/article/youre-simply-the-best-pko-bank-polski-app-takes-top-spot-in-global-ranking-4783

The business case for inclusive growth. (2018). Deloitte Global Inclusive Growth Survey.

The Economist. (2020). *Covid-19 and the crisis for higher education.* Report. London: The Economist.

The Economist. (2020a). *Leading From Afar. The new world of work calls for a more creative and adaptable approach to leadership.* London: The Economist Intelligence Unit Limited.

The Global Sullivan Principles. (n.d.). http://hrlibrary.umn.edu/links/sullivanprinciples.html

The Stanley Foundation. (2017). *The circular economy pathway to pursuing 1.5°C.* Available at https://www.stanley-foundation.org/resources.cfm?id=1630

Thietard, R. (2014). *Méthodes de recherche en Management.* Dunod.

Torugsa, N. A., O'Donohue, W., & Hecker, R. (2013). Proactive CSR: An empirical analysis of the role of its economic, social and environmental dimensions on the association between capabilities and performance. *Journal of Business Ethics, 115*(2), 383–402. doi:10.100710551-012-1405-4

Tran, K. T., & Nguyen, P. V. (2020). Corporate Social Responsibility: Findings from the Vietnamese Paint Industry. *Sustainability, 12*(3), 1044. https://doi.org/10.3390/su12031044

Transforming Our World. (2015). *The 2030 Agenda for Global Action United Nations.* A/RES/70/1. Available at https://www.unfpa.org/sites/default/files/resource-pdf/Resolution_A_RES_70_1_EN.pdf

Trojanowski, T. (2015). Przedsiębiorstwa wobec wyzwań zrównoważonego rozwoju. *Zeszyty Naukowe Politechniki Śląskiej. Seria: Organizacja i Zarządzanie, 77*, 239-247.

UN ECLAC. (2020). *The 2030 Agenda for Sustainable Development in the new global and regional context: Scenarios and projections in the current crisis.* Author.

UN. (2015). *Transforming Our World: The 2030 Agenda for Sustainable Development.* Seventieth United Nations General Assembly. Available at http://www.un.org/ga/search/view_doc.asp?symbol=A/RES/70/1&Lang=E

UNCTAD. (2018). *Circular economy: The new normal?* Policy Brief, No.61 UNCTAD.

UNDP. (2020). *Implications of the COVID-19 Pandemic for Global Sustainable Finance.* Working Paper. The International Network of Financial Centres for Sustainability United Nations Environment Programme. Available at https://unepinquiry.org/publication/implications-of-the-covid-19-pandemic-for-global-sustainable-finance/

UNESCO. (2016). *Education for People and Planet: Creating Sustainable Futures for All.* Global Education Monitoring Report 2016. Paris: UNESCO Publishing. Retrieved from: https://unesdoc.unesco.org/images/0024/002457/245752e.pdf

UNESCO. (2016a). *Contemporary learning crisis: education' failure in "creating sustainable future for all". In The Global Education Monitoring Report* (2nd ed.). UNESCO Publishing.

Unger, S., & Landis, A. (2016). Assessing the environmental, human health, and economic impacts of reprocessed medical devices in a Phoenix hospital's supply chain. *Journal of Cleaner Production, 112*, 1995–2003. doi:10.1016/j.jclepro.2015.07.144

United Nations (UN). (1975). *United Nations Environment Programme*. Report of the Governing Council on the work pf this third session. United Nations.

United Nations Global Compact. (1999). https://www.unglobalcompact.org/what-is-gc/mission/principles

UNSD. (2019). *The Sustainable Development Goals Report 2019*. Author.

Ushinsky, K. D. (2005). *Selected Works (vol. 4). Academic Press.*

Valero-Gil, J., Rivera-Torres, P., & Garces-Ayerbe, C. (2017). How is Environmental Proactivity Accomplished? Drivers and Barriers in Firms' Pro-environmental Change Process. *Sustainability (Switzerland)*, *9*(8), 1–15. doi:10.3390u9081327

van Eck, N. J., & Waltman, L. (2010). Software Survey: VOSviewer, a Computer Program for Bibliometric Mapping. *Scientometrics*, *84*(2), 523–538. doi:10.100711192-009-0146-3 PMID:20585380

Van Marrewijk, M. (2013). Concepts and definitions of CSR and corporate sustainability: between agency and communion. *Journal of Business Ethics*, 641–655.

van Marrewijk, M. (2003). Concepts and definitions of CSR and corporate sustainability: Between agency and communion. *Journal of Business Ethics*, *44*(2), 95–105. doi:10.1023/A:1023331212247

Vaslavskiy, Y., & Vaslavskaya, I. (2019). *Public-private partnership: institutional approach*. Aspect Press.

Vaslavsky, Y., & Vaslavskaya, I. (2019). Infrastructure public-private partnership projects: budget consolidation policy in Russia and government expenditures' efficiency increase. In B. S. Sergi (Ed.), *Modeling Economic Growth in Contemporary Russia* (pp. 199–228). Emerald Publishing. doi:10.1108/978-1-78973-265-820191007

Venkatesh, U., Mathew, J., & Chaudhuri, A. (2020). *Corporate social responsibility as an antecedent of brand valuation, Mandated Corporate Social Responsibility*. Springer.

Vincent, C., Neale, G., & Woloshynowych, M. (2001). Adverse events in British hospitals: Preliminary retrospective record review. *BMJ (Clinical Research Ed.)*, *322*(7285), 517–519. doi:10.1136/bmj.322.7285.517 PMID:11230064

Vishwanathan, P., van Oosterhout, H. J., Heugens, P. P. M. A. R., Duran, P., & Van Essen, M. (2019). Strategic CSR: A concept building meta-analysis. *Journal of Management Studies*. Advance online publication. doi:10.1111/joms.12514

Visser, W. (2010). *CSR 2.0: The Evolution and Revolution of Corporate Social Responsibility. In Responsible Business: How to Manage a CSR Strategy Successfully*. Wiley.

Visser, W. (2010). The Age of Responsibility: CSR 2.0 and the New DNA of Business. *Journal of Business Systems. Governance and Ethics*, *5*(3), 7–22. doi:10.15209/jbsge.v5i3.185

Visser, W. (2011). *The Ages and Stages of CSR. Towards the Future with CSR 2.0.* Social Space.

Vitolla, F., Raimo, N., & Rubino, M. (2019). Appreciations, criticisms, determinants, and effects of integrated reporting: A systematic literature review. *Corporate Social Responsibility and Environmental Management*, *26*(2), 518–528. doi:10.1002/csr.1734

Vygotsky, L. S. (1960). *Development of Higher Mental Functions*. Nauka Publisher.

Wade, C. L. (2002). *Racial Discrimination and the Relationship Between the Directorial Duty of Care and Corporate Disclosure* (Vol. 63). University of Pittsburgh Law Review.

Wagner, M. (2007). Integration of environmental management with other managerial functions of the firm: Empirical effects on drivers of economic performance. *Long Range Planning*, *40*(6), 611–628. doi:10.1016/j.lrp.2007.08.001

Walley, N., & Whitehead, B. (1994). It's not easy being green. *Harvard Business Review*, *72*, 46–52.

Waltman, L., van Eck, N. J., & Noyons, E. C. M. (2010). A Unified Approach to Mapping and Clustering of Bibliometric Networks. *Journal of Informetrics*, *4*(4), 629–635. doi:10.1016/j.joi.2010.07.002

Wang, V. X. (2014). *Handbook of Research on Education and Technology in a Changing Society*. Scopus. doi:10.4018/978-1-4666-6046-5

Wartick, S. L., & Cochran, P. L. (1985). The evolution of the corporate social performance model. *Academy of Management Review*, *10*(4), 758–769.

Wautelet, T. (2018). *The concept of circular economy: its origins and it evolution.* Retrieved from: https://www.researchgate.net/publication/322555840

WBCSD. (n.d.). *Moving beyond the "turbulent teens."* Author.

WCED (World Commission on Environment and Development). (1987). *Our Common Future. Un Documents: Gathering a Body of Global Agreements has been compiled by the NGO Committee on Education of the Conference of NGOs from United Nations web sites with the invaluable help of information & communications technology*. United Nations.

WCED. (1987). *Our Common Future. World Commission on Environment and Development.* World Commission on Environment and Development., doi:10.1080/07488008808408783

Webster, K. (2017). *The circular economy. A wealth of flows*. Ellen MacArthur Foundation.

WEF. (2018). *The Inclusive Growth and Development Report.* The World Economic Forum.

WEF. (2020). *The Future of Nature and Business*. New Nature Economy Report II. World Economic Forum.

WEF. (2020). The Global Risks Report 2020. Insight Report.

Weisz, U., Haas, W., Pelikan, J. M., & Schmied, H. (2011). Sustainable Hospitals: A Socio-Ecological Approach. *Gaia (Heidelberg)*, *20*(3), 191–198. doi:10.14512/gaia.20.3.10

Wernerfelt, B. (1984). A resource-based view of the firm. *Strategic Management Journal*, *5*, 171–180.

Wheeler, D., Colbert, B., & Freeman, R. E. (2003). Focusing on value: Reconciling corporate social responsibility, sustainability and a stakeholder approach in a network world. *Journal of General Management*, *28*(3), 1–28.

Whiteman, G., Walker, B., & Perego, P. (2013). Planetary Boundaries: Ecological Foundations for Corporate Sustainability. *Journal of Management Studies*, *50*(2), 307–336. doi:10.1111/j.1467-6486.2012.01073.x

Whitmore, A. (2006). The emperor's new clothes: Sustainable mining? *Journal of Cleaner Production*, *14*(3-4), 309–314. doi:10.1016/j.jclepro.2004.10.005

Wilkins, M. (2019). *The ESG Risk Atlas: Sector And Regional Rationales And Scores*. S&P Global Ratings. https://www.spglobal.com/_media/documents/ratingsdirect_theesgriskatlassectorandregionalrationalesandscores_41534468_may-15-2019.pdf

Williams, C. A. (1999). The Securities and Exchange Commission and Corporate Social Transparency. *Harvard Law Review*, *112*(6), 1197. doi:10.2307/1342384

World Bank. (2018). *World Development Report 2018: Learning to Realize Education's Promise*. World Bank.

World Bank. (2020). *The COVID-19 pandemic: shocks to education and policy responses.* World Bank Report.

World Bank. (2020). *The COVID-19 Pandemic: Shocks to Education and Policy Responses.* World Bank.

World Business Council for Sustainable Development. (n.d.). *Corporate Social Responsibility.* https://growthoriented-sustainableentrepreneurship.files.wordpress.com/2016/07/csr-wbcsd-csr-primer

World Commission on Environment and Development. (1987). *Report of the World Commission on Environment and Development: Our Common Future.* Author.

World Economic Forum. (2017). *The Inclusive Growth and Development Report.* Geneva: WEF.

World Economic Forum. (2019). *Transforming Infrastructure: Frameworks for Bringing the Forth Industrial Revolution to Infrastructure*. Community Paper. Geneva: WEF.

World Economic Forum. (2020). *The Future of Nature and Business.* New Nature Economy Report II. Geneva: World Economic Forum.

World Economic Outlook Update. (2020). A Crisis Like No Other: an Uncertain Recovery. Washington, DC: IMF.

World Economic Outlook Update. (2020, June). *A Crisis Like No Other, An Uncertain Recovery.* IMF.

World Health Organization (WHO). (2007). *Everybody business: strengthening health systems to improve health outcomes: WHO's framework for action.* https://www.who.int/healthsystems/strategy/everybodys_business.pdf?ua=1

World Health Organization (WHO). (2020). *World health statistics 2020: monitoring health for the SDGs, sustainable development goals.* https://apps.who.int/iris/handle/10665/332070

World Health Organization. (2002). *Health and Sustainable Development. Report.* WHO. Available at https://www.who.int/mediacentre/events/HSD_Plaq_02.7_def1.pdf

World Health Organization. (2015). *World Health Statistics 2015.* World Health Organization.

Worrall, R., Neil, D., Brereton, D., & Mulligan, D. (2009). Towards a sustainability criteria and indicators framework for legacy mine land. *Journal of Cleaner Production, 17*(16), 1426–1434. doi:10.1016/j.jclepro.2009.04.013

Xie, X. M., & Zhu, Q. W. (2020). Exploring an innovative pivot: How green training can spur corporate sustainability performance. *Business Strategy and the Environment, 29*(6), 2432–2449. doi:10.1002/bse.2512

Xu, Y. (2006). *Public Choice Theory.* Peking University Press.

Yankov & Zakrajsek. (2009). Credit market shocks and economic fluctuations: evidence from corporate bond and stock markets. *Journal of Monetary Economics.*

Yaryomenko, Yu. V. (1997). *Theory and Methodology of Research of a Multilevel Economy.* Moscow: Publishing House.

Yin, R. K. (1994). *Case study research: Design and method.* Sage Publications.

Yoon, K., & Hwang, C. (1981). *Multiple Attribute Decision Making: Methods and Applications.*

Zahid, M., Rahman, H. U., Muneer, S., Butt, B. Z., Isah-Chikaji, A., & Memon, M. A. (2019). Nexus between government initiatives, integrated strategies, internal factors and corporate sustainability practices in Malaysia. *Journal of Cleaner Production, 241*, 118329. doi:10.1016/j.jclepro.2019.118329

Zelazna, A., Bojar, M., & Bojar, E. (2020). Corporate Social Responsibility towards the Environment in Lublin Region, Poland: A Comparative Study of 2009 and 2019. *Sustainability, 12*, 4463. doi:10.3390u12114463

Zhang, B., Bi, J., Yuan, Z., Ge, J., Liu, B., & Bu, M. (2008). Why do Firms Engage in Environmental Management? An Empirical Study in China. *Journal of Cleaner Production*, *16*(10), 1036–1045. doi:10.1016/j.jclepro.2007.06.016

Zhang, X. (2016). *Research of China Systemically Important Banks Regulation of Negative Externalities*. Shanxi University of Finance & Economics.

Zhou, C. (2014). *Empirical Study on the Economic Externality of Chinese Insurance Industry*. Central South University.

Zhu, J., & Hua, W. (2017). Visualizing the knowledge domain of sustainable development research between 1987 and 2015: A bibliometric analysis. *Scientometrics*, *10*(2), 893–914. doi:10.100711192-016-2187-8

Zioło, M., Filipiak, M.Z., Bąk, K., & Cheba, K. (2019). How to Design More Sustainable Financial Systems: The Roles of Environmental, Social, and Governance Factors in the Decision-Making Process. *Sustainability*, *11*(20), 1-34.

About the Contributors

Kumari Anjali is a PhD research scholar with the research studies on Climate Change Mitigation at School of Sciences, IGNOU, New Delhi, India.

Iwona Bąk, PhD, is an associate professor at the West Pomeranian University of Technology Szczecin, Poland. Bąk is an expert in the field of quantitative methods, specializing in analyses regarding the use of quantitative methods in economic research, with a particular emphasis on the labour market and tourism, as well as regional development. Bąk is the author or co-author of over 100 articles published in scientific journals from the JCR list and also has practical experience in the implementation of projects carried out on behalf of public institutions.

Khawla Bouraqqadi holds a Master's degree in Money, Finance, Banking and Insurance from the Faculty of Economic and Social Juridical Sciences, Hassan I University, Morocco. She is currently pursuing her Phd studies in Management Sciences at the Faculty of Economic and Social Juridical Sciences in Casablanca. She is a researcher at the Laboratory "Finance, Banking and Risk Management", Hassan II University, Casablanca, Morocco.

Katarzyna Cheba, PhD, is an associate professor at the West Pomeranian University of Technology Szczecin, Poland. Cheba is an expert specializing in analyses regarding the use of quantitative methods in economic research, with a particular emphasis on international comparisons and regional development, with experience in working with advanced statistical packages STATISTICA, R program, etc. Cheba is the author or co-author of papers published in scientific journals from the JCR list and a member of many projects carried out on behalf of public institutions.

Beata Zofia Filipiak graduated from Faculty of Economic of University of Szczecin, Poland, in 1990, and obtained a PhD in economics and financial strategy from Faculty of Transport and Connectivity of the same university in 1995. Beata Zofia Filipiak worked in different financials institutions and obtained the qualifications of a tax advisor in 1998. She was involved in 25 scientific projects regarding: corporate financial strategies, financial strategies of LGU's and sustainable development and finance. Since 2013 is employed as a full professor at Institute of Finance of University of Szczecin. Beata Zofia Filipiak has authored and coauthored more than 200 publications including thirty monographs. Her research interests span from financial strategies, sustainable finance, financial analysis and financial aspects of sustainable development.

Abdelmajid Ibenrissoul is Professor in Management Sciences at the ENCG, University Hassan II of Casablanca, Morocco. He got a PhD in Economics (1997), a PhD in Organizational Engineering (1987) and a DEA in Mathematical Economics and Econometrics. He has held several scientific responsibilities. He is Director of the Research Laboratory Scientific Engineering of Organizations of the ENCG (since 2007) and President of the Research & Development Commission of SAR in Morocco (since 2014). He has also been the Director of Scientific Research at Mundiapolis University (2009-2018), the Director of the Observatory of Enterprise Competitiveness (2002-2007) and the Director of the Management Laboratory FSJES in Marrakech (1997-2003). He has directed about twenty doctoral theses in Management Sciences. From 2005 - 2007, he was the editor of the Economia journal. He has also published about twenty articles in scientific journals and he has published 2 books and has also participated in 3 collective books. In addition, he participated in several university commissions: he was a member of recruitment commissions for heads of universities (deans and general directors), member and/or president of commissions for the transition from Professor of Higher Education to Professor of Higher Education, member and/or president of university accreditation commissions, member and/or president of commissions for the recruitment of teachers - researchers, Member and/or president of commissions for the accreditation of laboratories and courses of study and member of the committee in charge of fusion research of the Hassan II Universities. He has also been a member of several integrated actions, organizer of symposia, congresses and forums University - Business, member of the MIMIR project (Modernisation of Institutional Management of Innovation and Research in South Neighbouring countries) bringing together 16 European and Arab universities and has held expert missions for the benefit of international and national organisations (World Bank, OCP, ONE, LYDEC, IRES, GIZ, Ministries, etc.).

Souhaila Kammoun holds a PhD in Economics from the University of Social Sciences of Toulouse 1, France. Her research interests focus on Innovation, Corporate Social Responsibility and Fintechs. She has published a number of research articles in international journals and collective books. She was a member of the PAQ-ES project committee, director of the Master's degree in Entrepreneurship and International Development (Tempus Project funded by the European Union) and member of the scientific council at IHEC of Sfax. She has held the positions of Head of the Department of Economics, Director of Studies and Vice-Director. She was also Director of IHEC of Sfax, Tunisia.

Nikhil Kant is pursuing PhD in Management from SOMS, IGNOU, New Delhi and is currently working as Assistant Registrar in IGNOU. He has varied experience of 08 years in leading Public sector Banks and 08 years in Administration & Finance in IGNOU. He has completed MBA, JAIIB, CAIIB, PGDFA, PGDDE and is UGC-NET qualified. Additionally, He is professionally trained in Soft Skills & Applications of IT tools such as Blockchain etc. and attends training workshops as resource person on invitation. He has several publications in International Journals and participation in Conferences/Seminars.

Marcin Kiestrzyn is a Ph.D. student at the Department of Sustainable Finance and Capital Markets at the Institute of Economics and Finance of the University of Szczecin; he is professionally associated with units of the health care sector, where he performs managerial functions. Marcin Kiestrzyn graduated from the Faculty of Economics at the University of Szczecin, Poland, in 2000. Marcin Kiestrzyn worked in the biggest hospitals in West Pomeranian Voivodeship in Poland at first in the analysis department, then in the accounting department. He was involved in a merger between hospitals and creating strategic plans in health care units. Today he is the chief accountant at the provincial hospital, where he is responsible for assets worth over $ 100 million. He oversees numerous investment and financial processes, being a member of the team implementing projects to improve the conditions for the provision of medical services. It cooperates with both public units and NGOs in the implementation of medical prevention programs. Participates in pro-quality activities, with particular emphasis on risk management in health care units. His research interests focus on finance and sustainability and the use of analytical tools in healthcare units. Its mission is to heal health care finances.

James Odia is a Professor of Accounting and Sustainability in the Department of Accounting, University of Benin, Nigeria.

Bartosz Oliwa, MA, is a PhD student at the Faculty of Economics, Finance and Management at the University of Szczecin. He obtained his master's degree in Finance and Accounting and European Studies - European Project Management. Co-author of a number of European projects in the financial perspective for 2007-2013 implemented in public administration, educational units and third sector organizations. Currently, he is involved in research on the Szczecin real estate market and evaluation of the local business sector, in particular SMEs. The main topic of the author's scientific interests is researching the role of financial markets in creating sustainable development.

Andrey Igorevich Pilipenko received his diploma of Higher Education from Leningrad State University (Faculty of Mathematics and Mechanics) in 1972. In 1984 he received his degree of Candidate of Science in Physics and Mathematics from the Institute of Physical Chemistry of the USSR' Academy of Science. In 1998 he received a degree of Doctor of Pedagogical Sciences from Russian Academy of Education. Being full professor for 40 years he has been working as a Professor at many Russian Universities: Lomonosov's Moscow State University, Russian Academy of National Economy under the Government of the Russian Federation, etc. He has been invited as a Professor by Gumilyov' Eurasian National University (Kazakhstan). He is currently a Professor at the "Institute of Management and Marketing" Department of the Russian Presidential Academy of National Economy and Public Administration. He has many publications, indexed by RISC (RF), Scopus, SSRN. His scientific interests lie in the areas of bifurcation effect' modeling in macroeconomics on the base of shocks theory, modeling factors of national financial stability, assessment of interference of monetary and fiscal policies as well as psychological and cognitive barriers in education.

Zoya Pilipenko received her Master's Degree in Economics from Lomonosov's Moscow State University in 2003. In 2004 she received her degree of Candidate of Science in World Economy, Finance, and Banking from Lomonosov's Moscow State University. In 2013 she received her degree of Doctor of Science in World Economy, Finance, and Banking from Lomonosov's Moscow State University. She worked as a financial analyst for the Insurance Company "Gefest," the Joint Stock Company "Sberbank of Russia," Central Bank of Russia. She has had teaching and research experience: 50 publications, indexed by RISC, Doi, Scopus. She has got certificates in Banking and Finance from practical seminars in Great Britain, Luxembourg, Austria, Italy, and France. She has got certificates in Banking and Finance from practical seminars in Great Britain, Luxembourg, Austria, Italy and France. She is currently a Head of the Group of Rating Agencies and Price Centers, Department of Financial Market Strategic Development, the Central Bank of the Russian Federation. Her scientific interests lie in the area of the shocks theory and the impulse model of cyclical economic development as well as peculiar properties of monetary policy' formation and implementation in connection with definite sectors of financial market.

Anna Spoz is Assistant Professor at the Department of Accountancy at the John Paul II Catholic University of Lublin. Manager, and lecturer of Postgraduate Programs Accounting and Tax and Management and Finance in Public Administration. She combines teaching and scholarly activities with work in the business. Author of many publications on finance, accounting, reporting, and management.

Irina Yu. Vaslavskaya has doctoral degrees in economics. She began her professional career as a senior, then a leading researcher of the Department of Scientific Research Institute of Economics, the Russian Academy of Science (2000-2013). She was invited as associate professor by many universities in Moscow, as well as by Kazan Federal University, the Russian Federation (2013-2015). Now she is a head of the Department of Enterprises and Organizations' Economics, Kazan Federal University (the Russian Federation) (2016-2018). She has numerous publications, indexed by RISC (the Russian Federation), Doi, SCOPUS. Her scientific interests lie in the areas of institutional economic theory, public-private partnership' organizational forms in Russia, state and public sector's functions in economic systems as well as factors of slowing economic growth at the globe.

Yan Vaslavskiy is a Ph.D. in political science; Associate Professor, Department of Political Theory, MGIMO University. 2015-2017: Director at the International Analytical Centre "Rethinking Russia"; 2013-2017: Director at the School of Government and International Affairs, MGIMO University; In 2012 held the position of APEC CEO Summit Program Director; 2010-2011: Deputy Director of the Global Policy Forum. Science editor of Political Atlas of the Modern World: An Experiment in Multidimensional Statistical Analysis of the Political Systems of Modern States (published by Wiley Blackwell in 2010). Member of the board of the Russian Political Science Association; member of the board of Research Committee #37 at International Political Science Association (RC #37 studies problems of political development).

Index

O

P

Q

S

T

U

W

www.ingramcontent.com/pod-product-compliance
Lightning Source LLC
LaVergne TN
LVHW060423300926
849162LV00006B/1505